The Growth and Culture of Latin America
VOLUME II

The Growth and Culture
of Latin America

The Continuing Struggle for Independence

VOLUME II

DONALD E. WORCESTER
Texas Christian University
WENDELL G. SCHAEFFER
Texas Christian University

Second Edition

New York
OXFORD UNIVERSITY PRESS
London 1971 Toronto

To Eric C. Bellquist
and Lawrence Kinnaird

Preface

As the twentieth century advances it has become increasingly difficult to encompass in a single, coherent volume the history of modern Latin America. The problem reflects the growing diversity of the vast region that is called Latin America. Great nations have emerged which, in the century to come, seem destined to be principal actors on the world stage, far exceeding in their extent, their population, their productivity, and their cultural achievements many countries on other continents whose stars have passed their zeniths after centuries of pre-eminence. At the same time, other parts of Latin America do not present the same pattern of evolution or change. Indeed, they change little at all, and their fortunes seem destined to decline as, overburdened by population, their limited resources prove increasingly unable to sustain existing standards of life and well-being.

The authors have attempted in this text once more to capture the changing picture, the growing diversity, the emerging trends, and the dynamic movement of this vast region. It is an impossible task that can only fall short of expectations. Nevertheless, it is hoped that by the use of theme concepts and the organization of chapters to bring out contrasts in development that a clearer understanding of the history of the region will result. Such a methodology differs sharply from a country-by-country treatment, and it differs as well from a strictly regional approach based on geographic propinquity. In the years to come greater use will necessarily be made of histories of individual countries. The authors hope that this text will help bridge the transition gap.

W. G. S.
D. E. W.

June 1970

Contents

IV THE ABORTIVE ALLIANCE: FRUSTRATIONS
    AND DISILLUSIONMENT

Maps

Glossary

Acción comunal. Community development program, Colombia.
Adelantado. Royal deputy and colony founder, Spanish America.
Aficionado. Sports enthusiast or fan.
Agiotista. Money-lender, usurer, Mexico.
Alcabala. Tax on sales.
Alcalde mayor. Governor of a province called an *alcaldía mayor.*
Aprismo. The philosophy of APRA or the Aprista party of Víctor Raúl Haya
    de la Torre, Peru.
Audiencia. A high court of colonial Spanish America and its jurisdiction.

Baldío. Vacant or public land.
Barriada. Shantytown area that has grown up around cities, Peru.
Barrios pobres. Shantytown areas around cities, Spanish America.
Blancos. One of two parties of Uruguay.
Bogotazo. The 1948 riot in Bogotá following the murder of Jorge Eliécer
    Gaitán.
Braceros. Farm workers.

Cabildo. Municipal government, colonial Spanish America.
Cabildo abierto. Emergency town meeting of leading citizens.
Cacique. Indian chief, political boss.
Callampa. 'Mushroom,' shantytown area around cities, Chile.
Callista. Supporter of Plutarco Elías Calles, Mexico.
Campesino. Rural peasant.
Canción ranchera. Song of the country folk, Mexico.
Capataz. Foreman, Brazil.
Casa de Contratación. House of Trade, Sevilla and later Cádiz.
Casa Rosada. 'Pink House,' presidential residence, Buenos Aires.
Caudillo. Chief, leader, military dictator.
Científico. Member of the group of Positivists surrounding Porfirio Díaz, Mexico.
Civilistas. Political party, Peru.
Co-gobierno. Student participation in university administration.

ix

Colorados. Uruguayan faction and political party.
Comité de fundo. Union of agricultural workers, Chile.
Conselho da India. Council of India, Portugal.
Consulado. Tribunal and merchants' guild.
Continuismo. The practice of politicians remaining in office after legal terms expire.
Corregidor. Governor of a province called a *corregimiento*.
Corregidor de Indios. Governor of an Indian community.
Creole. Person of European parentage born in the New World.
Cristeros. Fanatical pro-church group in Mexico.
Cuartelazo. Barracks revolt.

Descamisados. The 'forgotten (shirtless) ones' of the Perón era, Argentina.

Ejido. Communal village lands.
Encomienda. Grant of authority over a group of Indians with obligation to Christianize and protect them in exchange for tribute.
Estado Novo. The 'New State' proclaimed by Getúlio Vargas, Brazil.
Estancia, estanciero. Huge estate and its owner, Argentina.
Exaltados. Faction of the Liberal party, Brazil.

Farrapo. Vaqueiro rebel of Rio Grande do Sul, Brazil. Today any resident of Rio Grande do Sul.
Favela. Shantytown area in Brazilian cities.
Fazenda, fazendeiro. Plantation and its owner, Brazil.
Finca. Coffee plantation.
Fiscal. Attorney.
Fueros. Privileges given to corporate bodies such as the church and the army.
Fundo. Landed estate, Chile.

Gachupín. Unflattering term for peninsular Spaniards, Mexico.
Gaucho. Fierce horseman of the Argentine and Uruguayan plains.
Gaúcho. Brazilian equivalent of *gaucho*.
Golpe de estado. Violent overthrow of a government, *coup d'etat*.
Guano. Fertilizer composed of bird droppings, Peru.

Hacienda, hacendado. Landed estate and its owner, Spanish America.

Inquilino. Tenant farmer, Chile.
Irmandades. Semi-religious brotherhoods, Brazil.

Jefe Máximo. Number one chief, unofficial title of Plutarco Elías Calles, Mexico.
Junta. Committee, board of directors.
Justicialismo. Term Perón gave to his political philosophy, Argentina.

Ladino. Creole or mestizo group in Guatemala; Indians who adopt language and dress of the ladino group.
Lépero. Rabble of the cities, Mexico.
Lerdista. Follower of Sebastián Lerdo de Tejada, Mexico.
Ley fuga. 'Law of flight,' Mexico: prisoners were shot 'while attempting to escape.'
Limpieza de sangre. 'Purity of blood,' meaning that no ancestor was non-Christian.

Maderista. Follower of Francisco I. Madero, Mexico.
Mayorazgo. Entailed estate reserved for first-born son, Spanish America.
Mayordomo. Overseer.
Mazorca. Secret police of Juan Manuel de Rosas, Argentina.
Mestizo. Half-breed, Indian and Spanish.
Minifundio. Parcel of land too small to support a family.
Moderados. Political faction, Brazil.
Modernismo. Spanish American literary movement; Brazilian artistic and literary movement.
Mordida. 'The bite,' a petty bribe to an official for performing his normal work, Mexico.
Municipio. Township and immediate environs.

Nacionalistas. Members of Blanco party, Uruguay.

Obraje. Textile workshop.
Obregonista. Follower of Alvaro Obregón, Mexico.

Padroado. Patronage, Brazil. Right of government to nominate church officials.
Pampas. Extensive grasslands, Argentina (from Inca, *bamba*).
Patrón. Term to designate *hacendado* or *estanciero*: boss.
Patronato. Patronage, Spanish America. Right of government to nominate church officials.
Pax Porfiriana. Peace imposed on Mexico by Porfirio Díaz.
Pelucones. 'Bigwigs,' uncomplimentary term for conservatives, Chile.
Peninsular. Spaniard born in Spain.
Pensador. Thinker, intellectual.
Peronista. Follower of Juan Domingo Perón, Argentina.
Personalismo. Cult of the leader.
Pesquisa. Visit of an official inspector.
Pipiolos. 'Novices,' uncomplimentary term for liberals, Chile.
Porfirista. Follower of Porfirio Díaz, Mexico.
Positivism. Doctrine of Auguste Comte.

Quebracho. Medicinal bark used to treat fever; also used in tanning.
Quiteño. Resident of Quito, Ecuador.

Ranchos. Squatter settlements on hills around Caracas.
Regidor. Alderman or councilor, member of a *cabildo.*
Reino. Portuguese in Brazil who was born in Portugal.

Religión y fueros. 'Religion and privileges,' rallying cry of church and army, Mexico.
Rurales. Efficient but brutal rural police force in time of Porfirio Díaz, Mexico.

Sertão, sertanejo. Back country and resident of area, Brazil.
Sinarquistas. Fanatical, conservative, pro-church faction, Mexico.

Tribute. Head tax paid by Indian men.
Tumulto. Riot.
Tupamaros. Modern guerrilla organization, Uruguay.

Unitarios. Argentines who favored predominance of Buenos Aires.

Vecindades. Slum areas in modern Spanish American cities, the residents of which often identify with a common community of origin: neighborhoods.
Violencia. Costly civil war that began in Colombia in 1948.
Visita. Official inspection.

Yerba maté. Popular beverage in southern South America: 'Paraguayan tea.'
Yungas. Northeastern slope of the eastern cordillera in Bolivia, characterized by deep canyons.

Zapatista. Follower of Emiliano Zapata, Mexico.

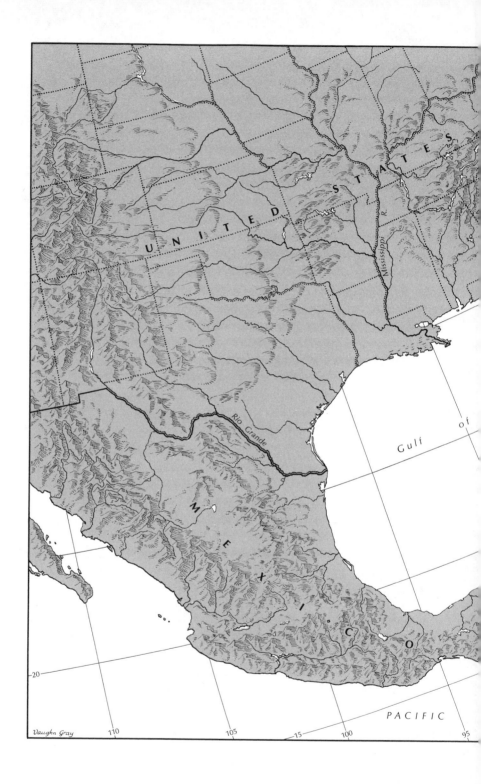

UNITED STATES

Mississippi R.

MEXICO

Rio Grande

Gulf   of

PACIFIC

Vaughn Gray   110   105   15   100   95

20

CENTRAL AMERICA AND THE CARIBBEAN

Miles
0   100   200   300   400   500

ATLANTIC
OCEAN

Bahama Is.
(Br.)

Mexico

C U B A

HAITI

DOMINICAN
REPUBLIC

JAMAICA

Caribbean   Sea

BR. HONDURAS

HONDURAS

GUATEMALA

NICARAGUA

EL SALVADOR

COSTA
RICA

Canal Zone
(U.S.)

PANAMA

COLOMBIA

OCEAN

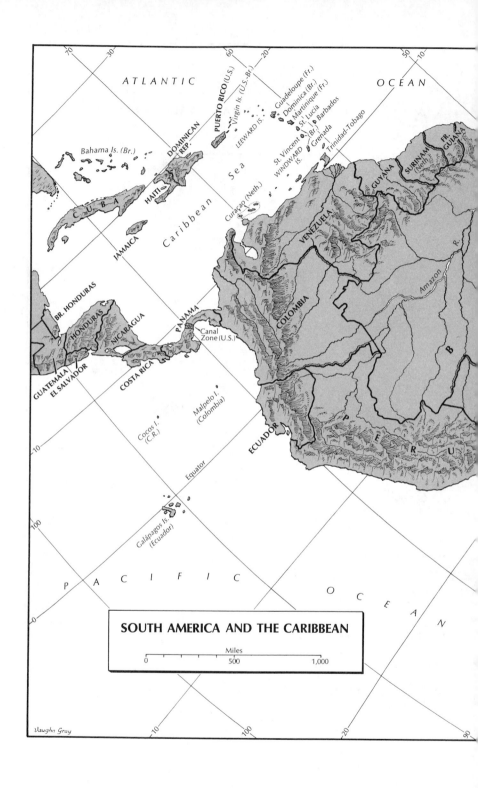

ATLANTIC   OCEAN

PUERTO RICO (U.S.)
Virgin Is. (U.S.-Br.)
Guadeloupe (Fr.)
Dominica (Br.)
Martinique (Fr.)
LEEWARD IS.
St. Lucia
St. Vincent
Barbados
(Br.)
Grenada
WINDWARD
IS.
Trinidad-Tobago

DOMINICAN REP.

Bahama Is. (Br.)

C U B A

HAITI

JAMAICA

Caribbean   Sea

Curaçao (Neth.)

VENEZUELA

GUYANA

SURINAM (Neth.)

FR. GUIANA

BR. HONDURAS

HONDURAS

NICARAGUA

PANAMA

Canal Zone (U.S.)

COLOMBIA

Amazon R.

B

GUATEMALA
EL SALVADOR

COSTA RICA

Cocos I. (C.R.)

Malpelo I. (Colombia)

ECUADOR

P
E
R
U

Equator

Galápagos Is. (Ecuador)

P   A   C   I   F   I   C

O
C
E
A
N

SOUTH AMERICA AND THE CARIBBEAN

Miles

0   500   1,000

Vaughn Gray

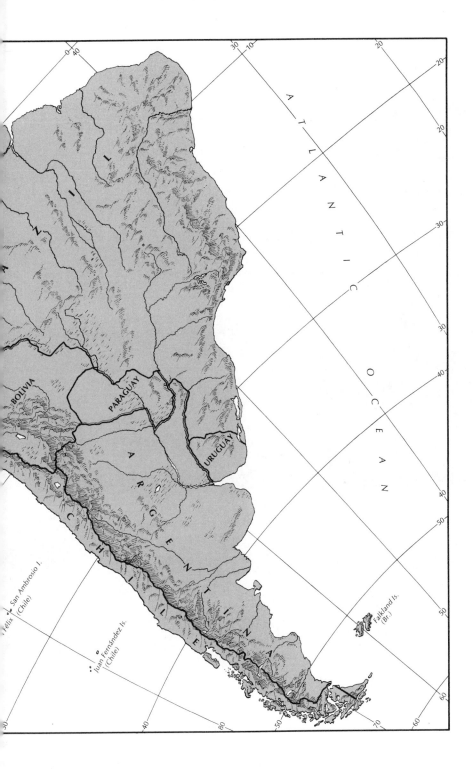

I THE STRUGGLE FOR POLITICAL STABILITY

I

The Heritage of Modern Latin America

> The leaders of the intellectual independence of Hispanic America sought a complete reformation of the . . . colonial heritage. Our heritage, they added, is the complete opposite of what we want to be and what we should be. We carry our defects in our blood; let us rid ourselves of this blood if necessary.*

Latin America is one of the world's great cultural regions. Although its various components share a major portion of the Western Hemisphere and at one time that portion was considerably larger than at present, Latin America is far from a homogeneous geographic entity. It is not a single political realm and its economic and social diversities are enormous. Only common elements in its cultural background justify the use of a single term with which to designate it. Any effort to bring the entire region into focus through the lens of a historian, a geographer, an economist, a political scientist, or a sociologist inevitably results in great distortions. Such distortions increase with the years as the common cultural background fades into the past and the modern world imposes new sets of values and new patterns of life.

The culture of Latin America is the product of many factors: human, physiographic, spiritual, economic, and historic. The state of technology of the arts and sciences, as well as of human organization, played a major role in many aspects of the region's establishment and evolution. It has had an overwhelming impact on modern development.

The Native Peoples

The aboriginal inhabitants of the Western Hemisphere, who owe their designation as Indians to the geographical ignorance of the early Iberian ex-

* From The Latin-American Mind, by Leopoldo Zea, p. 8. Copyright 1963 by the University of Oklahoma Press.

3

plorers, were a widely varied collection of peoples living in greatly differ-
ing states of civilization. The origins of these peoples are not completely
known, but certainly some crossed over from Asia in the vicinity of the
Bering Strait, probably at various times many centuries apart. It is also
possible that some came from the islands of the South Seas and others
from Africa. Archaeological evidence indicates that the American continents have been populated for many thousands of years, but there has been
nothing discovered to suggest that human life in its earliest forms was present in this region of the world. Differences in stature, physical features,
color, and other ethnological factors demonstrate clearly that no single
source accounted for the population that early European explorers encountered when they first set foot on the sands of the New World. Inhabitants
were to be found, however, in all parts of the two vast continents, and
their contribution to the race and culture of the future American civilizations was profound.

THE HIGHER CIVILIZATIONS

The four most advanced groups of peoples encountered by the early Iberian explorers were the Mayas and Aztecs of Mexico and Central America, the Incas of Peru, Bolivia, and Ecuador, and the Chibchas of
Colombia. Maya civilization was well past its apex when Cortés appeared
off the Mexican coast, and both the Aztec and Inca peoples were relatively
recent conquerors of older civilizations whose culture and civilizing accomplishments they had appropriated to themselves. Aztecs and Incas,
however, possessed a highly structured social and political organization,
lived in cities, and after quick subjugation became an integral part of the
Iberian imperial system to which they contributed labor, wives for the conquerors, and the basic structure of local social organization.

In the centuries following the conquest, the more civilized and sedentary
Indians intermixed with the Spaniards and Portuguese, performed most of
the labor in the fields and mines, and provided the basis upon which major
centers of colonial activity and power were erected. They adopted the
Catholic religion, modifying it in some cases in accordance with their own
ancient customs and beliefs, and became skilled artisans in the construction and decoration of the great religious edifices that became so important
a characteristic of Ibero-American civilization.

LESSER TRIBES AND NOMADIC PEOPLES

Many Indians belonged to less advanced tribes in some degree subject to the dominant Indian empires. Others were far removed from and had no contact with the Aztec or Inca systems. Still others were nomads of the plains and forests. The less sedentary peoples proved the most difficult to conquer or bring under the permanent rule of the Spaniards and Portuguese. Many of these fought against the invaders for generations until they faced extinction at the hands of the better equipped and organized armies that sought to pacify them. Some were induced to enter organized communal life in mission reductions operated by the religious orders, particularly the Jesuits. In the Caribbean islands, disease and harsh labor demands of the conquerors quickly decimated the Indian population. Within a few years after Columbus landed on the island of Santo Domingo, then known as Española, and established Spain's first American settlement there, the island was virtually devoid of Indian population. Similar declines in native population occurred on Puerto Rico, Cuba, Jamaica, and along the Brazilian coast. Vast numbers also died in the highland regions of Mexico and South America owing to disease and the harsh labor practices to which they were subjected.

Eventually all native peoples of the Spanish and Portuguese empires were brought under control, pacified, or destroyed. On the frontiers, however, such as the great plains of western North America, the interior of the Amazon valley, and the southernmost part of South America, numbers of tribes remained beyond the reach of civilized centers and the Spaniards and Portuguese saw little to be gained by efforts to subdue them. Often the missionaries were more effective in dealing with such peoples than the armies that occasionally were sent against them.

The Iberian Peoples

Spain and Portugal were the European progenitors of Latin America. The explorers and conquerors from these European lands indelibly fixed their imprint on the vast regions they incorporated into their imperial systems. The French, the Dutch, the Germans, and the English all participated at various times and places in the great enterprise, but the dominant European influence was Iberian. For three hundred years the Spaniards and the Portuguese held sway over their vast domains in the New World, pouring into them their efforts and devotion, fixing upon them their religion and the great artistic and architectural emphasis that was such an important concomitant of their religious practice. For three hundred years these people sought to extend their creed, their values, and their political power over every inhabitant of the territories they occupied, to incorporate all economic activity into a great mercantile system devoted to extracting the wealth of the Americas for the benefit of the two imperial crowns. The Iberian influence was pervasive in all areas of human activity, determined the social structure and its hierarchical characteristics, established and maintained governmental and administrative activities, and regulated the considerable array of interrelationships among the various groupings of castes and races constituting the population.

THE GENERATION OF THE CONQUEST

The Spaniards who first set foot on the soil of the New World and the Portuguese who shortly followed them were a hardy lot. Wars produce soldiers, and war had wracked the Iberian peninsula for centuries prior to the first voyage of Columbus; for the Christian inhabitants of the region had long been engaged in a bitter reconquest of territory from the Moors. The successful outcome of the Moorish struggle and the domination of Spain by a single monarch that the victory made possible created a powerful nation-state whose military prowess was soon the envy of all Europe. A generation of people inured to the hardships of combat and made bold and venturesome by their success readily enrolled in the task of discovering and exploring a whole new hemisphere.

The Portuguese of the same era were equally dedicated to empire-building tasks, but much of their effort was poured into the conquest of the East Indies and key footholds on the Asian continent. Only somewhat tardily did they press their claims along the Brazilian coast where they were obliged to contest with first French and then Dutch settlers for dominance of the region.

The conquerors of New World territories for Spain and Portugal were by no means a cadre of accomplished military officers. A few were. The great majority were adventurers seeking to better their position in the world, men of low estate who by acts of daring and heroism hoped to achieve a material fortune, lay claim to a higher rung on the social ladder, and make possible an eventual comfortable retirement at home. Only a small minority were fortunate enough to achieve such objectives; those who died in the attempt were numerous. The bones of Iberian aspirants to fame and glory were soon to be found from the sands of the western North American deserts to the jungles of the Amazon basin to the bleak plateaus and damp forests of Patagonia. A great many perished in the conquests of Peru and Mexico while others were lost in the perilous voyages to and from the New World. The manpower costs of creating vast overseas empires for Portugal and Spain were exceedingly great, but the benefits to the mother countries were incalculable and made possible one of the most fascinating and romantic chapters in the history of Western civilization.

The Africans

A far from romantic aspect of the conquest and settlement of the Americas was the role of the Africans who shortly arrived in ever-increasing numbers. They came not as conquerors but as slaves, mere chattels bought or captured along the West African coast and sold in the Caribbean islands and Brazil for the profit of a considerable group of international traders who soon made fortunes in the business. Most of the trade was carried on by the Portuguese, the Dutch, the British, and the French. Spaniards did not enter the competition for capture or purchase of slaves in Africa and for their transportation to the Western Hemisphere; they were excluded from Africa by the Papal Bull which established the respective conquest and settlement areas of Spain and Portugal in 1493. However, they provided the first and for many years the greatest market for the unhappy captives, particularly in those areas where the native Indians quickly died out or were found unsuited to the difficult labor in the mines and fields. Spain early legalized the slave trade to its colonies by a system of licensing, and favored slavers were permitted to meet the requirements of the rapidly expanding market.

Long before the end of the Spanish and Portuguese imperial systems, blacks from Africa had assumed a major role in the economic and social

life of great portions of the Americas. How many were actually transported into the colonies will never be known, but estimates run as high as
80,000 to 100,000 a year during the height of the nefarious trade. By the
time of independence, the number of blacks in the Spanish, French, and
Portuguese colonies certainly amounted to several million, but by far the
greatest portion of these were in Brazil, in the French islands in the Caribbean, and in the Spanish insular possessions. In the mainland areas of
Spanish jurisdiction, the blacks were concentrated in the port cities and
lowland areas around the Caribbean; in highland areas Indians predominated by far and were to continue to do so.

African contributions to the development of the New World possessions
of Spain, Portugal, and France were enormous. Quite apart from the fact
that black labor was cheaper and more reliable than Indian labor in much
of the region, the Africans frequently brought with them from their homeland knowledge and skills unknown to the American Indians and unprac-
ticed by the European colonists. In addition, they contributed vastly from
their culture, particularly in art, music, dance, and religious mysticism.
The blending of African religious beliefs with the Catholicism of the Europeans produced marked variations in religious practice throughout those
parts of the Americas where the black population assumed significant proportions.

The Portuguese and Spaniards were relatively relaxed in their treatment
of African subjects. Slavery was a significant commercial enterprise in
populating the colonies, but it did not long remain a highly sophisticated
commercial enterprise in the domestic economy, as was the case in British
North America. Slaves had defined rights and privileges and many obtained their freedom by purchase or through the generosity of their owners. Free blacks were everywhere in evidence and competed with Indians
and Europeans for economic opportunity and social improvement. This is
not to say that slavery in Latin America was less degrading than in British
America, and probably nowhere was the institution more oppressive than
in French Saint Domingue, but the relative ease with which Spanish and
Portuguese America moved from a slave economy to other systems of
labor organization suggests clearly a distinction in attitude toward the
black as an individual and the particular manner in which his labor was
commandeered.

The Latin American People

By the end of the colonial era, Latin America had already become a vast melting pot of races and nationalities. The principal elements were Indian, Iberian, and Negro, but the ratio of each of these elements to the others varied greatly. In the highland areas of both North and South America, the native Indians predominated, and in much of Mexico, parts of Central America, all of Bolivia, and the larger portions of Peru, Ecuador, and Colombia they constituted all but a small part of the population. In the Caribbean islands and in much of the coastal areas bordering this great American sea, Negroes outnumbered the white population, and the Indians had all but disappeared. Brazil presented the greatest mixture of races, with all degrees of interrelationship among Negro, Portuguese, and Indian, plus some other European stock as well. Add to these general combinations the cultural and physical differences of both the native Indian peoples and the various categories of Africans that entered the New World, and the result is one that leaves little ground for great pride in *limpieza de sangre* or purity of blood.

THE SYSTEM OF CASTES

The Iberian conquest of America was essentially a male adventure in which the women of Spain and Portugal played a relatively minor role. Alliances with native women throughout the entire region quickly produced the first and many subsequent generations of *mestizos* or mixed bloods. In the years of empire development and consolidation, women from the Iberian Peninsula joined the men in America in increasing numbers, but they were never sufficiently numerous to reverse the pattern of mixture that had been so firmly established from the outset. They did provide the basis, nevertheless, for the development of a *creole* class, people of European ancestry born in the American colonies. As time went on, many mestizos, whose Indian features were not prominent and who adopted European dress and manners, were able to enter the creole social group. The intermingling of races continued apace, but social practice soon established rigid categories of caste distinction based upon the degree of Negro or Indian ancestry a person possessed. Of equal significance was the distinction that very early emerged between persons born in America and those who first saw the light of day in the mother country.

Caste distinctions were rendered of particular significance by imperial legislation aimed at protecting the rights of the native population and exempting it from certain fiscal obligations. Of greater importance over the years, however, were the social and political distinctions that emerged and which were based in large part on accident of parentage and place of birth. Such distinctions had immediate economic consequences as well, for they determined who might be admitted into what employment, who might enter the priesthood, join the various corporate bodies that operated and regulated trade and commerce, or hold appointive or elective office in the imperial bureaucracies.

Probably no other single factor so exacerbated the relations between the Iberian kingdoms and their American colonies as the preferences enjoyed by the *peninsulares* and *reinos* and denied the creoles. Economic restrictions were evaded or went unenforced, the long struggle over slavery and personal service by the Indians was ameliorated by changing patterns of social and economic control, but the persistent disbarment of able and educated creoles from the principal offices of church and state created a running sore that could not be healed by the rare application of the balm of a significant creole appointment. The issue was even more strikingly accented in the closing years of the eighteenth century when the implantation of the intendant system as an administrative reform replaced creoles in the lesser provincial posts with new appointees from Spain. A few years later, the arrival of the Portuguese royal court in Brazil, with its vast retinue of reino nobility who quickly monopolized the important offices, demonstrated in that colony the width of the gulf separating the native born from the European.

ATTITUDES BASED ON STATUS

Three centuries did little to alter certain attitudes that prevailed in the Iberian colonies from the date of their founding. Men did not come from Spain and Portugal to till the soil, to labor in the mines, or to tend animals. They came as soldiers and conquerors whose domination of subject peoples quickly confirmed their already established aversion for physical labor. This aversion, far stronger among the Spaniards than the Portuguese, became institutionalized at an early date with the development of the system of *encomiendas,* whereby individual Spaniards were assigned large numbers of Indians for whose well-being and spiritual indoctrination they became responsible in return for the products of their physical labor. This system, to whose eradication the crown subsequently devoted great effort, gave way to other forms for organizing the labor of the subservient classes, ending eventually in an economy of debt peonage on vast *haciendas* or landed estates. In Brazil the *fazenda* or plantation became the center of economic and social life in the vast northeastern region until the discovery of mineral wealth created its urbanizing influence in the southern captaincies. The significant fact, however, was the continued dependence of the European and later the creole population on the labor of lesser classes: Indians, Negroes, and the many varieties of racial mixture. Even an ignorant peasant arriving from Spain or Portugal soon arrogated to himself the status of a superior being and refused thereafter to engage in the tasks or handicrafts by which he had earned his livelihood at home.

Labor shortages soon arose and plagued the colonial regions until the modern era. This was owing in large part to the rapid dying out of the indigenous population, ravaged by epidemics of European and Asian diseases to which they had no resistance, weakened by unaccustomed hardship and labor in the mines and fields of the conqueror, and slaughtered in the bitter struggles that attended the gradual subjugation of the South and much of the North American continents. Rapid expansion of the African slave trade, efforts to reduce still unconquered Indian tribes, and raids upon Indian settlements, such as those conducted by the Portuguese of São Paulo against the Jesuit mission reductions of Paraguay, attest to the constant struggle to develop and maintain a sufficient labor force to carry out the physical effort necessary to produce the crops and extract the minerals which constituted the bases of the colonial economy.

The holding of public office and the ownership of landed estates were viewed as honorable occupations by Spaniard and Portuguese alike, as was also membership in the clergy and particularly the holding of high clerical office. To engage in trade and commerce was demeaning, particularly among the Spaniards, and during the more than half a century that Spain and Portugal were united under the same monarchs, many were the Portuguese—particularly the 'new Christians' of former Jewish belief—who spread throughout the Spanish colonies as merchants and businessmen. Manufacturing, such as the weaving of cloth or the making of furniture, was an Indian occupation in which the workers were organized in rigidly disciplined *obrajes,* really sweat-shops, their tasks assigned and their output controlled by mestizos.

The learned professions were law, philosophy, and theology, and these subjects were taught in the universities. Rhetoric, grammar, Indian languages, and occasionally medicine, were also appropriate subjects of study. The sciences and mathematics were introduced only toward the end of the colonial era, but did not attain either the prestige or attract the attention that was the case with the more traditional areas of study. Prevalent attitudes among the intellectual elite, both European and creole, favored the philosophical and the highly theoretical discourse to the virtual exclusion of those areas of learning that could have had bearing on the daily lives of the people. Thus an effete elitism and a dogmatic religious orthodoxy prevailed among the conservative oligarchy that dominated the intellectual, social, and political life of the principal colonial capitals and provincial cities.

LITERATURE AND THE ARTS

Cultural development of the New World colonies of Spain and Portugal was quite appropriately conditioned at the outset by the tremendous events of discovery and conquest, the effort to Christianize millions of people of a wholly alien race and culture, and the crude and often barbaric life in the burgeoning centers of commercial and mining activity that sprang up in widely scattered parts of the vast region. At the very moment of the flowering of Spanish creative writing and artistic achievement, the Indies was still being discovered and settled; the European population was small and generally not of a literary or artistic bent; and the opportunities for intellectual creativity were limited indeed. Little was to be expected from the colonies, and little emerged.

In spite of such handicaps, however, a few Americans did distinguish themselves in the latter part of the sixteenth century and on into the seventeenth. Basically, the writers were Spaniards born in the colonies, except that one, the Inca Garcilaso de la Vega, was the son of a conqueror and an Inca woman who was a member of the royal family. His works, written in Europe where he spent all but the first twenty years of his life, were greatly influenced by the Renaissance intellectual life which he enjoyed. Most famous, however, was his *Royal Commentaries* recounting the history of the Inca people and the story of the conquest.

Much that was written in the seventeenth and early eighteenth centuries was heavily influenced by the religious faith of the people, and Latin was the language most frequently employed. Only bits and pieces of many items are known to exist today, for facilities for printing were in most places non-existent, and hand-written documents soon disappeared. Poetry was a common literary form, as was the writing of plays. Women as well as men participated in literary endeavor, and a few achieved considerable fame, although the appropriateness of women engaging in such activity was frequently questioned, particularly among the religious. As time went on, Spanish became the common language of literary expression throughout Spain's empire, as did Portuguese in the Brazilian realm of the Portuguese kings. By the eighteenth century, virtually all significant works appeared in the vernacular. Extravagance in form and style was the rule, as was typical of the baroque era.

Toward the end of the eighteenth century, the literary output of both the Spanish and Portuguese colonies flourished. Viceroys prided themselves as patrons of the theater and the arts, and the major capitals of the New World enjoyed a lively cultural activity. Important in this era was an increasing 'nativist' expression, particularly in poetic works, for it revealed an increasing identification with the emerging new country and the mixed culture on which it was based. Likewise, writers devoted increasing attention to rationalistic philosophy and the sciences, as befitted those who identified their efforts with the 'age of enlightenment.'

There is much to indicate that Latin American music of a distinct type emerged at an early date, and that some of it became popular in Spain and Portugal. Much of it was apparently related to the dance, and various forms of dancing of American origin were common in the mother countries. Only in the later years of empire, however, did these forms begin to incorporate Indian and Negro influences, except as they were performed among the lower classes.

The greatest achievements of Latin American art during the colonial era lie in the field of architecture, particularly in the construction and adornment of churches, monasteries, convents, and religious shrines. Not only were the finest skills employed in design of the buildings, but craftmanship of a high order was achieved in the carving and painting of religious figures. Some of the early techniques have never been improved upon and cannot even be duplicated today.

Architectural development in both Spanish and Portuguese America revealed a number of periods and styles. Early structures were simple and massive with little adornment, reflecting gothic and classicist forms. Subsequently, however, there emerged the baroque, most famous of all architectural forms in colonial Latin America, with ornate doors, archways, and windows, frequently showing Moorish influences. Thousands of churches and other religious buildings were constructed in this style throughout Latin America, and they stand to this day as monuments to the genius of their creators. In the eighteenth century, a further development of the baroque emerged, involving even more ornate structures than those built in the previous century. Particular emphasis was placed on exceedingly decorated altars, many of them heavily gilded and replete with the most intricate designs and figures. The finest examples of religious art and architecture carried over into the new republics as a heritage of their Iberian past are to be found in Mexico, at various locations in Quito, Ecuador, and in São Salvador de Bahia, Brazil.

THE PATTERN OF SETTLEMENT

The pattern of colonial settlement in North and South America reflected two basic factors, the land and its resources on the one hand and the native populations encountered on the other. Of course, the pattern of native settlement had already been influenced by the land for several thousand years. It is to be noted that none of the major Indian civilizations was situated in an area of extreme climatic variation. Also, only one of the centers of advanced Indian culture was located in the humid tropics, that of the Mayas in Yucatan and Chiapas, lowland regions of Mexico and northern Central America.

The South American continent and that portion of North America settled by the Spaniards have come to be viewed in modern times as not overly hospitable regions for human habitation. In the sixteenth century, however, the constant warmth and luxuriant vegetation of the Caribbean islands and borderlands, as well as the equally favored Brazilian coastal zone, no doubt seemed far more desirable than the bleak plains and dense forests to the north of Mexico and Florida, where winter cold brought snow and ice, and summer heat was scarcely less oppressive than that of the tropics. The northern region's fertile land, coal, iron, timber, and animal life were not readily apparent or held little appeal for the Iberian conquerors; the golden ornaments and settled communities of civilized Indians were far more attractive. Most of North America was left for the British and French to struggle over generations later.

The geographic features of those American regions occupied by Spain and Portugal presented enormous problems which only gradually were revealed to the colonists. Extremes in altitude proved quite as troublesome in their own way as did extremes in summer and winter weather. Heavy tropical rainfall and constant humidity provided an excellent breeding environment for a variety of strange diseases and tropical fevers with which medical science of that era was totally unprepared to cope. The same rainfall and the intense sunlight with which it alternated quickly leached away the fertility of the soil once it was turned by the plow. Heavy rainfall also produced innumerable streams that quickly eroded the upland areas and converted the vast river valleys into extended flood plains covered with water much of the year.

Most important, however, was the basic relation of mountains to lowlands, the presence of the vast *cordillera* of the Andes that stretches across the north and all the way down the western edge of the South American continent. This tremendous chain, highest in the Western Hemisphere, is partially matched in Mexico and Central America by the southern extension of the Rocky Mountains that provides a broad highland zone to nearly all the area. Both mountain chains are at various points interspersed by regions of high volcanic activity, and this, coupled with the frequent movement along fault lines of a geologically new formation, has produced spectacular natural phenomena with considerable frequency. Iberian settlers in the New World early learned to live—and die—with cataclysmic earthquakes, volcanic eruptions, and tidal waves.

In South America, where storm patterns move in opposite direction to those of the Northern Hemisphere, the Andes chain plays a dominant role in determining the climate of most of the continent. The trade winds from the Atlantic shed their rainfall against the eastern slopes of the mountains and feed the vast river systems of the Amazon and La Plata. West of the mountains, from southern Ecuador to central Chile, little rain ever falls, and much of the area is desert between the mountains and the sea. The Atacama desert of southern Peru and northern Chile is one of the driest in the world. At the same time, southern Chile is drenched with the rain of the northwesterly winds of the South Pacific, but little of this rainfall passes over the Andes to wet the barren slopes of Patagonia in the Argentine. The entire area is one of sharp contrast, and moderating influences are the exception rather than the rule.

The central portion of South America remains to this day largely unsettled. Its few inhabitants are primitive Indian tribes little touched by any form of civilization. After three centuries of Spanish and Portuguese rule around the periphery, much of the great South American continent remained unexplored by the beginning of the nineteenth century and was almost as little known as when Columbus first trod the shores of a distant Caribbean island. Mineral wealth and a ready availability of the labor force to exploit it were the key factors in the settlement of Spanish America. Thus the most favorable areas were the central highlands of Mexico and the Andean valleys of Peru, Bolivia, and Ecuador. It was from these points that the Spanish empire radiated. Portuguese power was derived from a string of coastal settlements along the Brazilian seaboard, and from these bases penetration into the interior was both tardy and limited to areas of mineral discovery. When the day of independence arrived, vast areas were incorporated into new republics with little regard for the resources they contained and only minor attempts to delineate precise boundaries.

The Political and Administrative Heritage

During three centuries of colonial rule, Spain evolved a complex system of governance and administration for its American possessions that to this day clearly merits recognition as one of the most remarkable organizational achievements of all time. Given the vast region over which the empire extended, the difficulties of communication and transport, the competition of enemy powers, and the many opportunities for wayward officials to turn against the regime and, for a price, seek protection elsewhere, the mere endurance of royal authority generation after generation would have constituted a signal accomplishment. This, however, was only the beginning. Millions of people were converted to a new religious faith, their cultural values modified, and their labor mobilized to exploit the resources of the land. Great cities came into being whose commercial activity, intellectual life, and physical appearance not only resembled that of major European centers but in some instances actually came to rival it. Institutions of government, religion, and society were implanted whose characteristics would condition the lives of people for centuries to come.

Portuguese accomplishments in Brazil were scarcely less impressive by reason of the fact that some of the governmental mechanisms employed were borrowed from Spain. The foundation of a great nation was laid on the South American continent. For a time that nation became the home of the Portuguese monarchy and thereafter moved on to surpass the mother country in almost every aspect of national development.

The pattern of political organization in the Spanish empire became fixed at a relatively early date. In Spain there evolved from the royal council a special body, the Council of the Indies, which assumed responsibility for the affairs of the American realms. It served not only as an administrative body, but also as a legislative authority and supreme judicial tribunal. The colonies themselves were divided into vast kingdoms ruled by viceroys sent out from the mother country. At first there were two such kingdoms, those of New Spain and Peru, but in the eighteenth century the additional vice-royalties of Nueva Granada and Río de la Plata were carved out of the vast territory that had been subject to the viceroy in Lima. The kingdoms were themselves divided into a number of lesser administrative units. In the later years of the empire, the principal subordinate unit was the captaincy-general, and these tended to be major areas enjoying considerable autonomy: Chile, Caracas, Guatemala, Cuba, and Santo Domingo. Of somewhat lesser status were the presidencies, and in the closing years of the empire these included Charcas (modern Bolivia), Cuzco, Quito, and Guadalajara. The vast northern region of New Spain (Mexico) was organized as a special military district known as a commandancy-general.

Just as important as the viceroys, captains-general, and presidents who headed the administration of their respective jurisdictions was another royal institution, the *audiencia*. Indeed, the first audiencia in the Indies was created at Santo Domingo a number of years before the first viceroyalty was established in New Spain. The audiencia was basically a court, with civil and criminal chambers to try the different types of cases brought before it. It consisted of a president, from four to eight judges, special criminal judges, and legal officers known as *fiscales*. By the end of the colonial period, there were fourteen audiencias located in the principal regions of the empire, including one at Manila in the Philippines. The last to be created prior to independence were those of Buenos Aires, Caracas, and Cuzco, and each of these had but three judges.

Normally, the viceroy, the captain-general, or the president of a jurisdictional region served as president of the audiencia in his capital city. As such, however, he did not control its decisions; he merely presided. The audiencias were established in part as a check upon executive authority, and their jurisdiction included cases alleging abuse of administrative prerogatives. Furthermore, the audiencias came to exercise substantial administrative powers, often assuming all governmental authority in a viceroyalty upon the death of a viceroy, and continuing to exercise it until the arrival of a successor, which might be several years later. Audiencias had certain legislative authority with respect to Indian affairs, were empowered to investigate the conduct and administrative acts of lesser officials and to sit in judgment as to their stewardship when they completed their terms of office. Often audiencas came into open conflict with viceroys or captains-general over matters of policy or administration, and as they were permitted to communicate directly with the Council of the Indies and with the king, final decision on many issues could only be obtained in Madrid. Such a division of authority served well the purpose of maintaining the supremacy of royal power and of those institutions in Spain to which portions of it were delegated.

GOVERNMENT AT THE POPULAR LEVÉL

Of far more immediate importance to the vast majority of the population, Indian, mestizo, and creole alike, were the lesser administrative offices whose incumbents' activities directly affected the daily lives of the lower classes. Men designated as provincial governors, *alcaldes mayores,* and *corregidores* numbered among their functions the duties of judge, tax collector, police administrator, inspector of Indian affairs, collector of Indian tribute, and, on occasion, chief military officer of their districts. Such positions were wide open to abuse and opportunity for personal enrichment, and many indeed were those who demonstrated few scruples in the treatment of their fellow men or in the protection of the king's interest. Few officials earned a more unsavory reputation than the *corregidores de indios,* men appointed to see to the welfare of Indian communities but who as often as not used their positions for purposes of ruthless exploitation.

The royal authority sought to control abuses of power and authority by a variety of laws and administrative devices for their enforcement. Officials were required to present financial statements upon assuming and leaving office, they were required to stand trial upon completion of their assignments at which hearing aggrieved individuals might bring charges of misconduct against them, they were forbidden to own property, engage in business, or to marry in the territory under their supervision. At any time a special investigation known as a *pesquisa* or a *visita* might be undertaken by higher authority, and some of the visitas ordered by the crown in connection with viceregal administration became famous examples of the exercise of corrective authority in the conduct of imperial affairs.

In spite of the many efforts to prevent the misuse of position, other practices tended to promote it. Such were the sale of lesser offices, which became prevalent in the seventeenth century and continued almost to independence; the contracting of tax collections to self-regulating guilds or monopolies, such as the *consulados* which dominated the commerce of New Spain, Panama, and Peru as well as that of Cádiz; and the gradual recognition of virtually hereditary rights on the part of some creole families to positions on municipal councils. Having paid for a position or a contracted benefice, the holder quite naturally sought to recover his investment and make as much profit as possible while he had the opportunity. The exploitation of public office for personal gain became a general practice, and those who failed to take advantage of their opportunities were likely to be considered naïve or stupid rather than admired for their honesty.

The laws of the Indies were replete with rules and admonitions concerning the welfare of the Indians, but seldom were they enforced or serious attempts made to carry out their spirit. The wide discrepancy between legal precept and everyday practice early became a fundamental characteristic of the Spanish legal and administrative system. This, as well as abuse of office for personal gain, became a common part of the culture. The tendency to correct one unenforceable statute by enacting an equally unenforceable new one may have salved the conscience of many a member of the Council of the Indies, but the tradition it fostered was an unhappy one to pass on to the new nations that emerged in the first quarter of the nineteenth century.

PORTUGUESE INSTITUTIONS

Portuguese administrative institutions were much less elaborate than those developed by the Spaniards. A *Conselho da India* comparable to the Council of the Indies was created in Lisbon in 1604, during a period in which the Spanish and Portuguese crowns were united, but it never assumed the power or significance of the older body in Madrid. A governor and captain-general had been appointed earlier, in the middle of the sixteenth century, to give an element of unity to the extended Brazilian settlements and better to equip them in co-ordinating their efforts against foreign interlopers, but many years were to pass before the region took on the aspects of a single domain. The numerous but widely scattered fazendas provided the nuclei of colonial life and society until the early eighteenth century when the discovery of mineral wealth and increasing urbanization created new centers of activity and major concentration points for commerce and industry.

Abuse of power was no less a problem in Portuguese America than in the domains of Spain. The decentralized administrative system was generally ineffective in coping with it, and such efforts as were made frequently ran counter to the selfish interests of the fazendeiros whose demands for cheap and abundant labor were seemingly insatiable. Conflicts between landholders and established authority in the coastal urban centers were common. Resort to violence in the settlement of such issues was frequent, and the entire colonial period was an era of considerable turbulence. Those who suffered most were the Indians, whose early disappearance in the coastal areas was marked by steady increases in the prevalence of African population and culture. Servitude was the common lot of the lower classes, whatever their racial origin, and those who benefited were frequently the lesser officials whose immediate contact with an exploited populace enabled them to gain advantage after advantage with a minimum of risk.

CHURCH AND STATE

A highly significant aspect of both Portuguese and Spanish administration was the unity of church and state. Royal officials were at the same time the representatives of both the secular and religious prerogatives of the crown. Officials of the church were employed in high governmental office as aides and counselors of the various monarchs, and they served in important posts in America. It was by no means uncommon for a high prelate to become a viceroy in the Spanish dominions, and members of the clergy of lesser rank participated regularly in civil as well as ecclesiastical affairs. The significance of this relationship can hardly be overestimated, for it gave religious sanction to royal authority and helped bind the allegiance of wayward individuals to the empire. An act against the king might well be interpreted as an act against religion and the church, and few indeed were those willing to challenge so imposing a hierarchy of temporal and spiritual power.

To the religious were entrusted important functions of a cultural and humanitarian nature, as well as responsibility for the spiritual well-being of the populace. Education was entirely in the hands of the church, religious influence predominating even in the universities where theology was a principal course of study. Hospitals, asylums, and other charitable institutions were all operated by one religious order or another, and in the later years of empire a number of the religious establishments entered vigorously into the economic life of the colonies.

Heresy was punishable through the Holy Office of the Inquisition, and church and state joined in the enforcement of religious orthodoxy. So intimately related were religious and secular administration that only the more knowledgeable and better educated could possibly draw the distinction. To the masses of the population they were one and the same. In this union were bound up the seeds of many a conflict in the years to come. The end of royal authority terminated the patronage relationship between the state and the Pope in Rome, and the liberalizing influences of the Enlightenment openly challenged the theocratic aspects of governmental authority throughout the Americas. A long and painful struggle between church and state was thus bequeathed to the independent nations of Spanish America. The lesser power of the church in Brazil spared that country a similar heritage.

THE ROLE OF THE MUNICIPALITIES

In the early days of empire, municipal government constituted a significant aspect of public life. As in contemporary Spain and Portugal, elected councils enjoyed considerable authority and freedom in the management of local affairs. Indeed, before the establishment of the audiencia and the office of viceroy, municipalities constituted the legal repositories of royal power. Appointed governors and *adelantados* were far too busily engaged in new explorations and conquests to concern themselves seriously with civil administration except when they needed legitimization of their actions. Thus for a brief time municipal government played a significant role in consolidation of the conquest and in giving legal sanction to steps taken to extend it.

In subsequent years municipal authority declined, local government functions were restricted to relatively minor housekeeping chores, and municipal office came to be viewed as so unimportant that it was permitted to pass into the hands of creoles. In many instances, the post of councilman (*regidor*) was sold to the highest bidder, and thereafter proprietorship became almost hereditary. This is hardly surprising, however, for the principal families of a community tended to monopolize local authority and office in Spanish and Portuguese America just as they did in the colonies of Great Britain and France.

Municipal authority was frequently reasserted in times of crisis and disaster, such as might be occasioned by foreign invasion, serious epidemic, or natural calamity caused by flood or earthquake. In these circumstances, recourse was often had to a *cabildo abierto,* an open meeting in which the leading citizens of the community joined those already constituting the town council in deciding what course of action to take. The use of such a popular meeting as a deliberative forum became extremely important in the years just prior to independence when the authority of the mother country had been challenged on the Iberian Peninsula by the armies of Napoleon, and British naval forces severed communications with the homeland for months and even years at a time. In more normal times, however, municipal councils did little beyond providing such local services as cleaning the streets, maintaining order, and operating public markets and slaughterhouses. Occasionally they would petition higher authority for special benefits or redress of some grievance.

The Management of Economic Affairs

From the early days of empire the American dominions of both Spain and Portugal, as well as those of France and England at a later date, were viewed as economic preserves of the crown. The prevailing system of mercantilism ordained that all trade and commerce with colonial regions would be the exclusive monopoly of the home country. In the case of Spain, this meant for many years the Kingdom of Castile. At the very opening of the sixteenth century, there was created the *Casa de Contratación* or House of Trade to control commerce and navigation with the Indies. This institution, functioning at the port of Sevilla and later at Cádiz, existed until the close of the eighteenth century and was primarily responsible for maintenance of the trade and communication monopoly with Spain's American possessions.

From the outset, economic enterprise in Spanish America was extractive in nature and involved the transfer of mineral wealth from the rich deposits of gold and silver in Mexico and Peru to the homeland. The process was much the same in Brazil, except that the products of colonial enterprise were fine woods and sugar until the discovery of diamonds and other mineral wealth in Minas Gerais at the opening of the eighteenth century. In return for the minerals and raw materials shipped to Europe, Spain and Portugal sought to sell to their colonies finished goods of domestic manufacture. This pattern of economic dependency became a rigid feature of colonial policy and was carried over into the independence period with little modification, although new entrepreneurs were involved and new products entered the commercial traffic. So rigid was the Spanish effort to guarantee a market for Spanish products in the American colonies that even the planting of grape vines and citrus trees was prohibited in the New World, a prohibition violated repeatedly.

Neither Spain nor Portugal was able to maintain its mercantile monopoly for long. Both lacked domestic industry to produce the products essential to the interchange. Soon both Cádiz and Lisbon were mere interchange points through which the American products flowed on their way to England, France, and the Low Countries; and the goods that moved westward in Spanish and Portuguese bottoms came from factories situated far to the north of the Iberian peninsula. As the years passed and both Spanish and Portuguese naval power declined, it proved impossible to maintain even the monopoly of transport. England became a principal trader with Brazil, and because of her dependence upon the British market for the sale of her wines, Portugal had to acquiesce in this arrangement. Spain, on the other hand, struggled to enforce her monopoly with diminishing success until the end of the colonial era. In the meantime, contraband had become a way of life in many of the colonies, and British, Dutch, French, and some Anglo-American vessels traded throughout the Caribbean area with little fear of Spanish interference in the later years of the empire.

Particularly significant in the mercantile system of Spain was its system of corporate organization. Commercial guilds, known as *consulados,* established themselves at an early date in the few ports open to legitimate commerce: Sevilla and later Cádiz in Spain, Veracruz and Acapulco in Mexico, Panama on the Isthmus, and Callao in Peru. Through their hands passed virtually all the legal commerce of the Indies, and their members grew rich, as did a number of Andalusian landlords who early served as their creditors. Other guilds soon came into existence to control, regulate, or monopolize such additional forms of economic activity as mining, sheep raising, and the important mule trade. Powerful vested interests soon dominated governmental policy and opposed any changes that would have weakened their stranglehold on Spain's mercantile activity. The guilds came to enjoy quasi-official status, providing government-type services and acting on behalf of the monarch in such important functions as the collection of revenues. Their resistance to modernization of economic and commercial policy in the eighteenth century seriously hampered the efforts of Spain under Carlos III to revitalize the imperial system, thus delaying needed reforms and hastening the day of the guilds' own demise.

The guilds were not corporations in the modern sense, but they set a pattern of monopolistic enterprise in principal sectors of the colonial economy. They pointed toward a pattern of corporate economic structure in which those engaged in similar or related activities tended to identify with each other in the promotion and defense of sectoral interests to the extent of discouraging competition, influencing government policy, and carrying economic community of interest into the social sphere. Protection of such interests in government policy and legislation was to remain a feature of the economic and political life of the new countries long after independence.

Both Spanish and Portuguese revenue systems focused imperial taxation on extractive industry and the movement of commodities in commerce. Sub-surface and mineral rights belonged to the crown, and exploitation involved payment to the royal treasury of a fifth of the value of the products removed. Import duties and transaction taxes, particularly one known as the *alcabala*—a sort of 10 per cent sales tax—were major sources of royal income, as was the tithe collected for support of the religious functions of the state. The sale of benefits, licenses, and offices produced lesser amounts of income. Indian tribute was a significant form of taxation during the later centuries of the Spanish empire as the encomienda disappeared. Effective taxation of real or personal property or of earned income was largely missing from the revenue structure.

Treasury practices and the tax structure passed with little change from the imperial systems to the independent nations that replaced them. Export taxes as a means of extracting income from the sale of raw materials abroad was a natural outgrowth of the mercantile system that had so long held the American realms in its grip. These grew in significance in the nineteenth century as agricultural products replaced minerals as the principal source of export earnings in most countries.

The Wars of Independence and Those Who Led Them

Late in the eighteenth century Spain began to arm her colonies for their own defense through the creation of troops of local militia. Heretofore significant bodies of military forces had been conspicuous by their absence except in northern and southern frontier areas after the early period of conquest. Repeated attacks by British naval forces and the fear of overland invasion by the French and British in North America suggested the necessity of better preparing for armed resistance in defense of the empire. Creation of militias was a risky step to take, for it involved the mobilization of creole regiments whose acquired military capability might possibly be turned against the Gachupín overlords. This at first did not seem a likely possibility, and the ejection of a British expeditionary force from Buenos Aires in 1807 by locally recruited troops under creole leadership was a reassuring event.

Opportunity for young creole gentlemen to embark upon a military career was not a significant possibility within the Portuguese and Spanish imperial systems. Military officers were, with few exceptions, chosen from the promising families of the Iberian peninsula. The creation of creole militias suggested the possibility of some modification in the traditional pattern, but the important chance to pursue a military career was opened wide to young creole aristocrats by the French Revolution and the Napoleonic Wars that followed. Numerous young men found their imaginations captivated by the stirring events that began in Paris in 1789 and soon propelled Napoleon's conquering armies to the Elbe, to Egypt, to the Danube, and throughout most of Western Europe, including Spain and Portugal. At first Spain's alliances with Napoleon made service with the French an acceptable form of military adventure; and the democratic character of French recruiting practices encouraged a few would-be soldiers among the Spanish American creoles to enlist. Francisco Miranda of Venezuela was one who served the French emperor on the field of battle, and he took advantage of his opportunity to drink deeply the French wine of 'Liberty, Equality, and Fraternity.' Soon he was thinking in terms of such benefits for his native land. Simón Bolívar, another Venezuelan aristocrat who happened to be residing in Europe during the early years of Napoleon's success, found his sensibilities profoundly stirred by the events he was witnessing, and soon he was willing to join Miranda in an attempt to overthrow Spanish authority at home.

On the other hand, Napoleon's invasion and conquest of all but a tiny portion of Spain created an entirely different set of circumstances. A creole fighting with the Spanish army against Napoleon was an able young Argentine, José de San Martín. He learned his military tactics exceedingly well, for he returned to Argentina to take command of an army of raw recruits which he trained to function as a first-class fighting force capable of defeating the finest troops that the Spaniards were able to throw against him up and down the west coast of South America.

Important as was the continuous warfare in Europe in the indoctrination and training of a few creole army officers, far more significant was the disruption of Spanish and Portuguese colonial rule that eventually ensued. Latin America was far from prepared to challenge Iberian control and authority at the turn of the century. Only a few hotheads dreamed of such a possibility. When Spain was overrun, however, and Napoleon's brother was placed on the throne in Madrid, the colonies were virtually forced to shift for themselves. Quickly self-governing *juntas* were formed, each declaring allegiance to their captive king, Fernando VII; and the major colonial capitals became the nuclei of new states. The Portuguese monarchy moved from Lisbon to Rio de Janeiro, and Brazil immediately became the focal point of the Portuguese empire, an impressive role that was soon to produce Brazilian independence and launch the country firmly on the course of stable monarchy.

Upon the restoration of Fernando to the throne of Spain in 1814, the many juntas that had 'pronounced' in his name were given short shrift. Instead, Spanish military forces were quickly reinforced and campaigns were launched to restore absolutism throughout the area. Bitter warfare ensued. The battle was essentially a struggle of the creoles against the peninsular Spaniards, with mestizo and Indian forces used as pawns by both factions. The major campaigns raged throughout Venezuela, Colombia, and Ecuador in the north, and in Chile, Peru, and Bolivia along the west coast of South America. Bolívar finally achieved victory in Nueva Granada and moved south to join up with San Martín, victor of the Chilean and Peruvian campaigns. San Martín withdrew after a brief meeting with Bolívar at Guayaquil, in Ecuador, and thereafter the forces from Nueva Granada under Bolívar and General Sucre completed the campaign of liberation in Bolivia. Spain made no attempt to carry her efforts at reconquest into the

Río de la Plata area except for minor and unsuccessful thrusts southward and downward from the heights of Charcas.

The independence movement in New Spain was of a different character. There the movement for independence early took on the aspect of a social revolution in which Indian masses led by priests fought against all established authority. Spanish forces put down the insurrection and held the country firmly for Fernando after his return to the throne. A conservative reaction against the social upheaval so narrowly averted provided strong support for royalist authority. Then suddenly Fernando lost control once again in Spain and was forced to submit to the authority of the Cortes and to the liberal constitution promulgated at Cádiz in 1812. The conservative forces in New Spain, fearful of another blood bath, merged their interests and under the leadership of Agustín Iturbide, declared Mexican independence.

The wars of independence in Spanish America created an entire generation of soldiers, for the campaigns that began in 1809 and 1811 did not end until 1826. An elite leadership with high patriotism and democratic ideals conducted the long campaigns that ended in victory for the republican forces. It soon passed from the scene, however. In its place there emerged in every important sector numbers of lesser military men, some who had served as officers under San Martín and Bolívar, others who had been only common soldiers. These men, creoles for the most part and some of mestizo origin, had tasted the fruits of victory and found the flavor to their liking. They stepped forward to lead the new and weak republican governments, and military power emerged with them as a dominant factor in the political life of the new countries.

2

The Responsibilities of Nationhood

> The land, it is true, belongs to large proprietors, but they do not form a
> class of men who, having a common and solid interest in the country,
> constitute a sort of natural aristocracy, concerned to preserve order, and
> make the government stable. . . . What is wanting in these countries
> is a sufficient number of citizens who have no personal ends to se-
> cure, and nothing to get out of the government, except good administra-
> tion. . . .
>
> JAMES BRYCE *

Problems of Independence

CO-OPERATION DURING WARS

The independence of the Latin American nations was achieved by a substantial amount of mutual aid and co-operation. Had such co-operation
been lacking, the various national uprisings might well have been crushed
one by one. As it was, Argentine troops participated in the liberation of
Chile and then, with Chilean aid, moved north against the Spanish in
Peru. Colombian and Venezuelan units struggled together against the large
armies that Spain sent to hold the viceroyalty of New Granada, and once
victory had been attained they turned southward toward Quito, Lima, and
the final defeat of the Spaniards at Ayacucho. Only in New Spain, Brazil,
and Argentina were the battles for independence won without substantial
aid from some other portion of the rebellious colonial domains. A further
exception must be made for Haiti and the Dominican Republic. There, at
one point or another, both British and United States forces became involved in the independence movements as a result of conflict with the
French; but both island republics in the final struggles achieved indepen-

---

* *South America, Observations and Impressions,* The Macmillan Company, New
York, 1929, pp. 532–33.

28

dence without direct foreign aid. A few regions, Central America, Paraguay, and Argentina, were not visited by the main bodies of European troops sent to hold the colonies. They owed their good fortune, however, to the successful action of the independence forces in those other areas where Spain, in particular, chose to concentrate her efforts to retain or reconquer her vanishing dominions.

Political and military co-operation was highly informal, however. No joint congress met to give orientation and central direction to the forces fighting in the field, or even to decide upon a declaration of independence. No commander-in-chief was chosen to lead the armies. Well-planned and co-ordinated military campaigns were the exception and not the rule. When the last important battle had been fought and the last Spanish flag hauled down, no precedent or firm basis for political co-operation had emerged, to say nothing of the possibility of political union. Instead, the colonial jurisdictional divisions—viceroyalties, captaincies-general, and presidencies—became the natural entities of separate statehood. This outcome, lamented by many Latin Americans at the time, was inevitable. Those who looked with envy upon the union effected among the former British colonies of North America failed to take into account the relative homogeneity of those neighboring states fronting upon the North Atlantic. They underestimated the centrifugal political forces arising from the scope, diversity, and grandeur of the vast domains that had belonged to the kings of Spain and Portugal. They overlooked how closely the North American union had come to failure in spite of geographic proximity and community of interest. Likewise, few at the time noted the comparative finality of Latin American independence, once it had been achieved.

RECOGNITION AND SECURITY

The United States began its independent existence surrounded by potential foes. To the north were the British settlements in Canada and Quebec. To the west and south were the possessions of Spain in Louisiana and Florida. France was known to have designs on Louisiana even after its transfer to Spain. To the east, across the Atlantic, was the erstwhile mother country, still powerful and still the mistress of the seas. Her failure to evacuate forts in the western territories as she had agreed to do and her constant agitations among the Indians raised serious questions as to whether reconquest might not be attempted should England find herself momentarily relieved of the pressure exerted by her traditional foes in Europe. The actions of British naval commanders on the high seas in forcing American sailors to serve under the royal flag did nothing to dispel the fears of the new republic.

With the defeat of the Spanish army at Ayacucho, on the other hand, the reconquest of Latin America became unlikely. No continental foothold remained to the Bourbon monarch. Neither Spain nor Portugal, nor even France, possessed a suitable base in the Western Hemisphere from which an attack upon any of the continental nations might be launched with any hope of real success. Except for minor outposts in the Guianas, in Honduras, and in those Caribbean islands still in the possession of European powers, Latin America formed a single geographic unit north to the Mexican border, a unit surrounded only by water. And on the water Britain stood guard, openly opposed to any move that might be undertaken by a concert of European powers against the independence of the Latin American states. Thus freed of any immediate peril to their new status, the new nations lacked external stimulus to cohesion and union. The independent peoples had far more to fear from each other than from alien encroachments from across the seas.

Naturally, the refusal of Spain, Portugal, and France to grant immediate recognition to the independence of their former colonies continued to be cause for some concern and left open the question of their eventual intentions. Such vague uncertainties were of little consequence, however, in influencing the political evolution of the new states. The political fragmentation that characterized the continents by 1830 became a fixed pattern, except in Central America where the forces of disunion had yet to run their course. External pressures receded ever further into the background and internal problems came to occupy the center of the stage.

TYPE OF GOVERNMENT

By far the greatest internal problem throughout all of Latin America was political, that of government. Each of the new states was more or less free to decide for itself the nature of its future governmental structure once the yoke of the mother country had been cast off. Nevertheless, many problems attended the making of this decision. What groups in the state were to be heard from? Who was to speak for these groups? Where were the voices to be heard? What were the principal choices and alternatives? To none of these questions were immediate answers available, except in Brazil, where independence caused no break in the continuity of government. In many respects, answers must be sought in the nature of the revolutionary movements and the course of the ensuing struggles, for these factors and events predetermined in major part the character of future political institutions and at the same time rendered academic many of the issues raised in the polemics of the era.

None of the major figures of the independence era lived to see his ideas put into effect. Hidalgo did not last long enough to make clear his plans for Mexico after independence. Morelos, on the other hand, expressed a number of ideas which were to remain part of the liberals' program for a century. He wished to see the end of privileged groups or classes, and equality between all racial groupings. He believed that Mexico required a powerful chief executive, but he also favored rule by law. Morelos has often been called an agrarian reformer, but his desire to break up the haciendas of the royalists was a war measure rather than a program for reform. Iturbide, who finally led Mexico to independence under the Plan de Iguala, was opportunist rather than a political theorist. He was probably more intrigued with the thought of being an emperor than he was convinced that constitutional monarchy was a desirable form.

Bolívar, though determined to eliminate all vestiges of monarchy, advocated a chief executive who was, in effect, an absolute ruler. At first Bolívar was hostile toward the church, but the overwhelming difficulties he encountered in governing New Granada induced him to co-operate with the clergy. His outlook was as practical as it was idealistic, for he knew his countrymen well, and he had no illusions as to their readiness for self-government.

Bernardo O'Higgins, who had received part of his education in England, was convinced that it was useless to change laws until Chilean society had been changed. Like Bolívar he believed that a dictatorship was necessary to prevent anarchy during the interim. His ideas concerning the abolition of primogeniture and entail, separation of church and state, and the promotion of commerce and education, were all adopted by later generations after being wholly or partially rejected during his own lifetime.

Bernardino Rivadavia of Argentina was another independence era statesman who had definite ideas of the course that should be followed. Like O'Higgins, he was respected but not loved, and he also faced opposition from all segments of society. He also articulated ideas that would be adopted later in the century, for he was ahead of his times.

José Bonifácio de Andrada of Brazil believed in a powerful rather than a democratic monarchy. He was convinced that Brazilians would not be able to govern themselves successfully until the Negro slaves were free and both Negroes and Indians had been incorporated fully into Brazilian life. The slaves were ultimately freed before the end of the century, and in the same period Cândido Rondon dedicated his life to bringing the wild Indians peacefully into the mainstream of Brazilian life.

As far as the Spanish colonies were concerned the first revolutionary undertakings stemmed directly from the Napoleonic invasion of Spain. Uprisings were originally oriented toward the maintenance of legitimacy with respect to the ruling family. Submission to the usurper, Joseph Bonaparte, was regarded as impossible. Had Fernando VII in 1808 followed in the steps of the Portuguese regent, João, and transferred the seat of his authority to the Western Hemisphere instead of submitting to the French invaders, it might have been possible to maintain intact the institution of monarchy in the colonial kingdoms, regardless of the outcome of events on the peninsula. Fernando, it has been noted, made no such move, but, along with his father, became the captive of the French emperor and turned a deaf ear to the clamor of colonial cabildos and juntas declaring their allegiance to him and renouncing the authority of the French-dominated government in Madrid.

Once restored to his throne Fernando made it perfectly clear that he had no intention of treating his American kingdoms as other than the subject colonies of Spain. The die was thereupon cast not only for independence, but against monarchy as well. The revolutionary juntas of Spanish America had separated, far more sharply than their forerunners in British North America, the two issues of submission to the mother country and her internal governing bodies and submission to the royal authority of the monarch. Both the British and the Spanish colonies reached the position at one point in their respective controversies where co-equal status with the mother country under a common monarch was regarded by many as a desirable solution to the conflicts arising out of colonial-metropolitan relations. The point was much clearer in Spanish America because the legitimate ruler had been deposed by a foreign interloper and the mother country conquered by the invader's troops. The monarch could simply have moved to another of his kingdoms. When, however, Fernando identified himself irrevocably with Spain and upheld her jurisdiction over the empire in the relationship of master to subordinate, the two issues merged as they had in British North America and independence from both mother country and king became the point of controversy.

A few revolutionary leaders favored the establishment of republican governments in Spanish America from the outset. An important republican movement existed in Brazil when independence was declared in 1822. In spite of the North American precedent, these people must have been considered extremists by a sizable percentage of their contemporaries, for the monarchical system was deeply rooted throughout the civilized world, and in Latin America it had the powerful sanction of religion to support it in the minds of even the humblest citizens. Consequently, it is not surprising that early steps were taken to preserve the institution of monarchy even though the Spanish king was rejected. Popular sovereignty was a useful theory that had taken firm hold upon the minds of many Latin American intellectuals, as is evidenced by the widespread use of the argument that once the monarch had been deposed sovereignty reverted to the people. Few, however, understood its real connotations or were willing to see the theory applied to domestic political life. Monarchy was still favored as a governmental form even by many who espoused popular sovereignty in theory and who had just participated in the overthrow of a king with the best of family credentials. Particularly was this the case with such thinking leaders as Bernardo Monteagudo, Manuel Belgrano, and José de San Martín of Argentina, Bernardo O'Higgins of Chile, and Lucas Alamán of Mexico. These men looked about them and perceived signs of social and political disintegration on all sides. In the establishment of a strong constitutional monarchy they and others thought they saw the possibility of arresting the steady drift toward social convulsion and political anarchy.

No sooner was the question of new monarchies seriously raised than the hopes of the monarchists were dashed to the ground. Eligible scions of Europe's royal families saw better than did their American supporters the risks and hazards, if not the utter futility, of accepting an American throne. A delegation from La Plata received a cold reception upon its arrival in Europe for purposes of negotiation with the royal houses. No one wished to set up his kingdom in a land where popular factions had shown their willingness to take government into their own hands. Neither were potential candidates anxious to fly in the face of the Spanish king by accepting the throne of one of his rebellious dominions. As the wars of independence dragged on and the republican forces of Bolívar possessed themselves of one Spanish stronghold after another in South America, the question of monarchy failed to hold much interest. In Mexico, the un-happy experience with the would-be emperor, Agustín Iturbide, served to demonstrate the futility of such a system both to the Mexicans themselves and to potential monarchs in Europe. By 1830 the issue of monarchy was quite dead and republicanism was triumphant in every country except Brazil.

The impossibility of maintaining a monarchical form of government in the new Spanish American states by no means meant that democratic re-publics were to be established. It meant, on the contrary, that for decades to come Latin America was to constitute a remarkable proving ground for costly experiments in self-government. These experiments again and again ended in failure in that they did not succeed in providing stable and effec-tive political systems. Of course, it cannot be assumed that under a mon-arch the new states would have fared any better. Brazil under monarchy did achieve a comparatively stable and effective political system and was able to make the transition from colony to independent statehood with ease. The fact that Brazil was blessed with two able leaders of the Bra-gança line gives no assurance that any other American country would have been equally fortunate, however. Thus, while the form and nature of the Spanish-American revolution did extirpate the seeds of royal authority, this in itself cannot be looked upon as a misfortune nor as a prime reason for the political confusion that followed. Indeed, thereby was eliminated a bone of contention that remained a disturbing factor in European political life for yet another century.

If kings were not to rule in Latin America, who was? To this question the revolutionary wars provided a real though temporary and not very sat-isfactory answer. In the early days of the revolutionary movements, cabil-dos and juntas formed of the prominent citizenry of the various communi-ties assumed the reins of government. These bodies could hardly be called democratic or even popular, for their composition favored the well-to-do, the military, the religious, and the intellectual elements to the exclusion of virtually all others. They were status rather than elective bodies. They soon gave way, however, to the military leaders who conducted the cam-paigns and fought the battles against the Spaniards. These were the real governors who emerged to rule the new nations of Latin America. But these too soon passed from the scene and political life descended to a bru-tish struggle for power among those who could muster sufficient military support to compete. This was the sorry picture coming into focus in Latin America by 1830.

Factors of Instability

The factors that made the road toward effective self-government in Latin America so tortuous are numerous and complex. Any listing of them is certain to be incomplete, and few will agree as to which were primary and which secondary in importance. Also, in retrospect, it is easy to confuse the issues of stable government and democracy, the basic requirements for which are not necessarily the same. In 1830, few Latin Americans were concerned with the practical application of the democratic ideal. It would have been enough if government could have been rendered stable and tolerably benevolent, minus the trappings of royalty and foreign domination. Thus, such commonly mentioned problems as large unassimilated Indian groups, general illiteracy, and lack of popular experience and education in self-government did not in themselves make stable government impossible, although they did present a milieu in which popular democracy was out of the question. This was well recognized by most of the revolutionary leaders, and few indeed were the serious advocates of handing political power over to the masses of the people.

IRRESPONSIBILITY

Probably the greatest single factor predisposing the new republics to unstable government was the absence of a real sense of responsibility at any point in the social structure after Spanish authority was withdrawn. The social system was, during the colonial period, essentially manorial, and so it remained after the independence wars were over. Wealth and social status were based upon the possession of land, large tracts of land upon which the aboriginal classes toiled in virtual servitude to the owners. The system, fostered in the days of the encomienda, nevertheless lacked many of the attributes of European feudal life. The pattern of property relationships did not constitute an articulated system once the Spanish monarch was removed from the picture. More important, however, was the fact that the possession of property had not, under the Spanish administrative system, carried with it political responsibility. Authority had been centered in the hands of peninsular Spaniards sent out to the colonies to enjoy the benefits of the chief administrative posts. Creoles, while they might and did become wealthy landlords and property owners, were excluded from most positions of political leadership. The cabildos, where the creoles were permitted participation, were of almost no importance, for their activities were so circumscribed by the rigid detail of Spanish legislation that the posts of regidores came to be regarded as largely honorific and were sold to the highest bidder, thus subverting not only the elective nature but the representative function of these municipal government bodies. In marked contrast to the native-born aristocracy of British North America, the creole aristocracy of Latin America played little or no political role in the colonial government. Its status was safeguarded for it by royal authority, and its only important struggle was against that very authority for a more generous share of royal benefices.

As already indicated, it was the creole aristocracy that furnished the leadership in the movement for separation from Spain. It was the cabildo, the political body in which they were represented, that first took up the question of self-government when the Napoleonic armies overran Spain, and the cabildos served as the legislative bodies of many of the colonies during the long struggle for independence. This proved, however, to be little more than a passing phenomenon. Leadership quickly passed to the chief military figures, and when the wars were over it was they who were calling the tune. The creole aristocracy, seemingly natural successors to political authority, were in utter confusion as to their political role. This upper layer of the social structure was itself unstable, a class ill-prepared to govern. It lacked experience, yes; but much more important, it lacked cohesion, purpose, and above all, a sense of responsibility.

The wealthy creole families made major sacrifices and substantial contributions in both men and money to the cause of independence. Sons and heads of families proved their courage on the battlefield and became popular heroes with the lower classes as a consequence, but few indeed were those willing to sit down to the gruelling task of giving their country an honest, effective government. There was perhaps more tragedy than wisdom in the statement of San Martín upon leaving Peru that 'the presence of a fortunate soldier, however disinterested he may be, is dangerous to newly established states.' An even greater danger to such states existed in the tendency for those who had shown constructive leadership during the revolutions to relinquish that leadership when the glory and glamour was past, letting it fall into the hands of those less capable and far less disinterested.

The wars of independence tore out by the roots the stabilizing influence of royal authority, leaving in its place a vacuum that the creole aristocrats were unable to fill. How quickly the revolutionary leaders passed from the scene. By 1830 virtually all were dead or in exile, either forced or self-imposed. In country after country government passed into the hands of lesser military chieftains whose principal interest seemed to be that of imitating the former Spanish rulers and amassing fortunes for themselves. The wealthy, the educated, the able, retired to their estates, eschewing the responsibility that their place in the social system and their role in the revolutionary wars had cast upon them.

This was a well-nigh fatal mistake if stable government were to prevail in the new republics. In 1830, and for several decades thereafter, virtually every country paraded military leadership in government; but the leaders were not those who had commanded the great revolutionary armies. Instead, they were the lesser officers, trained in violence, captivated by their own importance and the attractiveness of their uniforms, but lacking the noble purpose and the broad outlook of the principal figures who had directed the course of the revolutionary struggles. They did not form a corps of officers inured to the rigid disciplines of European military castes. The chaotic revolutionary struggles had not molded men into disciplined forces. Rather the wars had placed a premium on independent action, personal glory, and heroism for its own sake. Thus the young militarists were extreme individualists, in most cases incapable of working together with others of their own kind, and they were motivated by an intense interest in politics and a desire to exercise political power. The rough and undisciplined heroism that had characterized the Spanish struggle against the Moors and the early battles of the conquest centuries before was reborn in the new republics, and no stable forces, political or social, raised a hand to restrain it.

CASTE SYSTEM

The rigidity of the social caste system posed further difficulties that delayed the establishment of stable government. The distinction between the poor and the wealthy was too great, the gulf too wide to be easily crossed; no strong middle class existed to bridge the gap. Latin America was and has continued to remain essentially rural. City dwellers were composed in part of the land owners who resided away from their land, but whose interests remained irrevocably attached to the soil that constituted the source of their wealth; in part of the commercial people engaged in supplying the needs of those who could afford to buy; in part of small shopkeepers and hand manufacturers; and finally of vast numbers of hand laborers and servants whose livelihood was gained from the work they performed in the homes and shops of those more fortunately situated. Race joined with Old World social values to stamp indelibly upon these groups their respective roles in social and political life. The Indians predominated on the lower rungs of the ladder; and in the middle, seldom rising above the status of shopkeeper or small merchant, we to be found the mestizo and the poor white immigrant. The lines separating these social and economic groups, indistinct as they were in some cases, were not easily crossed. Had the lower or even the middle-level groups dared assert themselves, there were no channels of peaceful political expression, and a benign priesthood lost little opportunity to instruct the ignorant lower classes in the virtue of accepting their miserable lot.

In the countryside, the social and economic differences were even more sharply defined. There existed only the large estates and the ill-fed and ill-housed Indians who worked on them. In the more primitive regions were the Indian communities from which the corregidores of the past had long since extracted the last measure of self-respect in the interest of the tribute, the mita, and their own pocketbooks. Enforced military service in patriot and royalist armies during the revolutions only added one more burden to the already overburdened aborigines.

MILITARISM

In such a social environment constructive political leadership was lacking unless the creole upper classes were to furnish it. When they did not, other forces took over. The military was regarded as a noble profession. It offered an avenue to advancement that carried none of the social stigma associated with the trades and commerce. One did not have to be wealthy to enter it. In the new republics it was not sufficiently well organized to have an established hierarchical structure with the officer class at the top open only to the wealthy and the well-born. Personal valor and strength and above all, the ability to command others and attract a following offered promise of success. Coupled with a sortie into the political arena, military life even offered the possibility of wealth and social recognition for those who could never make the grade by any other means. Many were those who chose such a course, and great was the chaos they created and the havoc they wreaked upon their long-suffering countrymen.

Thus the political atmosphere of the new Latin American nations was charged with unrest. Those who might have provided stability and leadership shirked their responsibilities. Men schooled in the violence of the revolutionary wars, who were avid for power, who were seeking a means to break through the arbitrary restrictions of the old social order, these possessed themselves of the political power of their states. Government became a plaything in their hands, albeit a lucrative one provided they could successfully meet all challengers and maintain their positions of authority.

It was inevitable that the struggles of the military chieftains centered around the office of president. It was the office that controlled the military forces, the office from which appointments were made for the entire public administration, the office that dominated all government activities. With the death of the revolutionary cabildos, the role of legislative bodies in government became a mockery. Membership in the various national congresses was dependent more often than not upon the whim of the executive, and such bodies as did attempt to exercise legislative prerogatives soon learned that silence was the better part of valor. Legislative strength can exist only where strong and politically conscious groups seek expression of their interests through representation, and for this no precedent was to be found in Latin America. Furthermore, since no balance of social forces existed, the interests of the powerful and wealthy were better served by means other than debate. Without the participation of the prominent citizenry, the congressional discussions of national problems on the part of those with little social or economic power could be nothing more than a waste of breath. Thus the executive was left supreme.

Backed by the army and the police, ignored or patronized by the wealthy, the military officer who achieved the top executive office could propose and dispose as he saw fit. If the imprudence of his actions caused alarm, some other caudillo could easily be found who by means of intrigue and violence would take his place. In the meantime, the power of the state and usually its treasury were at his disposal. He might leave his office rich and respected, as a few were shrewd enough to do. More likely he would end his days in exile and poverty because he did not pick the opportune moment to retire. Nevertheless, more than one Latin American family owes its fortune and prestige to the fact that some obscure ancestor chose the military road to the presidency of his country.

It is a dark picture painted of a dark era. The years between 1830 and 1860 were far from happy ones for most of Latin America. They were years of retrogression and chaos, of almost constant warfare, both international and internal. The names of Santa Anna in Mexico, Santa Cruz in Bolivia, Carrera in Central America, Flores in Ecuador, and Rosas in Argentina will long be associated with the turbulence of this unfortunate epoch. These were the more successful. Many did not last long enough to be remembered except by the most meticulous historian.

CONFLICTS OF IDEAS

Interwoven in the pattern of power struggles throughout the Latin American countries during the first decades of independence were the conflicts over ideas, rights, and status. The problems that gave rise to these conflicts too had their roots deep in the soil of colonial life and were nurtured by the blood of patriots during the independence movements. The revolution from Spain, while perhaps prematurely consummated because of conditions in Europe, was no accident. Nor were the wars themselves simple struggles between creole and native forces on the one hand and Spanish soldiery on the other. Large American elements were active in both camps, and when the wars were over the opposing groups still remained. Issues that had divided the colonies on the question of independence continued to divide the new nations in their domestic politics. It would be absurd to assume that the influence of the French and American revolutions terminated once independence had been achieved and new governments established, for the ideas of individual rights and human liberties espoused in all three great revolutions were given constitutional embodiment throughout Latin America. The status of Latin American society, characterized as it was by great social and economic inequalities among the people, made the application of these ideas hazardous, difficult, and to some extent impossible. Nevertheless, most leaders gave at least lip service to equalitarian and democratic principles, and in spite of the great turmoil that prevailed in government and in part because of it, step after step was taken to break down the bastions of the old order. These steps did not create political democracy, but they eliminated a number of the legal and social impediments to democratic development.

The Spanish regime had been a centralist regime in which local interests had frequently been subordinated to the interests of larger units and to the empire as a whole. Independence was a signal for the local interests to assert themselves, as was clearly indicated by the pattern of statehood that emerged. The tendency to seek the smallest possible political denominator did not terminate at the confines of the new political jurisdiction, however; in many localities it carried to an extreme localism, justified and defended by reference to the successful federalism that had so recently come into being on the North American continent. In many cases, such as that of Brazil, Mexico, Argentina, and Colombia, vast territory and poor communications, coupled with considerable local variation in economic activity and tradition, made some form of local political autonomy seem most appropriate. Where conceded, and in the absence of strong national representative institutions, it had the disastrous effect of providing unimportant military chieftains a natural base for getting their feet firmly under them before undertaking the stepping-stone march to the national capital. At the same time, because government was hardly representative at any level, local autonomy did little to aid the cause of democratic development. It did provide the basis for much political disagreement and all too often for internal warfare.

ROLE OF THE CHURCH

Almost from the day of independence in each country, internal cleavages appeared as to what the role and power of the church should be. Aside from constituting a theoretical question stemming from eighteenth-century religious controversy, it was a very practical question. During the period of the empire, the viceroys had exercised the ecclesiastical patronage in the name of the king. Now there were neither kings nor viceroys. Upon whom would the duty fall? Ultramontanists asserted that the prerogative reverted to the Pope and his ecclesiastical representatives while others firmly espoused the natural carry-over of the regalist doctrine that the authority once held by the king passed on to the new state as his successor. Few were concerned with the possibility of a separation of church and state, for the functions of the two were inextricably intertwined. With a few very notable exceptions, the representatives of the church had supported the Spanish crown against the colonies in the independence struggles. They had opposed the revolutionary doctrines upon which the new governments were founded, for they foresaw that those doctrines would inevitably give rise to a challenge of the many privileges and special rights enjoyed by the church. Thus, in the eyes of many, the organization of the church was a carry-over from the empire, an extension of the system that the revolutions had been fought to extirpate. The slowness of the Vatican in recognizing the independent governments and the insistence of papal representatives on upholding the authority of the Pope in matters of church patronage did much to confirm this view. Consequently, many joined in attacking the church, some sincerely and from conviction, others in the hope of profiting from any steps the state might take to restrict the power and wealth of the religious organization. Vast numbers supported the church, believing in its sacred role and opposing the revolutionary ideas that in their minds verged on heresy. Many saw their own rights and privileges challenged along with those of the church, and common interest caused them to cast in their lot with the clerics. A major division of opinion ensued, an inextricable factor in the politics of the new republics.

Because no benefices could be filled until the Vatican recognized the new republics, and because many of the incumbents died or fled, there was a serious shortage in the clerical hierarchy, with disastrous effects on the lower clergy. In some areas the church's influence never was fully restored.

Under the conditions that prevailed after independence, all factions engaged in controversy naturally sought to widen the orbit of their influence and to affiliate or form alliances with other factions of similar or related interests. The maintenance of order through strong government seemed a more certain protection for the church than risking anarchy as a consequence of weak central authority. On the other hand, such major cities as Buenos Aires and Bogotá turned out to be strongholds of political liberals and anticlerical intellectuals who, when in power, utilized the central authority of the state to attack church privileges and prerogatives. Consequently, church alignments with other groups engaged in political controversy tended to vary with local circumstances. Strong central authority was favored if those in power were political conservatives sympathetic toward the church. If, as was the case in Colombia and the Plata region, the centralists were anticlerical, the church without hesitation threw its influence behind the more conservative advocates of federation from the provinces. In Central America, where federation was a centralizing tendency as contrasted with the separatism of the several states, the church opposed federalism and supported the separatists, for the federal or liberal party under the leadership of Morazán showed itself strongly anticlerical. As time went on, a pattern emerged showing two opposing groups—a pattern encountered generally throughout Latin America. One group was centralist in political orientation, somewhat liberal in its social outlook, and anti-clerical in its religious views. The other was federalist, conservative, pro-clerical, and highly militaristic. However, in the considerable number of countries where liberalism had little foothold and anticlericalism was but a minor issue, the church commonly supported the strongest and most dictatorial of centralist regimes. This arrangement most closely resembled the old order with royalist central authority and church power supporting and complementing each other.

The manifestations of developing political factions, while general, were not universal. Caudillismo, which emerged during this period and has continued in some regions of Latin America to the present day, was virtually dead in Chile by 1830, scarcely appeared at all in New Granada, and did not establish itself in Venezuela until a later epoch. The problem of centralization and decentralization in government was a most important issue in Mexico, Central America, New Granada, and Argentina, but of much lesser importance elsewhere, except in Brazil where the existence of a fairly stable monarchy tempered the issue measurably. In almost all areas the church issue was beclouded. Nowhere did anticlericalism at first mean anti-Catholicism, much less opposition to religion, although as the struggle continued, anti-Catholicism emerged. Opposition to the church meant opposition to certain aspects of its activities or to some of the activities themselves: the conduct of business enterprises, preoccupation with politics, the enjoyment of special legal privileges, control over the civil status of individuals and over education. Within the church the secular branch clashed with the religious orders, particularly with respect to the operation of schools. Ardent anticlerics and members of the Masonic lodges in Mexico and Brazil experienced no great difficulty in upholding the Roman Catholic religion even though the bishops were denouncing the lodges to which they continued to belong as heretical and ungodly. Latin America was experiencing an era of confusion characterized not only by political chaos but by chaotic thinking as well. Very little was clear, well-defined, or concise.

Much of the turmoil, however, was on the surface. History is written about those who make history, who bring about change and alter the course of human events. Little is said about those who continue at their daily tasks generation after generation in the humbler levels of society. The few years of revolutionary warfare had not erased the work of centuries. The adoption of new constitutions did not improve the living standard of the impoverished Indian or Negro, nor did it reduce the incidence of dysentery, tuberculosis, or venereal disease, which continued to decimate the population. The Indian continued to toil in his field or in the field of his hacendado, using the same methods of cultivation, the same tools, and reaping the same harvest as had his ancestors in the centuries preceding. The cobbles of the streets in the cities continued to resound to the crunch of the big wooden wheels of the oxcarts. The miserable waifs of the villages continued to huddle in the church doorways to protect themselves from the chill of the night. Religious processions proceeded regularly from the doors of the churches, made the rounds of the village streets, and returned to the churches followed by long streams of faithful adherents, some in the finery to which their status entitled them, others in the rags of the poor and humble. The strong current of every-day life flowed on, but its pace did not quicken.

ECONOMIC AND CULTURAL DECAY

In the three decades following the end of the revolutionary wars, little material progress or development was experienced in most of Latin America. Life was too hard and insecure to leave a margin for development and new construction. Enterprise languished, and everywhere men were on the defensive against the depredations of the political and military demagogues. In Mexico, the great silver mines that had poured forth their treasure in the days of the Spanish viceroys now stood idle, their shafts filled with water. In Central America, the orchards and fields, the indigo plantations, the rich lands of the monasteries grew weeds while the conscript armies of Morazán and Carrera roamed the countryside in a seemingly endless struggle for military and political supremacy. Venezuela and New Granada were all but prostrate after the devastating wars against the armies of Fernando VII. The wealth and prestige of the once great viceroyalty of Peru was gone, and the national treasury was reduced to dependence upon the sale of bird manure. The bleak highlands of the altiplano saw only the dust of the mounted legions and barefoot stragglers that formed the army of Santa Cruz. Argentina lay benumbed under the heavy hand of Rosas and his secret police, but Buenos Aires continued to grow.

Not only were social and economic life stagnant; the same was true of intellectual activity. Education and the arts were neglected, forgotten in the all-consuming struggle for political mastery. Able men from Argentina and Venezuela found refuge in Chile where the stimulus of their intellects contributed substantially to the welfare and development of that haven of stable government and national progress. Others fled to Europe from whose cultural centers they were able to return and contribute the more to their national literature by reason of their foreign experience.

During the long era of colonial rule, and particularly toward the latter part of the eighteenth century, the Spanish monarchs had shown much interest in the fostering of intellectual and cultural achievement in the Americas. They and their viceroys founded universities, patronized the sciences and the arts, encouraged the beautifying of cities and the construction of public buildings. During the wars of independence such things were quite naturally neglected. In the confusion that followed thereafter, an attitude of neglectfulness tended to become characteristic of many of the new governments. The new political leaders frequently had no interest in such matters, and those who did found little opportunity to exploit that interest. They were too busy maintaining themselves in power, and their public treasuries were drained by the corruption of their administrations and by the necessity of maintaining their military forces.

Any real progress was difficult for other reasons. Most decisions of policy were of necessity negative; that is, they were decisions of status rather than decisions of action. Economic development was 'fostered' if export duties on some product were lowered, or if import duties were raised in protection of some local industry. Education was 'fostered' if schools, closed during the revolutions, were permitted to reopen, or if teachers were permitted to teach with greater freedom than the previous regime had permitted. Finances were 'reorganized' if the public debt was refunded, or, for that matter, if public monies were honestly collected and disbursed for a short time. Progress consisted of words, legislative declarations, speeches, outlined objectives, meaningless reports—seldom of achievement. When a government did undertake some progressive measure, such as the construction of roads or the improvement of port facilities, the ancient bureaucratic machinery carried over from the colonial era often stood in the way. Designed as it had been to protect the king's patrimony from the machinations of wayward administrators, it served effectively to delay and block constructive activity by those who were honest, but it left the door of the treasury wide open to those who cared nothing for the rules or for the interests of the nation. In part these difficulties indicated that while the external yoke of Spain had been cast off, many of the administrative vices of the old regime still insidiously bound the new republics; in part they reflected the dearth of competent leadership.

ROLE OF GOVERNMENT

In Latin America, as in most other parts of the world, including the United States, government in the last century was not viewed as having a positive role to play in the economic or social affairs of the average citizen. It was expected to maintain order, provide a stable currency, uphold justice and the law, conduct foreign relations, and defend the homeland. These were minimum objectives and accorded well with the theory that the least government is the best government, a theory quite different from that of extreme paternalism espoused by the majority of Spanish monarchs. Reaction against the Spanish system and the reluctance of the propertied classes to participate in or accept responsibility for government made the minimum objectives seem adequate to important segments of the population. Unfortunately, when even these limited functions proved to be beyond the abilities of the struggling new nations, private enterprise and initiative could hardly be expected to venture into the field of national development. Conditions were too unstable and the risk of armed depredation and plunder was too great.

In a region where church and state were closely linked, chaos in government could not fail to react upon religious life and religious institutions. Whether it willed it or not, the church was inevitably drawn into political controversy. Its resources were at stake and its control over many traditional functions was threatened. To the complaints against it arising from its attitude during the revolutions were added those created by its support of fallen caudillos, opposition to Masonry, and insistence upon the maintenance of special courts and other privileges. In a number of countries the government turned upon the church and stripped it of much of its authority and no small portion of its property. Treatment was far from uniform from one country to another, but among the measures taken affecting the church were the abolition of special church taxes, abolition of church courts, confiscation of commercial and agricultural properties, secularization of cemeteries, and secularization of education. Many of these steps were justified and in the long run beneficial from the standpoint of those favoring the reduction of the political power of the church. On the other hand, certain important and useful activities suffered in the process. The maintenance of primary and secondary educational institutions had long been considered a church function throughout Latin America. Likewise,

CANADA

Ottawa

Chicago
New York
Washington

UNITED STATES

San Francisco

Los Angeles

New Orleans

Miami
la Habana
CUBA

DOMINICAN REPUBLIC
Ciudad Trujillo

MEXICO

México

BRITISH HONDURAS
Belize
HONDURAS
Tegucigalpa
Guatemala
GUATEMALA
NICARAGUA
Managua
San Salvador
EL SALVADOR
San José
COSTA RICA
Panama
PANAMA

Port-au-Prince
HAITI
PUERTO RICO

Caracas
VENEZUELA
GUAYANA
DUTCH GUIANA
FRENCH GUIANA

Bogotá
COLOMBIA

Quito
ECUADOR

Manáos

P-E-R-U

Lima

B R A Z I L

Natal

La Paz
BOLIVIA

São Paulo
Rio de Janeiro

P-R-G-Y

Asunción

Santiago

Rosario
Buenos Aires
Montevideo

LATIN AMERICA TODAY

0   800
MILES

the church, together with private charities, was expected to maintain hospitals, and to create and maintain the institutions for the helpless and the aged, for the poor and the destitute. While this was true elsewhere as well as in Latin America, the great social and economic distinctions and the very size of the lower classes, particularly the large impoverished Indian population, made the problems so great that the church could not begin to cope with them even under the best of conditions. The attacks upon the church and the depletion of its resources meant the inevitable curtailment of its service and educational activities at a time when the chaotic national governments were ill-disposed and in no way prepared to meet these important needs with state resources. Thus these functions, too, languished and atrophied.

However, the mid-nineteenth century was not a period of total gloom. At least two countries were fortunate enough to escape most of the difficulties that have just been described. Political stability was achieved at an early date, and during the years under discussion a firm foundation was laid for future development and national progress. This was true of Brazil and Chile, and to a lesser degree of Paraguay. Still another nation, Colombia, or as it was then known, New Granada, while convulsed by internal dissensions and repeated fruitless attempts to overthrow the government, nevertheless moved steadily forward in developing its national consciousness, in clarifying divergent political points of view, and in experimentation with organizational devices to meet the needs of a complicated geographic diversification that strained the very bonds of union time and again.

Both Brazil and Chile met well the rigorous tests of nationhood. Firm and enlightened leadership made possible the surmounting of early disorders in spite of the discordant clamors of numerous rebellious spirits. Brazil was indeed fortunate in that independence was accomplished gradually and without long and bloody warfare with Portugal. The country became virtually independent with the transfer of the Portuguese monarchy to Rio de Janeiro, so that when independence was proclaimed fourteen years later by the young Dom Pedro, no interruption in the affairs of internal government was necessary. Neither was there created by the severance a generation of self-seeking ex-soldiers to lead ignorant followers in endless struggles for power. Battles there were over local autonomy, but no single leader was strong enough to challenge seriously the Bragança kings, and those who might have united to overthrow the empire in the hectic days of the second Dom Pedro's infancy saw in the maintenance of royal authority the one firm hope of national solidarity, and to this they gave their support.

Chile, although the scene of extended and bitter revolutionary warfare, drew the early support of its prominent citizenry who were unwilling to cast the hard-won prize of self-government before the feet of self-seeking military demagogues. Astute and able men whose fame and fortunes were not made on the battlefield stepped to the helm and gave to their new state a stable political order that soon became the envy of the rest of the continent.

By mid-century, the independent Latin American nations had endured their most critical and difficult years. Encroachments from North America there had been, and as a result of these Mexico had lost half of her national territory. But the danger of permanent European conquest or domination was long since past. The principal problems were domestic, and toward the solution of these some of the countries had made important strides. In others internal disorder had become so fixed a pattern that it would take years to eradicate it. Such disorders had led and would lead again to international warfare among these nations of common Iberian ancestry. They had brought about and would again bring incidents and punitive intervention by European powers and by the United States. A foolish French emperor was yet to take advantage of chaos in Mexico to establish a short-lived satellite empire there. But these difficulties were part of the long process of achieving national stature. The future held vast possibilities, and those states that had passed their crisis and achieved the creation of a national consciousness were ready to move forward to the building of healthy and stable societies. They could now begin to give meaning to the philosophical concepts of liberty and equality about which so much had been said and written and so little done.

3

The Stability of Moderation: Chile, Brazil, and Paraguay

> Regardless of the form of government, republican society had changed but little in the twenty years which followed the beginning of the revolution; it continued to be almost the same as colonial society during the last years of Spanish control.
>
> LUIS GALDAMES *

Paraguay

DR. FRANCIA

Of all the Spanish American republics, only two achieved a relatively stable political structure shortly after independence. These were Chile and Paraguay. For Paraguay, the problem was simple, for old Doctor José Francia simply assumed the role of father and ruled the relatively small population of the isolated river republic as though they were his children. He accepted no interference, not even by the church, whose ultramontane manifestations he ignored and over whose officials he assumed powers greater than those formerly exercised by the Spanish viceroy in Buenos Aires.

Several factors account for the docility with which the rule of Francia was accepted. The man himself was an active leader whose local development programs produced results and whose stern demeanor inspired both respect and fear among the mestizos and Guaraní Indians who formed the bulk of the population. His army, recruited from the lower classes, developed an intense loyalty to the old caudillo and provided an ample force to

---

* *A History of Chile,* translated by I. J. Cox, University of North Carolina Press, Chapel Hill, 1941, p. 244.

check the ambitions of any creole landowners who might contemplate change in the political arrangements. Of significance also was the remarkable isolation in which the Paraguayans lived and which the paternalistic Francia did everything in his power to strengthen and perpetuate. Paraguay became almost completely self-sufficient, raising its own food and meat and manufacturing such clothing, utensils, and other light products as were necessary to carry on the rather primitive economy to which the people were accustomed. Foreign trade along the great river system that led to Buenos Aires and Montevideo was rigorously restricted to those goods and carriers in which the old dictator saw direct advantage to his continued domination of the country. This is not to imply that Francia was either an exploiter of his people or engaged in amassing a personal fortune. On the contrary, the dictator feared involvement in the warfare and strife that raged all around him in Uruguay and Argentina. He strove to protect the independence of his country and its peaceful existence. In his personal life he preferred the rigors of an almost spartan regimen.

Francia could scarcely be called a benevolent ruler. His was a personal depotism made somewhat tyrannical by the neurotic xenophobia he exhibited in all contacts with the outside world. Initiative and independence were crushed in the dictator's effort to maintain Paraguay as a hermit republic.

In 1840, Francia died. For a time it was not clear just how a peaceful transfer of authority might come about. For almost a year a military junta ruled the country pending the assembly of a congress and the selection of a new chief executive. Congress, reaching for executive stability without tyranny, saw fit to create a two-man executive similar in nature to a consular arrangement by means of which Francia had years before risen to power. As before, however, a strong man emerged to dominate. Carlos Antonio López, one of the pair of executive officers, assumed the leadership and shortly had congress place the government on a more formal basis with a written constitution providing for a president with a ten-year term of office. In 1844, López was elected under the new constitution and the country moved into a more progressive era without having suffered disruption or revolution during the transitional period following Francia's death.

Chile

O'HIGGINS

The political situation in Chile stabilized far more slowly than in Paraguay. As already noted, the period following independence was one of intense strife and almost continual bloodshed. Bernardo O'Higgins had been an able revolutionary leader, and no one has ever seriously questioned his sincere devotion to the welfare of his country. He was not, however, the proper man to soothe the fevered spirits of his fellow-citizens and calm the troubled waters of factional disagreement. Not only were his personal enemies numerous, but he viewed the needs of his country in such a puritanical frame of reference that he alienated many who would otherwise have been his friends. To pacification of the nation and the establishment of political stability he attempted to couple vigorous moral reforms. To restore law and order O'Higgins created strong police units to function over the countryside as well as in the cities, but their instructions were to suppress the use of alcohol as well as to put down sedition and arrest those involved in common crimes. The Chilean president was shrewd enough to realize that speed and sureness of punishment were strong deterrents to would-be criminals and insurrectionists alike. His system of drum-head courts dispensed a rapid and vigorous if sometimes not-so-just justice. But gambling and cock-fighting were considered to be serious crimes along with robbery and rebellion. By his puritanical efforts O'Higgins made himself the butt of many a joke and stirred up a fog of minor indignation. Far more serious consequences resulted from other reform measures that the president fostered, as when he attempted to secularize cemeteries and prohibit the entailment of estates.

All in all, the great Chilean patriot was no politician. His interference with burials angered the church, which was already ill-disposed toward the new republic and its independence leaders. His attempted abolition of entailments struck at the very core of the landholding system of the great families. Chile, perhaps to a greater extent than any of the other new republics, was characterized by an essentially feudal social and economic structure, resembling in many respects that of medieval Spain. Mineral wealth remained largely undiscovered and undeveloped during the long period of colonial rule, and an agrarian society came into existence in the great central valley. Lacking exportable products and cut off from the main stream of Spanish commerce, Chilean landholding families developed a high degree of self-sufficiency on the great estates that became their feudal domains. The crude agricultural implements which were used to till the soil were fabricated on the hacienda, as were household furnishings and much of the cloth in common use. The maintenance of law and order became the duty and the prerogative of the wealthy *patrón*. So did care for the well-being of the *inquilino* and his family. The inquilino was the peasant of Chile, tied to the estate on which he was born by the tenant relationship to the patrón, or landholder, and the bonds of tradition, family life, and personal dependence. When the inquilino or members of his family became ill, it was the patrón who saw to the necessary care. In time of death, marriage, or childbirth, the landholder and his family took care of the necessary amenities, providing for mourning or festivities as the case required. In contrast with other parts of Latin America, the laboring class was of essentially the same racial stock as the wealthy hacendado; for the native Araucanian Indian resisted conquest from the outset and moved southward into the forest lands beyond the Bío-Bío river rather than submit to the invader. Mestizos there were, to be sure, but in Chile the sharp racial distinction between the white proprietor and the Indian laborer existed to a far lesser degree than in Peru, Colombia, or Mexico, for there were far fewer Indians living within the area of white settlement.

The stability of the social structure and the wealth of the landholders depended on holding the large estates together. This was accomplished through the process of entailment whereby a stated heir, usually the oldest son, inherited the property and could not legally dispose of any portion of it. By the time of independence, the best land was monopolized and the system of ownership had come to constitute an economic and social evil depriving would-be agriculturists of any opportunity to acquire suitable land, even though much of it might not be in use. Consequently, O'Higgins' desire to institute reform in the system of land ownership was indicative of his farsighted statesmanship, but he attempted to do too much too rapidly. His puritanical attempts at moral reform lost him the support of the poorer classes, for they interfered with a cherished personal freedom. The inquilino cared little about the system of entailment, but he valued the pleasures of the cockfight and enjoyed an occasional bout with the demon alcohol.

Finally, O'Higgins committed a most serious mistake. His failure to give adequate attention to the collection and disbursement of revenues resulted in a financial deficit that left the soldiery unpaid. Only respect for a great revolutionary figure and the stern measures O'Higgins used to maintain law and order persuaded the populace to endure his government. The endurance proved temporary.

Between 1818 and 1831, constitution making became nearly a profession in Chile. Everyone of political importance had a hand in it. O'Higgins called a convention to draw up a constitution in 1822, and by controlling the selection of the delegates he was able to dictate almost the entire contents of the charter that emerged. Unfortunately, the document pleased only O'Higgins and it never became effective. Rebellion broke out in both the north and the south. Finally, an opposition group in Santiago gained sufficient strength and courage to call upon the now despairing leader to resign. O'Higgins went into exile in Peru, from which point he was able to judge the lasting effects of his revolutionary efforts and assess the failures and mistakes of his adventures as a politician and administrator. He continued in exile until his death in 1842.

O'Higgins' place in Chile was taken by Ramón Freire, a military leader who was able to establish his authority and shortly undertake the creation of another constitution. This time someone decided that federalism was the cure for Chile's ills. The idea had no basis in political precedent or reality, however, and no federalism resulted. Instead, the country was thrown into new turmoil out of which emerged a new convention and a new constitution in 1828. Constitution making had by now become an avocation, and as might have been expected the new piece of paper that fluttered in the 1828 breeze served only as another issue over which the many politicos and military factions could contend.

The period following O'Higgins' resignation and departure was an era of violence as well as an era of political uncertainty and administrative chaos. Until a major battle was fought at the Lircay river in April of 1830—a battle that ended with the complete defeat of Freire and his departure from the Chilean scene—there seemed little hope of rescuing the new nation from the hands of competing caudillos. Independence had come to mean anarchy. Several important stabilizing factors were emerging, however—factors that were to make possible eventual peace and stable national development. For one thing, the issues that divided the politically articulate elements of the population were gradually clarified. Basically there were those who wished to preserve society and national life much as it had been prior to independence, making only those changes that the maintenance of separate nationhood demanded. On the other hand were those who saw in national independence an opportunity to create a new order in society, to bring to fruition the ideals and aspirations of European and North American revolutionary extremists. This latter group proved that it well deserved the derisive title of *pipiolos* (novices) that the conservatives gave it by espousing just such causes as federalism in a country where regional or sectional differences and traditions scarcely existed and certainly had no significant political meaning. Likewise other changes that they advocated were doctrinaire in the extreme, considering the time and the environment and the basic necessity of establishing independent nationhood.

Conservative Rule

ERA OF PORTALES

The *pelucones,* or bigwigs, as the conservatives were called, were the realists of revolutionary Chile. Whatever one may think of their politics in retrospect, they were the group that best recognized Chile's immediate needs and they set about to create a governmental system that would provide the necessary stability, respect for law and order, and an increased though limited amount of individual freedom. In 1833 a new group met to revise the 1828 constitution, a group dominated by Diego Portales, a conservative businessman who had moved from a ministerial position into effective dictatorship of the country in the period following Freire's military defeat and exile. It proved impossible to arrive at a satisfactory revision of the 1828 fundamental law, and the convention ended by drafting an entirely new document. The fact that the new constitution went into effect and endured for over ninety years may be taken as an indication that the framers performed their service well. However, one needs only to compare the new document with the older ones to realize that the differences were of little consequence. Any one of the charters might have become the favored instrument had it been launched under the proper auspices and at a time when the populace was in a properly receptive mood. The key to the success of the conservative effort was the fact that strong leaders adopted moderate yet firm policies that were in basic accord with the reality of social and economic conditions as they existed in Chile in the 1830's.

Diego Portales was a most important factor in effecting the transition from the chaos of military caudillismo to progressive conservatism. As the head of Portales, Cea, and Company, the dominant mercantile house in Valparaíso and Santiago, he felt more sharply than the conservative landholder the need for a stable political system within which the commercial activities of the country could be expanded and developed. Likewise, he lacked many of the personal ties that linked many of the wealthy hacendados to each other and to various of the factions in the armed forces. Portales was, in reality, an upstart, a *nouveau riche,* whose great financial power gave him status that he could not claim by reason of birth or education. He had other attributes that stood him in good stead. He possessed boundless energy, firm decision, and courage. As is so often the case with successful businessmen he distrusted the intellectual and the theorist. In Chile in the year 1829, this distrust was also in Portales' favor; the intellectuals had proved they could talk and fight, but they had yet to demonstrate that they could administer a government.

Portales entered political office as a minister of several cabinet portfolios, including foreign relations, war, and navy, during the regime of a temporary junta created by congress in 1829. He quickly assumed a position of direct dominance of the government, and between 1829 and the inauguration of the new constitution in 1833, he was effectively dictator of Chile. His first major effort was to reduce the military to size by ridding the armed forces of all liberal-tinged officers who had supported either Freire or O'Higgins, as well as any others who might become troublesome to his civilian government. Then the entire public service was similarly purged. Liberal writers and the liberal press were silenced, and a conservative, aristocratic oligarchy moved to the ascendancy in public life. The regime continued to be dominated by Portales, but its policies accorded well with the desires of the church and the conservative landholders of central Chile. The constitution approved in 1833 was highly centralist, restrictive as to suffrage, and paved the way for strong presidential leadership of a conservatively oriented, two-house congress.

General Joaquín Prieto was the first Chilean president elected by the stable conservative regime. For a time Portales remained in the cabinet, but once Prieto was firmly in control of the government, he resigned and returned to live in Valparaíso where, as governor, he continued active in politics and proved a bulwark to the new administration. Prieto, at the insistence of Portales, adopted policies designed to make of Chile a strong commercial power in South America. The port of Valparaíso was greatly improved and its dock facilities enlarged. Favorable tax treatment was also used as a device to lure foreign merchants into the developing Chilean port first and, if possible, to the exclusion of the Peruvian port of Callao. The financial position of the government improved greatly with political stability, and for the first time since independence, Chile began to take on the characteristics of developing nationhood.

The reversion to a strongly centralized regime dominated by a conservative oligarchy was not a change that liberal elements could be expected to accept without question. A period of consolidation was required during the early stages of which the country might easily have been thrown again into bloody inter-party strife. Two factors worked strongly in favor of the conservatives, however. First, Diego Portales had been remarkably thorough in his early efforts to centralize control over the army in the government at Santiago and to destroy the loose relationships that enabled military commanders to develop what amounted to personal armies within the military establishment. Second, the government which Portales and Prieto provided was remarkably honest and reasonably efficient. Liberal sympathizers might decry the suppression of free expression and bemoan the absence of social and economic reform measures, but they could nevertheless take pride in a government whose positive and constructive measures gave tangible evidence of sincere devotion to the nation. Furthermore, opportunity soon arose to utilize the unifying cement of conflict against a common foreign enemy.

From Peru the ousted Freire plotted to overthrow the conservative government in Chile; but by the time his aspirations had reached the military stage the government was too well seated to be lightly brushed aside. Freire was soon defeated and became one of the political exiles on Juan Fernández island, far out in the Pacific. But Freire had received aid from the Peruvians, and had been conveyed to Chilean soil by Peruvian warships. Portales, now returned once more to Prieto's cabinet as minister of war, viewed with alarm the conditions he perceived beyond the desert and mountains of the northern frontier. One of Bolívar's old campaigners, General Santa Cruz, had made himself dictator of Bolivia, and in 1835 he brought about the unification of Peru and Bolivia under his authoritarian rule. Weak as were both Bolivia and Peru, their southern neighbors, Chile and Argentina, viewed this combination as a disruption of the balance of power and the potential threat of a more ambitious unification program. The support given by Santa Cruz to Freire, even though indirect, provided tangible evidence that the Bolivian dictator might view his role in history to be that of reconstituting as a single political entity the new republics that had once formed the viceroyalty of Peru. In any case, Portales counseled war, and late in 1836 Chile issued the declaration.

One can only speculate as to what elements constituted the complete matrix of Portales' interest in the conflict. Perhaps he and Prieto viewed a foreign military adventure as an antidote for internal political ills. Perhaps he was enraged by Peruvian measures aimed at blocking Valparaíso's development into the chief Pacific port of South America. Perhaps the desire to put an end to the potential threat of Santa Cruz was his and Prieto's only consideration. In any case, the military undertaking was viewed in Chile with strongly mixed feelings. No doubt some feared defeat, for the combined forces of Peru and Bolivia were far superior numerically to those of Chile. Others saw no threat in Santa Cruz and felt that their government was embarking upon an unprovoked military aggression. Feeling in opposition to the war ran sufficiently high that when martial law was declared it provoked considerable clamor and open sedition in some quarters. There was mutiny in the army, and Portales fell a victim of the tumult he had created, assassinated by soldiers of his own country.

The shock felt throughout the nation as a consequence of Portales' murder was profound. Portales had never been popular, but his ability and resourcefulness had earned him great respect. His death, quickly attributed by his friends to an enemy plot, served to rally the Chilean public behind the government. Prieto continued the struggle with renewed vigor, and by 1839 his field commander, General Manuel Bulnes, defeated the Bolivian dictator. The victory of the Chilean army promptly brought the downfall of Santa Cruz and collapse of the Peru-Bolivian confederation. Chile had been aided early in the war by an Argentine force sent into Bolivia by Rosas, but the final victory was achieved by Chileans alone after the Argentine forces had departed in defeat. Thus Chile could claim for herself full credit. The southern republic was well on the way to the development of a strong military tradition, and a new pride was engendered in the body politic.

Prieto had been elected to a second term in 1835, and thereby a tradition as to presidential succession was established; the 1833 constitution permitted the re-election of a president for one additional term after his initial five years in office, but further re-election was prohibited. Prieto took advantage of the full electoral opportunity permitted him by law, and for several decades others followed this same pattern without interruption. General Bulnes succeeded Prieto by the outgoing president's choice. Bulnes in turn, after ten years in office, secured the election of Manuel

Montt, his minister of education. Every five years, of course, the constitutionally provided election was held; but the restrictions upon the suffrage,
the good times that prevailed, and the general popularity of the outgoing
president assured his re-election or the election of his chosen successor.
Thus Chile was ruled by a conservative self-perpetuating oligarchy. Perhaps it might more appropriately be called an aristocracy, for it ruled generally in the interest of the nation. Political morality was maintained at a
high level, finances were soundly managed, and the national and international credit of the country was firmly established.

SOCIAL PROGRESS

Chile's conservative leaders were not so conservative that they took no interest in social progress and gradual change, even when change meant a
shift in the old political and social order. As early as Prieto's administration there was an active interest in education and a special administrative
department of the government was created to foster it. Only higher education was involved, however, for elementary instruction remained a function
of the church just as it did elsewhere in Latin America and in a major
portion of the United States. Even greater progress in education was made
during the administration of Bulnes when Manuel Montt was Minister of
Education. The latter set about founding numerous new educational institutions. Included were a reorganized National Institute in the capital, various secondary schools, and even a considerable number of primary
schools. Institutes for study of the special trades were also created for the
lower classes. As was true everywhere at the time and in many places
throughout the world even today, few were able to take advantage of the
educational facilities thus created. There were neither schools nor teachers
in sufficient number to approach even remotely mass education. The Lancastrian method of instruction, introduced in Chile during the presidency
of Freire, had as one of its principal innovations the extension of educational opportunities to larger numbers of students by enlisting the aid of
the more advanced to instruct the beginners. It involved primarily, however, a change in the mechanics of teaching that made possible the better
utilization of talent where instructors were too few. It did little to change
the social philosophy that recognized little value in educating the ignorant
masses beyond the rudimentary formalities of Christian doctrine. Manuel
Montt and a few other Chilean leaders were far advanced in their social

outlook, and they carried Chile ahead of her neighbors in the educational field, but even after the progress of the 1840's and 50's a genuine system of universal public education was something only dimly perceived in the far-distant future. There is little to indicate that the liberal politicians of Chile had any broader view of the educational role of the state than did Montt and his conservative supporters.

Bulnes and Montt, in contrast to Portales and Prieto, had little fear of new ideas or free expression of old ones. Under their administrations the restrictive measures of Portales were relaxed and ignored. Chile became a mecca for the intellectuals of other lands where the political environment did not favor their efforts. Andrés Bello of Venezuela was one of the first outstanding educators who identified himself with Chile and contributed in a major way to the intellectual climate of Santiago. There he for a time served as director of a colegio, edited a government periodical, and exerted his influence on behalf of cultural advancement and development. During the 1840's many more men of letters came to Chile, refugees from tyranny in other lands. They included such outstanding figures as Domingo Faustino Sarmiento and Vicente Fidel López of Argentina, Juan García del Río of Colombia, and Andrés Antonio Gorbea of Spain. Under their influence Chilean intellectual life was stimulated and a generation of native scholars prepared to move to the fore in the years to follow.

ECONOMIC DEVELOPMENT

Chile made considerable progress economically under the stable rule of the conservative aristocrats. The restrictive alcabala tax was eliminated and tariff laws were revised so as better to accord with Chile's economic needs. Mining became an activity of increasing importance owing to the discovery and exploitation of rich silver veins. Of greatest importance, however, was the tremendous increase in commercial activity. In late colonial times and on into the period of independence Chile had produced considerable agricultural wealth. Large sections of the country were ideally suited to orchard crops and much fruit was grown. The marketing system of the region was extremely poor, however. Not only was adequate transportation lacking in the matter of roads and waterways; marketing was simply not an organized activity. The large estates were virtual feudal manors subsisting upon their own products and the meager manufacturing skills of the workmen who resided there. Only the rich owners purchased in a wider market, and these purchases consisted largely of the luxuries imported from Europe. Prieto, Bulnes, and Montt each gave support to progressive measures aimed at tying the country together economically and opening the interior to commerce. Construction of roads was undertaken, and eventually, during the administration of Montt, the first railroads were built. Paralleling the development of land communication facilities was the development of ocean commerce. Extensive warehousing facilities built by Portales had lured many ships to Valparaíso during the 1830's. Then, in 1840, an American, William Wheelwright, started a steam navigation line between Chile and Peru. This same engineer was instrumental in beginning construction on the first rail lines a decade later. These commercial and facilitative improvements were of great importance, for by mid-century Chile was fast becoming a country of considerable commercial standing. Independence and able statesmanship strengthened a trend already under way in the closing days of the empire for Chile to replace Peru as the chief commercial center of western South America.

The discovery of gold in California in 1848 proved a tremendous boon to Chile. The many ships that now rounded the Horn on their way to the 'treasureland' of California stopped at the Chilean ports. Not only did Chilean products provision these vessels, but great quantities of foodstuffs were shipped to San Francisco to feed the hungry population there. The reopening of isthmian commerce and the construction of a railroad at Panama eventually caused a sharp reduction in the importance of Chile's new-found market, but the country had enjoyed a great commercial stimulation which left lasting benefits in terms of national development.

Forty years after independence, Chile had achieved much. The country was unified and relatively prosperous. Cultural life was well advanced; no other Spanish American republic could boast of an educational system comparable to that of Chile. The southern republic had engaged in successful foreign warfare and acquitted itself well. Political life, while subject to occasional violence, was remarkably stable. The ruling aristocracy passed the reins of presidential power from one leader to another decade after decade through the process of peaceful election, restricted and controlled though the suffrage was. Chile had taken the first important steps toward national maturity: the achievement of a stable social and political order. The republic prospered, and by mid-century new immigrants flocked in from Europe to share the benefits that it provided and to make their contribution to the developing nation. The newcomers were primarily Germans of a liberal bent who fled their homeland as a consequence of the social and political unrest attending the 1848 uprisings and subsequent repressive measures of the German principalities. The immigrants settled primarily in southern Chile around the city of Valdivia, and soon the countryside blossomed forth with new agricultural products—products grown on middle-class farms rather than on the grand estates of wealthy hacendados. A new and stabilizing element had been introduced in Chilean society.

Paraguayan Progress

THE SUCCESSORS OF FRANCIA

On a much smaller scale and with a considerably more primitive political system, Paraguay moved forward under the rule of Carlos Antonio López. As had Bulnes and Montt in Chile, so López encouraged educational development in Paraguay. The restrictive isolationism of Francia was replaced by a policy of commercial intercourse with the country's river neighbors. Wagon roads were cut through the jungles and the river ports were opened to all nationalities. Communications were further improved during the 1850's by construction of a telegraph system and the building of a short railroad.

Paraguay's problems were substantially different from those of Chile, or, for that matter, from those of almost any other of the new Latin American republics. The region had stood still or retrogressed in the late colonial period and there was little left of the creole population that had once made of Asunción a major river outpost of Spanish civilization. There were few great estates and few wealthy hacendados; much of Paraguay had been built originally on the basis of communal Indian settlements operated by the church, and these, disrupted and abandoned as a result of the intrigue between Portugal and Spain in the late colonial period, had reverted to wilderness. Paraguay did well to claim and to uphold its independent status, for it possessed few of the elements of nationhood. Nevertheless, López did a remarkable job of building a Paraguayan nationality upon the base prepared by Francia. One of his more important methods of welding the country together was through a widespread primary education system whereby the children, Indian, mestizo, and creole alike, gained the rudiments of an education. Hence came the oft-repeated boast of the Paraguayan of that era: 'I am Paraguayan: I can read.' Lacking in Asunción, however, was the intellectual flowering in the arts and sciences and in literature that became characteristic of Chile. Instead, the country came increasingly to resemble a great hacienda of which the president was the owner and whose interest in development was essentially that of improving one's own property and estate.

López had his problems, however. In 1855 a colony of French founded a settlement called Nuevo Burdeos at the edge of the Chaco region. López found himself in difficulties with France, which country protested the treatment received by the colonists. With Brazil López had a boundary dispute; with the United States there was an incident involving an attack upon an American naval vessel engaged in a river survey. With Argentina there was continuous difficulty, for the dictator Rosas refused to recognize Paraguay as an independent nation. In anticipation of an eventual attempt to conquer the region by either Brazil or Argentina, López set about to build and equip a sizable army and a small navy to sail on the river system. López developed a rather formidable little fighting force, and true to the patrimonial system of which he was the head, he placed his son, Francisco, in charge of it and made him minister of war. Thus Francisco was groomed to succeed his father and given the means of guaranteeing his domination of the country in the event of his father's death. In 1862, Carlos Antonio López died, and the congress assembled to elect Francisco for a ten-year term. Francisco was soon to destroy all that his father had created and to bring his race and his country very near to extinction. The patrimonial system had made possible an early stability in Paraguay, but it provided no broad basis for democratic development. There had been no institutionalization of law, order, and progress such as the Chilean conservatives had achieved.

Brazil

DOM PEDRO I

Just north of Paraguay, but far across the continent from Chile, another recently liberated nation had advanced at least as spectacularly as had Chile. Externally the conditions under which that progress was made were quite different. Brazil was a monarchy, the only monarchy in the Western

Hemisphere. In contrast to the narrow and extended coastal strip that formed the Chilean homeland, Brazil was a vast and diverse continental region far larger than the United States in 1830 and still larger than the great North American nation after the latter had filled out its continental frontiers at mid-century. Brazil was a land of marked regional variation, not only in the sense that geographic extent and difference in latitude and elevation created regional peculiarities, but also in the sense that the many population centers, remote from each other and poorly linked by non-existent or inadequate communication facilities, had each developed its own peculiar interests and outlook. Chile, on the other hand, while extended over many degrees of latitude, was characterized by a concentration of population within the confines of a relatively limited area of the central valley that paralleled the coast. Major centers were linked by ready access to ocean communication. Both countries, however, had by mid-century achieved remarkable political and social stability and were to be regarded as centers on the South American continent of cultural and intellectual advancement. No other Latin American countries could claim such achievement.

Brazil owed much to its erratic monarch, Pedro I. In spite of his many weaknesses, his devotion to the pursuit of the opposite sex to the neglect of duties of state and the good name of the monarchy, his autocratic refusal to permit more than a figment of popular participation in government; in spite of these drawbacks and to some extent because of them Dom Pedro I served as a rallying point for Bazilian patriotism. He it was who declared the independence of the Portuguese American state and who maintained the pomp and elegance of a European court amid the tropical splendor of Rio de Janeiro. He it was who held the Brazilian state together in the hour of its independence and who provided a unified and effective government in the years that followed. Then too, in spite of the raised eyebrows, the whispered rumors and the open criticism that Pedro's amorous antics caused, there can be little doubt that behind the façade of piety existed a frank admiration for the monarch's virility and bedroom accomplishments.

Dom Pedro's downfall was largely attributable to those whom he assumed to be his friends, the Portuguese gentry with whom he surrounded himself. If the Brazilians were to have a monarchy and pay the price of supporting it, they should at least enjoy the emoluments of office and the tokens of prestige that monarchy afforded. Suspicion grew as the years went by that the real interest of Pedro's friends, if not of the emperor himself, lay in the Portuguese homeland and the possibility of reconstituting a single realm. Likewise, the refusal of Dom Pedro to permit a broader participation in the affairs of state fortified republican sentiment, strengthened the adherents of federalism, and aroused a general animosity against the insolent favorites of the imperial court. The final cabinet crisis and desertion of the army that led to Dom Pedro's abdication was basically a reassertion of Brazilian nationalism and independence far more than a rejection of the emperor himself or of the institution that he represented.

Dom Pedro's position in the early days of April, 1831, just prior to his abdication, was weak. Nevertheless, he might have aroused sufficient support to put up a defense and attempt to retain his throne. The fact that he chose not to do so is to his credit, for his eventual defeat would have been only a matter of time and the institution of monarchy certainly would have gone down with him. As it was, by choosing self-denial and exile, the emperor was able to preserve the monarchy and to pass on to his young son the Amazon throne, giving to Brazil in the act of his abdication the most able executive leader in its history.

THE REGENCY

Dom Pedro II was less than six years of age when he became emperor, and it was necessary to name a regent. At first a committee was formed, but after four years of executive confusion the committee gave way to a single regent, a priest named Diogo Antônio Feijó. Padre Feijó was a powerful figure who had dominated the government as minister of justice since the abdication, but as regent he was less successful. He resigned after two years in office and was replaced by Pedro de Araújo Lima, a leader of the Conservative party.

The period of the regency was a period of great stress and strain for the young monarchy. It was virtually an interregnum, for no single firm hand was at the helm of state. The tides of republicanism and caudillismo surged about the infant prince and only by a thread was the empire held together. Even the monarchists were divided, for a strong group favored the recall of Pedro I to act as regent for his son. The possibility of the exiled emperor's return was never very real, and there is little to indicate that Pedro himself ever seriously considered such action. All his failing energies were devoted to securing for his daughter, Maria da Glória, her title to the Portuguese throne, a title usurped by Pedro's brother, against whom the exiled monarch plotted in Paris and whom he eventually ejected. Shortly after his successful campaign in Portugal, Pedro died, thereby removing one of the divisive factors in Brazilian politics. His American adherents joined their forces to those of the *moderados* who were supporting the constitutional monarchy and the regency. The new Conservative party that emerged from this union greatly strengthened the hands of those who were working to retain centralized government under an imperial court at Rio de Janeiro.

More of a threat to the monarchy than the out-and-out republican faction were the various proponents of federalism. The federalist principle found expression in two ways. Both the *exaltados,* a branch of the Liberal party, and the republican elements clamored for federalism in the press, and the former group used every opportunity to advocate it in congress. More serious were the provincial manifestations that expressed themselves in open rebellion. Revolt sputtered feebly in Pará and died out; but in Rio Grande do Sul it burst into open flame and consumed the resources of the province and the central government for over a decade. Intermittent strife broke out in Bahia and Minas Gerais. In the face of such opposition, the regency, conservative and centralist in political alignment, moved cautiously but effectively. In the congressional maneuvers at the capital it gave way. In 1834 the now famous *Acto Adicional* was adopted, granting representative legislative bodies to the provinces in place of the former consultative councils. The new assemblies were given considerable local authority, including the right to levy taxes and disburse funds. Provincial presidents continued to be appointees of the crown, however. The Additional Act, as an amendment to the Constitution of 1824, proved to be a sufficient concession in the direction of provincial autonomy to make possible a clearing of the air, and the issue of federalism gradually faded as a matter of immediate political significance.

The constitutional change might have proved quite ineffective in achieving stability had not the regency taken firm military action in the provinces at the same time that concessions were being granted in the capital. The efforts to put down forcibly the rebellion in Rio Grande do Sul were not immediately successful, and the struggle dragged on until five years after the new emperor had ascended the throne and taken up the reins of state. Finally, military pressure and increasing fear of Rosas in Argentina caused the *farrapos* (residents of the southern province) to consider the advisability of a reconciliation. Elsewhere, however, the regency was more immediately successful in meeting the seemingly never-ending crises of local insurrection. One by one rebellious movements in the provinces were crushed, and the supporters of federalism were forced to take what satisfaction they could in the limited local self-government provided them in the Additional Act.

DOM PEDRO II

Neither the concessions to local government nor the military successes served to quell the general feeling of discontent with the regency. The regency was an expedient made necessary by the infancy of the monarch, but it suffered the additional weakness that it was exercised not by a member of the royal family, but by a politician whose claim to the role rested upon personal prestige and the continued support of a conservative coalition. A steadier hand was needed, a hand with less personal interest in what it touched. Consequently, early accession of the young monarch was postulated by members of the opposition, led by Antônio Carlos de Andrada, a leading figure in the chamber of deputies. At first the regency opposed the move, fearing loss of control by the Conservative party. In the end, no other move seemed possible and the national assembly declared young Pedro of age and proclaimed him emperor of Brazil. Late in July of 1840, while still but fourteen years of age, Dom Pedro II took the oath of office and swore to uphold the constitution. Once again Brazil had a reigning monarch.

Had the new Brazilian emperor proved as autocratic as his father or as prone to play favorites, his accession to the throne would have provided little relief from the country's political difficulties. But Dom Pedro II was an entirely different kind of man. Young as he was, he was remarkably mature both physically and intellectually. That he was able to take the reins of government firmly in his hands and deal vigorously with the experienced politicians who surrounded him and who continued to struggle for national leadership was a great tribute to his common sense, his astuteness, and above all to the confidence he enjoyed in the eyes of the people. The new monarch did not allow affairs to continue drifting as they had in the last years of the regency. He set about to establish order in the provinces by military action and by political manipulation, and within five years even the dissident elements in Rio Grande do Sul had submitted to firm imperial rule. He replaced many provincial presidents with strong men of his own choice who were pledged to uphold law and order, yet he was generous in granting amnesty to those who had taken up arms against the regency.

Under Dom Pedro Brazil enjoyed many of the benefits of democracy, yet there was little doubt as to who was the real ruler. Life and property were reasonably secure, and personal liberty was certainly as great or greater than in any other country of Latin America. Popular participation in government was hardly to be expected on any significant scale, however. This was true not so much because the country was a monarchy, nor even because of any disposition on the part of the nation's leaders to prevent popular participation. Rather, the machinery of popular government was undeveloped. In a vast country of mixed races, dispersed population, and great ignorance and illiteracy, government remained the province of the aristocratic few. In the absence of a tradition of local self-government, there was little soil in which popular political forces could take root. Brazil experienced no counterpart of the democratizing movements that swept political control from the hands of the tideland aristocrats in the United States during the 1830's. Under a monarchy, of course, the stakes of political victory were not so high; and the centralized government of Brazil necessarily limited the advantages of political success at the provincial level.

Dom Pedro was shrewd enough to form no permanent alliances with either of the principal political factions. The liberals rode to power with the monarch's accession to the throne, but the conservatives were soon again in control of the national assembly—a control, however, to which they were unable to lay permanent claim. The emperor played one faction against another, one leader against opposing leaders; and while seeming to hold himself aloof he succeeded in keeping the balance of power firmly in his own hands. He did not provide great leadership in bringing about social or economic change, but he provided a stable political environment that facilitated sound national development on many fronts. Brazil was still a pioneer country, a rough country in which the pomp and display of an imperial court contrasted almost obscenely with the primitive crudity of life in the back country where the raucous influence of the gold-rush days was still to be felt. The anomaly of a stable monarchy in a frontier wilderness guided serenely along its course by a firm, kindly, unpretentious scion of a European royal family was not lost upon contemporaries. The crowned heads of Europe looked on and wondered.

The imperial court at Rio de Janeiro under the second emperor presented a marked contrast to the gaudy display of earlier days. Three years after ascending the throne Dom Pedro took as his wife an Italian princess, daughter of King Francis I of the Two Sicilies. Married by proxy, the young woman soon made the long journey to the royal husband she had never seen. She was warmly received by her new subjects as well as by the emperor, who took his marriage vows far more seriously than had his father. Throughout his long reign, Dom Pedro's domestic life was exemplary and the court gossips found little about which to waggle their tongues. The simple modesty that characterized family life at Guanabara Palace was also typical of state affairs. Dom Pedro had little interest in regal display, seldom appeared in uniform, and made little or no effort to popularize himself with the tools of glamorous exhibitionism so skillfully wielded by his parent. So lacking in color was he that in later years of his reign he was often referred to as the 'gray' emperor. What the emperor lacked in flashiness and popular appeal he made up in other ways. He was a native Brazilian with no ties to the fawning Portuguese nobility who in former years had sapped the substance of the royal treasury. The Brazilians were his people and were treated as such, and none had cause to question the honesty and sincerity of the emperor's concern for their welfare.

Perhaps during the first half of the nineteenth century Brazil was still too much of a frontier country to devote much attention to literature and the arts. Perhaps the transition from colonial status to national independence was too easily accomplished to evoke the talents of men who might have taken up the brush or pen in portrayal of the longings, sufferings, and aspirations of the people. The fact remains that little literary or artistic effort was forthcoming in the early days of independence or in the years that followed. Dom Pedro II was noted for his intellectual accomplishments and his interest in the sciences and arts. As a patron of intellectual and artistic pursuits he did much to raise the stature of Brazilian social life in the capital. But his efforts bore fruit in later years, and at mid-century the country could not claim, as could Chile, important strides in literature and education. As a home of exiles from all over the continent, Chile profited by the influx of talented men. Brazil attracted few such people. The country was absorbed in the physical aspects of living, the conquest of the wilderness, the mixture of races, the advent of new settlers from Europe.

In common with Chile, however, as well as with the United States, Brazil enjoyed during the early years of independence the concern and devotion of a public-spirited aristocracy. These leaders, conservative in outlook, were at the same time progressive in their approach to national development and realized that only through a government characterized by stable and orderly processes could the welfare of the nation be secured.

4

Tyranny and Confusion: The Dictatorship of Juan Manuel de Rosas

> . . . for this is not the first time in history when prodigality in the distribution of honors has stimulated public men until they reached the level of tyrants.
>
> JUAN MANUEL DE ROSAS

Four Argentinas

POLITICAL INSTABILITY

The first twenty years of independence were disastrous years for the Plata region. All the perils that seemingly could have attended the establishment of a new and independent nation proved mighty rocks upon which the Argentine ship of state pounded and crashed, apparently bent upon utter disintegration. One by one outlying provinces of the former viceroyalty slipped away to form independent governments of their own, aided in their escape by the constant warfare that raged across the pampas, up and down the great river valleys, and across the turbulent waters of the great estuary. Brazil was an avowed enemy; Britain was unfriendly and had aided in securing the independence of Uruguay; but most devastating of all was the turmoil that prevailed in the heart of the homeland. The struggle that divided the centralists and federalists seemed endless and hopeless. Neither side could gain a permanent advantage, and no leader emerged strong enough to unite the warring factions and turn the effort of the populace into constructive channels. The downfall of the centralist regime under President Bernardino Rivadavia spelled the end of porteño leadership. Federalists disliked Rivadavia and his policies at best, but his agreement with Brazil granting independence to the Banda Oriental and the loss of

70

the Charcas region to the Bolivarian forces of Generals Sucre and Santa Cruz provided the opportunity to discredit him completely.

The situation in the Plata region in the late 1820's and early 1830's was far more confused than is generally pictured. Only in recognition of this fact can otherwise apparent contradictions in motivations and events be explained. In a country with no developed sense of nationality and over-all unity, how could the granting of independence to a disputed frontier province prove so unpopular? Was not the federalist objective a high degree of autonomy or near independence for all provinces? Why would an ardent supporter of the federalist cause subject the country to the most tyrannical of centralist rule once he held the reins of power? Mere opportunism?

BUENOS AIRES

In reality there were four Argentinas. The first, and that which dominated the colonial viceroyalty and sparked the independence movement, was the port area of Buenos Aires. Its commercial and political interests favored continuation of the pre-eminent role enjoyed by the city prior to independence. As the center of political and intellectual leadership, Buenos Aires succeeded in directing the course of the new state after expulsion of the viceroy in 1810. For a time the intellectuals, the distinguished gentlemen of the assembly halls, the revolutionary leaders, had their day, but the chaos that was Argentina in the 1820's testified to their failure. No other Latin American country embarked upon the road to independent nationhood with such an array of distinguished leadership, yet lack of success in bringing about national unification and domestic tranquillity indicates only too clearly that the Argentine nation was as yet a dream founded upon a colonial administrative jurisdiction that had not stood the tests of time, community of interest, and mutual dependence. The sense of nationality lay buried deep beneath the soil of the pampas, and only a strong metamorphism could bring it to the surface. The porteño leaders were unable to provide the experience of transformation, for they could not see far beyond the interest of the capital.

The second Argentina lay far to the west in the sunny valleys along the foothills of the Andes mountains. This region, a principal population center in the early colonial period, had ceased to count for much politically or commercially during the previous century, but it still had its military leaders, or caudillos, who by giving support to one or another of the other factions were in position to influence the outcome of interregional struggles. The third Argentina was the river country north and west of Buenos Aires and including particularly the province of Santa Fé. This region was an increasingly important stronghold for the adherents of provincial autonomy and opposition to the domination of Buenos Aires. Finally, there was the fourth region, the province of Buenos Aires south from the port city. This area was gradually being wrested from the inhospitable Indians by the owners of large cattle estates, who with their gaucho followers conducted a more or less continuous campaign to push the frontier ever southward. These were the four Argentinas, each of which had its own peculiar interests and policies which it sought to protect or further. The degree to which unity among the four regions was lacking is attested to by the fact that foreign relations and commercial policy were largely in the hands of Buenos Aires, whereas internal taxation, education, and other matters lay within the control of each province, and military forces were largely the personal armies of the various provincial caudillos. General Sucre aptly wrote in 1825, in a letter to Bolívar, that no one could tell 'which people, which order of government was in control in Buenos Aires.'

The struggle between federalists and centralists was by no means a clear-cut conflict between the porteños and the provinces. On the contrary, there were ardent federalists in the erstwhile viceregal capital who saw in centralism a threat to the favored position of Buenos Aires. Centralism could mean, as Rivadavia had wanted it to mean, a single national budget and a single national tax structure that would have forced the capital city to share its resouces and particularly its customs receipts with the other sections of the national territory. Though certainly a minority, there were men in the provinces who would have given up a measure of local autonomy for the benefits of participation in the economic assets of the capital. The strategic position of the port city was crucial, for it enjoyed a near monopoly in foreign trade and provided the principal market for provincial products. The economies of the hinterland regions could be benefited or strangled depending upon the trade policies of the great river port. Consequently, the federalist-centralist issue was obscured by the more basic question of who was to control Buenos Aires.

GAUCHO LEADER

Following the resignation of Rivadavia in the summer of 1827, there was little immediate effort to hold the country together. The question of ultimate political organization was an open issue, and for the time being the various provinces went their own separate ways. Principal attention was focused upon Buenos Aires, province and port city. There in 1829 a strong figure appeared upon the scene—the figure of a crude but rugged man of the plains, an avowed federalist and by political orientation a conservative. Juan Manuel de Rosas was not a gaucho. He came from the city of Buenos Aires and from a fairly well-to-do family. When as a boy he went to live on a cattle ranch in the far south of Buenos Aires province, he went as the son of the owner and not as a wandering cowboy of the plains. Nevertheless, Rosas' early development was that of a frontiersman accustomed to the rugged life of a cattle raiser, and while still a young man he had achieved the distinction of being recognized as a prominent cattle baron and the master of grand estates. His frequent battles with the plains Indians, conducted at the head of his gaucho employees and fellow ranchers, brought him prestige and a reputation as a military leader.

Wealth and military prestige soon made Rosas a man to reckon with in provincial politics, and, coupled with his willingness to enter into the power struggles of the political leaders at the capital, gave him an importance in national affairs that could not lightly be dismissed. Rosas was a caudillo, a leader on horseback, a potential restorer of law and order in a conflict-weary and disturbed country.

GOVERNOR OF BUENOS AIRES

Rosas first emerged upon the political scene to participate in the struggles that took place upon the return of the unhappy troops which had been engaged in the Uruguayan war ending in 1828. He had previously supported a former provincial governor in crushing a minor uprising, but after the murder of Governor Dorrego by Lavalle, a disgruntled unitarian officer back from the wars, Rosas took a leading part in the general movement that unseated the usurper and drove him from the country. The legislature thereupon elected Rosas governor of the province for a three-year term. As governor the rising caudillo found himself plunged into a bitter civil war that raged for nearly two years between unitarians and federalists. It was a war that he knew how to win, and eventually Rosas restored peace in the province. He was also able, by agreements with the leaders in other provinces, to establish a pattern of inter-provincial relationships that ignored the question of whether or not there should be a national government. Before the world Buenos Aires province spoke for the Argentine confederation, but its authority to do so rested upon what were essentially personal agreements between Rosas and the caudillos of other provinces, such as Estanislao López in Santa Fé. Efforts of dissident federalists to secure the convocation of a confederation congress were skillfully blocked.

On governing the province for the first time, Rosas firmly altered the policies of the liberal *unitarios* whom he had succeeded, but his acts were generally characterized by moderation and gradualness. He abolished free trade and imposed tariffs on imported flour and grains, thereby favoring the wheat growers in his own province and Santa Fé. At the same time he opposed the idea of Argentina's need for new settlers and liquidated the colonization program of Rivadavia, who had established a special commission to attract northern European settlers to come to the country and take up farming. Rosas was himself the owner of a large estate, and his inclination was to build an economy based upon great landed properties belonging to the wealthy families that were his friends. Rosas' interests were still largely personal, however. His chief concern was for the maintenance of law and order in his own province and for the expulsion from public office of those whose policies of liberal reform and political unity betokened interference with the feudal independence of his own peculiar kind of society. With the unitarios defeated and driven into exile, Rosas resigned the governorship and returned home. Hostile Indians were stealing his cattle and overrunning his estates, and the owner's attention was required. For over two years Rosas, aided by his supporters and followers, waged a relentless campaign of extermination against the Indians of southern Buenos Aires province. As a consequence the frontier was pushed far to the south and vast tracts of Indian land were opened for new cattle estates.

DICTATOR BY INVITATION

Beginning in 1834, however, a new effort was made to bring Rosas back into politics. The provincial government was weak, and such governors as General Balcarce and General Viamonte were unable to maintain order or to hold the respect of the provincial legislature. In June of 1834 the legislature named Rosas governor again, but the caudillo was ill-disposed to accept. In fact, he stood firmly by his resolve through four successive offers. Others also refused, and finally the president of the legislature, Manuel Vicente Maza, took the position of chief executive on a provisional basis. In the meantime, affairs throughout the country went from bad to worse. The caudillo leaders of the other provinces warred among themselves, Tucumán and Salta in particular being in open conflict as a result of the rivalry of their governors. In March of 1835, Maza gave up all effort to govern in Buenos Aires, and for the fifth time since his retirement from office, Rosas was again offered the governorship, this time as absolute dictator in possession of all public authority and with no limit upon the term of office. Rosas agreed to accept, but on condition that a plebiscite be held to obtain approval by the people of the extraordinary delegation of authority that the legislature offered. Promptly the vote was taken in the city of Buenos Aires, and Rosas was confirmed in his position of absolute dictator of the province.

Quickly all aspects of Argentine political life changed. Rosas was dictator of but one province; but he soon made himself master of the entire confederation. By force, by intrigue, by alliance and compact, supported by a strong popular following among the middle and lower classes, Rosas was able to make his will prevail and his policies dominant. No one challenged his leadership.

Many have sought an explanation of the factors that motivated Rosas in his exercise of power and authority. A man of wealth and power at the outset of his political career, cajoled into the acceptance of public office, it was hardly to be expected that he would exercise the functions of governor and dictator in so arbitrary and ruthless a manner as history records that he did. Rosas was no intellectual and he had only a minimum of education. Apparently he distrusted those whose backgrounds were more genteel than his own. Yet he was one of those rare individuals who inspire in their followers an extreme loyalty to their persons but who at the same time drive from them and fear all those capable of exercising independent thought and judgment. Rosas rapidly became a tyrant. Political opponents were crushed and driven from the land, as were many others not engaged in politics but who found the atmosphere stifling and the risk to life and property too great to endure. Chile, Uruguay, and even Bolivia became refuges for an increasing number of Argentine citizens.

CENTRALISM VS FEDERALISM

Rosas entered upon political life as a federalist, and a federalist he remained in name. Nevertheless, his rule provided a degree of centralism
that the most ardent unitarian would have balked at imposing. Rosas' centralism was one of terror and fear. The efforts at repression and confiscation were at first directed at the unitarians, and the battle-cry of his regime, 'Death to the unitarians,' was adhered to closely. Death was meted
out to thousands of Rosas' political opponents. But soon no one stopped to
question whether the proposed victims of Rosas' tyranny were indeed unitarians; it was enough that they had incurred the wrath of the dictator or
of his fanatical followers. Rosas' adherents were organized into political
clubs in the various cities, and the dictator created a secret police known
as the *mazorca*.* Rosas was a monolithic figure and he built for himself a
monolithic state.

To those who have witnessed the political developments of the twentieth
century, the Rosas regime can hardly appear strange, but it certainly belonged to the wrong epoch and the wrong continent. Never before in the
Western Hemisphere and scarcely since has there existed such a political
system with all the trappings of totalitarianism. In the mazorca existed the
secret organization of the party elite bound together by a cult of adherence
to Rosas. Terrorism and denunciation produced death and exile for those
who fell under official disfavor or who were unfortunate enough to possess
property coveted by one of the cultists. Those who wished to protect themselves swore allegiance to the regime, displayed the red party colors, and
featured the picture of the political leader prominently in their homes and
places of business.

As might have been expected after the years of political chaos, the
church supported Rosas from the outset. Not only did he give promise of
restoring order and suppressing the anticlerical measures taken by Rivadavia, but he was known to favor the closest possible relationship between
church and state. Once in power, Rosas did embrace the church as a political ally; he nearly suffocated it. He restored many of the privileges that
the church had lost during the long period of confusion following the revolution when Argentine political leaders had been wont to bargain with the

* An ear of corn, used as a symbol of earthy unity. Rosas' enemies were prone to
use the term, *más horca,* meaning 'more gallows.'

papacy for diplomatic recognition of the new republic. He permitted the re-establishment of various religious orders that had earlier been excluded, including that of the Society of Jesus. He did not for a moment, however, relinquish his policy of regalism by which he, as head of the state, exercised authority over the church as well as over the civil government. During the period of his rule he literally purged the ranks of the religious in the interests of his government. Mariano Medrano, bishop of Buenos Aires, became the dictator's willing tool, and the clergy were forced to uphold the 'federation' and denounce the unitarians in the pulpit and in the confessional. Only the Jesuits showed an inclination to resist and adhere to the ultramontane view of religious organization. For failing to conform they were promptly excluded again from the country. Soon the church altars displayed Rosas' red colors, and his likeness appeared beside those of Christ and the Virgin Mary in the sanctuaries.

Rosas ruled Argentina from 1835 until 1852. His only real program was law and order for those who supported him and death and confiscation for those who dared raise a hand in opposition. His was a civil regime, for the military had no voice. The symbolism which he deftly utilized appealed to the masses and, supported by the church, Rosas enjoyed a considerable popularity among the ignorant of the lower classes. Foreign residents, pleased with the outward appearance of law and order, generally regarded his regime with benign toleration. Nevertheless, thousands of Argentines did not adhere to Rosas' government. Many sought refuge in Montevideo, from which neighboring river city they plotted Rosas' overthrow and attempted to rouse support for their cause in the Banda Oriental. The younger generation of Argentine liberals, however, attempted to work within the country through secret societies such as the Association of May, dedicated to fulfilling the political objectives of the May Revolution of 1810 for a free society and a liberal democratic government. One by one, however, the youthful leaders discovered that life in the Argentine capital was unhealthful for them, and their literary and intellectual abilities came to flower in Santiago and Montevideo where they joined earlier refugees from Rosas' despotism.

Outstanding figures in exile were such men as Bartolomé Mitre, Domingo Sarmiento, Juan Alberdi, and Esteban Echeverría. These men, each of whom contributed in a major way to the development of political liberalism in Argentina, were, with the exception of Echeverría who died prematurely, to play an important role in the creation of an Argentine nation once the era of confusion and disunity under Rosas had come to an end.

They had little to do, however, with bringing the federalist dictator's regime to a close. Action and strong allies were required to accomplish this feat. For the most part, the eligible leadership in the foreign capitals was disinclined to adopt tactics of violence, and the exiles were fearful lest an invitation to a foreign power to help in the overthrow of Rosas might be construed as an invitation to remain active in Argentine affairs long after Rosas was gone. Consequently, it was Rosas' own policies and actions that eventually brought about his downfall. His aggressive attitude toward neighboring Uruguay and Paraguay aroused not only the antagonism of those countries, but that of Brazil as well; and it created a situation in which it eventually proved possible for rival caudillos to draw support from these neighbors against the dictatorial regime in Buenos Aires.

SUCCESSES AND FAILURES OF ROSAS

Rosas' accomplishments were meager indeed. Twentieth-century dictatorships of the totalitarian variety have characteristically distinguished themselves by undertaking programs of physical improvement and by inauguration of measures designed to improve the economic lot of the lower classes, albeit at the expense of some scapegoat group. Upon such programs has rested the popularity of these regimes. Rosas provided a circus, but little bread. The country deteriorated during his rule in almost every way. Physical development languished and higher education virtually ceased as a number of institutions were closed and others subjected to a rigorous censorship. Economic life stagnated as investment capital turned elsewhere and potential immigrants sought more pleasant lands. Repeated blockades of the river capital by French and British warships in an effort to counteract Rosas' intervention in Uruguay did nothing to improve the trade situation; and even though the over-all trend of commercial activity was upward during the Rosas era, there were years in which it came to an almost complete standstill. In the end, Rosas' popularity faded and even his favored henchmen joined in plotting his destruction.

Rosas was aggressive in his foreign policy, but remarkably ineffective. In the first period of his governorship he attempted to make good the Argentine claim to the Malvinas, or Falkland islands, in the Atlantic. A small settlement was established there and an effort made to prevent sealers and fishermen from the United States from using the islands as a base. The result was a retaliatory attack upon the settlement by an American naval vessel. The Argentines withdrew and shortly the British arrived to make good a claim arising from an earlier coerced arrangement with Spain. The British stayed in spite of Rosas' protests, and the United States rejected the dictator's claim for indemnity for damage done the Argentine settlers on the ground of the disputed possession of the islands.

In 1837, Rosas joined with Chile in declaring war on the Peru-Bolivian confederation of General Santa Cruz, but his efforts were largely verbal owing to preoccupation with Uruguay and the absence of any real interest among the Argentine provinces in an Andean war. It was in the Banda Oriental that Rosas concentrated his military efforts, but even there he was not notably successful. Rosas claimed to be a federalist, and though his regime bore little resemblance to a federal system of government, the pretense served his purposes. Within the 'federation' were provinces that resisted his control. Among these Rosas numbered Corrientes, Paraguay, and the Banda Oriental, or Uruguay. Subjugation was in order and could be undertaken as a domestic rather than a foreign war. The possibility of reuniting the Banda Oriental to the former Spanish viceroyalty was a far more attractive undertaking, however, than the conquest of Corrientes or the isolated patriarchy of Doctor Francia; likewise, the possibilities seemed better, for Uruguay was torn with internal strife that Rosas could employ to advantage. Consequently, the struggling buffer state across the river was marked for special attention.

URUGUAY

Uruguayan independence had been nurtured in Buenos Aires during the years that the Banda Oriental formed the Cisplatine Province of Brazil. When Uruguay's famous 'Thirty-three Immortals' landed on the eastern shore in April of 1825 to raise the standard of revolution and liberty, unification with the Argentine provinces was clearly in their minds. In an assembly held in the little town of Florida, the revolutionists declared the eastern province incorporated into the United Provinces of the Río de la Plata, as Argentina was then known. The war that followed this invasion and declaration witnessed strong Argentine participation against Brazil, and the general success of the Spanish-speaking allies seemed to assure that incorporation would take place. Great Britain, ever concerned with the future of commercial activity in the Plata region, viewed with misgiving the possibility of an Argentine victory that would place that country

firmly astride the mouth of the great river in position to shut off all river
trade not beneficial to Buenos Aires. At the peace conference in 1828, the
British representative, acting in the role of intermediary, insisted that the
disputed territory be set up as an independent nation with no direct political attachment to either of its powerful neighbors. This arrangement was
provided in the terms of settlement, and to assure that all parties were in
agreement, both Brazil and Argentina were induced to approve the constitution of the new state. Thus did Britain seek to prevent further struggle
over the region and, incidentally, of course, establish for herself a quasi-
protectorate on the great Plata estuary.

By the time Rosas had assumed power in Buenos Aires, the Uruguayan
leaders, Juan Antonio Lavalleja and Fructuoso Rivera, had proved their
basic similarity to the rest of mankind by engaging in armed disagreement
as to who should rule the new republic. By 1836, a third contender, Manuel Oribe, placed in the presidency as a compromise choice, had shown
sufficient attachment to the Lavalleja faction to spur Rivera to organized
revolt. A permanent pattern of factional disagreement was emerging. Into
this struggle stepped Rosas.

Rosas threw his support behind the *blanco* * faction of Oribe. The
blanco leader, following in the steps of Lavalleja, was at least friendly to
Argentine overtures of union, particularly when he found himself in need
of Rosas' support against the *colorado* † forces of Rivera. Unfortunately
for Oribe, Rosas' assistance proved of negative value. The revolt had
begun in 1836, and in 1837 Rosas had serious difficulty with the French
over his highhanded treatment of certain French nationals and their property. As a consequence of the dispute, a French fleet was sent to blockade
Buenos Aires. Rosas' new European enemies were delighted to have the
opportunity to deal him a further blow by aiding the rebellious colorado
forces of Rivera in Uruguay, and they made available more modern arms
and ammunition. By October of 1838 Oribe was obliged to resign and flee
the country, taking up residence with his mentor in Buenos Aires. Rivera
became president of Uruguay, promptly declared war on the Argentine
dictator, and with the assistance of French troops drove all of Rosas' army
back across the river.

Rosas' downfall was eventually sealed in the Banda Oriental. The long
struggle over this region, begun in the early days of colonial rule in the
Plata basin, seemed destined to continue unabated far into the republican

* So known for their party color, white.
† Likewise so called for the party color, red.

era. The British effort to erect a buffer state resulted only in the creation of a power vacuum into which the competing forces of Argentina, Brazil, and even Paraguay were drawn. Rosas, as many a colonial governor before him, threw countless human and material resources into the battle, and in doing so he lost his hold on the parent country. Constant warfare raged from 1839 until 1852, and the latter part of the period is known in Uruguayan history as that of the Great War. It was characterized by a nine-year siege of Montevideo by the combined forces of Rosas and the Uruguayan blancos supporting Oribe. Ranged against the blancos and their Argentine allies were the Uruguayan colorados and the Argentine province of Corrientes, joined later by forces from Santa Fé and Entre Ríos as the grip of the dictator in Buenos Aires began to slip. Numerous battles were fought, and for a time it looked as though Rosas might succeed in subduing his recalcitrant 'province,' but in the end the tide surged strongly against him.

Rosas was particularly inept in dealing with the two European powers that showed most interest in the Plata region, England and France. The motives of both powers were certainly open to question, and there can be little doubt that they were willing to take what advantage they could of disturbed local conditions for the benefit of themselves and their nationals; but by his arbitrary actions and by over-extending himself in relation to his resources, Rosas placed himself at their mercy. During the siege of Montevideo, the two European nations jointly blockaded the mouth of the Plata river with their fleets, supplied the beleaguered citizens of the Uruguayan capital, and forced their way up the Paraguay and Uruguay rivers to open the hinterland to their commerce. Such action destroyed much of the effectiveness of Rosas' military measures, encouraged the river provinces to slip out from under Rosas' domination, and made virtually impossible a complete victory over the Uruguayan colorados.

The Uruguayan war carried on by Rosas was much more than a simple struggle undertaken to subdue a wayward 'province.' It was a conflict affecting the entire Argentine federation in a direct military way. Rosas' ability to dominate provinces other than Buenos Aires was subject to continuous challenge. Montevideo was a hotbed of intrigue on the part of Argentine centralists in exile from the day that Rosas established his dictatorship. Various Uruguayan politicians and military leaders participated openly in plots against the dictator, and soon they were in league with federalist recalcitrants from the back country provinces along the foothills of the Andes. During the long conflict governors of Corrientes, Tucumán,

Salta, Catamarca, La Rioja, and Jujuy, all at one time or another joined in the efforts to overthrow the government in Buenos Aires. General Juan Lavalle was a principal leader in the 'liberation' forces, and organizing an army with the aid of President Rivera in Montevideo, his movements ranged throughout the northern provinces and westward as far as Córdoba. There, in November of 1840, he suffered a major defeat at the hands of General Oribe, the ousted blanco president of Uruguay and principal commander in Rosas' army. Clearly, the conflict was all mixed up. Leaders on both sides of the river made common cause with allies on the opposite side, and throughout the war Argentines and Uruguayans alike fought for each other's causes and in each other's armies with little or no distinction. It was one big civil war among a people whose provinces were too disunited to form a nation but sufficiently well united to make common cause in an effort to settle the problems and determine the fate of all. Uruguay was scarcely yet a nation, nor did its people really so regard it. It was, during the wars of the Rosas era, for all practical purposes just another province neither more nor less closely linked to the Argentine confederation than Corrientes, Santa Fé, or Córdoba. Time and the experience of working together had not yet created in the minds of the people the concept of separate nationality.

URQUIZA

The long struggle was finally brought to an end by a combination of circumstances that produced the resignation of Rosas and his exile to England. The most important blow was dealt the dictator by Justo José de Urquiza, long-time follower of Rosas and governor of Entre Ríos province. Urquiza, a strong man politically and a provincial caudillo in his own right, turned against his dictatorial superior in Buenos Aires and allied himself with the Uruguayan colorados. His official pronouncement was made on May 1, 1851, after a long period of ever-mounting disagreement between the Entre Ríos governor and Rosas over control of commerce by the porteños. The proclamation itself set forth the idea that the high hopes for peace and order with which the Argentine people had greeted the advent of Rosas had been dashed to the ground by the evil actions and sinister intentions of the dictator. A call was issued for 'liberty, organization, and war against despotism.' Quickly Urquiza formed his alliances for the inevitable struggle. Corrientes was already with him, as were the colorados of Uruguay; but now Brazil too was brought into the compact in exchange for minor boundary concessions along her frontier with Uruguay. This time the forces against Rosas were determined to succeed, even though it meant incurring the risk of further Brazilian intervention in the Banda Oriental.

Urquiza soon raised a large army with units from each of the compact members, including Brazil. First he moved to relieve the siege of Montevideo, a feat accomplished with no great difficulty. Then with an army of some 30,000 men he negotiated a difficult crossing of the Paraná river at Diamante and moved on into Santa Fé province. In February of 1852 the major battle of Urquiza's campaign was fought at Monte Caseros, where after intense fighting Rosas' army fled in defeat. Urquiza's victory was complete, for the dictator's military forces disintegrated as an organized body, and only straggling units of disgruntled soldiers fell back upon the capital. They would fight no more. Rosas took pencil in hand and wrote his resignation and promptly departed for England, where by reason of the confiscation of his properties he lived in poverty until his death in 1877. Unlike his modern imitators such as Juan Domingo Perón, he had not taken the precaution to establish a sizable bank account abroad.

General Urquiza occupied Buenos Aires and appointed a new provisional governor. He then set about the difficult task of organization that confronted him in his effort to establish a federal government. Most of the extraordinary powers over foreign affairs, vested in the Buenos Aires governor by the federal pact of 1831, were assumed by Urquiza, even though his only official position was that of governor of Entre Ríos province. This arrangement was displeasing to many in the port city, where the victor of Monte Caseros was regarded not only with suspicion but also with a considerable amount of contempt. He was, after all, only an up-river provincial who insisted on continuing to wear Rosas' red colors. The pot continued to boil, and it rapidly became evident that Buenos Aires was hardly the place to lay the foundation for a new federal system. In accordance with an agreement drawn up by the provincial governors in May of 1852, a constituent congress assembled in Santa Fé in November of that same year. No delegates from Buenos Aires appeared.

Gradually the air was beginning to clear. Urquiza, as one of his first acts after the overthrow of Rosas, had declared a general amnesty, and many of the exiled unitarians swarmed back to Buenos Aires. They gradually took over control of the city and province, and although they rebelled against Urquiza they were in no position to contend with him at

Santa Fé. Instead, they remained aloof, setting up their own independent state while the remaining thirteen provinces of Argentina worked out a new political organization. The centralist porteños were determined to dominate the entire country, and if that was not possible they would go their own way alone. Chief among them was Bartolomé. Mitre, who as a deputy in the provincial legislature and later as a principal collaborator of Governor Pastor Obligado provided statesmanlike leadership in the political group that ruled the port city.

In Santa Fé, the federalists were in complete control. Among them were men of outstanding ability and character, Urquiza himself, Juan María Gutiérrez, a poet and literary figure of considerable note, and Juan Bautista Alberdi, an able political theorist. Alberdi, in his book *Bases y puntos de partida para la organización política de la República Argentina,** captured the spirit of strong liberalism within a workable federal system that characterized the Santa Fé constituent assembly's work. Alberdi wrote much of the constitution that was approved by the assembly in 1853, patterning his basic concepts after those of an earlier American political theorist, Alexander Hamilton. The constitution was to endure for many a year.

The era of Rosas was now past. Gone were the oppression, the mazorca, the little red flags, and the stultifying condemnation of intellectual independence. Nurtured in exile and tempered by the bitter strife of civil war, the Argentine spirit was free once more to soar above the bloody pampas and the misty marshes of the great rivers. Able and dedicated men still allowed their personal jealousies and petty regional interests to divide them. More battles would be fought, to be sure, but it was only a matter of time until a great and united Argentine nation would emerge, for the one valuable heritage of the Rosas dictatorship was a sense of Argentine nationality.

The Rosas tradition did not disappear completely from the minds of men, for it was revived almost a century after his fall. In the 1940's and 1950's Juan Domingo Perón and his *peronistas* would return to the cult of Rosas, especially to the powerful nationalism, the support of the working class, and a tendency toward tyranny. For almost the first time Argentine writers began to treat Rosas as a potential national hero rather than as a blot on Argentine history. His revival was temporary at that time, however, for it depended on Perón's success. When Perón, too, was driven from the country, Rosas went into eclipse once more.

* *Bases and Points of Departure for the Political Organization of the Argentine Republic.*

5

Caudillismo and Anarchy: The Bolivarian Republics

Del rey abajo ninguno—Below the king, no one is better than I.

OLD SPANISH PROVERB

Break-up of Gran Colombia

FORCES OF DISINTEGRATION

With the death of Bolívar all the liberator's dreams of a great and power-ful nation in northern South America were dashed asunder by localism and petty self-interest. Each of the major segments of Gran Colombia went its own way to form a separate nation. Venezuela succeeded to the terri-tory formerly governed by the Spanish captain-general in Caracas; Ecua-dor claimed jurisdiction over the region of the former presidency of Quito; and New Granada was formed from the central territory of the earlier vice-royalty. Peru was already a separate nation having no further tie with the northern neighbor from which the forces of its liberation had emerged. Bolivia, too, stood forth in the ragged garb of her independent statehood, but for a time political and military links with Peru were maintained as ef-forts to achieve stability encouraged a certain amount of mutual interven-tion.

In New Granada the transition from the larger to the smaller state was made less difficult by continuation in office of much the same group of public officials in power at the time of Bolívar's death. Nevertheless, for a period of two years it appeared that a sort of national lethargy might per-mit the republic to suffer almost total dismemberment. General Juan José Flores, a former military leader under Bolívar, headed the movement to make Ecuador independent, and he became the new country's provisional

85

president. After a centralist constitution was adopted in 1830, Flores was elected to a four-year term as president by the new congress; and, as virtual dictator, he set about establishing a northern frontier that would include in his jurisdiction as much of southern New Granada as political persuasion and military conquest could make possible. Flores invaded the Cauca valley; he occupied Pasto, Popayán, and Buenaventura. These areas had been represented in the Ecuadorian constituent assembly held at Riobamba. For a time it appeared that the highland valleys, part of which had been included in the old Quito presidency, would merge peaceably with Ecuador, and largely by their own choice. There was little to indicate that anyone in Bogotá was remotely interested in the fate of the southern regions of Gran Colombia. The province of Chocó voluntarily declared for union with the Flores regime. Eventually, however, the New Granadans awakened to the fact that they were in peril of losing some of their richest provinces, and sent an army against Ecuador. Flores might have achieved victory had his own position been more secure; but so unsettled were conditions in Quito and so tenuous a hold did the general have on Guayaquil that he was obliged to disengage his forces and return to the capital to suppress his political opponents. There followed a series of diplomatic negotiations in which Flores was bested. The Cauca region was recognized as belonging to New Granada and the Carchi river was established as the boundary from the mountains to the coast.

New Granada was too weak and disunited to press further any attempt to reincorporate the Quito region in the larger republic, nor was there any serious interest in so doing. A new constitution, adopted in 1832, proclaimed the territory of New Granada to include the disputed southern valleys, but it laid no claim to Quito or Guayaquil.

ROLE OF CHURCH

One issue did assume significance, not so much in the countries that had formed the outskirts of Bolívar's shadowy empire, but in the heartland of New Granada. That issue was the question of just where the church was to fit in the new order of independent nationhood. The old Spanish empire had been far more than a political system; into its fabric had been woven all the institutions of human society. Once the fabric was torn asunder, the resulting pieces possessed many loose threads that had to be tied firmly back into the cloth lest each segment become completely unraveled. The early Iberian weavers had selected a major portion of their yarn in Rome.

The degree to which church and state had been intermingled in the empire made it difficult for secessionist nations to adjust to their new status. Did the republican government succeed to the religious prerogatives of the Spanish king, or did the duties and responsibilities of the monarch pertaining to religion revert to the Pope in Rome once the king's voice in American affairs had been silenced? This was a major and all-important question. It had little to do with religious freedom, and most of the traditional discussions of liberalism *versus* conservatism are in large measure irrelevant. Prompt resolution was necessary, however, for the very nature of the new states was involved, as was also the reality of independence. In such areas as Bolivia, Peru, and Venezuela, the lack of political stability and the preoccupation of the caudillos with matters military permitted the issue to be resolved for a time at least by default. The church became the arbiter of its own destiny, and for a military chieftain to challenge its right to do so was to invite disaster. In Gran Colombia and subsequently in New Granada, however, where intellectualism and true liberalism had been outstanding features of late colonial society, the issue was inescapable and was faced almost as soon as political independence was firmly established. The struggle over its resolution permeated all other forms of political controversy for more than two decades after the death of the liberator.

In 1824 a Law of Patronage was enacted by the government of Gran Colombia. By this law, the new government reserved to itself the full patronage authority with respect to the church—that is, the authority to nominate the principal religious officials of the country. Inasmuch as the government was not recognized by the papacy, the actions taken by it in religious matters were in a sense provisional. The Pope could not act upon the nominations or presentations of the Gran Colombian congress without recognizing the legitimate authority of the revolutionary government. Recognition he could not grant without creating a whole set of problems for himself in Spain. The Pope could not appoint the various religious officials himself, however, for he had no way of enforcing his decisions. In these circumstances, the local church hierarchy received and accepted office from the republican government, but papal confirmation had to await an eventual adjustment in relationships between Rome and Bogotá.

The patronage issue was for a time the prime issue of church-state relationships. The clerical group and their supporters opposed government control over the selection of church officials. They would have preferred to have the church free to control within its own organization all religious personnel, their selection, and their advancement. They were in no sense willing to concede the other side of the coin, however, and permit church-state separation. They insisted on continuation of the tithe as a tax and through it financial support of the church by the government. Likewise, they demanded prohibition of non-Catholic religious activity and asserted their exclusive right to continue performing the varied semi-religious temporal functions that had historically fallen into the church province. These functions included the conduct of all education, public and private; the performance of all welfare services; operation of hospitals and all institutions for the homeless and aged; control of marriages and funerals; and operation of cemeteries. It must be recognized, of course, that many of these functions have only become uniquely civil rather than religious in the twentieth century. They were, and to some degree remain, church functions throughout the Christian areas of the world. In Spanish America, the union of the Roman Catholic Church and the state had promoted a complete monopolization of the indicated functions by the church and support of the activities by government-imposed taxes paid over to the church. A further matter of no small significance was the extent of economic power exercised by the many religious orders through ownership of land and the conduct of agricultural and commercial activities. The integration of church and state had fostered a high degree of 'socialism.'

New Granada

Bolívar was, in his last years, in many ways a more conservative Catholic than others of the Gran Colombian political leaders. Santander was the firm and stable statesman who saw clearly the course of moderation and followed it doggedly. He insisted steadfastly upon governmental control of religious patronage, upon the creation of secular educational institutions, and upon limiting the jurisdiction of the special religious courts that exercised control over the clergy in civil matters. He was damned by the clergy as a 'liberal' and by the liberals as pro-clerical. Thus was vindicated the wisdom of his course.

In 1838 José Ignacio de Márquez was elected to succeed Santander in the presidency of New Granada. He believed in freeing education from the restrictions of religious dogma, as had Santander, but he also had strong views concerning the economic power of the church, particularly that of various religious orders. The church itself was divided on this issue, as the secular clergy, that is, those who performed religious services for the public and who did not belong to monastic orders, were jealous of the power and wealth of the various orders. Márquez moved against several missions operated by the orders and transferred them to the secular clergy, and in so doing he had the support of the chief secular prelate in the affected area, the bishop of Popayán. The stroke was aimed primarily at assuring a more definite dedication of the church's resources to religious and educational purposes, but it produced a revolt against the government, led by priests. While the uprising was quickly crushed, and principal political, military, and religious leaders joined Márquez in the effort, the incident was merely the opening shot in a long struggle over the religious issue. Indeed, it soon became questionable whether religion was an issue or a pretext, for caudillos in various parts of the country rose in revolt claiming to be acting in support of the church. Astutely, the bishop of Bogotá, Manuel José de Mosquera, noted in a pastoral letter that religion was being used as a pretense for disturbing the peace and he denounced those who would on such a basis justify revolution. Nevertheless, revolt seethed throughout the country, and for a time Márquez seemed powerless to control it. General Pedro de Alcántara Herrán commanded the government forces. Joined with him was another outstanding leader, General Tomás Cipriano de Mosquera. Together, and with the help at one point of President Flores of Ecuador, these men were finally able to restore peace. However, the struggle lasted nearly four years, disrupted the economic and social life of the country, bankrupted the national treasury, and settled nothing but the personal ambitions of a few men. In the midst of the disorders, Santander died, and thus was lost the one great stabilizing figure linking the new republic to the glorious period of the revolution. Also during the conflict, a new election brought General Herrán to the presidency, but for more than a year he was forced to absent himself from the capital conducting military campaigns against the revolutionists.

The administrations of Herrán and Tomás Cipriano de Mosquera, who succeeded Herrán in 1845, were periods of more stable national life. A new constitution was adopted in 1843, centralist in nature, and tending toward parliamentarism in that members of the president's cabinet were given seats in congress and members of congress were permitted to hold positions in the administration. With respect to the religious issue, the bond formed between the government leaders and the secular religious hierarchy during the preceding struggle held firm, and, for a time at least, church and state drew closer. Inasmuch as peace prevailed, commerce revived and flourished, aided by commercial treaties with other countries, including Spain. Roads were built and a treaty with the United States authorized that country to construct a railroad across the Isthmus of Panama. The national debt was sharply reduced, a new monetary system established, and the Bogotá mint refurbished.

A guiding hand in New Granada's progress was that of Mariano Ospina Rodríguez, a wealthy conservative of an aristocratic Antioquian family. Holding various public offices, he was able to wield tremendous influence on public policy and to do much to further national development. His efforts were particularly significant in the field of education where he was successful in reorganizing university education, founding normal schools in nearly all provinces, and placing the entire educational program of the country on a sounder and more disciplined basis. Indeed, the Jesuits were brought back in 1844 to take over responsibility for much of the revised educational program. In other fields Ospina was able to undertake a program of distributing large tracts of public land to private settlers and landholding companies. Whatever the social wisdom of the new landholding arrangements, much otherwise idle land was made productive, and with the introduction of coffee growing, an important new piece of the foundation was laid for the future economy of the country.

Although anesthetized somewhat by all the obvious material and social benefits produced by the peaceful years of Herrán's and Mosquera's administrations, New Granadan intellectual liberalism was far from dead. Unlike most of the military leaders of other Bolivarian countries, New Granada's presidents and other prominent public figures were for the most part well-educated and widely traveled men. They were aware of and receptive to social and political shifts on the European scene. Many, including President Mosquera, were aroused by the wave of liberal revolutions that swept Europe in 1848. For New Granadan liberals it was a fresh and welcome breeze which, once felt, inspired a rededication to ideals and principles espoused during the days of the American, French, and Spanish American revolutions, but since almost forgotten. Those in control of the government represented the landholding classes, the church, and the military. Their views, although enlightened and generally progressive, were essentially conservative and on some matters reactionary. It was with considerable justice that they called themselves and were referred to by their political opponents as 'Conservatives.' Mosquera was clearly one of these, but in the background of his character was an element of radicalism that gradually came to the fore and caused him to view with some favor the efforts of political and social reformers. Certainly he took no action to suppress or quiet them.

ANTICLERICALISM

In 1849 congress as usual had to select the president inasmuch as no candidate received an electoral majority. Their choice was José Hilario López, who was supported by virtually all who opposed the older conservative elements. It was a victory for Cundinamarca, the province of the capital, and the port regions over the church-dominated provinces of the south. In the later years of Mosquera's administration the old religious and territorial differences had begun once more to crystallize. Now López set forth upon what was in essence an extremely radical program to break the power of the church. To the consternation of his friends and family, ex-President Mosquera supported this radical move. Within a brief time all manner of measures had been taken to curtail church authority and power. It was cut off from the national treasury, the tithe tax abolished, and it was forced to turn to the provincial governments for support. The Jesuit order was again expelled, the church fueros were abolished, and an official act was passed separating church and state. In other areas, also, López moved to satisfy his radical supporters. All slaves were freed, virtually complete freedom of the press was permitted, and a convention was called to draft a new liberal constitution granting complete religious freedom and providing general manhood suffrage. Other steps were taken, both by statute and constitutional provision, to strengthen provincial and local governments and to increase their financial resources and autonomy.

Naturally, such sweeping and radical changes were hardly to be inaugurated peacefully. In 1854 and 1855 the country was swept by revolt and disorder, but even the conservative ex-presidents came to the support of legitimate government however much they disagreed with its policies. Internal peace was restored. The liberal movement, with considerable popular backing, continued on its course of reform, albeit at a slower pace. The religious issue was still dominant, but at mid-century in New Granada other factors were beginning to emerge as major points of national controversy. A stronger agricultural base underlay the economy, light industry flourished, and economic issues assumed increasing importance. Surrounded by countries in which caudillismo and anarchy prevailed, New Granada had not escaped unscathed from such evil influences. The far richer and deeper cultural and intellectual heritage of the former viceroyalty, however, served to hold men to reason and orderliness. There existed a true sense of nationality and a sense of patriotism for which men were willing to sacrifice personal ambition. This degree of national maturity remained but a vague promise in the other Bolivarian republics.

EARLY DEVELOPMENT OF NEW GRANADA

During the crucial period of controversy with Flores, New Granada was ruled by a constituent assembly and by a provisional vice-president, Dr. José Ignacio Márquez. To Márquez fell not only the difficult task of securing a settlement of the southern boundary question, but also that of organizing the government under the new centralist constitution. The provisional president, chosen by the constituent assembly, was Francisco de Paula Santander who was at the time residing in exile in New York. Santander now returned to New Granada and a popular election confirmed him in the post of president for a four-year term. Don Joaquín Mosquera became his vice-president and Márquez retired from his provisional role. Thus at last Santander was president in his own right and assumed the duties he had so long exercised in Bogotá as vice-president of Gran Colombia during Bolívar's absence in the south. Now, however, the country was greatly reduced in size and suffered from bitter factionalism brought on by Bolívar's final debacle and the political disintegration that followed.

Santander as president was a man of stern aspect and rugged determination. In popular appeal he was almost the antithesis of Bolívar. He was admired and respected for his integrity, his devotion to duty and to the program he fostered in the interest of the young nation over which he presided. He demonstrated almost none of the flamboyant gallantry and social grace, however, that had constituted so basic a feature of Bolívar's appeal. Perhaps disillusionment and frustration had soured Santander. Certainly the crucial break with his old and trusted friend, Bolívar, had come about only after great emotional crisis—a crisis that could not fail to leave a deep mark on the sensitive and somewhat introverted statesman. In any case Santander ruled with a sober determination and inflexibility of principle that left no room for frivolity. Indeed, the harsher aspects of his character emerged and seemed to dominate his conduct in office. Political enemies, the former supporters of the late liberator, were offered no token of conciliation or gesture of forgiveness. Neither were they permitted any role in the new government. Exile or the firing squad was their reward for renewal of political activity. Santander's efforts to purge the army of sympathizers with the late president produced a bitter reaction that finally erupted in plots to overthrow the government. These Santander suppressed and in 1833 a number of the conspirators were publicly executed in the main square of Bogotá. Soon it was obvious that the ranks of the president's enemies were growing rapidly. A general factor in addition to the harsh measures taken against the Bolivarian factions was the unwillingness of the chief executive to take advice. Suggestions were interpreted as personal criticisms, and criticism became, in Santander's mind, synonymous with treason.

In spite of the many difficulties faced by the president, including that created by his own personality problems, Santander's administration produced a number of notable achievements. A peace agreement was worked out with Ecuador and Venezuela whereby each recognized the independence of the others and each assumed a share of the national debt of the former Gran Colombia. Ratification of this agreement was delayed until after Santander's retirement, but the basic terms of settlement were worked out through his efforts. The president retained a firm hand in matters of religion, asserting strongly the right of the government to exercise the patronato. Likewise, in the face of considerable clerical opposition, the government embarked upon a program of public elementary education for both boys and girls. Santander, who had traveled both in Europe and North America, had developed a strong interest in all aspects of education, and he fostered in New Granada the Lancastrian system of instruction. Many were happy when Santander's term of office drew to a close, but few could deny that the young nation had made substantial progress toward stability and prosperity under his firm, if rigorous, rule.

VENEZUELA UNDER PÁEZ

To the east, in the new republic of Venezuela, Bolívar's old friend and occasional trouble-maker during the days of Gran Colombia, José Antonio Páez, dominated the political scene. Páez was the first president elected under the constitution adopted in 1830, and his administration was a relatively stable one. Although a conservative he was sufficiently moderate in his views to avoid the bitter animosities that troubled Santander in New Granada. On the other hand, apart from providing an atmosphere in which the pangs of separation from Gran Colombia quickly disappeared, there was little for which the government could claim much credit.

As a successor to Páez, the Venezuelan congress selected the rector of the university as president. In the election no person had achieved a majority of the votes cast, thus throwing the burden of decision on the legislators. The selection of José M. Vargas was not received with great joy throughout the country, not because anyone particularly disliked the distinguished scholar, but because intellectuals simply were not regarded as possessing the requirements of vigor and strength to exercise the prerogatives of chief executive. Military men particularly were distrustful of intellectualism—a phenomenon by no means rare nor limited in its currency to Venezuela. Shortly a military coup ensued and Vargas was forced to turn over his duties and responsibilities to the vice-president and leave the country. A more successful and thoroughgoing revolt was prevented by the intervention of Páez, who, as commander of the government troops, restored order. However, Vargas was not returned to the presidency. Páez' views were not notably at variance with those of his military friends, but he had no wish to see the government become the plaything of military adventurers.

In 1838 Páez was again elected president, and during his second term the country's progress in terms of economic well-being was considerable. International trade increased sharply, thus adding to the government's revenues at a time when expenditures on the military were being reduced. New immigrants came to the country from Central Europe, cart roads were built, a national bank was established, and other tangible improvements were noted. The slave trade in African natives was terminated by agreement with England. The administration of Carlos Soublette, who followed Páez, was likewise marked by general prosperity throughout the country and was unmarred by serious threat to the internal peace.

During the years of relative calm after independence, and particularly during the period that Páez was most active in national affairs, an air of complacency seemed to prevail in most matters of public interest. True, there were advocates and supporters of greater decentralization in government, of withdrawal of state support from the church, of secularization of education, and of many other ideas that would have involved considerable change. By and large, however, no one pushed such matters vigorously, and the attitude of the government was not discouraging to those inclined toward the expression of liberal or radical views. As time went on, however, there emerged a genuine opposition movement, the leaders of which regarded the progressivism of Páez as nothing but ultraconservatism. Chief spokesman for the liberal group was Antonio Leocadio Guzmán, a publicist and editor of *El Venezolano,* a journal founded primarily as a medium for the expression of political opposition to the leadership of Páez and the conservative families from which he drew his principal support. The liberal group was hardly revolutionary, nor did it associate itself with the liberal impulse that had produced a revolution from Spain and spearheaded the anticlerical struggles in New Granada. Rather, the liberal movement found expression in carping criticism of the government. In the background lay the jealousies and antagonisms of family factions that more truly than any intellectual differences provided the divisive factors in Venezuelan social and political life.

In 1846 a new family entered the political jousts with the election of José Tadeo Monagas as president. Supported by Páez and the conservative faction, Monagas was expected to continue the tradition of moderate progressivism. He had been opposed in the election by the owner of *El Venezolano,* Guzmán, who became so vitriolic in his attacks that Soublette had had him arrested and condemned to death. Monagas softened the penalty to exile, but shortly the outspoken editor was back and serving as Monagas' vice-president. Some of his friends were appointed to high office. It was apparent that Monagas was joining the opposition. In congress there was talk of impeachment, and as a consequence the legislative body was dissolved and the dissolution enforced by the army. Páez started a revolt, was defeated, and sent into exile in the United States.

Now the era of peace was almost at an end. Páez' grip upon the country was not only weakened; it was broken. Men spoke of liberalism and conservatism, of radicals and oligarchs, but these were mere words. Federalists opposed centralists, but the positions taken reflected the jockeying for power of families and factions rather than sincere convictions of how best the government should be constituted and organized. There was revolution in France, in Germany—a true liberal movement was in progress. It carried into Chile, the Argentine, and into New Granada, wherever genuine intellectualism responded to trends in contemporary thought and political action. Its impact in Venezuela was slight; for there the minds of men were sterile. Intrigue was rife and critics were outspoken, but this was only the froth stirred up by personal rivalries; beneath all this the country plodded on its lethargic way to market and home again. For over a decade the Monagas family directed the affairs of state. The third in line, José Tadeo again, evidenced new ambitions. He forced through the controlled congress a new constitution, centralist in concept and permitting the president to succeed himself to a six-year term. This move united the various factions against him, and early in 1858 he was forced from office and replaced by a provisional junta which called a new constituent assembly.

Soon it became apparent that the various family factions could not agree. Calling themselves 'conservatives' and 'liberals' they struggled over the issue of centralism *versus* federation until debate degenerated into a resort to arms. The country was torn with revolution. In 1861 Páez was recalled from exile to restore order, which he was able to do only after months of bitter fighting. A new constitution was drafted, this one providing for provincial autonomy in a federation. Páez retired again from the scene, and when the new arrangement proved to be no improvement over the former, the aged statesman could no longer summon the strength to return and quench the fires of revolt that flared anew. For ten years the country was prostrated by conflict and warfare, all to no purpose beyond satisfying the personal ambitions of warring caudillos. Finally, in 1872, one man emerged more powerful than the rest. He was Antonio Guzmán Blanco, son of Antonio Leocadio Guzmán of editorial fame. He was to rule as Venezuela's prototype caudillo for the next twenty years. Bolívar's homeland had strayed far from the path of the great liberator. From the grave in Caracas, to which the body of Bolívar had been transferred in 1842, the voice of the great statesman could not be heard.

Peru and Bolivia

Far to the south, Bolívar's legacy proved no less a burden than in the successor states of the dismembered Gran Colombia. The failure of the Gran Colombian dream is often attributed, in part at least, to the liberator's absence during the period of greatest crisis. However, the regions favored with his presence during those crucial years of the late 1820's failed even more dismally to live up to the great plans of the Venezuelan general. Bolívar's ultimate aim was certainly the creation of a powerful federation of all the states of northern South America. His many writings and many of his letters and public decrees point to such a goal. Only in the light of such an objective can one make out the elusive explanation of the liberator's extended preoccupation with Peru and Bolivia.

Bolívar's strange constitution, which was foisted on both Bolivia and Peru, provided excellent material for the general's critics and in a sense came to symbolize all that was wrong with his grandiose schemes. The lifetime presidency, coupled to a cumbersome three-house legislative structure, was impossible enough in itself, but when Bolívar assumed the presidency in Peru and his principal general, Marshal Sucre, reluctantly assumed that role in Bolivia, the impracticability of the entire program became patently apparent. To Peruvians and Bolivians alike it seemed that the benefits of their independence were to be enjoyed exclusively by their Venezuelan and Colombian liberators. The continued presence of Colombian armies did nothing to allay such suspicions. Thus when Bolívar was absent in 1827 to deal with the Venezuelan crisis created by the separatist tendencies of General Páez, Peruvians quickly overthrew the provisional government of General Andrés Santa Cruz and established one more to their own liking. Colombian troops, discouraged by irregular pay and long absence from home, joined in the mutiny and were quickly sent home. A new constitution was framed and Peru assumed responsibility for its own government without the aid of a liberator. Soon a struggle was underway with Colombia over title to the border provinces of Mainas and Jaén, and an army was sent to invade Guayaquil. The Peruvians met defeat at the hands of Marshal Sucre, but the last vestiges of friendly collaboration between Peru and Colombia were at an end. The southern portion of Bolívar's dream of federation was already exploded before Gran Colombia fell apart.

The affairs of Peru and Bolivia remained related and confused in the aftermath of the Bolívar era. The two regions had been closely united for centuries, from the Conquest to the late eighteenth century, when the Audiencia of Charcas was detached from Peru and incorporated into the newly created Viceroyalty of Río de la Plata. When Spanish domination ceased the old ties were reasserted, and strife-torn Buenos Aires was forgotten. Peruvians sought to dominate Bolivia and Bolivians sought to dominate Peru. None succeeded. Marshal Sucre was the first victim of this conflict. In 1828 he faced not only mutiny among his own Colombian troops but rebellion in Bolivia and invasion from Peru. He resigned from the post he had reluctantly accepted, and departed.

Sucre, far more than Bolívar, was the creator of the Bolivian nation. He not only commanded the army that won the last great battle against Spain at Ayacucho but also called into being Bolivia's first legislative body and, over Bolívar's opposition, supported the nation's assertion of independence. It was Sucre, too, who finally persuaded Bolívar to accept that action and endorse Bolivian independence. Sucre wisely regarded his task as temporary, for he intended to exercise control only until the Bolivians themselves were ready to take over. Although he was forced to resign he was neither shocked nor bitter. He had come as a hero and he departed as one, even though he was wounded in the uprising that precipitated his resignation.

With Sucre out of the way, Peruvian forces occupied the principal cities of Bolivia and imposed a number of terms to be complied with before they would leave. One condition, of course, was the departure of all Colombian soldiers from Bolivia, a move that a majority of the Bolivian leaders looked upon with favor. Other conditions involved the acceptance of Sucre's resignation, the calling of a constituent assembly to draft a new constitution, and financial settlements to defray the costs of occupation. It is difficult to determine the exact nature of Peruvian motives at this point. Certainly they wished to see all Colombian influence—meaning that of Bolívar, in particular—eliminated from both Peru and Bolivia. The possible incorporation of Bolivia into Peru was certainly not altogether absent from the minds of Peruvian political and military leaders, and there is little doubt that individual military commanders used the occupation as an opportunity to foment among the Bolivian populace some sentiment for annexation. Before matters could run their course, however, the Peruvian troops quit Bolivia to engage in the war with Gran Colombia and attempt the conquest of Guayaquil. The Bolivians were suddenly left to their own devices.

Neither Peru nor Bolivia was really prepared to undertake self-government. Both owed their independence largely to external forces. Neither had, in the process of gaining independence, developed outstanding leaders and statesmen comparable to those of Colombia, Chile, or Argentina. Rather, they fell back upon those military leaders brought to the fore during the era of Bolívar, and as was the case in Ecuador and Venezuela where similar military leadership prevailed, the legislative branches of government scarcely got off to a start. In Bolivia particularly, several attempts to get action out of the representative assembly after the departure of Sucre ended in such dismal failure and disorder that the body, called into being as a conventional assembly, went down in history known as the 'asamblea convulsional,' the assembly of convulsion. A major and related problem in Bolivia was the absence of any real sense of social or political unity among the Spanish-speaking population, to say nothing of course of the Indian masses who constituted the great majority of the Bolivian people but who had no role whatsoever in public affairs. The various figures who moved in the limited political circle were known as supporters of Sucre or Bolívar, of Peruvian ambitions, or of some other essentially alien individual or influence apart from development of a true Bolivian nationality. The man who finally emerged to bring some semblance of order to Bolivian national existence was a native son who had been a soldier under Bolívar, had headed the Peruvian interim government that ruled for a brief period during Bolívar's absence in 1826 and 1827, and who, when chosen to be president by the Bolivian congress, was in Chile engaged on a diplomatic mission for Peru. Thus in the generation of independence was leadership mobile and transferable. General Andrés Santa Cruz assumed the presidency of Bolivia in May, 1829, and thereupon undertook to stem the tide of anarchy that was sweeping his homeland and his adopted Peru as well.

Era of Santa Cruz

RULE IN BOLIVIA

For two years Santa Cruz ruled Bolivia as a dictator without a constitution and without any more legal claim to his office than his appointment by a congress called into being by a military agreement with Peru. Nevertheless, he enjoyed great personal popularity and the confidence of all elements that were politically articulate in Bolivia. When he took over as president, the treasury was empty, the economy of the country disrupted, the mines unproductive, and law and order non-existent. By 1831 Santa Cruz had been able to replenish the treasury by loans and taxes, to restore mining activity to some degree of productivity, and to build the armed forces of the country into a body capable of maintaining order and defending the country against foreign encroachment. It was then time to elect a constitutional assembly to draw up a new constitution and to place the presidential office on a legitimate basis. This was done. The various actions of Santa Cruz were ratified, a constitution was adopted providing for a two-house popularly elected legislative body, a chief executive assisted by a council of state, and an independent court system. Santa Cruz then set about, through the use of special committees, the development of basic legislative codes, such as the criminal code, code of civil procedures, commercial and mining codes, and others. This was an extremely important step, for a new country without a basic code structure and unused to the system of common law and judicial precedent common in Anglo-Saxon countries, had little or no basis upon which to perform the normal judicial and regulatory functions of government. Santa Cruz and his committees used French and Spanish precedents primarily, as eventually did most of the countries of Latin America, even though much French legislation was neither particularly good nor well suited to the Bolivian situation. Nevertheless, as a result of Santa Cruz' efforts, Bolivia became one of the first newly independent American states to possess a fairly complete codified legal structure.

ACHIEVEMENTS

Santa Cruz took other important steps to give his country some of the basic elements of nationhood. He founded universities in Cochabamba and La Paz, organized the medical and legal professions, and undertook to develop the rudiments of a secondary education system. Such constructive efforts served to add appreciably to the popularity of the president and to justify Marshal Sucre's confidence in the man, for Sucre had recommended him to the Bolivian political leaders at the moment of his retirement from the country. Santa Cruz, however, was a man of broad political convictions whose experience, as already indicated, included intimate association with the affairs of Peru. Like his earlier illustrious associates, he did not wish to be bound by the provincialism manifesting itself in the pattern of national jurisdictions that had emerged in the Andes region. Undoubtedly his success and general popularity in Bolivia influenced Santa Cruz to believe that he could provide the leadership for a grander structure within which both Bolivia and Peru might enjoy the benefits of unification. Conditions in Peru certainly indicated that a guiding hand was needed, for after the Peruvian armies had been turned back from Guayaquil by Sucre, all semblance of stability seemed to have departed the country that had so long served as Spain's principal kingdom in South America. President José de La Mar was shortly overthrown by the outstanding Peruvian army leader, General Agustín Gamarra, but Gamarra in turn was unable to establish himself firmly. By 1833 Peru was in the throes of general disorder and anarchy with rival claimants for power established in various parts of the national territory. These Peruvian difficulties played directly into the hands of Santa Cruz who treated with first one and then another of the Peruvian caudillos in an effort to gain support for his program of federation.

SANTA CRUZ CONFEDERATION

The motives of Santa Cruz have been subjected to severe criticism by both contemporaries and historians. Some assert that he was vain, lustful for personal power, avaricious in a financial sense, and in general a thoroughly reprehensible character. That he ruled Bolivia in a completely dictatorial manner is hardly to be questioned. Nevertheless, there is strong testimonial to the effect that however dictatorial, Santa Cruz' government was both moderate and progressive and only in a minor sense tyrannical. Further, it must at least be stated that his plan of confederation had the distinct merit of uniting Peru and Bolivia without subordinating either of the two countries to the other. True, the plan did subordinate both nations to his own personal rule, but no one can seriously deny that vigorous leadership was needed if the unification plan was to have even a faint hope of succeeding.

Whatever his motives, Santa Cruz requested and received from the Bolivian congress extraordinary authority to embark upon his unification program, and in 1835 his armies entered Peru to support General Orbegoso, one of the Peruvian claimants for power from whom Santa Cruz had received a promise of support in uniting the two countries. In two difficult battles the Bolivian army defeated both Generals Gamarra and Salaverry, and all Peru fell to Santa Cruz. There followed special congresses and agreements, and in the end a confederation was formed uniting north Peru, south Peru, and Bolivia in a three-way confederation. Each unit was provided with its own congress and executive officers, and Santa Cruz was chosen by the plenipotentiaries as protector, or chief executive, of the confederation. His term of office was to be ten years with re-election permitted.

There was much to be said for the confederation in that, had it endured, one of the causes of future international difficulty in the western region of South America might have been avoided. Of prime importance to Bolivia, and a matter of much discussion during the pre-federation maneuvers, was the matter of Bolivia's access to Pacific ports. In this period Bolivia possessed coastal territory between Peru and Chile. The region was largely desert and its harbors were less than satisfactory. It was eventually to prove an important source of nitrate and to attract Chilean investors and developers, thereby creating an international crisis that exploded into war and cost Bolivia her access to the sea. In the time of Santa Cruz, however, the question was one of access to ocean commerce, and the route to Arica and Cobija was not suitable. Commerce might move more easily over the older established trade routes through Peru to the ports of Mollendo and Callao. Peru, however, was inclined to press its geographic advantage and impose severe burdens on Bolivian commerce through its territory. Unification could well have ended such difficulties and made possible the movement of goods by routes uninfluenced by the artificialities of political boundaries. Furthermore, it might well have discouraged subsequent Chilean adventures in the nitrate fields of the Atacama desert. The Peru-Bolivian confederation was not to last, however.

CHILEAN OPPOSITION

Both Chile and Argentina viewed Santa Cruz' creation with strong disfavor. For a time the Bolivian leader attempted to calm his troubled neighbors with assurances of peaceful intentions, and even when Chilean expeditionary forces were sent against the confederation after a declaration of war, Santa Cruz preferred to negotiate rather than fight. Such efforts were unavailing, however, for Chile in particular was determined that the unification of her two northern neighbors should not endure. At the same time, it quickly became obvious that Santa Cruz had over-extended himself, for with the possibility of Chilean intervention latent opposition to the confederation dictator appeared in all quarters, including Bolivia. Defeated in battle by the Chileans at Yungay, Santa Cruz was quickly discredited. In February, 1839, the whole structure he had created crumbled around him. He fled to Ecuador and the confederation came to an end. Indeed, so bitter were the dictator's enemies that even in Bolivia they expressed approval of Chile's action in breaking up the confederation, outlawed Santa Cruz, and confiscated his personal property holdings. After contests for power in both countries, General Gamarra took over the presidency of Peru and General José Ballivián assumed the corresponding position in Bolivia. The era of Santa Cruz was at an end.

Not so the struggle for domination between Peru and Bolivia. President Gamarra blamed Bolivia for the problems created by Santa Cruz, and in 1841 he invaded the highland country during a struggle between Ballivián and a rival claimant for the presidency. The rival, General Velasco, immediately united his forces with those of his opponent, and in the battle that followed the Peruvian forces were routed and Gamarra killed. For a time, at least, the Peruvian threat to Bolivian independence was ended, and each country went its own way.

In Bolivia Ballivián was a national hero. He was formally chosen president by convention in 1843, at which time a new constitution was also proclaimed. Ballivián governed the country through a series of insurrections until the end of 1847. He then resigned his position and left the country on a diplomatic mission to Chile. His departure was forced, however, for conditions had reached such a state that he was in constant danger of assassination. Immediately upon his departure, political disorders spread throughout the country. Ballivián was the last of a series of men, beginning with Sucre, who had provided some semblance of orderly and constructive government for the new republic. Indeed, Ballivián accomplished more of lasting benefit in terms of physical improvements and extension of public services than did his more famous predecessors, but even his efforts to set a pattern of progressive national development came to naught in the long period of almost utter chaos and anarchy that began in 1848.

OLAÑETA

The early history of independent Bolivia is a history of violence, intrigue, and half-way successful efforts by three outstanding men to give the nation leadership in its formative years. Strangely in the background is another figure, almost lost in the shadows of forgotten records and dust-covered documents. The man, Don Casimiro Olañeta, was the nephew of a Spanish general who fought against the independence movement. Perhaps a monarchist at heart, as was his better-known counterpart in Mexico, Lucas Alamán, Olañeta exercised considerable influence in Bolivian affairs

throughout the entire period until the departure of Ballivián and even afterward. Now a minister of state, then a court justice, later an ambassador
to Chile, Olañeta was deeply involved in the intrigue that marked the rise
and fall of each of the three outstanding presidents of the era beginning
with Sucre. An educated man, he wrote ably but caustically to persuade
prominent men of his day in favor of or in opposition to the chief political
figures. He appears to have had few scruples. In the fall of Sucre, his fine
hand is seen encouraging the Peruvian Gamarra to invade Bolivia. He supported Santa Cruz and served as his ambassador in Chile, yet quickly and
nimbly shifted to the opposition as the Protector's position weakened. In
the closing days of Ballivián's presidency, Olañeta's evil pen was at work
to bring about the downfall of the last of Bolivia's early constructive leaders. In part, at least, this back-stage detractor was responsible for the numerous sharp and bitter about-faces that came to characterize Bolivian
public life and that made it all but impossible to resolve political questions
on any other basis than force and violence.

Peru

RAMÓN CASTILLA

As Bolivia tumbled into the abyss of unrestrained lawlessness, Peru settled
down to enjoy the benefits of its first stable government since independence. The death in battle of President Gamarra had touched off a new series of internal struggles for political power that lasted until 1844. In that
year, a young mestizo caudillo from Tarapacá, Ramón Castilla, achieved
victory over his competitors and control of the government in Lima. The
following year he was named constitutional president of Peru for a six-
year term, and under his firm and able leadership the country enjoyed a
period of relief from internal strife and undertook a number of important
economic and commercial improvements. It had been discovered that the
accumulated tons of bird excretions that virtually covered the Chincha islands in the bay of Pisco were an excellent source of nitrates. This product
came into great demand in Europe, as did nitrates from the enormous salt
beds of the Atacama desert region. Overnight, export of guano (bird deposits) became a most profitable business, and this desirable traffic was
augmented by activities in the desert mineral fields. Castilla's government

extracted and exported the guano fertilizer as a government monopoly and thereby brought millions of dollars into the national treasury each year. Basically an honest man, Castilla put the huge revenues to good use in stabilizing the fiscal system and in making payments on foreign loans contracted during the revolutionary era.

For a time, at least, the stability and financial soundness of the Peruvian economy seemed assured and private investment increased. New buildings arose, roads were constructed, and a railroad line was built linking Lima with the near-by port of Callao. Other improvements of a similar nature were undertaken and the country prospered. Castilla nevertheless occasionally had time to roil the troubled waters of Peru-Bolivian relationships.

At the end of his term of office, Castilla retired and a much lesser man, José Rufino Echenique, was made president. Echenique could not avoid the temptation to convert to his personal use and that of his friends some portion of the handsome government revenue, and soon the whole moral tone of the government service declined. Public confidence disappeared and domestic commerce languished. Soon a revolutionary plot was under way, headed by Castilla, and Echenique was overthrown and exiled. Castilla resumed the presidential office after a *pro forma* election and continued in that position until 1862. Again the country prospered and numerous improvements were fostered, this time in a less material sense. The few remaining slaves in Peru were freed, the Indians were relieved of paying tribute, and a feeble attempt, at least, was made to provide some facilities for public education. Also during Castilla's second term of office a new constitution was drawn up and adopted, providing as had earlier basic laws for a national unitary government of separated executive, legislative, and judicial powers. At the same time the presidential term was reduced from six to four years and immediate re-election prohibited.

The long period of relative tranquility was discouraging to ambitious local political leaders, however. Castilla ruled with a firm and almost dictatorial hand, and he was able to keep things under control until he retired from office. Signs of unrest were apparent when a revolt occurred in Arequipa in 1856, an insurrection in which the Peruvian naval forces joined. Indeed, reduction of the presidential term and the ban on re-election provided by the 1860 constitution were further indications that Castilla's long rule was becoming tiresome. His departure from office signaled a return to corrupt and chaotic government.

Ecuador

FLORES REGIME

Farther north, in Ecuador, independence provided no better guarantee of a secure life for the people than it had in Bolivia and Peru. Juan José Flores, the first president, ruled with a heavy hand that offered no relief from the political and religious exploitation that had aroused liberal opposition to the Spaniards in 1809 and 1810. Opposition was ever present, particularly in Guayaquil where separation from Quito seemed to have a continuing appeal. Likewise, outspoken liberals, who wished to curtail the authority of the church and permit greater freedom of expression, posed a constant threat to Flores' regime. The principal liberal leader, Vicente Rocafuerte, who had a strong following in Guayaquil, proved particularly dangerous. Flores arranged with him to alternate presidential terms, and for eight years the agreement was kept. In 1843, however, Flores, after serving his allotted four-year term, broke faith and secured re-election for eight years under a new constitution. Rocafuerte was pacified with a handsome pension, but other liberals were not so easily placated. They revolted and threw Flores from office and into exile, leaving the country without effective leadership. Liberal zealots commited numerous anticlerical acts and these were reciprocated by acts of violence on the part of church supporters. Soon the country was in complete disorder, racked by widespread and continuous violence. Individual caudillos controlled this or that section of the national territory for brief periods and then lost out to rival claimants. Trouble arose with New Granada and Peru. For fifteen years there existed no Ecuadorian government worthy of the name. Finally, in 1860, Flores saw an opportunity to return from exile and join forces with Gabriel García Moreno, a strange, ultraconservative intellectual who had formed a movement to restore order in the country and bring about political reform along lines in keeping with the conservative tradition of imperial Spain. Inasmuch as a military effort was needed Flores proved useful, for García Moreno was a writer, a university rector, a lawyer, and a politician, but no soldier. Together, the two men ousted the local caudillo in Guayaquil, who had attempted to turn over that port city to Peru, and moved on to take over the country. Quickly Flores was brushed aside, and the long regime of García Moreno began.

GARCÍA MORENO

By 1860 caudillo government had become the rule in all the outlying regions touched by the Bolivarian epic. It was government by the military with a vengeance, and it had led to anarchy, violence, and chaos, interrupted for greater or lesser periods by the stable regime of an outstanding man. In none of the countries, Peru, Bolivia, Ecuador, or Venezuela, did substantive issues or programs provide the basis for political activity nor did they significantly influence the selection of men for public office. True, in some of the countries people called themselves conservatives or liberals, but these labels had little bearing on how men thought or acted. More often they distinguished one group of landholders from another. Those whose wealth and influence were concentrated near the capital were centralist and conservative. Those whose power lay in the provinces favored decentralization, which represented a change from the established pattern; they were *ipso facto* liberals. Such matters were essentially personal and proprietary. To the long parade of military upstarts who strutted across the national stage, most of whose family connections were somewhat vague, even these considerations meant little. Power and wealth were their objectives, and the issues that concerned them were the personal battles with their military rivals. Without system or tradition, with no firm rooting in the minds and hearts of men, the republican form of government served only as a phrase written into each succeeding constitution. Who, after all, would constitutionally describe his government as military despotism intermixed with anarchy! As for popular democracy, no one even dreamed of that in a country populated largely by subservient Indians.

It was perhaps no accident that for years following the Bolívar era, the affairs of Peru and Bolivia were strangely intermixed. The two regions had been closely united for centuries until the audiencia in Charcas was attached to the viceroyalty of Río de la Plata late in the eighteenth century. Once Spanish domination was at an end, the old ties were reasserted and Buenos Aires, torn with its own problems, was quickly forgotten. Peruvians sought to dominate Bolivia and Bolivians sought to dominate Peru. The first victim of this development was Marshal Sucre, who, in 1828, was faced with rebellion in Bolivia, invasion from Peru, and mutiny among his own Colombian troops. He was forced to resign and return northward. Sucre, far more than Bolívar, was the creator of the Bolivian nation. As

Bolívar's field commander, his was the army of liberation and he the hero of the last great battle with the Spaniards at Ayacucho. He it was who, in opposition to the expressed wishes of Bolívar, called into being the first legislative body of Bolivia and supported its declaration of independence. It was Sucre who with great difficulty persuaded the liberator to accept that decision and endorse Bolivian independence. It was he who gave to Bolivia its first independent government. Had he given up his ties with Bolívar he might have been able to maintain his position as head of the new state; but he wisely refused to regard himself as other than an interim chief executive bound sooner or later to hand over to the Bolivians control of their own destinies. Thus it was that although his departure was forced it was not unexpected. His tragic death in Ecuador was but another event in the long record of discord that was to characterize the relationships of the southern Bolivarian republics for generations to come.

6

The Age of Santa Anna

> The new rulers of independent Mexico were the military. . . . . Law was
> their will; assassination and betrayal were their weapons; their price
> was the wealth of their country.
>
> LESLEY BYRD SIMPSON *

Ephemeral Empire

The former viceroyalty of New Spain presented a dreary picture indeed in
the decades immediately following independence. Throughout its whole,
vast extent there was no order, no peace, no security. The greatest and the
richest of Spain's former dominions had become the most miserable of independent states. Probably in no other region of Latin America, with the
exception of French Saint Domingue, had the wars of independence so utterly destroyed the fabric of society. In no other place had the excesses of
the old order provoked dissenting priests into leading hordes of ignorant
and untrained Indians in an orgy of plunder and rapine and to their eventual slaughter at the hands of Spanish soldiery. Nowhere else did the struggle degenerate so completely into a mad mêlée of warring factions fighting
without purpose, without understanding, without identification of principles or objectives. A struggle that began as an assertion of freedom from
the misgovernment of Spain and the oppression of the military and religious oligarchy became so confused that independence was finally achieved
under a counter-revolutionary movement in opposition to the 'radical' constitutional system proclaimed by the Spanish monarchy in 1820.

* *Many Mexicos*, University of California Press, Berkeley, copyright 1941, 1946,
1952, p. 199.

109

ITURBIDE

Independence, of course, did not put an end to the difficulties. It only cut the last weak cord that tied the vast region to the rotting tree of empire and the one remaining source of order and stability. Agustín Iturbide, whose defection from the Spanish cause at Iguala turned the tables on Spain, found himself in a very dubious position. An avowed monarchist, he had just thrown his army against the remaining feeble forces of Fernando VII. A strong supporter of the Catholic Church and the privileges of the clergy, he had just allied himself with the anticlerical republican revolutionaries; and, as an ally of the republicans, he proclaimed the continuance of monarchy and the virtues of the old order. Had Iturbide been a man of great ability and political astuteness, he might have gotten away with his utterly opportunistic anomalisms and united a majority of the factions behind him. He was no such man. On the contrary, he was a vain autocrat of little tact and no patience. His personal ambition led him to believe that with the army behind him he could succeed in any unscrupulous act of deception and betrayal. He overlooked the fundamental difficulty of keeping the support of the army without money.

The aged viceroy O'Donojú had accepted the Plan of Iguala under duress. The Spanish government rejected it. At this juncture, Iturbide found himself looking down what appeared to be an open road to the emperorship of his headless monarchy. He had little support from the Bourbon sympathizers, who could see no sign of the required royal blood in the upstart mestizo. Likewise, the numerous republicans rejected his royal pretensions, for they were in no mood to countenance monarchy whoever the king or emperor might be. But these groups were paralyzed by the lack of either program or leadership. Iturbide was strong enough to form a provisional junta and a committee of regency, both of which he headed. A congress was called into being with due care exercised that the membership was predominantly monarchist in sentiment. Iturbide immediately encountered difficulty with his congress, however, for it was truly a do-nothing legislative body. It failed to provide needed fiscal support for the military and was particularly disinclined to support the ambitions of Iturbide for a crown. Bourbon monarchists and republicans drew together in their common distrust of the regency chairman. There was serious danger that lack of action and general dissatisfaction with the government would bring about the downfall of the regime. Frustrated and desperate, Iturbide decided to move things along a bit in his own way.

The regency chief had sufficient army support to stage in the capital an impressive parade and demonstration. The chanted theme of the participants was 'Viva Agustín Primero.' The cry was soon taken up by the rabble and a large crowd gathered in front of the regency building demanding the appearance of the prospective monarch. The 'reluctant' chief acceded to the popular clamor and consented to accept the crown. The coronation took place in July of 1822.

Mexico's upstart 'emperor' quickly set about strengthening his grip on the country. Congress, which had been frightened by the Mexico City mob into voting for Iturbide's coronation, remained cold to the executive's proposals. It would vote no taxes and it would not work seriously on a constitution. Finally, Iturbide imprisoned fifteen members of the legislative body, dissolved the congress and reconstituted it with fewer and more tractable deputies, but to no effect. Thereupon he began ruling openly as dictator and the sole and final authority in the government.

One of Iturbide's first steps as 'emperor' was to attempt to secure recognition of his authority throughout all the mainland region that had been New Spain. The captaincy-general of Guatemala had proclaimed its independence from Spain in the late summer of 1821 after word arrived of the events transpiring in Mexico. Iturbide had sent an invitation to join in the new Mexican state, and deputies from the former captaincy-general were present in Iturbide's congress. Difficulty arose, however, when it became apparent that a monarchy was to be retained and that Iturbide was to be the emperor, for republican feeling ran strong throughout most of Central America. Adherence to Mexico, furthermore, was by no means an entirely acceptable course of action to all provinces of the former captaincy-general. Leaders in Salvador openly opposed such a step, and those in Honduras, Nicaragua, and Costa Rica were little more enthusiastic. In Nicaragua and Costa Rica, inter-city squabbles loomed large in local affairs and the question of association with the central region of the former viceroyalty received little attention. Iturbide, nevertheless, sent an army to enforce his imperial authority, but it made little headway beyond Guatemala. It was stalled near San Salvador when word came that the 'emperor' had found it convenient to seek employment elsewhere and that a republican regime had been proclaimed in Mexico City. The Mexican army thereupon withdrew, and a general assembly was called in Guatemala City to decide upon a future course of action. At the assembly, the five provinces determined to join in the formation of an independent federation to be known as the United Provinces of Central America. Only the remote region of Chiapas, which had in the past been a part of the Guatemalan captaincy-general, remained with Mexico. Both Mexico and the United Provinces were far too preoccupied with their own internal problems to do more than mark for future dispute the issue of the political fate of the primitive jungle district between them.

Mexico made no move with respect to the Spanish insular possessions, which were left to shift for themselves. Neither Puerto Rico nor Cuba was sufficiently strong to cast off Spanish dc nination unaided, for the mother country held them far more firmly than she had Santo Domingo, which had been absorbed by Haiti in 1821. As noted earlier, abortive uprisings had been easily crushed in Puerto Rico in 1815; and after Spain in 1820 restored the liberal Constitution of 1812, the privilege of having a colonial assembly and representation in the Spanish Cortes calmed revolutionaries in both Puerto Rico and Cuba. Liberalism in Spain was short-lived, and when, in 1823, the king regained his autocratic authority and restored rigid control over the internal affairs of the colonies, restlessness became rife, particularly in Cuba. Puerto Rico was too isolated to make much pretense of revolt, and Cuba was too heavily garrisoned with Spanish soldiery to leave independence leaders much hope of success.

Mexico was quite unable to provide assistance to any other region of the empire in its struggle for independence, not even to the islands that had formerly been under the nominal jurisdiction of the viceroy at Mexico City. The crusading spirit that brought Bolívar and San Martín together in Peru from opposite ends of the South American continent had no counterpart in the independence movements north of Panama. The ambitious 'emperor' Agustín was unable to hold the continental realm together; much less was he able to embark upon an insular campaign.

Iturbide's reign was short. Having no claim to regal status, he did his best to make up for this lack by show and extravagance. He created a new nobility whose members immediately became the objects of ridicule and buffoonery. The treasury was already bare, and to finance his pretentious display of imperial pomp, Iturbide turned to the expedient of exacting forced loans from the wealthy—a measure designed to win him few friends. His high-handed methods, his extreme clericalism, his utterly ridiculous pretensions, and his wanton waste of public funds in the midst of poverty converted more monarchists into republicans than the exhortations of political theorists could ever have done. Iturbide even committed the cardinal sin of forgetting his military supporters. Some of them he snubbed; most of them he left unpaid. When the congress would vote him no funds, he flooded the country with worthless paper scrip. Conditions quickly went from bad to worse, and the machinery of state ground to a halt.

Too late did the would-be monarch realize his mistakes and seek to conciliate his detractors. In vain he searched for supporters; none remained. In December of 1822, an able and opportunistic military leader whom the 'emperor' had snubbed, the commandant at Veracruz, saw his opportunity and pronounced against the 'empire.' The commandant, Antonio López de Santa Anna, was a mere upstart, and his pronunciamiento would have appeared absurd had the atmosphere been less volatile. But others were of like mind, and the faltering Iturbide was helpless to check the rising tide of opposition. In February of 1823 he resigned and accepted a pension voted in token of his services to the country and granted on condition that he leave Mexico and not return.

Iturbide went to Italy, but in exile he showed even less wisdom than he had demonstrated at home. He planned to return. Within two years, ignorant of the fact that his enemies were aware of his designs and had moved to forestall him, Iturbide landed on Mexican soil. He was arrested immediately, and his subsequent execution was carried out within a matter of days. Would-be Mexican emperors of the future would have done well to ponder this lesson.

Age of Santa Anna

With the departure of Iturbide, Mexico entered upon a period that has come to be known as the 'Age of Santa Anna,' certainly the most dismal period in all Mexican history. Vain, arrogant, shrewd, and beset with a profound sense of boredom that verged on psychosis, Santa Anna amazed the world by his comings and goings, his military exploits, his skill at political manipulation. For over thirty years he dominated the Mexican political stage, and under his guiding hand the once magnificent colonial kingdom reached the nadir of national calamity. In vain have historians and students of government sought to explain the strange hold that this prince of caudillos maintained on the minds and emotions of his countrymen. No less than eleven times did he step to the center of the stage to direct the destinies of Mexico, and eleven times he let his people down. Yet in each new national crisis some fool was always ready to call back the 'hero' of Manga de Clavo.* Perhaps the greatest tribute ever paid the man was the decision of a museum curator to hang his autographed picture upon the wall of the Lee Chapel museum in Lexington, Virginia, where the likeness of the dashing Mexican general looks down upon the skeleton of Robert E. Lee's famous horse.

Santa Anna did not lead the movement that overthrew the government of Iturbide. Although he had been the first to pronounce for a republic, he remained at Veracruz and prepared to flee the country if others did not come to his support. The chief figure to emerge from the chaos of Iturbide's downfall was Guadalupe Victoria, the popular general who had played an important role in the revolutionary army of Morelos. Guadalupe Victoria had broken early with the would-be emperor and had been residing in self-imposed exile in the mountains above Veracruz, but with the first mutterings of revolution he came forth and headed the army of 'liberation.' He became Mexico's first president.

In Mexico, society was still divided into a multitude of corporate bodies held together by similar occupation or function. Unlike European nobility, the creole aristocrats did not exercise any civil jurisdiction or any political power. Each corporate entity—each group or class—defended its own interests. None of them thought in terms of national good.

The new congress, summoned after the downfall of the 'empire,' drew up Mexico's first republican constitution. The document represented the views of the extreme liberals who dominated the congress, and provided for a decentralized federal system of nineteen states and several territories. Mexican federalism was a by-product of the provincial deputations called for in the Spanish Constitution of 1812. Father Miguel Ramos Arizpe, who had served in the Cortes of Cádiz, was an ardent supporter of the provincial deputations, and he became the 'Father of Mexican federalism' in the Constituent Congress of 1823–24.

The three branches of government—executive, legislative, and judicial —were patterned closely after those of the United States, except that the president and vice-president were to be chosen by the state legislatures rather than by an electoral college, and the president was not permitted to succeed himself. An important innovation was introduced in that the church was deprived of its monopoly over education.

The new constitution was an absurdity in Mexico. Its idealism was ex-

* Manga de Clavo was Santa Anna's estate in Veracruz.

cellent, but the realities of Mexican social and political life belied its underlying assumptions. The states, for the most part artificial creations of the law, were not homogeneous political units. They possessed no traditions of self-government nor had they any experience in the use of legislative bodies. The majority of the population in all the states was composed of illiterate Indians and mestizos accustomed only to a life of servitude and social segregation. Their participation in government as independent voting citizens would have run counter to the fundamental scheme of social existence and to their very outlook on life. They could only blindly respond to the exhortations of the clerics or follow the instructions of the local caudillos and politicos who plied them with pulque and herded them in drunken hordes to the polls. Many, still living in the back-country wilds where the rudiments of the Spanish language had not even reached them, were completely outside the orbit of political life.

Of fundamental importance was the absence of any sort of political consensus. No group or class seemed willing to place the interest of the new nation above what it conceived to be its own selfish interest. Compromise, the very essence of republican and democratic government, was utterly alien to the spirit of even the most altruistic of political leaders.

Given these difficulties, the new government did remarkably well for the first four years. Guadalupe Victoria, upon being chosen to the presidency, had sufficient military backing to maintain himself in office and serve out his term. He was not strong enough, however, to face realistically the problems that confronted his administration. The most pressing problems were financial. With commerce and industry disrupted by the years of revolution and chaos and with Indian tribute abolished, revenues were wholly inadequate. Expenditures, two-thirds of which were absorbed by a bloated military establishment, far exceeded available resources. Faced with this dilemma, the government under Guadalupe Victoria's leadership turned to a disastrous expedient. It borrowed from abroad. Loans were negotiated with London bankers at exorbitant discount rates and the money squandered in useless military expenditures. Thus was inaugurated a sequence of financial manipulations that created crisis after crisis. Viewed in retrospect, it is difficult to see who were the bigger dupes, the foreign money lenders or the Mexican politicians. The government was seldom able to pay even the interest on its loans, and the foreign investors, unable to collect their accounts, turned to their governments to have political pressure exerted on the irresponsible officials of the Mexican republic. Financial default became the standing issue of Mexican diplomatic negotiations, and in the end it was a major factor in attracting foreign military adventurers to Mexican soil. The consequences of Guadalupe Victoria's policies were hardly to be foreseen during his four-year term of office, but the precedent of irresponsibility in fiscal policy was firmly adhered to by his even more irresponsible successors.

The government's weakness lay in the fact that it was utterly dependent upon the military, and the military were a pack of gluttonous wolves interested only in their regular feed. Victoria's government was opposed by the church, by the landowners, and by the conservative Scottish-rite Masons. The president did not care to risk certain revolution by attempting to tax the wealth of these groups. He found himself in a vicious trap and took what seemed the only course open to him. His path was made much easier by the intrigue of foreign agents. H. G. Ward, the British chargé, d'affaires, and Joel Poinsett, the American minister, competed strenuously for influence over the new government. The tactless Poinsett, working in alliance with the York-rite Masons, made himself so obnoxious that his recall was requested, but not until he had become deeply involved in Mexican politics. Lucas Alamán, a powerful conservative aristocrat, was strongly favorable to British interests during the many times he was in the government as a minister of state, and to his pro-British sentiment was due in part the success enjoyed by Ward in tying the new government to the coat-tails of British financiers. The British played a vigorous game of sterling diplomacy, and their interest grew apace with favorable trade agreements and heavy investments in Mexican mining stock and other commercial enterprises. Mexico took her first steps toward becoming an economic dependency of alien powers.

Mexican liberal leaders such as José María Luis Mora were concerned with creating free political institutions where none had existed before. In Spain the regime of privileged corporate bodies had been destroyed both by Joseph Bonaparte and the Cortes of Cádiz, but it remained deeply entrenched in Mexico. This tradition of privileged corporate groups, together with the custom of centralized power, made the creation of a constitutional regime extremely difficult. Mexican liberals maintained great faith in the miracle-working powers of constitutions until 1827. This ephemeral optimism was a reflection of the liberals' tendency to identify themselves with the United States, where the adoption of a federal constitution was followed by rapid economic progress.

In the election of 1828 General Manuel Gómez Pedraza, a former officer of the Spanish army, was chosen president by the state legislatures.

The vote was ten to nine, each state having one vote. Gómez Pedraza was a strong conservative with support from the church and the Scottish-rite Masons, and the liberal-republican opposition whose defeated candidate had been an old revolutionary general, Vicente Guerrero, refused to accept the electoral verdict. Guerrero pronounced against the president-elect.

For four years little had been heard from Veracruz. Now the young commandant decided once again to take a hand in national politics. Santa Anna pronounced in support of Guerrero, insisting that he would not stand idly by and see the Inquisition re-established by the conservatives. Gómez Pedraza attempted to crush the uprising and he might have been successful had he not broadened his attack to crush other political adversaries who were not in revolt. Other factions pronounced and the president-elect left the country. In January of 1829 the retiring Victoria handed over the government to Guerrero. Again Santa Anna had triggered the overthrow of the national government, but his role in the hostilities had been inconsequential. He was not yet a hero.

Santa Anna soon had a better opportunity. Fernando VII noted the chaos prevailing in Mexico, and he decided to send an army to restore order in what he considered to be still his colony. The army was landed at Tampico where it took the fortress, only to be abandoned by the fleet that had brought it. Santa Anna rushed from Veracruz to accept the surrender of a fever-ridden expeditionary force with no line of retreat. Now he was a hero, and the country began to take notice of him.

The Spanish attempt to recover the former colony touched off a new series of reprisals against Spanish-born residents of Mexico City. It was an opportunity for more looting and destruction, and the mob rose to the occasion. A considerable exodus occurred among the Spanish merchant class, and the economy of the country was further weakened by the resulting decrease in commercial activity. Guerrero was unable to maintain order and reaction set in against him. His vice-president, Anastasio Bustamante, plotted his overthrow, and in 1830 a defection of the army permitted Bustamante to take over the government. Guerrero fled, only to be delivered up to the authorities for execution by an Italian sea captain at Acapulco in exchange for 50,000 pesos. Santa Anna talked loudly but remained in Veracruz.

Bustamante ruled Mexico for two years, but he was a tool of the reactionaries. Lucas Alamán directed national policies, and for the first time since the overthrow of Iturbide the conservatives enjoyed the fruits of office. A military dictatorship was imposed that ruled by terror and violence in the name of religion and the privileges of the military caste. Santa Anna bided his time and when the inevitable reaction set in, fanned by the execution of the revolutionary hero, Guerrero, he made a new pronouncement. Others followed and Bustamante retired, leaving the government in the hands of the man who had been constitutionally elected in 1828, General Gómez Pedraza. In the turmoil that followed during the spring of 1833, Santa Anna was chosen president.

Beginning with his pronouncement against Iturbide in 1822, Santa Anna's campaign for the presidency had been a long one. Perhaps the Veracruz commandant was not really campaigning after all. When the day of his inauguration arrived, he stayed home at Manga de Clavo. His vice-president, Valentín Gómez Farías, took office as acting president, and Santa Anna let him have a free hand, or, more aptly, all the rope he needed to hang himself. Santa Anna was a coquet who enjoyed power only for the sheer love of wielding it. He had no desire to administer the affairs of state, for he had no objectives in view, no program to accomplish. He wished only to toy with the government and with the lives and fortunes of the sycophants who waited eagerly for their cues. He wanted to be begged, wheedled, and cajoled until finally, bored with his flatterers, he would turn and destroy them and look for some new diversion. What a man to choose for president of a struggling new republic!

GÓMEZ FARÍAS

Gómez Farías was no sycophant. He was an able liberal leader determined to place the Mexican governmental house in order. Supported by a liberal congress, he embarked upon far-reaching reforms. He struck at the resources of the church by making the payment of tithes voluntary, by assuming control over church patronage, by closing the Indian missions in California, and by limiting the jurisdiction of the ecclesiastical courts. Like other 'liberals' he wanted to deprive the church of its prerogatives and still preserve the state's right of patronage. Then he turned to the problem of reducing the military to size, proposing to decrease their number and curtail the special judicial immunities they enjoyed.

Gómez Farías lasted about a year. Santa Anna stood aside and allowed matters to take their course, interfering only occasionally. In the meantime, the conservative political factions became increasingly incensed. Army officers and the church united their voices in the cry of *religión y fueros,* or 'religion and privileges.' Someone had to be found to deliver them from the liberal regime that was attacking the very foundation of their privileged existence. They turned, of course, to Santa Anna; and after sufficient coaxing he responded. In the spring of 1834, the 'savior of religion' threw out the man he himself had placed in power and assumed absolute control of the government. All along he had been the master, but every so often he felt called upon to reverse the whole political system lest anyone forget who was calling the tune. So degraded had political life become that Santa Anna had little difficulty in reasserting his power. The liberals who had originally supported him for the presidency were crushed and demoralized. Gómez Farías and other leaders were hounded into exile; the only remnant of their reforming efforts was the law making tithing voluntary.

It is not important to detail here all the political shifts and maneuvers that took place in the years immediately following the return to power of the conservatives in 1834. Santa Anna did not long remain in office but retired again to his Veracruz estate. He much preferred to play cat and mouse than to rule the country, always pouncing again just when the mouse was about to make good its escape. One by one the mice died, and the country grew weaker and weaker.

DISINTEGRATION

Between 1835 and 1848 conditions in all of Mexico went from bad to worse. The same was true in Central America. It was a period of political fragmentation and economic collapse. There was imminent danger that the entire region would break down into a multitude of anarchic little states, and indeed there were times when even ineffective government virtually disappeared and only roving bands of barefoot soldiery dared venture upon the roads of the countryside.

It is not really surprising that Mexico was unable to retain her vast domains. Every outlying region was lightly held, and the continuous struggle for control of the central government left little time for attention to affairs in the states and territories. It was on the northeastern frontier that the first signs of disintegration appeared. Anglo-Saxon settlers from the United States began to enter the territory of Texas as early as 1824 under a concession granted by the Mexican government to Stephen Austin, an American frontiersman of venturesome spirit who was interested in the rich land

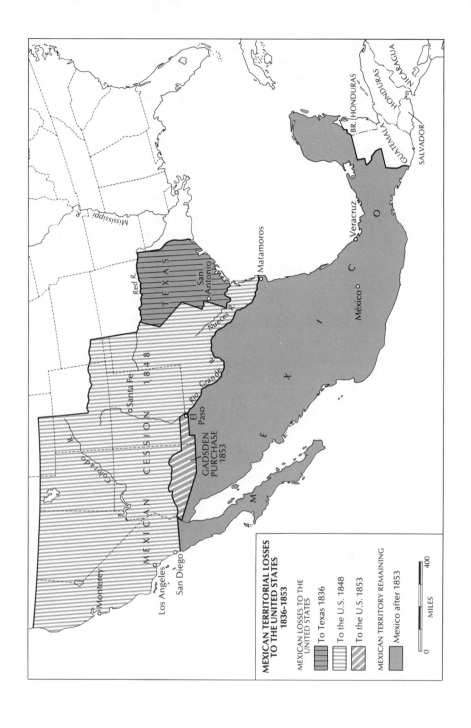

MEXICAN TERRITORIAL LOSSES TO THE UNITED STATES 1836-1853

MEXICAN LOSSES TO THE UNITED STATES

To Texas 1836

To the U.S. 1848

To the U.S. 1853

MEXICAN TERRITORY REMAINING

Mexico after 1853

MILES
0   400

Mississippi

TEXAS

San Antonio

Red R.

Nueces R.

Matamoros

Veracruz

México

MEXICAN CESSION

1848

Santa Fe

Colorado R.

Rio Grande

El Paso

GADSDEN PURCHASE 1853

Monterey

Los Angeles

San Diego

MEXICO

GUATEMALA

BR. HONDURAS

HONDURAS

NICARAGUA

SALVADOR

along the Brazos river. Mexico was at first anxious to have its northern land settled, but as time went on the increasing hazard to national sovereignty in the region became apparent. There were few Mexicans in Texas when the original concession was made, and the English-speaking settlers lived unto themselves. They were even exempt from taxation under the terms of Austin's agreement, as well as under those of later grants.

LOSS OF TEXAS

As the alien population continued to mount Mexican leaders began to perceive the danger. Many of the settlers were unruly characters seeking escape from their creditors or from the sheriff in the United States; they could hardly be expected to mend their ways upon becoming Mexican subjects. Others brought slaves with them, even though slavery in Mexico was nearly unknown. An almost constant squabble over land claims gave rise to disorder and caused Mexican officials much concern. Steps were therefore taken to curb the influx of American settlers and restrict the influence of those already established in Mexico.

The Mexican congress enacted several laws intended to discourage further settlement. One enactment abolished slavery throughout the republic and another prohibited the entry of non-Catholics. An attempt was made to collect customs duties at the frontier. When these measures proved ineffective and a survey by a prominent Mexican official indicated that slavery continued to prevail and that non-Catholics were still entering the country in large numbers, more drastic action was taken. In 1830 a decree was issued prohibiting further colonization from the United States, and troops were sent into the Texas region to enforce the law and insure the collection of customs duties. In addition, Mexican settlers were urged to enter Texas to counter-balance the large Anglo-Saxon population. These measures, while more effective than any of those previously taken, had the immediate effect of inflaming the Texas settlers to the point of rebellion.

Mexican leaders had good reason to be alarmed about the future status of the 15,000 or more Americans living inside the Texas boundaries. That prominent leaders in the United States had designs upon the region was well known. While Minister to Mexico Joel Poinsett had indicated the possibility of purchase; others were inclined to argue that the Texas territory was part of the vast tract of land included in the ill-defined Louisiana Purchase which brought the Mississippi valley and land to the west into the

United States in 1803. Lucas Alamán was particularly distrustful of the intentions of Mexico's northern neighbor, and his fears were transmitted to many of those around him. British agents and diplomats in Mexico City, ever vengeful in their attitude toward the United States and jealous of the growing power of the former British dominions, missed no opportunity to play skillfully upon Mexican misgivings. The cold fact of the matter was, however, that once settlers from the United States had moved into Texas in large numbers and established their homes there, nothing short of a miracle could have prevented the loss of that region by the Mexican republic. Not even Santa Anna was adept at performing this kind of miracle, although it must be said that he tried.

The inevitable might have been postponed had Texas been granted separate statehood in the Mexican federal system. Stephen Austin realized this and went to Mexico City to argue the case for autonomy, but he was jailed for his trouble. When open resistance to Mexican authority broke out in San Antonio, Santa Anna recruited an army and headed north.

In February of 1836 Santa Anna reached San Antonio in command of an ill-equipped and ill-trained Mexican army. He found the Texans disorganized. Austin, released from prison in Mexico, had rushed to Washington in the hope of securing aid from the United States. A group of 150 settlers and adventurers had formed a defensive force. Too few in numbers to face Santa Anna in open combat, they turned an old mission building, the Alamo, into a fortress and prepared to defend it. The Texans were commanded by William Barrett Travis. Santa Anna surrounded and attacked the Alamo fortress, but was at first repulsed. Finally, after a brief siege, the Mexican army broke through the Texan defenses and a fight to the death ensued—a fight in which every last defender died. No quarter was given, and there is little to indicate that any was asked.

In the meantime, a rump convention held in eastern Texas had issued a declaration of Texan independence. A government was formed and a military commander was named to defend it. The commander was Sam Houston, a true adventurer capable, when sober, of directing frontier warfare in true Western style. Now the issue was finally drawn, and Santa Anna had the choice of returning to Mexico to boast of his accomplishments in San Antonio or of adding to his exploits by crushing rebellion throughout the Texas territory. He chose the latter course and soon came to regret his decision. His first efforts were highly encouraging, for Texans fled eastward before his armies in complete confusion, and it appeared that the erstwhile Yankees might be driven from Mexican soil without so much as a major skirmish. Near the San Jacinto river, however, Houston prepared for battle, and the foolish Santa Anna, confident that he held the initiative, took few precautions against a Texan attack. Shortly before his dinner hour Santa Anna was rudely awakened from a siesta by heavy gunfire and shouts of 'Remember the Alamo!' There was no opportunity for defense, and the Mexican army was quickly decimated or captured while the great general fled the scene of battle dressed in his red carpet slippers.

Santa Anna's defeat was climaxed by his capture the day after the battle and his narrow escape from on-the-spot execution. Finally, however, he was spared and sent to the United States to discuss his problems with Andrew Jackson. Unfortunately for Mexico, the American government finally sent him home. Texas was in fact independent, barred from entry into the United States by northern fear of adding new slave territory to the Union, and separated from Mexico by a gulf of hatred that would endure for years. The Mexican government firmly refused to recognize Texas' claim to independence, but it made no serious effort to reconquer the region by military action. Mexico was encouraged in its refusal by the sorry state of Texan affairs and the failure of Texan military undertakings against Mexican settlements in New Mexico and Tamaulipas. The Texas republic appeared to be destined for a short career.

Central America

In other parts of the former Spanish viceroyalty matters were little better. From its inception the confederation in Central America was torn by controversy. At first the major issue was the authority of the church and the relationship it should bear to the republican authorities. Liberalism in religious matters centered in Salvador where efforts were made to secularize education and where a local priest, Matías Delgado, secured the creation of a separate diocese and an appointment as its first bishop. The archbishop at Guatemala City opposed this arrangement vigorously. Manuel José Arce, elected president of the confederation in 1825 as a candidate of the liberal forces, soon indicated that his sympathies lay with the archbishop, and his earlier backers felt that they had been betrayed. In 1826, passions inflamed by the exhortations of the clerics reached the boiling point; the vice-governor of Guatemala, a liberal, was assassinated by an incited mob. Open warfare followed.

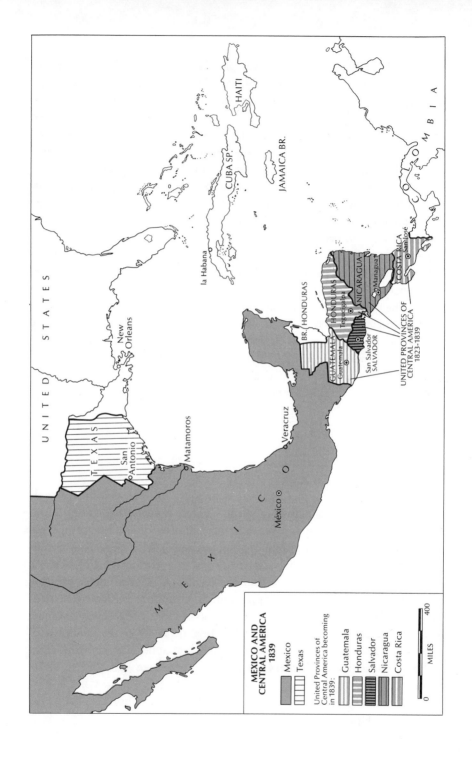

MEXICO AND
CENTRAL AMERICA
1839

Mexico

Texas

United Provinces of
Central America becoming
in 1839:

Guatemala

Honduras

Salvador

Nicaragua

Costa Rica

MILES

0   400

UNITED   STATES

New
Orleans

la Habana

CUBA SP.

HAITI

JAMAICA BR.

T E X A S

San
Antonio

Matamoros

Veracruz

M E X I C O

México ⊙

BR. HONDURAS

GUATEMALA

Guatemala ⊙

San Salvador
SALVADOR

HONDURAS

Tegucigalpa ⊙

NICARAGUA

Managua ⊙

COSTA RICA

San José ⊙

UNITED PROVINCES OF
CENTRAL AMERICA
1823–1839

O L O M B I A

MORAZÁN

There emerged during the ensuing struggle a distinguished yet tragic figure who was to devote his entire life to the causes of liberalism and Central American union. The man, Francisco Morazán, was a Honduran by birth, but in the seemingly endless military campaigns in which he was forced to engage he became increasingly identified with the liberal faction of Salvador. He drew support in varying degrees from Honduras, Nicaragua, and Costa Rica. He had a small group of followers in Guatemala, which he entered in 1829 at the head of a liberal revolutionary army determined to re-establish order throughout the confederation and to expel the archbishop and his supporters—including Arce—who were felt not only to have disrupted the peace within the confederation but to have betrayed the republican movement in interests of the church and restoration of the Spanish monarchy. Morazán became the chief executive of the confederation in fact, and he was officially elected to the presidency by the congress when complete order was restored.

The period between 1829 and 1837 was characterized by tremendous efforts at reform within the confederation. Morazán ruled as a virtual dictator, but he enjoyed great popularity as a military hero and vigorous political leader. He was intensely hated by the church and all the conservative political forces that opposed the many changes he inaugurated. Under his leadership the liberal congress decreed the end of all religious orders and dis-established the church; at the same time he declared that religious freedom should prevail throughout the confederation. Many buildings and other properties that had formerly belonged to the church were taken over by the state and used for other purposes, including public schools. Efforts were made to bring new immigrants to the country, and some attention was given to the development of roads. Even the old Spanish legal codes were revised to accord with the new republican regime.

Many problems troubled Morazán and his liberal followers in congress and in the administration, however. The major centers of confederation activity were in the northwest, in Guatemala City and San Salvador. Honduras, Nicaragua, and Costa Rica, as states within the confederation, enjoyed a high degree of autonomy, but their own internal problems increasingly absorbed their attention and tended to isolate them from the mainstream of central government activity and controversy. Morazán's problems with

Guatemala and Salvador were sufficiently vexing to keep him completely occupied. At one point the capital was transferred to San Salvador to reduce the influence of Guatemala and to provide a more central location within the confederation. This only served to create further friction, and a continuous effort was necessary to preserve order by putting down incipient revolts and movements toward secession.

Throughout Morazán's administration the church continued its battle to influence the minds of the people in favor of restoration of the old order. Natural phenomena were pointed out to the ignorant Indians as manifestations of divine wrath at the atheistic and sacrilegious activities of the liberals. No Indians in Central America were more ignorant and superstitious and more docile in the hands of the priests than those of the Guatemalan back country. It was among these Indians that the religious finally found a willing tool and able leader in the person of an illiterate pig-driver. In 1837 a cholera epidemic ravaged the countryside, and unscrupulous clerics spread the rumor that the liberals and foreigners were poisoning the water. Supported by the church, Rafael Carrera left his pigs to assume the role of divine emissary to lead his people against the liberals and foreigners who, he was told, were bent upon destruction of religion and the Indian race.

RAFAEL CARRERA

Soon all of back-country Guatemala was inflamed and Carrera was able to take Guatemala City, where he promptly instituted a reign of terror. Many liberals fled to the old capital, Antigua, where they awaited the coming of Morazán from San Salvador to restore order. At first Morazán was successful. He defeated the Indian forces in the streets of Guatemala City, but he could not reconquer the hinterland. Blocked for the time being, he returned to San Salvador, where he remained until expiration of his presidential term in 1839. The confederation was falling apart, and the states took steps toward secession, encouraged in this move by the federal congress whose members saw little hope of preserving the union.

Morazán was unwilling to see the confederation dissolved. Organizing an army of Salvadoreños, he headed west to do battle once again with Carrera. He set up his headquarters temporarily at Ahuachapán, and near there he inflicted defeat upon a conservative contingent sent against him. Moving on to Guatemala City, he saw his luck run out, for Carrera defeated him badly. Now Morazán's fickle following vanished into thin air.

His former friends turned their backs on him and refused him welcome even in San Salvador. After two years of exile in South America he was induced to come to Costa Rica where he was shortly betrayed and executed. The year was 1842; the confederation was at an end and its most able proponent and defender was dead.

With the disintegration of the Central American confederation, each of the five participant states went its own way. Discussions of reconstituting the union were held from time to time by representatives of the affected nations, but they all came to naught. Rafael Carrera ruled Guatemala for over twenty-five years. Possibly well meaning, he was far too ignorant to carry out any manner of constructive program. He was sufficiently shrewd, however, to maintain himself firmly in office and to prevent the conservatives and clerics from dominating him completely. His was a dictatorial regime in which liberalism and liberals had no part, and the country made little progress in any direction.

Foreign Pressures

Internal disorder within any country invites international difficulties. Property becomes less secure, including that held by aliens; and it is common practice for all powers, particularly the major ones, to intercede in behalf of their nationals when the welfare of such nationals is threatened abroad. The disorder prevailing in Mexico and Central America caused serious property loss to many alien residents, and European powers took up the claims of their citizens and attempted collection through diplomatic channels. France made such an attempt in Mexico in 1838.

The question of damage claims cannot be regarded as basic in the many maneuvers of France, England, and the United States in the Caribbean area during the middle of the nineteenth century. The two European countries were predatory hunters after territory, economic and political advantage, and international prestige. Political leaders in the United States were not wholly innocent of pretensions along these lines. The struggle between the slave-holding and the non-slave-holding states of the Union had its international ramifications. Southern leaders looked upon Cuba, for instance, as ripe for annexation to the United States as new slave territory. Efforts were made to purchase the island from Spain on more than one occasion after 1845, and twice, in 1850 and 1851, filibustering expeditions to free

Cuba from Spain were organized by Cuban independence leaders on United States soil with financial support from pro-slavery factions within the country. Britain and France furthered their imperialistic designs on a far more official basis, however. Their warships cruised the Caribbean waters and France exerted almost continuous pressure upon Haiti while Britain extended her influence and control southward along the Atlantic coast of Central America from her base at Belize.

Mexico

PASTRY WAR

In 1838 French warships blockaded the Mexican port of Veracruz in an effort to force the Mexican government to recognize claims of French citizens for compensation for property damage which they claimed to have suffered as a consequence of the general disorder prevailing in the country. One of the claims, and only a very minor one, was for 800 pesos on behalf of a French baker in Tacubaya whose pastries had been confiscated one night by an unruly group of Mexican army officers. The Mexican president, Bustamante, refused payment of what he considered quite correctly an exorbitant claim of 600,000 pesos to cover a variety of minor losses, including that of the baker. Finally the French admiral fired upon the old fortress of San Juan de Ulúa and forced its surrender. The Mexican government declared war upon France, and the famous 'Pastry War' ensued.

No more able leader could be found to lead the Mexican army against the French than Santa Anna. Here was a chance to vindicate himself for the debacle at San Jacinto. The French took the whole affair rather lightly, and from their position in control of the fortress and the harbor they seemed quite content to let Santa Anna control the city. Again the frustrated Santa Anna went to sleep. He was rudely awakened by the approach of a French landing force conducting a small raid into the city. Santa Anna fled in his underwear. Soon he came back as the French were returning to their boats, and at the head of his troops he attacked. Then, as one historian has so incomparably described the event, 'the god of luck took him by the hand and led him into the path of a French cannonball.' * Santa Anna lost his left leg below the knee. Now all was vindicated! San Jacinto was forgotten! Mexico's hero was a hero again.

* Simpson, *op. cit.*, p. 215.

Guaranteed payment of the 600,000 pesos, the French squadron withdrew. The war was over and Santa Anna was ready for new adventures in the wonderland of political activity. Shortly he was again president of Mexico, and his in-again, out-again approach to the acceptance of political responsibility continued. Each sojourn in the presidential palace, however, cost the country enormously. Increased taxes, illegal levies, forced loans, all produced new funds for the general to squander in personal display and ostentation. True, the dictator undertook some rather important public works activities in Mexico City; but in addition to paving a few streets he also erected a monument to himself and had constructed a costly cenotaph for the severed portion of his leg, which was brought from Manga de Clavo and paraded through Mexico City to its new resting place.

WAR WITH THE UNITED STATES

Now once again in the midst of Mexico's distress the issue of Texas came to the fore. Northern resistance to annexation in the United States was weakening, particularly as Britain was showing more than a casual interest in the tottering republic. Finally, in the spring of 1845 annexation was approved by the United States Congress. Mexico promptly broke off diplomatic relations with her northern neighbor, but with an empty treasury and generals 'pronouncing' from every quarter, her ability to wage war was far from impressive. For a time matters drifted without any overt act or a genuine declaration of hostilities. Perhaps the crisis would pass. Those who hoped for peace, however, reckoned without considering the objectives of James K. Polk, the new president of the United States, or the foolhardiness of the 'hero' of San Jacinto, Antonio López de Santa Anna.

Ambitious expansionists in the United States had long looked covetously at the vast expanse of territory stretching westward from Texas and including the far Pacific coast region known as California. Mexico's claim to Santa Fe and the surrounding area of New Mexico dated far back to the early days of Spanish colonization in the New World, but the Pacific coast territory had been effectively occupied and settled only in the latter half of the eighteenth century. California remained sparsely populated with the principal towns located along the line of the mission chain founded by the Franciscan fathers. The missions, following the secularization laws of Gómez Farías, had gone into decline, and Mexico's hold upon the region was tenuous at best.

Life for the scattered cattle ranchers who dwelt in the rolling hills along the Pacific was idyllic indeed. They were few in number and their vast land grants extended for miles in all directions. With the breakdown of Mexican governmental institutions, they ceased to be bothered by arbitrary edicts and exactions of transitory politicians who swarmed in and out of Mexico City. The hacendados conducted their own affairs in autonomous complacency. Such a situation was most inviting to land-hungry European powers, and England particularly showed considerable interest in acquiring California. The possibility of a French venture along the Pacific was not out of the question, and Russia, with numerous outposts in the far northwest corner of the continent, likewise could not be overlooked as a potential west-coast neighbor of the United States. American statesmen, looking into the future and dreaming of a nation of continental dimensions, could not fail to see the disadvantages of any European power acquiring a new foothold along the Pacific coast. If Mexico was too weak to hold California, the better part of wisdom called for the United States to occupy it. President Polk was poignantly aware of the need for prompt action, and the acquisition of California became one of the key objectives of his foreign policy.

The Texas issue played squarely into the hands of the American expansionists. Firmly the United States set about settlement of the Texas issue by linking it to the purchase of California. While diplomatic relations between Mexico and the United States remained severed, President Polk made what he hoped would be a conciliatory gesture and sent to confer with President Herrera of Mexico a special envoy with the rank of minister, John Slidell. His mission was to negotiate a settlement on the various matters of disagreement between the two governments. In exchange for Mexican recognition of the annexation of Texas to the Union and the establishment of a suitable boundary line, he might offer to absorb a considerable amount of outstanding claims by American citizens against the Mexican government and to purchase California for a substantial sum of money that would go far toward replenishing the Mexican treasury.

Polk reckoned with little understanding of Mexican politics and no understanding of a people's patriotic sensitivities. Perhaps he thought that all Mexican presidents had as few scruples as Santa Anna. José Joaquín Herrera had come to the presidency in 1844 as a result of a revolt of the moderates against Santa Anna. Although the 'hero' had been temporarily exiled, Herrera's position was far from secure. He dared not show any sign of weakness, such as a willingness to compromise over the Texas issue. He refused to treat with Slidell, even though there were indications that he would have liked to do so. Slidell was sent home. Even this action did not satisfy the Mexicans, and General Mariano Paredes overthrew the government. He would lead his country to war. But this was a miscalculation; only one man could lead the country to war against the United States. Santa Anna answered the call.

The dismissal of Slidell by Herrera produced a strong reaction in the United States, and American troops were sent to the Río Grande, into a region beyond the Nueces river which the Texans claimed but never occupied. Paredes, then still president in Mexico, regarded this as an act of war and ordered the American advance to be resisted by force. A detachment of American soldiers was attacked and some killed, others captured. President Polk asked Congress for a declaration and the war was on. This was April, 1846.

General Zachary Taylor moved into northern Mexico from Texas. He captured Matamoros and then Monterrey. Saltillo also fell, and there he set up his headquarters. In the meantime, California was taken over by the American navy after a transitory republic was set up under the leadership of John C. Frémont, a visitor from the United States. An expeditionary force prepared to land at Veracruz under the command of General Winfield Scott. Mexico's position seemed hopeless.

In league with Gómez Farías, again returned from exile, Santa Anna proceeded to organize an army by impressment, while funds were raised by a forced levy upon the church. Again Santa Anna headed northward with a large army of untrained and ill-equipped soldiers. In February of 1847 he met Zachary Taylor at Buena Vista, far north of San Luis Potosí. There Santa Anna drove his soldiers into the greatest battle of his life. His men overran line after line of Taylor's defensive network. When night came and a heavy storm interrupted the battle, Taylor and his remaining forces were fighting for survival, for Santa Anna's army was in position to annihilate the invaders. Fortunately for Taylor, Santa Anna did not realize the extent of his advantage. His troops had suffered staggering losses and were ready to drop with fatigue and hunger. Under cover of darkness the Mexican army melted away to the south, but Taylor made no move to follow.

Having returned to the capital claiming victory, Santa Anna turned on Gómez Farías in exchange for support from the church, and then prepared to face Scott who was moving on Mexico City from Veracruz. A skirmish in the mountains ended in Mexican defeat, and the defenders retired to prepare a new line before the capital city. A representative of the United States State Department, Nicholas P. Trist, attempted to negotiate with Santa Anna, but with no success. Finally Scott's army advanced and, after several days of bloody fighting, took the capital. The battle was a bitter one. Many of the Mexican units fought tenaciously, some to the death of the last man. But not Santa Anna. Jealous of his subordinate commanders, he fled the city with a fresh contingent and prepared to carry on guerrilla warfare.

TREATY OF GUADALUPE-HIDALGO

Mexico was tired of war and it was tired of Santa Anna. He was deposed and after being given safe-conduct by the American army, was exiled to Jamaica. A new government, headed by the chief justice of the supreme court, Peña y Peña, established itself at Querétaro and made peace with the invader. By terms of the treaty of Guadalupe Hidalgo, Mexico ceded to the United States Texas, California, and all the territory between them claimed by Mexico. In exchange, outstanding financial claims against the Mexican government were canceled and the Mexican treasury received a payment of $15,000,000. On March 10, 1848, the treaty received final ratification by the United States Senate and the war was over. Mexico had lost nearly half of her national territory—the least populated portion to be sure—and had suffered a humiliating defeat at the hands of her northern neighbor.

Now, indeed, Mexico was near to a state of anarchy. In Yucatán the Indian henequen workers had risen against their masters and bitter racial warfare was in progress. The wild Indian tribes of the northern Sierra raided settlements and villages at will. But the moderates were in power in Mexico City, and there they remained. Herrera was brought back to the presidency, and in 1850 he was succeeded by Mariano Arista, who had been properly elected in the first peaceful transfer of executive power since independence. These men attempted to give Mexico a better government, and they were able to restore some sort of order in fiscal matters. British pressure over defaulted obligations was eased by pledging three-quarters of the customs receipts to bond service, and by attacking the army in its moment of weakness it was possible to bring about a drastic reduction in military expenditures. These measures were scarcely signs of progress; they were in reality manifestations of exhaustion.

Between 1848 and 1857 Mexico began to change drastically. The alteration was deep-seated and not at first evident on the surface. With the moderates in power and the constitution of 1824 in effect, the authority of the central government was relaxed and that of the several states grew stronger. This in itself was not significant; what was significant was the change in political leadership at the state level that accompanied this resurgence of state autonomy. A new generation was rising to the fore, a generation that had reached maturity in the midst of national degradation and shame, a generation that had witnessed the perfidy of the revolutionary caudillos, the church, the propertied classes, and the parasitic *agiotistas,* or usurers. These groups had consistently for thirty years placed their own interest above that of the state; they had opposed all social progress in an effort to preserve their privileged status and to profit by the corruption of Santa Anna and his ilk. Had circumstances been a little more favorable they might have sold the whole national territory to the United States to buy the protection and order which they themselves were too selfish or too incompetent to provide.

Resurgence of Liberalism

After the war with the United States, the liberal program had two principal goals: to achieve individual liberty, economic as well as political, and to liberate Mexico from the regime of corporate privilege. For Mexico to achieve genuine nationhood, it was necessary for citizens to give their undivided loyalty to the state. The state could not share its citizens' allegiance with any corporate body—church, army, university, or Indian community. To achieve their objectives, the liberals sought secularization and reform of education, abolition of the fueros, and similar changes that were anathema to the conservatives.

Liberalism had long had a spokesman in Gómez Farías, but he had proved himself inept at politics, foolish and naïve in his dealings with Santa Anna, and with little real support in any quarter. The new generation would build afresh. In Oaxaca a pure-blooded Indian, Benito Juárez, became governor. This man who came from the hills to the city as a domestic servant had, with the aid of a creole benefactor, procured for himself an education and entered the legal profession. He married well and entered politics. As governor of Oaxaca he earned for himself an outstanding reputation for honesty and efficiency, and particularly he gained a strong following among the lower classes. At no time did he forget his own humble beginning. Juárez was but one of a group of new liberal leaders. In Michoacán another important figure secured the governorship. Melchor Ocampo, an able intellectual, gave evidence of real administrative ability and an understanding of the ills that beset his people. Brilliant literary figures, Guillermo Prieto and Ignacio Ramírez, attracted attention in Mexico City with their poetry and satire, and soon a nucleus for revolutionary liberalism had been formed in the capital. As these new figures in Mexican affairs became articulate, memories of Morelos and Hidalgo stirred in the minds of the people. Clearly something was afoot that boded no good for the conservative oligarchy.

By mid-century, conservative ideas were widely held, and the liberals were on the defensive. The conservatives held that independent Mexico had rejected its colonial heritage and embraced alien cultural values which made the country ungovernable. They held that Mexico's proper independence day was when Iturbide entered Mexico City, not the day when the Grito de Dolores was uttered. They urged their countrymen to disavow the ruinous liberal principles and return to those that were in keeping with their Spanish past. Lucas Alamán even doubted the advantages of independence. For nearly a decade after the war with the United States, Iturbide enjoyed a respect denied him while he lived.

Throughout the long, tragic era of Santa Anna, one able conservative had seen with dismay the steady disintegration of his country. Lucas Alamán had always remained a monarchist at heart. Distrustful of the United States, he had foreseen the loss of Texas and California and attempted to guide Mexico into closer relationships with European powers, particularly England. Now in his declining years, he devised a new plan to achieve a stable political system and at the same time guarantee the preservation of the conservative social and political tradition. Mexico should again become a monarchy and Europe should supply the king. But first, the conservatives must seize power. It was a simple matter to foment a new revolution, for now all the old elements of reaction—the church, the landowners, the army, and the money lenders—were thoroughly aroused by the wave of liberalism that seemed to be sweeping the country. Early in 1853 the government of Arista was turned out of office. Of course, an interim dictator was needed until a European monarch could be found, and of course the old oligarchy turned to Available Antonio. Santa Anna was recalled from exile and installed as president for one year. This time it would be different, for the 'hero' would be carefully watched and Alamán would rule from behind the scenes. The plan worked for almost two months. Then Alamán died. Santa Anna promptly reverted to character, looted the treasury, negotiated new loans, expanded the army, and instituted a wave of terror to drive every liberal from the country. In short order, Ocampo and Juárez found themselves living in New Orleans. As long as the funds held out, Santa Anna was firmly in the saddle.

SALE OF THE MESILLA TRACT

Shortly the treasury was empty, and true to their history, the great property owners and the church saw no reason to contribute to the support of the regime they had foisted on the Mexican people. Someone else could pay the army's wages, and sure enough the United States came to the rescue. In fixing the boundary by the Treaty of Guadalupe-Hidalgo, the negotiators had failed to take into account the American need for a low pass through the mountains for railroad construction. Claims and counterclaims. Yes, Santa Anna would sell the Mesilla valley for ten million dollars! The Gadsden Purchase was completed in 1853, and Mexico transferred to the United States a portion of land along the Mexico-Arizona border. Now Santa Anna had enough money to keep himself in power for two more years. His action had angered many, however, and provided useful ammunition for his enemies. The sale of national territory is an act ill-suited to enhance the popularity of any politician, but the use to which Santa Anna put the new funds added personal insult to the injury of national pride. He spent it largely on himself.

Truly a revolution was brewing. This time, however, it was not a question of a dissatisfied general. The plotters against Santa Anna included men from less common walks of life. There was Morelos' former chieftain, Juan Alvarez, and a former customs collector, Ignacio Comonfort. These men, in the spring of 1854, proclaimed at Ayutla a plan for revolution having as its objective the return to power of liberal leaders and the drafting of a new constitution. Santa Anna attempted to crush the movement, but its leaders vanished into the mountains only to reappear in a different location. Now began the process that spelled the end of the reactionary government. In the northern states political leaders one after another declared for the Plan de Ayutla and expelled Santa Anna's administrative officials. In August of 1855, the man whose political and military adventures had marked an era of Mexican social and governmental decadence departed the presidential office for the last time. In part he was frustrated and bored; more pertinent, however, his perceptiveness enabled him to predict as had Louis XV, *'Après moi, le déluge.'* Santa Anna, fearing that his line of retreat might be cut off at Veracruz, hurried away into exile in South America. Twenty years later he died in Mexico City, having been permitted to return by a stronger man who had no reason to fear a spent old general with a wooden leg.

Three months after Santa Anna's departure, a liberal army under Juan Alvarez entered the Mexican capital and a generation of national ignominy moved rapidly to its bloody climax. Now came bitter civil war—the War of the Reform. The liberal movement of 1855 was of a vastly different character than any such movement since the days of Hidalgo and Morelos. Indeed, it was closely related to the earlier social upheaval that accompanied the struggle for independence. Among those who played leading roles were Indians and mestizos. Representatives of these downtrodden classes seized the reins of government and their numbers filled out the ranks of the armed forces. Alvarez surrounded himself with such men as Melchor Ocampo and Benito Juárez, the former liberal governors of Michoacán and Oaxaca. Other strong liberals included Guillermo Prieto, Santos Degollado, and Miguel Lerdo de Tejada, all men whose assumption of high political office struck terror in the hearts of the conservative landholders and the clergy.

That the new regime was intent upon drastic social change quickly became apparent. In late November of 1855 the new government passed the 'Ley Juárez' ending the privileged ecclesiastical courts of the church. Shortly thereafter came the 'Ley Lerdo,' an enactment intended to force religious corporations to sell all their land. Both laws created a storm of protest, and in the hope of allaying somewhat the fears of the opposition, Alvarez stepped aside to turn the presidency over to the more moderate Ignacio Comonfort. This proved to be a mistake, for Comonfort was too easy with those who plotted his downfall. Finally he fell a victim of conservative intrigue, and his weakness and vacillation enabled the conservative forces to seize the capital and drive the liberal government into the provinces. There followed three years of devastating war.

La Reforma

CONSTITUTION OF 1857

The liberals adopted a new constitution in 1857 before they were driven from the capital, and the constituent congress that created it wrote in the basic reforms that had first found expression in the Ley Juárez and the Ley Lerdo. It went even farther. It included provisions establishing secular education and allowing nuns and priests to renounce their vows, but it failed to include any provision prohibiting the exercise of religions other than the Roman Catholic. The war quickly became a religious war, for the church, including its temporal head, Pope Pius IX, denounced the constitution and all those who supported it. Excommunication was decreed for all who swore allegiance to the new fundamental law, and from that point onward no compromise was possible.

The entire country was thrown into turmoil when the first president under the new regime, Ignacio Comonfort, was tricked into turning over the government to General Félix Zuloaga, a tool of the conservatives, late in 1857. Benito Juárez became president of the liberal government with headquarters first in Michoacán and later in Veracruz. The conservatives continued to hold the capital, and the battle was joined. Plunder, rapine, assassination, murder of prisoners, and wanton destruction of property were practiced by both sides. It became impossible to carry on the economic life of the nation, and soon hunger joined the struggling armies to assist in the slaughter. Each side was forced to desperate measures, and the extreme views that came to characterize the opposing forces served only to intensify the conflict. Now the church poured treasure into the conservative coffers and the liberals took the only retaliatory measure open to them; they nationalized all real property of the church and abolished the tithe. Other drastic measures were aimed at ending the existence of religious corporations and suppressing all religious orders. These steps gave at least some semblance of legality to the plunder and destruction of churches and monasteries by the liberal armies. For three centuries the church in Mexico had grown rich and powerful. With power and wealth had come corruption and exploitation of the lowly Indian and mestizo masses. With the War of the Reform the day of reckoning finally arrived.

BENITO JUÁREZ

As the war dragged on, the stern, silent figure of the Zapotec Indian, Benito Juárez, became the mainstay of the liberal forces. Forced to flee to Veracruz by way of Panama, he set up headquarters there and directed the guerrilla activities of his followers throughout the country. Step by step the liberal government under his guidance decreed the Laws of the Reform that stripped the church of its status and legalized the confiscation of its wealth. His position was particularly advantageous, for by holding Veracruz he deprived his enemies in the capital of access to commerce and customs revenues. General Miguel Miramón, the conservative chieftain, failed in his attempts to capture the port, for the liberal defenses were strong and the Indians Miramón brought from the high plateau to attack the port city quickly fell prey to the lowland fevers.

Gradually the tide began to turn. Miramón could not be everywhere at once, and although he won victory after victory, the liberal forces surged back like an incoming tide the moment his back was turned. In the north the liberals triumphed. Under an able liberal general, Porfirio Díaz, they conquered the south. Slowly the conservative armies melted away, and after several sharp defeats Miramón saw that the end was near and fled the country. On January 1, 1861, the liberal army entered the capital and the war was over. Days later, dressed in a black suit and riding in a black carriage, Juárez rode quietly into the city. He had achieved a great victory. Without leading a single army into battle he had unobtrusively guided the liberal government through its darkest hours and held the movement together until victory was assured. Could he, a civilian, now rule the country?

Now fortune averted her face as Juárez rode by. Never had Mexico been so completely prostrated. The treasury was empty. Customs revenues were pledged to foreign bankers, and internal commerce and industry were so completely disrupted that no revenues were to be derived from taxing those sources. The great wealth of the church had been dissipated in the bitter war, and a tax upon the transfer of its former properties produced little. In fact, the whole reform movement had fallen dismally short of attaining its objectives. The church was temporarily subdued, yes; but its vast property holdings had been snatched up by a new class of wealthy landholders, many of them foreigners. In the outlying states a new set of caudillos had come into existence as a result of having taken for themselves the wealth of expropriated properties. Mexico was no nearer being a country of small independent landholders than before the revolution. Some guerrilla fighting still continued, and within a matter of months Juárez lost two of his most able supporters to the conservative guerrilla, Márquez. Both Mechor Ocampo and Santos Degollado were captured and shot. Juárez seemed unable to act positively. He would abide by the constitutional processes at all costs, even if those processes tied his hands. Congress talked and talked.

During the war the conservative government under Miramón had engaged in two nefarious financial transactions in a desperate effort to raise money. It had confiscated 700,000 pesos being held for British bondholders by the British legation in Mexico City, and it borrowed 750,000 pesos from a Swiss banker, Jecker, who took as security fifteen million pesos' worth of Mexican government bonds. On the liberal side, Degollado had seized a San Luis Potosí silver train belonging to British mine-owners. The foreign property owners held Juárez responsible for making good these losses, plus a long list of other alleged claims arising out of the conflict. The financial position of the Mexican government was far too weak to stand any such burden. Juárez, though willing to recognize legitimate claims, adopted the realistic position that the creditors would have to wait until the government's financial position strengthened. He declared a two-year moratorium on the payment of foreign debts.

Throughout the war, Mexico escaped foreign intervention by the narrowest of margins. Spaniards openly aided the conservatives in every way possible without getting directly involved. The British had also shown a marked preference for the clerical party and had recognized Miramón's government. Only the United States favored Juárez and the liberals, and supplied them with arms through the port of Veracruz. Now that the war was over the danger of intervention actually increased, for Britain, France, and Spain immediately demanded reparations for loss of life and property by their citizens during the conflict. The British bondholders demanded payments from the customs duties. Furthermore, hope for support from the United States was gone; that country was involved in a bitter civil war of its own.

French Intervention

England, France, and Spain, quick to take up the claims of their citizens against a weak foreign power, agreed upon a punitive expedition to remind the irresponsible Mexican officials of the importance of meeting their international obligations. The British had little desire to embark upon military action against Mexico, and they tried to forestall France and Spain by making a separate agreement with Juárez giving British officials supervisory authority over the collection of Mexican customs. The Mexican congress, however, rejected any such arrangement, and the British went ahead under their commitment to France and Spain.

Early in 1862, the allies landed at Veracruz and presented their demands. Quickly it became apparent that the French had more in mind than the collection of a few million pesos. They intended to change the government of Mexico. France now had an emperor, Napoleon III, whose ambition it was to make a place for himself in history equal to that of his uncle, Napoleon I. He might have undertaken to do so by extending French influence and power in Europe, but colonial venture would entail fewer risks.

Other factors were at play. The Mexican conservatives and the church were quite willing to call upon the French to support them against their liberal countrymen. With the triumph of Juárez, Mexican exiles streamed into Paris—a procession of bishops, priests, formerly wealthy playboys, and disgruntled politicians. One had become a favorite of the French empress; another, Santa Anna's old comrade-in-arms, General Almonte, was eager to sell his country to the French in exchange for the Mexican presidency. The exiled 'patriots' were easily duped into believing that the French were their champions and upon successfully occupying Mexico would return to them their confiscated properties and estates. Mexico would again become a monarchy with a genuine European prince upon the throne.

When early disagreement arose among the allies as to the objectives of the punitive expedition, Britain and Spain withdrew. They had no desire to further Louis Napoleon's ambitious undertakings in Mexico. The French, using Almonte as a provisional president, waited in Veracruz for a general uprising of the conservative forces which their patriot informants had promised would take place. Finally, the despotic guerrilla, Márquez, arrived with a small contingent of half-starved irregulars. That was all. The French decided to move on Puebla. There their small force of 6000 men was badly routed by Ignacio Zaragoza, one of Juárez' most able commanders. They fell back upon Veracruz to regroup.

Now Napoleon realized that the 'patriots' to whom he had listened had overplayed their case. He had a real project on his hands. The French promptly dropped their pretense of playing along with the exiles and went about their attempted conquest in earnest. A large force was sent to Mexico and a new commander, General Forey, was placed in charge. Almonte was cast aside and the enlarged French army moved on Mexico City. After a brief siege Puebla fell, and shortly thereafter the invaders entered the capital. Juárez had wished to defend Mexico City, but he had neither an army nor capable generals. Zaragoza was dead of typhoid, and his other able commander, González Ortega, together with Porfirio Díaz, had been captured at Puebla. Juárez and his government fled northward to San Luis Potosí and eventually on to Monterrey. Early in June General Forey entered the capital triumphantly. The church held solemn Masses amidst great rejoicing while the conservative sycophants stood around waiting for restoration of their properties. Both the clergy and the hacendados were amazingly naïve. They failed to note the large number of Frenchmen who had possessed themselves of redistributed property under the Ley Lerdo and the 1857 constitution. Great was their shock when General Forey issued a decree confirming the new property holders in their titles to former church estates. They too had been tricked.

MAXIMILIAN

Quickly now the French expanded their conquest northward and westward from the capital. A plebiscite was held to confirm Napoleon's selection of Archduke Maximilian of Hapsburg as Mexican emperor. Time passed, and it was the spring of 1864 before the new emperor accepted his throne and set forth with his wife, the former Belgian princess Carlotta, to establish his court in Mexico City. The whole affair was one grand farce. Napoleon expected to get his investment back, all the various European bondholders expected to get their reward, yet in order to finance the new royal court in Mexico City, Maximilian had to borrow still more heavily in France. Mexico's paper debt grew enormously. Maximilian was a gentle well-meaning tool of the French who had been duped into believing he was assuming a throne at the request of his future subjects. He breathed sweetness and light, but when he arrived in Mexico his breath caught in his throat. The French controlled everything, the customs, the treasury, the army, and the economy of the country. He was helpless and ignorant. He did not understand that the country lacked even the barest rudiments of an administrative machinery, that none of his well-intended enactments as emperor had the slightest chance of implementation. Then he made the same mistake that Napoleon and everyone else concerned had made: he thought that Mexico was rich. It was grindingly poor. There was no Aztec treasure to fill the coffers of Napoleon as it had those of Carlos V, neither was the country productive as in the days of Revillagigedo. Increasingly the French emperor began to rue his bargain, while the Mexican emperor tried desperately to ingratiate himself with his subjects.

In 1865 the Civil War ended in the United States, and mysteriously surplus war matériel began to find its way across the Río Grande and into the hands of Juárez' soldiers hiding in the mountains and along the border. At the same time efforts were made through diplomatic channels to persuade Napoleon of a war hazard should his army be left much longer in Mexico. The French prepared to withdraw their troops and write the entire adventure off as a mistake. Such preparation was by no means retarded by Prussia's quick and decisive victory over Austria in the Seven-Weeks War of 1866—a war that resulted in Prussia's replacing Austria as the polarizing power for German unification among the South German states. Gradually French troops were withdrawn from the northern regions, and as fast as they left, Juárist guerrilla armies sprang into existence behind them. The inevitable failure of the French undertaking was now apparent to all—all, that is, except Maximilian and his wife Carlotta. Carlotta returned to France to beg further assistance from Napoleon, but he could promise her nothing. Desperate, she turned to the Pope in Rome, but he could remember only the property that Maximilian had not restored to the church. Carlotta went rapidly insane and had to be taken home to Belgium.

Early in 1867 the French army withdrew. Every effort was made by the French commander and by Napoleon to persuade Maximilian to leave also, but the 'Mexican' emperor would stay with 'his' people. A small group of conservatives continued to support him in the hope that Juárez' armies could be turned back. But one by one the states and cities fell before the advancing liberal forces until only a few points remained. Maximilian went with his army to Querétaro where the liberal armies under

General Escobedo quickly surrounded them. In the meantime, Porfirio Díaz moved up from Oaxaca and captured Puebla. The line of retreat to Veracruz and Europe was cut off.

The emperor might still have escaped, but he chose no such way of ending his reign. Possibly it never occurred to him that in Mexico wars are sometimes deadly serious. Perhaps his recollection of what happened to the would-be emperor Iturbide was a little hazy. Or perhaps, as was said of him, he knew better how to die than to govern. At any rate he would stay. In May the royal army surrendered, and the fate of the emperor, as well as that of the old conservative generals Miramón and Mejía, was placed in the hands of the Zapotec Indian from Oaxaca. These men deserved little sympathy and they received none, in Mexico. Ignoring the pleas and protests of both European and American governments, Juárez carried out the sentence of the Mexican military court: death. The emperor, together with Miramón and Mejía, died before a firing squad in Querétaro June 19, 1867.

Now at long last a calm descended over Mexico. The bloody process of cleansing the country of the evil heritage of Santa Anna and his traitorous supporters was at an end. The church's control of the mental and physical resources of the nation was broken, temporarily at least; and a new generation of property owners had arisen as a result of the land redistribution of the reform. The cleansing process had been thorough; not only had the poor Indian soldiers died by the thousands, generals also died, and so had a Hapsburg emperor. Juárez presided over a prostrate land and a people bled white in the struggle to achieve nationhood.

SUGGESTED READING

M. Burgin, *The Economic Aspects of Argentine Federalism, 1820–1852*, Cambridge, Mass., 1946.

I.F. Cady, *Foreign Interventions in the Río de la Plata, 1835–1850*, Philadelphia, 1929.

F. E. Calderón de la Barca, *Life in Mexico*, Boston, 1843 (later editions).

R.G. Caldwell, *The López Expedition to Cuba, 1848–1851*, Princeton, 1915.

W.H. Callcott, *Santa Anna: The Story of an Enigma Who Once was Mexico*, Norman, 1936.

A. Edwards, *The Dawn: Being the History of the Birth and Consolidation of the Republic of Chile*, London, 1931.

J.L. de Grummond, ed., *Caracas Diary, 1835–1840*, Baton Rouge, 1951.

B. Harding, *Amazon Throne, The Story of the Braganzas of Brazil*, Indianapolis, 1941.

W.H. Jeffrey, *Mitre and Argentina,* New York, 1952.

A.K. Manchester, *British Preeminence in Brazil, Its Rise and Decline,* Chapel Hill, 1933.

M.W. Nichols, *The Gaucho,* Durham, 1942 (later edition).

R. Roeder, *Juárez and His Mexico,* 2 vols., New York, 1947.

W.O. Scroggs, *Filibusters and Financiers: The Story of William Walker and His Associates,* New York, 1916.

O. Singletary, *The Mexican War,* Chicago, 1960.

A.C. Wilgus, ed., *Argentina, Brazil, and Chile Since Independence,* Washington, 1935.

—— *South American Dictators During the First Century of Independence,* Washington, 1937.

GENERAL READING

R. Alexander, *Communism in Latin America,* New Brunswick, 1957.

—— *Labor Movements in Latin America,* London, 1947.

G. Arciniegas, *Latin America, A Cultural History,* New York, 1966.

F. de Azevedo, *Brazilian Culture,* New York, 1950.

J.M. Bello, *A History of Modern Brazil, 1889–1964,* Stanford, 1966.

S.F. Bemis, *The Latin American Policy of the United States,* New York, 1943.

H. Bernstein, *Modern and Contemporary Latin America,* New York, 1952.

R. Burr, *By Reason or Force, Chile and the Balancing of Power in South America, 1830–1905,* Berkeley, 1965.

J.P. Calogeras, *A History of Brazil,* Chapel Hill, 1939.

A.N. Christiansen, ed., *The Evolution of Latin American Government,* New York, 1951.

H.F. Cline, *The United States and Mexico,* Cambridge, Mass., 1953.

W.R. Crawford, *A Century of Latin American Thought,* Cambridge, Mass., 1944; 1961.

J. Cruz Costa, *A History of Ideas in Brazil,* Berkeley, 1964.

L. Galdames, *A History of Chile,* Chapel Hill, 1941.

J.W. Gantenbein, ed., *The Evolution of Our Latin American Policy,* New York, 1950.

C.C. Griffin, ed., *Concerning Latin American Culture,* New York, 1940.

E. Gruening, *Mexico and Its Heritage,* New York, 1934.

J. Henao and G. Arrubla, *A History of Columbia,* Chapel Hill, 1938.

P. Henríquez-Ureña, *Literary Currents in Hispanic America,* Cambridge, Mass., 1945.

M.P. Holleran, *Church and State in Guatemala,* New York, 1949.

R.A. Humphreys, *The Evolution of Modern Latin America,* New York, 1946.

C. Jane, *Liberty and Despotism in Spanish America,* Oxford, 1929; New York, 1966.

J.J. Johnson, *The Military and Society in Latin America,* Stanford, 1964.

—— *Political Change in Latin America: The Emergence of the Middle Sectors,* Stanford, 1961.

T.B. Jones, *South America Rediscovered*, Minneapolis, 1949.

G. Kubler, *The Indian Caste of Peru, 1795–1940*, Washington, 1952.

R. Levene, *A History of Argentina*, Chapel Hill, 1937.

E. Lieuwen, *Arms and Politics in Latin America*, New York, 1960.

R.W. Logan, *The Diplomatic Relations of the United States With Haiti, 1776–1891*, Chapel Hill, 1941.

———— *Haiti and the Dominican Republic*, New York, 1968.

W.D. and A.L. Marsland, *Venezuela Through Its History*, New York, 1954.

J.L. Mecham, *Church and State in Latin America*, Chapel Hill, 1934.

D. Perkins, *Hands Off; A History of the Monroe Doctrine*, Boston, 1941.

M. Picón-Salas, *A Cultural History of Spanish America*, Berkeley, 1962.

D. Pierson, *Negroes in Brazil, A Study of Race Contact at Bahia*, Chicago, 1942.

F. Pike, *The Conflict Between State and Church in Latin America*, New York, 1964.

———— *Freedom and Reform in Latin America*, Notre Dame, 1959.

R. Poppino, *International Communism in Latin America, A History of the Movement, 1917–1963*, New York, 1964.

S. Putnam, *Marvelous Journey: Four Centuries of Brazilian Literature*, New York, 1948.

A. Ramos, *The Negro in Brazil*, Washington, 1949.

Y.F. Rennie, *The Argentine Republic*, New York, 1945.

S. Rodman, *Quisqueya, A History of the Dominican Republic*, Seattle, 1964.

P. Romanell, *Making of the Mexican Mind*, Lincoln, 1952.

J.R. Scobie, *Argentina—A City and A Nation*, New York, 1964.

L.B. Simpson, *Many Mexicos* (various editions).

T.L. Smith, *Brazil: Peoples and Institutions*, rev. ed., Baton Rouge, 1963.

A. Torres-Rioseco, *The Epic of Latin American Literature*, New York, 1942.

C. Wagley, *Introduction to Brazil*, New York, 1963.

H.G. Warren, *Paraguay; An Informal History*, Norman, 1949.

A.P. Whitaker, *The Western Hemisphere Idea: Its Rise and Decline*, Ithaca, 1954.

G. Wythe, *The United States and Inter-American Relations: A Contemporary Appraisal*, Gainesville, 1964.

L. Zea, *The Latin American Mind*, Norman, 1963.

II THE FEW AND THE MANY

7

Popular Government on Trial

> The patriarchal organization of colonial society has shown . . . an astonishing capacity for survival. The economy of all the Latin American countries is primarily an agrarian economy in which landownership means control of the major instrument of production. The dominance of the *hacienda* . . . has not only fostered the stratification of society; it has tended to perpetuate a concentration of political power in the hands of small minorities.
>
> ROBIN A. HUMPHREYS *

Measurement of Progress

The modern world is possibly obsessed with the idea of progress. Progress implies change from a less desirable to a more desirable condition or state of affairs. Life itself is a process of continual change from childhood to old age; and inasmuch as throughout the greater portion of his span of years man's outlook is toward the future rather than the past, the element of progress is associated with the process of change. The growing child becomes stronger, more self-reliant; as he learns more about the world in which he lives, he becomes better equipped to support himself and to cope with life's problems. Eventually a wife and family are acquired, possibly a home and considerable property. Within the commonly accepted framework of human values, each of these steps marks passage from a less desirable to a more desirable state of affairs. In certain Eastern cultures, old age is the most venerable state of all; and certainly the pattern of Western Christianity treats old age as but a final step before progression to an even higher status in the world to come.

Progress has been equated with the acquisition of material goods almost

* *The Evolution of Modern Latin America,* Oxford University Press, New York, 1946, p. 83.

149

universally, in spite of the fact that certain religions see virtue in poverty. All civilizations of which there is record have been characterized by an unequal distribution of material goods, and invariably those persons possessing the greater amount have been the object of veneration or envy. All humanity strives, however feebly and ineffectively, to increase its material well-being. Success in this endeavor is considered to be a mark of progress, whether achieved individually or collectively.

The idea of progress has long been associated with man's most complex institution, the state. States are held to progress as the peoples who compose them achieve greater material well-being, as they are enabled to live in greater harmony with one another, as their numbers increase, and as they acquire larger portions of the earth's surface. The concept of progress pervades every aspect of human existence.

As the historian Toynbee has so cogently indicated in his studies of civilizations, however, progress is not a continuous process. There are periods of rise and there are periods of decline in the histories of all civilized societies. The achievements of one people or one nation are frequently gained at the expense of others. Nevertheless, because of the ever greater productivity of modern man and because of his ever increasing knowledge of the physical world and his ability to manipulate it to his seeming advantage, the sum total of human endeavor still seems to accord with the concept of progress.

As already suggested, progress can be measured only in relation to some given set of values. If poverty were truly regarded as a virtue, the acquisition of wealth would be considered an act of retrogression. If productive activity were not regarded as desirable, the man who did nothing would be considered as contributing most to society. It must not be overlooked that in a society where such values as these were reversed, man could not support his present numbers and millions would die. Nature provides sanctions that have conditioned the formation of human values.

Some consideration of values is fundamental to any interpretation of history. Those of the historian are probably far less important than those of the people who made the history. Part of the historian's task is to record faithfully changes in the value pattern of those about whom he is writing. The independence of the Latin American peoples marked a great change in value patterns in that self-government became more desirable than attachment to Spain and all that membership in the Spanish imperial system implied. Many did not make the shift and preferred the old order to what they regarded as doubtful benefits of the new. Thereby was precipitated the conflict and the wars of independence. Once separation from Spain was a reality, further value adjustments were called for and new conflicts arose.

The period from 1860 to 1930 was characterized by deep and far-reaching changes in the aspirations of the Latin American peoples. New sets of values were created and old ones discarded. Progress came increasingly to be measured by the degree to which new scientific developments were put to use in the new countries. The construction of railroads and telegraph lines were tangible evidences of progress that any could see and appreciate. The production of more material goods and the acquisition of wealth through commerce were viewed with favor by many who in times past had thought the ownership of land the only road to wealth and higher status in society. In increasing numbers men attached importance to a more equitable distribution of material goods and to the moral, spiritual, and political benefits of independent nationhood. Progress came gradually to be equated with the extension of education, with greater freedom to express opinion, with the maintenance of law and order without oppression. Finally, the masses of Indians, mestizos, farm laborers, peons, and laborers in the cities began to adopt values similar to those of the upper classes. They sought land, education, economic opportunity, and enough to eat. Progress became a vital consideration of the many, not merely of the few.

Already by mid-century change was in men's minds. The European revolutions of 1848 saw a resurgence of liberalism that once again battered at the ancient structure of the landholding aristocracy. The stirrings in Europe were observed and faintly echoed in Latin America, but they were not understood. Germany and France were undergoing a basic shift in the locus of economic power as industrialization created a new wealthy class of manufacturers and businessmen. These alterations in the balance of economic and political power had affected England somewhat earlier; now they were manifested throughout Western Europe. They were soon to appear in the United States and contribute to the fires of a violent civil war. Latin American liberals stirred uneasily, and although they came into political power in a number of countries, they proved incapable of doing more than erecting a new façade behind which the ancient colonial social order carried on as before. There was no industrialization and no rising new class to challenge effectively the old oligarchy; instead there were developed new agricultural commodities and new products of the pampas and forests that served only to concentrate greater wealth in the hands of those who owned the land. A major difficulty, of course, was the apparent absence of those basic requirements for industrialization: coal, iron ore, and power. Missing also, however, was any element in the Ibero-American cultural pattern that placed high value on scientific inquiry, on mechanical creativeness, or on the practical kinds of knowledge essential to advance in the age of mechanization which the Western World was entering.

LIBERALISM

Although Latin American liberalism somehow remained a fetish for lack of a broader social and economic base, it was not devoid of accomplishment. Physical progress was indicated by the construction of roads and buildings, and intellectual development was achieved through the creation of new educational facilities at elementary, secondary, and university levels. A sense of national consciousness emerged in nearly all countries, and with it came greater political stability, a somewhat broader participation in government, and a more extensive use of the trappings of democracy. Nevertheless, as time went on and 'liberalism' and 'conservatism' proved to be nothing more than labels bandied about by competing groups with essentially the same social and economic outlook, the gulf grew wider and wider between the few who governed and the many whose welfare they held in their hands. Gradually a deep current of social unrest became evident, and in Mexico it swept all before it in a vast tide of social revolution carried forward in the tradition of Hidalgo, Morelos, and Juárez. Elsewhere, the same current was in varying degrees apparent, and it was to become a major influence in the modern era.

IMMIGRATION

Europe's social and economic changes during the nineteenth century had other direct consequences in Latin America. Millions in Europe, awakened to the hope of a better life and seeing no possibility of achieving it in the land of their birth, turned to the Western Hemisphere as a land of new and greater opportunity. Soon passage was sought on every available ship sailing for the United States, where, it had been reported, land could be had simply by occupying it. The rise of new and sparsely populated nations had long since excited the interest and imagination of English, French, German, Italian, and Spaniard alike. The chaos which followed the creation of the Latin American nations was disillusioning, however, and few were incautious enough to risk life and property in the face of the political disorders that characterized the region. Most emigrants from Europe preferred to take their chances in the United States. When particular Latin American nations became more stable, and the opening of the great grasslands of southern South America became increasingly profitable, millions of people migrated to Argentina, Chile, Uruguay, and Brazil. The vital need for immigrant labor and capital was acknowledged by Argentina in particular, and agents were sent to major European capitals to recruit new residents. Alberdi, one of Argentina's great statesmen, expressed a conviction of many of his countrymen when he said, 'To govern is to populate.' An extensive colonization program was developed to open up vast new sections of territory, and the population of Argentina increased rapidly.

At the same time that the southern South American nations were experiencing rapid population increase through European emigration, steps were being taken to rid the great plains and the frontiers of the last remnants of hostile Indian groups. The result was a sharp decrease in the Indian populations of Argentina and Chile while the European component increased. Argentina, Chile, and Uruguay took on increasingly a European complexion, and their resemblance to other Latin American nations decreased proportionately.

Immigrants brought with them new tools and new methods of agriculture. The Germans who settled around Valdivia in southern Chile introduced dairy farming on a sizable scale. The English who came to Argentina not only brought with them capital to build railroads, but they also introduced such inventions as windmills and barbed wire, and soon large sections of the pampas were transformed from open range for swift, lean cattle and fierce gauchos into a land of endless wheat fields and complacent English shorthorns. In the face of these bewildering obstacles to his ancient freedom, the lawless, ungovernable gaucho succumbed, as did the nomadic, buffalo-hunting tribes of the great plains of North America. The result was fortunate for both Argentina and her gaucho tradition. The one grew into a prosperous and fairly stable nation; the other became a subject for literary endeavor. Aided by poetic license and abetted by the enchantment of time and distance, the gaucho became a national hero and the epitome of Argentine nationalism, instead of the bloodthirsty, hardhearted outcast and skinner of other peoples' cattle which his contemporaries had known him to be.

Other effects of immigration were no less marked. The newcomers, who increasingly were of Italian and Spanish stock in Argentina, to be followed later by sizable numbers of Poles, Swiss, and Germans, soon monopolized many industries and forced creoles to abandon many of their ancient methods of production and commerce. Buenos Aires became a great and cosmopolitan city and the entire nation was faced with serious problems of assimilation. By 1915 at least one-third of the inhabitants of Argentina were foreign born; and in 1930 the proportion was still about one-fourth. By this latter date, however, when restrictions were placed on immigration, the number of newcomers arriving annually had already dropped to an insignificant amount.

Brazil was also affected by immigration, although not with the same final result as in Argentina, Chile, and Uruguay, where the population was substantially 'Europeanized.' In some Brazilian regions, such as Rio Grande do Sul, immigration played a potent role in economic development; elsewhere the influence of the newcomer was less important. Abolition of the slave trade in 1850 stimulated the desire for immigrant laborers, and the imperial government consistently encouraged Europeans to come to Brazil. The construction of railroads made for an easier adjustment to Brazilian life, but the abolition of slavery in 1888 removed the greatest obstacle to settlement by Europeans. The rapid growth of São Paulo and of the coffee industry in that area was both a product of and a stimulant to immigration. Brazil's greatest influx, which came after the abolition of slavery, brought more than a million and a quarter new residents as contrasted with the six million that were pouring into Argentina. Brazil's new population came primarily from Italy, Portugal, and Lebanon, although important numbers arrived from Germany and Poland as well. In both Brazil and Argentina, and to a lesser extent in Chile and Uruguay, the Germans and the English came to exercise an influence far out of proportion to their numbers. They not only introduced more scientific uses of agricultural and mineral resources, but also exercised dominant roles in banking, commerce, and in commercial transportation.

After the First World War, increasing numbers of eastern Europeans and Orientals entered Latin America. Chinese coolie labor had been introduced in Peru years before to work on railroad construction projects. Now Japanese colonists came in large numbers to settle in Brazil, Chinese settled in Mexico and Cuba, and East Indians emigrated to the southern shore of the Caribbean, particularly to Dutch Guiana, the coastal cities of Venezuela and Panama, and to the island of Trinidad.

Most of Latin America had few advantages to offer the potential emigrant from Europe. Wherever the large native population included substantial numbers of semi-assimilated Indians, the European was placed at a

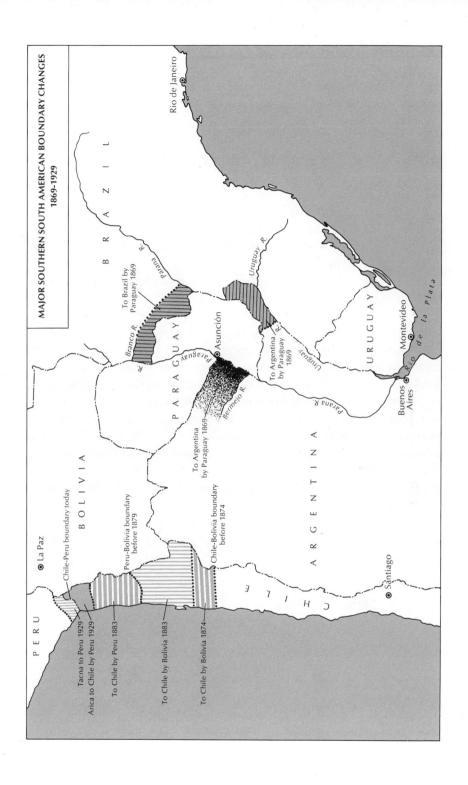

MAJOR SOUTHERN SOUTH AMERICAN BOUNDARY CHANGES
1869-1929

PERU

● La Paz

Chile-Peru boundary today

Tacna to Peru 1929
Arica to Chile by Peru 1929

To Chile by Peru 1883

Peru-Bolivia boundary
before 1879

BOLIVIA

To Chile by Bolivia 1883

Chile-Bolivia boundary
before 1874

To Chile by Bolivia 1874

● Santiago

C H I L E

A R G E N T I N A

B R A Z I L

Rio de Janeiro

Paraná R.

Branco R.

To Brazil by Paraguay 1869

R.

P A R A G U A Y

Paraguay R.

● Asunción

To Argentina
by Paraguay 1869

Bermejo R.

Uruguay R.

To Argentina
by Paraguay 1869

Uruguay R.

Paraná R.

U R U G U A Y

Montevideo ●

Buenos
Aires ●

Río de la Plata

disadvantage in seeking employment. A large labor force was already present. If the immigrant desired to farm, as many did, the best land was already occupied by the owners of large haciendas. Even in Argentina, where vast tracts of land were open to the early immigrants, land values rose rapidly; soon newcomers were obliged to become farm laborers or tenants, for unoccupied land quickly disappeared. The size of individual holdings was a major problem, and it became obvious that Argentina was not soon to become a land of small farmers. In general, during the latter half of the nineteenth century the percentage of landless increased in spite of great agricultural expansion throughout major portions of Latin America. In a region that remained predominantly agricultural, this development boded ill for the future.

While large-scale immigration was rapidly giving to the southern countries of Latin America a distinctly European cast, the continuous intermixture of Indian and Spanish races, begun during the centuries of colonialism, was producing a largely mestizo population in Mexico, Central America, and the Caribbean region generally. Brazil, too, became increasingly mixed, but the components were more varied and included a substantial Negro element. In Peru, Ecuador, Paraguay, and Bolivia the process of racial amalgamation was much less thorough, and the large Indian population remained essentially an element apart, racially, culturally, and economically, from the much smaller but dominant European and mestizo groups. In Central America, Guatemala followed the pattern of Peru and Bolivia, with the descendants of the ancient Mayas clinging doggedly to a traditional isolation that even the Roman Catholic Church found frustratingly impenetrable. Various sections of the former Spanish empire were, in the period of independence, growing farther apart from one another racially, culturally, and economically. Political attributes proved infinitely more tenacious.

Foreign Interest

TECHNOLOGY

New residents were not all that approached Latin America from across the seas. As Europe and the United States became increasingly industrialized, the economic power of the leading nations expanded at a tremendous rate. New outlets were sought for the investment of capital, and Latin America appeared to offer excellent possibilities for development. The desirability of investment in the region was considerably heightened by the availability there of raw materials and other resources that were not elsewhere abundant. Argentine hides and beef, Chilean nitrates, Brazilian rubber and coffee, Paraguayan quebracho extract, Mexican oil, and numerous lesser products were valuable commodities in the markets of Europe and North America, and great effort and money were expended in making them available. Foreign promoters and investors poured large sums into Latin America to construct railroads, telegraph lines, docks and harbors. Others invested in mining, agriculture, and commercial enterprises on a large scale. The introduction of electrification was also the work of foreign entrepreneurs. Technological advance in many regions seemed to accomplish miracles, considering the obstacles which geography, climate, and the shortage of skilled workers presented. Naturally, some regions and some countries benefited more than others, but in all areas the pioneering investor and developer were welcomed by liberal and conservative alike. In most cases, foreign companies relied exclusively upon their own nationals to fill responsible positions, leaving opportunities for Latin Americans only in unskilled or semi-skilled labor. The policy was understandable; extensive training programs in most regions would have been necessary before native managers and technicians could have been made available, and the development projects were not inspired by philanthropy. However, since most of the new industries were extractive in nature, and since Latin Americans found employment in them only as a source of cheap labor, few of the Latin American countries received great direct benefit or found their economies substantially strengthened. As was true of politics, so it was with economic development; it was the few who benefited and the many who looked on with envy, the envy heightened by the realization that the few were frequently foreigners.

ECONOMIC PENETRATION

Spurred on by the urge for material progress, Latin American governments turned heavily to borrowing. The relative political stability, achieved as the echoes of the wars of independence died out, gave foreign investors an undue measure of confidence in the governments with which they negotiated loans. Borrowed funds were all too often used to erect government office buildings or to pave streets over which only oxcarts rumbled. In such cases productivity was not increased, and neither were the governments' revenues with which to repay the loans.

Economic progress was essential to the welfare of each of the Latin American nations, but few of the statesmen of the period discovered appropriate and beneficial ways of accelerating all currents of economic life. Economic panaceas introduced from abroad were adopted with wholehearted enthusiasm and lack of caution. The apparent prosperity thus created did not permeate the basic economic reality of the poverty of the great majority of the populations, and social progress lagged far behind. Some governments, pathetically eager to benefit from the magic of modern technology, co-operated with foreign entrepreneurs by providing cheap and docile labor. Thus arose the aphorism said of Mexico in the time of Porfirio Díaz: 'She was the mother of the foreigner and the stepmother of the Mexican.'

Other evils were equally costly. Too often the largest part of any loan went into the pockets of the few in power, leaving nothing for the nation but a debt. Government loans had to be repaid like any others, and future generations were saddled with burdens for which there was nothing to show but increased opulence on the part of the favored few.

The impact of foreign enterprise and technological advance was of great benefit in some countries. In the seventy years after 1860 Argentina developed into a great and productive nation, as to a lesser degree did Chile, Brazil, and Uruguay. In each instance, technological improvement and foreign capital played major roles. But in other areas where telegraph lines were erected to link the principal cities and nothing was done to stimulate industry, messages carried by the new communication media were more often of political portent than of commercial interest. Railroad lines in Argentina transported grain and cattle, but in Central America their traffic was more likely to be in troops. Indians carrying their poultry to market now sometimes rode, but for the heavier items the pack mule and the oxcart still were used. It is not to the credit of the mule or the oxen that the steam locomotive failed to drive them out of business.

While the nations of southern South America were experiencing tremendous population influx from Europe and marked transformation of their economies through economic development, less fortunate nations bordering on the Caribbean were being introduced to the fact that economics and international politics are bedfellows. International rivalry in the Caribbean area was as old as European penetration into the region; but in the period immediately associated with the wars for Latin American independence, almost continuous warfare in Europe preoccupied the major powers and precluded their interference in the American revolutionary struggles. With peace re-established in Europe, however, Britain and France turned westward once more; soon the Caribbean was again a major center of international competition. The nature of international competition had nonetheless undergone a change. While land-grabbing colonialism was not entirely discarded, as evidenced by British interest in Texas and along the coast of Guatemala, Honduras, and Nicaragua as well as a renewed French interest in Haiti, penetration by the great powers increasingly took on an economic complexion. Investments and loans preceded political pressure and threats of occupation. Such considerations accounted for French and British interest in Mexico.

INTER-OCEANIC CANAL

The sudden expansion of the United States westward after the war with Mexico added an entirely new dimension to Caribbean rivalry. American interest in the area grew apace with the discovery of gold in California and the great rush of thousands to the Pacific Coast. In the era before railroads spanned the North American continent, travel by sea was by far the simplest, and the long Isthmus of Central America was at once recognized as an obnoxious barrier and an economic challenge. Cornelius Vanderbilt organized a transportation company to take advantage of the San Juan river route across Nicaragua, and soon a treaty between Colombia and the United States made possible construction of a railroad across Panama. The railroad was built between 1850 and 1855. In the meantime, the United States and Great Britain both sought access to a canal route, with Britain in the forefront by reason of laying claim to a protectorate over the Graytown region of Nicaragua which included the mouth of the San Juan river.

The United States was fearful that a canal route might become the exclusive property of another power and attempted to avoid this possibility by advocating neutralization of any route. In 1850, this objective was achieved in large measure by successful negotiation of the Clayton-Bulwer Treaty with Great Britain. By the agreement neither power was to hold exclusive control over the Nicaragua route or to take dominion over any part of Central America. Any canal route was to be neutralized in time of war or peace and was not to be fortified. No canal was immediately undertaken, and soon attention was focused on other matters.

In the United States the long struggle over the slavery issue began to have international repercussions. In an attempt to retain control over the American congress, slavery advocates became involved with abolitionists in bitter competition to add new states to the Union. Southern glances were cast in the direction of Cuba and Santo Domingo and some fell upon Central America. In 1854, an American filibuster from New Orleans by the name of William Walker organized in San Francisco an expedition to aid the liberals of León, Nicaragua, in a struggle they were having with the conservatives of Granada. Walker had made earlier forays into the Sonora and Lower California regions of Mexico, but had achieved nothing for his efforts. In Nicaragua he was more successful, and soon he was in control of the country and had himself made president. Early objectives seemed to imply an intent to offer the region to the United States for annexation, but any such thought rapidly fled Walker's mind once he found himself in control of the small Central American nation. Walker sought international recognition for his government but could not secure it, even from the United States. Instead, other Central American nations united their efforts to unseat him and destructive warfare ensued. Walker soon made the serious mistake of incurring the disfavor of Vanderbilt and his transportation company and he was forced to flee the country. In 1860 he tried to return but was captured by the British and turned over to the Hondurans who promptly executed him. Although Walker came to no good end, his expedition had struck fear to the hearts of all Central Americans—fear of the United States and what appeared to be its aggressive intentions.

Shortly thereafter France was eliminated for the time being from Caribbean competition by the disastrous consequences of Napoleon III's adventures in Mexico, but British and American interest persisted. End of the slavery issue eased somewhat the risk of American land grabbing, but other forms of imperialism soon appeared. As early as 1854, President Pierce of the United States made an abortive effort to open the possibility of purchasing Cuba from Spain. He sent an agent to Madrid, who, failing there, met with the American ambassadors to Great Britain and France at the city of Ostend in Belgium to discuss the problem of purchase. A declaration was issued by the conference participants that promptly became known as the Ostend Manifesto. It stated in terms clear enough for anyone to understand that if Spain were unwilling to sell Cuba the island would be taken from her by force. The statement was promptly repudiated by the American secretary of state, and soon the Civil War intervened; but the Latin American world had been given notice that Cuba was considered a desirable prize in the United States.

CUBA

In 1868 Cuba was torn by revolution against Spain, prompted in part by Spanish difficulties at home, but more directly the result of unrest that had been seething in the island for years. The Spanish administration had learned little by the loss of a great empire on two continents, and relations with the remaining American possessions were never smooth. The revolutionists proclaimed independence, and soon American sympathizers, particularly disgruntled soldiers from the recently defeated Confederacy, flocked to their aid. Ships from the United States carried supplies to the rebellious patriots, and the Spanish government retaliated by declaring a blockade of rebel-held sections and capturing a vessel, the *Virginius*, flying the American flag. Although the ship was sailing under American colors illegally, the incident nearly precipitated a break with Spain, for many of the crew were Americans and the Spanish captain-general executed a number of them. Finally the revolution was suppressed; but American interest in Spain's Caribbean possessions did not abate and expansionist politicians continued to advocate seizure of the islands. American investments in nations bordering on the Caribbean continued to expand even if the 'jingoists' could not promote territorial adventures.

Peace in Cuba did not prove of long duration. Spanish promises of reform and insular representation in the Spanish Cortes at Madrid proved illusory. Agricultural development of the island favored peninsular-born landholders, who made huge profits selling sugar to the United States. Increased investments by American citizens failed to benefit materially the ordinary Cuban. Dreams of independence continued to fan the embers of insurrection and exiles in New York, Puerto Ricans as well as Cubans, prepared plans and solicited funds for a new revolutionary effort. In 1895, Cuba was once more torn by rebellion. Patriots united under the leadership of Máximo Gómez, an ardent advocate of independence, and soon large portions of rural Cuba were in the hands of revolutionists whose policy it became to strangle their Spanish adversaries by wholesale destruction of property. The Spaniards concentrated women and children in the cities and attempted to put down the insurrection by vigorous forays into the countryside. For over two years the struggle wore on. Much property, including that of Americans, was destroyed, and the Spanish government seemed incapable of bringing the situation under control. All the while sympathy for the patriot cause mounted in the United States, fanned by reports of the cruelty of the Spanish general, Weyler, and by the interventionist policies of certain American newspapers, particularly the Hearst press. The American congress took the lead in advocating recognition of the state of war in Cuba, an action that would have given *de facto* governmental status to the insurgents so far as relations with the United States were concerned. President Cleveland and his successor, McKinley, both held back in an effort to avoid war with Spain. In January of 1898, however, disorder spread to la Habana, and an American battleship, the *Maine,* was sent to the principal Cuban harbor to provide a refuge for United States citizens who might be in danger, and, incidentally, to present a show of force to the Spanish government. A few days after its arrival in la Habana the battleship was suddenly blown asunder by causes that to this day have not been satisfactorily determined. In the heat of the moment no one took time to investigate the matter seriously. The Spanish government denied responsibility, but the American press paid little heed to such protestations of innocence. Over 250 Americans had been killed, and forceful intervention in Cuba was demanded.

SPANISH-AMERICAN-CUBAN WAR

On April 11, President McKinley sent a message to congress offering that body the choice of decision as to whether the time for war had come. The response was a series of resolutions demanding the withdrawal of Spain from Cuba, empowering the president to use the armed forces to cause such a withdrawal, and disclaiming any desire on the part of the United States to control or exercise jurisdiction over Cuba. In spite of a last-minute offer of the Spanish government to suspend hostilities in the island, war was undertaken. Both Cuba and Puerto Rico were quickly occupied by United States armed forces, and in the distant Philippines the American navy met and defeated the Spanish Far Eastern fleet and occupied Manila. Quickly the Spanish government sued for peace, and by the end of the year a treaty had been signed terminating the war. Cuba, Puerto Rico, and the Philippine Islands were at the complete disposal of the United States. Promptly the attention of all Latin America was focused on the American government. Would Cuba be given her independence or would she become a United States possession?

The answer, when it finally came after over two years of military occupation of the island by United States forces, was not quite so simple. Cuba

would be made independent under its own newly drafted constitution provided certain conditions were met. These conditions, commonly referred to
as the Platt Amendment because they were first stated in a congressional
amendment to a United States army appropriation bill, placed basic limitations on Cuba's sovereignty. They limited Cuba's freedom to enter into
agreements with other foreign powers, they placed certain limitations on
the borrowing power of the Cuban government, they reserved the right of
the United States to construct a naval base on the island, and, most important, they gave to the United States authority to intervene in the island to
preserve order and guarantee its independence. As for Puerto Rico, it was
annexed to the United States, as were the Philippine Islands.

Cuba became independent in 1902 and the island's first president,
Tomás Estrada Palma, was inaugurated with great ceremony. He entered
upon the administration of a country that had benefited materially by the
brief period of United States occupation. Roads had been built, many steps
had been taken to improve sanitary conditions, and a system of popular
education had been established. These benefits were far from one-sided,
however. An eminent Cuban physician, Dr. Carlos Finlay, had reached the
determination as a result of investigations by himself and his associates
that yellow fever was carried and spread by the Anopheles mosquito. By
eliminating this variety of mosquito, yellow fever could be controlled and
eventually eliminated. This discovery was soon to prove immensely beneficial to all of tropical America where yellow fever and malaria were endemic. United States Army doctors made use of this important knowledge
to combat these dread diseases in Panama during and following construction of the inter-oceanic canal.

Cuban independence remained illusory, for the semi-dependence upon
the United States under the Platt Amendment encouraged American investment that expected special concessions and protection, distorted Cuban
political life by opening the door to foreign intervention whenever local
authorities lost control of the situation, and created a permanent issue for
the use of all factions opposed to the status quo. A major intervention occurred in 1906 and lasted until early 1909, during which United States officials governed the island. Subsequent interventions were of lesser significance and duration, and in 1934 the Platt Amendment was abrogated by
the government of Franklin D. Roosevelt in accordance with his 'Good
Neighbor' policy for developing better relations with Latin America. Unfortunately, a pattern of economic and political domination was already
firmly established, and later events were to demonstrate that neither Cuba

nor the United States was able to make use of the many beneficial relationships that propinquity and mutuality of interest might have made possible.

Largely because of growing American commercial interest and investment in Latin America, a step toward closer relationships with the region was taken in 1889 by the then secretary of state, James G. Blaine, who succeeded in organizing a Pan American Conference, the first since one Bolívar had attempted to convene at Panama in 1826. Bolívar's conference was not fully attended and little came of it, but Blaine was able to get started a series of gatherings, held generally at five-year intervals, which brought together representatives of all Latin American nations and the United States. As a device for cementing friendly relations among the participating powers, the early conferences achieved only minor successes. Latin American statesmen were far more influenced by the deeds of the United States than by the friendly protestations of its diplomatic officials. Even the public statements of American government spokesmen were not always designed to inspire confidence. Within a few years after the first conference, President Benjamin Harrison rattled the sabre at Chile over an incident involving the behavior and treatment of American sailors in a Chilean port, and for a time the possibility of war was rumored. The incident left a legacy of ill-will and distrust. Then in 1895 Secretary of State Richard Olney issued an insult to all Latin Americans in terms and tone which were ominous. In writing of the Monroe Doctrine, he declared: 'Today the United States is practically sovereign on this continent, and its fiat is law upon the subjects to which it confines its interposition. . . .' Amid the echoes of portentous official declarations of this type, the words of friendship spoken in the conferences did not carry far.

The fact that after 1900 the United States moved rapidly into the ranks of capital exporting nations probably had less effect on American foreign policy than often asserted. Nevertheless, the rapid expansion of commercial and financial activities in Latin America coincided with the revival of Manifest Destiny, the concept that had been used earlier to justify expansion westward across the North American continent. A few vocal expansionists soon advocated turning the same slogan to useful purpose in the Caribbean area.

At the same time that the United States' interest in the Caribbean mounted as a consequence of the Spanish-American War, political and economic conditions of two island republics reached a crisis. In both the Dominican Republic and Haiti government was characterized by continuous chaos, wanton pilferage of the public treasury, and frequent revolution. Heavy loans had been negotiated abroad, and revenues were insufficient even to meet interest payments and carry on other government functions. Investors in the United States and Europe clamored for government intervention in their behalf. The United States became fearful that some European power, particularly Germany or France, might use local conditions as an excuse for intervention and perhaps more. At the same time, the Cuban adventure had demonstrated that much could be accomplished through the imposition of honest collection of revenues. These factors pointed toward an arrangement similar to that provided through the Platt Amendment for Cuba. Within a few years President Theodore Roosevelt had installed American military government in the Domincan Republic and instituted a system whereby an American official was to act as receiver of customs until foreign indebtedness, at least, had been retired. In 1915 President Wilson took similar steps in Haiti, while armed intervention in Cuba had been repeated and prolonged. The conclusion was inescapable that all three island republics were little more than United States protectorates. Roosevelt made the point clear in his so-called corollary to the Monroe Doctrine, by which he asserted that if European powers were precluded from interfering in the Western Hemisphere to protect the financial and other interests of their nationals, then the United States, in whose behalf the Monroe Doctrine operated, was under obligation to protect their interests for them. Incidentally, of course, the private interests of American nationals were not overlooked. Indeed, charges were soon made by distressed nationals of the island republics that United States intervention was simply a method of exploiting the islands on behalf of foreigners. Improvements in sanitation and education were ineffective medications to apply to the wounds of injured pride and loss of national independence.

Throughout Latin America thoughtful people viewed the situation with growing alarm. Yankee Imperialism and fear of the Colossus of the North became the lingua franca of political utterances from the Río Grande to Patagonia. The theme was played particularly by social and political reformers who in country after country saw unscrupulous caudillos and politicians grow rich by accepting the apparent largesse of North American banks and private speculators. Would default signal the landing of American marines in Peru or Venezuela? Many fearfully thought that it would, and certainly the evidence they could marshal was impressive.

By far the gravest reactions stemmed from United States activities on the mainland. In 1903 Roosevelt 'took' the Panama Canal. In 1878 a French firm, the DeLesseps Company, secured from Colombia a concession to construct a canal at Panama. The project failed owing to sanitary and engineering difficulties and poor financial management, but the arrangement had raised a storm of controversy in the United States and caused the American government to attempt to secure an alternate route through Nicaragua. The old British treaty, however, stood in the way of an American undertaking until finally, in 1901, a new agreement was ratified that terminated the Clayton-Bulwer Treaty. Promptly, a treaty was negotiated with Colombia by which the United States was to take over the rights and property of the defunct French company and obtain a perpetual lease of a six-mile strip across Panama. Unfortunately, the Colombian senate refused to ratify the agreement. A sum of $40,000,000 was at stake, that being the amount to be paid to the stockholders of the New Panama Canal Company, successors to the bankrupt DeLesseps Company. The French concession was soon to expire, and upon expiration all rights to the property of the French company would revert to the Colombian government. It seemed worthwhile to delay the transaction. President Roosevelt thought otherwise. Conveniently, a small group of Panamanian conspirators staged a revolution on November 3, 1903, and conveniently American naval vessels were on hand to prevent the landing of Colombian troops to put down the rebellion. Washington immediately recognized the new government of the independent Republic of Panama and proceeded to sign a canal treaty with its representative, a mystery-shrouded character by the name of Bunau-Varilla, who just happened to be in Washington. The fact that Bunau-Varilla was principal owner of the new canal company, formed to buy up large blocks of the defunct DeLesseps Company stock for a pittance in the Paris stock market, merely added spice to the whole affair. His interest in consummating sale of the French rights and properties before their reversion to the Colombian government was something more than Panamanian patriotism.

The Colombian government rightfully protested and demanded both an indemnity and an apology. For years all such requests were rejected, and anger against the United States burned deeply throughout Latin America. But the canal was built and opened to commerce in 1914. Its eventual construction fulfilled a dream as old as the Hapsburg kings of Spain who had made exploratory surveys of canal construction possibilities as early as the sixteenth century.

In 1913, United States marines entered Nicaragua, ostensibly to protect the lives and property of American citizens endangered by a bitterly fought revolution. Again an American receivership of the customs was established, and a British loan was refunded through New York bankers while new loans were extended for various Nicaraguan government purposes. A canal contract was negotiated, and the right of the United States to construct a naval base on the Gulf of Fonseca was included in the agreement, formalized in the Bryan-Chamorro Treaty of 1916. United States marines remained in Nicaragua, except for a few months in 1926, until finally withdrawn in 1933. So bitter was resentment against the United States for this intervention that in the later years of the occupation an unworthy bandit by the name of Sandino became an international hero by harassing the marines from his mountain 'hide-out' near Jinotega. His ability to escape capture became legendary, and news correspondents from afar sought to interview him. A Spanish correspondent even wrote a book in his praise. But throughout Latin America the good name of the United States was besmirched and blackened.

The long period of direct and forceful intervention by the United States in Latin American jurisdictions produced a reaction far more violent than is easily remembered today. It quickened the thinking of thousands of men, heightened the political urgencies of the epoch, and watered the seeds of an intense nationalism that soon enveloped the entire Western Hemisphere. Foreign investors, particularly those from the United States, appeared not as benefactors but as harbingers of political pressure and intervention, omens of the coming loss of sovereignty. Outward tokens of resistance to the anticipated or actual encroachments of the United States became an urgent necessity for governments of many Latin American nations. 'Yankeephobia' flowed from the pens of Latin America's most gifted writers, who warned their readers again and again to beware the 'Colossus of the North.'

ANTICLERICALISM

Thus between the middle of the nineteenth century and the great world depression that began in 1930, Latin American civilization was deeply stirred by broad currents of change. Economically, great advances were made in agriculture and the extractive industries; socially, some regions experienced growing racial intermixture while others were transformed by the influx of new European stock; politically, liberalism finally achieved its day in court, while the increasingly aggressive activities of the United States aroused fear of intervention and fanned the flames of a growing nationalism. Crossing and mingling with all these currents was yet another which had a continuing impact—anticlericalism. Its implications were intellectual, emotional, economic, and political, and at least some of its roots went far back into the eighteenth century. Those who attacked as well as those who defended were Catholics, and church doctrine was not the primary issue. The changes demanded, many of which had their advocates in the independence era and have already been noted, were in the realm of the church's temporal activities. Reformers protested the ownership of land by the church—land that was not used for religious purposes, but which, once it had passed into church hands, was never again available for private ownership and development. The least developed countries were least disturbed by the church issue, for continuous struggles among rival caudillos tended to preclude attention to social reform. By playing one military autocrat against another, the church was often able to retain its temporal power without serious challenge. Such was the case in Peru, Bolivia, Ecuador, and most of Central America. In Chile, Colombia, and Mexico, however, the church issue had already assumed momentous proportions and become a main feature of political controversy. Likewise in Argentina and Brazil the church problem was never very far below the surface and frequently emerged as a factor in partisan political strife.

Liberal parties throughout Latin America generally adopted platforms that included curtailing the authority and economic power of the church. Counter-movements frequently were begun in the name of religion and defense of the faith, but real motives were the maintenance of power by the clerical party and their usual allies, the landholding aristocracy. The most successful reactions against the general trend in favor of anticlerical liberals were those led by García Moreno in Ecuador and Rafael Núñez in Colombia.

Brazil, a land generally free of sharp church-state antagonisms throughout most of its history, witnessed a clash over the emperor's asserted rights stemming from the colonial *padroado,* or patronage. The Brazilian liberal party saw the time ripe for separation of church and state, but the emperor did not choose to fly in the face of public opinion. The effects of the controversy that ensued were not far-reaching, but the popularity and prestige of Dom Pedro II were damaged, not only by his attitude toward clerical officials who resisted his authority, but because he turned back on the course the liberals had chosen for him.

In Argentina, where essential reforms were begun in the revolutionary aftermath, and in Chile, where both church and state exercised a fair degree of moderation, the position of the church was stabilized without resort to violence, but in Mexico and Colombia much blood was shed eventually over the clerical issue. In Paraguay and Uruguay, despotic governments were able to inflict their will upon the church with little opposition, for there was no large privileged group to whom the church could turn for support.

Before 1930 some of the principal currents of social, economic, and political change had begun to merge. Many of the nations developed distinct national characteristics that differentiated them from their sister republics. Argentina, vigorous, proud, and European in orientation, displayed an increasing tendency to regard herself as the champion of Latin American rights against encroachments by the United States. In this role she was occasionally supported by Chile, and the 'new' nations of South America gradually displayed the attributes of leadership on their continent— potential world powers of future eras. Despite generally harmonious economic relations with the United States, Brazil occasionally took a position alongside Argentina. The reasons for this course were not obscure. One needed only look to the Caribbean to discover that a large portion of the former Iberian empire of Spain had fallen into abject subordination to the United States.

ECONOMIC COLONIALISM

World War I brought forcibly to the attention of many Latin Americans the full reality of their economic colonialism; and the economic, political, and social disorders of the post-war period were emphatic evidence to support their convictions. In a number of the smaller countries, the decade of the 1920's witnessed an unsurpassed orgy of foreign misinvestment. Popular reaction set in against a system that permitted such gross extravagance and dissipation of national wealth by the few who controlled. At the same time the 'liberal' trends which had appeared strong early in the twentieth century now gave evidence of having run their course, undermined and destroyed by the neglect of the many by the few. Too often, it appeared, programs of land reform, social welfare, and free elections were merely useful slogans employed to capture political office. Reforms were the subjects of debate, not the bases of action. The lofty optimism and impractical idealism of earlier times gave way to cynicism and pessimism. Pressing social and economic problems remained unsolved, too frequently for want of champions who could resist temptation. Those who remained loyal to their ideals, however, found their hopes frustrated and their efforts wasted in the labyrinth of anachronistic administrations.

The beginning of the world trade depression was soon to accentuate the economic disorders, bring discredit to governments unable to cope with the situation, and engender disillusionment with the apparently wasteful and fruitless activities of representative government. Together with the other currents of unrest, this widespread dissatisfaction stimulated a nationalism aimed at freeing Latin America from foreign economic and political domination and distributing natural resources for the benefit of the many at home rather than the few across the seas. Unfortunately no clear-cut programs were immediately forthcoming. Mexico had a vigorous program, but by 1930 it had failed to prove its merit. Sensing that the Latin Americans stood at a crisis in their history, European and even Asiatic powers entered upon an extensive courting program, to which the United States soon also became a party, each offering a solution in terms of ideology, economic assistance, and cultural transformation.

ART AND LITERATURE

The various currents influencing men's thoughts during the period from the mid-nineteenth to early twentieth century produced dramatic changes in literature and the arts. At the opening of the era Latin American intellectuals were still strongly under the influence of European and particularly French romanticism, which stressed the symbolism of things and appealed to the emotions and the individualism of man. Picturesqueness and beauty of thought and idea were emphasized as opposed to realism and perfection of form. Latin American contributions in the arts and literature were essentially imitative and had no real basis in Latin American culture and society. After the turn of the century, the mood of Latin America began to reflect the long period of growth and change since independence. The clash of economic classes, the rise of mechanistic science, and the emergence of a spirit of skepticism combined to create a realism that challenged the concept of inevitable romantic progress. Strife and struggle were everywhere in evidence, and positivism was replacing the naturalistic philosophy that had conditioned the intellectual climate of the late eighteenth and early nineteenth centuries. Latin American writers picked up the new mood and made what is probably their first genuinely original contribution to world literature, modernism. The modernistic movements of Spanish America and Brazil were not at all the same, but both produced remarkable literary works that had deep roots in Latin American life as it was being lived. Latin American culture came increasingly to be valued for its own sake. Principal writers whose works reflected the awakening of interest in their own culture included Rubén Darío, the restless Nicaraguan poet, José Martí and Casal of Cuba, Amado Nervo and Gutiérrez Nájera of Mexico, Valencia and Silva of Colombia, and José Enrique Rodó of Uruguay.

Two of the works produced by the modernists were particularly outstanding. Darío's *Azul* was a collection of poems and short stories published in 1888, which had tremendous influence on writers in Spanish America and Spain. Rodó's *Ariel,* a small volume published in 1900, analyzed the nature of democracy and the pitfalls in the path of its development—mediocrity and materialism—which reminded him of Caliban, a brutish slave in Shakespeare's *Tempest*. Rodó feared that the process of democratic development would push society toward the lowest common denominator, and that much that was good would be lost in the process. *Ariel* had a profound impact throughout Spanish America, for it pictured the United States as dominated by materialism and devoid of real culture, whereas Latin America was pictured as having a far greater appreciation for cultural values. The idea proved a soothing balm to the growing sense of economic inferiority of many Latin Americans, and to this day the impact of *Ariel* is still discernible in the thinking of multitudes who know as little about the United States as did Rodó.

Another innovation in modern Latin American literature was the appearance of women writers, principally poets. Worthy of mention were Delmira Agustini and Juana de Ibarbourou of Uruguay, Alfonsina Storni of Argentina, and particularly Gabriela Mistral of Chile.

Since 1900, the most significant literary achievements have been in realistic novels. Spanish American writers have shown an increasing interest in social conditions, and brutally realistic books have been written on the plight of the Indian, on the Mexican Revolution of 1911–19, and on the pathetic attempt of a mestizo or mulatto to rise above the level of the society into which he was born. Masterpieces on the Mexican revolutionary period are Mariano Azuela's *Los de abajo* (1916) and Martín Luís Guzmán's *El águila y la serpiente* (1928).

Brazil's greatest literary figure of the nineteenth century was Joaquim Maria Machado de Assis, who was both poet and novelist. Among the romantic novelists, Alfredo D'Escragnolle, Viscount Taunay, won the most lasting fame. His most famous work, *Inocência,* published in 1872, concerned rural life in Mato Grosso, and was one of the forerunners of the realistic movement. The Brazilian work that has received the most widespread recognition, however, was *Os sertões,* by Euclides da Cunha, a book translated into English under the title of *Revolt in the Backlands.* It is a remarkable description of the Brazilian back country and its people, and centers around the rebellion of Antônio Conselheiro and his sertanejo disciples in the 1890's.

Growing out of the bitter social revolution that swept Mexico from 1911 to 1919, the currents of which continued to flow strongly on through the 1920's and into the present era, came outstanding literary and artistic endeavor. José Vasconcelos wrote incitingly and bitterly against foreign economic domination and the imperialism of the United States, while José Clemente Orozco and Diego Rivera depicted the great social struggle of the Mexican lower classes in murals that have become world famous.

Throughout all of Latin America, the strong currents of social, economic, and political change were reflected in a larger awareness of social and economic problems. Writers and artists were inspired by awakened national pride, but they also reflected a growing feeling of frustration and inferiority in those nations whose progress had not been great and whose material advances were but tokens in comparison with those of the United States and Western European powers. Evidence of maturity and less-confused thinking marked the close of the epoch, when popular demands shifted from panaceas offered by aliens to nativist solutions to the problems of the few and the many. It was no longer easy for those in power to continue on the reckless path which their predecessors had trod. The most insistent demands were for a more equitable distribution of land and wealth and the end of economic colonialism. The strong undercurrent running through these demands was that the natural resources of Latin America should be enjoyed by Latin Americans.

8

Southern South America: Rapid Growth and Political Experimentation

Protect . . . private enterprises for the construction of railroads. Shower them with advantages, with privileges, with every favor imaginable, without hesitating at the means. . . . Let treasure as well as men come from abroad to live among us. Surround it with immunities and privileges so that it will take out citizenship and stay.

JUAN BAUTISTA ALBERDI *

Argentina, Uruguay, and Chile in 1860

In 1860 Argentina, Uruguay, and Chile were still relatively poor and sparsely populated regions, having been among the poorest parts of the Spanish empire in South America. The wild Indians of the southern frontiers had yet to be subdued, except in Uruguay; cattle ranges were open and unfenced, and livestock was more remarkable for its fleetness and toughness than for the production of meat or wool. The area of tilled land was extremely small. A few thousand immigrants had come since independence to struggle for a living in the empty hinterland, or to engage in commerce and industry in the cities. Trade and economic activity were not greatly improved over their condition in the colonial period. Short railroad lines penetrated the interior in a few places in Argentina and Chile, but Uruguay had yet to build her first line, and many fertile regions in all three countries were totally without suitable means of communication. Oligarchies of the few families of great landowners dominated economic and political life; the bulk of the populations was landless, illiterate, and poverty-stricken.

* *Bases y puntos de partida para la organización política de la República Argentina*, Buenos Aires, n.d. (1853).

173

Argentina and Uruguay were yet to acquire the political stability and unity which had given Chile an initial advantage over her neighbors, and which made possible a gradual weakening of the power of the landed oligarchy through the rise of new economic forces in the major cities. The Liberal party had been regenerated by the rise of a middle class; this middle class demanded liberty in politics and thought as essential to social progress.

While Chilean liberals fought to curtail the power of the president and the church, in Argentina the main division was still between Buenos Aires and the other provinces. In 1861 General Bartolomé Mitre led the porteño troops against the confederation in an indecisive action at Pavón. His opponent, General Urquiza, regarded the result as a moral defeat, and retired to Entre Ríos. Following President Derqui's flight Mitre became not only governor of Buenos Aires but the provisional head of the confederation. Modern Argentina at last took shape, and provincial defections declined, to disappear altogether after the federalization of Buenos Aires in 1880. Settlement of the 'capital question' was the most important political achievement of nineteenth-century Argentina. In Uruguay, meanwhile, the blancos and colorados still fought desperate wars for control of the government.

ECONOMIC AND SOCIAL CHANGES

Between 1860 and 1930 Chile and Argentina, and later Uruguay, underwent remarkable transformations and made striking advances in economic development, population growth, and social and political maturity. In all three countries powerful liberal movements developed whose aims included redressing the balance between the many and the few in the governments, and broadening the economic bases by the building of railroads and other means of transportation and by reviving or establishing livelihoods in addition to agriculture. In some of these economic designs all groups agreed in principle. One handicap common to all three countries was scarcity of population; encouragement of immigration was not new, but the period from 1860 to 1930 marked the high point in population growth by the introduction of foreigners. Intellectually, a resurgence of interest in Europe occurred, and French culture again rose to a preferred position.

AGRICULTURAL COLONIES

In the years immediately following independence hopeful Europeans had come to the coastal towns as merchants and shopkeepers, and a few had acquired agricultural or pastoral lands. Disillusionment followed, and the stream of European immigration was diverted away from southern South America by social conditions, economic insecurity, and physical dangers arising from political chaos. Probably the most constant obstacle to attracting immigrants, however, was the system of latifundia, which restricted the prospect of acquiring land.

The problem of obtaining land was most acute in Uruguay, although much of the land made available for colonization in Chile was unattractive. In both of these countries European immigration played an influential role despite its smallness. Many of those who emigrated to Uruguay moved on to Argentina once their hopes of obtaining land had been dashed, or their lives and property imperiled by one of the numerous uprisings against the government. The Italians, most numerous of those who came to Uruguay, remained for the most part in Montevideo. In Chile the Germans were most numerous; they settled primarily in the south, and were especially influential in the growth of dairy farming and in the development of Valdivia.

Immigration to Uruguay and Chile continued to come in a small but fairly steady stream, until World War I caused a complete interruption. After the war immigration was resumed, but it had almost ceased before the hemisphere-wide movement to close the gates to Europeans and Asiatics occurred about 1930.

It was in Argentina that immigration played its most striking role in Latin America. When the rift between Buenos Aires and the other provinces was healed, Argentina entered into an epoch of remarkable growth. Agricultural colonies of Swiss had been founded during the previous decade, and many others followed once their success had been assured. In most of the new Argentine agricultural settlements the colonists were able to obtain land, either as an outright gift or at a nominal price. Between 1869, when the first census was taken, and 1895, the population increased from less than two million to nearly four. By the latter date a fourth of the population was foreign born.

By 1900 the era of agricultural colonization was past, for the new uses made of the land in growing crops for export led to a rapid rise in land values. Thereafter it became extremely difficult for immigrants to obtain titles, and the colonization program necessarily was abandoned. Immigration continued, however, and reached its peak in the decade before the beginning of World War I. Immigrants who wanted to engage in agriculture either rented land as tenant farmers or became sharecroppers.

Most numerous of the immigrants to Argentina were the Italians and Spaniards, who supplied three-fourths of the total. Most influential in proportion to their numbers were the British, whose capital and commercial connections gave them enormous prestige, while English livestock rapidly replaced criollo stock on the ranges after the development of the refrigerated ship.

By the close of the century the immigrant Italians, Spaniards, French, Belgians, British, Germans, and Swiss had become firmly established and at home in Argentina, as landowners, merchants, shopkeepers, and operators of hotels and restaurants. In commerce and related occupations they were far more numerous than native Argentinians, who were forced to adapt themselves to changing methods of business or lose out. They gave Argentina a vigorous middle class, but a middle class that had, before 1912, little voice in the government.

Economic Improvement

In both Chile and Argentina there were groups interested in improving the livestock industry and agriculture, but their first efforts aroused little enthusiasm. The Argentine *Sociedad Rural* was founded in 1866, but when its first livestock show was held, in 1875, the majority of the estancieros remained aloof. In the following year the first shipment of refrigerated beef to Europe was made, and the Sociedad Rural soon became a powerful force in improving the livestock industry. The first Chilean agricultural exposition was held in 1869, but in Chile, too, the lethargy of many of the great landowners was at first difficult to overcome.

Increasing revenues enabled the Chilean government to engage in various projects of physical improvement but many of those undertaken did not enhance the country's capacity to produce. Funds were allocated for forts and garrisons needed to defend the Indian frontier, for beautifying the capital, and for introducing streetcar lines and extending the railways.

At the same time, however, private Chilean capital moved into the nitrate and guano fields of Bolivia and Peru. Over-expansion, the failure of revenues to reach expected proportions, and a costly Indian uprising in 1868 led to a severe depression in the 1870's. The crisis was heightened by the seizure of Chilean nitrate and guano properties by Peru and Bolivia, and by the War of the Pacific which followed.

The Chilean government, too, engaged in many government-financed public projects during the 1880's, while the rise of a native capital enabled the growth of private enterprises to keep pace. The speedy exploitation of the territories taken by conquest from Bolivia and Peru more than doubled governmental revenues in five years, and future prospects seemed even more promising. The government optimistically undertook new and more grandiose public projects, and strived to make Chile more attractive to aliens and their wealth. The construction of roads and bridges, and the technical skills provided by foreigners, greatly facilitated mining and agriculture, and, as in Argentina, the benefits of the physical improvements were widely appreciated.

CHILE AND ARGENTINA

Argentine economic development, too, was retarded by war, a costly and prolonged conflict with Paraguay, 1865–70. Although the country gained some war profits by the sale of supplies to the Allied forces, principally Brazilian, President Mitre's leadership was diverted from more appropriate domestic problems, and the lands taken from Paraguay were little compensation for the cost in effort, lives, and money, in comparison to the rich prizes that fell to Chile as spoils of the War of the Pacific.

After the Paraguayan War had been concluded Argentina entered upon a period of economic growth unparalleled in South America. Economic development became a national passion; foreign capital was welcomed, and surplus English wealth was poured into a multitude of enterprises such as municipal streetcar lines and gasworks. Promoters like William Wheelwright of Massachusetts won wealth and fame as railroad builders. The coming of immigrant and alien capital and the rapid expansion of agriculture and the livestock industry soon made Argentina the most prosperous country in Latin America. The opening of vast lands to the south following the destruction of the plains Indians in 1880 and the final settlement of the capital question in the same year, combined to give added impetus to

European home-seekers and speculators. At the same time the government followed a policy of encouraging foreign companies by granting overly generous concessions to those engaged in national projects such as the building of railroads.

In the 1880's commerce surpassed all previous records; railway lines were extended in many directions, and Argentine landowners enjoyed the pleasant sensation of suddenly acquired wealth. For much of the physical improvement Argentinians bestowed their gratitude indiscriminately on foreign promoters and companies. But because of the government's guarantees of minimum interest on investments for railroad construction and operation, in a distant day of calmer reflection many Argentinians realized that they rather than foreigners had, in the final analysis, supplied most of the money, and that their railroads and tramways had been dearly bought. At the moment, however, the broadening economic horizon which these improvements opened to Argentinians made them aspire to even grander projects.

Both governments, however, made the same crucial financial error. During earlier crises both had resorted to the printing press and the issuance of inconvertible paper money. This currency was still in circulation, and its value continually decreased, to the detriment of commerce. For a few years the Argentine government converted the paper pesos into stable gold notes, but abandoned the project in 1884. The paper peso began a more rapid decline in value, and threatened to carry the merchants to ruin. The cattlemen and wheat growers, however, approved of inflation. They sold their products abroad for stable European currencies; and they soon discovered that their pound notes and francs were more valuable as the peso declined. The government was still their instrument, and it did not jeopardize their pleasure by ending the inflation. It was, in fact, accused of secretly issuing additional paper pesos to encourage inflationary trends; this charge officials did not admit or deny.

In both countries inflation caused a marked increase in the cost of living, while wages rose too slowly to keep pace. The merchants were particularly troubled. Their desperation increased as they saw the governments blithely continue to pour vast sums into the building of railroads while making plans for future expenditures of a similar nature. No attempt was made to stabilize the currency. In Argentina the unfavorable balance of trade rose sharply, and in three years the public debt more than doubled. The government seemed unconcerned over its financial condition even while negotiating new loans to pay the interest due on old ones! In 1890 commerce virtually ceased, bringing ruin to the merchants and hardship to many others. The government fell, and because of the financial panic, immigration which might have benefited Argentina was diverted to southern Brazil for several years.

The crisis in Chile was heightened by the clash between president and congress. Inflation and high prices made the situation of the poorer classes critical, for their welfare had become increasingly associated with the demand for Chilean nitrates and copper. Much remained to be done in broadening the economic base, for poverty, drunkenness, and vagrancy were widespread. The growing tension caused by rising prices and the threat of a crash reacted against President Balmaceda's vast program of public works and the expenditures it involved, and in the civil war that broke out against his rule, his opponents fought with great bitterness.

In contrast to the political decline following the triumph of the advocates of parliamentary government in 1891, Chilean economic expansion continued. Foreign trade increased, and government revenues were ample despite waste and fraud. The apparent prosperity, however, did not permeate all classes, and labor unrest grew in proportion to the number of men engaged in mining and industry; the rural peasantry remained politically inarticulate.

Both Chile and Argentina made rapid recoveries from their economic and political crises of 1890, and by the end of the century foreign trade had risen to new highs, permitting the governments to turn once more to relatively unproductive but pleasing projects such as beautifying the capitals, laying out parks, and paving streets. The Avenida de Mayo in Buenos Aires began to have a Parisian flavor, reflecting the Europeanization of the Argentinian's outlook in the preceding two decades. The newly rich landowners of the 1880's had discovered the delights of Paris and the Riviera, where their liberality made Argentine wealth a legend. European, and particularly French, influences on Argentine life multiplied.

URUGUAY

In the twentieth century Uruguay, having at last achieved political equilibrium, rose rapidly in the economic scale. She had not attracted alien capital to the same degree as had Argentina, and Uruguayan statesmen such as José Batlle y Ordóñez were determined to retain control of the country's natural resources and major industries. To provide Uruguayans with credit needed for business enterprises, the government expanded the activities of the Bank of the Republic and acquired control of the Mortgage Bank of Uruguay. Both institutions played an increasingly important part in the economic expansion of the country. Uruguayan economic development now followed an unusual course, for the government took an active role.

Uruguayan landowners and merchants began in the 1870's to devote greater interest to their private affairs and less to politics, stimulated in part by the example of Argentinians. These individuals soon regarded the customary civil disturbances with strong disfavor, and they brought pressure on the government to preserve order. As a result of their pressure the governments became more authoritarian and took sterner measures against disturbers of the peace. But even the most strenuous efforts of soldier-presidents could not immediately stamp out the custom of decades, and Uruguay continued to be politically unstable. Economic advances were made in spite of political instability.

The Uruguayan government went into business itself, particularly in competition with foreign companies. It produced electricity, operated port facilities, and manufactured cement. Other industries were taken over in whole or in part. The Uruguayan program of governmental participation in economic activity is especially noteworthy, for it has been adopted in part by many Latin American governments since that time. Uruguay, despite her late start and her limited resources, marked out a path of moderate economic nationalism which attracted widespread emulation. The efforts of Uruguay were fairly successful in keeping her natural resources under the control of nationals, but as in Argentina and Chile, rural agricultural workers remained almost untouched by the forward sweep of commerce and industry.

The rise in demand for wheat and beef, copper and nitrates, during World War I, temporarily aided Argentina, Uruguay, and Chile. By the end of the war Argentina was no longer a debtor nation. All three suffered during the abrupt decline in demand in the readjustment of the 1920's, and Chile was particularly hard hit by the growth of the synthetic nitrate industry in Europe and a fall in the price of copper. One favorable step was taken to salvage the nation's currency after years of delay; the Central Bank was established, and the peso's more violent fluctuations were curtailed by backing it with gold.

Foreign investments continued to rise in Chile and Argentina, and at a slower pace in Uruguay. By 1929 the United States alone had 600 million dollars invested in Chile; the Chilean government continued borrowing money abroad until the world depression dried up the sources. The hostility toward foreign capital pervading all parts of Latin America was heightened by the depression, and the new economic nationalism reacted against the governments of Argentina and Chile, for they were blamed for the fact that many key industries and resources were the property of aliens.

END OF INDIAN RESISTANCE

Related to the problems of population growth, expansion of effective area, and attraction of foreign capital, was the continued existence of warlike Indians in the south of Argentina and Chile. These Indians were a centuries-old problem, for they had never been conquered nor effectively controlled, and they were not culturally adaptable to peaceful integration. Costly military establishments maintained a tenuous line of resistance. When, for any reason, the troops were needed elsewhere, the Indians overran the frontiers.

Both countries resolved to end the Indian problem. In Argentina the final destruction of the Ranqueles awaited General Julio A. Roca's war of extermination in 1879, while the Araucanians of southern Chile remained troublesome until the veterans of the War of the Pacific were sent against them in the 1880's. In both cases the Indian problem ended, and a vast new territory was opened for settlement. Uruguay faced no similar problem at this time, for her warlike Indians had been subdued and destroyed or absorbed before mid-century.

CHURCH—STATE STRIFE

The conflict between church and state, characteristic of the period, was present to some degree in each of the countries. The colorados of Uruguay passed anticlerical legislation, but the blancos did not become a clerical party. The authority of the church dwindled rapidly in the 1880's, when civil marriage was made compulsory and divorce legalized, and the registration of births and deaths was taken over by the government. Financial support from the government was drastically curtailed, leaving the church weak and unable to participate effectively in political strife.

Differences between state and church in Argentina were settled early by the government asserting and maintaining the right of patronage formerly exercised by the king of Spain. The constitution of 1853 specified Roman Catholicism as the official religion, but conceded toleration to other faiths. Argentina has been relatively free of church-state contention until very recent times.

The clash between church and state in Chile was more heated, for the liberals soon began agitating for abolition of the ecclesiastical courts, and of the church's right to register births and deaths, perform the marriage ceremony, and control education. One segment of the Conservative party came to the support of the church. The intensity of the struggle was caused by the conviction of the liberals that the church was an obstacle in the way of change, and they were determined to weaken its power. The first inroads into clerical authority were the abolition of the clerical courts and the opening of cemeteries to non-Catholics. Not satisfied with these measures, the liberals renewed their efforts, and the partisans of the church resisted desperately. In the 1880's further laws were passed, largely under the lead of José Manuel Balmaceda, which carried out most of the anticlerical program except for separation of church and state. The constitution of 1925 added this last feature.

EDUCATION

In the development of educational institutions and in national cultural activities, the period from 1860 to 1930 was particularly fruitful. Argentina and Chile, because of their earlier progress toward political stability, gained a vast lead over Uruguay. It must be remembered, in considering the expansion of public education, that public education was for the poor. The wealthy generally did not send their sons to public schools.

The promotion of public education was one of the ideals of the planners of independence. Bernardo O'Higgins of Chile, Bernardino Rivadavia of Argentina, and José Artigas of Uruguay were all strong proponents of the idea. Every Chilean government regarded the extension of public education in the nation's interest, despite the opposition of many members of the conservative oligarchy. Argentine education, and that of Uruguay, languished in the long era of political disorders. It was only in 1868, with the election of Domingo F. Sarmiento to the presidency, that rapid strides were made in Argentina.

Sarmiento, self-educated and of provincial background, was the greatest champion of education and civilization Latin America had produced. 'Mister Me,' as he was called because of his lack of modesty, vigorously set about educating and civilizing his countrymen. To him the enemy was ignorance, and the gaucho its epitome. Education would solve all problems once the gaucho and the caudillo had been cast into oblivion. One of his first acts as president was to order a census taken, the first of its kind in Argentina. He learned that the country had nearly two million inhabitants, a third of whom lived in the city and province of Buenos Aires. Only 12 per cent were foreign born. It did not take an official count to inform him that the vast majority of Argentinians lived in poverty and ignorance.

An admirer and friend of Horace Mann, Sarmiento sought to emulate him in reforming education in his country. He won noteworthy success in establishing a primary school system and in implanting his educational philosophy. With the aid of his minister of education, Nicolás Avellaneda, he doubled the number of public schools, and Argentina was able to boast the highest proportion of children attending schools of any South American country. In six years the number of students rose from 30,000 to 100,000. The literacy rate increased from 22 per cent in 1869 to 50 per cent in 1895. By 1930 it was above 80 per cent, the highest in Latin America.

Secondary education in Chile received a similar impetus under the lead of Diego Barros Arana, director of the National Institute and one of the greatest Latin American historians of the nineteenth century. For the first time instructors were required to specialize in certain fields of learning instead of attempting to teach all. Historical studies flourished, and the natural sciences were divided into separate courses. In the same period an agricultural school was founded. But even as late as 1920 only half of the children of school age were attending schools, and technical training was still inadequate for the country's needs.

Attempts to secularize education in Chile and to lay greater stress on the sciences were violently opposed by the pro-clerical wing of the Conservative party, who regarded the trend as anti-religious, and who also preferred to retain university positions in the form of political patronage. For a brief period in 1872 their views prevailed, and they were able to force through a law giving seminaries conducted by religious groups the right to grant certificates which must be accepted by the university. An auction of these certificates made the law an embarrassment, and it was repealed.

The first genuine accomplishments in furthering education in Uruguay came only in and after the era of professional soldier-presidents, beginning in 1875. In 1877 the average attendance in public schools was only about

12,000. In the next few years the number of schools and students was greatly increased, and the quality of instruction was improved. In 1900 there were less than 500 primary schools in Uruguay, and no secondary schools outside Montevideo. By 1930 the number of schools had tripled, but outside Montevideo educational facilities were available for only a third of the children. The late nineteenth century was, however, a time of marked upsurge in intellectual activity, and one in which interest in politics was gradually displaced by other pursuits.

LITERATURE

In literature romanticism was giving way to realism, still under French influence. Argentina and Uruguay produced a number of noteworthy poets, particularly Estanislao del Campo, author of *Fausto,* and José Hernández, whose epic poem *Martín Fierro* glorified the vanishing gaucho, and was a reply to Sarmiento's earlier *Facundo.* Juan Zorrilla de San Martín was one of Uruguay's chief romantic poets, and also one of the early poets of the modernist school. Eduardo Acevedo Díaz and Carlos Reyles have been ranked among the best of Uruguay's novelists of the period. Alberto Blest Gana inaugurated the realistic novel in Chile. The Indianist theme inspired many writers, including the poet Pablo Neruda of Chile. After the rise of modernism in 1888, it, too, had many followers in all three countries.

Chilean historical writers of the period were outstanding, foremost among them Miguel Luis Amunátegui, Benjamín Vicuña Mackenna, and Diego Barros Arana. José Toribio Medina, historian and bibliographer, also made a monumental contribution to scholarship in his many volumes. Bartolomé Mitre, Juan B. Justo, and Joaquín V. González were among the best-known Argentinians concerned with improving the intellectual life of their country. Mitre, statesman, historian, and publicist, founded the eminent newspaper, *La Nación,* which shared with *La Prensa,* also of Buenos Aires, a reputation for excellence extending far beyond the limits of Argentina. Justo, a militant socialist, fought for the improvement of political life and for the consolidation of democracy. González, statesman and educator, founded the National University of La Plata, and wrote fifty volumes in the fields of politics, law, history, teaching, and literature.

One of the most influential of Latin American writers of the period was José Enrique Rodó of Uruguay, whose small book called *Ariel* was widely read by the youth of his generation. As already indicated, Rodó gave his countrymen a comforting if inaccurate picture of their spiritual nobility, typified by Ariel, in sharp contrast to the baser materialism of Caliban— the United States. *Ariel*'s following finally dwindled, but Rodó was still remembered for his literary criticism and for his influence on style.

The establishment and improvement of newspapers was another noteworthy feature of cultural development. *La Nación* and *La Prensa* of Buenos Aires both appeared by 1870. There had been only two noteworthy daily papers in Chile in 1860, but before the end of the century the number had increased to thirty, for the desire to obtain news of the War of the Pacific greatly stimulated the habit of reading daily papers. In 1872 freedom of the press was guaranteed by law.

Major Wars

SPAIN

Foreign relations were marred during the epoch by two major wars among Latin American nations; and a minor clash between Spain, on the one hand, and Chile and Peru, on the other. The conflict with Spain, 1865–66, was caused by resentment over Spain's brusque treatment of Peru. Chileans were indignant at Spain's seizure of the Chincha islands from Peru, and regarded the incident as a threat to all of the Pacific Coast nations. A mob attacked the Spanish legation in Santiago. The Chilean government offered an explanation to the Spanish admiral, José Manuel Pareja Septién, and considered the incident closed. In September, 1865, however, while Chileans were celebrating the anniversary of their national independence, the Spanish squadron appeared before Valparaíso and Pareja demanded a twenty-one gun salute. The Chileans responded with expressions of patriotism and a declaration of war.

To carry on a naval campaign against the Spanish flotilla, Chile had only one mediocre sloop, the *Esmeralda,* and the splendid traditions established under the aegis of Lord Cochrane during the wars of independence. The *Esmeralda* left her refuge in Chiloé and captured the Spanish schooner, *Covadonga.* On learning of this humiliation, Pareja committed suicide. His successor ordered a blockade of Chilean ports in an effort to recover the *Covadonga* and to restore Spanish pride. Before retiring from the Pacific, the Spanish warships bombarded the undefended port of Valparaíso.

The conflict with Spain demonstrated once more to Latin American nations the need for collective defensive measures, and to Chileans the need for a naval force to defend their long coastline. The government ordered the purchase of two warships of most recent design, and built fortifications for Valparaíso. Chilean statesmen promoted the old idea of a Spanish American confederation. In 1865 this policy was implemented by offensive and defensive pacts with the governments of Peru, Bolivia, and Ecuador, but the project ended there. The new Chilean warships were soon to be used against Peru, for the foreign threat was quickly forgotten.

In the Plata region Uruguay, the much-chewed bone of contention between Argentina and Brazil, figured in the start of a major war. The blancos and the colorados, in their customary battles for the presidency, frequently sought help from Argentina or Brazil. In 1863, for example, the colorados under Colonel Venancio Flores, supported by aid from Buenos Aires, attacked the blanco regime of Bernardo P. Berro.

PARAGUAYAN WAR

The disorders which had prevailed in Uruguay since her independence led to frequent violations of the Brazilian border. Separatist movements in nearby Rio Grande do Sul made the Brazilian government especially sensitive to Uruguayan political discord, but its many complaints were unavailing. In 1864 Brazil again presented strong demands to the Uruguayan government to restore and preserve peace along the frontier, a demand which the hard-pressed blancos could not meet. When they failed to control the raiders or to give satisfaction, the imperial government massed troops near the southern border.

President Mitre of Argentina attempted to prevent the outbreak of war, but Brazil's decision to make reprisals and the continued dissension in Uruguay made his effort fruitless. Francisco Solano López, dictator of Paraguay and commander of the largest army in South America, now perceived an opportunity to indulge his ambition to become arbiter of the continent. He protested the Brazilian action, promised support to the blancos, and demanded to know Brazil's intentions. His pretensions were slighted by Brazil, and his delusions ran rampant. He reacted by sending his troops into undefended Mato Grosso. Had he gone immediately to the aid of the blancos he might have died a hero. They resisted stubbornly, meanwhile vainly waiting for the aid he had loudly promised.

Argentine participation in the conflict was not long delayed. Solano López requested permission to cross Corrientes to reach Uruguay, but was refused by Mitre. He retaliated by secretly declaring war on Argentina; the declaration was not announced until a munitions ship en route from Argentina was thought to be safely in Paraguayan waters. By the exercise of discretion, Solano López might have won the support of Entre Ríos and other anti-porteño provinces; instead, he made an oblique contribution to Argentine unity by giving the contesting factions compelling reasons for uniting against him.

The Paraguayan War had little to commend it from any standpoint. The unattractive character of Solano López and his brutality toward his countrymen and even toward members of his own family has made it difficult to recognize him as a national hero, the epitome of Paraguay's will to survive. Because Francisco Solano López has generally been condemned by those who wrote about him, it has been easy to ignore the terrible responsibility that Argentina and Brazil shared for the devastating conflict. The soon-published 'secret' treaty between them made it clear that their intention was to partition Paraguay. Knowledge of this treaty stiffened Paraguayan resistance and turned opinion everywhere against the allies.

The conquest of Paraguay proved far more costly and protracted than had been anticipated. The heroic and unexpected resistance of Paraguayans and misunderstanding among the allies prolonged the unequal conflict for five years. In 1868 Mitre, who had been forced to neglect domestic affairs to command the allied army, returned to Buenos Aires, and Argentina's active participation in the fighting declined. The Duke of Caxias, Brazil's ranking officer in the campaign, took charge of the war. The allied naval squadron, largely Brazilian, played a significant role in the transport of troops and supplies, and in several decisive engagements, such as the reduction of the fort at Humaitá. Efforts to end the war by negotiation were negated by Emperor Dom Pedro's insistence on the removal of Solano López as a preliminary step, and the sanguinary conflict ended only with the death of the Paraguayan dictator at the hands of Brazilian troops. The cost of the war in human life was appalling, and it served no useful purpose.

WAR OF THE PACIFIC

Before the War of the Pacific began, in 1879, Chile and Argentina seemed on the verge of hostilities over their mutual boundaries at the southern extremity of the continent. Feelings rose high, as if the territory involved were of great value, and in 1878 both countries sent naval squadrons to the Strait of Magellan. In both nations there were many persons who regarded warfare between Chile and Argentina as unthinkable, and the governments agreed to negotiation. In 1881 they reached an agreement whereby Chile was left in possession of the strait. The dividing line agreed on was along the highest peaks of the Andes, erroneously believed also to be the continental watershed. The question arose again when it was discovered that the highest peaks did not divide the waters, and again there was a threat of war. Once more, however, the problem was amicably settled, as was a controversy over the boundary in the Puna of Atacama.

While the earlier issue with Argentina remained threatening, differences arose with Bolivia over exploitation of guano and nitrate deposits in the Bolivian province of Antofagasta. In 1866 Chile had acknowledged Bolivian sovereignty north of the 24th parallel, south latitude, and the two countries agreed to divide equally the revenues derived from taxes on minerals and guano taken from the area between the 23rd and 25th parallels. Chileans opened mines in Antofagasta, and their enterprise was responsible for a sudden increase in nitrate production in this zone. The first Bolivian railroad was a part of the same project, for it was needed to transport minerals from the mines to the port.

In 1874 the Bolivian government agreed not to assess any new taxes on Chileans in exchange for Chile's cession of all claims north of the 24th parallel. The Bolivian government was not long in the control of any group or party in this period, and the treaty was violated a few years later by the imposition of new taxes.

Relations between Chile and Peru were strained at the same time, also over nitrate exploitation, on this occasion in the Peruvian province of Tarapacá. Chilean companies refused to co-operate in a Peruvian plan to raise the price of nitrates. In 1873, fearing the consequences of taking action against Chile, Peru and Bolivia signed a defensive-offensive alliance. This treaty frequently has been called secret. There seems little doubt, however, that Chilean officials were aware of it, although the Chilean public did not take notice of it until it was employed in arousing a patriotic effort against the signers. Soon after the treaty had been made, Peru decreed the nitrate industry of Tarapacá a state monopoly, and set the price it would pay producers. Another law forced Chileans to sell their holdings to the government. In 1875 they surrendered their buildings and equipment on a promise of compensation, a promise which was not kept.

In 1878 a newly arisen Bolivian dictator, Hilarión Daza, decided to try similar action against the Chilean Nitrate Company of Antofagasta. His act of levying a heavy tax violated a treaty, while Peru had not been bound by any agreement. The Chileans refused to pay, and in February, 1879, the day the company's holdings were to be sold at auction, Chilean soldiers occupied Antofagasta.

Because of her treaty with Bolivia, Peru found herself suddenly involved in a war in which she had nothing to gain and much to lose. The Chilean government was asked to withdraw its troops and negotiate the dispute; on Chile's refusal Peru mobilized and Bolivia prepared for war. In April, denouncing the so-called secret treaty, Chile declared war on the allies.

If numbers alone were an important consideration, Chile's action appeared suicidal, for her army was outnumbered nearly four to one by the combined forces of the allies, and Peru's recently acquired ironclad cruisers were thought superior to those of Chile. Chilean progress since independence, however, was a factor to be considered. The contest proved unequal, as many expected, but the superiority lay with Chile. Antofagasta was easily held, and Bolivia could do little more than join forces with Peru.

On the sea the campaign was especially significant. Peru and Chile each boasted two formidable cruisers of recent design, in addition to outmoded sailing vessels. The Chilean cruisers were the *Cochrane* and *Blanco Encalada,* named after heroes of the wars of independence; the Peruvian cruisers were the *Huáscar* and the *Independencia.* Chile sent the old sailing ships *Esmeralda* and *Covadonga* to blockade the port of Iquique, where they were found by the Peruvian cruisers. In the actions that followed the *Huáscar* rammed and sank the *Esmeraldo,* whose crew established a Chilean tradition by going down with guns manned and colors flying. The *Independencia,* in a similar attack on the *Covadonga,* struck a reef and was lost. For Peru the engagement was costly, for she lost her best warship; Chileans, on the other hand, were greatly stimulated by the heroism of their men and the destruction of the most powerful enemy vessel. Peru, nevertheless, carried the war to the coast of Chile with considerable success, until the *Huáscar* encountered the *Cochrane* and *Blanco Encalada* and was forced to surrender after a battle that made history as the first major clash of ironclads on the high seas. After this victory, Chile controlled the sea, and by October, 1879, the way was prepared for an invasion of Peru.

Chile immediately launched an attack against allied forces in Iquique. The province of Tarapacá fell in a single battle, the repercussions of which were felt in the allied capitals. General Mariano Prado resigned the presidency of Peru, and Daza was deposed. Tacna and Arica were taken, and the coast of Peru blockaded. An attempt to negotiate peace made on board a warship of the United States failed because the allies refused Chile's demand for cession of Antofagasta and Tarapacá. Warfare was resumed, with the Chileans determined on the conquest of Lima.

Late in 1880 a large Chilean force landed on the Peruvian coast south of Callao, and the march to Lima began. The Peruvians rallied to defend their capital with desperate but futile sacrifice. In January, 1881, their resistance was shattered, and Lima fell. The War of the Pacific was over, but for two more years guerrilla activity kept Peru in a state of anarchy, and the problems engendered by the war endured for half a century. Not until 1883 could a peace treaty be signed. By this treaty, signed at Ancón, Peru ceded to Chile the province of Tarapacá and yielded possession of Tacna and Arica for ten years, after which a plebiscite was to be held to determine future ownership. A separate peace was made with Bolivia; title to Antofagasta became Chilean, leaving Bolivia completely landlocked.

AFTERMATH OF THE WAR

The 'Question of the Pacific,' as the unsettled fate of Tacna and Arica was called, disturbed relations between Chile and Peru until 1929. Attempts to hold the proposed plebiscite failed, largely because the aggressive actions of Chileans in the provinces made Peruvians fear that a fair election would not be held. In 1911 Peru severed diplomatic relations with Chile. Numerous attempts to bring the two countries together failed. United States President Herbert Hoover took an active interest in the dispute, and he helped persuade the two countries to restore diplomatic relations and to reach a solution. In 1928 they exchanged envoys once more, and in the following year the issue was finally resolved. Arica remained a part of Chile, and Tacna was returned to Peru, along with an indemnity.

In 1891 Chile became embroiled in a dispute with the United States. Feeling against the North American power was strong, for the Congressionalist party, victors in the recent civil war, regarded the United States as having favored liberal José Manuel Balmaceda. During the war a congressionalist ship, the *Itata,* bringing munitions from the United States, had been intercepted by a United States warship. Patrick Egan, United States minister to Chile, incurred further disfavor by giving asylum to political refugees when the civil war ended.

BALTIMORE AFFAIR

Under these circumstances, with the unsettled conditions caused by the bitter civil war and the known hostility toward the United States, the captain of the *U.S.S. Baltimore* unwisely permitted a liberty party ashore at Valparaíso. The seamen apparently sought the entertainment customarily provided by port cities, and became embroiled in street fights with Chileans. The Valparaíso police either were reluctant or unable to disperse the mob, although Chilean army and navy officers acted quickly to escort some of the seamen to safety. Before all could be returned to the *Baltimore,* two had been killed and several injured.

The incident was unfortunate but not surprising, considering the state of tempers as a result of the civil war. The repercussions, however, were astonishing. Egan placed the blame entirely on Chilean officials, even before an investigation had been made to determine where the fault lay. His tactless demands were coolly received, and he heightened the tension by the irritation he displayed at what he regarded as procrastination on the part of the Chilean government. President Benjamin Harrison, who could have easily settled the dispute with little friction, chose instead to employ it for political ends in the approaching election in the United States, and the affair grew beyond reasonable proportions. A peremptory demand for an apology and reparations was sent Chile in January, 1892. Without waiting for a reply, Harrison delivered a war message to Congress. Chile offered an indemnity to be determined by the Supreme Court of the United States, and the incident was officially closed. It left Chileans with strong feelings about the United States which were neither flattering nor easy to dispel.

Resurgence of Liberalism

One of the strongest currents in the southern South American nations was the rising tide of liberalism. Liberal predominance was achieved first in Chile, for Argentina's political maturity was delayed by the provincial caudillos and the capital question. The nineteenth-century Uruguayan parties, the blancos or *nacionalistas,* as they began to call themselves, and the colorados, represented areas rather than principles. The blancos were the party of the rural landowners, and the colorados the party of Montevideo. Only after a spirit of compromise began to develop through agreements giving the colorados control of the national government and the blancos control of their own districts was it possible for Uruguay to free herself from the plague of revolts.

CHILE

Already in 1861 the liberals had won initial triumphs in Chile, for President José Joaquín Pérez had been acceptable to them and he formed his cabinet from all political groups. The most extreme of the liberals now demanded immediate enactment of anticlerical legislation and a weakening of the power of the president. They succeeded in 1871 in limiting the presidential term to prevent a president from succeeding himself, although he could be elected after an intervening term. In the same year Federico Errázuriz Zañartu, a liberal conservative, assumed the presidency. The enactment of anticlerical legislation began.

Also during this administration the electoral system was reformed to remove elections from control of the municipalities, and indirectly, of the chief executive. They were placed under boards of leading citizens. The cumulative vote was introduced for election of members to the chamber of deputies in an effort to give minority parties representation corresponding to their strength. Each voter now had as many votes as there were deputies authorized for his district, and these votes could be cast for one or more candidates. The experiment proved less successful than its authors anticipated, for the proliferation of political parties that followed filled the chamber with many groups of nearly equal strength, none commanding a majority and none feeling deeply its responsibility to the nation.

Social legislation was not a part of the liberal programs of the nineteenth century. Instead liberals sought to extend the franchise where necessary to their rise to power, to reduce the church to political impotency, and to forward the physical improvements which were expected to enhance national prosperity. These movements were supported mainly by the middle class, and they were by no means radical. On many questions there was little difference of opinion between liberals and conservatives. The most critical issue between them was the role of the church. Some Chilean liberals supported measures intended to weaken executive control, such as making the president's cabinet responsible to the chamber of deputies. In the 1880's a Chilean law provided for overriding a presidential veto by a two-thirds vote of both houses. In the same decade judicial and administrative officials were restricted in their authority to arrest individuals, a law intended to prevent arbitrary confinement of opponents of the government during political campaigns. The vote was extended to include all literate males twenty-five years of age, without property qualifications. Despite all these advances, the government's candidate for the presidency invariably won.

BALMACEDA

As the liberals accomplished their program step by step, the Chilean government became less and less effective. Able and energetic President José Manuel Balmaceda, 1886–91, faced a continuous succession of cabinet crises. There was no majority party in the congress, and his coalition cabinets changed with bewildering frequency. Relations between the president and congress became embittered, and government painfully difficult. Balmaceda tried to co-operate with the chamber of deputies by appointing ministers satisfactory to the volatile majority of its members, despite the fact that the constitution did not provide for ministerial responsibility to the congress. When this recourse failed, Balmaceda reverted to the former practice of choosing ministers from his own following.

When the time came to decide on a successor, Balmaceda attempted to follow precedent by appointing the man of his choice minister of the interior in order that he might be able to control the outcome of the election. His opponents in the chamber rebelled at this action and fought him through their control of taxation and the voting of appropriations. Even by yielding to their demands, however, Balmaceda could not resolve the quarrel, for congress adjourned without voting a new appropriation for the coming year. Irresponsibility in the legislature was shockingly great, and personal animosities loomed larger than legislative duties.

The opponents of the president had criticized him vociferously for his economic policies, even as Juárez Celmán of Argentina was being censured for supporting inflationary trends and for reckless government spending. In 1890 Juárez Celmán resigned in the face of revolt and financial chaos. Balmaceda did not succumb so readily. After congress adjourned, instead of calling a special session to provide an appropriation bill, he unconstitutionally declared the previous year's bill in force for the coming year. He did not stop there. Convinced that it was impossible to govern constitutionally, he assumed dictatorial powers.

The revolt of the Radical party against Juárez Celmán was easily put down, although the president's prestige was ruined. That which arose against Balmaceda was far more effective. The Congressionalist party acted quickly to win the adherence of the navy, and sent it north to seize control of the nitrate provinces acquired in the War of the Pacific. By thus appropriating to itself the principal source of governmental revenue, the Congressionalist party was well prepared to finance the conflict. The war continued from January to August, 1891, when the congressionalist army captured Valparaíso and Santiago. Balmaceda committed suicide in the vain hope of placating his vengeful enemies and sparing his friends. When the destructive war was ended Chile entered into an era of unsuccessful parliamentary government. The victory was an apparent triumph for liberalism, for domination by the president was replaced by that of the legislature. In effect the change meant merely the triumph of governmental irresponsibility.

ARGENTINA

In the days of prosperity, speculation, and inflation of the 1880's, the opponents of the Argentine administration gathered together to form the Unión Cívica Radical, later the Radical party, composed of middle-class merchants and politically conscious descendants of immigrants. It demanded the extension of suffrage and honest elections in order that this group might wrest control of the government from the estancieros. It was not, as its name implies, radical. It was bitterly resisted because it represented landless 'foreign' elements, and its abortive revolt against Juárez

Celmán merely caused the conservatives to tighten their grip on the government.

By 1900, freedom of suffrage and honest elections seemed to the radicals no nearer than in 1890. It was not property qualifications that prevented the immigrant and commercial classes from participating in the government, but fraud and force. Government endorsement of a candidate, as in Chile, made his election certain, for if control of the polls did not suffice, there was the added safeguard of counting the votes. As the desperation of the Radical party grew, it turned increasingly to Hipólito Yrigoyen, an enigmatic backroom politician of Basque descent, and a nephew of Leandro N. Alem, one of the founders of the party. By 1900 Yrigoyen's influence was preponderant, for he carefully eliminated his rivals. When the early leaders of the Radical party, such as Alem, Senator Aristóbulo del Valle, and Bernardo Irigoyen, fell from grace, he coldly ignored them.

YRIGOYEN

To Yrigoyen it appeared that his party might never gain control of the government except by rebellion, but his tactics embraced that method only as a last resort. To emphasize that the country was ruled by a minority clique, the radicals abstained from voting.

In Argentina, meanwhile, the extravagant hopes of the reformers were dashed by the autocratic regime of Yrigoyen. He, who had long inveighed against undemocratic methods of government, surrounded himself by officials accustomed to accepting his complete domination without chafing. Yrigoyen's administration was more personal than any Argentina had seen for more than half a century. Those who had expected a regime of reform were mistaken in their man; Yrigoyen did not favor drastic changes. He made only mild reform gestures in comparison with Batlle. Retirement funds were provided for by law and labor unions were allowed greater freedom than before. Yrigoyen recommended the passage of laws providing for arbitration of labor disputes and collective bargaining, but he did not seem greatly concerned with getting them enacted.

Yrigoyen's political methods were those he had formerly fought so bitterly, and he directed his party's energies toward capturing control of provincial governments by questionable methods. To his credit was a noteworthy reorganization of the universities, which not only improved them but brought higher education within reach of students of the lower middle class. His promises had aroused far greater expectations, however, and there was profound disappointment on the part of many enlightened politicians. The conservatives loathed him for stirring up the hopes of 'foreigners' and laborers.

The nadir of Yrigoyen's first term was a labor massacre of January, 1919. Unrelated strikes broke out in a British metalworks and among maritime workers, and pickets skirmished with the police. One of these clashes caused a flare-up in feeling against the government, and mobs formed in the streets, bent on indiscriminate destruction. The police, apparently on instructions from the president, shot to kill, and they fired on anyone found in the streets. The Regional Argentine Workers' Federation ordered a general strike for twenty-four hours, and the city population became panic-stricken. Before the carnage and rioting subsided, hundreds had been killed, and destruction ran into thousands of dollars.

What finally brought the radicals to power was not revolt, however, but a peaceful and astonishing transition. In 1910 Roque Sáenz Peña, son of a former president, won the presidency determined to reform electoral laws and end the boycotting of elections. In 1911 the 'Sáenz Peña law' was passed making voting secret and compulsory. Other changes allocated to the minority party a third of the seats in the chamber of deputies regardless of its voting strength. The Sáenz Peña law gave Yrigoyen an unparalleled opportunity.

The first elections under the new law were for deputies to congress, and the radicals won a clear victory. But the crucial test did not come until the presidential election of 1916. Yrigoyen's years of patient building up of a disciplined following were rewarded, for the first free and genuinely representative election in Argentine history gave him the presidency. When he took the oath of office he was surrounded by a delirious, optimistic mob. But throughout the demonstration the people's choice remained unsmiling.

Yrigoyen's second administration in Argentina coincided with the presidency of Ibáñez in Chile, and ended in the same manner. When he was elected for the second time in 1928, Yrigoyen was more than eighty years of age, and quite unable to govern. Unscrupulous members of his party soon discovered that Yrigoyen would sign any paper put before him, and they made haste to empty the treasury. Thus, at a time when the country urgently needed a government that could deal incisively with the complex economic problems of falling exports and fluctuating currency, it was under a senile president and a host of plundering politicians.

Protest from within the party and from without rose to such a crescendo that at last it reached the ears of the old caudillo himself. On September 5, 1930, Yrigoyen resigned in favor of his vice-president, but by this time matters had gone too far for the agitated country to accept anyone closely associated with the Radical party. The next day General José Félix Uriburu marched into Buenos Aires at the head of a column of troops, and the epoch of Yrigoyen and of pseudo-liberalism abruptly ended.

BATLLE Y ORDÓÑEZ

Neither the parliamentary regime of Chile nor the radical administration of Yrigoyen made social and economic reform a major part of its activity. It was in Uruguay that a South American government first undertook to improve social and economic conditions by positive legislative action. The fact that Uruguay seized the initiative seems astonishing, for the internecine strife between blancos and colorados had barely been terminated when the country became one of the most advanced in the world in terms of social legislation.

Foremost in spearheading the drive was José Batlle y Ordóñez, a well-educated journalist with a passion for social reform. He had been in office only a year when Uruguay's last serious civil war broke out in 1904. The control over six departments consigned earlier to the nacionalistas made effective government difficult, and Batlle was determined to govern effectively. He suppressed the revolt, but only after much destruction of life and property. The rebels lost their previous position, but were granted amnesty and a promise of reform.

To eliminate the possibility of similarly destructive revolts in the future, Batlle improved army training and discipline, and had wireless installations placed in rural garrisons to prevent their isolation. More important as a step toward stabilizing the country was his effort to remove the cause of rebellions. The conduct of elections was made more satisfactory, and the nacionalistas received a greater share in the government, which helped to reconcile them and at the same time relieved their sense of frustration.

In 1911 Batlle began a second term as president, and it was at this time the major reforms were introduced. The government established the State Insurance Bank to compete with foreign companies, and certain types of insurance became state monopolies. In order that Uruguayans would not need to depend on alien capital to finance economic enterprises, the Bank of the Republic expanded its activities, and the government purchased control of the Mortgage Bank of Uruguay. At the same time the administration took other steps to prevent the domination of the Uruguayan economy by foreigners.

In the field of social reform Batlle's program made even more drastic changes. The abolition of capital punishment, the establishment of an eight hour day and a forty-eight hour week for laborers, old age pensions, compensation insurance for workingmen, and minimum wages for rural laborers were enacted into law despite strenuous opposition.

Batlle's influence left other lasting impressions. His toleration of his opponents made political persecutions unfashionable, and freedom of the press came to be regarded as a vital liberty. For the first time university education was placed within reach of all economic classes. A spirit of cooperation for national development replaced the venerable factionalism of earlier eras.

Batlle's prestige and purposes remained strong in the administration of Feliciano Viera, who followed him in 1915. Although Viera's term coincided with World War I, Uruguayan attention was not diverted from domestic affairs. Diplomatic relations with Germany were severed, and in other ways Uruguay expressed favor for the Allied cause; otherwise the war's effect was no more than that of any international crisis affecting world trade. More important for Uruguay was the promulgation of a new constitution.

The Uruguayan constitution of 1917 was the result of compromise between the nacionalistas, who favored a parliamentary regime, and the colorados, who were divided in their desires. Under the new constitution the president retained control over foreign affairs and national security, while a national council composed of members of both parties was charged with his former administrative duties. The president was to be chosen by direct vote rather than by congress, and proportional representation was introduced into local elections. The secret ballot and compulsory voting were also required.

After 1917 the honest management of elections and minority representation in the government removed most of the former grievances which had led to strife. The government continued to engage in business enterprises, most of which were successfully managed. In 1928 it opened a national meat-packing plant for the purpose of assuring better prices for producers. Preparations were made for a government corporation to manufacture and sell alcohol, and for another to compete with private companies selling petroleum.

The Chilean counterpart of Yrigoyen and Batlle, as spokesmen for the opponents of the landed oligarchy and proponents of change, was Arturo Alessandri Palma, who won tremendous support by advocating laws favorable to labor. He campaigned for the presidency in 1920 as the candidate of the Liberal Alliance, and his appeal was directed not only at the middle class but at labor as well. In the bitterly contested election Alessandri won by a slender margin, while his party gained a majority only in the chamber of deputies. The conservative majority in the senate forced his cabinets to fall one after the other and effectively blocked his legislative program. The economic situation of Chile became critical, for European countries were protecting their new artificial nitrate industries. Chilean unemployment increased, and those in distress looked vainly to Alessandri for relief.

With economic ruin and governmental ineffectiveness the major problems facing Chile, the congress voted in 1924 to establish salaries for the members of both houses. The measure was necessary if governmental responsibility was to be shared by honest men without private wealth; previously congressmen had been unpaid, and the seats had been literally auctioned to members of the wealthy class. It was not the proposal itself but the precedence given it over more urgent business that caused interference by young army officers.

Possibly inspired by events in Spain and Italy, a committee of officers approached the president in September, 1924, and demanded a new cabinet composed of army officers. This thinly veiled threat of force intimidated the congress, and pending reform bills were quickly passed in profusion, and almost without consideration or dissent. Alessandri resigned and left the country, and a provisional government of high-ranking, conservative officers was installed. Their reactionary policies were no more pleasing to the young officers than those of former governments, and in January, 1925, the young officers seized the government and set up a junta composed of friends of Alessandri, whom they invited to return. The most powerful member of the cabinet was Colonel Carlos Ibáñez, Minister of War.

One of the first acts of the provisional government was the promulgation of a new constitution which restored presidential power to its former status, at the expense of the unworkable parliamentary system. Members of congress were not permitted to hold cabinet posts, nor was congressional approval needed for ministerial appointments by the president. Other changes were introduced, including separation of church and state.

The apparent ambitions of Ibáñez made the presidency uninviting to Alessandri after his return, and he resigned before the end of 1925. Emiliano Figueroa Larraín, a compromise candidate, replaced him, but Ibáñez retained his power. Governmental factionalism and class antagonism made many Chileans desire a dominant chief executive on whom they could rely to prevent social upheaval. In 1927 Figueroa Larraín resigned, and a month later Ibáñez was elected president.

As president, Ibáñez represented a return to the type of chief executive typical in Chile before 1860, but his program was one of social reform and labor legislation. Agrarian reform, however, was scarcely contemplated. Loans from Europe and the United States were used to promote an extensive program of public works which, together with the stabilization of the peso, made possible a modest improvement in the living conditions of urban laborers.

Foreign investments in Chile had risen enormously in the 1920's, and by 1930 the hostility to foreign capital which had appeared in all parts of Latin America reacted against Ibáñez, who was accused of permitting foreigners to influence the government through their financial power. Copper, nitrates, and other critical resources were owned primarily by aliens, and for this condition Ibáñez was blamed. As the impact of the world trade depression caused acute unemployment in Chile, agitation against the government became violent. In 1931 rioting by university students set off a wave of insurrections and strikes throughout the country; Ibáñez, unable to preserve order without resorting to greater violence, resigned.

The period from 1860 to 1930 was one of population growth, economic development, and urbanization for Argentina, Uruguay, and Chile. Their literacy rates rose impressively, and their cultural contributions achieved widespread recognition. It was also a time of political ferment, with a rising middle class, influenced by or composed of European immigrants, challenging the old order of the landholding conservatives. By 1920 the liberals had won control of the governments, but except in Uruguay their rule was disappointing to the lower middle class and labor. One of the most crucial problems, that of the landless, was scarcely discussed. In each of the countries two or three thousand families still owned up to 80 per cent of the agricultural land. By the end of the period the condition of labor was generally much improved, but the gulf between the few who owned the land and the many who worked on it was still immeasurable. Those who owned the land chafed at loss of control of the government; and the inadequacies of the liberal regimes, combined with a world-wide economic depression, prepared the way for a conservative return to power. Chilean and Uruguayan experiments with parliamentary government and with the dual executive proved visionary. Reaction to the discredited parliamentary regime in Chile led to the rise of an autocratic army officer who pushed through social legislation instead of endlessly debating about it. The failures of the Radical party in Argentina, on the other hand, caused a reaction which enabled the conservative minority, with the aid of the army, to return to power. In Uruguay it was not lack of social and economic reform that led to interference with the constitutional regime, but the difficulties engendered in a time of economic crisis by optimistic experimentation with divided executive authority.

9

Indo-America: An Era of Stagnation and Retrogression

> In respect of civil rights, there is no legal distinction between the Indian and the white. Both enjoy the same citizenship for all private and public purposes, to both is granted the equal protection of the laws, equal suffrage, equal eligibility to office. This is to some extent a guarantee to the Indian against ill treatment, but it does not raise him in the social scale. He seldom casts a vote; not, indeed, that it makes much difference in these countries whether the citizen votes or not, for a paternal government takes charge of the elections. . . . No one has yet preached to him the gospel of democracy; no one has told him that he has anything to gain from action as a citizen. . . . There is, therefore, not yet any 'Indian question' in South America. There ought to be an Indian question; that is to say, there ought to be an effort to raise the Indians economically and educationally. But they have not yet begun to ask to be raised.
>
> JAMES BRYCE *

The "Indian" Countries

Peru, Bolivia, Ecuador, and Paraguay differed in many ways from Argentina, Uruguay, and Chile, and the differences were accentuated during the period from 1860 to 1930. Each of the former countries had a population basically Indian, and because of the presence of a large, servile class of laborers, because of the extreme concentration of land ownership, and because of the chronic political disorders, immigrants found little to attract them in these regions. The 'Indian' countries, nevertheless, were not altogether untouched by the currents running through the rest of the continent. To a greater or lesser degree anticlericalism, the rise of liberal movements, and the passion for physical improvements through the attraction of

* *South America, Observations and Impressions,* The Macmillan Company, New York, 1929, pp. 469–70.

202

foreign capital infected them. The gulf between the few who owned the wealth and dominated the countries and the many who lived and toiled in poverty and ignorance was tremendous; and because the many were blighted additionally by the handicap of being the children of the conquered, their rise to an intermediate status was almost beyond hope. In these countries the heritage of the conquest and of the colonial era remained powerful and resistant to currents of social change.

The subordinate role of the Indians was a major obstacle to the achievement of national prosperity and cultural maturity, for unless all the population was allowed and encouraged to progress to the extent of its abilities, the economic and cultural productivity of these countries was limited to the accomplishments of a small group. Alien capital could acquire control of the natural resources with little competition from domestic capital. In addition to this enormous problem of raising the Indians to a status beneficial to themselves and to the countries at large—a problem that was not met frontally by any of the nations involved—Paraguay, Bolivia, and Peru suffered devastating setbacks by engaging in losing wars with their neighbors.

In 1860, Peru, Ecuador, Bolivia, and Paraguay were all in or on the verge of periods of political disorder, and political strife was one of the most consistent overtones of the epoch. Faction-torn Peru soon found herself facing serious difficulties with Spain over her refusal to receive a 'royal commissioner' sent, along with a naval squadron, to press claims for damages done to Spanish subjects. The title of the agent indicated that Spain still regarded Peru as a rebellious colony. Affronted by this insult to national honor, the Peruvians rejected the unwelcome visitor. The Spanish squadron retaliated by seizing the Chincha islands, source of guano and of more than half of all governmental revenue.

President Juan Antonio Pezet, who was willing to negotiate in order to avoid a war for which his country was unprepared, was overthrown in 1865 by those who favored a more aggressive attitude. Peru now declared war on Spain and joined an alliance composed of Chile, Ecuador, and Bolivia. Governments were short-lived for the next few years, but in 1868 Colonel José Balta emerged victorious from the many-sided struggle for power. By that time the Spanish fleet had made a damaging but fruitless assault upon Callao and left the Pacific. In 1871 Peru signed a truce with Spain, and in 1879 Spain belatedly acknowledged Peruvian independence. In the meantime the senseless conflict had heightened domestic confusion and retarded efforts at economic development.

PERU

Balta restored order and attempted to bring the Peruvian economy up to date by letting contracts for the construction of railroads, dock facilities, and similar improvements. His intentions were generally meritorious, but his accomplishments did not always deserve praise. He made foreign loans for which he pledged future deliveries of guano. The projects for which the money was spent were not in themselves productive of governmental revenue, and private industry did not expand at a rapid pace. Consequently, the outlay for interest on the loans grew while government income was shrinking.

The influx of foreign capital through official loans encouraged prodigal expenditures by the government, and much of the money was sidetracked from its intended use by corrupt officials. The country's financial future was made increasingly precarious by the continued practice of borrowing against future shipments of guano. This recourse had obvious attractions for the ephemeral governments; they received the cash and were able to dispose of it, while later administrations were left to face the day of reckoning.

To aid the expansion of agriculture and to speed the construction of railroads, the government admitted about 85,000 Chinese coolie laborers between 1861 and 1875; these Chinese were soon reduced to a condition little better than slavery on the coastal plantations, in violation of the contracts under which they had come. Henry Meiggs, fresh from his triumphs at railroad building in Chile, transferred his operations to Peru, where his success made him the social lion of Lima.

Before the end of his term, Balta was assassinated, and a new political epoch began. His successor was Manuel Pardo, the first civilian president of Peru and one of the few candidates ever to defeat the official choice. Pardo's victory reflected the triumph of the newly wealthy class of professional men and merchants and planters, who formed the *Civilista* party in opposition to the conservatives and the military. Balta's assassination was part of a desperate attempt to maintain military control, and he was punished for accepting the outcome of an election which went against the party in power! Such was the state of Peruvian politics at the time.

Peru suffered even more from the war than Bolivia, for her navy was destroyed, her land invaded, and thousands of her men killed, in addition to the loss of her richest nitrate province. Guerrilla opposition to Chile continued in the interior for several years, and it was not until General Miguel Iglesias assumed the presidency that Chileans could find a government willing and able to accede to their terms, formalized by the Treaty of Ancón in 1883.

The War of the Pacific was a grave setback to both Peru and Bolivia, for it greatly retarded economic development and political maturity. The injuries caused by the loss of the war were not always tangible, for the damage done to morale was manifested in many ways. In both countries attempts had been made to establish civilian administrations to replace the military despotisms, and statesmen had appeared who advocated economic and social change. The war upset both countries immeasurably, and made their financial plight even more precarious than before. The defeat and loss of territory, on the other hand, seemed to have a salutary effect on political life, for the dangers of dissension were driven home forcibly, and political factions accepted compromise more readily than before.

Financial chaos jeopardized the first essay at civilian government in Peru. The guano exports were no longer a source of governmental revenue, for the entire sales proceeds for years to come had been mortgaged to alien creditors. To make matters worse, artificial fertilizers were replacing guano in European markets. By 1876 it was necessary to suspend payment on the foreign debt, and Peru was mired in an economic morass from which it took several decades to extricate herself. Pardo attempted to reduce government spending. At the same time he sought to curtail the influence of the army in political life by disbanding certain troublesome units and by creating a national guard, and by stimulating greater interest in politics among civilians. He tried to raise educational standards by bringing in foreign educators, and he negotiated a treaty with China in an effort to humanize the Chinese coolie traffic.

The government was assailed for the financial chaos, and Pardo was hard pressed to discover methods for reviving the economy. The drop in the price of nitrates led him to formulate plans for a government monopoly of nitrate sales. Chilean companies operating in Tarapacá and the Bolivian province of Antofagasta, however, refused to co-operate in the plan to raise prices artificially. Peru and Bolivia signed a military alliance, aimed specifically at Chile, for both regarded Chilean economic penetration as a common problem. In 1875 the Peruvian government created a monopoly of the nitrate industry and expropriated Chilean and other foreign holdings. The disastrous War of the Pacific began when Bolivia inaugurated similar policies.

Little advance in political life had been made in Bolivia since independence. Semi-military factions had battled for power, and none of them had accomplished more than a hasty reaping of the fruits of victory before being expelled in turn. The few attempts at social or political reform, such as that of José María Linares, a civilian president, were doomed to failure by the ephemeral nature of the administrations. Similarly, presidents who sought to reduce factionalism by conciliatory measures merely courted disaster, for tolerance of opponents was regarded as weakness and an invitation to revolt.

In 1864 Mariano Melgarejo, one of the most notorious examples of the violent caudillo, captured the government in a typical barracks revolt. An ignorant but shrewd soldier, Melgarejo had discovered that Bolivians would follow an audacious leader, and in time of battle he fortified his courage by generous applications of alcohol. His often-interrupted regime was one of lust, violence, and misgovernment. In 1866 he surrendered Bolivian rights to territory on the coast to Chile, and the following year ceded a large tract to Brazil. He debased the currency and despoiled the Indians of their tribal lands, greatly increasing the social and economic ills of the country. Melgarejo dominated the scene until 1871, when he was ousted by another barracks revolt.

The presidency continued to change hands frequently. In 1876 General Hilarión Daza seized power, and he soon found himself at war with Chile over his violation of the nitrate taxing agreement of 1874. The recklessness with which he precipitated the war indicated that Bolivians little appreciated the advances Chileans had made.

Bolivia's role in the War of the Pacific was insignificant and humiliating. Chilean troops easily overran the province of Antofagasta, and after their invasion of Tarapacá in 1879, Daza was overthrown. The Chilean victory at Tacna in the next year virtually ended Bolivian participation in the war. The loss of the coastal territory left Bolivia without access to the sea, and regaining an outlet has been the most consistent theme of her foreign policy since that time. A truce was made with Chile, but it was not until 1904 that a treaty was finally signed. Chile received title to Antofagasta, and Bolivia received an indemnity.

ECUADOR

Ecuador, too, had been badly torn by revolt and counter-revolt since independence, and had no national government at all in 1860. The most powerful of the various caudillos was Guillermo Franco of Guayaquil. A contest for power ended with the triumphant emergence of the conservative lawyer Gabriel García Moreno. The country he undertook to govern was in deplorable condition. Roads were almost impassable, foreign commerce was negligible, and the majority of the people lived in poverty and oppression surpassing that of the colonial era. The Indians of the highlands eked out a miserable existence from an unfriendly soil whose products went largely for the sustenance of others while in the lowland port regions disease took a frightful toll. Property was everywhere insecure, and economic enterprise was conspicuous by its absence. To many Ecuadorians a despotic government that could restore and preserve order seemed far more attractive than chronic anarchy.

GARCÍA MORENO

García Moreno, a religious zealot, assumed the disagreeable task of trying to form a government capable of maintaining order throughout the country. His methods were reminiscent of those of Rosas in Buenos Aires a few years before. Opposition was liquidated without such formality as trials. Revolts were furiously suppressed, and holders of liberal views were hunted out and executed or driven into exile. Gradually the entire nation took on the somber aspects of a monastery whose dreary, black tone bore little resemblance to the colorful era of colonial rule.

For fifteen years García Moreno remained the ruler of Ecuador. He permitted others to serve in the capacity of president between his own administrations, but he never relinquished control. The dictator might well have been a chief inquisitor himself, so complete was his fanatical devotion to the church. Experiences in France during an earlier period of exile—he had witnessed the revolutionary upheavals there in 1848—had set his mind inexorably against all vestiges of liberal doctrine. He regarded anticlericalism as a primary cause of disorder, for to him the church was the most vital institution in life. He brought back the Jesuits to Ecuador and gave them a prominent role in education. In fact, all education was placed in church hands, as was authority over all matters pertaining to literature and the arts. The church became the sole judge as to what books might be imported or published, and no literature was permitted to circulate without religious blessing. The theocratic dictator signed a concordat with the papacy giving the church a status even more powerful than it had possessed in the colonial era. García Moreno expected his support of the church to be reciprocated, and he endeavored to rid the clergy of many long-standing abuses and to purify its ranks to the end that priests and members of the orders would be at least as devoted to the holy cause as he. In 1873 he consecrated his tiny country to the 'Sacred Heart of Jesus.'

In spite of his efforts, García Moreno was never completely able to crush all opposition. Revolts were frequent, and to secure a firmer grip on the machinery of government, the dictator introduced a new constitution lengthening the president's term of office to six years and permitting immediate re-election. Even with this basic law he found it impossible to govern the country constitutionally. Opposition became more desperate, and the dictator's methods of suppression grew more and more severe.

The long period of García Moreno's rule, although far from peaceful, was more orderly than any previous era since independence. Some material progress was to be noted. A road was completed from Guayaquil to Quito. New schools were opened by the Jesuits and the French Christian Brothers. Political corruption was not tolerated, and the government's financial condition improved to the point that payments on the national debt were resumed. But animosity to the regime eventually became uncontrollable, and from neighboring countries plots to overthrow the theocratic state were continuously hatched. García Moreno's career was finally ended by assassination. Far away from the scene, Juan Montalvo, Ecuadorian journalist and one of Latin America's most gifted essayists, exclaimed on hearing of the dictator's death: 'My pen has killed him!'

For most of the twenty-year period after García Moreno's death the conservatives held the government, although sporadic uprisings, barracks revolts, and new constitutions disturbed the peace. Under Antonio Flores, 1888–92, Ecuador enjoyed an interlude of domestic peace and a fair measure of civil liberty. His successor became involved in a national scandal by permitting Chile ostensibly to transfer a warship to Ecuador while actually selling it to Japan for use against China. In the uproar that followed revelation of this act the liberals perceived an opportunity to drive the badly divided conservatives from power. Their victory brought in a new regime under General Eloy Alfaro in 1895.

ALFARO

General Alfaro remained the dominant figure in his country's political life until his assassination in 1911. To Alfaro liberalism was more than the fetish it had been to his predecessors. Although his extreme anticlericalism was a reaction to García Moreno's policies, and made him anathema to the conservatives, his moderation and tact for a time prevented a 'religious' war from engulfing Ecuador. During his first term, however, a patronage law was passed giving the government greater control over clerical affairs.

In 1906 a new constitution, the twelfth since independence, was promulgated, and it aroused the conservatives to fury by omitting to make Roman Catholicism the state religion. Conspiracies and insurrections were frequent and Alfaro, again in the presidency, adopted severe measures to restore order. His problems were complicated by the threat of war with Peru over a boundary dispute. Despite the many difficulties, domestic and foreign, Alfaro energetically pushed to completion the project of building a railroad line from Quito to Guayaquil. This railroad was an important factor in subsequent political and economic progress, for it not only opened the interior to foreign trade but tended to lessen the regional strife between coastal and mountain factions.

The outbreak of World War I caused a temporary economic setback, but trade revived rapidly after 1916. The conflict between church and state subsided, and was no longer a source of civil disorder. One of the most significant accomplishments of the period was brought about during Alfredo Baquerizo Moreno's administration when, with the aid of the Rockefeller Foundation, sanitary improvements freed Guayaquil of yellow fever and bubonic plague. The port, once feared as a graveyard of foreign seamen and shunned by ship captains, became safe at last. Commercial expansion followed, and the country benefited by increased governmental revenues, part of which were used to build schools.

The issuance of unredeemable paper money in Ecuador led, as elsewhere, to depreciation and to hardship among the merchants and labor. In 1922 and the following year, riots were frequent owing to the rise of prices and the failure of wages to increase. The growing agitation of laboring groups and the fear of revolt induced the government to make concessions.

One of the concessions to the radical wing of the Liberal party was permitting the election of an extreme liberal, Dr. Gonzalo Córdoba, in 1924. The measure failed to mollify the opposition, owing in part to the illness and incapacity of Córdoba, and in 1925 the vice-president who succeeded him was driven from office. In the following year, after an interval of military rule, Dr. Isidro Ayora became provisional president. He attacked financial problems by adopting currency stabilization measures suggested by Professor Kemmerer of Princeton University. A short time later the world trade depression made further efforts futile.

As elsewhere in Latin America the depression produced intense political unrest in Ecuador. Hunger and privation increased alarmingly, and the government was held responsible for the nation's ills. The brief period of progress and promise came to an end in 1931, when Ayora resigned and the government once more became a bone of contention between political factions and the army.

PARAGUAY

Paraguay's political life since independence had been vastly different from that of her Andean neighbors, for she had known only two rulers in nearly half a century. In 1862 the second of these dictators, Carlos Antonio López, died, leaving the country in the control of his son, Francisco Solano López. While the father's methods may be classed as borderline benevolent despotism, the son's were far more despotic than benevolent. Despite the cultural influence of a visit to Europe, he apparently acquired little more on the trip than a mistress, a red-haired Irish adventuress named Elisa Lynch, and an overwhelming desire to emulate Napoleon Bonaparte.

Solano López began building up an army which would make him the arbiter of South America, and he had at his complete disposal the Guaranís, a courageous people thoroughly disciplined by centuries of rigid control. Where the depraved dictator ordered them, the Paraguayans obediently went, and that the nation survived his rule at all is astonishing.

The Paraguayan War began in 1864 with Paraguay's attack on Brazil. Because of the unsavory character of Solano López, he has generally been blamed unquestionably for the war. He had expected to receive aid from Urquiza, who also opposed Brazilian interference in Uruguay, but he alienated Urquiza by his ill-considered invasion of Corrientes, an attack upon Argentine territory made because Mitre refused him permission to cross.

The Paraguayan War was appallingly costly to all combatants, but especially to Paraguay, and in the final years her armies were manned by young boys or women. The allied casualties were also high, for the Paraguayans literally fought to the death. The population of Paraguay was reduced by more than half, and of the remainder only about one in ten was male. At the conclusion of the war, Paraguay escaped complete partition only because the victors could not agree. In 1870 a new constitution was drawn up for the purpose of preventing the rise of dictatorships in the future. As had been proven elsewhere, however, a basic law could not be effective if it ran counter to traditions and social conditions, and Paraguay did not change overnight into a democratic republic because of a new constitution.

Brazilian troops, who had borne the brunt of the fighting toward the end of the war, remained in Paraguay until 1876, partially to preserve order. Indemnities demanded by the victors could not be paid, nor were they ever seriously pressed. Misiones territory was ceded to Argentina, and a large section of the northern frontier passed to Brazil. Argentine claims to the Chaco were submitted to the arbitration of President Rutherford B. Hayes, whose award in 1878 was favorable to Paraguay. Grateful Paraguayans renamed a town Villa Hayes in his honor.

It was many years before Paraguay was to have a government nearly as effective as those of her first two dictators. Barracks revolts were frequent, and few presidents completed their constitutional terms of office. The uprisings fortunately were for the most part of local origin, and the country at large was little disturbed by them. Paraguay slowly and painfully began to recover from the devastation of war. Foreign immigrants and capital, although on a small scale, provided impetus for the development of commerce. Cattle raising and the exportation of yerba maté and quebracho extract became important, and by the end of the century Paraguay had made surprising strides toward recovery.

New Era

PERU AFTER THE WAR OF THE PACIFIC

In Peru, also, the road to recovery was long and difficult. The civilista administration of Nicolás de Piérola 1895–99, was a time of substantial economic advance. By diminishing the political influence of the army and by attempting to put an end to interference at the polls, Piérola attracted the growing liberal elements to his support, and with their aid he made a mild move against the church by legalizing civil marriage. Commerce was aided by stabilizing the currency and backing it with gold, and by various public construction projects. Election control was eased, and the power of the civilistas increased, for their great wealth enabled them to control the outcome by resort to bribery rather than force.

The civilistas remained in power until 1919, when Augusto B. Leguía deposed José Pardo shortly before the end of his term. Under the civilistas' twenty-five year regime, considerable progress had been made in reviving the national economy. One of their most significant accomplishments was the contract negotiated with the W. R. Grace Company for paying interest to holders of Peruvian bonds. The government's revenues had been barely sufficient for ordinary expenses, and payments on its tremendous foreign debt were long in arrears. Under the arrangement made with the Grace Company, the foreign bondholders were given control of the state railways for sixty-six years, the right to extract three million tons of guano, and the promise of 80,000 pounds sterling annually for thirty-three years. This was in exchange for assuming the payments on Peru's foreign debt.

In bettering social conditions the civilistas accomplished little, for social reform was not their primary interest. Guillermo Billinghurst's mild attempt to improve the lot of Indian rubber-gatherers in the Amazon area helped to bring about his overthrow. Indians were still politically beyond the pale, but the lower middle class and urban laborers were becoming articulate and making demands. As in Chile and Argentina, they importuned the aristocratic government for benefits which were not granted. They became the bulwark of Leguía's Democratic party. Merchants and professional men, whose humble origins precluded a rise in the Civilista party, also rallied to the Democratic party, partly owing to conviction and partly because of the greater opportunity it offered them.

These groups were mildly anticlerical, and in 1915 they pushed through a Toleration Act permitting the exercise of other faiths than Roman Catholicism. It was these same middle and working classes who stood behind Leguía when he ran for a second term in 1919. Leguía had been elected as a civilista in 1908, but had broken with the party a year later. Like Alessandri of Chile, Leguía was determined to improve social conditions in his country. In the election of 1919 he received a majority of the votes cast, but his partisans feared that his opponents intended to prevent his taking office. They seized the government and deposed Pardo before his term expired. Peru was at last ready for a regime of social and economic experimentation backed by a strong and resolute government.

FALL OF LEGUÍA

Leguía's second administration began with the promulgation of the first new constitution since 1860. The constitution of 1920 was designed to make effective the changes that Leguía and his supporters contemplated. A graduated income tax was introduced; compulsory arbitration of labor disputes and compensation for labor accidents were required. Freedom of religion was granted, but at the same time the government surrendered its claim to the right of ecclesiastical patronage, and the church was able to appoint its own officials.

Leguía's attempt to introduce sweeping social and economic changes met with strenuous resistance. His authority was upheld by military and police forces, and the wave of post-war prosperity aided his cause, for the government was able to spend vast sums on public projects. Copper mining and petroleum production contributed to national revenues. Transportation facilities were greatly extended and improved, and Lima was modernized. Education, which had occasionally been a matter of temporary interest to the government, was expanded under the guidance of commissions from the United States. In spite of the harsh aspects of Leguía's rule the country made rapid progress in economic expansion. Relations with the United States were especially cordial, and surplus American wealth flooded the country. Governmental extravagance was unfortunately encouraged by the availability of money, and unwise and dishonest financial practices made the situation explosive when the world depression ended the easy access to alien capital. As was the case elsewhere, the benefits of 'economic progress' were generally limited to the few in power, although the Indians were given some hope for the future. In foreign affairs the most notable event of Leguía's rule was the settlement of the ancient Tacna-Arica dispute, an event already described in connection with Chile.

The downfall of Leguía, like that of many of his contemporaries in Latin America, was caused largely by the government's inability to cope with an economic depression that was world-wide in scope. His government was undeniably censurable for some of its acts, for it had permitted the increase of the national debt to more than ten times its size when Leguía took office, and a shockingly large part of the borrowed funds had been sidetracked to reward the faithful or placate the hostile. When new loans became unavailable, bankruptcy followed. Political agitation became so great that Leguía resigned. He and his sons were tried and found guilty of misappropriating public funds, and he died in prison a year later. His successors faced growing political unrest and financial chaos.

BOLIVIA

After the War of the Pacific the Conservative party of Bolivia remained in power until 1899 by carefully controlling elections, despite the increasing dissatisfaction of the liberals. The revival of silver mining aided economic recovery, and the extension of railroads began to end the degenerating influence of isolation and provincialism in many districts. The relative stability of the government aided economic development, for most of the liberal uprisings were localized, and the barracks revolts of former days did not recur.

In 1899 the liberals came into power by revolt over a matter of local concern, the location of the national capital. In the past Sucre, the Chuquisaca of colonial days, had been the official capital, but because of its isolated location many presidents had governed from more conveniently located cities. There had occasionally been proposals to transfer the capital, and the people of La Paz insisted on their city as the most appropriate choice. When the congress voted to make Sucre the permanent capital, the rival factions of La Paz forgot their differences and joined forces under Colonel José Manuel Pando to assert their claims forcibly. The La Paz contingent won the contest, and the capital was moved. Other groups then took advantage of the turmoil and seized the government.

The so-called liberal regime lasted from 1899 to 1920, and in political techniques differed little from its predecessors. Under Ismael Montes, El Gran Presidente, who served from 1904 to 1909 and 1913 to 1917, the most lasting improvements were made. This period was remarkable for the absence of civil disorders so characteristic in earlier times. The country's economic condition changed rapidly, and Bolivia's first foreign loans were negotiated for the purpose of building railroads. By means of revenue raised by a special tax and by using forced labor of Indians, the government pushed to completion a network of roads. Formerly isolated regions were brought into contact with the capital and the currents of world trade. A line between La Paz and Mollendo, on the coast of Peru, gave Bolivia access to the sea, as did another from La Paz to Arica, which Chileans built in accordance with the treaty ending the War of the Pacific.

The liberals introduced the usual reforms aimed at the clergy. Civil marriage was legalized, special courts abolished, and cemeteries were secularized. Opposition to these changes was fairly mild, and it did not lead to the violence which occurred in some other regions.

National revenues were greatly augmented by the development of tin and copper mining and a corresponding demand for these metals in Europe and the United States. The expansion of the Brazilian rubber-gathering industry in the Amazon basin led to a dispute over Bolivia's Acre territory. In 1903 Bolivia sold the region to Brazil for 200,000 pounds sterling and a railroad to be built around the cataracts of the Madeira river. Since the rubber market collapsed a few years later, the Bolivians may have come out of the dispute better than it first appeared. The money received from Brazil was especially important in the government's railroad building program.

In 1920 the Republican party, a newly formed opposition group composed of dissident liberals, overthrew the government. The republicans welcomed American capital, and the foreign debt grew rapidly. The uses to which the loans were put did not consistently promote economic improvement, and when the depression set in Bolivia had pledged nearly all her customary revenues in advance. In 1930, service on the national debt was suspended, and in the wake of financial chaos president Hernando Siles was ousted in favor of a military junta.

Paraguayan liberals finally captured control of their government in 1904, and a succession of their presidents held office briefly during the next two decades. Only Dr. Eduardo Schaerer completed his full term during this period, and only his administration differed significantly from those of the conservatives. He brought relative order and stability to the turbulent country, and its commerce was aided by completion of the railroad from Asunción to Encarnación on the Paraná river. The government established the agricultural bank to aid farmers and passed laws to enable others to acquire farming lands.

In the 1920's Paraguay entered the same phase of national physical improvement which was to be found throughout the continent, and the country seemed at last to be well on the way toward subordinating its less fortunate customs when it was shocked by the world depression. President José Guggiari declared martial law in 1929 to prevent rioting, but the difficulties could not be overcome, and in 1931 he was forced to resign. Although he resumed office and finished his term, the liberal regime in Paraguay, too, was at an end.

By the close of the period Peru, Bolivia, Ecuador, and Paraguay had made hesitant advances similar to those which had occurred among their more prosperous neighbors, but they were still far behind Argentina, Uruguay, and Chile in this regard. The Andean countries had yet to make a genuine effort to improve national prosperity by raising the economic and social level of the Indians. Because of the racial issue attempts at social reform were little more than gestures, for the ruling cliques were apprehensive lest the Indian masses, once freed from ancient restraints, would overturn the social order. In some of these countries, however, writers and political leaders took up the cause of the Indians with a seriousness and determination rarely shown before.

The conditions which had retarded economic and cultural growth in the Indian countries also handicapped their literary output, and it was generally below that of Argentina, Uruguay, and Chile. There were, nevertheless, a number of noteworthy writers, such as the Peruvians Manuel González Prada, who campaigned vigorously for social justice, Ricardo Palma, the folklorist chronicler of Lima, the poets César Vallejo and José María Eguren, and the novelist Ciro Alegría. Ecuador produced the eminent essayist and polemic writer, Juan Montalvo, and the Indianist novelists Jorge Icaza, Fernando Chaves, and Enrique Gil Gilbert. In Bolivia, too, there were followers of the Indianist theme, most prominent of whom was Alcides Argüedas, author of *Raza de bronce.*

IO

From Despotism to Social Revolution:
The Caribbean Borderlands

> The majority of Latin American countries are agricultural. Over 75 per cent of the economically active population of Mexico are engaged in some kind of agricultural work. . . . Before the 1910 Revolution . . . 2 per cent of the population owned 75 per cent of the land.
>
> LUIS QUINTANILLA *

Economic and Political Problems

The countries of Latin America bordering or near the Caribbean sea had much in common in the decades between 1860 and 1930. These were the nations most seriously threatened with economic and political penetration by the Western European powers and the United States. These were the nations which, with one exception, lay athwart the narrow land mass that was the chief obstacle to inter-oceanic commerce between the Atlantic and the Pacific. Here the economic and social pressures of domestic life were heightened by the ever-present fear of foreign exploitation. No vast influx of new people swelled the population to alter the social balance and expand national productivity. All the old problems of the past were ever present while new ones were being added with alarming rapidity. Alien enterprise was everywhere in evidence, but its beneficiaries were far removed and its impact served more to embitter than to soothe the passions of those affected by its handiwork.

* *A Latin American Speaks,* The Macmillan Company, New York, 1943, pp. 76–78.

LIBERAL ASCENDANCY

The seemingly universal conflicts between liberals and conservatives, between centralists and federalists, and between church and state were clearly in evidence. So, too, was the tendency to violence in achieving political change. As the era opened, liberal forces were in the ascendency from Mexico City to Caracas, but their achievements proved ephemeral, and either they collapsed violently or melted away before conservative counter-attacks. Racial animosities were also keen, for the process of amalgamating heterogeneous Indian groups and Spaniards was in evidence but far from complete. The multitude of caste and class lines based on the extent of European ancestry were sharply drawn, and the disunion that prevailed prevented government and economic development from becoming co-operative ventures supported by, and for the benefit of, all groups. Nevertheless, the almost total separation that characterized the racial structure of the Andean republics to the south had obviously gone far toward breaking down. Had not Mexico had a pure Indian as president? Was not the mestizo the dominant strain in much of Central America and considerable portions of Colombia and Venezuela? Clearly the countries of the Caribbean borderland were in process of rapid change, a change little less startling than that taking place on the vast pampas of the Argentine, on the grasslands of Uruguay, and in the central valley of Chile. But the direction of change was far less evident, and the era closed without sufficient evidence to indicate what form the developing nations would eventually assume.

FOREIGN PRESSURES

Perhaps the most striking development peculiar to the Caribbean countries was the heavy and disturbing foreign pressure to which they were subjected. At first this pressure came from European nations in the form of old-style imperialism, as evidenced by the French misadventure in Mexico; but this mode of interference was rapidly replaced by the more subtle pressures following in the wake of foreign investments, pressures more often private than official, and for that reason more disconcerting. At times the interference was inspired by the strategic interests of the United

States, as in the acquisition of the isthmian canal route and in the safe-
guarding of that route. Such interventions were likely to be blunt and
forceful, neither subtly disguised nor considerate of Latin American sensibilities. After the Spanish-American War, when the United States undertook the political rehabilitation of Cuba and annexed Puerto Rico, pressure from the burgeoning North American power became intense, and
astonished Latin Americans suddenly discovered that their ancient 'sea of
destiny' had become an American lake. It was an era of resurgent Manifest Destiny when, as it appeared to Latin America, presidents of the
United States such as Theodore Roosevelt and secretaries of state such as
Richard Olney walked softly but talked loudly, carried big sticks, and went
far, especially in their encroachments upon the sovereign rights of Caribbean governments. While strategic considerations seemed foremost to the
United States government—and such considerations were not wholly mis-
understood in Latin America—later cases of intervention seemed to stem
from a quixotic determination to do good to others no matter how violently they resisted. To worried Latin Americans it appeared unmistakably
clear that wherever Americans and their dollars were about to be separated as a consequence of chaotic political conditions United States marines were prompt to appear. When to the propensity to intervention was
coupled a policy of refusing to recognize governments coming to power by
other than constitutional means, there seemed little doubt that the 'Yankee
Colossus' was setting itself up as the arbiter of the political destiny of
Latin America. For financial and commercial reasons, the withholding of
recognition was an extremely potent weapon that few governments in the
Caribbean area could long withstand. Long before steamships began passing through the Panama Canal, numerous countries learned the shocking
news that they had lost the venerable right to mismanage their own affairs.

CIVIL WARS

The era was ushered in amid civil wars between liberals and conservatives
in Mexico, Nicaragua, Costa Rica, Colombia, and Venezuela, while several Central American countries were involved in struggles against caudillo despotism, Cuba still sought vainly to achieve independence, and
Santo Domingo was being readmitted to the Spanish empire. In Mexico,
the War of the Reform ended with triumph for the Juárez liberals who

were promptly ousted by the legions of Napoleon III. In Colombia, the liberal forces of Tomás Mosquera captured Bogotá in 1861, while to the east federalist liberals gained a partial victory in Venezuela where, in 1864, by pushing through a new constitution, they created a confederation known as the United States of Venezuela. Truly it was an inauspicious opening for an era of progress.

VENEZUELA UNDER GUZMÁN BLANCO

At opposite ends of the borderland region, events soon conspired to bring an end to the confusion of domestic strife and to inaugurate a long period of political tranquility. In Venezuela the weakness of the confederation soon became manifest, and the country remained strife-torn until 1872 when a resolute and able leader gained sufficient power over his rivals to establish a dictatorship. Antonio Guzmán Blanco was essentially of the 'liberal' stripe, which meant little more than that he took a firm anticlerical stand and undertook important public works to bring railroads and telegraph lines to the country. He did nothing to stabilize the political institutions of his country or to further the practice of democratic government. Rather, he based his regime on popular appeals to the lower classes and a vigorous effort to befuddle his opposition. Although permitted only a two-year term of office by the constitution, the dictator was able to maintain control of the government even when out of office and get himself back in the presidential chair as soon as he was eligible again. Such an arrangement he managed to keep functioning for sixteen years. In the meantime, commercial activity increased rapidly, many men grew rich, and the country appeared to prosper. None prospered so much as did Antonio Guzmán Blanco, however. In fact, he was so proud of himself and his achievements that he had monuments erected to himself in conspicuous places throughout the country.

The Venezuelan dictator took many steps to break the power of the Roman Catholic Church. He legalized civil marriage, abolished monastic orders and confiscated their property, and even expelled a papal representative from the country. A Grand Master of the Masonic Order, Guzmán Blanco so opposed control of the church from Rome that he even considered establishing a national church independent of the Pope, a threat which he did not attempt to carry out, however. Instead, he was content to scandalize the clergy by encouraging Protestant missionaries to come to Venezuela. Naturally, opposition to the dictator became a religious issue that was fully exploited by his enemies.

By 1888 opposition to Guzmán Blanco had become intense. While he was absent from the country mobs gathered in the cities and began overturning the many statues of him and demolishing other reminders of his tyrannical rule. The dictator displayed his usual political sagacity in this crisis; he decided that it was time for him to retire from public life and enjoy his remaining years in Paris. Needless to say, he had prepared himself well for retirement by financial chicanery and plunder of the public treasury.

Guzmán Blanco's long rule was not without material benefit. Under the dictator's watchful eye a vast number of public works projects had been completed, including a railroad line, the paving of streets in the cities, and construction of many parks. At the same time government revenues mounted as international commerce increased, and a major portion of the national debt was retired. Over against such manifestations of progress was the fact that the country remained the patrimony of a few families who lived in ostentatious splendor while the great majority of the people—the lower classes—continued to serve in poverty and ignorance, without hope and without opportunity to improve their lot. The economic gulf between the few and the many widened appreciably. Also, in spite of material improvement, the country made little intellectual progress. Education was neglected generally, and few people even among the wealthy demonstrated more than a superficial acquaintanceship with literature, the arts, and the sciences. Social life was stodgy and represented little more than a feeble effort to seek relief from boredom through an occasional private party or dance. Religious observances provided some diversion for the poorer classes.

After the overthrow of Antonio Guzmán Blanco, Venezuela returned to a period of chaos and disorder while would-be wearers of the dictator's shoes struggled to get possession of them. Finally, one of Guzmán Blanco's old friends, Joaquín Crespo, succeeded in establishing order. With the aid of a new constitution he was able to maintain control of the country until his retirement in 1898. He was inclined to much the same course and policies as his more famous predecessor, and the outstanding event of his administration was a dispute with Great Britain over the boundary between British Guiana and Venezuela. The dispute dated back many years, and even in Guzmán Blanco's time had provoked a severance of diplomatic relations with England; but it came to a head in 1895 when some British officials were detained for trespassing on Venezuelan soil. Crespo appealed to the United States for support, and President Cleveland responded by invoking the Monroe Doctrine in a note which his secretary of state sent to Great Britain. For a brief period, relations between England and the United States became strained, but finally all parties agreed to abide by the decision of an international boundary commission which awarded most of the disputed territory to Britain. Strangely, once the United States had entered the controversy, the chief issue became that of British acceptance of United States doctrinal claims of paramount interest in the Western Hemisphere. All parties eventually compromised, but impending difficulties in South Africa no doubt influenced the British government toward a conciliatory attitude in the matter.

Far to the north and west another Caribbean borderland nation slipped quietly into the hands of a master dictator at about the same time Guzmán Blanco came to power in Venezuela. With the downfall of Maximilian, Juárez returned to Mexico City and in 1867 was elected president. In spite of prompt and substantial reductions in the armed forces, his popularity continued. Disgruntled ex-generals and would-be caudillos 'pronounced' from time to time, and the Indian tribes of the northwest engaged in continuous marauding expeditions, but gradually loyal juarista forces subdued the opposition and peace returned to the famine and misery-ridden country. Juárez set about making the doctrines of the 1857 constitution a reality. A program of free secular education was inaugurated, and town councils and owners of large haciendas were required to build schools. The program was entrusted largely to Gabino Barreda, an able educator imbued with positivist doctrines. By 1874 some 8000 schools were functioning and attendance reached almost 350,000, about one-fourth of those of school age. At the same time vigorous efforts were made to replenish the national treasury and to get back on the long road to national solvency through an honest administration of revenues.

Many approved of Juárez, but there were others who did not. Chief among the opposition was Porfirio Díaz, a general who had fought with Juárez against the French intervention. Díaz felt that his services—actually less than spectacular—had been insufficiently rewarded. He had no love for civilian government in accordance with the constitution and the law; he was an adherent of military dictatorship. In 1871, he came forth from his estate in Oaxaca to run against Juárez for the presidency. The vote was split by the candidacy of Sebastián Lerdo de Tejada, and no candidate received a majority. Congress had to decide, and it selected Juárez, who had received a plurality. Díaz pronounced, declaring the election illegal. He chose as his slogan, 'Effective Suffrage and No Re-election!' His brief rebellion was quickly suppressed, but a strong following remained led by army chieftains who wanted the spoils of public office. Then suddenly on July 18, 1872, Juárez died.

No one could take the Indian president's place. Lerdo de Tejada tried, and although he was an able man who had designed many of the juarista reforms, he failed. He lacked Juárez' popular following, his mystic grip upon the common people of Mexico and many in the upper classes as well. He remained honest, not turning the government over to anyone, even his own followers. He went ahead with Juárez' program, and while conditions in the country gradually improved his enemies organized against him. Díaz went abroad to plot, but in 1875 he returned and soon a new pronunciamiento was heard, the Plan of Tuxtepec. Civil war ensued, but Lerdo's position was hopeless. Late in 1876 he departed into exile and Porfirio Díaz took over the country.

Díaz was, of course, a liberal. He had been a supporter of Juárez. But Juárez had recognized him for the military opportunist that he was, an object of suspicion. All Juárez' suspicions were well justified, as Díaz soon proved. As a liberal, Don Porfirio became the answer to the prayers of all Mexican conservatives from Iturbide to the present. In contrast to Agustín I, he was shrewd and intelligent; unlike Santa Anna, he never became bored with his job; and in common with Lucas Alamán, he was a champion of orderly progress.

The first and most essential task was to pacify the turbulent land, to make the roads safe from bandits, and to reduce the incidence of local revolts. The *pax porfiriano* imposed on Mexico gave the troubled land its longest interlude of order and stability since colonial times. Only then was it possible for economic development to begin. Pacifying Mexico was no simple matter, and it was Porfirio Díaz' first achievement.

Díaz remained the master of Mexico for thirty-four years. True, he modestly stepped aside—not very far—to permit Manuel González to serve as president from 1880 to 1884; but otherwise the old refrain of effective suffrage and no re-election became a standing joke to which only a later generation could give any meaning. Díaz took care of his military friends by bringing them back to a share in the spoils, but he did not trust any of them. Shrewdly he played one against another while keeping them all amply supplied with pesos. He organized his private little band of paid assassins who proved quite capable of taking care of anyone who became 'dangerous' in a political sense. The country became a paragon of order, but the order was not that of law; it was the order of Don Porfirio solely.

As dictator, Don Porfirio turned his back on Mexico. His more outspoken opponents might say he held her while the foreigners raped her. The wealthy creole landholders found themselves in favor once more, and even the clergy soon discovered that Díaz looked the other way while the anticlerical laws enacted under Juárez and during the period of the Reform were openly ignored. Once again the church acquired property, religious schools appeared, and the religious orders set up their establishments once more. Of far greater significance, however, was the welcome extended foreigners. Not only were foreign capitalists invited to invest in a pacified Mexico, but even the ranks of the priesthood were swelled with religious from Latin Europe. Mestizo and Indian elements found themselves cast aside or held in subservient status. Only that which displayed a European cast achieved social and cultural standing. All that smacked of nativist origin was disdained.

Díaz was a liberal in that he believed in progress and development. He would turn Mexico into a modern nation, a concept which he measured only in terms of physical improvements. In the social evolution that had been so fundamental an element in the program of Juárez, he had no interest. Indeed, it soon became evident that he opposed it. The Mexican lower classes would provide the labor, foreign investors would provide the funds, and Díaz would see that peace prevailed throughout the land. To this end he organized the terribly efficient *rurales,* a band of rural police composed of military stooges and ex-bandits. To keep them subservient to his personal control he paid them well, provided them with elaborate uniforms, and allowed them to plunder the property of his enemies. The rurales became a famous police force, feared by all Mexicans who dared express opposition to the government, who dared disturb the peace, or who happened to stray away from work projects or the fields of a wealthy hacendado. Banditry disappeared, foreigners were treated with courtesy and respect, property was secure, and those who could not see beneath the surface to the mass of suffering humanity looked on and approved.

At first Díaz' methods shocked the country and the world. In 1879 a *lerdista* plot was discovered in Veracruz, and some alleged plotters were seized by the governor. He asked Díaz for instructions and received the terse telegram: 'If they are caught in the act, kill them in cold blood.' Jails were soon filled to overflowing, but Díaz had no wish to construct new centers of incarceration. The *ley fuga* or 'law of flight' was everywhere invoked; that is, prisoners were disposed of out of hand on the grounds that they were 'trying to escape.' Eventually the ley fuga would be invoked against a president and vice-president of the nation.

Díaz' harsh regime had the look of benign paternalism to many foreigners who themselves never encountered difficulty in Mexico but were greatly impressed with the pace of economic growth, the orderliness of the countryside, and the cleanliness of the cities. Thousands of miles of railroad track were laid, streets were paved, mineral production tripled, and plantation agriculture and new textile mills added to national exports. The capital city was beautified by improvements in parkways and boulevards, if not by the construction of the unlovely Palace of Fine Arts. A new water system was provided Mexico City, and sewerage and drainage works were undertaken—a major need in a city built upon a former lake bed. Strenuous efforts were made to hide all the ugliness and evil of Mexico's poverty. The rag-clad, barefoot *lépero* of the capital was driven from the streets or into forced service in the fields. At the same time luxurious and ornate homes were built by wealthy landholders, foreign businessmen, and political favorites of Díaz.

Particularly disastrous for the rural peon was the passage of many estates into foreign ownership. Americans in particular, unused to the old-style paternalism of the Spanish hacendado, were prone to treat their employees as paid laborers and nothing more. They saw little cause to assume the paternalistic responsibilities that control of the destinies of many peon families had long implied. Laborers were expected to live on their miserable wages and look after themselves, something to which most were wholly unaccustomed. This difficulty, coupled with absentee ownership, encroachment on communal lands, and the repressive efforts of the rurales caused great suffering and hardship. Debt slavery became general, and peons were slated to work forever to pay off the principal and interest of small loans advanced them.

In spite of great economic expansion, Díaz had difficulty keeping the Mexican treasury in a healthy condition. It was not until 1894 that the budget was first balanced, and all obligations were met on a current basis. The event was especially significant for the *porfiristas,* as the Díaz followers were known. Now they felt secure, for every man had his price.

Surrounding Díaz during the last fifteen years or more of his regime was a group of young intellectuals, the *científicos,* whose acknowledged leader was José Ives Limantour, son of an immigrant Frenchman, who became the financial genius of the porfirista regime. The científicos constituted the first genuinely bureaucratic class to emerge in Mexico after independence. Government employment had become the refuge and the economic basis of the Mexican middle class, and Limantour and the small group around him were the cream of the crop. Their efforts made public administration more honest and efficient, but they abjured only the cruder methods of acquiring wealth through political power. Under the tutelage of the científicos the Díaz regime was harnessed more securely to the interests of alien investors. Their goal was government by a creole oligarchy, their methods were heartless efficiency in the collection and management of revenues, and their political philosophy was borrowed from the positivism of Auguste Comte.

As secretary of the treasury Limantour took a number of steps that were of economic benefit to the country, such as abolition of the alcabala, that ancient obstacle to commerce and relic of the colonial era. He also secured government control of the railroads by purchasing a majority of the stock with public funds, but in the transaction científicos made vast profits. The growing strength of the bureaucratic oligarchy caused unrest among many of Díaz' supporters, however, for in the years after the turn of the century the old dictator, seemingly secure in his position, allowed more and more power to slip into the hands of his chief officials. These men, cold and obsessed with their projects of financial manipulation, gave little thought to keeping Díaz' political fences mended. They seemed to think the regime could go on forever.

In the meantime, the status of the lower classes grew steadily worse. The mining industry passed into the hands of American companies. The *baldío* (vacant land) laws of 1883 and 1894 led to the transfer of upwards of 134,000,000 acres of public land to foreign speculators and favored Mexicans. Land survey companies were authorized to locate and survey baldíos in exchange for one-third of the land surveyed. About one-fifth of the area of the republic was thus transferred from public to private control. Other measures led to the 'Second Conquest,' the looting of Indian village lands. Troops and rurales were sent against Indians who resisted, and those who were not killed were sold into slavery in Quintana Roo. All but a few Indian communities lost their lands. As a consequence, concentration of land ownership reached a new peak. Just before Díaz' downfall in 1911, nearly half of Mexico was owned by fewer than 3000 families, and about 95 per cent of the ten million persons employed in agriculture owned no land at all. Industrial laborers were generally better off than the debt-enslaved peons, but their attempts to organize into unions were brutally suppressed. Since foreign interests owned the majority of the mines and oil fields as well as the textile mills, it was not surprising that Mexicans began to identify foreign capital with oppression. By 1900, American investments alone in Mexico were more than one billion dollars, and English, French, and Spanish capital had also found the country a fertile field. Díaz had succeeded in expanding the economy of Mexico, but the condition of the great majority of Mexicans had sunk below what it had been at any time during the colonial period.

Culturally, the Age of Don Porfirio was one of stagnation, although a few notable writers were produced, such as Justo Sierra and Francisco Bulnes, and the poets Gutiérrez Nájera and Amado Nervo were of first rank. Sierra's *Evolución política del pueblo mexicano* (*Political Evolution of the Mexican People*) was a thoughtful and interpretive history. In general, however, intellectualism languished and artistic endeavor consisted of unproductive attempts to imitate the tawdry extravagance of France during the Second Empire.

Díaz brought poverty and misery to his people during his long rule. Physical development and vast profits for a few were small compensation for the loss of human dignity and personal security by the Mexican citizen of humble status. But abroad Don Porfirio was a hero. He had brought peace and 'progress' to the land of Santa Anna, and that indeed was an accomplishment! His chest was covered with the medals bestowed upon him by his foreign admirers. He was the grand old man who had enabled thousands of aliens to grow rich and live in luxury with a retinue of docile servants in his beautified capital. The world would soon know the true extent of Mexico's progress.

Central America

South and east from Mexico the five republics of Central America weathered the long years from the collapse of the confederation till the worldwide economic crisis of 1930 with little internal change. Each of the countries went its own way and each was torn to a greater or lesser degree by the activities of caudillos and the interminable conflicts over the status of the church. Few notable figures emerged in political life, intellectual and artistic achievement was, with one notable exception, of minor significance, and economic advance consisted largely of the gradual entrance of

American investors in the banana industry along the eastern coast of Guatemala, Honduras, and Costa Rica. Guatemala was for long years ruled by a military dictator, Manuel Estrada Cabrera, who held the country firmly in his iron grasp from 1898 to 1920. Honduras, thinly populated and isolated, remained as in colonial times the most backward and undeveloped region of Central America. El Salvador, fronting only on the Pacific ocean, escaped the pressures of European and American powers struggling for control of the Caribbean. Likewise, and for the same reason, this, the smallest of the Central American republics, escaped almost entirely foreign economic penetration. After the turn of the century the gradual development of native-owned coffee plantations along the volcanic slopes from Santa Ana to San Vicente added greatly to national economic productivity and foreshadowed the creation of an extremely rich class of coffee planters after the great depression of the 1930's. Other progress was marked by the building of railroads linking San Salvador, the capital, with Guatemala on the west and with the Honduran frontier on the east. British investors provided the capital and owned and operated the lines.

COSTA RICA

Costa Rica remained essentially isolated, with no direct means of communication by land with neighbors on either side. As such, she escaped the military aspects of the occasional conflicts that arose among the five countries when some strong man conceived the idea of reuniting Central America by force. Justo Rufino Barrios of Guatemala was the first to make such an attempt in 1885, and for his pains he met death on the battlefield. Costa Rica was involved in the coalition against him, but Nicaragua and El Salvador carried the burden of the conflict. Conflict arose again in 1906, and although Costa Rica sided with El Savador and Honduras against Guatemala, the principal contestants were the northwestern republics. Costa Rica, largely devoid of Indian population, exhibited many European characteristics and gradually developed an agricultural economy based on rather extensive participation in land ownership by the rank and file. Principal crops were corn, as in almost all Latin American countries, and bananas and coffee. The country remained comparatively tranquil domestically, and self-government came gradually to exhibit as high a degree of free popular participation as in any of the Latin American nations. Strong men were held in check by the relative strength of the legislative body, a rare phenomenon in the region and one that still persists with considerable vigor.

As already indicated Nicaragua early became a principal recipient of foreign pressure by reason of her geographic resources: a large lake only thirteen miles from the Pacific ocean and a semi-navigable river connecting the lake with the Atlantic. By reason of the attention focused on the area, Nicaraguan affairs attracted far greater attention outside of Latin America than did those events taking place within neighboring countries. The William Walker filibustering expedition in the late 1850's struck fear to the hearts of men in every Central American capital, and the struggle between Great Britain and the United States for control of the Nicaraguan canal route was watched closely throughout the region. In 1893, a tyrannical liberal, José Santos Zelaya, seized the presidency, and his sword-rattling for the next fifteen years disturbed the entire Central American area and even aroused fears in the United States that he would sell canal rights to Japan to flaunt his dislike and contempt for the North American power. The possibility of such a development can hardly be said to have lessened America's willingness to intervene on behalf of the Nicaraguan conservatives in 1913. Supported by the United States marines, conservatives were able to dominate the government until 1928 when a really free election was held under American supervision. The liberals were promptly returned to power with the election of José María Moncada.

CENTRAL AMERICAN CHARACTERISTICS

By 1930, the Central American nations had taken on distinctive characteristics and atmospheres that set each apart sharply from all the others. In Nicaragua the age-old struggle between León and Granada had provided a geographical twist to the party alignment, but the emergence of Managua as the major city and capital of the republic greatly reduced tension and provided some hope for a more peaceful future. United States intervention and domination branded the nation as an American satellite and earned for it the contempt of its neighbors, particularly since strong factions had encouraged and profited by the continued presence of the foreign marines.

Nicaraguans cherished their independence, and many were willing to fight for it; but even after the last marine was withdrawn early in 1933, ties with the United States remained close and Americans continued to be held in high regard by a substantial portion of the population. This was a phenomenon that other Central Americans were never quite able to understand.

Guatemala's distinctiveness stemmed from her picturesque and mountainous landscape, her large and racially unique Indian population which remained unassimilated, and her pretensions of superiority and leadership. As the seat of the former captaincy-general, Guatemala never became fully reconciled to a status of no better than equality vis-à-vis her neighbors to the south and east. It was no accident that in the struggles which from time to time disturbed the peace of the isthmian region Guatemala frequently found herself aligned against a combination of her neighbors.

Chief rival to Guatemala for leadership in Central America was El Salvador, a situation carried over from the internal struggles of the confederation. Densely populated and with the process of racial amalgamation virtually complete, El Salvador was in position to play a potent role in Central American affairs should it be possible to raise the great bulk of her people out of their misery and poverty. In the early part of the century, however, after coffee became a major crop, land ownership became increasingly concentrated and the gulf between the few who owned and profited and the many who toiled and subsisted deepened appreciably.

Honduras remained essentially primitive with her largely mestizo population scattered over the mountainous countryside. As the United Fruit Company acquired large banana plantations along the northern coast social and economic life in the region acquired the characteristics of a large company settlement that set the region apart from the remainder of the republic. The company went its way and so did the small mountain town of Tegucigalpa, the Honduran capital and principal population center of the republic. Neither interfered in the affairs of the other and the country remained divided, exhibiting little evidence of national cohesion or unity.

Costa Rica, with her predominantly European population, had no real Indian problem. Her population, including an increasing number of immigrants from Germany and Austria, concentrated in the cool mountain valleys from Alajuela to Turrialba, worked hard to build their country and to enjoy the pleasant life which a tranquil region afforded. Popular education was emphasized and the literacy rate was pushed higher and higher. The small nation took on the aspects of a middle-class community that would not have seemed out of place if tucked in some mountain valley of Central Europe. Only the teeming and steaming port cities of Limón and Puntarenas belied the illusion.

Probably the most famous Central American of the era was Rubén Darío, the Nicaraguan poet whose verses captivated the entire Hispanic world. His influence was that of an oasis in an intellectual desert, however, for few other Central Americans interested themselves deeply in literature or the arts. There were no centers of higher education worthy of the name in the entire region.

THE ISLANDS

In the Caribbean islands life was even less secure than in Central America. Social, economic, and political conditions in Haiti were deplorable, and education was completely neglected. Not until 1860 were relations restored with the papacy and regularized in a concordat which made possible the rehabilitation of the clergy. Educational institutions were founded by the Christian Brothers and other orders, but these could do little to dissipate the ignorance of generations. Not until the twentieth century, when American intervention occurred, were serious efforts made to improve health, education, and transportation. National finances were organized and taken out of the hands of covetous officials, and a police force was trained, in the hope that it could preserve order in lieu of an army.

The Dominican Republic, under constant threat of intervention from Haiti and by European powers as well, ended her precarious independence in 1861 by voluntarily returning to the Spanish empire. Spanish rule was no more satisfactory, and in 1865, after a destructive war, independence was restored. Like Haiti, the Dominican Republic remained politically and financially chaotic. For a short time the government hoped for annexation by the United States, but although President Ulysses S. Grant favored the move, the Senate opposed it. Under Theodore Roosevelt the United States assumed management of Dominican customs and the financial condition of the government improved. In 1916, a year after intervention in Haiti, American marines landed in the Dominican Republic.

Cuba and Puerto Rico, still colonies of Spain, were torn by various unsuccessful attempts to win independence, particularly the bloody Cuban Ten Years' War, beginning in 1868. Trade relations with the United States improved meanwhile, and American interest in Cuba remained strong. In

1895 Cubans rebelled once more, led by the eminent writer, José Martí, and Thomás Estrada Palma, later president. In 1898 the United States became a party to the conflict, after the unexplained sinking of the *Maine*. Cuba was granted independence, though the United States retained the right to intervene, and Puerto Rico was annexed.

As an independent nation Cuba's early political experiences were far from peaceful and gratifying to those who fought so bitterly for independence. The sugar industry became prosperous while high prices prevailed, but graft in government remained an insoluble problem. Political life continued to be unsettled, leading to intervention by the United States in 1906, and to the landing of marines on several occasions to protect lives and property of American citizens. In 1924 Gerardo Machado assumed the presidency, and he maintained himself in power by tyrannical means until his overthrow in 1933.

Colombia

The other great region of the Caribbean borderland still languished in the throes of religious and sectional factionalism. The liberal-minded conservative president of Colombia, Mosquera, did not go far enough to please the truly liberal factions which were stimulated to action by the French revolution of 1848. In the election of 1849, no candidate received a majority, and as had happened so often before, final choice was thrown into the lap of congress. That body, under strong pressure from liberal supporters who swarmed into the building where the deputies were meeting, finally selected the liberal candidate, General José Hilario López. For the first time a new party took over control of the government. It embarked on a drastic and radical reform program aimed at converting Colombia into the image of the Second Republic in France.

Almost immediately after López took office, pressure was exerted to expel the Jesuits, who had been readmitted to the country only a few years before. Amid sharp religious antagonisms, the black-robed fathers were once again driven from the country, and the government quickly turned to other measures designed to reduce the authority and power of the church. In 1853 a new constitution abolished church exemptions and privileges, deprived it of state support, and declared complete freedom of religion throughout the nation. It also abolished slavery, decreed freedom of the press, established manhood suffrage, and provided for the secret ballot. It provided for the election of provincial governors, a step designed to provide a larger amount of 'home rule.' Truly, the constitution was an innovation.

Opposition to liberal rule was severe, and revolt flared quickly. Fortunately for the country, even the older factions preferred constitutional rule to military despotism and the barracks revolt. Revolution was suppressed, and soon the decentralizing steps of the 1853 constitution were carried even farther. Colombia became a confederation of virtually autonomous states over which the national government came to exercise less and less control. Disorders became widespread; and the Granadine Confederation, as the arrangement came to be called, seemed on the point of anarchy. Still the liberals were able to remain in power, and it was not until 1884 that the curtain was finally rung down on their chaotic rule.

The liberal regime took a variety of steps to improve the national economy. Roads and railroads were constructed and telegraph lines linked the principal regions, but commercial progress was minor. The regime, decentralized and ineffective, was unable to maintain order, banditry was everywhere a scourge, and military bands struggled for control of the provincial or state governments. Politics and strife struck the dominant note, and in such an atmosphere little economic and material progress was possible.

In 1880, a new figure emerged on the Colombian scene in the person of Rafael Núñez. One of the earlier extreme liberals who had become greatly interested in European socialist doctrines, he was rudely shaken from his former tendencies by his experiences in the presidency from 1880 to 1882. He watched the chronic turmoil of his country with growing distaste until he became convinced that it was his duty to bring an end to the confusion. He began organizing a party of his own dedicated to reconstruction of a strong central government that could re-establish law and order and make possible greater national development. In 1884 Núñez was re-elected and his new Nationalist party, composed of moderates from among the conservatives and liberals, dominated the council he assembled to prepare a new constitution. In addressing the group Núñez denounced the political changes of the liberal regime as entirely destructive. He called for a highly centralized government and a return to church control over education. The constitution was written in keeping with his wishes and was put into force in 1886. The president's power was greatly enlarged, his term of office was extended to six years, and he was authorized to appoint provincial governors and to issue decrees to supplement the laws passed by congress. Roman Catholicism was made once more the state religion, and education was to conform to the doctrines of the church.

Núñez remained in power until his death in 1894. In 1888 he negotiated a concordat with the papacy which restored to the church the privileges and authority it had enjoyed in the colonial period, except that the Inquisition was not reinstituted. The government agreed to compensate the church for the property it had confiscated earlier.

LOSS OF PANAMA

The liberals were no more willing to accept exclusion from the government than the conservatives had been, and revolts during Núñez' rule were frequent. The most serious uprising began after his death. It broke out in 1899 and lasted until 1903, completely disrupting the country and giving a watching world the impression of hopeless disorder. It was a struggle of wayward provinces against the capital, of Freemasons and liberals against the church and the conservatives, of would-be caudillos against the legitimate government. The revolt was finally suppressed, but the loss of life and the destruction of property had been great. Panama had been the scene of a major disaffection, and the event lent credence to the views of Theodore Roosevelt that the region might easily be constituted a separate nation more favorable to his canal project. In 1903 he acted on this premise. As discussed in an earlier chapter, Colombia was unable to prevent the secessionist move, and she lost her province and all possible benefits of having a canal constructed across her territory. Panama became independent and an American protectorate.

The loss of Panama had a sobering effect upon political factions in Colombia. It made them more restrained when national stability was at stake. In 1906, during the administration of able, energetic, but impetuous Rafael Reyes, a law was passed providing for minority representation in the congress and the cabinet, and this helped to pacify the liberal opposition. In 1910 the constitution was amended to restrict the franchise by imposing literacy and property or income qualifications. The conservative regime was thereby strengthened, and the liberal and democratic tenets espoused by the opposition were dealt a serious blow.

During the years between 1910 and 1930, Colombia enjoyed relative peace under conservative administrations with which the liberals occasionally co-operated. It was under such conservative administrations, in fact, that most of Colombia's social legislation was passed. Measures were enacted in this period providing for pensions for school teachers, compensation for labor accidents, and improvement in public health conditions. Income taxes were also adopted in an effort to broaden the revenue base.

Once peace was re-established, a program was initiated to recall the worthless paper pesos in widespread circulation as a consequence of virtual financial collapse. Gold was auctioned off for bundles of the pesos, and enormous piles of them were burned. Much paper of dubious value remained in circulation, however, to the continued detriment of commerce. In 1922, after several unsuccessful attempts to reach a better understanding with the United States, a treaty was ratified whereby Colombia was to be paid twenty-five million dollars as compensation for the loss of Panama. There was no expression of regret forthcoming, however, as to the manner in which the loss had occurred. In the following year the first installment was paid, and it greatly aided the government in introducing a new and more stable currency.

Economic progress in Colombia was slow. It was gradually discovered that the country was richly endowed with natural resources. The highland valleys of the south provide excellent agricultural lands, and the lower reaches of the mountains throughout the country are suitable for coffee growing. Indeed, coffee was planted widely and soon became the chief export commodity. The country is rich in minerals, including petroleum, gold, lead, mercury, manganese, iron, and various precious stones. It is the world's chief source of emeralds. The forests of Colombia abound in valuable woods. Geographic obstacles, however, have impeded large-scale development. The rugged terrain, with altitude varying from sea level to 18,000 feet, has made transportation difficult from the days of the Spanish conquest, and even though Bolívar was able to perform wondrous feats with troops of cavalry, the movement of goods has never fared so well. Steam navigation of the Magdalena river enabled limited areas to be served by ship, but the river has always been capricious and accidents have been frequent.

During the years from 1860 to 1930 Colombians remained generally poor. By the beginning of the great depression, Colombia had some eight million inhabitants, but the great majority of those engaged in productive activity worked in agriculture at a subsistence level. The country was a land of small towns and villages separated by high mountains. Only four cities —Bogotá, Medellín, Barranquilla, and Cali—developed into major population centers. Of these, only Medellín attracted industrial growth. Bogotá remained a political center, Barranquilla a port, and Cali became the chief distribution point for a large agricultural region. The unhappy experiences of other Latin American nations, plus antagonism against the United States after the Panama incident, made Colombians suspicious of foreign capitalists and investors. Alien capital was not strongly encouraged in Colombia, and for the most part citizens of the country have shown an inclination to see their resources lie untouched rather than watch foreigners carry them away. In 1920, however, a German aviation company, 'Scadta,' was given a concession to operate the first air line in Colombia and in South America.

In 1922 the liberals made a strong bid for the presidency after failing to enter candidates in some of the earlier elections. General Pedro Nel Ospina, the conservative candidate, won, nevertheless, and served until 1926 during a period of national prosperity. Coffee and petroleum produced considerable wealth, and loans from private investors in the United States were used for railroad construction and other public works. Inflation caused prices to rise, and when world trade collapsed the conservatives found themselves badly divided and disorganized. The liberals, who had at first been indifferent toward the election of 1930, perceived an opportunity to win, and their candidate, Dr. Enrique Olaya Herrera, was elected on a platform of social and political reform. Thus at a time when many other Latin American nations were ousting liberal regimes in favor of more incisive despotisms, Colombia peacefully made the transition from conservative to liberal rule.

Colombia produced many able men who were masters of the literary arts and whose greatest contributions were made during the second half of the nineteenth century. Probably the greatest poets of the era were Gregorio Gutiérrez González and José Asunción Silva, both widely known. José Joaquín Ortiz and Julio Arboleda deserve mention, as do also Diego Fallón and Rafael Pombo. In 1867 José María Vergara y Vergara published a work on national customs and folklore, a prose work that brought him fame and appointment to the Spanish Royal Academy. The Restrepo family, ever active in literary circles, continued to have illustrious representatives. Antonio Gómez Restrepo developed a notable work on Colombian literature which he published in 1926. In general, however, fewer men made significant contributions to Colombian literature after the turn of the century than in the preceding fifty years.

Venezuela

While Mexico was being exploited by the porfiristas and Colombia was torn by revolution and anarchy, Venezuela passed from the hands of one tyrant into those of another. A revolt in 1899 enabled Cipriano Castro to establish himself as dictator. He attempted to continue the road-building and other public works projects inaugurated by former rulers, but frequent revolts led to more destruction than construction. Castro ruled for nearly ten years, but by 1908 opposition to him was so bitter that he turned the government over to his vice-president, Juan Vicente Gómez. Castro departed for Europe for reasons of health, and indeed his health would have suffered had he remained in Venezuela. He had gotten his country into serious difficulties with several European powers and the United States over failure to meet obligations and his inability or unwillingness to protect the lives and property of alien residents. England, Germany, and Italy had jointly blockaded the seaports in an effort to force collection, and for a time it appeared that Germany might have somewhat broader objectives. Even after the Hague Court had settled the claims of the major powers, greatly reducing many of them, the Netherlands undertook a new blockade. All that Castro did seemed to produce only trouble.

JUAN VICENTE GÓMEZ

Juan Vicente Gómez proved himself a man of many talents, including the ability to maintain himself in power from 1908 till 1935, when he died in office from natural causes. He won support from abroad by agreeing to meet all of the country's external obligations and keeping his word. Foreign capital was extended a ready welcome, and within the period of his rule oil production, which had amounted to a mere trickle when he first assumed office, mounted to astronomical proportions. Value of foreign trade jumped from less than 50 million dollars in 1910 to nearly 250 million in 1929. Proceeds from oil royalties and duties filled the government's coffers and the pockets of Gómez and his friends and relatives. The national debt was entirely liquidated, roads were built to link the major portions of the country, and railroad mileage was extended greatly. Obviously Gómez was a man who believed in progress.

Unlike Mexico under Díaz, however, Venezuela under Gómez was not handed bodily over to aliens. Aliens were satisfied, however, as long as they were permitted to tap the country's vast oil reserves in the region of Lake Maracaibo. Gómez did not trouble the miserable back-country population or take away their land. He was content to confiscate and operate the business and commercial enterprises of the country, and he allowed oilfield workers to benefit by the high wages they received. In other ways his rule was utterly despotic. He destroyed every semblance of constitutional government, even though he did pause occasionally to tinker with the written charter. His enemies were ruthlessly imprisoned, tortured, and slaughtered. Gómez could spot a potential trouble-maker miles away, and his preventive measures were swift and entirely effective.

As the years passed Gómez became immensely rich. He built for himself a huge mansion, so elaborate indeed as to arouse almost as much laughter and ridicule as anger among those who feared and hated him. Gómez was an ignorant and crude man who lacked the sensitivities that might have prevented him from making such a tawdry display of his wealth. His vast horde of relatives, including innumerable children, legitimate and 'natural,' were permitted to enrich themselves also at the country's expense; but with so many evidences of physical 'progress,' who should complain? The intellectual climate was stultifying, the press was rigidly controlled, and all opposition seemed hopeless. Nevertheless, when Gómez died in 1935, the news provoked one of the wildest celebrations ever witnessed in Venezuela. Between moments of rejoicing, mobs sought out Gómez' most obnoxious adherents and killed them.

In spite of harsh and oppressive dictatorship throughout most of the Hispanic nations bordering on the Caribbean, in spite of heavy foreign pressure, in spite of exploitation from within and without, the lower classes remained generally passive. The ignorant Indian or mestizo knew his place and kept to it. Not so in Mexico.

Mexican Revolution

Class differentiation is an inevitable concomitant of human civilization, judging by all the lessons of history and anthropology, nonsensical communistic theories notwithstanding. Human differences—physical, intellectual, psychological, and accidental—account for the evolution of class structure. The great American ideal, so close to reality in the United States in the twentieth century, would place the whole concept of class on a purely rational basis. The individual would be free to move upward or downward in accordance with his abilities, supported in the process by relative equality of opportunity. Such social objectives have never been entirely alien to liberal Latin American thought, but the process of achieving them has been slow indeed. Occasionally, however, a violent effort has been made in Mexico. Such was the case in the revolutionary struggles of Hidalgo and Morelos, and in the long War of the Reform in the time of Juárez. A new effort was made beginning in 1911, and it toppled the porfirista regime to the ground.

In 1900 a small group of intellectuals in San Luís Potosí had begun agitating for democracy, free enterprise, and restrictions on the church. They initiated the 'Precursor Movement' of the Mexican Revolution, an attack on the evils of the Díaz regime. The movement, at first directed by the upper and middle classes, was broadened to include the protest issues of labor and the rural peon. In the preceding decade the economy had changed rapidly: the opening of new factories was at its peak, and agriculture was transformed by the introduction of modern machinery and transport facilities. Thousands of small farmers lost their farms and became low-paid laborers on land that was once theirs. They bitterly resented such changes, and their resentment was directed especially against aliens. Economic nationalism was a key factor in the revolutionary ferment before 1910.

The hacendados, too, were dissatisfied with economic conditions, the decrease in exports, and the difficulties of obtaining credit. Many of them joined the conservative wing of the opposition movement. In the Plan of San Luís Potosí the socially prominent families sought the support of the middle class and the workers against the Díaz administration. In the hard times of 1909, professional men suffered drastic financial and social decline. Many lawyer-intellectuals, such as José Vasconcelos and Antonio Díaz Soto y Gama, joined the anti-Díaz movement.

Another group opposed Díaz in more violent terms—the Partido Liberal Mexicano. It was composed of lower and middle-class elements who were radical in outlook and prepared to engage in violence. The PLM, headed by the avowed anarchist Ricardo Flores Magón, was the spearhead of the Precursor Movement. It aroused the workers and the agricultural peasantry to a bitter effort to revolutionize society.

Porfirio Díaz had failed to provide for a successor; and as the 'Grand Old Man' grew increasingly senile, the question of presidential succession became an urgent issue. Bernardo Reyes, mestizo governor of Nuevo León, and Limantour, idol of the científicos, were potential candidates. In an interview with an American journalist named Creelman, Díaz announced that he planned to retire in 1910 and would welcome the formation of an opposition party. His words were undoubtedly meant for consumption in the United States, but they were received with enthusiasm all over Mexico. Free elections and reform were demanded by intellectuals throughout the country. Díaz, old and out of touch with conditions, was unconcerned by the clamor. He sent Reyes off on a diplomatic mission, and no potential leader seemed left to oppose him. But so weakened had his position become that the old dictator was to be overthrown by a mild-mannered little vegetarian, Francisco I. Madero, who had written a book in which he gently suggested that the Mexicans should be allowed to choose their vice-president.

FRANCISCO I. MADERO

Madero was virtually overwhelmed with supporters and launched bodily into a role for which he had few of the necessary qualifications. The first attempts at rebellion were fiascos, and Madero decided to abandon the affair. He had found that Díaz' opponents were badly divided and unable to compromise their differences. One possibility was non-violent change, as he had advocated. The other was violent revolution with socio-economic goals, the program of Flores Magón and the PLM. Many intellectuals were not satisfied with either alternative and tried to find a middle course.

Madero had not become widely known until 1909. Up to that time he had been absolutely opposed to violent revolution for, as he admitted, he had a 'veritable horror of bloodshed.' Madero was convinced that Mexico's problems were primarily political. Only on the eve of the revolution did he make even a half-hearted effort to attract labor and peasant support for his cause.

By 1910 only the overthrow of Díaz had been agreed upon by the major revolutionary groups. Otherwise, there were few common and many conflicting goals. The *maderistas* proclaimed 'Effective Suffrage and No Reelection.' For PLM and the followers of Emiliano Zapata, a peasant leader of the south, the cry was 'Land and Liberty.' They regarded the revolution as a movement of rural and urban workers against the middle class.

When Madero set November 20, 1910, as the day for the revolt to begin, his followers had insufficient time to collect arms. Because he had consistently emphasized non-violence, his supporters were ill-prepared for the fierce fighting that ensued. The only revolutionary group with arms and battle experience was the PLM, and in the first year of fighting PLM victories kept the anti-Díaz movement alive. Madero saw his cause embraced by sterner men, the vaqueros and bandits of Chihuahua led by Pascual Orozco and by the local Robin Hood, Pancho Villa. The capture of Ciudad Juárez by Orozco convinced Díaz that it was time to retire. He chose, however, to negotiate with the moderate maderistas rather than with the PLM leaders. Madero would have been willing for Díaz to continue as president, but Dr. Francisco Vázquez Gómez convinced him that Díaz had to go.

The Ciudad Juárez agreement between Díaz and Madero called for an election in October, 1911. Suddenly the rotten timbers of the dictatorship crumbled in a manner astonishing to Díaz and Madero alike. On May 25, 1911, Díaz resigned and left the country to spend his remaining years in France. Hopeful Mexicans awaited Madero, who seemed from a distance to be the man needed to redress the wrongs of centuries. Instead they faced a decade of rapine and guerrilla warfare fought by the contenders for the mantle Madero found to be ill-fitting.

Even before the election was held, groups began breaking away from Madero and rebelling against his leadership. Two of the early defectors were Vázquez Gómez and Bernardo Reyes, both of whom adopted agrarian reform slogans. The rising strength of the lower level revolutionaries became a powerful force.

Madero had no program but the overthrow of the Díaz regime. His understanding of Mexico's problems and aspirations was slight, to say the least, for he naïvely assumed that once Díaz was gone things would right themselves. The long-suffering Mexicans hungered for land as well as liberty from tyranny. A large proportion simply hungered. Most important to Madero was the immediate establishment of political democracy, a concept which not even he understood. While he remained impractically idealistic, his brother Gustavo set about bossing Mexico in the established tradition. Soon disillusionment with the Madero regime surpassed the early enthusiasm for it. Emiliano Zapata, who epitomized the Indian's undying yearning for land, was the first to rebel. It was not long before revolts swept from one end of the country to the other.

VICTORIANO HUERTA

Profoundly disturbed by the sudden changes in the Mexican administration, foreign businessmen and capitalists began to look for an official who could re-establish order and guarantee them the same protection they had enjoyed under Díaz. They considered a number of candidates before arriving at their choice: heavy-drinking, slow-thinking, sadistic General Victoriano Huerta.

Huerta's rise to power began when Madero sent him to quell revolts instigated by Bernardo Reyes and Pascual Orozco. After his success against the rebels, Huerta anticipated a handsome reward; instead he was retired. He became a bitter and unscrupulous foe of Madero. Other revolts broke out, but none was serious until the American ambassador, Henry Lane Wilson, began conniving with the opposition. Under his guidance the downfall of Madero was engineered.

Wilson's messages to the state department in Washington contained frequent and violent attacks on Madero and urged United States intervention. In the meantime, Madero's loathing of violence prevented his ordering the execution of rebels, and rebellion became safe. Soon his army was undermined, and when the final attack came in January of 1913, he made the fatal mistake of placing Huerta in command of his troops.

DEATH OF MADERO

In February Huerta seized Madero and the vice-president, Pino Suárez. Francisco Madero's brother, Gustavo, was literally drawn and quartered while Huerta was significantly occupied elsewhere. Huerta, Félix Díaz, an ostensible rebel with whom Huerta had secretly been co-operating, and the American ambassador drew up a plan to save Mexico. A few nights later,

Francisco Madero and his vice-president were shot, reportedly while 'attempting to escape.' Huerta took over the Mexican government and the American ambassador notified his government that a wicked despotism had fallen.

Before disposing of Madero, Huerta had required his resignation to maintain a semblance of legal form. To secure the resignation Huerta promised both Madero and Pino Suárez safe conduct from the country, but he made no pretense of keeping his pledge. Wives of the doomed men pleaded with the American ambassador to intercede to save their husbands, but Henry Lane Wilson dismissed them on the ground that he could not interfere in Mexico's internal affairs! After all, Madero had even harbored the thought of taxing idle lands.

After the murder of Madero and Pino Suárez on February 21, 1913, workers and peasants rushed to enlist in the armies of Zapata, Villa, Carranza, and Obregón. The revolutionary leaders became more and more radical because of this increased support. The zapatistas fought for agrarian goals; the villistas tried to follow the Madero line; industrial labor organized rapidly and supported Carranza until 1916. Intellectuals were generally moderate in outlook when the revolution began, but events pushed them steadily to the left. They fought among themselves rather than uniting behind a single leader. After the revolution most of them became more conservative. One who did not was Ricardo Flores Magón, who remained anarchist to the last. He died in 1922 in a prison in the United States.

HUERTA'S RULE

Huerta's seventeen-month rule was one of the most sordid tyrannies that ever befell a Latin American country. His almost pereptual state of intoxication and his characteristic brutality made governing the country chiefly a process of plunder and extermination of enemies. His ministers, handpicked by the American ambassador, resigned or were shoved aside. Over a hundred members of congress were jailed. Murder became the chief public function. Huerta controlled the area around Mexico City, but in the south Zapata remained unconquered and was busily engaged in redistributing the land to his Indian followers. In the north new opponents arose.

VENUSTIANO CARRANZA

Venustiano Carranza, governor of Coahulia, refused to recognize Huerta and called for his removal. He announced his *Plan de Guadalupe,* simply a restoration of the principles and constitution of 1857, and joined forces with Álvaro Obregón, governor of Sonora. Other allies were found in the persons of Pancho Villa and Pablo González in Chihuahua. A slow march on the capital began, and the real revolution got under way.

Carranza was a simple man and in no sense vicious. Obregón was able and astute and possessed a deep understanding of what was wrong with Mexico. His Yaqui Indian troops had been victims of Díaz' spoliation. Villa was a plundering bandit and little more. Both Carranza and Obregón distrusted him and he them. As the move on the capital progressed, a systematic pillage of town and hacienda began, and none of the leaders took serious steps to check it. Captured hacendados were promptly shot along with other members of their families after the women had been turned over to the soldiery. Death was dealt on every hand, and Villa and his lieutenants reveled in an orgy of blood. Carranza shuddered and Obregón frowned and would have no part of it, but the unpaid and ill-disciplined army had to be kept satisfied. The great estates continued to go up in smoke while their owners were left for the well-fed buzzards and their cattle were sold across the northern frontier for additional arms.

Mexico was offered a sorry collection of leaders. Carranza's greatest recommendations were his distinguished appearance and his basically gentle nature. In reality he was quite undistinguished, ignorant, and jealous of subordinates who demonstrated unusual ability. He did have enough respect for human misery to hold the vicious Villa back from entering Mexico City when finally the revolutionary armies approached the capital. For this 'betrayal,' Villa never forgave him. Obregón, by far the most promising of the northern rebels, lacked prestige, and the fact that he frowned on looting weakened his chances of becoming a popular hero to his troops.

In the south, the *zapatistas* proceeded with their crude but effective program of land distribution, that of killing off the hacendados and dividing their land. They were not concerned with more remote problems. In many ways, Zapata was the most attractive of the rebel chiefs, for he had a commendable goal in the rehabilitation of his people.

Foreign interest in Mexican problems increased dangerously. British investors who had received favors from Huerta supported him enthusiastically, but American concessionaires and owners of mines and ranches called for intervention. President Woodrow Wilson of the United States reviewed the record of Huerta and found it loathsome. Belatedly he recalled his ambassador, Henry Lane Wilson, and urged Huerta not to be a candidate for the presidency. The American president was simply and not too politely ignored. Wilson took more drastic action. In 1914 he took advantage of the arrest and brief detention of a few American seamen at Tampico and ordered the navy to seize Veracruz. This ill-considered act aided Huerta more than it injured him, for it nearly united the Mexican factions in opposition to the Yankee invader. The error was quickly rectified, however, for President Wilson recognized the belligerency status of the forces of Carranza and Obregón and began selling them arms. This step quickly spelled doom for the besotted tyrant, Huerta. Heavily supplied with equipment for which they had traded the confiscated cattle of wealthy hacendados, Obregón and Villa raced with their troops down the Gulf of California coast and across the central valley, each hoping to reach the capital first and take over the government. Obregón's forces won, thanks to Carranza's interference with Villa. Huerta fled the country. Villa, however, considered himself betrayed, and turned his army against Carranza's, and for a time their struggle became the principal conflict.

By issuing a series of reform decrees in 1915, Carranza greatly strengthened his political position. Obregón, hoping to bring about some semblance of order, threw his support to Carranza whom he considered to be the lesser of two evils. This gave Carranza the ablest Mexican general. Both Carranza and Obregón, because they made political pronouncements and gave evidence of a desire to reform Mexico's social structure— however vague their objectives—were regarded as dangerous men. Conservatives and foreign capitalists gravitated toward Villa, who obviously was a type who could be bought. Their cause was lost. Obregón defeated Villa in a series of vicious and devastating battles, scattered his motley army, and returned him to his boyhood occupation of banditry in Chihuahua.

THE VILLA INTERVENTION

In October, 1915, President Wilson recognized Carranza as *de facto* head of the Mexican state. Villa was furious. He vented his anger and disappointment on all American citizens on whom he could lay his hands. He even raided the New Mexican town of Columbus across the border in the

United States. This act prompted Wilson to send General Pershing into northern Mexico to capture Villa dead or alive. Such a measure greatly weakened Carranza's position for a time, for it faced him with a new American invasion of Mexico. He was, however, in no position to oppose, and Villa was as much his enemy as an enemy of the United States. Pershing's expedition was a ridiculous failure, for he had not the slightest chance of capturing the wily Villa.

CONSTITUTION OF 1917

In 1916 Carranza, who fancied himself the heir of Juárez, called for an assembly to revise the constitution. Although he contemplated nothing more striking than a provision to increase the authority of the president, a small group of radicals, led by General Francisco Múgica and Andrés Molina Enríquez and backed by Obregón, incorporated in the new constitution some of the basic ideas distilled from the revolutionary ferment. Article 27 was written as a masterful attempt to undo all the evils of the porfirista regime with respect to the alienation of Mexican lands and resources. National ownership of mineral and subsoil rights, recognized from the colonial period, was reaffirmed and declared to be inalienable. The ownership of surface land was limited exclusively to Mexicans and largely to individuals, except under very stringent conditions. The church was prohibited from holding property and corporate ownership of agricultural land was proscribed. The usurpation of Indian *ejidos,* or communal village lands, was to be reversed. Most of the land concessions granted since the days of Juárez were declared null and void.

Article 123 included most of the known guarantees for labor, and although no laws were passed immediately to make the principles operative, the article embodied the goals of the revolutionaries on behalf of the industrial worker.

The anticlerical principles of the Juárez epoch were reaffirmed, and a number of more stringent restrictions were added. In addition to proscribing church ownership of property the constitution gave to state legislatures the authority to regulate the number of priests permitted within each state and required priests to register with the civil authorities. Because of the political activity of the church party on behalf of Díaz and Huerta, it now suffered once again the bitter consequences of defeat.

Even though Carranza had little sympathy with or understanding of the aspirations of the revolutionary leaders, and did not attempt to invoke any of the offending articles, opposition to the constitution of 1917 was enormous. It stemmed from the foreign interests, from the conservative landholders, from the church; but the Mexican middle and lower classes who understood applauded. Priests, hacendados, and foreign owners of mines and oil fields prepared to have the distasteful articles obliterated before any government should try to put them into effect. No fears were aroused by Carranza's actions, for he ignored the land problem except when his own followers wanted rewards, and he threatened striking workers with the firing squad.

Partisan forces in Chihuahua and Morelos still held out against government troops, but in 1919 Zapata was assassinated. This removed one of the most colorful and devoted of the revolutionary leaders, but his program of land reform was already accomplished and no one moved to interfere.

During 1919 the question of a successor to Carranza raised a furore, but Obregón was the only candidate with hope of success. He had the support of labor, and labor had suddenly become a powerful factor in Mexican politics. Labor unions were formed and consolidated into a national federation dominated by Luis Morones, an able figure dedicated to the revolutionary principles of the new constitution. The *Confederación Regional Obrera Mexicana,* or CROM, was controlled by an executive committee, the *Grupo Acción,* composed of trusted associates of Morones. Morones could throw the entire labor movement behind Obregón.

Carranza, despite his opposition to re-election in the past, was reluctant to surrender his power. Yet his term, which dated from 1917, was expiring. The Obregón faction found an occasion to revolt when Carranza threatened to use federal troops to break a strike in Sonora, in April, 1920. It immediately became apparent that Carranza was no match for Obregón, and the various regional chieftains quickly deserted the one and swore loyalty to the other. Carranza fled for Tampico, but his guide murdered him en route. By the time Obregón assumed the presidency in November of the same year, the country was more nearly pacified than it had been in the past decade. It was a peace of exhaustion, but a number of old wounds had been healed. The zapatistas were permitted to retain their lands in Morelos; Zapata's assassin had been shot; and Villa had been distracted from his normal trade by the gift of a cattle ranch in Durango.

ÁLVARO OBREGÓN

Obregón began putting into effect some of the ideas of the revolution, although in most outward aspects his government was a replica of its predecessors. He had no intention of making immediately sweeping changes that might as easily be reversed. Mexico's first need after domestic peace, he believed, was a more efficient economy. He maintained control by skillfully balancing his supporters and opponents. Agrarian reform, which he regarded as dangerous to the economy, was permitted to continue at a slow pace as a safety valve, but it was not encouraged. The most noteworthy accomplishments of his administration were due to the heroic efforts of José Vasconcelos in the field of popular education.

The rural school system established by Vasconcelos and supported by Obregón was one of the most important factors in consolidating the ideas of the revolutionaries. The rural school teacher became the successor of the sixteenth-century missionary in spreading the new gospel of Mexico for the Mexicans. A tremendous task remained to be done, for more than a million Indians knew no Spanish at all, and most of them regarded anyone from outside the village with suspicion and hostility. These people had to be assimilated into the new Mexican nation.

Foreign capital presented the gravest problem to Obregón for the revolution was pledged to recover Mexico for the Mexicans, and foreigners apprehensively awaited the first signs of danger in this direction. The taxes levied on the oil industry were violently denounced, but since the proceeds were used to resume payments to foreign bondholders, a significant element of foreign opposition was placated. Obregón finally declared that Article 27 of the constitution would not be applied retroactively, and in August, 1923, the United States recognized his regime, barely in time to prevent a serious civil war over the presidential succession.

The revolt of Adolfo de la Huerta was serious enough for three months, but in the end Obregón triumphed and was able to turn the presidency over to Plutarco Elías Calles, the president-elect, without incident. This was in 1924.

PLUTARCO E. CALLES

Calles, whose early career gave little promise of future greatness, at first devoted his remarkable energies to social reform. As president he ruled as personally as any of his predecessors, and although many of the revolutionary ideals were put in practice, political control became more and more concentrated in his hands. Educational improvement was continued, and the government organized and financed various projects to improve sanitation and to irrigate rural areas where rainfall was insufficient. Land redistribution, which had lagged under Obregón, received active support; progress still was made at a snail's pace, however. Labor organization proceeded rapidly, and Luis Morones became as powerful as any general and more wealthy than most.

The church was Calles' most determined opponent, and in 1926 its hostility became critical. Calles replied to clerical threats by deporting priests and closing churches and Catholic schools. Priests were forbidden to appear on the street in clerical garb, and they had to register with civil authorities as the constitution prescribed. A futile religious strike began which lasted for three years. Rebel bands of fanatical clerical supporters calling themselves *cristeros* sought to embarrass the government by acts of sabotage, such as the dynamiting of trains. Counter-measures of military chieftains were little more conducive to peace, and thousands of innocent persons suffered. Not a few priests paid the supreme penalty for their devotion.

Outside of Mexico, the world was shocked by this persecution of religion, and as such it was reported by church officials and the clerical party. Relations with the United States eased materially, however, when Dwight W. Morrow replaced Ambassador Sheffield in the Mexican capital. Morrow was probably the first American ambassador to Mexico who had a genuine appreciation for the efforts of the Mexican people to overcome their miserable heritage of a century of foreign and domestic exploitation. He also had a sincere respect for Mexican sovereignty and exercised a judicious restraint in interfering in the internal affairs of the country to which he was accredited.

In 1928, the question of presidential succession again threatened to precipitate a civil war, for many ambitious politicians saw their hopes dashed by the apparent plan of Calles and Obregón to alternate the presidency between them. Those who pronounced against the government were quickly disposed of, so that Obregón was left without serious competition and was overwhelmingly elected. Before he could take office, however, he was assassinated by a religious fanatic. Many thought that Calles had engineered the deed, but it was not proved. Actually, it was in the crisis following the assassination that Calles displayed his most statesmanlike qualities. He announced that thereafter Mexico should be governed by laws rather than ruled by men, and his words had a calming effect in spite of their patent insincerity. The congress selected Emilio Portes Gil, an *obregonista,* to serve as provisional president, and a return to anarchy was avoided.

By 1929 many of the old revolutionaries, including Calles, Morones, and scores of others, had become wealthy through the spoils of office. Little by little their revolutionary zeal deserted them until they came to regard reforms with displeasure. Calles, who had ostensibly retired from political life, began to interfere excessively in the administration of Portes Gil. The various political factions were welded into a single party, the National Revolutionary party, or PNR. It held its first convention in 1929 for the purpose of nominating a successor to Portes Gil. The choice was Pascual Ortiz Rubio, a man suggested by Calles. Despite a whirlwind campaign by Vasconcelos, Ortiz Rubio's opponent, the party candidate won by a tremendous majority, and Vasconcelos vanished into self-imposed exile to write his memoirs.

The control which Calles exercised over Ortiz Rubio brought the revolutionary reforms to a temporary end. From his palatial home in Cuernavaca, the *jefe máximo* ruled Mexico by means of a private telephone line into the National Palace. The administration of Oritiz Rubio came to a sudden if not surprising end in 1932. On the day after Oritiz Rubio had dismissed several *callistas* from his cabinet, the president read in the morning paper of his resignation, announced by Calles. Wealthy Abelardo Rodríguez was appointed to finish the term.

Many Mexicans felt that the revolution had been betrayed, that the still vital and necessary reforms had all been sidetracked. Calles was obviously running the country through his stooges and filling his pockets ever fuller in the process. The left wing of the PNR began determined agitation for change. Finally the callistas made a gesture toward placating them. The 1934 candidate for the presidency would have to satisfy the new generation and those demanding further progress toward the revolutionary ideals, but he would also have to be a man who would remain basically loyal to the one-time revolutionaries who had now 'retired.' In choosing Lázaro Cárdenas for this role, Calles grossly underestimated both the man and the power of the reform forces. With the election of Cárdenas a new era of the Mexican revolution opened. Soon Calles was living in exile in the United States and a new reform movement was sweeping all before it. The revolution had come of age.

I I

Brazil: The Waning Empire
and the Old Republic

> Comparatively few show themselves sensible of the tremendous problems which the nation has to face, with its scattered centers of population to draw together, its means of communication to extend, its public credit to sustain, its revenues to be scrupulously husbanded and applied to useful purposes, above all, its mass of Negro and Indian population to be educated and civilized. Nowhere in the world is there a more urgent need for a wise constructive statesmanship.
>
> JAMES BRYCE *

Empire at High Tide

By mid-century Brazil appeared bound on a course quite different from those pursued by most of her Spanish American neighbors. The period of the regency had given the country an unhappy acquaintance with republicanism and federalism, and the experiences of near-by Argentina only fortified Brazilian faith in the monarchy. After his coronation young Dom Pedro II had gradually rejected attempts of court cliques to manage his affairs, and had established himself as the real ruler of Brazil. His remarkable character was to be one of the potent forces molding Brazilian life, and one of the reasons for an easy transition to republicanism in 1890. His chosen role was that of moderator between the political forces striving for power. During his long reign Brazilians enjoyed civil liberties unparalleled in the rest of the continent, and the men who held high offices displayed an enviable political morality. The emperor himself set the example by a life of sobriety, moderation, democracy, and intellectual curiosity which did little justice to some of his lusty forebears. But neither the emperor

* *South America, Observations and Impressions,* The Macmillan Company, New York, 1929, p. 419.

nor his statesmen were prepared to solve economic problems constructively, and Brazil's material progress remained shackled to slave-based agriculture.

Dom Pedro exercised his constitutional powers fully. Had it not been
for his interference there would have been few changes in the complexion
of the chamber of deputies, for the party controlling the ministry decided
the outcome of elections. Dom Pedro transferred the ministry from the
conservatives to the liberals, or the reverse, when he felt that a change was
in the nation's interest, and elections were subsequently held which reflected this change in the assembly. The contending parties did not greatly
appreciate the emperor's impartiality, for they felt that he could not be depended on for constant support. By 1862 a balance had been achieved between the conservatives and the revived Liberal party, and the empire politically was at high tide. From this point onward a strong democratic
current developed, and the conservative flood began to recede. As it ebbed
the fate of the empire was decided. Even in the 1860's some men voiced
the belief that Dom Pedro would be the last emperor of Brazil.

EDUCATION

As far as education was concerned, Brazilians continued to concentrate on
law, and law colleges of necessity served a supplementary cultural purpose.
All of those who studied law did not find employment in the legal profession; law became the basic training for politicians, diplomats, journalists,
teachers, poets, and novelists. The ecclesiastical approach to education of
colonial days was thus replaced by a secular, juridical spirit. Through the
law schools the influence of French and English philosophers reached the
ruling class. The law schools, and especially that of São Paulo, became
deeply involved with politics, and most of the liberal movements of the
epoch first found articulate expression there.

With the law colleges serving to prepare the cultural elite, technical
studies were largely neglected. Two medical schools founded in the time of
João VI had survived, but their days of most fruitful achievement were
still in the future. The need for a school of mines was voiced early in the
century. In 1832 a law was passed creating a course of mineralogical studies in Minas Gerais, but it was not put into effect until 1876, after the
visit of Louis Agassiz and Charles Frederick Hartt from the United States.
The lack of men with scientific training necessary for fully comprehending

the material needs of the country was seriously felt. Although the empire and the Old Republic which succeeded it produced brilliant jurists, eloquent orators, impassioned poets, and extraordinary statesmen, they failed to provide men who could develop an effective program.

LITERATURE

In literature romanticism was giving way to a Brazilian version of French naturalism by 1870. A realistic reaction had set in with the poems of Castro Alves, the 'poet of the slaves.' Castro Alves did not portray the slaves themselves in picturesque terms, but he gave telling poetical expression to their misery. His aid to the cause of abolition was tremendous, for he created a widespread sentiment against slavery. The first naturalistic novel to appear in Brazil was *O mulato,* by Aluísio de Azevedo, which concerned a young man's reactions to racial prejudices in society. The greatest Brazilian writer of the nineteenth century, however, was the mulatto Joaquim Maria Machado de Assis, novelist, poet, short story writer, and playwright.

Other Brazilians whose writings have won respect far beyond their country's borders are Joaquim Nabuco, abolitionist, historian, essayist, and literary critic; João Capistrano de Abreu, historian; and Rui Barbosa, who was not only an internationally renowned jurist but the greatest living authority on the Portuguese language. Shortly after 1900 there appeared two books which have had a profound impact on Brazilian literature of the twentieth century: the already mentioned *Os sertões,* by Euclides da Cunha, and *Canaan,* by José Pereira da Graça Aranha. Both of these works are characterized by a deep national consciousness.

POLITICS

During the lifetime of Dom Pedro the electoral process was under almost constant attack, and such reforms as were made failed to alter the situation appreciably. The most significant effort to make the chamber of deputies represent the will of the electorate rather than that of the ministry was the Saraiva Law of 1881. Among other changes the law established direct election of deputies, and extended the franchise. It provided for supervision of elections by committees representing both parties and for the removal of troops from the vicinity of the polls. The law was a worthy attempt at improvement, and it was fairly effective between its enactment and 1886. In that year former practices were revived by the conservatives in a desperate but futile effort to turn back the tide of abolitionist sentiment which threatened to engulf them.

The statesmen called by Dom Pedro to direct Brazilian affairs were usually men of high caliber. The monarchy was appreciated and effectively supported by a small group of men with keen insight, members of the aristocratic planter class which had dominated political life since independence. Republican sentiment never entirely died out, and it appeared sporadically in isolated insurrections. The overthrow of Napoleon III and the establishment of a republic in France had echoes in Brazil. In 1870, on the day after the birthday of Dom Pedro, the Republican party issued its manifesto. Its membership remained small for the next decade, but it soon boasted a number of capable men. In this same period the positivist philosophy of Auguste Comte gained adherents in Brazil, especially among the military.

ECONOMIC AFFAIRS

The economic structure of the empire favored the continuance of domination by the landed class, for business was despised and generally left to immigrants and foreigners. It was not until the last days of the empire that many Brazilians cautiously entered industry, despite the spectacular and unique career of the Baron of Mauá in constructing railroads. The oligarchy of landholders dominated Brazilian political life until its ascendency was challenged by other classes less bound by ties to the monarchy. These began to appear by 1860, but they did not immediately make an effective bid for political power.

By 1860, through the activities of foreigners, modern business had come to Brazil. Banking houses had been established in the 1850's, and they provided credit for various enterprises such as railroad building. In 1854 railroads began connecting the coastal cities with the interior centers of population. Telegraph lines were extended to many parts of the country, and in 1874 a trans-oceanic cable began carrying messages between Brazil and Europe. Steamship navigation on the rivers opened the way for commercial development of previously isolated areas.

The greatest figure produced by the empire in the fields of industrialization, railroad building, and banking was Irineu Evangelista de Sousa,

Baron and Viscount Mauá. Mauá, unfortunately, found the government unreceptive to his daring and multitudinous enterprises; and the government was apprehensive of his power, which was not based on the traditional ownership of land and slaves. Mauá frequently complained of the lack of imagination on the part of ministers of state, but the ultimate cause of his ruin in 1875 stemmed from the chaotic aftermath of the Paraguayan War, and the general decline of the slave-based economy.

Commerce based largely on the products of the fazendas of the north and the coffee plantations of the south grew immensely after 1866. The upsurge of commerce gave new life to the coastal cities, which were increasingly oriented toward Europe. The decay of the rural aristocracy was accelerated by the attraction of the cities for the young men from the fazendas, for after their educations had been completed few chose to return to the country. Instead, they stayed in the cities and followed careers of diplomacy, politics, journalism, and the liberal professions.

Immigration to southern Brazil began to modify society there even before the abolition of slavery. In the two decades after 1864 between twenty and thirty thousand immigrants came annually. By 1886 the number coming each year had more than doubled, and in the next ten years more than a million foreigners arrived in Brazil. Between 1864 and 1935 four million came. Half of these were Italians and Portuguese; half a million were Spaniards. Germans, Austrians, and Japanese came in smaller numbers. Because of the fact that a part of these immigrants congregated in frontier communities of their own making, their assimilation was sometimes slow. Most of the foreign frontier colonies remained isolated, for the line of dense settlement did not sweep past and engulf them. They usually had to provide their own schools, and naturally continued using the language of their ancestors. It was not the fault of these immigrants if they did not become Brazilianized quickly; this tardiness, however, did not become recognized as a problem for government attention until the major wars of the twentieth century.

Abolition

Although foreign trade flourished the development of industries to meet domestic needs for manufactured articles did not make satisfactory progress until World War I. For as long as fazendeiros and lawyers dominated the government protectionism was not advocated with much enthusiasm.

As new bases of wealth appeared, a new class began the struggle to wrest control from the powerful grasp of the fazendeiros. This class gradually became aware that it could not succeed without breaking the power of its opponents, and this power was traced to the ownership of slaves. Abolition became the most vital issue between the two forces, and other goals were momentarily forgotten while the crucial issue was settled. Through the efforts of Joaquim Nabuco, Rui Barbosa, and others, the Liberal party reluctantly embraced the cause of abolition, but its members saw in the crusade only the moral and human aspects.

After 1865 Brazil found herself almost alone among her hemispheric neighbors retaining the outmoded institution of slavery. Dom Pedro, who seems always to have favored abolition, was willing to proceed toward the goal in a cautious and moderate fashion so that it could be accomplished without bringing ruin to the slaveowners. For a time it appeared as if this policy would succeed, but progress was delayed by the Paraguayan War and the bitter resistance of the slaveowners.

The unfortunate conquest of Paraguay needs little further said of it in so far as military campaigns are concerned. Although it turned Brazilians forcefully away from ideas of armed intervention and imperialism, for the most part its effects were exceedingly detrimental. In addition to the loss of 50,000 men and severe damage to the nation's economy, the war postponed solution to many important domestic problems.

Because of the need for Uruguayan and Argentinian co-operation during the war Dom Pedro's government shunned agents sent by Maximilian to establish close and friendly relations between his ephemeral empire and Brazil. The statesmen of Uruguay and Argentina were outspoken against the intervention in Mexico, and some thought Dom Pedro had gone too far even in recognizing Maximilian, despite the fact that he refused to establish diplomatic relations with the French-supported imperial government.

The abolitionist sentiment in the meantime had built up considerable momentum. The Rio Branco 'law of free birth' of 1871 declared all children born of slave parents to be free after a term of service to their masters, and the eventual end of slavery was assured. But by the time the law was enacted the abolitionists were no longer satisfied with such a slow solution to the problem. In 1885 slaves over 65 years of age were granted their freedom, an act which merely aroused the abolitionists to fury. Several states with few slaves freed all within their borders, and voluntary manumission kept pace. Soon the demand for complete and unqualified emancipation became irresistible.

While the abolitionist campaign was striking at the vitals of the emperor's main support, a lost bout with the church damaged his prestige considerably. The strife between church and state in the 1870's was primarily political. The emperor claimed and exercised powers over clerical affairs granted to him by the constitution, and stemming from the royal patronage of the colonial period. Papal edicts were not to have force in Brazil except by his authorization, and he disagreed with the papal ban on masonic activities. In Brazil, liberal priests had previously regarded masonry as a bulwark of Christian liberalism, and some were members. On the matter of abolition the Masons and the church ultimately agreed. The masonic order had supported the cause from its inception.

In 1871 the Masons of Rio de Janeiro held a celebration in honor of the Rio Branco law. During the ceremony a priest delivered a sermon in terms which indicated his masonic affiliation. When challenged by the bishop of Rio de Janeiro, he refused to forsake his masonic sympathy, and was suspended. The masonic lodges resolved to attack the 'ultramontanism' of the church. The Grand Master of one branch of the order was Baron Rio Branco, Prime Minister of the empire.

The masonic issue spread to other parts of Brazil despite the fact that Dom Pedro had not sanctioned the papal edict against the Masons. Other bishops took advantage of the quarrel to strike a blow at regalism. In the torrid outpourings on both sides, the colorful, symbolic language of the champions of the church, who spoke of 'shackles and crumbs' and the 'blood of Christ,' reached the masses more effectively than did the arguments of the regalists. The bishop of Olinda suspended one of the *irmandades,* semi-religious brotherhoods, which refused to expel its masonic members, and the bishop of Pará took similar action. The matter ultimately came before the Council of State, and the bishops were ordered to lift the interdicts. On refusing they were sentenced to four years at hard labor, which sentence was commuted to simple imprisonment. It was widely felt that the government had gone too far, and in 1875 Dom Pedro retreated. The triumph of the church was a further step in the imperial decline, for the clergy no longer supported the throne.

The aid of the church in the battle against slavery was enlisted by Nabuco on a visit to Rome, and in 1888 Pope Leo XIII announced his support of the cause of the enslaved anywhere in the world. At the same time he canonized Father Pedro Claver, the 'apostle of the Negroes' in seventeenth-century Cartagena. Dom Pedro was in Europe, and his daughter Isabel was serving as regent when the chamber finally passed a law ending slavery without compensation to slaveowners. The suddenness of emancipation and the failure to compensate the fazendeiros seriously disrupted Brazilian economy and brought ruin to many planters. The traditional domination of the northern landowners in the economic and political life of the nation had already been jeopardized by the growing prosperity of the coffee growers of São Paulo, and the emancipation of some 300 million dollars' worth of slaves was a serious blow. In the south immigrant labor helped the coffee planters to weather the storm with less injury.

Although Dom Pedro had supported the abolition movement with moderation, his failure to oppose it or to arrange for reimbursement of slaveowners cost him the loyalty of the fazendeiros. The rift with the church had already alienated most of the clergy. The army had long felt that he had not bestowed upon it the honors and rewards which its services merited. Thus while still popular with the rank and file of Brazilians, Dom Pedro was left with only indifferent support by organized groups.

One of the ironies of the abolitionist movement was that the laws of 1871 and 1885 were both passed by conservative governments. It was known in advance in both cases that the laws must be passed, and the decision as to which party would be in power was the emperor's. Both of the major parties were deeply offended, the conservatives at having to officiate at their own execution and the liberals at being robbed of the fruit of their labors. A few of the most ardent abolitionists such as Nabuco, Barbosa, the brilliant mulatto engineer, André Rebouças, and the freedman orator, José do Patrocínio, were unconcerned over the political results. The republicans cheered emancipation, for they correctly regarded it as the first step toward the establishment of a federal republic.

After Abolition

FEDERALISM

Immediately after abolition had opened the floodgates for reform, the idea of federalism swept the country, championed by Rui Barbosa. Nabuco remained a staunch monarchist, and vainly tried to save the throne by the only possible remedy—the establishment of a federal empire. His suggestions were considered too bizarre for serious attention, and he won no support for the idea. Barbosa was less concerned with the type of government than with its federalism, and although he did not call himself a republican his writings gave the party some of its most effective arguments. Dom Pedro was not oblivious to the danger to the throne, but he merely rejoiced that at last the slaves had been freed.

At the time of abolition the Republican party was still numerically small and had no seats in the chamber of deputies. Most of the republicans, it appeared, were content to permit Dom Pedro to serve out his lifetime as emperor. Many persons who did not embrace republicanism were apprehensive about the succession passing to the emperor's oldest daughter, Dona Isabel. She seemed bigoted in matters of religion, had been outspoken in behalf of abolition though warned it would cost her a crown, and was married to a French prince who appeared aloof and condescending because he was slightly deaf and extremely shy.

END OF THE EMPIRE

The overthrow of Dom Pedro came as the culmination to factional disputes between civilians and the military for supremacy. The plot which led to his banishment began simply as an effort to oust a ministry which had chastised several army officers. Marshal Deodoro da Fonseca, acknowledged leader of the military clique, hoped to force a change in the ministry favorable to the army. The republican spokesman among the military, Benjamim Constant, a professor of mathematics at the military school and a positivist, became one of the engineers of the plot, and the goal was raised to a higher level. What started as a mere barracks revolt to unseat a ministry bagged bigger game by merely raising its sights.

The downfall of the empire in the face of the universal acclaim for its ruler has the outward appearance of a paradox. On the surface it did not appear that Latin America's most stable and democratic regime was in any danger. But the gradual shifting of economic power from the old fazendeiro class to new business groups employing free labor had splintered the pillar on which the monarchy leaned. The quarrel with the church, the grievances of the military, imagined and real, the very neutrality of the emperor toward political change, and the prospect of his being succeeded by an overly religious woman and her foreign-born husband left the monarchy with few ardent supporters and created an atmosphere in which a few companies of disgruntled troops could topple the throne. The empire had become merely a hollow shell with a polished exterior. The overthrow of the empire was accomplished by a fraction of the army, without opposition; the majority of Brazilians had no conception of what took place before their eyes and remained merely as bystanders.

The downfall of the empire was engineered in a simple fashion. The uprising against the ministry had been planned for November 20, 1889, but rumors that the government might arrest Deodoro caused precipitous action on November 15. The cabinet was seized. Dom Pedro came leisurely to the capital from Petrópolis to name a new ministry. By the time Dom Pedro arrived the republic had already been proclaimed. The advice and guidance of Benjamim Constant was primarily responsible for Deodoro's change of plan.

The empire of Dom Pedro II, pushed so ignominiously into the discard in 1889, had served Brazil well and probably deserved at least to die before its funeral was held. In the political development of Brazil it represented a successful effort at unification. Its success enabled the republic to emerge secure from the rocks and shoals of fragmentation and caudillism. Dom Pedro gave Brazil half a century of domestic peace and pride, and he balanced as best he could the two main forces organized into political parties. Brazilians enjoyed a fruitful apprenticeship in self-government unhampered by tyranny or censorship. Because of the unifying power of the monarchy, the republic inherited intact all of the area that had been Brazil.

THE REPUBLIC PROCLAIMED

On November 17 the royal family was unceremoniously embarked on a ship for Europe; Deodoro was extremely apprehensive lest the emperor's plight should precipitate civil war. A provisional government was created, dominated by the army but including many prominent civilians such as Barbosa. A federal republic was proclaimed, and this act was followed by a multitude of decrees aimed at introducing the new order; the electorate was enlarged, church and state were separated, and titles of nobility were abolished.

Recognition of the new regime was soon forthcoming from Latin America. Uruguay, Argentina, and Chile acknowledged the republic during the remaining months of 1889, and other Latin American nations followed their lead. The United States took similar action in January, 1890. France delayed recognition until June, and in the interim tried to negotiate a favorable settlement of an old boundary dispute between Brazil and French Guiana. The boundary problem was not immediately solved, but the principle of arbitration was accepted by both nations. Most European nations withheld recognition until Brazilian elections had taken place.

The republic inherited a number of additional boundary questions. In 1889 Argentina and the imperial government had agreed to submit the ancient dispute over Misiones territory to arbitration. After Argentine recognition had been accorded the provisional government, however, it attempted to display its gratitude by an overly generous division of the territory regardless of claims. In January, 1890, a treaty was negotiated in Montevideo, but public disapproval in Brazil over abandonment of both Portuguese and Brazilian gains reminded the government that foreign policy was not the place to exhibit its philanthropy, and the treaty was not ratified.

The financial organization of the new government was undertaken by versatile and energetic Rui Barbosa, who inherited the chaos and confusion stemming from the last days of the empire. His opponents blamed him for all of the financial ills of the republic, but impartial investigations have revealed his measures to be wise if not miracle-working. He did not remain long at the post, and his successor sought to solve the currency problem by the common resort to paper, ink, and the printing press. Before long a whirlwind of feverish speculation swept the country; when the wind settled many paper fortunes and Brazil's foreign credit were no more.

Domestic peace was frequently disturbed during the infancy of the republic. Civilian politicians chafed under the unaccustomed restraints imposed by military rule, and they devised ways to embarrass and discredit the government. Deodoro, long used to commanding, was neither patient nor restrained in the exercise of his authority. Monarchists were usually blamed for all disturbances even where none was remotely involved.

THE CONSTITUTION

One of the early acts of the provisional government was to begin drafting a constitution. Inspiration was drawn not only from the imperial constitution, but also from those of the United States, France, and Argentina. The power granted to the federal government to intervene in the affairs of states made the national regime potentially dictatorial, yet the same power had existed under the empire. When the delegates to the constituent assembly arrived to begin work, they were given a preliminary draft of the document. Attempts on the part of the assembly to make modest changes were coolly received by Deodoro. Church and state were separated, with the church retaining its property, and conflict between church and state disappeared.

Despite the many difficulties and the runaway emotions of the epoch, the constitution was promulgated in February, 1891. Its critics have pointed out various flaws and defects which they blame for its failure to function perfectly. The reasons, however, are to be found more in the ascendency of a small group of ambitious men than in the constitution itself. The hostility between the civil and military factions was an obvious obstacle to the success of any government. After 1930, however, the federalism of the republican constitution came to be regarded by many as an aberration.

When the constitution had been adopted a struggle for the presidency ensued between the strong-government group headed by Deodoro and the civilian faction supporting Dr. Prudente José de Morais Barros, a paulista republican. Deodoro won, for many Brazilians felt that the turbulent times required a firm hand at the helm of state. Marshal Floriano Peixoto was chosen vice-president. The choice was not that of the electorate, but of the constituent assembly.

The immediate tasks of the new government were concerned with pacifying the country and healing its economic ills. In neither of these labors did it win notable success. Unity was lacking; feeling between the civilian and military factions ran so high that the assembly spent eight months vainly trying to elect a presiding officer! Deodoro's martial impatience was not geared to accommodate such sloth, and he finally ended the bickering by abruptly dissolving both houses and assuming dictatorial powers. Although unconstitutional acts frequently did not cause even a slight murmur, on this occasion Deodoro faced a storm of protest so threatening that he resigned to avoid causing a civil war. He was succeeded by the enigmatic vice-president, Floriano Peixoto, who in the week preceding the overthrow of the empire had assured the ministry that it could count on the loyalty of the army.

FLORIANO PEIXOTO

Peixoto's political abilities proved considerably greater than those of his predecessor, and although his methods were no less drastic and often frankly unconstitutional, his regime gave the infant government the strength it needed for survival. The constitution called for a special election after Deodoro's resignation. Peixoto ignored it, declaring that the enemies of the republic were plotting to restore the monarchy. His most urgent problems, however, were raised not by monarchists but by vociferous military factions.

Civilian Rule

Within a few months a score of military revolts had broken out in Amazonas, Maranhão, Rio de Janeiro, Mato Grosso, São Paulo, and Rio Grande do Sul. Only a few of these insurrections were serious, for the opposition to the government remained scattered and disunited. The most formidable challenge to Peixoto's authority was the naval revolt of 1893; for the naval conspirators worked out plans for a joint campaign with the rebels of Rio Grande do Sul, and attempted to prevent munitions from reaching government forces from abroad. The standard of revolt was raised by Admiral Custódio José de Melo, whose main purpose was to depose the tyrannical Peixoto and end army domination of the government.

Peixoto met the naval revolt with unexpected courage and resourcefulness, coupled with deceit and subterfuge. To the chagrin of the navy the rebel army from the south failed to arrive. Greater disappointments were in store, for the foreign warships in Rio de Janeiro harbor, and particularly those of the United States, refused to recognize and permit the blockade since their governments had not accorded the rebels the status of belligerents. The navy was thus deprived of its only advantage, and its revolt was doomed to certain failure.

In the south the rebels of Rio Grande do Sul found the road to the capital effectively blocked at São Paulo. Advance turned into retreat, and retreat to rout. The collapse of the insurgents was followed by a period of terrorism in which suspected rebels and known enemies of the administration were hunted down and persecuted.

Relations with Portugal were strained to the breaking point because Portuguese warships granted asylum to some of the naval rebels who feared for their lives. On their way to Portugal the ships stopped at Buenos Aires, and some of their Brazilian refugees escaped. Peixoto was highly incensed, for he expected them to join his enemies in Rio Grande do Sul. He severed diplomatic relations with Portugal.

The terror continued until November 15, 1894, when Peixoto astonished his countrymen by unhesitatingly surrendering the presidency to his recently elected successor, the civilian Prudente de Morais. Many writers have flayed Peixoto for his tyranny and severity, but his firmness had given pause to frivolous conspirators and had held the country together during a critical epoch. As a result, he left the republic on a more solid basis than it had been when he assumed its leadership.

During the interval of national calm, 1895–96, the dispute with Argentina was settled by the arbitral award of President Grover Cleveland, whose decision was favorable to Brazil. The boundary disagreement with France over French Guiana was submitted to the arbitration of the Swiss government. Soon national attention was again claimed by purely domestic issues.

In 1897 a serious rift between Prudente and his vice-president, Victorino Pereira, appeared over questions of policy. Opponents of the government were quick to perceive and exploit an opportunity to harass the president. The government became so shaky that it swayed dangerously in every current, and was pushed to the brink of ruin by a few hundred fanatic *sertanejos* in the backcountry of Bahia.

The people of the *sertão* were always little touched by the affairs of coastal Brazil. In their arid and forbidding land life was hard and somber at best, and the melancholy sertanejos were receptive to miracle-workers. A large following had become fanatically attached to a mysterious, bizarre old man whose life had been spent wandering through the sertão. Known as Antônio Conselheiro, Anthony the Counselor, he had finally settled with his nondescript horde of bandits and would-be saints at an abandoned ranch called Canudos.

Rumors that the monarchists were stirring up the sertanejos prompted the governor of Bahia to send a small force to disperse the miserable rabble. Before this apparently simple task had been concluded the national government had seen its troops twice defeated, and had finally undertaken a full-scale campaign. The fighting was bitter, for the followers of Antônio Conselheiro literally fought to the death. Probably the most far-reaching effect of the wretched affair was that it inspired Euclides da Cunha to immortalize the episode in Brazil's most famous book—*Os sertões* (*Rebellion in the Backlands*).

Elsewhere the government's enemies were more real and no less determined. Numerous plots continued to be hatched, and in parliament the opposition to the president almost equaled his support. In November, 1897, an attempt to assassinate Prudente reacted in his favor. The assassins failed, and public opinion rallied to the president, making his final year in office comparatively peaceful. Factionalism and militarism were not dead, however, but merely quiescent.

The civilian presidents of the next decade faced fewer insurrections, but the financial problems of the country were only slightly less vexatious and perplexing. Foreign credit had flown in the hectic years of speculation and fluctuation after the empire's fall, and it was no simple matter to lure the timid bird back to a secure roost. Manuel Ferraz de Campos Sales, Prudente's successor, personally negotiated with London bankers while president-elect. The result of his efforts was the funding loan of 1898, by which the house of Rothschild provided £8,500,000 to the Brazilian government in exchange for bonds bearing 5 per cent interest.

The success of Campos Sales and his minister of finance, Joaquim Murtinho, in restoring financial order had a salutary effect upon the nation's economy. Domestic and foreign commerce increased, and industry showed signs of expansion.

Francisco de Paula Rodrigues Alves, the next president, followed financial policies similar to those of his predecessor. In addition, he pursued two worthwhile objectives of somewhat local interest—the improvement of sanitary conditions in the capital and the modernization of its port facilities. The transformation of Rio de Janeiro from a pest-ridden provincial city to a modern capital world famous for its beauty was the work of Lauro Müller, Pereira Passos, and Dr. Oswaldo Cruz. Yellow fever vanished and the incidence of bubonic plague and smallpox was drastically reduced. The improvement of Rio de Janeiro was a major triumph for the administration, for it gradually aided the material growth of the country in general. The benefits were soon extended to other parts of the nation, although many regions were left unchanged. Railroad building was promoted by Müller, and the exploitation of the nation's natural resources was given added stimulus. On the other hand, very little was achieved to improve the condition of the landless or of the urban laborers. More than 70 per cent of the nation's agricultural land was concentrated in large holdings.

In the field of diplomacy the republic carried on in the successful tradition of the empire. One of the greatest figures in the conduct of foreign affairs was the Baron of Rio Branco, whose father had been a distinguished minister of Dom Pedro. In 1902 Rio Branco became minister of foreign affairs, which office he held until 1912. He had an active part in the peaceful settlement of several boundary disputes, and in 1903 persuaded Bolivia to sell Acre territory to Brazil. One of his first official acts was to raise the Brazilian legation in Washington to the rank of embassy, and Joaquim Nabuco was sent as first Brazilian ambassador to the United States. In 1907 Rui Barbosa was representative of Brazil at the Second International Peace Conference at The Hague. Barbosa, by a magnificent display of erudition and humanitarianism, became one of the outstanding delegates at the conference and the acknowledged spokesman of the smaller nations. When the sessions closed Barbosa had won for his country the esteem of the major powers of Europe.

In 1909 the mineiro president, Dr. Afonso Augusto Moreira Pena, died in office, leaving his vice-president, Nilo Peçanha, to complete the term. Moreira Pena had continued the program of national development, and had paid particular attention to stabilizing the currency. The army and navy had been made more effective by the purchase of improved weapons and warships. The naval program revived Argentine fears of Brazilian aggression.

ARMY RESURGENCE

The election of 1910 was one of the most bitterly contested in the brief history of the republic. The most powerful political figure of the era was Pinheiro Machado, the caudillo of Rio Grande do Sul, who literally dictated the election of Marshal Hermes da Fonseca, nephew of the late Deodoro. Hermes had displayed modest administrative ability as war minister under Moreira Pena, but his strength lay more in the thwarted aspirations of the military and the conservatives who championed a return to military rule than in his political acumen.

The opposition joined in the formation of the *Civilista* party, and held the first democratically elected nominating convention in Brazilian political history. The choice for a presidential candidate was Rui Barbosa, the learned and eloquent Bahian, who campaigned in a vigorous and unprecedented manner. In his speeches he deplored the threat of militarism and the rule by cliques and factions. The outgoing president, Nilo Peçanha, gave his support to Hermes da Fonseca, and the government's intervention in the election was decisive.

Hermes' promise of a regime of order and justice was soon shattered by an epidemic of revolts, for the men who had placed the conservatives back in power were impatient for their rewards. Disaffection appeared once more in the navy, and for a time the government was unable to do more than yield to the demands made upon it.

The economic problems of the era were too complex for easy solution, for they were influenced by conditions and events beyond the borders of Brazil. Immigration was encouraged by the government, however, and the greater availability of labor made possible a rapid expansion of the railroads and some private enterprises. The coffee planters were soon confronted by the problem of overproduction, while the rubber boom of the previous twenty years ended in a dismal crash because of the competition from oriental rubber plantations.

Subsidies to save the coffee planters and rubber producers failed. They served merely to increase the national debt. A return to the expedient of printing unconvertible paper money was no more successful, and once more it was necessary to seek a funding loan in England. Dissatisfaction with the government's vacillating financial policies became violent, and as the election of 1914 approached, resentment against the machinations of Pinheiro Machado rose.

Under ordinary circumstances Pinheiro Machado might easily have succeeded to the presidency, for he was the choice of Hermes and controlled a strong bloc of his own. But he was identified too closely with the errors of the regime, and the paulistas and mineiros, who were accustomed to alternating the presidency between them, regarded him as an unscrupulous interloper. The conflict shaping up in Europe threatened to have a catastrophic effect on the Brazilian economy, especially if factionalism were intensified. Pinheiro was persuaded to withdraw from the race for the sake of domestic peace, and a compromise candidate was found in the vice-president, Wenceslau Braz Pereira Gomes, a mineiro who was not held responsible for or closely associated with the misfortunes of the administration.

The outlook for the government of Wenceslau Braz was not encouraging, for the problems raised by World War I were added to the usual domestic issues. The Brazilian economy staggered under the impact of the blockade and counter-blockade of the warring powers. Foreign trade, which usually provided the principal source of government revenue, was drastically reduced, and distress was universal.

A reduction of government expenditures helped bring a solution to the financial problems nearer, but the search for new sources of revenue to replace export duties failed. Once again the government returned to the time-honored resort of printing unconvertible paper money. The economic dislocation caused by the outbreak of the war proved temporary, for the Allies began purchasing vast quantities of processed foods from Brazil in 1916, and the economy quickly recovered.

DOMESTIC STRIFE

Political unrest added to the president's difficulties early in his regime, but the revolts were suppressed without undue excitement. Fears of sabotage and insurrection by the German settlements after Brazil entered the war on the side of the Allies led to an expansion of the president's wartime powers. Martial law was declared in supposed danger zones, and federal troops were stationed in strategic areas to maintain order. The anticipated uprisings did not materialize.

In the post-war election political compromises once more defeated the perennial candidate, Rui Barbosa, who was anathema to the army. In 1918 Rodrigues Alves was elected to a second term, but he died a few months after taking office. A special election was held, and the choice fell on Epitácio da Silva Pessoa of Paraíba, who had remained aloof from the partisan clashes between civilian and military factions, and who was distinguished as head of the Brazilian delegation to Versailles.

Pessoa irritated his military supporters by appointing civilian ministers of war and navy. Since the policies of these two men were not inspired by the military, they were criticized indiscriminately by the officer clique. Some militarists began to feel that the only way to secure what they regarded as their rightful place was through seizing the presidency by force.

Like many another Latin American nation in the early 1920's Brazil borrowed vast sums abroad, especially from the United States, for the purpose of promoting internal improvements. The administration was vigorously assailed by paulistas and mineiros for what seemed to them sheer extravagance. Discontent again became widespread, and the campaign for a successor to Pessoa found emotions high and tempers short.

The official candidate was Artur da Silva Bernardes, a mineiro. Nilo

Peçanha, who was now associated with disgruntled army officers and desperate office-seekers, announced his candidacy. Hermes da Fonseca cast his line into troubled waters in behalf of Peçanha, but came away empty-handed. After the election of Bernardes, Hermes and the Military Club of Rio de Janeiro began interfering more forcefully in political battles, even to the extent of countenancing insubordination in the army. Domestic peace once more hung in the balance.

As far as internal affairs were concerned Bernardes' administration was virtually one long military campaign. Factional quarrels and strife in the states led to an abusive use of the state of siege and of federal interventors, for Bernardes was determined to keep his enemies in check at all costs. In July, 1924, there occurred the most critical challenge to his authority when a revolt broke out in São Paulo. A state of siege was declared, and federal troops dispersed the rebels in less than a month's time.

While Bernardes had concentrated upon containing his political and military rivals, the long-inarticulate, destitute laborers of plantation and city had acquired champions at last. Brazilian radicals of varying hues, including a young army officer named Luís Carlos Prestes, who had turned to Marxism, began to capture the attention of the illiterate, impoverished masses. When the government belatedly became aware of these activities, federal troops drove Prestes and others into exile. The seeds which had been planted had fallen into earth made the more fertile by the severity of economic conditions and the lack of promise on the part of the administration. Thereafter the government was obliged at least to make some pretense of improving the lot of urban and rural laborers, although the statesmen of the Old Republic did little more than discuss the problems. Concentration of land ownership was one of the most acute causes of distress, but this delicate matter was carefully skirted.

In 1926, when Bernardes' term drew to a close, he avoided political strife by naming his successor from among the paulistas. His choice, Dr. Washington Luís Pereira de Sousa, was elected with little opposition.

The major concern of Washington Luís was coping with the insoluble problems brought on by the world-wide economic depression. The drastic drop in international trade had especially severe repercussions in Brazil, so great was the dependence upon foreign markets. As the demands for Brazilian coffee and sugar decreased abruptly, privation and distress spread over the land. Loans from the United States failed to stem the tide and the government faced imminent bankruptcy. The undue dependence upon import and export duties left the administration with few resources, but it did not seek to save itself by introducing other forms of taxation which would have been unpopular with the ruling class.

As his hectic term approached its end Washington Luís crowned his career with a political blunder that cost him the last days of his rule. He felt that only another paulista would carry to a successful conclusion the economic program he had begun. Tradition, however, demanded that his successor be a mineiro. Casting caution aside he ignored the claims of the mineiro heir-apparent, Antônio Carlos, and declared in favor of Júlio Prestes, governor of São Paulo.

The outraged mineiros immediately sought to learn the temper of opposition groups elsewhere, and to find a rival candidate they could sponsor. Their choice was enigmatic Getúlio Dorneles Vargas, governor of Rio Grande do Sul, and an outspoken critic of the administration. The *Aliança Liberal* was formed by uniting the opponents of the government to promote Vargas' candidacy.

Enthusiasm for the Aliança Liberal surged high during the campaign and election, but when the votes had been counted the government announced Júlio Prestes the victor. Vargas and his supporters did not conceal their conviction that he had been defrauded of the presidency, and prepared for revolt. In October, 1930, they seized government installations in Rio Grande do Sul. The march to Rio de Janeiro was quick and eventful. On November 3 Vargas picked up the reins of government hastily dropped in flight by Washington Luís. The individualistic, generally liberal, but ineffectual career of the Old Republic was a part of history. Its social and political morality were soon to be scoffed at by men who stood for socio-economic changes, and who placed greater emphasis on efficiency than on liberty.

SUGGESTED READING

C. Beals, *Porfirio Díaz, Dictator of Mexico,* New York, 1933.
M. Bernstein, *The Mexican Mining Industry, 1890–1950,* Albany, 1965.
G. Blanksten, *Ecuador: Constitutions and Caudillos,* Berkeley, 1951.
P.H. Box. *The Origins of the Paraguayan War,* Urbana, 1930.
F.R. Brandenburg, *The Making of Modern Mexico,* Englewood Cliffs, 1964.
A. Brenner, *The Wind that Swept Mexico,* New York, 1943.
E.L. Bridges, *The Uttermost Part of the Earth,* New York, 1949.
A.W. Bunkley, *The Life of Sarmiento,* Princeton, 1952.
W.H. Callcott, *Liberalism in Mexico, 1857–1929,* Palo Alto, 1931.
C.E. Chapman, *A History of the Cuban Republic,* New York, 1927.

J.D. Cockcroft, *Intellectual Precursors of the Mexican Revolution, 1900–1913*, Austin, 1968.

E.C. Corti, *Maximilian and Charlotte of Mexico*, 2 vols., New York, 1898.

I.J. Cox, *Nicaragua and the United States, 1909–1927*, Boston, 1927.

C.C. Cumberland, *Mexican Revolution: Genesis Under Madero*, Austin, 1952.

E. da Cunha, *Rebellion in the Backlands*, Chicago, 1943.

W.J. Dennis, *Tacna and Arica*, New Haven, 1931.

C. Gauld, *The Last Titan, Percival Farquhar, American Entrepreneur in Latin America*, Stanford, 1964.

R. Gilmore, *Caudillism and Militarism in Venezuela, 1810–1910*, Athens, Ohio, 1964.

C.W. Hackett, *The Mexican Revolution and the United States, 1910–1926*, Boston, 1926.

C.H. Haring, *Empire in Brazil*, Cambridge, Mass., 1958.

L.F. Hill, *Diplomatic Relations Between Brazil and the United States*, Durham, 1932.

M. Jefferson, *Peopling the Argentine Pampas*, New York, 1926.

F.A. Knapp, Jr., *Life of Sebastián Lerdo de Tejada, 1823–1889*, Austin, 1951.

C.J. Kolinski, *Independence or Death, The Story of the Paraguayan War*, Gainesville, 1965.

A.H. Luiggi, *65 Valiants*, Gainesville, 1965.

A. Marchant, *Viscount Mauá and the Empire of Brazil*, Berkeley, 1965.

M.C. Meyer, *Mexican Rebel, Pascual Orozco and the Mexican Revolution, 1910–1915*, Lincoln, 1967.

R.R. Miller, *For Science and National Glory, The Spanish Scientific Expedition to America, 1862–1866*, Norman, 1968.

C. Nabuco, *The Life of Joaquim Nabuco*, Stanford, 1950.

M.W. Nichols, *Sarmiento, A Chronicle of Inter-American Friendship*, Washington, 1940.

E. O'Shaughnessy, *A Diplomat's Wife in Mexico*, New York, 1916.

E.T. Parks, *Colombia and the United States, 1765–1934*, Durham, 1938.

D.M. Pletcher, *Rails, Mines, and Progress*, Ithaca, 1958.

R.E. Quirk, *The Mexican Revolution, 1914–1915*, Bloomington, 1960.

S.R. Ross, *Francisco I. Madero, Apostle of Mexican Democracy*, New York, 1955.

T. Rourke, *Gómez, Tyrant of the Andes*, new ed., New York, 1948.

C.W. Simmons, *Marshal Deodoro and the Fall of Dom Pedro II*, Durham, 1966.

W. Stewart, *Henry Meiggs, Yankee Pizarro*, Durham, 1946.

F. Tannenbaum, *The Mexican Agrarian Revolution*, New York, 1929.

M.C. Thornton, *The Church and Freemasonry in Brazil, 1872–1876*, Washington, 1948.

A. Tischendorf, *Great Britain and Mexico in the Era of Porfirio Díaz*, Durham, 1961.

M.I. Vanger, *José Batlle y Ordóñez of Uruguay*, Cambridge, Mass., 1963.

M.A. Watters, *A History of the Church in Venezuela, 1810–1920*, Chapel Hill, 1930.

S. Welles, *Naboth's Vineyard; The Dominican Republic, 1844–1924*, 2 vols., New York, 1928.

N.L. Whetten, *Rural Mexico*, Chicago, 1948.

M.W. Williams, *Dom Pedro the Magnanimous, Second Emperor of Brazil*, Chapel Hill, 1937.

G.S. Wise, *Caudillo: A Portrait of Antonio Guzmán Blanco*, New York, 1951.

J. Young, *The Brazilian Revolution of 1930 and the Aftermath*, New Brunswick, 1967.

III THE CONTEST FOR
HEGEMONY AND THE RISE
OF INDIGENOUS NATIONALISM

1 2

The Struggle for Economic Independence, 1930-60

> Fundamentally, subsidiaries of foreign industrial enterprises operate in Latin America not because they consider it a very protable area of investment—although it usually is—or because consumption in Latin America has enjoyed very brilliant prospects, but because through such operations they thus ensure the market for themselves, forestall possible competition from other countries and local industries, and even reduce their tax burden at home.*

Economic Collapse and Political Disillusionment

WORLD DEPRESSION

The great economic depression crept like a dense fog over the world in 1930. Its stifling dampness rapidly enveloped the countries of Latin America creating confusion and chaos. Old values were discredited and a deep unrest stirred among the population. Poverty and want, never strangers to most of the world's people, gnawed deeply into the vitals of society and stirred men to acts of desperation. In Europe vicious little men came forward with schemes to reshuffle the deck of social organization and thereby change the entire course of history. Seemingly the forces of liberal democracy had run their course and that course had ended in world economic collapse in which even the privileged few fared little better than the many who had waited in vain for the benefits of capitalist productivity to trickle down to them. The exponents of free enterprise and laissez-faire liberalism appeared baffled and helpless. They could only counsel patience until things righted themselves. But people would not wait.

* Víctor L. Urquidi, *The Challenge of Development in Latin America,* Frederick A. Praeger, New York, 1964, p. 104.

277

The desperation in Latin America spread extreme disillusionment, for it brought home to every nation its utter dependence upon economic forces over which it exercised little or no control. The difficulty had been glimpsed earlier during World War I when old trade lines were greatly disrupted by events in Europe, but readjustments were rendered relatively simple by tremendous expansion of the American market and by the orgy of reckless investment that characterized economic activity during the 1920's. Now no war could be blamed; the system itself seemed at fault. Now, as if by evil design, the value of Latin American exports suddenly declined nearly two-thirds. Agricultural and mineral surpluses piled up in the fields and warehouses, but almost no one wanted them at any price. At the same time the sources of foreign capital dried up and money became desperately scarce. The fine paved boulevards and great stone buildings constructed with borrowed funds during the reckless years of the 1920's stood empty and silent; they produced nothing but mounting interest charges. The anachronistic reliance of governments upon import and export duties for revenue left them bankrupt as ships stood idle at the wharves and goods could not be moved. Foreign and domestic obligations could not be met, and at the very moment when government expenditures were most urgently needed to stimulate recovery there were no funds to be spent. The loss of earnings from unemployment further restricted the already feeble purchasing power for manufactured goods. At no point did it seem possible to lay an arresting hand upon the downward spiral.

POLITICAL CHANGES

The almost immediate reaction to all these difficulties was a change in government. Old-style liberal regimes were overthrown in Argentina and Brazil. Confusion reigned in Chile since no one seemed able to establish a stable regime. In Peru the long-standing dictatorship of Leguía was overthrown and that of Gómez in Venezuela was threatened. In Colombia the Liberals won their first election in many years, and political unrest swept through Central America. In the years immediately following 1930 numerous political changes took place throughout Latin America, and on the whole the swing was toward the military dictators and away from both the conservative right and the liberal democratic left. Extreme left-wing groups were ominously active in Chile, Brazil, El Savador, and Mexico, but generally they were kept in check by the firm rule of the military and the more palatable nationalistic socialism that gradually emerged to resolve the problems of economic colonialism.

ECONOMIC NATIONALISM

In spite of the series of shifts from right to left and from left to right, certain fundamental changes in outlook soon became evident—changes indicating that the disturbances of the depression had been more than surface phenomena. They had roiled the waters deeply, and previously latent forces of nationalism now surged like a great wave across a continent and a half. In virtually every capital men turned with bitter indignation against all manifestations of foreign economic domination and sought some means of rebuilding a national economy less dependent on what transpired in the great manufacturing centers of Europe and the United States and in the financial marts of New York and London. In the same sweeping wave of change, the masses of the people came forward to assert their demands for a greater share in the national patrimony. Such demands, scarcely articulate in the sense of defined movements and programs, were nonetheless real as indicated by the increasing restlessness of urban labor, a rising interest in Indianist propaganda, and a growing fear that the seeds of Soviet communism were beginning to sprout in the fertile Latin American soil. Scholars throughout the hemisphere engaged in studies of the basic problems of their respective countries, and attention became increasingly focused on poor land distribution, idle land, illiteracy, inadequate production, outmoded methods, and particularly the almost total absence of nationally owned and operated industries. In those countries of sizable Indian populations, emphasis was given to the fact that many of these people still lived in the utmost ignorance amid filth, disease, and poverty, and that their tremendous contribution to the national entity had been neither appreciated nor permitted to attain its full potential. To act on these problems meant significant change in the role of government, for only by the exercise of governmental powers could any real change be brought about.

Ideological Competition

TREND TOWARD CONTROLLED ECONOMIES

The trend toward greater governmental activity in fields previously reserved for private initiative was world-wide. In the United States the Democratic party, under the leadership of Franklin Delano Roosevelt, gave birth to the New Deal, a tremendous program of governmental activities aimed at reviving the domestic economy and protecting the nation against future dangers of economic collapse. Major projects in the field of public works were coupled with large welfare outlays and the initiation of insurance and social security benefits to protect the working population from the economic disabilities of unemployment, physical handicap, and old age. Business was subjected to a high degree of regulation in matters of financing, trade practices, hours of work, and wage rates. Such measures were intended to strengthen the private enterprise system by giving it better balance and protecting it from internal abuse. In Europe government had long been more active in economic matters than in the Western Hemisphere, but now that activity was intensified. Italy had long boasted a form of state socialism involving close co-ordination between government and private economic life. The system, known as fascism, attempted in theory to convert the state into a vast holding company in which industry, labor, and the consuming public were all represented. From this was derived the corporate state concept in which the fundamental distinction between public and private activity tended to disappear and the state became the supreme concentration point of all activity, all loyalty, and all national energy. The idea was ideally adapted to Hitler's scheme for revitalizing Germany and converting that nation into a tremendous military machine to serve his purpose of European and perhaps world conquest. Thus the National Socialist or Nazi party, which came to power in 1933, placed the state above all other considerations and civil liberties and economic freedom quickly disappeared.

The statism of Soviet Russia had been in existence since the revolution in 1917, and in theory and practice it involved the almost total elimination of private rights and private property. The state and the Communist party became the only forms of social organization. These systems, fascism, nazism, and communism, differed markedly from the program of increased government activities in the United States, England, and other democratic nations where the role of the state was viewed only as aiding and providing a suitable environment for individual citizens to choose and pursue freely their own destinies. Indeed, nations imbued with democratic traditions and ideals tended to regard government as a necessary evil that posed a threat to individual liberty whenever it got too big or too active. Consequently, although there was a great deal of precedent for positive government controlling and regulating the economy, democratic countries moved in the direction of greater public authority reluctantly and with misgiving. Such issues were troubling the entire Western world at the same time they were presented in Latin America.

IMPERIAL COMPETITION

The opposing political and economic ideologies of Europe were somehow viewed as exportable commodities. In reality the systems mattered little to Germany and Italy, or even to Russia. Rather, each of these powers was attempting with purely imperialistic objectives to bring other nations under its domination or into its system of political and military alliances. The alleged possession of a system or ideology to solve economic and social ills was merely a propaganda device to ensnare the unwary. Nevertheless, at the very moment when the Latin American nations were deeply engrossed with the problem of recasting their economic and political institutions, skilled salesmen from across the seas pressed upon them the apparent advantages of close political, economic, and ideological ties with nazi, fascist, or communist powers. It would be naïve to state that such salesmen were without influence. Counter propaganda from the United States also had its effect.

REJECTION OF OUTSIDE INFLUENCE

Despite the intensive competition for influence over the course of Latin American development, however, most Latin American social and political movements after 1930 were basically nativist in origin and their genesis could be traced to ideals and events stemming from the rich history of the region. Wisely, not a single republic, in spite of severe economic stress, saw much to be gained by placing minority groups in concentration camps, murdering the well-to-do, or hitching its wagon to the imperialistic star of a European power bent on world domination. Indeed, it was obvious to most thinking Latin American leaders that, apart from trade, all that any of the various 'isms' had to offer them was a new and subservient colonial relationship to a European power. Part and parcel of the movement that swept Latin America during the third and fourth decades of the twentieth century was the rejection of colonialism in any guise, including that of economic domination. As a consequence, the economic power and aggressiveness of the United States, recently associated with the 'big stick,' a whole series of interventions in the Caribbean, and the financial manipulations of 'dollar diplomacy,' were viewed with much the same suspicion as were the economic and political machinations of Germany, Italy, Russia, and Spain. Many elements in the United States have continued to find this phenomenon quite incomprehensible.

That governments should undertake a more positive role in determining the course of national economic and social development involved no significant departure from Latin American tradition. Republican governments, by and large, apart from a running struggle with the church over their respective domains, had been generally inclined to leave to private initiative the establishment of industries and the extension of agriculture, as well as numerous welfare and philanthropic activities to alleviate poverty and care for the indigent. Such limitation of the field of government action was in marked contrast to the almost extreme paternalism of the Spanish and Portugese imperial systems. It marked a preoccupation with problems of government organization and political stability rather than serious convictions that the role of government should be minimized. Throughout the entire nineteenth century, liberal groups in nearly all countries had advocated all sorts of reforms that only government action could bring about, but conservative landholders, the church, and the military interests had demonstrated general satisfaction with things as they were, and drastic reform efforts had been blocked almost everywhere. Nevertheless, the empire precedent existed, and from time to time reform advocates, such as Juárez in Mexico, had attempted to utilize political power to remold the social structure.

MEXICO FOR THE MEXICANS

One of the most immediate precedents available to the neo-nationalists of the depression era was embodied in the Mexican Constitution of 1917 and the program of national regeneration espoused by the Revolutionary party. Mexico, during the long rule of Porfirio Díaz, had been as intensively and extensively subjected to foreign economic domination and exploitation as any country in the Western Hemisphere, and the social upheaval that followed Díaz' overthrow released the same passions and bitterness now brought to the surface fifteen years later all over the Latin American region by the great depression. The Mexican program itself had long roots reaching back to Juárez and Morelos in political aspiration, back to the colonial regime in reaffirmation of national ownership of subsoil rights and the social responsibilities attendant upon the ownership of property, and back to the pre-conquest era of both Spain and Mexico in regard to the communal landholding unit known as the *ejido*. On the other hand, the influence of European social philosophies was apparent in reforms designed to encourage, strengthen, and even coddle the labor movement and to take over and operate as government enterprises such key industries as railroads, financial institutions, and, eventually, petroleum production and distribution. At the same time, the old liberal anticlericalism of Lerdo and Juárez was manifested by a tremendous assault upon the church and its control of the educational system. The impact of the socialistic aspects of the program was most drastically felt during the six-year administration of President Lázaro Cárdenas from 1934 to 1940. Cárdenas' administration achieved the realization of a long-cherished objective when oil properties of foreign concessionaries were expropriated by the government in 1938. This act, affecting primarily United States and English interests, represented the boldest manifestation of the nationalist goal—Mexico for the Mexicans. Fifteen years later the same fundamental issues and objectives were involved in Bolivia's expropriation of foreign-owned tin mines.

BRAZIL'S NEW STATE

Brazil's most striking changes came during the long administration of Getúlio D. Vargas, 1930–45. The *Estado Novo* or New State which he proclaimed in 1937 brought intensified nationalism and centralism to replace the easy-going, liberal regime of the federalistic Old Republic. Vargas himself remained undoctrinaire, but elements of corporatism appeared in the new political system and the government stepped forward firmly in the economic sphere. Industrial development proceeded rapidly, stimulated by World War II, the demands of the Allies, and the encouragement of the United States. The Vargas program, like that of Perón and his predecessors in Argentina, was greatly aided by the artificial prosperity stemming from wartime conditions and the rebuilding of Europe after 1945.

PERÓN'S JUSTICIALISM

The Argentine solutions to the problems posed by world-wide depression and the evils of economic colonialism were slower to emerge than those of either Mexico or Brazil. For a time all that took place after the overthrow of Yrigoyen in 1930 was a return to the extreme conservatism of the military and landholding oligarchy. Some of the militarists, among whom Perón was a latecomer, found a degree of professional kinship with certain of the German Nazi clan, but this made them neither Nazis nor pro-German. Rather, it provided an opportunity for pulling Uncle Sam's beard as a gesture of defiance against the sheepherder proclivities evident in American foreign policy.

The real 'revolution' in Argentine affairs took place after 1945, when Juan Domingo Perón was firmly in the presidential saddle and his wife, 'Evita,' was holding the reins. A strong political following was built among the laboring classes, the *descamisados* or shirtless ones. Labor unions associated with the peronista movement were encouraged and patronized; independent unions were crushed. A vast amount of welfare and so-called social benefit legislation was enacted, all exacting a considerable toll from the businessman. Unofficial exactions were made on behalf of Evita's charities and 'cultural' projects, and penalties for non-compliance were often more severe than those applied in cases of tax evasion. More significant than all the exactions of a corrupt political machine, however, was the monopolization by the government of virtually all foreign trade, particularly the export of staple commodities. The government purchased grain and beef from producers at prices it had itself fixed, and then sold at the highest obtainable price in an extremely favorable sellers' market abroad. Slowly but steadily, important segments of the old landholding, cattle, and grain-raising aristocracy were brought to their knees. Proceeds of such practices were devoted to major works and development projects, expanded welfare activities, and military preparedness. At the same time the government supported the creation of an Argentine merchant marine and forced British owners to sell rail and street transportation systems.

In one sense the peronista movement, belatedly termed 'justicialism' and defined as a middle ground between capitalism and state socialism, represented the reassertion of porteño domination of the provinces, but the porteños in control were those who provided a circus for the masses. All this was not out of keeping with Argentine tradition, but it was the tradition of Rosas and not that of Mitre or Sarmiento. Like Rosas, Perón established regimentation in education, industry, and society. The press was subjected to rigid control and the defiant *La Prensa,* one of Latin America's great newspapers, was driven to the wall. As in the time of Rosas, the Eastern Republic of Uruguay soon became the home of thousands of Argentines in exile.

In Uruguay, swept by the same economic difficulties in the early 1930's, the government entered freely into business in competition with foreign companies, in large part to guarantee better marketing conditions for national producers. Banking and insurance became fields restricted to Uruguayan concerns, and while private enterprise was generally encouraged, the activities of aliens were closely supervised to prevent foreign domination. At the same time a considerable array of welfare and social security legislation was passed to benefit the working classes and public employees.

CHILE'S DEVELOPMENT CORPORATION

Chile went through a series of shifts in governmental policy ending during the mid-thirties with a liberal government supported by a parliamentary coalition in which the so-called radical and the genuine left-wing elements had a major influence. To cope with the problem of extreme depression in the mining and nitrate industries, Chile experimented with government-owned development corporations, but more than new organizational devices were needed to operate successfully an industry whose product had been replaced by a cheaper synthetic one manufactured elsewhere. However, in 1939 under the administration of President Pedro Aguirre Cerda, there was created the Corporación de Fomento (CORFO), the Chilean Development Corporation, an institution endowed with sweeping powers and government funds for the industrialization of Chile. This institution, created with a much broader purpose than earlier public business-type institutions, produced a national development plan and then set about executing it. Soon the Chilean government, through the Corporación de Fomento, was deeply involved in all types of productive enterprises from the generation of electricity to the construction of steel mills. It joined private and government capital in a host of ventures all designed to industrialize the nation, develop its natural resources, and relieve its dependence on foreign industry for the manufactured goods it consumed. In many respects the public business corporation was a great success, for through its efforts many new industries came into existence. The Chilean model was studied and copied by other Latin American nations, but none of them was able to emulate it. It represented a striking experiment in state enterprise, but it by no means solved Chile's major economic problems nor terminated the nation's dependence on world trade for its economic life.

APRISMO IN PERU

During the 1920's Peru had given birth to a nationalist and socialistic movement that had far more of an intellectual and philosophic basis than any other major Latin American reform movement of the modern era. A forerunner was Manuel González Prada, a distinguished literary figure and journalist who died in 1918 at the age of seventy. A confirmed socialist, González Prada enjoyed a wide acquaintanceship beyond the borders of Peru and exerted considerable influence over a number of rather able young intellectuals. One of these, José Carlos Mariátegui, associated himself for a time with another young man, Víctor Raúl Haya de la Torre, in the organization of a movement known as the *Alianza Popular Revolucionaria Americana,* better known as APRA. These two men produced a body of doctrine and a program aimed at building in Latin America a new social system socialist in economic outlook and Indianist in its emphasis on ancient cultural values and the evaluation of the Indian to a more significant position in national life. In part the movement was international, and organizational activities were carried on in Brazil, Argentina, and other countries beyond the borders of Peru. The appeal to the Andean Indian groups was understandable, but in such predominantly European areas as Argentina the popularity of the movement rested largely upon its promise of improving the living conditions of the laboring classes and particularly upon its violent anti-imperialist and anti-foreign doctrines.

Mariátegui and Haya de la Torre soon broke over basic philosophic issues and the former drifted over into complete conformity with the Communist party line. Haya de la Torre became the outstanding leader and champion of *aprismo* in the hemisphere. He traveled widely in Europe and established intellectual ties with British, German, and Russian socialists; but while he borrowed many concepts of social and economic organization from socialist and communist theorists, he did not become the tool or agent of European revolutionaries. Rather, he rejected many of the core ideas of socialist doctrine to view Indo-America as a unique and distinctive region requiring unique and distinctive solutions to its many problems. Haya de la Torre could identify no industrial proletariat in whom the powers of the state should be vested; industrialization was hardly begun yet in Latin America. Instead he saw the plight of the downtrodden rural Indian and a middle class struggling to come into existence. A class struggle within Latin America was meaningless when the true enemies of Indo-American development, as he saw them, were the foreign capitalists who wished to keep the region in a state of perpetual dependence as a source of raw materials, while keeping to themselves the benefits of industrialization. Consequently, his program was one of stimulating industry through government action and promoting better conditions for the Indians through land reform and co-operative agriculture. His political program, contrary to the monopolistic statism of Soviet communism, involved the preservation of intellectual freedom, individual liberties, and democratic institutions.

Aprismo attracted wide attention prior to 1930 even though numerically its supporters outside of Peru were few. In Peru, the organization's bid for political power came in 1931 when Haya de la Torre ran for the presidency. Although defeated, he continued his efforts to build a powerful organization by the cellular techniques and conspiratorial secrecy characteristic of socialist revolutionary activity. His efforts were bitterly opposed by Peruvian governments in power, and the apristas were for years denied recognition as a genuine Peruvian political party. At the same time, aprismo was under constant attack by the Soviet brand of communists for being deviationist and for refusing to acknowledge Russia as the source of true orthodoxy. As a consequence the two movements never united and instead drifted farther and farther apart. Indeed, during the critical years of the 1930's they largely canceled each other out as revolutionary forces in northern South America. Finally, in 1945, modified and tempered in doctrine and program by the long struggle for survival in Peru, apristas for a brief time shared power in a government that they had supported at the polls. In 1948 that government was overthrown by a military coup, aprismo was driven underground, and Haya de la Torre was forced to seek asylum in the Colombian embassy. There he remained for almost five years while a Peruvian guard patrolled the exits to prevent his escape. His plight became a subject of international controversy until safe conduct was finally guaranteed him and he was permitted to depart for Mexico.

Strong nationalist and quasi-socialistic movements stirred the currents of Latin American life. Individuals and parties espoused such causes in every country from the Rio Grande to Patagonia, but with widely varying degrees of success. During the war years and in the period just preceding, Nazi activities were a disturbing factor where large colonies of Germans were to be found. German agents were particularly active in southern Chile and in southern Brazil, as well as in Argentina, but few took them seriously. Communism constituted a far more dangerous and consistent threat because of its potential appeal to the ignorant and impoverished masses. Its agents were active in every country. It became a particularly persistent force among the miners of Chile, and it developed a small but highly articulate following in Brazil. Soviet agents, financed through the Russian embassy in Mexico City, plowed the fertile fields of Guatemalan ignorance and poverty. Latent hatreds of the United States and of American business concerns were exploited to the full, and communism spread openly and with official approval through the bureaucracy. Some visionaries and others who were but corrupt opportunists went along with the movement, but they were thrown out of office by revolution in 1954 and the conspiracy was driven underground. The revolution, strongly supported by American intelligence efforts, was initiated from Honduras and quickly put a conservative leader in charge of the government. Not so obvious was the steady penetration of the Cuban labor movement by communist agents and converts.

There existed in Latin America a genuine fear of communism, but that fear remained inchoate and was limited to relatively small groups, principally among the propertied class. It seldom fostered hysteria. Movements to overthrow governments by force were an old story, but one directed from outside the hemisphere seemed to run counter to the whole trend of Latin American development. Sophisticated officials and intellectuals, far more accustomed to dealing with the advocates of European brands of radicalism and revolutionary socialism than their conservative, business-minded counterparts in the United States, showed little fear of socialism, as such. Many accepted a pragmatic mixture of private and state ownership in the economic sphere and saw no incompatibility between them. They thought themselves able to separate social revolutionary doctrine from external imperialism. Little did they understand the Russian dedication to world-wide revolution or the subtle means employed to bring it about.

Equally important, perhaps, was the Latin American's ingrained cynicism concerning human motivation. Every man was viewed as seeking his own personal advantage. In this light the communist revolutionary was just as weak and corruptible as anyone else. The Latin would die for glory and honor, and personal martyrdom was not excluded, but only a fool Russian or a crazy German would sacrifice his life for the personal advantage of a Stalin or a Hitler. Regimentation was known to breed reaction, and in Latin America discipline was a scarce commodity. Individual freedom was highly prized. Much of the turbulence of Latin American political life stemmed from this philosophy. So did high absenteeism and indifferent application in mass production industry. But it was thought to provide an excellent insulation against a communist movement that required strict discipline and self-abnegation from its adherents. So it seemed until the rise of Fidel Castro.

ECONOMIC NATIONALISM

All the varied programs, reform movements, and assertions of economic nationalism occurring after 1930 had a pronounced effect on the climate of the Latin American economy. Foreign private capital was all but denied entry and existing investments were forcibly liquidated. Country after country enacted legislation restricting the freedom of monetary exchange and limiting the profits that could be taken out. Other laws required foreign corporations to employ high percentages of native personnel in every establishment; this was an effort to force the training of domestic technicians and to bring local talent into the management of important business activities. No such measures could immediately influence economic activity except in a negative and depressing way, for the conditions of investment were seemingly rendered less favorable and certainly less stable and certain. At the same time, efforts through diplomatic channels and at each international conference were made to secure adherence to the rule that foreign governments, particularly the United States, would have no right to intercede through exertion of political and diplomatic pressure on behalf of their nationals who became involved in business difficulties in Latin America. The only recourse of such people would thus be the same as that of local businessmen: resort to local courts in the respective country. In principle, at least, the rule was gradually accepted.

Virtually every Latin American nation was faced with the problem of trying to move in seemingly contradictory directions at the same time. Industrialization was sought while the necessary capital was discouraged from entering the region. Domestic as well as foreign business concerns were faced with a mass of social legislation that in some places fostered aggressive unionism and in others placed serious impediments in the path of traditional business operations. Progressive income taxation was tried to narrow the gap between extreme wealth and extreme poverty and to give the governments a more stable source of revenue than that provided by the traditional import and export duties, but such measures, if effectively enforced, would have had a depressing effect on private capital formation. In some countries the breaking up of large landed estates clearly disrupted agricultural enterprise at the very time that increased agricultural production was a major national goal. Behind many of these obvious contradictions, however, lay the firm conviction that old social and economic evils must be rooted out at whatever cost to make way for a more soundly based future development from which all elements in the nation would eventually benefit.

Economic independence for Latin America was only a relative possibility. As an absolute it was neither attainable nor desirable. Individual countries were confronted with insurmountable geographic and material limitations. Some must always be hewers of wood and carriers of water. The real struggle was not for independence as such, although greater independence was most certainly sought, but for a greater and more diversified productivity capable of sustaining on a higher level the growing Latin American population. Such objectives generally called for an increased volume of exports under conditions that would permit the accumulation of public and private development capital in Latin America. Thus the proceeds of export sales were to be spent in Latin America for domestically produced consumer goods and outside of Latin America for production goods to be installed in new Latin American industrial plants.

Domestically, increased production in every line was necessary to reduce the volume of consumables that had to be imported, particularly foodstuffs. Thus, as in every industrialization effort, the pleasures of immediate consumption were to be sacrificed in expectation of greater consumption at some future date. This is a difficult pattern to force on any people, but particularly so when there is a scarcity of domestic savings available for investment, when there is a strong proclivity to invest savings and profits in land or secondarily in commerce rather than in the production of new commodities; when there is a strong tendency toward conspicuous consumption on the part of the wealthy classes; and when a large portion of the export profits is owned by foreigners who have not the slightest intention of investing or even spending their earnings locally. From difficulties such as these, rather than from a desire to exploit the foreign investor, arose such regulatory devices as capital export limitations, exchange control, import licensing, domestic personnel employment requirements, and similar measures. More drastic steps were those limiting the nature and scope of foreign-owned enterprise and outright forced sale and expropriation.

Faced with such difficulties, a sizable number of the foreign investors, particularly those in the transport, utility, and mining fields, showed anything but enterprise and foresight. Many were definitely unco-operative. Their chief objective seemed to be the derivation of the maximum possible return while providing the absolute minimum of service with obsolete and inefficient equipment. A vicious circle was fostered by the claim that, given the risk of expropriation and further restrictive legislation, outlays for capital improvement or expansion could not be justified. No better path could have been chosen to increase the very risks that were feared. On the other hand, some foreign corporations, particularly those in the petroleum and fruit export business, were able to dispel much of the local antagonism toward them by energetic measures on behalf of their labor force, including such benefits as higher wages, housing projects, free medical service, and social security systems. Others joined confidently in the development program, investing capital in the production of manufactured goods for internal rather than external markets. Still others created new marketing facilities trading in domestic as well as imported goods. As foreign capital became increasingly interested in the Latin American domestic market, rather than in extracting products to be sold abroad, conditions more favorable to Latin American industrialization were created. Indeed, many economists believed that the key to the entire development effort was the creation of an effective domestic market based upon modern distribution and sales practices and a wider and greater distribution of purchasing power. New industries could not long survive if their products could not be sold in Latin America, for outside the region they could not yet compete with the more advanced industries of Europe, North America, and Japan. Indeed, many required protection and even subsidy in the domestic market. Eventually efforts were to be made to create common market areas among groups of Latin American countries.

THE LABOR MOVEMENT

In countries where economic nationalism flowered most luxuriantly and the government actively intervened to promote national development, few phases of national life escaped attention. Industrialization was viewed as but one of many factors in the total development process. Labor groups soon demanded recognition of rights equivalent to or even better than those accorded workers in Western Europe and the United States. Collective bargaining was fostered in Mexico, Chile, and Argentina, sometimes with such strong government support that it got out of hand. Most countries made some attempt to protect the worker by wage and hour laws, severance pay rights, and job and pay protection for women before and immediately after childbirth. Generally, however, the administrative machinery proved hopelessly ineffective in carrying out the legal intent. Growth of the labor movement was far from free; it was inextricably involved with politics. While some governments promoted rapid labor organizations, the majority permitted unionism only under rigorous controls. Consequently, many so-called unions were nothing more than mutual benefit societies, and efforts to convert them into genuine trade union organizations were considered communistic and were vigorously opposed by both government and management. As appendages of political organizations, unions were torn with all the schisms and divisions of partisan activity responsible leadership was prevented from developing, and unions were distracted from proper goals and their efforts dissipated. In extreme cases unions were made completely subservient to the government, and labor's strength in such cases was used for ends not at all in keeping with the desires of workingmen.

By and large, the most neglected group in Latin America remained the large body of agricultural workers. Many still lived on a purely subsistence basis on plots of land belonging to great hacendados who utilized their services for two or three months during the year in harvest season. This was generally the case in the great coffee-growing regions of Central America and in the coffee regions of Brazil and Colombia. Tenant farming became increasingly prevalent in the northern pampas region of Argentina where the high cost of land made individual farm ownership economically prohibitive except for the wealthy landholder whose fortune dated back to earlier days. Share-cropping remained common throughout all of Latin America. In no country were the various benefits available to industrial workers extended to the small farmers or the agricultural workers.

LAND REFORM

Land reform was a constant rallying point for political reformers, particularly those concerned with the status of the Indian. Only in a few countries was anything done to bring it about. Mexico's program to break up the large estates and to foster communal agricultural colonies financed by government loans was by far the most outstanding, but though it achieved a social goal, it failed as an economic measure. Everywhere land reform was fought by the large agriculturalists and great estate owners, even though much of their land may have been idle.

Merely breaking up the large estates and dividing the land into small plots is no answer, for this usually means greatly reduced production. Unless the grants of land are accompanied by low-cost credit, equipment, seeds, and other necessities, the new proprietors will live at a subsistence level, and will not produce anything for sale in the cities or for export.

More important than land tenure is land use, intensive cultivation of the arable land. If the land is to be made as productive as possible, it means the use of modern equipment and techniques, and these are too expensive for small farmers. But if the land is cultivated intensively and agricultural labor is paid a living wage, who owns the land is not as serious a factor as it would be otherwise. A decent wage for agricultural labor would greatly expand the domestic market, and make various industries profitable.

Co-operative agricultural improvement programs financed jointly by the various governments and the *servicios* of the Institute of Inter-American Affairs, then an agency of the United States government, in some areas introduced better farming techniques and improved crop strains. Emphasis, however, was generally on experimentation, to the exclusion of educational extension programs; and even in the few cases where extension was emphasized the programs scarcely scratched the surface of a tremendous need. More successful, perhaps, was the work of the Rockefeller Foundation in its program to introduce highly productive hybrid corn types in Mexico and, subsequently, in Colombia. Everywhere, however, the plight of the small farmer was desperate, his ignorance abysmal, and the effort to assist him inadequate. It was small wonder that agricultural productivity, except with certain specialized crops destined primarily for export, was very low.

Discussion of industrial possibilities and progress is significant, but it must not becloud the fact that all of Latin America remained predominantly agricultural, with the great majority of its population living in small villages in the rural areas. It was estimated that 65 per cent of all South Americans were directly dependent upon agriculture for their livelihood, and the percentage can scarcely have been lower in Central America, the Caribbean islands, and Mexico. Of those employed in agriculture only a small portion were concerned with the production of the great export crops: wheat, coffee, bananas, cacao, sugar, and beef. Even in Guatemala, where coffee and bananas accounted for 90 per cent of the country's exports, three times as much acreage was devoted to growing corn and beans for local consumption than was used for production of the export crops. In Bolivia and Chile, where minerals were the principal exports, far more than half of the populations derived a living from agriculture rather than from mining and its subsidiary activities. Only in a few cases, such as Puerto Rico and Cuba, was the general population heavily dependent upon imports for basic dietary requirements.

ILLITERACY

Other basic problems were encountered in the fields of education and health. Illiteracy was an ever-present, pernicious condition in all of Latin America with the exception of two or three countries such as Argentina, Uruguay, and Costa Rica. Vigorous anti-illiteracy programs were conducted in nearly all countries, and tremendous strides were made in extending elementary education even in rural areas. But these steps barely touched the real problem. The content of the educational program needed to develop not only the simple abilities of reading and writing, which are the mere tools of greater achievement, but it needed also to include the basic knowledge of commonplace phenomena that would enable the individual to adapt himself to and utilize the tremendous achievements of a modern technological civilization. Industrialization required this in order to develop a skilled labor force; it was equally essential in any large-scale improvement of agricultural practices. It was precisely for this reason that community education programs in Mexico and Puerto Rico placed time-honored academic subjects lower on the scale of importance than such matters as personal hygiene, homemaking, agriculture, and rudimentary mechanics.

HEALTH

In the same sense, health remained a tremendously important factor in national development, completely apart from the humanitarian factors involved. The Latin American loss in human productivity from undernourishment and disease was beyond measure. Again, medical and nursing professions were woefully understaffed and highly concentrated in the larger cities. A large-scale public health program was required in nearly every country to make a serious impression on the problem. Again, the Institute of Inter-American Affairs was active in this field, as was the World Health Organization of the United Nations, but funds were insufficient and other needs competed with equal force for the limited amounts that were available. Nevertheless, major progress was made in the elimination of malaria, and yellow fever was virtually eradicated except in remote regions of the upper Amazon basin. The same countries that were most energetic in effecting other social and economic reforms gave most attention to creating government health and social welfare programs emphasizing medical care.

Inadequate housing was an obvious and contributory factor in health and educational deficiencies. Consequently, public housing on a mass scale became a major platform in nationalist reform programs all over Latin America. In spite of significant efforts in a number of countries, the vast housing complexes that sprang up around major cities all over the region failed to keep pace with the burgeoning population. Crudely constructed shacks made of boxes and crates, tin sheets, and tarpaper were built by squatters on any available land in and around the growing cities, and the crowded slums they formed housed far more people than the public housing structures erected by the governments. This situation became increasingly acute toward the end of the 1950's. Private effort could not begin to cope with a problem of such magnitude and in which there was so little prospect of profit, but it became increasingly clear that even government programs were hopelessly ineffectual.

Economic Improvement

GRADUAL RECOVERY

Few measures taken by Latin American governments along the lines of progressive nationalism and moderate state socialism following the many revolutions of the early 1930's had much immediate effect in improving economic conditions. Nevertheless, economic conditions in Latin America gradually improved, as a result of general world recovery, in some cases faster than in the United States. Influences from outside the hemisphere predominated, particularly the tremendous economic recovery of Western Europe under the stimulus of German war preparations. Raw materials again came into demand, and European purchasers turned to Latin America for them. The reviving German economy needed markets for its export industries, and goods were poured into Latin America under a whole series of barter agreements. Such measures, restrictive of free international commerce, were denounced by the United States; but they were clearly beneficial to the participating countries. Barter trade was better than no trade. Soon Germany had assumed a major role in the foreign commerce of Latin America. By 1938 it was supplying 16 per cent of Latin America's imports and taking 11 per cent of its exports. In the same year Great Britain provided only 12 per cent of Latin America's imports, but it accounted for 19 per cent of its exports. The United States, taking 33 per cent of Latin American exports and providing the same percentage of imports, continued to dominate the total trade picture as it had for many years. Italy and Japan were also active in the Latin American market, but to a much smaller extent.

With the outbreak of World War II trade boomed to tremendous proportions, even though the export market on the European continent was lost, for the Allied powers quickly absorbed the goods that could no longer be shipped to Germany, France, Italy, and the northern countries. Some goods continued to reach Germany through Spain, however. At the same time, a flight of investments from Europe poured funds into principal Latin American capitals, particularly Buenos Aires. A large part of such funds was held in idle cash, but substantial amounts became available for local investment. In Brazil, and to a lesser extent in certain other countries, mutual defense arrangements with the United States brought extensive development of military installations, large payrolls in affected locations, and numerous subsidiary benefits of a commercial nature. Soon nearly every Latin American nation had piled up a substantial dollar balance which for the time being could not be spent owing to the shortage of manufactured goods during the war years. Thus, in Latin America recovery merged quickly into a form of prosperity that encouraged the storing up of reserves to carry over into the readjustment period that was certain to follow once international peace was re-established.

READJUSTMENT

Peace in 1945 did bring readjustment, but owing to continued prosperity in the United States and the tremendous effort to foster European recovery, the readjustment was not nearly as drastic as many had feared. It was a disappointing period for Latin America, however. Capital goods, with which many of the American republics had hoped to promote their own industrialization after the war, remained unobtainable or so high-priced as to discourage their purchase. Gradually the pressure for consumer goods ate up the accumulated reserves while economic reconstruction as a concern of the United States government seemed to bear only a European tag. Opportunities slipped away, and growing disappointment and disillusionment burst forth in a wave of vehement protest at the 1948 Inter-American Conference in Bogotá. During the period of the New Deal and the war years that followed, the majority of the Latin American countries had been drawn rather close to the United States as a consequence of her 'Good Neighbor' policy. Although no firm commitments were made, many hopeful leaders in the American republics had come to expect that after the war the United States, by granting governmental credit and trade priorities on production goods, would make a significant contribution toward the industrial and social development of its southern neighbors. The seemingly more urgent demands for assistance in Europe and Asia, however, precluded all but a few token manifestations of American interest in Latin American economic development.

Some areas of Latin America were stimulated to new economic activity by Sears, Roebuck, and Company, which began its Latin American enterprise in 1942 with a store in la Habana, and in 1947 with another in Mexico City. In 1949 Sears' first store in South America was opened in Rio de Janeiro; others were established in Caracas, 1950, in Bogotá, 1953, and in Lima, 1955. In each case local industries were organized to provide sources of supply, even though this had not been the company's original plan. The company found it satisfactory to arrange partnerships with local suppliers and to train natives for jobs at all levels, including managerial. Of its more than 500 employees in South America in 1960, fewer than 50 were from the United States. The Sears stores have had a far-reaching impact on manufacturing and marketing practices wherever they have located.

PREFERENCE FOR GOVERNMENT LOANS

It might appear that the countries of Latin America had done an about-face with respect to their views on foreign investment and that once again the alien capitalist was welcome. On the contrary, what was sought after World War II was investment on an entirely different basis than that which characterized the activities of foreign companies prior to 1930;

inter-governmental loans were requested. That is, the modernization and industrialization effort was to be made primarily under governmental auspices in nearly every country, and the necessary funds were desired from government lending agencies in the United States such as the Export-Import Bank. After formation of the United Nations organization and creation of the International Bank for Reconstruction and Development, more commonly known as the World Bank, the latter agency became the chief source of developmental credit for Latin America. In most countries the private foreign investor continued to be viewed with suspicion and distrust. As the United States government felt its lending resources strained to the utmost, however, primary effort involving both loans and outright grants was channeled into those areas immediately menaced by communistic Soviet imperialism. Latin Americans were advised to review their thinking and their policies with respect to admitting and encouraging private capital. With the advent of a Republican administration to power in 1952, the possibility of the United States financially supporting government-owned industry or even major developmental public works projects declined appreciably. Republican policy, expressed repeatedly but subtly, when stripped of verbiage informed Latin Americans that they could either accept private capital for private development or do without.

In 1948 the Latin American nations, over American opposition, persuaded the U.N. to set up an agency, the Economic Committee for Latin America (ECLA), to study economic problems and recommend measures to be taken. Under the Argentine economist Dr. Raul Prebisch, ECLA assembled mountains of data and made many recommendations, few of which were actually carried out.

In 1958 President Juscelino Kubitschek of Brazil proposed a solution to Latin American economic problems by a pooling of resources and the creation of an Inter-American Bank. Its purpose, as he saw it, would be to stimulate and assist economic development and the general raising of living standards. American officials agreed, though without any expression of enthusiasm, to support the creation of the lending agency as Kubitschek visualized it, but they had a far different concept of the amounts of money that the United States should or could provide. The Inter-American Development Bank was established the next year. Soon the United States government's concern over Castro's Cuba and its relationship to the USSR had become so intense that it was willing to reconsider its contributions. The bank's funds were greatly enlarged as a result, partly as an answer to those who had accused the United States of neglecting Latin America in favor of Europe and Asia, and partly in an attempt to apply a sovereign remedy to the causes of communism in Latin America.

In the meantime, all was not going well with the economies of the American republics. Growing consumer demands far outstripped official efforts to control imports and keep international payments in balance. The currencies of Chile, Brazil, and Mexico declined steadily on the international market. Other countries saw their currencies fluctuate erratically. A few nations, such as Venezuela with its tremendous oil exports and El Salvador with its coffee crop, continued to enjoy dollar surpluses while investing sizable amounts in national development programs through both private and governmental channels. Argentina, though short of dollars, enjoyed a favorable sterling balance as a result of its exports of foodstuffs to Great Britain. It was even able to extend credits to Paraguay and Bolivia.

In general, the major nations of Latin America accomplished a great deal in their struggle to raise the levels of national productivity and achieve some degree of economic independence. They were seriously hampered by the lack of adequate managerial skills, by obsolete and ineffective administrative practices in government and in public corporations, by much dreaming and little sound planning, and by social traditions that hampered the mobilization of domestic capital and that continued to discourage able young men from entering into business and commercial activity. Even the skilled trades were regarded as menial. Change was demanded on the one hand, while on the other an undying effort was made to preserve the status quo. The result was often the form of change without its substance. Great pride was shown in national trade schools whose benefits were available to only a handful of students. New enterprises provided with the most modern equipment functioned at a level of efficiency that hardly justified their existence; their products often could not compete even in the domestic market with those of foreign manufacturers. Modern and beautiful cities hid from the casual observer the most wretched of urban and rural slums, and the glittering Cadillacs of the hacendados told nothing of the miserable peonage of the agricultural worker.

In spite of the many contradictions and sharp contrasts—contrasts inevitable in a civilization boasting the gadgetry of the twentieth century and the social organization of the nineteenth—tremendous changes have taken place in all of Latin America since 1930. Where a moderate degree of industrialization came, as it did to Mexico, Brazil, Chile, Peru, Argentina, Venezuela, and Puerto Rico, it brought into being new economic and political classes. These classes challenged the ancient social order, and their gradually increasing purchasing power provided great hope for a market that would enable the industrialization programs to succeed. Middle-class urban attitudes began to break down the powerful ties of the patriarchal family, and women increasingly stepped from the stultifying seclusion of the servant-operated home into useful employment in commerce, industry, and government. New and vigorous leadership was injected into economic and political life, a leadership fired with an intensive nationalism that gradually transcended the stereotypes of the ancient caste-ridden social system.

Cultural Development

Some of the most satisfying consequences of the great changes emerging in Latin America are to be found not in new factories, new highways, greater agricultural production, or in higher levels of consumer purchases; rather they are artistic, literary, and aesthetic in character. Few artists of the modern era have received such universal acclaim as José Clemente Orozco and Diego Rivera of Mexico, the former for his depth of feeling and portrayal of abstractions through vivid symbolism, and the latter for impressionism with a social revolutionary—even communistic—punch. Both men were products of the Mexican revolution and its nationalistic, reformist, and Indianist spirit. In architecture, extreme modernism in design has characterized the new spirit of progress. It is particularly to be noted in São Paulo, Brazil, and in Mexico City, where huge office buildings displayed story upon story of glass even as the United Nations building was being erected in New York City. Residential structures throughout the hemisphere, but particularly in the Caribbean area, reveal a remarkable appreciation for functional beauty ideally adapted to informal tropical living. Conventionalists have been prone to criticize much of the modern Latin American architectural efforts as being garish and in poor taste, and certainly utility often has been too little considered or sacrificed for effect. Nevertheless, much of it is truly indigenous, original, and a faithful expression of the modern nationalistic spirit, even the flaws of poor planning and stark contradiction.

BRAZILIAN MODERNISM

In February, 1922, "The Modern Art Week Exhibition" was held in São Paulo. It represented the culmination of efforts to break with tradition in art and literature, and it was the poets who took the lead in establishing a totally new artistic attitude. The forces that produced the explosive week had been building since the last days of the empire, and were best reflected in the work of Negro poet João da Cruz Costa, whose short and tragic life ended in 1898. It was not until 1920 that young Modernist writers found in Cruz Costa's verse what they were groping for and made him their hero. The man who did most to arouse writers and artists and turn them to Modernism was Oswald de Andrade, who urged them to find new inspiration.

At the same time Victor Brecheret and other young sculptors were breaking with the past and striking out creatively and with great originality in new directions. Anita Malfatti was doing the same in her painting. None of the early Modernists was well-received by most of his contemporaries. Anita Malfatti's paintings were scorned and criticized until she lost confidence in her work, but the tumult aroused many to her defense, and she became known as the 'awakener of the Modernist Movement.'

Above all the Modernists wished to create, in the language of Brazilians and liberated from the confining rules of Portuguese grammar, truly native expression. The one word that came closest to describing their basic sentiment was 'freedom.' The movement passed through several phases. The first 'destructive' phase was from 1922–30; the 'serious and socially concerned' phase, 1930–40; the 'aesthetically formal,' 1940–50; and the 'Concretist experimental' phase, 1950–60. The movement seemed on the verge of dying out at times, but it always revived.

In the field of classical music, modern Latin America has displayed little originality. But to stop with such a statement would indeed be absurd. Perhaps no other area of the world has had such a tremendous impact in the realm of modern popular music as has Latin America. Mambos, rhumbas, tangos, boleros, and sambas from the American republics have captivated the dancing feet of millions from New York to Singapore. The plaintive *canción ranchera* of Mexico and the rhythmic calypso of the Caribbean islands are wonderful examples of a spontaneous folk music that the modern radio and phonograph have carried far beyond its locale of origin. It was through such media that the spirit of modern Latin America contacted and influenced the average citizen in other parts of the world.

In 1960 there was no doubt that the American republics contained within their midst rising forces that were dynamic, virile, and potentially capable of solving the difficult problems with which they were faced. Latin America remained one of the greatest areas of racial fusion known to the modern world. The process of amalgamation was necessarily slow and even painful at times, but the synthesis began to emerge. Latin American states revealed themselves as a group of high-spirited and proud nations struggling to achieve greater national unity based on regional cultural, economic, and political self-sufficiency. They were striving to escape the foils of anachronistic institutions and to resolve their problems through a pragmatic and rational approach that avoided the extremes of dogmatism and safeguarded the freedom and dignity of the individual. The Latin Americans were in the process of building a culture which in every way they could call their own. And in February of 1960, in the Treaty of Montevideo, Argentina, Brazil, Chile, Mexico, Paraguay, Peru, and Uruguay created the Latin American Free Trade Area (LAFTA) in order to promote commerce and economic development by reducing tariffs and by stimulating intra-regional exchange. In this way they hoped to create a genuine Latin American economy over which they could exercise a substantial measure of control.

13

Mexico: A Study in Dynamics

The balanced approach, to which Mexico owes so much of its recent
stability and spectacular prosperity, can be quickly sketched. In it agriculture has a full partnership with industry.*

Toward Political Stability

The Mexico of 1930 had advanced far beyond the chaotic society that
spawned Iturbide and Santa Anna, yet it was only on the threshold of its
greatest era of progress. One need only recall the agonizing trials of Morelos and Juárez, the selfish machinations of Santa Anna, and the suffocating
rule of Porfirio Díaz to appreciate fully the remarkable changes in Mexican life since 1910, and particularly since 1930. It is against this somber
background that the Mexico of 1930 to 1960 must be viewed. It is not appropriate merely to catalog areas still needing improvement. The story of
modern Mexico is one of remarkable achievement in the face of overwhelming obstacles, not the least of which was a tradition of cavalier military intervention in politics. What is important is how far Mexico has
come since independence, not how far she may yet have to go.

THE OFFICIAL PARTY

Political life improved enormously after 1930. In the interval between the
assassination of Álvaro Obregón and the accession of Lázaro Cárdenas in
1934, Plutarco Elías Calles, who had become wealthy and conservative,
ruled the country through three presidents, Emilio Portes Gil, Pascual
Ortiz Rubio, and Abelardo Rodríguez. More important, however, was the

* Howard F. Cline, *Mexico, Revolution to Evolution: 1940–1960*, Oxford University Press, London, for the Royal Institute of International Affairs, 1963, p. 233.

304

creation of an official political party to cope with the crisis caused by Obregón's assassination. The new party, the *Partido Nacional Revolucionario* (PNR), was a loose coalition of regional chiefs under Calles, the *jefe máximo*. Calles astutely undermined the regional bosses and increased the authority of the new party. Though it was only an informal organization, it proved effective in maintaining power over the nation.

LÁZARO CÁRDENAS

To many Mexicans who still believed in the unfulfilled aims of the Revolution there was a feeling of betrayal, and revolutionary sentiment grew too powerful to be safely ignored by Calles and his friends living on what was called the 'Street of the Forty Thieves' in Cuernavaca. Counter-activity to Calles became dangerously strong, and it was necessary for him to pick a candidate who would appear to satisfy demands for fulfilling the goals of the PNR yet who would be manageable rather than independent of Calles. While the PNR drew up its Six Year Plan to implement the revolutionary goals, Calles chose General Lázaro Cárdenas to represent him in the presidency.

Even during the presidential campaign it appeared that Calles might have misjudged his man, for Cárdenas campaigned as if his opponents actually had a chance to defeat him. He visited remote regions never seen before by a presidential candidate. His travels gave him a feeling for longstanding regional problems, and what was perhaps equally important, enabled rural Mexicans to talk to their future president and to become acquainted with a name other than that of Calles. Cárdenas was, in fact, campaigning against Calles, for until the jefe máximo could be dethroned there was no prospect of instituting genuine reforms. Cárdenas' activity during the campaign was part of his astute program for winning control of the country from Calles.

Two of the most powerful of the anti-callistas were Narciso Bassols and Vicente Lombardo Toledano, who prepared the way for the Cárdenas program by reorganizing education and labor. Bassols inaugurated a program of education aimed at instilling a new, socialistic attitude toward government and property. He and his system were bitterly denounced as atheistic, and the life of the rural schoolteacher became perilous.

In less than two years after taking office, Cárdenas had skillfully drawn to himself the main clusters of power, and was ready for the crucial test with Calles. The callistas had until then frustrated his efforts by various acts, including an attempt to stir up a church revolt by persecutions of Catholics. In the contest Cárdenas proved abler than his rival. He organized the PNR and brought it under his control; he increased the pay of enlisted men in the army, so that they looked to the president for betterment rather than to the generals; and he redistributed more land to the peasants than had been done in the entire period before 1934. Lombardo Toledano's new labor organization, the CTM, replaced the nearly defunct CROM of Morones, and gave Cárdenas powerful support.

By April, 1936, Cárdenas was ready to challenge Calles and Morones, and the two were sent by airplane to Texas, the traditional route of political exiles. After this dramatic political achievement Cárdenas governed Mexico without a serious rival, his power resting firmly on labor, the agricultural peasantry, and the army, no one of which was allowed to prevail over the others. The method of divide and rule was traditional in Mexico, but the Cárdenas regime was unique in its diminished reliance on regional chiefs and its efforts to create dependence upon the government and the party rather than on individual leaders.

PRM

In his reorganization of the official party Cárdenas sought to eliminate vestiges of callista power and to orient it toward carrying out the Revolution's major goals. Four functional 'sectors' replaced the regional chiefs: the military, labor, agrarian, and a 'popular' sector. Co-ordination was achieved at local, state, and national levels by means of committees representing the four sectors. The party, renamed the *Partido de la Revolución Mexicana* (PRM), was now far more representative of a consensus of the nation's main interest groups than it had been previously. All offices were apportioned before elections, and in each case all four sectors supported the party's candidate regardless of the sector he represented or the office he sought. This was a departure from earlier custom, when men of one 'corporation' supported only their own candidates. Now elective offices at all levels were divided among the four sectors prior to elections. Although committees selected the candidates, the president, as head of the party, had the last word as to who was to run. The National Executive Committee had already heard the opinions of state and local party groups, and it advised the president. Because of this centralization of political activity, the regional bosses lost control of the groups within their own domains.

Apprehensive of the military because of its history of intervention in politics, Cárdenas created two potential rivals to the army—the *Confederación Trabajadora Mexicana* (CTM), a nationwide labor union, and the *Confederación Nacional de Campesinos* (CNC), a similar organization of rural workers. Each formed a potential militia, and Cárdenas kept control by skillfully preventing the two from uniting.

As head of the party, the president mediated or decided issues between the sectors. Even though the losers might regard his actions as arbitrary and inimical to their interests, they did not often bolt the party. To do so would have cost them the well-known advantages of belonging, and might have brought on some form of reprisal. The PRM did not ignore the views of the groups that composed it, however, and it functioned smoothly in comparison to earlier political organizations.

In 1945, during the presidency of Manuel Ávila Camacho, the Revolution was 'institutionalized.' The official party was changed once more, to the *Partido Revolucionario Institucional* (PRI). The framework introduced by Cárdenas was retained with one very significant exception—the military sector was eliminated. Army officers with political ambitions were not excluded, but they had to work through one of the elements of the 'popular' sector.

The number of interest groups embraced within the party increased after 1945, and it was decentralized somewhat by giving the state units greater authority. More and more people began to participate in politics, and the party became increasingly responsive to public opinion. The president remained the titular head of the party, but his rule was no longer absolute. His main task was balancing interests, settling disputes, and preventing interruptions of the development program. The ex-presidents formed an unofficial nominating committee for the party's presidential candidate.

The PRI extended party representation to most of the country, and the many diverse and dissimilar elements within a sector meant that a spirit of compromise developed of necessity. Only the church, industrialists, bankers, and great hacendados did not have representation in any sector. As a result, any or all of them occasionally supported opposition parties.

The PRI was successful both in winning elections and in governing Mexico. It took into account the opposition parties and whatever they sup-

ported that attracted public attention. The PRI incorporated such popular
issues, thus enhancing its own future success and destroying the chances of
an opposition party to win an election. After 1940 the official party emphasized industrialization and increased production rather than land or
labor reforms. Industrial and agricultural production increased at a rapid
rate, to the benefit of the promoters and a growing salaried middle class
rather than of agricultural and urban labor. Because PRI maintained support for long-range developmental projects, such programs were no longer
merely 'six year plans' limited to the tenure in office of a particular president. PRI's ability to balance conflicting interests peacefully within the
party became a major reason for Mexico's economic progress and political
stability.

OPPOSITION PARTIES

Although no opposition party had any real hope of defeating the official
party, a number of splinter groups campaigned in each major election, and
some of them held together despite overwhelming defeats. The *Partido de
Acción Nacional* (PAN), established in 1939, was begun as a conservative
party of business and professional men centered primarily in Guadalajara
and Monterrey. In 1952 PAN leaders tried to attract remnants of the outlawed Sinarquistas, but without noteworthy success. The *Partido Popular*
(PP) was a radical party which occasionally elected a few congressmen.

AGRARIAN REFORM

To appreciate the determination of Cárdenas and his supporters to eradicate the hacienda system it is necessary to recall its role in the Mexican
economy. In 1910 about one per cent of the population owned most of the
land, which was divided into many great haciendas. Three-quarters of all
rural communities, which embraced more than half of the rural population,
were located on haciendas. But the patriarchal system, which had been
useful in extending the agricultural frontiers in time of insufficient population, was neither creative nor enterprising, and it had long since outlived
its usefulness.

   Article 27 of the Constitution contained the goal of the Revolution with
regard to land: to recover that which had been granted in enormous tracts

to companies and individuals, to break up the hacienda system, to free agricultural labor from peonage, and to promote the prosperity of agricultural communities. It was also intended as a weapon to give the state an advantage in its struggle with long-standing foes—the hacendados, the foreigners, and the church as a temporal political force.

In 1935 the hacienda villagers were given the right to apply for and to obtain lands, a reflection of the Cárdenas administration's determination to face the hacienda issue squarely. More than 20,000 communities were granted lands; of these about 500 were in the form of community units called *ejidos,* such as that of Laguna, where 600,000 acres of rich land in Durango and Coahuila were organized into a co-operative project for 30,000 families. Similar projects were instituted in the henequen-growing region of Yucatan and in many other regions.

The problem of making large semi-communal holdings compatible with small private farms was at first difficult, and there was much friction and some violence. The ejido had the advantage of government protection throughout the Cárdenas administration, but large and small private holdings continued to exist. They were not eligible, however, for the financial aid that was available to ejidos.

OIL EXPROPRIATION

Toward the goal of recovering Mexico for the Mexicans the most spectacular action was the expropriation of foreign oil properties in March of 1938. This step followed a two-year strike of oil workers, and refusal by the companies to accept the decision of arbitral boards even though upheld by the Mexican Supreme Court. The expropriation was a symbolic triumph of Mexican nationalism backed by labor. It created more problems than it solved, for the government relied heavily on oil taxes and on the silver-buying policy of the Roosevelt administration. The government assumed a tremendous debt to the oil companies, while the United States temporarily ceased buying Mexican silver in retaliation. The oil companies withdrew their technicians, and foreign nations boycotted Mexican oil. Although Expropriation Day, March 18, is a national holiday celebrating the beginning of Mexican economic independence, the great difficulties with the oil industry discouraged the expropriation of other foreign-owned industries.

PEMEX

The state corporation, *Pemex,* organized to manage the oil industry after 1938, was handicapped by the lack of technicians as well as by labor troubles. In 1946 President Miguel Alemán appointed Antonio Bermúdez, an astute businessman, as head of Pemex. Bermúdez called in foreign wildcatters to search for new fields. By 1952 oil production equaled that of earlier years, but there were still many obstacles to overcome before Pemex could serve the nation most effectively. The industry developed by the foreign companies had been for the purpose of exporting oil, so that most of the refineries were located near the coast. It was necessary to lay pipelines and otherwise to reorient the industry to enable it to serve the nation first. Pemex often sold its products at less than the cost of production, so that in effect it operated at a loss. It diversified by adding the production of petrochemicals, and it relieved the nation of having to import many industrial items not produced domestically before.

FOREIGN PRESSURES

Another activity of the Cárdenas administration which met with considerable unpopularity at home and abroad was its support of the Spanish Republic against Francisco Franco, and its offer of a refuge to Spanish republicans. Many of them took advantage of the offer, and Mexico's economy and intellectual life were enriched by their coming.

Other foreign pressures were felt in Mexico. A falangist movement arose patterned after that of Spain. Red Shirts and Gold Shirts fought to gain political power and to halt the Cárdenas reform program, which they regarded as far too radical. In 1938 Cárdenas faced a rebellion led by General Saturnino Cedillo, political boss of San Luis Potosí, who had risen from poverty and ignorance to wealth and influence by the means peculiar to Mexican generals of a bygone era. By 1938 Cedillo was the only local caudillo who still retained a private army. For a time Cárdenas had kept Cedillo in his cabinet, the better to watch him.

Cedillo's abortive revolt followed the demand that he surrender his private army and leave San Luis Potosí. Government troops easily crushed the uprising, and the caudillo, perhaps the last of his kind, was slain.

Cárdenas broke with tradition by sparing his prisoners, and the church demonstrated a new attitude toward politics by supporting Cárdenas against Cedillo.

EDUCATION UNDER CÁRDENAS

The extension of public schools, efforts to integrate the Indian into national life, and promotion of a feeling of national consciousness were among the important accomplishments of the Cárdenas administration. The government gave solid support and encouragement to anthropologists and archaeologists in an attempt to make known the achievements of the pre-Columbian era and to give the Indians pride in their heritage and a sense of belonging. The educational program begun in the 1920's under the tutelage of José Vasconcelos received a change of direction and a new impetus. Cárdenas favored acculturation rather than assimilation, the acceptance of parts of Indian culture rather than the rejection of it in its entirety. The rural and Indian schools and the cultural missions were the instruments employed to reach the long-neglected rural peoples, mestizos and Indians. The teacher and the missionary had to bring to entire communities, not merely to children of school age, all that had been lacking for generations.

The cultural missions also served for a time as teacher-training schools, but they later surrendered this function to schools designed specifically for that purpose. Agricultural schools were associated with the teacher-training programs, to prepare teachers more adequately to meet the needs of the impoverished rural communities. The system of rural education was an effective innovation that began the long, slow task of raising the rural standard of living.

NACIONAL FINANCIERA

To aid and stimulate private industry has been the main work of *Nacional Financiera,* a semi-autonomous body created by Cárdenas in 1933 primarily to sell rural real estate. In 1934 it was authorized to create a Mexican stock market, and it also served as a fiscal agent of the government. Nacional Financiera was encouraged to organize and administer any enterprise that would contribute to the PRI's developmental goals. Until 1940 it was primarily concerned with agricultural credit, but after that year it gradually became concerned with total economic development. In 1940 its charter was revised to authorize it to promote investment in industry and to provide financial backing whenever commercial credit was unavailable or insufficient. In 1947 Nacional Financiera became the sole agency empowered to negotiate loans abroad. Its role in Mexico's industrial and agricultural development has been vital, and its success is reflected in the most rapid increase in production of any nation in the hemisphere from 1940–60. One of the most significant aspects of this astonishing growth is that it was financed largely by Mexico, for only about 20 per cent of the funds used came from abroad. There was still too much invested in real estate rather than in production. Between 1940 and 1950, nevertheless, foreign investment in Mexico tripled, and it doubled again in the next decade. But the foreign investors did not dominate industries as formerly. In 1949 foreigners were prohibited from owning more than 49 per cent of the stock in any Mexican enterprise. United States firms became minority stockholders in Mexican corporations, and provided capital for expansion and operation as well as patents and technological assistance.

OBSTACLES TO INCREASED PRODUCTION

As in most Latin American nations one of the principal obstacles to successful industrialization was the absence of an adequate domestic market. In Mexico this problem was acute, for while two-thirds of the workingmen were engaged in agriculture, they were unable to produce enough to feed the nation, and agricultural workers had little to spend for manufactured goods.

Deforestation had increased soil destruction, and at the same time it was necessary to expand cultivation to hillside areas, with the result that soil erosion became a critical problem. Corn or Indian maize was the staple food crop, and nearly two-thirds of the land under cultivation was devoted to its production. The yield per acre, however, was extremely low. Wheat was next in importance among food crops, and its production was no more satisfactory. The problem of providing enough food for her growing population was one of the most critical Mexico faced at the time she began seriously to industrialize.

There were physical as well as financial difficulties, to which were added inherent resistance to change on the part of the rural peasantry. Ancient customs and beliefs were difficult to uproot, and it was against these that the rural and Indian schools struggled.

From the time of Cárdenas the government and the economy became closely related and interacting. This association led to the nationalization of the oil industry, the railroads, and large areas of agricultural lands. The government's purposes were political and social rather than economic, based on the desire to give Mexicans a strong sense of nationalism as well as the right to determine their own future. To accomplish this it was necessary to eradicate foreign control of basic industries and then to create an economic system that would carry out the aims of the Revolution to bring material well-being to all rather than to the fortunate few.

After Cárdenas

POLITICAL LIFE

Because of the tradition of government seizure by ambitious men, the government was obliged to perpetuate itself in power or invite insurrection. It conducted elections and permitted free speech, for political democracy was one of the cardinal aspirations of the Revolution. No opposition party came forth with a more attractive program to challenge the official candidates, and none of them was a serious threat. Most opposition candidates did not expect to win; their greatest hope was to create a moral justification for revolt. If the army could be alienated and the government driven from power, an opposition candidate would be in a position to hold an election in which he and his followers would win control of the government. The military uprising was merely a means of transferring power from one group to another. One strong deterrent to rebellion in Mexico was knowledge that the United States would support the legal candidate with military aid.

The various changes in the official party had no widespread effect on Mexican political conditions, except that more compromising was accomplished within the party than had been possible between parties. Cárdenas had relieved government employees of involuntary exactions for the support of the party treasury, and the government itself had assumed responsibility for financing the official party. The existence of a single major party made the country dependent upon the government for socio-economic change, and later modifications merely emphasized the government's role. The effective party control made it possible to permit splinter parties to organize and campaign without fear of their success.

The government widened the base upon which its power rested by its leadership in social and economic reorganization, attracting to its support the benefited groups in both urban and rural life. It also took on the responsibility for directing the national economy, a burden made the more difficult by failure to inaugurate appropriate changes in administrative machinery and in political morality. Efficiency and integrity did not keep pace with the growth of governmental responsibilities, nor did the processes of representative government. Congress remained largely a rubber stamp, while the president, as the most powerful figure in the nation, implemented his program by decree with the permission of Congress. The real political issues were thrashed out by personal negotiation with political leaders representing the powerful sectors that composed the official party. In this environment, the sounds issuing from the legislative halls had a hollow ring.

The device of a government-sponsored party proved to be an effective device for retaining control and avoiding rebellions. It did not mean that elections were any less reflections of popular expression than they would have been if no official party existed. As compared with the era of Porfirio Díaz, the change made for greater stability and democratization in political life. The most obvious accomplishment in this direction was the principle of no re-election. The president could no longer succeed himself though his party remained in power. Legally he had the right to run for the presidency again after an intervening term, but after the assassination of Obregón no president availed himself of the opportunity.

By creating a more stable civil service and by eliminating the worst aspects of the ancient spoils system, the government acquired greater effectiveness and continuity in administrative departments. In the corps of civil servants it also gained one of its most devoted groups of supporters.

The government's power was strengthened by its support of organized labor, and it was partially because of this fact that the state influenced the process of industrialization. The government was a party to every labor discussion or contract. When Article 123 was written into the Constitution Mexico lacked a sizable industrial laboring class; most of the small group that might be so classed were in the employ of aliens. Governmental support of labor was in effect action against foreign capital, and no local interests were injured or threatened by the creation of labor organizations.

Government concern for labor was twofold: to improve the situation of the working man and to increase the authority of the state.

Every gain in power by the unions was reflected by a greater gain by the government. The union, the collective labor contract, and the Boards of Conciliation and Arbitration gave the government great weight in the councils of industry. The Boards of Conciliation and Arbitration became increasingly important as they were granted additional powers from time to time, so that they came to possess a judicial competency in labor disputes.

The rise of organized labor added a new force to Mexican political life, a force which came to challenge the army in strength and influence. But as long as the threat of rebellion in the states remained alive, the government had no choice but to continue relying heavily on the loyalty of the army. Organized labor and the agricultural communities rallied to the government's support in times of crisis, and dependence on the army diminished. The unions and the ejidos have given the president strong support among the masses of Mexicans, a support that was neither courted nor obtained previously.

The PRI remained a coalition of moderate elements of the left and the industrial right, labor, agrarian groups, and the bureaucracy. Leadership of the country for a Mexican president depended upon his ability to hold this coalition together. His task was to harmonize the diverse interests of these groups sufficiently well to keep them united. The basic course of the government was determined by this method, and for the president the task was never easy.

One of the means of controlling the states available to the central government was provided through the tax system. The bulk of taxes collected was claimed by the government; the states and municipalities had to depend on their good standing with the government to gain financial favors. Within the states the political bosses, if they remained loyal to the regime, were all-powerful, and little could be done without their consent.

IMPACT OF WORLD WAR II

The amount of money in circulation increased considerably during World War II, owing to the favorable balance of trade that resulted, the money spent by the United States to restore Mexican transport, the funds brought in by European refugees, and the money sent home by Mexican workers in the United States. Despite optimistic claims, however, little new wealth was created at the time. Industrial output did not increase after 1942, although its value doubled or tripled because of inflation. The immediate result was merely harder times for the average Mexican workingman and his family.

The government was able to reduce its indebtedness, to spend vast sums for public works, and to settle the claims of the oil companies. In 1942 the minister of finance negotiated an adjustment of the external debt with the International Committee of Bankers for Mexico. The dollar debt was converted to a peso debt, at a peso to the dollar. Because of the later devaluation of the peso the obligation was substantially reduced.

Mexico's government-sponsored housing program undertook the construction of huge apartment houses, complete with schools, playgrounds, medical clinics, and fire departments. In 1949 the *Centro Urbano Presidente Alemán,* one of the first completed, was opened for occupancy with facilities for more than one thousand families. Others were completed later.

CHURCH AND STATE RELATIONSHIPS

The conflict between church and state that embittered so much of the nineteenth century in Mexico appeared occasionally after 1930, though without the extreme attitudes on both sides characteristic of earlier clashes. To the followers of the Revolution the church was identified with foreign interests instead of the social program found in the revolutionary doctrines. Once it opposed the Revolution, the church found itself in a situation from which there was no dignified and graceful exit. The bitter strife that broke out in the era of Calles and the cristero rebellion continued until 1935, when Cárdenas quietly modified the government's policy toward the church without making any overt changes in law. Soon afterward he persuaded state governors to follow his lead, and the tension died down. Relations between church and state improved considerably thereafter, although there have been few legislative changes except for modification of Article 3 of the Constitution to remove the features most objectionable to the church.

One of the focal points of opposition to the PRI was the *Sinarquista* (with order) movement, a Christian Front organization motivated by various fanaticisms including religious, totalitarian, and anti-democratic. The shortage of food during the war gave the sinarquistas the opportunity to charge the government with shipping food to the United States while Mexicans starved. Even though the United States was sending foodstuffs to Mexico, by carefully nourishing latent Yankeephobia and other hatreds the sinarquistas created a fairly large following. Their activities, like those of the cristeros before them, led to the outbreak of religious fanaticism which included attacks on Protestants. The sinarquistas made bids for political power at the state and national levels, but merely to prepare the way for revolt. The loyalty of the army to the PRI was the main safeguard against sinarquista insurrection. Because of the violence it instigated, the sinarquista party was outlawed.

GOVERNMENT IN BUSINESS

From the administration of Cárdenas the government became a partner in the economy, and it assumed the responsibility of achieving and maintaining a high rate of growth. Miguel Ávila Camacho, a somewhat colorless general who was dubbed 'The Unknown Soldier' in the presidential campaign, governed from 1940 to 1946. He did much to calm the growing unrest of the conservatives which had been aroused by Cárdenas' 'socialistic' policies, and he also soothed the church. Under his guidance the Revolution took new directions. The agrarian program, especially the ejido system, had failed to contribute to the nation's food supply, partly because the plots were too small for anything but subsistence farming. The new projects had economic rather than social bases: ejidos were still created, but the family allotments were larger. The greatest stress, however, was on increasing the area of land under cultivation, especially by developing irrigation systems. Small and medium-sized individual farms were now encouraged by providing them the same financial aid as the ejidos, aid that was previously denied them.

The major emphasis of Ávila Camacho's administration was on industrialization, despite the fact that some Mexicans feared its social consequences. In April, 1941, the Law of Manufacturing Industries went into effect, providing tax exemptions to industrial enterprises. The Mexican business leaders designed a basic plan for the simultaneous development of industries and modernizing of agriculture. In February of 1946 the Law for the Development of New and Necessary Industries was designed to raise the standard of living of all Mexicans by producing at home many items previously imported. Each economic sector had its responsibilities and its sacrifices to make for the general welfare. The agriculturists had to feed the nation and produce a surplus for export, and supply the raw materials that otherwise would have to be purchased abroad. Industry was to purchase agricultural products, provide employment for farm workers whose places were taken by machinery, and supply manufactures at reasonable prices. Labor was to avoid disputes and interruptions of work. Consumers in general had to accept inflation. Together the farm and the factory would raise the living standards of all.

Mexico's balanced approach—industrialization together with modernization and expansion of agriculture—was successful. The rate of growth accelerated, and the government-business partnership and joint planning proved eminently workable. Oil and mining declined steadily in relative importance, but the national budget grew larger each year, and in keeping with the party's aims education and developmental projects received larger shares of it than the armed forces.

EDUCATION

All classes in Mexico regarded education as a primary national goal and the key to fulfilling the aims of the Revolution. Education came to be assigned a larger share of the national budget than the military, and teachers came to outnumber soldiers. Although a great deal was accomplished in improving education and making it available to all classes in all localities, there remained a number of serious deficiencies, and some children had no opportunity to attend elementary schools. Among the ministers of education have been some of the best minds, from José Vasconcelos to Jaime Torres Bodet, who served under both Ávila Camacho and López Mateos.

There was a continuous effort to tailor education so that it would help the nation achieve its basic goals. In this regard the public school served the causes of unity and democracy. The extraordinarily high birth rate meant that new schools and teachers were constantly needed. One of the basic problems of education in Mexico was that about half of the population was scattered in rural and often isolated hamlets.

In 1929 the ancient university in Mexico City was granted the privilege of running its own affairs (autonomy), and in 1945 it was reorganized as a public corporation, the *Universidad Nacional Autónoma Mexicana* (UNAM). In 1953, four centuries after it was founded, the university moved to a new campus, the *Ciudad Universitaria* or University City.

Technological studies are provided by the National Polytechnic Institute, created by the Cárdenas government in 1936, and the Institute of Technology in Monterrey, which was established in 1942 by a group of businessmen and industrialists of that city to provide technicians for the expanding industries.

AGRICULTURE

The governments after the Cárdenas administration had to decide between alternative policies with regard to agriculture. The most popular choice was obviously to stress political agrarianism and provide land for the landless. Less popular but more vital for the nation's economic future was to stress improvement of agricultural production by means of irrigation projects, scientific agriculture, and mechanization. Most of the governments reached a compromise between these alternatives. Every administration distributed land, but in larger plots than before, and with an emphasis on the best use of the land for the national benefit. As a result, the living standards of rural peoples slowly rose.

Before the Cárdenas administration about 17 million acres of land had been redistributed. His total was about 41 million acres, but the disappointing results caused a new approach after 1940. It was a political necessity to continue redistributing some land, but more emphasis was on the creation of new land resources, such as the opening of millions of acres of arable land to cultivation along the Gulf coast. The amounts of land redistributed by presidents after Cárdenas were considerable: under Ávila Camacho more than 16 million acres, under Alemán more than 12 million, under Ruíz Cortines more than 8 million. In his first two years (1958–60), López Mateos redistributed nearly 8 million acres, but there was not much land left available for this purpose.

Between 1939 and 1960 the amount of land under cultivation was increased by almost half. By the 1950's maize, the chief ejido food crop, was produced in such quantities that a surplus was available for export. In the 1940's coffee production was expanded, so that by 1960 Mexico was the third highest exporter of coffee in the hemisphere. She had also become the second greatest exporter of cotton. In 1960 agriculture supplied 60 per cent of the value of all exports.

MIGUEL ALEMÁN

The elections of 1946, 1952, and 1958 were relatively peaceful. Miguel Alemán, the PRI choice in 1946, was the first civilian elected to the presidency since Carranza. Alemán concentrated his efforts on industrialization, the modernization of the faltering transport system, and the reorganization of Pemex to increase its efficiency. He increased the powers of Nacional Financiera to enable it to take further action to improve the economic system. The result was not only a rapid industrial growth, but a considerable increase in agriculture and in school facilities. Toward the end of his term financial scandals, labor unrest caused by his freezing of wages and use of troops to prevent strikes in the oil industry, and discontent among agriculturists greatly diminished Alemán's popularity. He had, however, made enormous contributions to Mexico's economic progress, for he took over the economic and social programs planned by his predecessors and implemented them.

RUÍZ CORTINES

In 1952 Adolfo Ruíz Cortines promised to clean out the corruption that had entered the government, and to continue the various economic projects. He did both, and his administration was one of the most honest and constructive of all time. He made each government official file a financial statement on entering and leaving office, and he dismissed any official who was proved guilty of peculation. Ruíz Cortines also took up the cause of the rural poor, who had been somewhat overlooked in the push to industrialize. He began the shift of peoples from the desert regions of the North to the newly opened lands in the rainy South. In 1953 women were given the right to vote for the first time, and the fear that they would revive the former political influence of the church proved unfounded.

LÓPEZ MATEOS

In the campaign of 1958 there was renewed hostility between radicals and conservatives. Adolfo López Mateos, the highly successful secretary of labor under Ruíz and the PRI choice, was regarded as slightly left of center in political outlook. He continued the developmental programs of his predecessors.

About half of Mexico's electricity was still produced by private and foreign companies when López Mateos assumed office. The remainder was generated by the Federal Electricity Commission. López Mateos saw the need for doubling electrical energy as quickly as possible, to meet the growing needs of industries. Since electric power was regarded as a vital element in economic development, its increase seemed a proper government program. Early in 1960 the government purchased the American and Foreign Power Company, a United States firm, and then acquired 90 per cent of the stock of the Mexican Light Company, which was owned by Canadians.

IRON AND STEEL

Successful industrialization requires adequate domestic supplies of iron and steel. The Monterrey Iron and Steel Works, which began production in 1903, was the first modern plant of its kind in Latin America. Mexico has ample reserves of coal and iron ore in Durango and Coahuila. In 1951 the Altos Hornos plant began producing iron and steel at Monclova in Coahuila. In 1960 it merged with the foreign-owned La Consolidada company, so that the main steel plants were owned by Mexicans, and they produced almost enough steel to supply the growing domestic market. In Latin America, Mexico came to rank second, next to Brazil, in iron and steel production.

FOREIGN POLICY

Mexico had long been fairly active in international affairs, particularly those concerning the Western Hemisphere. At the Rio de Janeiro Conference of 1942, Mexican Foreign Minister Ezequiel Padilla had played a vital role by his eloquent support of hemispheric solidarity. The differences between Mexico and the United States were settled in the same period, when Mexico agreed to pay for confiscated land and for expropriated oil properties. A new trade treaty with the United States restored the silver-purchasing policy that had been interrupted after the oil expropriation. In April, 1943, President Roosevelt went to Monterrey to confer with Ávila Camacho. He was the first U.S. president to visit Mexico.

The Mexican government has strongly supported the United Nations. Jaime Torres Bodet served as the Secretary General of UNESCO, and in 1952 Luis Padilla Nervo was President of the Sixth General Assembly.

Under López Mateos Mexico assumed an even larger role in hemispheric and world affairs. Mexico strongly upheld the juridical equality of states, large and small, and a reflection of this attitude was the raising of all Mexican diplomatic posts to embassy rank. Mexico adhered strictly to the accepted principles of international law. Her foreign policy in general was based on the desire to 'promote moderation, cordiality and tolerance and mutual understanding,' and to uphold the dignity of man. She desired freedom, independence, and equality for all nations. These were not new goals for Mexico, and they were reaffirmed regularly by presidents from Cárdenas onward. The main principles of international relations for Mexico have been non-intervention, singly or collectively, and the self-determination of peoples. From the time of Cárdenas Mexico continued to have no relations with Franco Spain.

One aspect of the cordial understanding with the United States was that Mexico would decide her own stand on international issues, and even though it proved often different from the stand taken by the United States, relations were not strained. Mexico opposed military assistance agreements with the United States, but the two nations maintained a satisfactory understanding on military matters concerning hemispheric defense.

THE DECLINE OF MILITARISM

In the early years of World War II the Mexican army became a professionally trained corps. Military interest in politics declined according to the degree of professionalization, though it stemmed in part from the reorganization of the official party under Cárdenas, for he eliminated the power base of regional generals. After the 1940's the Mexican army remained 'non-political,' and some authorities stated categorically that militarism was dead in Mexico. Whether or not this was an optimistic and unrealistic view only time would tell, but at any rate the military became only one of several powerful interest groups instead of being the only one, as it had been in the past. The army changed from being the chief cause of instability to a vital influence for stability, which was one of the most significant accomplishments of the PRI and the government.

ART AND LITERATURE

In the period following 1930, Mexico's artists such as Diego Rivera, David Alfaro Siqueiros, José Clemente Orozco, and Miguel Covarrubias gained international reputations. Alfonso Reyes, son of General Bernardo Reyes, was the leading poet and essayist until his death in 1959. The poet and essayist Octavio Paz, whose *Labyrinth of Solitude* (1950) was a penetrating analysis of the Mexican character, was Reyes' primary successor. Novelists Carlos Fuentes and Luis Spota chose as themes Mexico's changing social values, and both won recognition at home and abroad. Leopoldo Zea, author of *The Latin American Mind* (1949) and many other works of an intellectual nature, was one of the leading thinkers of the era. Another was Ramón Xirau, whose book *The Pendulum and the Spiral* (1959) explained the meaning of history to his countrymen. There developed a group of excellent historians, anthropologists, and sociologists who won recognition throughout the hemisphere and beyond.

RAILROADS

The various foreign-owned railroads of Mexico were consolidated and nationalized, partly through expropriation in 1937 and partly through government purchases in 1946 and 1950. Beginning in 1946 the government modernized equipment for the main lines, and eventually Mexico began manufacturing her own freight cars. Much of the modernization and improvement of the railroads was promoted and supervised by Nacional Financiera.

WATER RESOURCES

Much of Mexico's territory has either too much or too little water. In 1948 President Alemán raised the agency for water resources to cabinet rank as the Ministry of Hydraulic Resources, and it completed a number of enormous and costly projects before 1960. In this period it reclaimed nearly four times as much land as had been reclaimed since 1926, when the government first undertook reclamation. The water resources program is one of the largest of its kind anywhere in the world, and it has served as a school for technicians from many other countries with similar problems.

Among the various projects was the construction of the Miguel Hidalgo Dam in the Río Fuerte Basin of Sonora, the Falcón Dam in the lower Rio Grande valley, and the Miguel Alemán Dam in the Papaloapan river basin —all completed between 1956 and 1960. In 1953 the government began shifting farm populations from the arid north region to the rainy coastal areas as the land was cleared and ready for use. In the Papaloapan project more than 200,000 acres were cleared, and homes were erected for settlers. The Alemán Dam, the largest in Latin America, provided water for irrigation as well as electricity for the settlers. In the north the Falcón Dam, the Yaqui Alto Canal, and the Miguel Hidalgo Dam opened fertile but arid regions to intensive cultivation. By September, 1955, President Adolfo Ruíz Cortines was able to announce that for the first time Mexico did not need to import basic foods.

By 1960 Mexico's economy was vastly changed from what it had been in 1940, although the contrast between wealth and poverty was sharper in 1960 than in 1940. In that year two-thirds of the working population was involved with agriculture, while the country imported large amounts of foods. In 1960 the national population had increased by 12 million over 1940, yet agricultural production had now made it possible to feed the ever-growing population and have a surplus for export. Agricultural production had increased an astonishing 250 per cent, yet the percentage of the working population involved in agriculture had shrunk from two-thirds in 1940 to about 54 per cent in 1960. Land under cultivation meanwhile had expanded from 37 million to 50 million acres, largely through various irrigation and land-clearing projects. Improvement in agricultural techniques and increases in per acre yields were also factors in the increased production. From 1944 on, the Rockefeller Foundation made important contributions to the development of highly productive new strains, and to the introduction of modern techniques, insecticides, fertilizers, and similar aids. The enormous increase in agricultural production was, therefore, the result of both expansion of acreage under cultivation and a greater per acre yield in crops.

FOREIGN TRADE

Mexican officials made a continuous effort to stimulate the production of items that were being imported in large quantities, with the result that by 1960 40 per cent of Mexico's imports were in the form of capital goods rather than consumer items. Mexico's foreign trade expanded considerably during World War II and after. Between 1939 and 1958 mineral exports declined in percentage of the total value of exports from 69 per cent to 29 per cent. By 1960 Mexico was second in cotton exports and third in coffee among Western Hemisphere nations. Mexico's import and export trade continued to be largely with the United States, but the bulk of her cotton went to Japan. Agriculture supplied 60 per cent of the value of exports, having risen while mining declined.

Although Mexico imported by value more than she exported, tourism helped create a favorable balance. By 1960 tourism produced more revenue than mining or oil, and as an economic activity it ranked after agriculture, manufacture, commerce, and service industries. As a result President López Mateos raised the Bureau of Tourism to just below cabinet rank. The *braceros* or agricultural laborers who worked in the United States also contributed to the favorable balance between the cost of imports and the profits of exports by sending much of their earnings home.

POPULATION GROWTH AND URBANIZATION

Mexico's population increased at the high rate of 3 per cent a year, which meant that economic growth had to be at a more rapid rate or the standard of living would have remained static or actually declined. In this regard Mexico was extremely successful. Between 1950 and 1957 the population increased by 21 per cent. In the same period petroleum production rose 160 per cent, electrical power 150, agricultural production 100, industrial manufacture 75, and mining 40 per cent. The increase in national income was not equitably distributed, however, for urban and rural workers benefited little compared to others. But unlike many Latin American countries, Mexico began collecting personal and corporate income taxes, which together provided one-half of the national budget.

The movement from country to city was rapid, even though the isolated rural hamlets did not disappear. More than half of the population still lived in rural communities of less than 2500 in 1960, but Mexico City had become one of the largest urban centers in the world, ranking sixth (after Tokyo, London, New York, Shanghai, and Moscow), and it became the second largest in the Western Hemisphere. Mexico City's dominating position in the nation was evident from the fact that the combined populations of all other Mexican cities of more than 100,000 totaled only about half that of the capital, which in 1960 was about 4.5 million. In the two decades after 1940 the city grew by 3 million. Other Mexican cities grew at the same time, so that in this period the number of cities with populations of 100,000 or more rose from three to sixteen. These changes gradually altered Mexico's way of life. By 1960 the upper and middle classes composed about a third of the total population. Men were, as a result of the economic and social changes, able to raise their statuses. The middle class, for example, tripled in size between 1940 and 1960.

In the three decades after 1930, Mexico changed more than in the previous years since independence. Although it seemed for a short time before 1930 that the goals of the Revolution had been subverted, Lázaro Cárdenas, in one of the most astute political maneuvers in Mexican history, disposed of Calles and returned the nation once more to the course that the Revolution had marked out for it. He reorganized the official party so that no one man could again sidetrack the nation from progress toward its basic goals. As a result of his efforts and those of his successors, Mexico rose to a prominent position among the Latin American nations that were trying to modernize their economies and societies. In many ways Mexico moved far along a course that new or underdeveloped nations might profitably imitate. By 1960 Mexico had initiated a number of critical projects for solving her most crucial problems, and the future seemed much brighter than it had in 1930.

14

The Restless Caribbean: An American Lake

> It must first be said that there is no area of the world more strategically important to the United States than the Caribbean, if that term is used to include Colombia and Venezuela, as well as Mexico, Central America, and the islands. In the strategic sense, the boundary between North and South America is the Amazon Basin, and between 1904 and 1954, the Caribbean was a "closed sea." *

The countries of the Caribbean region—Mexico, Central America, the islands, Colombia, and Venezuela—lie within the orbit of direct United States influence. Within the region, the point of greatest strategic importance to American military planners has for half a century been the Panama Canal. The international roles of the Caribbean nations were, until very recently, determined largely by the state of their relations with the United States. In the years between 1930 and 1960 defense of the area and of the Panama Canal figured more prominently in these relations than any other single factor until the rise of Fidel Castro in Cuba.

Before the pronouncement by President Franklin D. Roosevelt of the 'Good Neighbor' Policy and its subsequent implementation during the years of his tenure in office, the Caribbean was the region in which United States diplomacy was stigmatized as 'big stick' and motivated primarily by pursuit of the almighty dollar. After 1933, however, not only did public policy with regard to the Caribbean nations change for the better with apparent abandonment of old-style intervention, but the activities of American companies and individuals engaged in economic enterprises also became more enlightened. Corresponding to the voluntary change in attitude on the part of the United States was an increasing determination on the part of most of the governments of the region to extricate themselves from positions of economic subservience to foreign interests, a determination which resulted in measures that subjected American intentions to severe

* From *Latin America in World Politics* by Norman A. Bailey, p. 53. Copyright © 1967 by Norman A. Bailey; reprinted by permission of the publisher, Walker and Company, New York.

strain again and again. Expropriation of foreign-owned property was matched only by restriction on the use of those properties left in foreign hands.

The international problems of the Caribbean states were those of small nations lying in the shadow of a great power. It is not surprising that the principal countries of the area showed a strong predilection for hemispheric organization on the basis of equality among the member states. To the Caribbean countries, international organization served the purpose of protecting the small from the large. Despite occasional flare-ups among their number, countries of the area sought to preserve the newly established principle of non-intervention, regardless of the occasions that challenged the rights of private property, whether owned by domestic or foreign interests. Colombia and Venezuela were especially active in promoting international co-operation, and they took the lead in submitting proposals to strengthen inter-American organization in defense of such principles. At the Buenos Aires Conference of 1936, for example, Colombia proposed the creation of an association of American states, a concept that finally reached fruition at the Bogotá Conference of 1948, when the Organization of American States (OAS) was created. During World War II and the years immediately preceding it, Colombia and Venezuela both strongly urged the creation of inter-American juridical committees. At la Habana Venezuela offered the Declaration of Reciprocal Assistance and Co-operation, which measure was adopted as an important step in strengthening the inter-American system against outside interference.

Friction among the Caribbean nations was lessened slightly if at all by the advance of international organization. Venezuelans continued to look askance at the activities of Colombians. Central America and the island countries had their own peculiar feuds, in addition to sporadic resistance to the activities of the North Americans. Great Britain and Guatemala continued to argue over the status of Belize, a British colony on the Caribbean coast claimed by both parties. The cause of Central American union, espoused by many for generations, progressed only slightly until the 1950's when a new spirit of co-operation became manifest among the five governments capable of bringing it about. Discussions in 1934 and 1945 accomplished little, but in 1951 representatives of the five nations meeting in San Salvador adopted a document, subsequently known as the Charter of San Salvador, providing for creation of an Organization of Central American States (ODECA). Initially the agreement fostered consultation on mutual problems and looked toward measures of cultural and economic co-operation, but it became the basis for the later creation of other arrangements for a free trade zone and significant steps toward economic integration. It was not until 1957, however, that concrete action began to reshape the economies of the Central American area. In the interval, relations among the five states placed severe strains upon the maintenance of common purpose on more than one occasion and suggested how delicate was the fabric with which the weavers of union were working.

Regional Unrest

Subsequent to World War II, a series of incidents in the Caribbean area provided the inter-American system with most of its peace-keeping problems. The Organization of American States, created by the Act of Bogotá in 1948, had as one of its key responsibilities that of seeking to maintain peace in the hemisphere. On several occasions it received appeals for assistance from the island republics and Central America. Most of the clashes would have been considered purely domestic affairs had it not been for the exiles, refugees, and soldiers of fortune who drifted from one fracas to another with the ubiquitous phalanx known as the Caribbean Legion. Developed initially under the leadership of José Figueres of Costa Rica, whose National Liberation Party (PLN) assumed a vanguard role for liberal democracy in Central America, the Caribbean Legion became an active force in a number of efforts to overthrow dictatorial regimes in the islands as well as on the mainland. Principal targets were the dictatorships of Rafael Trujillo in the Dominican Republic, Marcos Pérez Jiménez in Venezuela, and Anastasio Somoza in Nicaragua. These in turn were soon embarked upon measures of a counter-revolutionary nature. Many charges were made by the various governments that their opponents were harboring their exiles and aiding them in attempts to overthrow existing administrations, charges that frequently seemed to be well-founded. Thus Costa Rica charged Nicaragua with aiding revolutionary forces and Haiti accused the Dominican Republic of intervention. Venezuela leveled accusations against the Dominican Republic, which in turn issued blanket charges of its own against Costa Rica, Venezuela, and Cuba of actions aimed at throwing Trujillo from power. An examination of these various charges and the findings of the Council of the Organization of American States suggested that a sizable number of the Caribbean governments applied the principle of non-intervention only against the United States.

In January of 1950, the Council of the OAS decided to apply the provisions of the Rio de Janeiro treaty to the persistent hostilities among the Caribbean nations, and a special fact-finding committee was created to make a study. Tension was heightened by the fact that Trujillo's compliant congress granted him authority to declare war, a gesture intended to intimidate countries harboring the numerous enemies and exiles from his regime. He was informed by the OAS that it possessed sufficient machinery for settling quarrels peacefully. The fact-finding committee found evidence of misconduct on all sides, and called on Haiti and the Dominican Republic specifically to mend their ways and live up to their celebrated Joint Declaration of mutual friendship made on June 9, 1944. The OAS Council received assurances from both governments, as well as from Cuba and Guatemala, that they would abide by their commitments to the inter-American system. Trujillo's war powers were repealed, and it appeared that peace would reign once more.

The 'watchdog' committee considered its work done, and it soon disbanded. Shortly thereafter the Dominican Republic seized near its coast landing craft manned by an assortment of Cubans, Guatemalans, and Dominican exiles whose obvious intent was to sneak ashore and initiate an uprising. Charges and counter-charges flourished once more. In 1951 the Dominican Republic freed five Cubans and three Guatemalans as a gesture toward peace. The underlying problem of the floating province of political exiles and refugees, however, remained unsolved.

In 1950 Guatemala had been accused of harboring the Caribbean Legion, which had actually located its headquarters in Cuba. In various of the abortive invasions of the Dominican Republic, the Legion was said to have used Guatemalan rifles, planes, and other military equipment. Trujillo and Somoza were the principal foes of President Juan José Arévalo of Guatemala and of his minister of defense, Jacobo Arbenz, who succeeded to the presidency in 1951.

The years of turmoil and unrest in the Caribbean were indicative that the problems of instability, political oppression, and social dissatisfaction were far from ended. The more neighborly policies of the United States seemed to invite greater activity on the part of international agitators and soldiers of fortune. The Caribbean Legion never numbered more than a hundred or so men, and their politics ranged the gamut from the extreme right to avowed communist adherence. However, when backed by sympathetic governments, as was often the case, the capacity of a small group of activists to create international incidents was substantial. Few of the states were doctrinaire in their external relations; moreover, in the brief civil strife that occurred in Costa Rica in 1948 when José Figueres rebelled in a successful effort to secure the presidency for the legally elected moderate liberal, Otilio Ulate, the leftist forces were aided by Nicaragua and Honduras while the moderates were helped by Guatemala.

Central America

Political conditions in Central America have ever been turbulent, and the period from 1930 to 1960 was no exception. In all but Panama (which is not generally considered part of Central America) and Costa Rica, strong men seized power in the 1930's and held it for years. In the most populous country, Guatemala, whose largely Indian population played little or no part in political life, General Jorge Ubico ruled from 1931 until his overthrow in 1944. In 1931 Maximiliano Martínez established a virtual dictatorship in the smallest republic, El Salvador, and he too ruled until 1944 when a general strike brought about his downfall. The year 1932 saw the rise of Honduran dictator, General Tiburcio Carías Andino, who remained in power in his poverty-stricken and underpopulated country until he voluntarily stepped down in 1948. In Central America's largest country, from which United States marines finally departed in 1933, General Anastasio Somoza toppled the legally elected government of Juan B. Sacasa in 1936 and took over the presidency, which office he either occupied or dominated until his assassination in 1956.

RADICALISM AND REACTION IN GUATEMALA

After the ouster of Ubico on July 1, 1944, there followed several months of chaotic military rule. Then in December a constituent assembly was chosen and a new president elected. Juan José Arévalo, a university professor who had been teaching in Argentina, became president, and under the new Constitution of 1945 he set about righting the many wrongs that had so long kept his country in a state of backwardness and poverty. He tried to bring the Indians into the social and economic life of the country by abolishing forced labor and promulgating a new labor code, as well as by seeking to extend to them the benefits of an educational system. He promised land reform and the break-up of large estates. Opposition soon appeared from the military and landowners, and Arévalo had all he could do to remain in office until the end of his term. His reform program languished. In the meantime, communist organizers were busily at work among the laboring people of the capital and within the bureaucracy, seeking to build a strong party base.

In March of 1951 Arévalo stepped down in favor of his elected successor, Lieutenant Colonel Jacobo Arbenz Guzmán, a man whose sympathy for the communist organizers was unmistakable. In 1952 he succeeded in obtaining enactment of an Agrarian Reform Law aimed at confiscation or expropriation of thousands of acres of agricultural lands, ostensibly to redistribute them to the Indians. Among the properties seized were 200,000 acres belonging to the United Fruit Company, and only nominal compensation was promised. The United States Government promptly protested such action.

United States–Guatemalan relations were further complicated by the obvious official encouragement of anti-American demonstrations in the Guatemalan capital, as well as by the increasingly open sympathy displayed for the small but vigorous force of communists in the country. All foreign holdings in Guatemala were imperiled, for the intelligent policies of some foreign countries in the previous decade had not erased from the minds of many Guatemalans the conviction that all such companies were in league with the forces of an evil imperialism. Any unfavorable comment by officials of the State Department concerning communism in Guatemala was promptly interpreted as pressure on behalf of the foreign fruit interests.

More alarming to Washington than land reform was the increasing evidence of developing ties between the Guatemalan government and communist regimes in Eastern Europe, climaxed in May of 1954 by the revelation that an arms shipment was on its way to Guatemala from Poland. Fear of an outright communist takeover mounted. However, many Latin Americans found it difficult to appreciate the concern of the United States or of Guatemala's immediate neighbors over the impending importation of communist military supplies. They did not conceal their suspicion that American apprehension was based on the attacks on foreign-owned holdings.

The situation in Guatemala in early 1954 was paradoxical. Economic and social reforms were being carried out in an apparently democratic climate, although political repression was increasing. A legalized communist party, the Guatemalan Labor Party, was the strongest political group in the country and was clearly influential in the highest government circles, yet the economic development effort was being carried forward within a capitalistic, free enterprise economy. The political power of the communists among the masses of the people seemed weak, but President Arbenz was clearly using the communists as a weapon against the United States. This situation was soon to produce his downfall.

The Tenth Inter-American Conference held at Caracas in March of 1954 provided the scene for an open confrontation between Guatemala and the United States. American Secretary of State John Foster Dulles sponsored a resolution warning international communism to keep hands off the Western Hemisphere. The wisdom of such an initiative was certainly open to question, for it placed the United States in the unenviable position of finding itself vigorously attacked by the Guatemalan foreign minister, Guillermo Toriello, who won wide applause by denouncing 'imperialism' and 'foreign monopolistic interests,' favorite whipping boys of governments intent on measures of economic nationalism at the expense of foreign investors. Many of the delegates obviously enjoyed the spectacle of tiny Guatemala frustrating and irritating the powerful United States, and the reception given Toriello's fulminations against the time-honored terms of 'big stick,' 'dollar diplomacy,' and 'monopoly' indicated that Latin America's conditioned response to these bugbears had not disappeared.

The anti-communist resolution condemned international communism as a threat to the peace of the Americas and provided for consultation among the American republics if one of them should come under the domination or control of the movement. The Guatemalan delegate voted against it, and both Argentina and Mexico abstained from voting at all. Thus the resolution passed, as did another proposed by Panama in opposition to racial discrimination. However, the Guatemalan representative abstained from voting on that issue because the preamble stated that racial discrimination not only was opposed to democratic principles but promoted continuation of a climate favorable to communist propaganda.

Even before the Caracas meeting, the increasing difficulties in relations between the United States and Guatemala had given rise to consideration of a possible American embargo on the importation of Guatemalan coffee. This would have constituted a severe blow to the economy of the Central American republic, since the United States was the principal purchaser. However, the idea was rejected on the grounds that such an economic sanction could have been interpreted as a form of intervention in the internal affairs of the country. Nevertheless, the Guatemalan delegate at Caracas chose the occasion to propose a resolution to prohibit economic boycotts in the hemisphere, a move useful only for anti-United States propaganda.

Guatemala's immediate neighbors were made increasingly uneasy by the events taking place in the spring of 1954, particularly when it became known that arms from communist countries were to be imported. Perhaps as great as the fear of what Guatemala might do with those arms was concern that their very presence in Central America might cause a new and major American intervention. They well understood their geographic inclusion inside the Canal Zone defense perimeter of the United States.

The United States, however, had developed a new set of techniques for dealing with problems such as those created by Jacobo Arbenz. Its Central Intelligence Agency secretly supported a small band of revolutionaries being organized across the border in Honduras by a relatively unknown exile, Colonel Carlos Castillo Armas. In June, Castillo Armas ordered his rebel force to march on Guatemala City. Rumors flew wildly among the Central American capitals of possible support from other neighbors for the rebel forces. Arbenz found himself virtually without support from either his communist friends or the Guatemalan army. He fled the country and Castillo Armas quickly took over the presidency. Friendly relationships with the United States were promptly restored.

Reaction to these events in other parts of Latin America was mixed. In Mexico a society calling itself the Friends of Guatemala was organized. It charged that the communist issue was merely a smoke screen to cover up action on behalf of American companies that feared nationalization of their properties. The right-wing *Sinarquistas* of Mexico accused the United States of sending arms to Guatemala'a neighbors 'under the pretext of protecting a democracy that does not exist and a security that is not menaced and in reality for defending the illegitimate interests of North American monopolies that have robbed the riches of brother peoples.' A few Mexicans defended the United States' role in supporting the Castillo Armas invasion, but in Chile demonstrators burned the American flag.

The government of Castillo Armas was clearly reactionary and politically unenlightened. Arbenz had betrayed the liberal and democratic reform movement begun after the ouster of Ubico, but Castillo Armas sought to turn back the clock. New reform laws were decreed, but the failure to carry them out left the Indians and poor farmers without benefit from his administration. His major concern seemed to be the elimination from public office of all who might once have harbored a liberal or revolutionary idea.

Castillo Armas was assassinated in July, 1957, by a palace guard, but because of his growing unpopularity his passing was little mourned. Two unsuccessful attempts to elect a president were followed by congressional action to end the confusion. Because he had gained a substantial plurality in the voting, although not a majority, congress named General Miguel Ydígoras Fuentes president. Ydígoras promised a democratic administration, and for several years democratic rights were upheld. Numerous exiles, many of them former supporters of Arbenz, were allowed to return. Rumors spread that Ydígoras was banking vast sums of money abroad, money possibly looted from the social security fund, and his popularity quickly faded. In spite of such stories, as well as trouble with an obstructionist congress, Ydígoras was able to maintain a tight grip on the presidential office. His policies were basically conservative, and the country marked time under his rule. From the outset, he took a firm stand in opposition to Fidel Castro in Cuba, and this did little to increase his popularity at home at a time when most of the hemisphere was applauding the overthrow of the hated Batista regime. He was later to make his opposition to Castro more tangible.

As the Guatemalan case demonstrated, the role of the United States in the Caribbean, no matter how enlightened it might be or might become in the future, will never be easy. American officials learned in the post-World War II period to fear the possible spread of communism wherever and whenever a dictatorial regime is overthrown. While frequently favoring basic social and economic reforms in countries where a few wealthy landlord families control almost all the national wealth, they saw that liberal and democratic reform movements suffered from instability and were easily infiltrated by communist agents with more on their minds than the welfare of the *campesino*. Prior to 1960, many Latin American intellectuals, such as Leopoldo Zea of Mexico, and statesmen such as Lázaro Cárdenas, had great difficulty accepting the sincerity of America's concern. They believed that the United States was using the 'Cold War' and the communist threat to check movements that ran counter to American political and economic interests. This belief was and remains deep-seated, and many were prepared to produce evidence, some purely circumstantial, in support of the Latin American case. State Department officials have often found dictatorial regimes easy to deal with, and as a result they have been accused of favoring such governments over democratic but less pliable administrations. Central America's most famous example of the favored dictatorship is that of the Somoza family in Nicaragua.

THE SOMOZA PATRIMONY IN NICARAGUA

In 1930 American marines were still in Nicaragua and still unable to cope with the bandit-patriot, Augusto César Sandino, and his band of guerrillas. Public opinion in Latin America and the United States was increasingly critical of the occupation, and President Hoover sought a graceful exit. In 1932 Juan Bautista Sacasa, a leader of the Liberal party, was elected president; the Nicaraguan National Guard under the leadership of Anastasio Somoza seemed sufficiently strong to maintain order, and Hoover ordered the marines home. Within two years Sandino had been lured to his death and the country seemed at peace at last.

Anastasio ('Tacho') Somoza was a nephew of President Sacasa, but the family tie did not prevent him from throwing his uncle out of office in 1936 and taking over the leadership of the country. For twenty years he controlled the presidential office, either occupying it himself or placing in it someone responsive to his wishes. He ruled the country as if it belonged to him, and before his career was ended by an assassin's bullet in 1956, a large part of it did. Tacho was given credit for maintaining stable government and for promoting the economic development of the country, but little development took place that did not directly add to the growing wealth of the Somoza family. Actually, the country progressed far less than did some of its less stable neighbors, and when Somoza died he left behind a legacy that might more aptly be described as exploitation than development. Throughout his career, however, Somoza made a point of maintaining the most friendly relations with the United States, and as a result he received many favors.

When Anastasio Somoza was assassinated at a political rally in León, his son Luis took charge of the country and was shortly elected to the presidency. Another son, Anastasio ('Tachito'), took charge of the National Guard. Both sons had received their higher education in the United States and they continued the policy of their father in maintaining the most cordial relations with that country. Luis Somoza Debayle did not rule in the manner of his father, however. He was disturbed by the accusations of oppression and brutality so long made against the Somoza regime, and he determined to permit greater freedom in the political life of the country and to relax somewhat his family's control of virtually all phases of Nicaraguan economic life. Perhaps of greater importance were Luis Somoza's assurances that upon completion of his term of office in 1963 his family would withdraw from politics, and that the next election would be a fair and honest one in which the secret ballot would be introduced. These pledges were received with considerable skepticism both at home and abroad. Events proved such skepticism to have been well-justified, although Luis may have been quite sincere when first he expressed such intentions.

LIBERAL PROGRESSIVISM IN COSTA RICA

Central America's least turbulent country did not escape political difficulties of her own in the period between 1930 and 1960. Nevertheless, she avoided the extremes of revolution and oppression experienced by some of her neighbors. In 1940 a strong reform movement was initiated under the sponsorship of President Rafael Calderón Guardia, based primarily on the strengthening of labor unions and the labor movement generally. In 1944 Teodoro Picado Michalski succeeded to the presidency and it soon became clear that he viewed benevolently a growing communist influence in the labor unions. In reaction to the leftist trend of governmental policy, the moderates made a strenuous effort to recover control of the country in 1948, nominating as their presidential candidate a well-known liberal publisher, Otilio Ulate. Ulate won the election, but he was not permitted to take office. Opposition in congress declared the election void and ordered Ulate arrested.

At this critical point there appeared on the scene a young landowner and farmer, José Figueres, who organized a small militia which he designated an 'Army of National Liberation.' From a stronghold in the mountains south of Cartago he waged open warfare against the forces of Dr. Calderón Guardia and his supporters who controlled the capital. Figueres had little difficulty in overcoming the motley combination of extreme rightists and extreme leftists clinging illegally to governmental power. He quickly established his control of the government by means of a junta which he dominated until peace was restored. Then, in 1949, he turned the presidency over to the legally elected contender, Otilio Ulate.

The rise to political prominence of José ('Pepe') Figueres marked a significant moment in the political and international affairs of the Caribbean area. A liberal leader who strongly supported social and economic change by means of the free operation of democratic processes, Figueres opposed

both the *caudillo*-type rule of the Somozas and the Marxist–Leninist doctrines of the communist revolutionaries. He found himself in accord with
the reform efforts of Arévalo in Guatemala and Rómulo Gallegos in Venezuela, but he disliked strongly the dictatorial regimes of Trujillo, Somoza,
and Pérez Jiménez. His election to the Costa Rican presidency in 1953
gave him a strong position from which to improve conditions in his own
country while at the same time encouraging liberal movements among his
Caribbean neighbors. Soon he was an international figure to be reckoned
with, and he demonstrated few scruples about mixing in the affairs of
those countries whose governments he viewed as despotic.

As president, Figueres pushed his own development program, which included broadening social welfare, development of public housing, and the
fostering of industries such as meat-packing to relieve dependence on the
unstable banana trade. Unlike every other country in Central America, Costa
Rica is characterized by widespread land ownership among the population,
and steps toward industrialization were viewed as important not only to
raise the productivity of the country but also to counter the increasing
problem of *minifundia,* that is, the division of landholdings into units too
small for economic operation.

Nationalization of some industries brought on charges of socialism, but
Figueres seemed little bothered by such criticisms. His was a pragmatic
policy, not a doctrinaire one. Outspoken criticism of dictators, however,
including his near neighbor, 'Tacho' Somoza, led to unflattering exchanges
and outright hostility. Only the quick and forceful action of the Organization of American States prevented warfare between Costa Rica and Nicaragua early in 1955.

Figueres' domestic and international adventures alarmed enough voters
to elect a conservative foe of reform movements to the presidency in 1958.
Mario J. Echandi was chosen over the Figueres-supported candidate, Francisco J. Orlich. As president, Echandi made no genuine effort to reverse
the many policies of his predecesor or to take the government out of the
many business enterprises on which Figueres had embarked it. A congress
supportive of Figueres' National Liberation Party was prepared to block
any conservative initiatives Echandi was inclined to take. In the meantime,
Figueres gave major attention to the organization of the National Liberation Party on an institutional as distinct from a personal basis. As a result,
by 1960 the party's hopes and those of Francisco Orlich were again on the
rise.

PANAMA'S STRUGGLE FOR IDENTITY

Panama's independence and sovereignty were ostensibly enhanced in 1936 by a treaty with the United States in which the American protectorate over Panama was abandoned; the right of intervention was renounced; and the annual payment for lease of the Canal Zone was substantially increased. At the outbreak of World War II, nevertheless, Panamanian President Arnulfo Arias showed strong sympathies for the Axis powers and was clearly anti-American in his outlook and policies. Shortly, he was ousted from office by pro-United States groups and the American government was bitterly denounced in many parts of the hemisphere for alleged complicity in the revolt. After 1946, Police Chief José Remón became the dominant figure in Panamanian politics, and in 1952 he became president.

José Antonio Remón did much to improve the status of his country in the few brief years he held office, for in 1955 he was assassinated shortly after returning from a visit to Washington. His record of accomplishments included an improved tax structure in Panama and the negotiation of a far more favorable treaty with the United States over the status of the Canal Zone than any previous agreement in the history of his country. The annual lease fee was more than quadrupled to $1,930,000, valuable property of the Panama Railroad was transferred to the Panamanian government, and the hated 'gold' and 'silver' wage scale differentials between American and Panamanian laborers working in the Zone were terminated. Although the treaty went into effect after Remón's death, it constituted a monument to his remarkable capabilities in seeking to resolve long-standing differences between his country and the United States.

In the election of 1956, Ernesto de la Guardia was the victor. He numbered among his supporters both arch-nationalists and communists, and soon he was trying to outdo his predecessor by exacting even greater concessions from the United States. Guardia openly incited Panamanian agitation for complete surrender of the Canal Zone by the United States, and his followers were further aroused by the Suez crisis and Egypt's ultimate success against Britain and France. There were numerous violent demonstrations. On one occasion late in 1959 it seemed likely that there would be an outbreak of unrestrained fighting between Panamanian and Canal Zone forces.

In the face of insults and provocations, American President Dwight Eisenhower remained calm and willing to make concessions. Panamanians still had many grievances, including the fact that the Panamanian flag had never flown over the Canal Zone, though they regarded it as part of Panama's national territory. They asserted that the uniform wage scale agreed to in the treaty signed in 1955 had never been put into effect, and a host of other issues were raised, many of which had little to do with the Canal Zone or its status. At the end of the decade, tensions remained high and most issues remained unresolved, at least from the Panamanian point of view. New troubles were in store for the years to follow.

The presidential election of May, 1960, had one unique quality—it followed an administration in which the president had served out his entire term, a feat that Panamanians under the age of thirty could not recall in their lifetimes. Roberto F. Chiari, the victor, sought to establish cordial relations with the United States and frowned on the destructive anti-Yankee demonstrations. He advised his countrymen to forget their nationalistic fixation on the canal and to develop industries and businesses that would raise the standard of living for all. He also called for a major miracle—the elimination of corruption in government and a thorough regeneration of political life. Many Panamanians applauded Chiari's goals, and watched and waited for the miracle to occur.

EL SALVADOR: STABILITY AND PROGRESS UNDER MILITARY GUIDANCE

In 1931 El Salvador's elitist oligarchic rule gave way to a military dictatorship. The immediate cause was an alleged communist uprising in the western department of Sonsonate. Frightened by the possible threat to property and social stability, the coffee aristocracy which had long dominated the political and economic life of Central America's smallest republic acquiesced in a military take-over by General Maximiliano Hernández Martínez, a professional military officer. Quickly Martínez restored order and stability to the country, and the fears of the property owners subsided.

The rule of General Martínez lasted until 1944, when a general strike forced his resignation. In the interval, however, El Salvador achieved rather substantial physical progress. The Inter-American Highway was completed and paved from border to border; many schools were built and the educational system extended throughout most of the country. Government services were performed with relative efficiency, and the steady extension of coffee cultivation brought to the country a favorable trade balance and a sound currency. Martínez was, in one sense, a man of the people, for he appealed to the masses of the population while protecting the economic interest of the propertied classes. His eccentricities and spiritualistic nostrums appealed to the ignorant populace and caused him to enjoy a substantial following among thousands who felt an empathy with the man even though the tangible benefits of his concern for them were difficult to discover. In the end he lost touch with the changing imperatives of his era, and his ruthless suppression of opposition alienated intellectual leaders and many of his military subordinates.

Martínez' departure into exile was followed by a period of instability finally terminated in 1948 when a military junta took over the corrupt government of Salvador Castañeda Castro, and called for a constituent assembly and election of a new president. The military junta was composed of a group of younger army officers whose dedication to reform and improved social and economic conditions for the majority of the population set in motion a pattern of political leadership almost unique in the hemisphere. In 1950 a new constitution was adopted and Colonel Oscar Osorio, who had presided over the military junta, was elected to a six-year presidential term. The election was conducted in circumstances that assured fairness and honesty and marked a high point in El Salvador's political development.

Osorio's presidency was a period of outstanding achievement. Great efforts were exerted to strengthen the economy and improve the status of the lower classes. Public water systems were constructed; housing projects were erected on a substantial scale and in widely separated parts of the country, not simply in the capital. A hydro-electric dam on the Río Lempa doubled the nation's supply of electrical energy, and this in turn spurred the development of a variety of new industries, primarily in the capital area, that achieved regional importance later in the decade when the Central American Common Market began to emerge from the planning stage. New efforts extended and improved the nation's system of highways, educational facilities were expanded, and a significant program of governmental reorganization and administrative modernization was undertaken with highly beneficial results.

El Salvador's government presented the unusual example of a military regime alert to the growing demands of a poverty-stricken population for an improved standard of living and greater economic and social opportunity. Opposed to communist ideology and revolutionary destruction of the social order, the leadership chose a moderate but steadily progressive course to bring about constructive change. Thus the revolutionary influences emanating from Moscow, occasionally from Guatemala City, and later from la Habana, were effectively countered.

In 1956 José María Lemus succeeded Osorio as president. Although he continued the programs initiated by his predecessor, in whose administration he had served as minister of interior, he proved too inflexible and unimaginative to meet recurring crises brought on by dissatisfied leftists and university students. The progress of improvement slowed and Lemus became preoccupied with heavy-handed measures to curb the opposition. In October, 1960, he was driven from office by a short-lived radical regime that was itself shortly replaced by a new military junta. The new junta quickly indicated its intention to move ahead on the same path charted by Osorio and his associates some years before.

THE POVERTY OF HONDURAS

The regime of dictator Tiburcio Carías in Honduras ended in 1948 when the old man voluntarily relinquished office to his hand-picked successor, Juan Manuel Gálvez. Carías had ruled for sixteen years, and little could be said for his government other than that it provided a respite from the political instability that preceded and followed his tenure in office. The country remained basically underpopulated and impoverished, dominated in the Caribbean coastal area by American banana producers and in the isolated mountain towns and cities by local *caciques* and political chieftains. Honduras for years was the world's principal producer of bananas, but the sale of this crop produced little benefit to the country. Apart from the wages paid to the workers and a small part of the profit shared with the government, income from the sale of bananas was distributed abroad. Most Honduran farmers continued to eke out a miserable livelihood by subsistence agriculture conducted in the most primitive fashion. Industry scarcely existed, and government employment and related services provided the basis for the economic life of the capital, Tegucigalpa.

Gálvez proved to be an able liberal rather than the conservative heir of Carías that most people expected him to be. Political life was freed from the stifling restraints under which it had so long been held, and discussion of national issues and problems in the press became commonplace for the first time in years. Gálvez provided in the national budget for modest expansions in education, road construction, and welfare services. He sought to encourage foreign investment leading to the beginning of industrialization, and his efforts to promote agricultural diversification raised coffee to a more significant status in the export economy. A prolonged controversy with the United Fruit Company troubled the latter days of his administration, but in the end he was successful in obtaining more favorable wages and working conditions for Honduran banana laborers. Perhaps the Honduran labor unions deserved the credit for this accomplishment more than did the president, for a prolonged strike was necessary to bring about a settlement. Unfortunately, Panama Disease and other illnesses attacked the banana plantations in these same years, greatly reducing production and causing the fruit industry to transfer much of its operations to other Caribbean areas and on to Ecuador in South America. Soon Ecuador had replaced Honduras as the world's principal producer.

Gálvez' opposition to Jacobo Arbenz in Guatemala assured him American support in the form of financial assistance. It was from Honduran soil that Castillo Armas launched his successful invasion to drive Arbenz from Guatemala.

An indecisive election in 1954 resulted in the seizure of power by a would-be dictator, Julio Lozano Díaz, whose arbitrary measures displeased everyone, including the army. In 1956 he was removed from office by a military junta which ruled for a little over a year and then turned the government over to Dr. José Ramón Villeda Morales, a prominent physician from Tegucigalpa who had been chosen president by a constituent assembly elected in 1967. Villeda Morales, a liberal in the style of Figueres in Costa Rica, was widely acclaimed both inside and outside of Honduras as a person likely to lead his country far along the road to political maturity and national development. By 1960 he was in the midst of his term and seemed to be fulfilling many of the expectations that were raised by his selection for the presidential office.

Northern South America

The anti-communist issue was not the only one which split the Tenth Inter-American Conference at Caracas in March of 1954. Costa Rica, long hailed as one of the most democratic of Latin American nations, refused to send a representative. In a letter to the Organization of American States, President Figueres made clear that communism was not the only present danger to Latin America; he pointed out that dictatorship of any type was equally threatening and a more persistent and widespread menace. Although he pledged that his country would adhere to any resolutions adopted for strengthening American solidarity and defense of the hemisphere, conditions in Venezuela convinced his government that it should not be represented at Caracas.

VENEZUELA'S STRUGGLE FOR A MORE DEMOCRATIC WAY OF LIFE

The conditions to which Figueres alluded had been of considerable concern to the friends of democracy and of civil liberties throughout the hemisphere. Following the death of the old tyrant, Juan Vicente Gómez, in 1935, a new constitution was drafted during the provisional presidency of General Eleázar López Contreras, but it provided no significant improvement. State legislatures and municipal councils were to elect the national congress, and congress in turn was to choose the president. This arrangement continued the same old system that assured conservative control of the government and discouraged the emergence of a popular figure and national political leader as a contender for the chief executive office. López Contreras' rule was politically oppressive, and potential political leaders were exiled.

In the 1940 election López Contreras was able to dictate the selection of his successor, and the magic wand of power touched another army general, Isaías Medina Angarita. Medina Angarita served during the years of World War II, and this period witnessed an enormous increase in the prosperity of the country, primarily as a consequence of increased oil exports to support the Allied war effort. The inflow of new wealth stimulated the growth of private industry while at the same time enabling the government to undertake many physical improvements such as new roads, more school buildings, and better communications facilities. A new agreement with the oil industry was negotiated that increased royalties paid the government, thus assuring increased funds for the expansion of public services. Equally significant, however, was the president's relaxed attitude in the area of political liberties. Exiles returned and parties were permitted to organize. During this period an outstanding liberal intellectual, Rómulo Betancourt, assumed leadership of a new political force known as *Acción Democrática* (AD), which party soon became the most prominent in the country, numbering among its supporters the principal intellectuals, labor leaders, many of the growing middle class, and numerous younger army officers. When, toward the end of his term, it seemed likely that Medina Angarita would dictate the election of a conservative successor, Acción Democrática joined forces with a group of the younger military officers and overthrew the government.

Rómulo Betancourt became head of a seven-man junta, five of whom were civilians. Thus Betancourt became the first civilian to rule the country in over a hundred years. Quickly a new constitution was drafted and adopted, one providing for direct election of the president. Universal suffrage was adopted, thus permitting women to vote for the first time. Many other changes were brought about by legislative action. Taxes on oil profits were increased, a program of land distribution was inaugurated for the benefit of the poor peasant, and major steps were taken to extend an effective educational system throughout the country. Also, an effort was made to improve the work skills of the population by encouraging immigration from war-ravaged Europe. The regime of the junta was moderate and liberal rather than revolutionary; its goals were the achievement of long-needed social and economic reforms under a representative political system. After adoption of the new constitution in 1947, an election was held for president early in 1948, and the overwhelming victor in an open and free election was Rómulo Gallegos, Venezuela's best-known writer and intellectual leader. He was the candidate of Acción Democrática.

Rómulo Gallegos assumed office February 15, 1948. Ten months later he was ousted by a new military dictatorship headed by Lieutenant Colonel Carlos Delgado Chalbaud, who immediately imposed an oppressive and arbitrary rule, suspending constitutional guarantees and then the constitution itself and all the organs of government created by it. Rómulo Gallegos' regime had been too liberal and provided little opportunity for honest graft on the part of military leaders. Acción Democrática was proscribed and driven underground, its leaders exiled. The clock was turned back, and Venezuela once again found itself living under a ruthless dictatorship.

In 1950 Delgado Chalbaud was assassinated by a jealous fellow officer, and soon a new military figure, Colonel Marco Pérez Jiménez, a member of the junta from the same Andean province of Táchira that had spawned Juan Vicente Gómez, emerged as strong man of Venezuela. In 1952, apparently deluded by his imagined popularity, Pérez Jiménez held an election, but before all the returns were in it was clear that his candidates were running far behind his foes, even though Acción Democrática was not permitted to participate. He had all the ballots seized and declared a smashing victory for his official party and named himself provisional president. His friends promptly voted a new constitution in keeping with his views and a year later elected him president for five years. He was the military dictator to whose country 'Pepe' Figueres refused to send a Costa Rican delegate in 1954.

Pérez Jiménez relied heavily on the army, and he bought its loyalty by building a luxurious officers' club and by indulging the troops in abuses of civilians and other non-military forms of recreation. His spies were everywhere and no one was safe in his privacy or his property. Because of the Korean War and United States import policies, Venezuelan oil exports mounted once again, and the government received half of the profits, or at least theoretically it did. Tremendous amounts went into the pockets and bank accounts of Pérez Jiménez and his friends. Oil was almost the only export, but Venezuelans not employed in the industry benefited little. The dictator assigned one-third of the budget to 'public works' such as the enormously costly highway between Caracas and the port of La Guaira, superhighways in and around Caracas, and new buildings constructed on a most elaborate scale. Squalid slums spread unchecked around the capital while the dictator provided lavish parties for himself and his associates.

In 1957 Pérez Jiménez announced cancellation of the elections scheduled for the following year, and instead he held a plebiscite in which people were asked to vote for his continuance in office. Who would dare cast the red card of opposition? In the meantime, an underground movement against the dictator had spread, for Venezuelans wanted no more of his rule. After an air force rebellion failed in January, 1958, a general strike was more successful. On January 23 Pérez Jiménez and his family left for the Dominican Republic and luxurious exile in Miami. He did not go unprepared and in poverty, for he had thoughtfully deposited or invested abroad an estimated $200 million which he had acquired in the time-honored methods of Venezuelan dictators since the time of Guzmán Blanco.

An unfortunate aspect of the Pérez Jiménez rule was the favor he sought and secured in Washington. General Eisenhower, as President of the United States, conferred on him the highly regarded Legion of Merit, and in so doing expressed support for the tyrant in terms so flattering as to turn the stomach of any democratic Venezuelan exile. To make matters worse, his hated police chief, Pedro Estrada, whose hundreds of tortured political prisoners languished in filthy Venezuelan jails, was offered a warm welcome and elegant reception upon a visit to Washington. It should have been no surprise to Vice-President Richard Nixon that he was greeted with spittle and stones rather than flowers when he visited Caracas after the decorated dictator was comfortably residing in the United States.

After Pérez Jiménez' departure, Admiral Wolfgang Larrazábal became interim chief, and exiles flocked back from abroad, including among their number Betancourt and Gallegos. Larrazábal, who showed symptoms of presidential fever but resisted the temptation to seize power, wooed the masses and posed as a moderate leftist. He showed little irritation, therefore, when the Nixon visit turned out to be something less than a friendly chat.

In an election called for December, 1958, Larrazábal represented a radically oriented coalition, while Rómulo Betancourt was the candidate of Acción Democrática and the winner. Betancourt polled 59.2 per cent of the popular vote. The candidate of the Social Christian Party (COPEI) was Rafael Caldera, and although he obtained but 16.2 per cent of the vote in contrast with Larrazábal's 34.6 per cent, his emergence on the political scene was to have considerable future significance.

Before turning the presidential office over to Betancourt in February, 1959, Larrazábal recast Venezuela's basic agreement with the oil companies by forcing them to pay the government 60 per cent of the profits rather than 50 per cent as formerly, an action Betancourt had promised to take if elected. Extreme nationalists demanded confiscation of the foreign oil company properties, but cooler heads were well aware that if nationalization occurred Venezuela would not be able to sell her oil.

With Betancourt officially in office, Venezuela, in the second half of the twentieth century, at last undertook to create a tradition of civilian rule. The army was quiescent, at least temporarily, shamed and silenced by the sordid excesses of the Pérez Jiménez regime it had helped force on the country. In June of 1960 an attempt to assassinate Betancourt almost succeeded, but the source of this outrage was the Dominican Republic where ex-dictator Pérez Jiménez was living on friendly terms with Rafael Trujillo, the 'dean' of Latin American dictators. The Organization of American States censured Trujillo as a result of the plot, but this was only one incident in a long series of actions designed to bring down or discredit the Betancourt government. Some were inspired by the extreme right and others by the communists in Venezuela; others had their origin in Castro's Cuba as well as the Dominican Republic.

The Betancourt government moved rapidly to extend educational, health, and welfare services throughout the country while at the same time pressing ahead on major industrialization and regional development projects, particularly in the river basin of the Orinoco, a long-neglected area east and south of the capital. Soon the school population had more than doubled, and civic education was a major focus in the application of both human and fiscal resources. Betancourt was determined that the following decade would not be a repetition of the last.

'LA VIOLENCIA' IN COLOMBIA

Colombia weathered the great economic depression of the 1930's without loss of political stability. Indeed, unlike most of her neighbors, in 1930 Colombia established a Liberal regime through the electoral process, and the Liberals remained in power until 1946. During this period an extensive program of social legislation was passed in the interest of labor, and a significant extension of the educational system was achieved. The most articulate and implacable foe of the Liberals throughout their ascendancy was Laureano Gómez, an arch-reactionary publisher who urged the kind of Hispanicism and Catholicism that appealed to a highly conservative segment of the population. During the Second World War, Gómez lauded the Nazis and scourged the United States.

In spite of strong conservative opposition, the legislative record of the Liberal governments during the 1930's was impressive. The constitution was amended to make possible taxes on personal income and capital, the Catholic Church was disestablished and its control over education ended, and social security laws were passed for the first time. Mass poverty and ignorance remained endemic throughout the country, however, and the gulf between the few wealthy landowners and the Indian and *mestizo* masses grew wider.

In 1932 a serious incident occurred that for a time threatened war with Peru. A Peruvian force seized the little Amazon valley settlement of Leticia which five years before had been ceded to Colombia by treaty. A Colombian force was sent to oppose the interlopers, and a serious clash occurred. A mediated settlement favorable to Colombia and accompanied by an apology from Peru was finally achieved with the help of the League of Nations.

Journalist Alfonso López had represented Colombia in the dispute over the Leticia seizure, and in 1934 he became the Liberal party candidate for the presidency. The Conservative party staged only a token campaign, and the Liberals won both the presidency and the control of congress. The impressive changes in the constitution and in legislation already mentioned were the immediate consequence and by 1938 Colombia enjoyed a most respected image throughout Latin America. She seemed to have turned the corner, replacing a long tradition of violence with stability, order, economic progress, and freedom. Eduardo Santos succeeded López, and he was in turn replaced by López in 1942. At this time foreigners were high in praise of the Colombian political system, which appeared to function smoothly and effectively. However, the Liberal party had grown complacent and somewhat corrupt. A socialistic faction within the party led by Jorge Eliécer Gaitán became increasingly popular in the cities, where he appealed to the lower classes and to dissatisfied labor. The Liberal ranks were split.

Laureano Gómez, the Conservative leader, attacked the López administration through his newspaper and tried to convince Colombians to return to a course in keeping with Hispanic tradition and Catholic doctrine, as he interpreted these. Everything seemed to go wrong at once. The country was divided by extreme views; labor was militant and eager for battle, though not certain which side would suit it best; and the middle class was stung by rampant inflation. In 1944 the president and some of his cabinet were shamefully kidnapped and held for a few days in Pasto. The following year the confusion was heightened by the end of World War II and the economic dislocations which this event unleashed. López, no longer a national hero, resigned.

Provisional President Alberto Lleras Camargo, a distinguished writer and Liberal party diplomat, tried to save the country from complete chaos, but the country would not be saved. Lleras called elections in 1946, but the Liberals split their vote between moderate Gabriel Turbay and the radical Gaitán, and Conservative Mariano Ospina Pérez won a plurality along with the presidential office.

Ospina offered the Liberals several cabinet posts, which they accepted, but this cordial gesture availed little. Colombia, in the throes of rapid industrialization and suffering acutely from inflation, would not be soothed. Public disorder increasingly threatened and angry threats and charges were exchanged by the constituted authorities and their many opponents. In the midst of this troubled situation, the Ninth Inter-American Conference assembled in Bogotá in the spring of 1948.

The Conference had little more than convened in April of that year when Jorge Eliécer Gaitán was murdered on the street in daytime in full view of many people. There was a virtual explosion, as crowds rushed through the city killing well-known Conservatives and destroying public and private property. The government fled the city, Gómez left for Spain, and the violence continued unchecked. This riot, the *bogotazo,* inaugurated a decade or more of civil war that Colombians named *'La Violencia,'* as if it were a disease. In the elections of 1950 the Liberals abstained from voting and arch-reactionary Laureano Gómez, back from his asylum in Spain, was elected. Gómez knew that the majority of Liberals loathed him, and he preferred to reciprocate this sentiment rather than win over any of his opponents. He maintained a state of siege and kept the prisons full.

Ospina Pérez had imposed censorship prior to the 1950 election, and Gómez continued it in violation of long Colombian tradition. He incited religious fanatics to attack Protestant missionaries, many of whom were beaten, some fatally. Because a large part of the army was Liberal in political persuasion, Gómez sent troops to participate in the Korean War side by side with the hated Yankees who, with other members of the United Nations, were trying to prevent the take-over of South Korea by North Korean communists.

By 1952, all of Colombia's apparent political gains had vanished, and many of her economic gains with them. In that year Gómez was stricken by a heart attack, and the army began sharing his power, but it did not abate the oppression and violence. The entire country was in a virtual state of war, a war to the death between Liberals and Conservatives. Towns known for their Liberal or Conservative coloration were open to attack and destruction by their opponents. In June of 1963 the army finally deposed and exiled Gómez, and its head, General Gustavo Rojas Pinilla, replaced him.

In spite of a long-standing aversion to military intervention in politics, Colombians breathed a sigh of relief and greeted Rojas Pinilla as a deliverer. Their relief and greetings were premature. Rojas made few policy changes, although he relaxed somewhat the strict censorship of the press and eased the pressure on non-Catholics. He did nothing to provide badly needed schools, to improve the lot of the unhappy urban masses, or to restore economic stability, although a flurry of speculation followed the change in government leadership. Rojas Pinilla's chief interest seemed to be collecting cattle ranches and engaging in other forms of personal enrichment. All parts of society turned against him and he was greeted in public with jeers. On one lamentable occasion a huge crowd in the Bogotá bull ring hissed his daughters, and Rojas ordered police to fire on the hecklers.

No one knows how many people were killed and wounded, but estimates ran as high as several hundred.

The final insult to the country came in 1957 when Rojas called a constituent assembly which elected him to another four-year term. Nationwide opposition, a general strike, and widespread looting worried the army, and a group of generals deposed Rojas and sent him off to Europe. Lleras Camargo met with Laureano Gómez in Spain to negotiate a settlement between the warring political parties. In the Declaration of Sitges, a small town near Barcelona, the two leaders agreed to divide power between the Liberals and Conservatives for a period of twelve years. Each party was to receive half of the seats in the national and departmental legislatures as well as in the municipal councils, and this arrangement would extend as well to commissions, judicial offices, and key administrative posts. The presidency would be alternated between the two parties, with the office to go to the Conservatives for the first four years. Other commitments extended the right to vote to women, provided that one-tenth of the budget was to be allocated for education, and supported Catholicism as the official religion. A historic plebiscite on December 1, 1967, produced what nearly amounted to unanimous approval by the voters of the 'National Front' compact, which was extended to sixteen years.

A number of difficulties remained to be overcome, however, before *convivencia* became a reality. The Conservatives could not agree on a choice for the first president, so eventually they passed the first presidential term to the Liberals with the proviso that Lleras Camargo be the candidate. Reluctantly he accepted, and in May of 1958 his election was overwhelming. In keeping with the agreement, Lleras divided cabinet seats between the two parties, and carefully adhered to all other terms of the compact.

The arrangement appeared to function well at first, and the state of siege, imposed after the *bogotazo* ten years before, was finally lifted. The Violencia gradually diminished in intensity, but it was far from over. Armed bands with no particular political allegiance continued to roam the countryside murdering innocent victims, kidnapping prominent figures to hold for ransom, and committing other acts of brutality and violence. Rojas Pinilla returned to stand trial before a reluctant Colombian senate in January, 1959. The judgment deprived him of his pension for having abused his authority, and the supreme court later sentenced him for financial misdeeds to a period in prison, but he was soon free and talking of re-entering politics.

Dictatorship and Revolution in the Islands

Prior to and throughout the period of World War II, the United States continued to maintain its paramount position in the Caribbean. When war first broke out in Europe, the foreign minister of Panama invited the governments of the inter-American system to a meeting in Panama City for mutual consultation. The Declaration of Panama that emerged was a general statement of neutrality toward the warring powers, but of greater long-run significance was pronouncement of a neutral zone within two hundred or more miles from the coasts of the American continents and within which no hostile acts were to be committed by any belligerent nation. It was agreed that the various countries party to the declaration might collectively or individually patrol their adjacent waters to make certain that no act of war occurred within them. A number of years later various Latin American countries found this concept a useful one in proclaiming that their territorial waters extended two hundred miles to sea.

The United States was particularly concerned as to the security of the Panama Canal, and a friendly Colombian government took steps to assure it that airfields within its territory might not be used by the Axis powers for launching a possible attack on the canal. Its German-dominated airline was converted into a new company owned jointly by Colombian and American capital, and in other parts of the region German interests were gradually liquidated, including German-owned coffee plantations in Guatemala.

Another significant step was the leasing by the United States of island bases in the Caribbean from Great Britain in exchange for fifty destroyers. Included in the agreement was the mainland colony of Guiana. Another inter-American agreement made at la Habana in 1940 anticipated the possible need to take French and Dutch colonies under protection by the Western Hemisphere countries to prevent their being used as bases by the Germans who had overrun the mother countries. Such action never became necessary, however.

After the war, the growing menace of communist infiltration replaced the comparatively feeble Nazi efforts to influence the American nations. The United States remained ever watchful and assisted significantly in removing the first major communist thrust in Guatemala in 1954. The problems that emerged a few years later in Cuba offered no comparable solution.

Cuban political life between 1930 and 1960 went through a variety of phases and some hopeful experiments as well as recurrent dictatorships before the triumph of Fidel Castro. In 1931 dictator Gerardo Machado y Morales suppressed a revolt against his tyrannical regime, but his power was slipping and he was expelled from the country two years later. A period of confusion followed in which a new strong man finally emerged. This was Fulgencio Batista, an army sergeant who led an enlisted-men's revolt in 1933 against senior military officers and their weak puppet president, Dr. Carlos Manuel de Céspedes. Batista stripped the army of its old officer corps and set up a five-man junta to rule the country. The United States refused to recognize the new government and the possibility of military intervention once more loomed on the Caribbean horizon. Batista had his junta turn over the government to a professor in the medical school of the National University, Dr. Ramón Grau San Martín, whose liberal and reformist proclivities were immediately manifested in a series of new laws. The American ambassador, Sumner Welles, opposed the new regime and was able to persuade his government to withhold recognition. In January of 1934 Grau San Martín had to resign, squeezed between United States displeasure and Batista's impatience. In the same year, the United States as part of President Roosevelt's 'Good Neighbor' Policy, renounced its right to intervene in Cuba under the Platt Amendment that the framers of the Cuban constitution had been forced to incorporate in the document as the price of independence. Ambassador Welles well understood the undesirable role that this amendment had played in Cuban politics for three decades.

Batista, enjoying the support of an army whose officers only a few months before had been enlisted men and owed their new rank to him, strengthened his hold on the government and installed another president, Dr. Carlos Mendieta y Montúfur, who was no more successful in preserving order and administering the country than Grau had been. In 1935 Mendieta resigned. Batista remained behind the scene as president-maker until 1940, when a new constitution was adopted and he had himself elected president. In 1944 Batista permitted Grau San Martín to take office after an election in which he had supported another candidate, Carlos Saladrigas. Batista's and Grau's administrations both benefited enormously from the high sugar prices that prevailed during World War II, as well as from a friendly United States that needed military bases and was prepared to pay for them. American loans were also available for physical construction and development programs on the island. Batista's administration is generally credited with having provided a period of stable progress with relative freedom. Grau's government, on the other hand, was viewed as increasingly corrupt and his Auténtico party split in part because of this issue in 1946. Nevertheless, in 1948 Grau's choice, Carlos Prío Socarrás, succeeded him in the presidential office by electoral victory.

The period of Prío Socarrás' administration was punctuated with frequent acts of political violence, although the president made a strong effort to maintain democratic freedoms and political processes. Communists were active in the labor movement, as they had been since the 1930's, but the basis of Prío's support was being eroded away by disaffections within his own Auténtico party. Just before the scheduled election of 1952, Batista stepped back into the picture and toppled Prío from power, installing himself once more as Cuba's strong man. Although he had been one of the candidates for the presidency in the upcoming election, Batista had learned that an army revolt was to be staged whether or not he agreed to lead it. Lacking voter support, Batista accepted, and the revolt succeeded with little opposition. If the charges made against his two immediate predecessors were true, graft and corruption had flourished unchecked during their administrations. Batista set out to prove what small-time operators Grau and Prío had been.

Although Batista hinted at enacting reforms, he suspended the Constitution of 1940, suspended civil liberties, and drove his opponents into exile. Students and political leaders complained and agitated, but Batista silenced them with harsh and repressive measures. In July, 1953, two disaffected brothers, Fidel and Raúl Castro, staged a futile attack on an army barracks in Santiago; they were fortunate not to be shot when they surrendered.

Batista kept himself in power until the end of 1958, suppressing all opposition with a vigor and brutality not evident in his earlier years of power. Nevertheless, the country appeared prosperous, industrialization increased, and tourism expanded greatly as la Habana became a center for the operations of international gambling syndicates, much to the profit of the grasping dictator. The Korean War maintained a steady demand for sugar and kept the price high. Thus Cuba's principal industry prospered, although few of the benefits trickled down to the impoverished and under-employed cane cutters.

In spite of the veneer of prosperity, a great restlessness and widespread resentment pervaded Cuba. This dissatisfaction was expressed in constant plotting against the government, frequent bombings, and other acts of de-struction and violence that Batista blandly attributed to communist agents. He now outlawed the communist party (*Partido Socialista Popular*) whose legalization under a different name he had assisted years before. In De-cember of 1956 the Castro brothers, returning from Mexico where they had fled in 1955 following release from prison, led a band of eighty-two insurrectionists ashore in the province of Oriente. All but a dozen or so were killed by Batista's troops, but the survivors were able to make their way into the Sierra Maestra range where they proceeded to organize a guerrilla force in opposition to the Cuban dictator. The Twenty-Sixth of July Movement, as Castro's rebellion became known in memory of the fu-tile attack on the Moncada barracks at Santiago in 1953, sparked popular imagination and aroused public sympathy from the outset.

From his mountain refuge, Fidel Castro, aided by his brother and an Argentine economist and guerrilla warfare expert, Ernesto ('Che') Gue-vara, opened a propaganda war against Batista and welcomed a stream of volunteers from all over the island. The bearded, khaki-clad rebels became the symbol of resistance to dictatorship, and a legend was already growing around Fidel long before he came out of the mountains in December, 1958. By this time he had won over the agricultural peasantry and the middle class, and he was gaining ground with urban labor whose commu-nist leadership had initially scoffed at Castro as an impractical lawyer and intellectual leader of the bourgeoisie. When Castro and his rebel army came out to give battle, Batista's military forces were totally demoralized by two years of frustrated effort to put an end to the guerrilla movement. The army collapsed. On January 1, 1959, the former army sergeant fled to enjoy his foreign bank accounts and to manage his foreign properties pur-chased earlier in anticipation of a forced 'retirement.'

Castro was received everywhere with the wildest enthusiasm, and his beard, cigar, and shapeless khaki uniform became adored symbols to many Cubans, who listened to his four-hour harangues with heroic patience and attention. Castro quickly cleaned house, and large numbers of Batista henchmen who had not been able to flee the country were shot by firing squads. The execution of so many opponents was not customary in Latin

America, for who could predict when the tables would be reversed? Neither was the practice of allowing television cameras to carry the garish public trials and their grisly aftermath to the public. It soon became clear that this was no ordinary revolution in the Latin American tradition, for the executions meant that the Castroites would fight to the death before giving up power and allowing their opponents to repay them with a new set of firing squads.

Manuel Urrutia was named president, but he soon resigned, protesting the extent of communist participation in the government. Oswaldo Dorticós Torrado replaced Urrutia, and Fidel Castro became premier while his brother, Raúl, became chief of the armed forces. The Partido Socialista Popular was not only given legal status again, but it became the only recognized party. Instead of reinstating the Constitution of 1940, which had been one of the key points in Castro's revolutionary campaign, a special Fundamental Law was promulgated early in February, 1959. Moderate and anti-communist supporters of the Castro revolution soon found themselves brushed aside and well-known communist leaders moved into significant positions throughout the government.

Soon a steady stream of Cuban refugees began arriving in Miami. Castro began vitriolic attacks on the United States and announced that the property of American companies and citizens would be nationalized. In mid-1960 President Eisenhower urged the United States Congress to curtail the program for purchasing Cuban sugar at subsidized prices. It would not be long before diplomatic relations between Cuba and the United States would be severed.

THE MISERY OF HAITI

Haitians had few causes for rejoicing in the three decades prior to 1960, even though American intervention ended in 1934. Sténio Vincent ruled the country from 1931 to 1941 by controlling the Haitian Guard, the constabulary trained by the American marines before their departure. Under Dumarsais Estimé, who was 'elected' in 1946, Haiti made some efforts at sweeping away economic and social privileges of the small group of landed elite. He began a road-building program, organized collective farms, and constructed model villages financed by the country's first income tax. In 1949, however, he was deposed by Colonel Paul Magloire because he sought re-election, and in the following year Magloire was elected president.

Magloire obtained foreign financial and technical aid for economic development, health, and education. His administration appeared to be fair and public-minded, but in 1956 a group of army officers ousted him for reasons not entirely clear. After a year of meddling maladministration, the army junta staged an election. François ('Papa Doc') Duvalier, a Haitian doctor and voodoo expert, was the winner.

Duvalier's regime was notably bloody and repressive in a land where the people have always suffered at the hands of their rulers. Schools and churches were closed if students or priests murmured in protest against the harsh regime. The country grew poorer and more oppressed, but Papa Doc's only genuine programs seemed to be the retention of power and elimination of the mulattoes.

TRUJILLO'S DOMINICAN DOMAIN

From 1930 on through 1960 the Dominican Republic served as the personal and private domain of Rafael Leonidas Trujillo Molina. By gaining control of the Dominican Guard he was able to achieve control of the country and to have himself re-elected repeatedly to the presidency except at intervals when he let his puppets play in the office. Trujillo's rule was almost entirely negative, for while he brought about improvements in agriculture and commerce the benefits of increased productivity were promptly absorbed in the family fortune. Politically, the dictator's rule represented tyranny and repression. He and his family and friends became multi-millionaires. Hundreds of Dominicans took refuge in exile, while many others disappeared or were 'accidentally killed' in automobile accidents or other incidents under mysterious circumstances. The Dominican exiles were involved in many desperate attempts to invade the country but without success; large numbers lost their lives for their trouble.

Under Trujillo the Dominican Republic was operated as a private business. Its foreign loans were repaid and its currency stabilized, and it was uniquely free of inflation. Trujillo was an able estate manager, but he kept his workers in ignorance and without hope for improvement. The torture and liquidation of the dictator's enemies were an apparent necessity to maintain control and prevent all challenges to his authority. Much that was known of this aspect of Trujillo's rule was in the form of rumors. His many American commercial friends doubted that they were true.

In 1956 Trujillo committed an act so brazen and brutal that it was almost unbelievable. In March of that year a Basque refugee named Jesús de

Galíndez, who was known to be writing a doctoral dissertation on the Trujillo era, mysteriously disappeared from Columbia University in New York City. Many months later the story was pieced together. Dominican agents had contracted with an American pilot named Gerald L. Murphy to fly a chartered plane to the Dominican Republic. Some months later Murphy disappeared mysteriously in the country shortly before he planned to return to the United States. Murphy had told his friends about bringing Galíndez to the island, and they repeated his story to United States authorities. There was a great outcry against Trujillo. His paid publicity agents in New York and some Washington politicians who had received enormous fees from him for very minor services, were unable to stem the outburst by extolling his virtues. The double murder was the beginning of the dictator's downfall, but the end was several years away.

In June, 1960, Trujillo's agents attempted to assassinate President Rómulo Betancourt of Venezuela, an old enemy. Explosives were prepared for detonation in a car that was parked along the route that Betancourt was expected to follow. As the president's car neared the parked vehicle, the explosion was set off by remote control. Two men were killed and Betancourt was badly burned. By now world opinion was so inflamed against Trujillo that the Organization of American States overcame its opposition to any form of intervention and imposed economic sanctions against the Dominican Republic. By 1960 Trujillo's enemies had taken renewed heart and were again busy plotting his destruction.

AMERICA'S PUERTO RICAN SHOWCASE

The most unique situation of any of the former Spanish colonies in the Caribbean region developed in Puerto Rico, the island retained by the United States as a permanent possession after the Spanish-American War. After languishing in neglect for years, Puerto Rico entered an era of rapid development under the guidance of Rexford Guy Tugwell, who was appointed as governor by Franklin D. Roosevelt. Economic progress was assisted by the boom period of World War II, when Puerto Rico became an important military and naval base, but it did not end with the cessation of hostilities. Assisted by Tugwell, energetic Puerto Rican leadership initiated and carried out a highly successful campaign of industrialization based upon the attraction to the island of a host of mainland business enterprises and manufacturing plants. At the same time, creation of hotel and recreational facilities attracted thousands of tourists who found in Puerto Rico an island paradise under the American flag and close to the main population centers of the United States East Coast.

In 1948 Puerto Rico was permitted to elect its own governor, and Luis Muñoz Marín was chosen. In July of 1952, the island became a 'free commonwealth' associated with the United States, its people retaining United States citizenship. Despite the clamor against colonialism in other parts of the Caribbean, Puerto Rico chose by the ballot box to remain a close relative of the United States when granted the right to decide on her future and manage her own affairs. In Governor Muñoz Marín, the island commonwealth had one of the most astute statemen in the Caribbean region. Under his administration Puerto Rico expanded its industrialization program, and within a decade the island's economic, social, and political conditions had improved remarkably.

A small, highly nationalistic group of Puerto Ricans continued to agitate for complete independence, but they did not attract a large following. Another group desired full statehood, but Muñoz Marín urged patience until the country was ready to bear its full share of federal taxes.

Puerto Rico was much changed from its days of dependence on the sugarcane crop. The industry, ingenuity, and enthusiasm of its businessmen and statesmen were bringing about its transformation from plantation to a modern diversified economy. The well-being of the people increased tremendously.

THE TROUBLED WATERS OF THE AMERICAN LAKE

By 1960 it had become increasingly apparent that the sometimes calm waters of the Caribbean were greatly agitated. The British colonies and dependencies throughout the region, widely scattered and economically weak, began in 1957 an effort to form a federation. Guyana, on the northern edge of the South American continent east of Venezuela, did not choose to participate. Still under British rule, its local government in that same year passed to a rising political group, the People's Progressive Party, led by Dr. Cheddi Jagan, son of an East Indian plantation foreman in Guyana. Jagan was widely suspected of communist sympathies, as was his American-born wife, Janet, and it appeared that should Great Britain grant independence to the colony, as the Jagans demanded, a communist foothold on the South American continent might well emerge. Guyana's reluctance to participate in a Caribbean federation seemed in part a racist fear of Negro domination on the part of Jagan's East Indian minority. It might also have interfered with a socialist take-over, which seemed within reach. Guyana's refusal to join the federation, plus Jamaica's dissatisfaction with the location of the capital in Trinidad, did not augur well for the future.

Trujillo's despotism could clearly last but little longer in the Dominican Republic, and Papa Doc Duvalier's grip on Haiti could easily slip. The abrupt departure of either dictator would leave a power vacuum dangerous to the easy domination of the area by the United States, for communist agents were certain to be found fishing in such troubled waters. Cuba was rapidly moving in the direction of establishing the first full-fledged communist state in the Western Hemisphere, a situation not likely to improve Russian-American relations in the midst of the Cold War. America's domination of the Caribbean was obviously approaching the crisis of a challenge.

15

Brazil: Destiny Not Quite Manifest

> Nationalism . . . corresponds to what pushes us forward and breaks
> with what held us back. Between the new and the old the choice is not
> difficult. Between the past and the future, no doubt exists. We choose
> the future.*

The Revolution of 1930

The year 1930 marked a turning point in Brazilian history as dramatic as
the changes from empire to republic. Politically, the easy-going liberalism
and federalism of the Old Republic succumbed to a world-wide trend toward centralism and executive domination that came in the wake of the
great depression. Economically, the drive for diversification and industrialization sought to lessen the monocultural dependence on coffee. Manufacturing made tremendous gains. Socially, long-neglected urban labor at last
had a champion to hand down much-needed and overdue reforms that the
complacent parliamentarians of the earlier regime had hardly even discussed. A drive to open the empty Brazilian West began, and the settlement of the Amazon valley became a government dream yet to be fulfilled.

The Brazilians themselves regarded many of these changes with mixed
feelings, for not all of the developments and results were clearly seen as
gains in the light of long-standing aspirations for a truly democratic and
representative government. Advances in certain directions meant retreat in
others; the balance sheet did not appear the same to all Brazilians, for
what was progress for one class seemed to constitute retrogression for another. Those who held to the positivist motto of 'Order and Progress' were

* Transl. from Nelson Werneck Sodré, *Raizas Históricas do Nacionalismo Bras-
ileiro,* Ministério da Educação e Cultura, Rio de Janeiro, 1960, p. 35; in E. Brad-
ford Burns, ed., *A Documentary History of Brazil,* Alfred A. Knopf, New York,
1966, p. 375.

delighted with the nation's orderly accomplishments. Those who held human values above all others condemned some of the changes and called the Labor Code a fraud. Brazil must make a choice, said the cynics: order *or* progress.

In 1930 Getúlio D. Vargas, governor of the southern pastoral state of Rio Grande do Sul, came into power by revolt during the world-wide economic crisis. Rio Grande do Sul was the home of Brazilian positivism, which had long been the state's official philosophy. Under Rio Grande's positivist state constitution the governor was all-powerful and the legislative assembly did little but approve the budget.

As leader of the Liberal Alliance against Júlio Prestes of São Paulo, Vargas saw the government of paulista Washington Luís Pereira de Sousa declare Prestes winner of the election. His followers refused to accept the results of what they considered to be a rigged election, and many states resented the growing power of São Paulo. Oswaldo Aranha, later to become a distinguished diplomat, played a prominent role in organizing rebellion. In October Washington Luís was easily swept from office before his term had expired. The army stepped in at the last moment, but reluctantly turned over the government to Vargas when he arrived in Rio de Janeiro.

Vargas immediately consolidated and centralized his power by replacing all state governors with intervenors responsible to himself. Without regularizing his regime or returning to constitutional rule, he began energetically to pursue the goals of the Liberal Alliance. He created a Ministry of Labor, Industry, and Commerce, and reorganized that of Education and Health. Illiteracy was estimated to be as high as 80 per cent, and was obviously a problem in need of even more urgent attention than it received.

The Brazilians, long accustomed to constitutional rule, chafed under the provisional regime, and they became insistent in their demands that a constituent convention be called. In 1932 the paulistas, who had seen the presidency snatched from their hands, rebelled. When Brazil's aviation pioneer, Alberto Santos-Dumont, learned that airplanes were being used in the fighting, he was so distressed that he took his own life. Both sides interrupted the fighting for one day out of respect for him.

After the rebellion had been quelled, with much cost and effort but few fatalities, Vargas bowed to the demands, and called for the election of delegates to a constitutional convention in 1933. The product of the convention's labors was a series of compromises between federalism and centralism, the Constitution of 1934. It introduced the corporate state concept, for one-fifth of the legislators were to be elected from among employers and employees in agriculture, labor, industry, commerce, and transportation. The delegates were also authorized to elect the president, and Vargas was the obvious choice. He was dissatisfied with the constitution and made plans to replace it with one more to his liking. He worked skillfully to discredit the legislature, and in this the members were helpful.

The Estado Novo

His opportunity came in 1937, when the time approached for a presidential election. The constitution prohibited re-election, which was one reason Vargas disliked it. As the election neared he systematically discouraged all of the potential candidates except Plínio Salgado, an active writer and leader of the fascist, green-shirted *integralista* organization. The fascists of Europe rejoiced, but before election day arrived Vargas had abolished all political parties, canceled elections, and replaced the Constitution of 1934 with one his aides had prepared. The incubation period was over, and the *Estado Novo* or New State was abruptly hatched. The explanation for this coup was that it was necessary to save the country from falling to the communists.

The new regime accentuated the trend toward executive domination by granting vast powers to the president and reducing those of the states. Federalism retreated before the principles of order, unity, and national defense imposed by the president. The Estado Novo constitution, which was never actually promulgated, recognized private property and private initiative, but the government's right to interfere in the economy was greatly enlarged. A progressive labor policy was implied, but a policy that the government would formulate without the aid of labor. Though he was clearly a dictator, Vargas remained popular with the masses, who had not lost any of their rights because they had few to lose.

After November 10, 1937, Vargas ruled as a benevolent dictator and legislated by decree. The last article of the constitution declared that the document would begin to be in force after a national plebiscite, and such a plebiscite was never ordered. The preceding article stated that 'In the entire country the state of national emergency is declared.' During a state of emergency the constitution was suspended. Earlier articles dealt with such a condition. Since the declaration of a national emergency was part of the constitution, only an amendment could remove it. But a constitutional amendment required action by the legislative body envisaged by the constitution, and elections could not be held until after the plebiscite. The crucial article, and the actual constitution under which Vargas governed Brazil, was No. 180, which declared: 'Until the National Parliament meets, the President of the Republic shall be empowered to issue decrees on all matters of legislation for the Union.'

The socio-economic program outlined by other articles of the constitution, however, represented the goals of the administration, and the government attempted to live up to that program. With the executive and legislative branches fused by Article 180 of the constitution, Vargas was able to issue a multitude of decrees. One of his first efforts was to create a fairly competent corps of civil servants.

The green-shirted integralistas, bitterly disappointed at having the prize snatched from their outstretched hands, attempted to assassinate Vargas in 1938. The attempt failed, and Vargas learned that the German ambassador was implicated in the plot. The integralistas were crushed; Salgado fled to Portugal; and the German ambassador was handed his hat. Vargas emerged from the crisis more securely in power than before.

From this time until 1945 Vargas ruled Brazil without effective rivals though not without opposition. His regime worked smoothly, and the ever-present force was subtly veiled. Vargas was an astute and undoctrinaire politician, and a capable administrator. He kept opposition in check, and won the support of many Brazilians for his program of developing transportation, for wider education of the mass of people, for political unity on a national scale, and for his labor policies. In these goals he was favored even by those who loathed his destruction of democracy, civil liberties, and representative government.

The threat of war in Europe led Vargas to expand and modernize Brazilian military forces, particularly the air arm, which was placed under the new Ministry of Aëronautics. German and Italian commercial air lines were eventually expropriated by the government, and operated by Brazilian personnel. As Brazil's military strength grew, Argentina's envy and concern also mounted.

INDUSTRIALIZATION

It was in industrial development, however, that the country made its most astonishing gains. Before the New State, industry provided only about 30 per cent of Brazilian production, but by the end of the Vargas administration the value of industrial products surpassed that of agriculture, and the country no longer relied on foreign sources for most of its consumer goods.

Most of the wartime industrial activity was centered in São Paulo and the Federal District. The São Paulo textile industry was particularly stimulated by the war, and Brazil emerged as one of the leading producers of cotton goods, with an export market in South America and South Africa. Her production of silk and other fabrics also rose.

In São Paulo many other industries were developed and most of them, like textile production, were favored by the availability of locally produced raw materials. All of these were not stimulated by the war, for many were actually retarded by the difficulty of acquiring machinery and by the shortage of shipping space. Unless the industries were essential to the war effort of the Allies, they were unable to obtain allocations of equipment and raw materials necessary for rapid expansion. Much of the wartime development was limited to special projects such as the Volta Redonda steel plant, cement-producing companies, and the national airplane-motor factory. By the end of the war nearly all Brazilian industries faced a critical problem of replacing outdated or worn-out machinery.

The development of steel production was one of the most noteworthy accomplishments during the period of wartime scarcity. Iron and steel were in great demand, and the metallurgical companies took on many new activities in the processing of crude metals. New blast furnaces and rolling mills were constructed, and by 1945 production approached domestic demands for certain types of crude and partly processed iron.

In 1941 the government established the *Companhia Siderúgica Nacional*, the National Steel Company, which began constructing mills at Volta Redonda on the Paraíba river in the state of Rio de Janeiro, within three hundred miles of the fabulously rich iron deposits of Itabira in Minas Gerais. In 1946 the mills started producing.

The aircraft industry, too, was largely war-inspired. The production of copper, aluminum, cement, and glass was accelerated by wartime needs and shortages. The mining of strategic minerals such as manganese and chromite was also speeded up because of the military requirements of the United States.

The government's role in planning the Brazilian economy was carried out through a co-ordinator of economic mobilization rather than by means of a governmental development corporation as was the practice in most of the Spanish American countries. A Ministry of Production was established to maintain control of industry and labor. Various nationalistic devices were employed to avoid the experiences of other nations that had encouraged foreign economic activities without regard to the promotion of domestic enterprise.

Measures restricting foreign participation in the Brazilian economy were introduced into the Constitutions of 1934 and 1937. Foreigners were required to obtain specific authorization from the government to establish corporations or public utility companies unless a majority of the officials were Brazilian. Deposit banks and insurance companies could not be opened unless all of the shares were owned by Brazilians. Foreigners were excluded from newspaper and magazine publishing, and from liberal professions not guaranteed by treaty. Foreigners could not constitute more than a third of the employees or receive more than a third of the wages in any of a number of specified enterprises unless the government acknowledged a shortage of suitable native labor.

The government went far in favoring industrialization by granting exemption from customs duties for equipment and raw materials and by reducing tax rates. It also required the use of certain percentages of domestic products. A fairly high tariff protected a number of activities. These restrictions undoubtedly discouraged private capital from going to Brazil, but the government preferred to rely on more easily controlled official loans.

The lack of a domestic petroleum industry and the necessity of relying on imported oil were major obstacles to Brazilian industrialization. In 1938 Vargas set up the National Petroleum Council, and it began geological surveys, securing technical aid from American oil companies. The constitution provided that oil was national property. To obtain the oil needed from abroad until domestic production might fulfill the needs, the government negotiated a treaty with Bolivia, but it was necessary to construct a railroad connecting Santa Cruz de la Sierra in Bolivia with Corumbá in Brazil. In 1952 Brazil spent some $230,000,000 on oil imports, about a fifth of what was earned by coffee exports.

The development of hydroelectric power in various Brazilian rivers was encouraged by Vargas and carried on by his successor, General Eurico Dutra. The biggest project undertaken was at the Paulo Afonso falls on the Rio São Francisco, begun in 1949 and completed in 1953. It doubled the supply for the states of Pernambuco, Alagoas, Paraíba, Sergipe, and Bahia.

It is not necessary to catalog all of the industrial development achieved by Brazil in the fifteen years of the Vargas era. There can be no doubt that the development was phenomenally rapid. Coupled with it was a similar effort to bring about agricultural diversification and to reduce the dependence upon coffee. The government undertook the extension of cultivation in the hinterland along the entire coast, and in the Amazon valley. After the war a program of Japanese colonization in the Amazon was inaugurated with the idea of creating a small farming population that would produce rubber, jute, and other tropical products.

FOREIGN RELATIONS

Vargas, the super-nationalist from the ultra-provincial state of Rio Grande do Sul, had a great deal to learn about foreign affairs after driving Washington Luís from office. He displayed an interest and astuteness in promoting foreign friendship and respect for Brazil, and his efforts in this direction were ably conducted by Oswaldo Aranha. Aranha won wide acclaim in international circles, and supported Vargas' cause with unusual skill. In 1933 President Justo of Argentina paid an official visit to Brazil. In the following year Vargas returned the honor, at the same time calling on President Gabriel Terra of Uruguay. Aranha served as ambassador to the United States from 1935 to 1937, and the friendly relations between the two countries were greatly strengthened by his presence. Aranha was able to dispel much of the suspicion current in the United States that Vargas leaned toward the Axis, and to convince American statesmen that Brazil was firmly devoted to the principle of American solidarity. The air was cleared further when Franklin D. Roosevelt visited Vargas in Rio de Janeiro in 1936. Later, when Vargas decided to support the Allied cause, he was able to point to his crushing of the integralistas as evidence of anti-fascist activity at a time when the major democracies were thinking in terms of appeasement.

As the war in Europe became imminent, Vargas was in a dilemma as to which side might be expected to win. His attitude toward the contenders seems to have been based solely on this consideration, although he was suspected of inclining toward the Axis. After Italy attacked France in 1940 Vargas declared that the future belonged to 'vigorous young peoples,' and that only 'stubborn liberals' resisted the march away from 'decadent systems.' Friends of Brazil in the United States were shocked and dismayed, and it was not easy for his supporters to rationalize away the unfavorable impression he created. But the United States was determined to remain on friendly terms with Brazil, and the speech was forgotten.

After the war in Europe broke out there was never any doubt as to the sympathy of the majority of Brazilians for the Allies, though Vargas himself remained noncommittal and perhaps undecided. He did not lead his country into the war against the Axis; his decision happened to be in accord with public opinion. Once he had decided on the course to pursue, however, he followed it with his customary vigor and thoroughness. In almost all of his decisions with regard to foreign affairs and international commitments Vargas displayed far greater sagacity and vision than did his contemporaries in Buenos Aires. Thanks to Vargas or his advisers Brazil left Argentina far behind in the diplomatic race. She gained enormous prestige as well as crucial military and economic assistance by her course, while Argentina steadily lost ground. Brazil's position in Latin America and among the small nations of the world benefited tremendously because of her diplomatic course during and after the war.

POLITICAL RETROGRESSION

The other side of the Vargas ledger was far less favorable, especially from the standpoint of political progress and civil liberties. Freedom of the press, which had been slowly circumscribed after 1930, disappeared in 1937. The Department of Press and Propaganda (D.I.P.), was created in 1939, and it was housed in the building formerly used by the then defunct Chamber of Deputies. Press censorship worked smoothly in Brazil, but behind the pleasant facade was the ugly threat of force. The D.I.P. controlled newsprint supplies, and censorship was imposed *ex post facto*. Newspapers were ostensibly free to print what the editors wished, but if their columns displeased government officials, their supplies were cut off. Foreign newsmen were given a champagne-and-dancing-girls treatment which generally succeeded in giving everything they saw a pleasant aspect. Those who could not see the situation as the government wished them to were soon on their way home. The D.I.P. was blasted by many Brazilian writers after it lost power.

Censorship of the press was generally handled with sufficient care and subtlety to avoid scandalizing Brazil's friends abroad. The threat of cutting off newsprint was much more effective and less noticeable than actually passing on each copy before it was printed. Perón of Argentina acknowledged the success of this practice by adopting it himself in 1946. But even in 1944, when Americans were greatly concerned over the attacks on Argentina's famous dailies, *La Prensa* and *La Nación,* no voice was raised in protest against the loss of freedom of the press in Brazil. This difference in attitude toward similar events in Brazil and Argentina caused Perón to comment: 'Every time we are called fascists by the American press, we look to the northern neighbor and smile.'

When the Brazilian government decided to enter the publishing field itself, to make its views appear in a more favorable light, it confiscated *O Estado de São Paulo,* one of the most excellent Latin American papers. The paper belonged to a family bitterly opposed to Vargas. The confiscation was justified on the grounds that an arms cache had been discovered in the newspaper building; apparently the arms were placed there by government agents for the police to find.

The use of secret police and of a Tribunal of National Security, which served as a 'star chamber' and could be relied on to find political opponents guilty, was a method which many Brazilians found intolerable. But so skillfully did Vargas keep the opposition scattered and helpless that he had little to fear from it.

As a result the Brazilian bureaucracy became virtually a closed corporation, and there was no way to check on the uses made of public funds. Lack of a healthy opposition encouraged graft and waste, though Vargas himself had no patience or sympathy with such activities. No Brazilian was permitted to rise to a position of power and popularity from which he might successfully challenge Vargas' rule. All potential rivals, including Oswaldo Aranha and João Alberto Lins de Barros, were kept in check.

The absence of elections and the excessive centralism of the Vargas regime stifled the embryonic democracy of the Old Republic. The only forms of democracy in which Vargas was purportedly interested were economic and social, but the Constitution of 1937 nevertheless denied labor the right to strike. One of the unfortunate consequences of the suppression of opposition and the control of public opinion exercised by the government was that many highly qualified men became reluctant to take part in public service.

Toward the close of the war the pressure on Vargas to restore some semblance of representative government and democracy became strong, for a Brazilian expeditionary force was taking part in the European campaigns along with the Allied armies. In March, 1945, Vargas yielded; he restored freedom of the press and released political prisoners, including the communist leader Luís Carlos Prestes. Plínio Salgado, exiled integralista champion, was permitted to return from Portugal. Political parties were allowed to organize once more, and a presidential election was scheduled.

Before the election was held, doubts as to Vargas' willingness to surrender his power aroused fear and suspicion in the army. When he appointed his brother Benjamim chief of police of Rio, a delegation of high-ranking officers called on him and suggested that he return to his native Rio Grande do Sul. Vargas complied. Various explanations have been suggested as to the army's motives. One was that Vargas was planning to entrench himself with the aid of Prestes and the communists, and his ousting, therefore, was aimed primarily at the latter. There is another view that holds to the belief that the army was anxious to restore its influence in the government, and Vargas' presence constituted a serious obstacle. At any rate he resigned in favor of Chief Justice of the Supreme Court José Linhares, who ran the government during the election. Unlike Perón and Pérez Jiménez, Vargas had not enriched himself at the country's expense, and he did not have to flee for his life. He simply returned home and won election to the senate.

DUTRA

General Eurico Dutra won the election, Brazil's first in more than a decade, and the first in which the extended suffrage incorporated in the Constitution of 1934 was employed. Women voted for the first time. Dutra took office in January, 1946, and before the end of the year a new constitution had been promulgated. It preserved the social-democratic character of its predecessor of 1934, devoted much space to the rights of labor, and returned to the federalism of earlier days.

The communists, despite their long suppression, made a surprising recovery in the election, and Prestes won a seat in the senate. In 1948, however, the party was outlawed and Prestes and others were expelled from the national legislature, to go into hiding once more.

In general, President Dutra continued the policies of economic nationalism and promotion of industrialization that had been fundamental to the Vargas administration. The army's influence was restored, but the army did nothing to check the growth of industry and trade. New projects were undertaken or encouraged by the government, such as the vast flood control and hydroelectric program in the Rio São Francisco valley. In the last year of Vargas' rule the Ford Motor Company had turned over its $18 million investment in the Amazon valley—Belterra and Fordlandia rubber plantations—to the Brazilian government. In 1947 Brazil joined Peru, Colombia, Venezuela, Bolivia, and Ecuador in organizing the Hylean Institute for developing the resources of the enormous Amazon region.

RETURN OF VARGAS

In 1951 Vargas was returned to the presidency, as the candidate of the Labor party. His economic policies continued the trends he fostered earlier. In addition the government made a full-scale effort to integrate the Amazon region into the national economy. For nearly ten years a constitutional provision had assigned 3 per cent of total federal, provincial, and municipal revenues to Amazonian development, but little had been done to put the provision into effect. The budget of 1954 included an appropriation of about $25 million for use in the Amazon region. About a third of it was devoted to a program of agricultural, industrial, and transportation improvements. The first goal of the government was to stimulate food production to the point that the region would be self-sufficient in this respect. An intensive research program was also maintained. Japanese farmers already produced enough jute to supply the Brazilian market, and other families were brought from Japan for the purpose of developing rice cultivation on a similar scale.

Economic Growth

Brazilian industrial output doubled in the decade after 1945, but the rapid and unequal growth raised many problems. In June, 1953, Oswaldo Aranha was named to the post of minister of finance, and a few months later he announced a program of financial reforms aimed at restoring economic stability and bringing about a better balance. His plans included tariff revision, a new national tax code, and consolidation of the public debt. Inflation, however, was the key concern.

One of the Brazilian methods for improving the productivity and skill of laborers was a national program for training apprentices in free schools. By 1947 sixty different courses were available in the state of São Paulo, including textiles, woodworking, and masonry, but little was accomplished elsewhere. The industrial Social Service, created in 1946, carried the program a step farther by educating workers socially with a view to improving their general well-being. By 1950 more than a million men were receiving the benefits of these programs.

In the spring of 1953 a vast, new improvement program for Brazil, financed in part by foreign loans, was under way. The aid was administered by the Joint United States-Brazil Economic Development Commission, which functioned as part of the United States' Point Four program of technical assistance. A five-year plan for speeding up Brazil's economic maturity was laid down, and it was expected to require some $400 million worth of foreign credits and a larger sum supplied by Brazil. Among the many projects approved were railway rehabilitation, installation of new power plants and expansion of others, purchases of agricultural machinery, and construction of port facilities. A subsidiary activity of the commission was arranging scholarships for Brazilian students in American universities to provide training in transportation, economics, education, health, agriculture, and public administration.

The long-range aims of the program were to improve basic services such as transportation, electric power, and port facilities, to increase exports and to stimulate production to replace imports, and to encourage the production of capital goods.

In making the difficult transition from a basically agricultural nation to an industrial one, Brazil rose well above other Latin American countries. Not all of her problems were solved, for she was still troubled by the shortage of foreign exchange, by the excess of imports over exports, and by a residue of commercial debts abroad. Inflation, too, was still a serious problem. The production of electrical power was far below needs, and the transportation system was equally inadequate. But the advances made after 1930, and especially after the war, were extraordinary. Brazil created the greatest steel, textile, and rubber industries in South America. Although cement production was vastly expanded, it still could not keep up with the heavy demands caused by the thriving construction business. In the 1950's the national income nearly doubled, as did the number of factories and the number of men employed by industry.

STEEL PRODUCTION

The Volta Redonda steel plant steadily increased its capacity and its output, but the nation's demands also grew. It was organized on a mixed company basis typical of much of Brazilian industrial expansion. The government owned a majority of the common stock, with states, municipalities, and private investors owning the remainder. The company was a financial success from the start, but only by reason of its operation in a protected market. A new loan from the Export-Import Bank permitted an expansion of facilities to double steel production, and a further expansion was planned to bring production to the level of domestic needs. Coal was still one of the principal problems of the steel industry, for about half of that used had to be imported.

THE AUTOMOBILE INDUSTRY

The assembly of motor vehicles from Europe and the United States became an important activity in Brazil—more than 250 small firms produced automotive parts and accessories. The tire industry was greatly stimulated by the increase in the number of automobiles and trucks in use, and in 1950 Brazil imported natural rubber. Although a million and a half tires were produced in 1951, they did not satisfy the demand. To meet the increased needs for rubber the government encouraged rubber producers in the Amazon valley, and established plantations in São Paulo and Bahia.

As the use of trucks and of passenger cars became more widespread, the building of highways took on added significance. In 1946 Brazil began a large-scale road-building program; by 1960 more miles of road had been laid than had existed previously in the entire country. A national plan was followed in the laying out of thoroughfares, and a fund was created for the purpose by a single federal tax on fuel and lubricating oils. Despite the rapid progress made in road building, the program had far to go before the country's needs could be met. In 1953 there were only 45,000 miles of surfaced roads, and more than 70 per cent of these were concentrated in the eastern and southern coastal regions, primarily in São Paulo and Rio de Janeiro. To assist Brazil in meeting the need for more and better roads in other parts of the country, the Joint Commission drew up plans for a tremendous road-building program.

The development of the petroleum industry was placed under a mixed company, Petrobras, of which the government was the main shareholder, and which enjoyed a monopoly in prospecting and drilling for oil. Foreign companies were excluded, although some government officials feared that the cost of importing oil would become an overwhelming burden before Petrobras could discover and develop enough fields to meet the country's requirements.

AGRICULTURE

The extraordinary progress of industrialization in Brazil tended to obscure the fact that the country was still basically agricultural. More than 60 per cent of the population depended on farming for a livelihood, and coffee was still the most important cash crop. Brazil produced about one-half of the world's supply, and coffee constituted nearly three-fourths of the value of Brazilian exports. Over half of the exported coffee went to the United States.

The Brazilian government followed a policy of establishing institutes for each of its principal agricultural commodities. Its purpose was to promote production and consumption, and to control prices and marketing policies with a view to lessening the harmful fluctuations that had occurred in the past.

LABOR

After the re-election of Vargas following Dutra's administration, organized labor made new gains with the support and favor of the government. The number of unions and of union members increased rapidly. Vargas, the candidate of the Labor party, stated his aim as the 'cordial and harmonious co-operation between capital and labor on a basis of equality.' The Ministry of Labor still exercised a powerful control over the unions, but congress granted unions the right to affiliate with international labor organizations.

According to Brazilian law labor disputes were to be taken to special labor courts, and these bodies upheld claims for pay raises of 40 per cent over 1950 levels to meet the rise in cost of living. Labor laws also upheld the principle of job security, vacations with pay, social service benefits, medical and dental care, disability pay, and old age pensions. Minimum wages were established for different regions, and the law required pay for the seventh day after six days of work. The eight-hour day became mandatory, and a code of safety regulations was put in force in factories.

The principal problem of labor was the high cost of living caused by inflationary trends. Unemployment was not a problem, for there was still a greater demand for skilled labor than could be met, and there was also a shortage of farm labor.

RAILROAD DEVELOPMENT

Railroad transportation remained a vital need, for most of the existing 23,000 miles of track were laid to bring raw materials to the ports, and consequently were concentrated in the coastal areas. The first three projects begun by the Joint Commission were concerned with the railroad problem. The need of rehabilitating old lines was so great that the Commission placed that task ahead of construction of new ones. In addition to the repairs and purchases of new equipment, branch lines were extended. The Northwest of Brazil Railroad was extended from Pôrto Esperança to Corumbá in western Mato Grosso, which gave Brazil a trunk line to the Bolivian border and a connection with the Brazil-Bolivia Railroad. This series of railroads linked the Brazilian port of Santos with the Chilean port of Arica on the Pacific.

An oil refinery was built at Corumbá to refine crude oil from the Bolivian fields of Santa Cruz. The Corumbá plant was intended primarily to serve the undeveloped region of Mato Grosso, which figured prominently in plans for increasing food production. One of the encouraging signs of progress to Brazilians was the fact that their own industry was able to make important contributions toward providing the equipment and materials needed for railroad rehabilitation. The freight car building firms, for example, were able to turn out 500 cars a month and, with plate produced at Volta Redonda, to make tank cars, wheels, and other rolling stock.

Along with road and railroad construction Brazil developed an extensive system of domestic and international air lines that helped to link the widely scattered cities more closely, and gave Brazilians easy access to the major nations of the world. Between 1942 and 1960, with the help of government subsidies, the air lines increased by more than eight times the mileage served.

GROWTH OF SÃO PAULO

One of the most astonishing developments in Brazil between 1930 and 1960 was the growth of the city and state of São Paulo. The city became the third largest in South America and the commercial center of Brazil. The state of São Paulo led the nation in both industry and agriculture, produced about half of the national .wealth, and was the source of about half of the exports. Paulistas also paid nearly half of the income taxes collected by the government. It was not surprising that they regarded their accomplishments with considerable pride.

CONSTRUCTION INDUSTRY

The construction business grew enormously because of the large number of people moving into the industrial cities. Brazilian architects such as Oscar Niemeyer and Lucio Costa won world-wide acclaim for their pioneering in architectural design, particularly with regard to office buildings and apartment houses. There was a corresponding boom in real estate, for land was still regarded by many Brazilians as the safest investment, and real estate profits enjoyed lower tax rates than those of industry. The annual investment in construction rose to more than twice the amount devoted to agriculture.

DEVELOPMENT OF PARANÁ

The planting of coffee trees in the frontier state of Paraná caused a spectacularly rapid filling up of that once empty state. Immigration from within Brazil and from foreign countries increased its population by more than 70 per cent in ten years. Its coffee production rose at a similar rate, from 2 per cent of Brazil's total crop in 1930 to one-quarter in 1955. With new coffee trees being planted at the rate of 25 million a year, Paraná surpassed São Paulo in coffee production by 1960.

Mechanization in agriculture was introduced on a small scale in Brazil, particularly in the coffee areas of São Paulo and Paraná, under the Agricultural Mechanization Enterprise (E.M.A.). Part of the first task was clearing new lands for use by coffee planters. E.M.A. began as a joint Brazil-United States project, but soon became entirely Brazilian. *Sementes Agroceres* (S.A. or S.A.S.A.) was a similar organization for producing better grades of seeds and livestock. Progress was made especially in the development of hybrid corn for various regions, and in some cases it increased production by as much as 50 per cent.

Financial troubles continued to plague the government, particularly inflation and the declining value of the cruzeiro. In August, 1954, the currency was indirectly devaluated by a decree permitting exporters to exchange 20 per cent of their foreign currency earnings at the free market rate rather than to surrender all earnings to the Bank of Brazil at the official buying rate. The policy of granting bonuses to exporters, instituted by Oswaldo Aranha in 1953, remained in effect. The decision to modify the system was caused by the sharp increase in the issuance of paper money, which lowered the gold reserve for each cruzeiro, and by the falling off of coffee sales at the minimum price fixed by the government.

End of the Vargas Era

Events that led directly to a termination of the Vargas regime were precipitated by the 'Tonoleros Street Affair.' Carlos Lacerda, outspoken editor of the *Tribuna de Imprensa* and arch-critic of the Vargas administration, was frequently escorted about the city by off-duty Air Force officers who feared for his life. On the night of August 5, Lacerda and Major Vaz returned to his home on Tonoleros Street. An assassin opened fire and wounded Lacerda. Major Vaz returned the fire and was killed. The police made no progress toward finding the assassin, so the air force stepped in on the grounds that a 'military crime' had been committed. The murder weapon was a .45 automatic, a gun that by law was restricted to the armed forces. The air force soon found the killer, and learned that he had been hired by a member of Vargas' own palace guard, which occupied the floor beneath the president's quarters at Catete Palace. It was soon known that the chief of the guard was involved in influence peddling on an astonishing scale. When Vargas, whose honesty was unquestioned, learned of the illegal acts of men he had long known and trusted, he was visibly shaken. 'I have the feeling I have been living over a sea of mud,' was his only comment. Rumors that Vargas planned to declare a state of siege heightened the tension, and mobs roamed the streets demanding that he resign.

On the night of August 24 the cabinet met in an all-night session in an attempt to solve the dilemma of what Vargas should do. Some suggested that he take a ninety-day leave; others mentioned resignation. Toward morning, since there was no consensus, Vargas agreed to a ninety-day leave and left for his quarters. Meanwhile the armed forces chiefs were also meeting separately, awaiting the decision. By this time the air force had won over the army and the navy to its point of view. When the officers learned of Vargas' decision, they sent a terse message to the cabinet. It was too late for a leave of absence; Vargas must resign. Vargas' brother Benjamim hurried to Catete Palace with the ultimatum. Vargas sent him away on some errand and then took his own life.

Not long after the death of Vargas his short, hand-written suicide note was made public. Later in the day a much longer polemic was published, a 'political testament' Vargas had written earlier in the week. It blamed Brazil's troubles on 'international groups.' Brazilians instantly translated this into 'United States,' and rushed to attack U.S. consulates as well as such harbingers of evil influence as Coca Cola trucks. The Brazilians were emotionally agitated by the events of the week and by Vargas' dramatic exit. The crowds which had been demanding that Vargas resign now struck out blindly against his enemies, guided only by a few professional agitators.

JOÃO CAFÉ FILHO

Vice-President João Café Filho succeeded to the presidency and began at once to form a coalition cabinet in hope of restoring peace to the troubled country. The towering economic problems still loomed over the land, and their solution was not brought closer by the bitter factional strife. Oswaldo Aranha, finance minister under Vargas, resigned. The post of finance minister, exposed as it was to all manner of attack, was the most difficult to fill.

The Brazilian Labor party, which Vargas had led, soon abandoned the coalition with Café Filho's Social Progressives and declared 'absolute independence' of the government. It restricted its members from accepting cabinet posts. With only the frail support of his own party, Café Filho had little influence in the congress. At the same time another split raised the specter of continued strife and dissension, for military leaders became sharply divided over the action taken against Vargas. The legacy of bitterness and recrimination added to Café Filho's troubles. He could do little but call for morality in public affairs.

KUBITSCHEK

Before the election of October, 1955, Café Filho warned that the country was too disturbed, and suggested postponement. The election was held, nevertheless, and Governor Juscelino Kubitschek of Minas Gerais, candidate of the Social Democrats, won a plurality by selecting João ('Jango') Goulart as his vice-presidential running mate and gaining the support of the Labor party. Goulart, a protegé of Vargas and minister of labor, was the Labor party candidate for the presidency. Kubitschek and Goulart also received the communist vote. Other contenders were General Juarez Távora of the Democratic Union party, Plínio Salgado, and Adhemar de Barros of São Paulo.

For a time there were rumors of army intervention to prevent Kubitschek from taking office. Café Filho suffered a heart attack and turned the executive duties over to Deputy Carlos Luz, who was next in the official line of succession. Soon there were rumors that Luz was conspiring to deprive Kubitschek of the presidency. This time the army did step in, at the orders of Marshal Henrique Teixeira Lott. It removed Luz and replaced him with Senator Nereu Ramos, who was next in line. To add to the confusion Café Filho attempted to reclaim the presidential office, while Luz refused to accept his own dismissal. Acting in its capacity of 'moderating power,' the army supported Nereu Ramos, and ended speculation by announcing that Kubitschek would be inaugurated on January 31, 1956, as scheduled. Before 1946 the army had assumed the moderating power that once belonged to the Emperor. Article 177 of the Constitution of 1946 named the military as the 'guarantor of the constitutional powers of law and order.'

Kubitschek entered office with great enthusiasm and grand plans for making 'fifty years' progress in five.' Brazil's financial situation was by now so desperate that he apparently considered it futile to try to improve it. He went ahead with his sweeping plans, particularly the construction of a new capital at Brasília, far in the interior of Goias. Brazilians had thought of relocating their capital for nearly a century and a half, in order to give it a more central geographical position. It was an extravagance the nation could ill afford, but it was to be Kubitschek's monument, and he pushed the work despite all obstacles. On 'Tiradentes Day,' April 21, 1960, before his five-year term had ended, he had many of the government offices moved to the unfinished capital, over the protests of everyone who had to leave Rio de Janeiro for the wilds of Goias. During Kubitschek's administration the cruzeiro plunged from about 96 to the dollar to about 227. The Brazilian population was now around 60 million, and the country was hard pressed to raise enough food. Many problems plagued the nation, and no one came forth with effective solutions.

THE ELECTION OF 1960

The presidential election of 1960 was the first in Brazil's history in which the opposition candidate won. The voting was almost entirely on the basis of personalities, since Brazil's national political parties had been destroyed by the adoption of the federal system in 1889–90, and they had never recovered. There were three 'laws' that governed Brazilian politics: the law of the miraculous, the law of the vacancy, and the law of the scapegoat.

According to the 'law of the miraculous,' if one governmental system failed there was always another one to fall back on; this had the effect of sidetracking serious efforts to solve difficult problems. The 'law of the vacancy' was a formula for men who were politically ambitious. Those who were with a radical party one day might appear as leaders of a conservative party the next, if the latter lacked a party leader. It is the opportunity that counts, not the ideological bent of the party, providing it has one. This custom meant that voters often had no notion of the basic beliefs of the candidates, and might vote for men whose views were actually inimical to their interests. The 'law of the scapegoat' was used in times of economic stress. The attempted solution was blamed for the failure even though it alone did not cause the failure. As a result, the government would search for another solution rather than try to correct what was wrong.

Brazilians have long had a tendency to adopt foreign economic or political systems without regard to their appropriateness for Brazil. The 1891 Constitution, for example, was based on that of the United States. Many Brazilians do not regard communism as a threat, for they feel that economic development is the important problem. Some have felt that it would be possible to adopt some of the principles and techniques of communism without becoming a satellite of the USSR.

Kubitschek's administration and his tolerance of political opposition made it possible to conduct the 1960 election under tranquil conditions, and his obvious respect for election procedures temporarily lessened Brazilian cynicism concerning political activity. Kubitschek's critics, however, asserted that his actions were not based on conviction but on his plans to run for the presidency again in 1965, since the constitution did not allow him to run in 1960.

The victor in 1960 was Jânio Quadros, who had served ably as governor of São Paulo, and who had made use of the Christian Democrats, the Brazilian Socialist party, the Republican party, the Liberal party, and the National Labor party as well as others in his rise to the presidency. He had nothing but contempt for any of them, and he made it clear during the campaign that even those that supported him could expect nothing of him once he took office. The reason for the existence of so many parties was that the Constitution of 1946 legalized proportional representation. According to the Electoral Code, any party that had 50,000 members in at least five electoral districts would have representation in the national congress. Once a party was qualified and registered with the Supreme Electoral Tribunal, it did not need to worry about the size of its membership. Parties were merely tools for forming governments, for they had little influence on the government; they functioned only at election time.

In the election Quadros appealed directly to the voters rather than through any of the parties that supported him. The government candidate was colorless Marshal Henrique Teixeira Lott, former minister of war. Neither he nor Quadros had previously been connected in any way with the party that nominated him. This was not a serious problem, for most voters were not bound to any party. In the campaign in some states the PTB supported a Quadros-Goulart ticket for president and vice-president; in others, where Lott had a following, it favored a Lott-Quadros ticket. In this way the party tried to ensure its candidate the vice-presidency, and the strategy was successful. The communists supported the conservative Lott rather than the social reformer Quadros. Lott, they believed, would bring the country close to chaos, and this would be to their advantage. Quadros, on the other hand, was expected to introduce social reforms, which would weaken the communist program.

After his victory Quadros made it painfully clear that he intended to ignore the congress as well as all political parties, and to appeal directly to the public. His relations with the legislative branch were, therefore, stormy and unproductive. Quadros made a serious miscalculation, for he was certain that the armed forces would maintain him in power, if only to prevent Goulart from assuming the presidency. He continued his strange policy, with disastrous results for the nation.

16

European South America:
Argentina, Chile, and Uruguay

The aspirations and desires of the lower classes had been stimulated without simultaneous growth of the . . . capacity to support such ambitions.*

Argentina, Chile, and Uruguay were traditionally beyond the sphere of United States' influence and, in matters of trade and in cultural interests, were more strongly swayed by European currents than by the affairs of the North American colossus. That they should be especially sensitive to European happenings was understandable, for Europe had long been their chief market and France their cultural ideal. Added to this natural tendency to face toward Europe was the Argentine effort to create a southern bloc, dominated by herself, to offset the economic and military preponderance of the United States.

All three countries were severely shaken by the world depression, for they relied heavily on exports to Europe. Political agitation and resentment engendered by economic ruin caused forceful changes in the governments and fostered a powerful spirit of uncompromising hostility toward foreign capital. The inept Radicals of Yrigoyen gave way to a temporary regime of army officers and restoration of conservative domination in Argentina. Chilean strong man Carlos Ibáñez, despite his economic and social reforms, was opposed violently for his tyranny and financial extravagance and was forced to resign. On the other hand, Uruguayan President Gabriel Terra found the divided executive powers unsatisfactory in time of crisis, and he restored presidential powers at the expense of the vaunted administrative council.

* James R. Scobie, *Argentina*, Oxford University Press, New York, 1964, p. 235.

Argentina

Economic recovery was the immediate problem in Argentina, and although government effort produced modest headway, political leaders seemed powerless to accomplish much more. Complete recovery and a return of prosperity depended upon the revival of industry and trade far beyond Argentina's borders, and years passed before such a revival became general. General Agustín P. Justo, who won the Argentine presidency in 1931, rescued the cattle industry at the expense of other segments of the economy by means of the Roca-Runciman Pact with England in 1933. By this agreement, Argentina was obliged to purchase her manufactured products in Great Britain if she wished to maintain her traditional beef and wool outlets in the British Isles. Argentine industry had to stand aside, and by subsequent agreements the British-owned transport system in the capital was protected by the suppression of local competition. In 1934 an income tax was introduced, and other measures provided for greater control of foreign exchange to limit the free flow of international payments. National boards were established to give the government a measure of control over grain and cotton. These acts signaled the end of Argentina's historic free trade policy, the policy which for so many years had favored producers of foodstuffs for the export market.

For a time after the election of Roberto M. Ortiz in 1937 it appeared that the Argentine Radical party would soon return to power. Ortiz, to the chagrin of his Conservative supporters, seemed determined to restore honest elections and government by the majority. He intervened in provincial elections to ensure honesty and to uphold secrecy of the ballot. Radical hopes rose and the Conservative minority grew desperate.

The hopes of the Radicals were dashed violently in 1940, however, for Ortiz became seriously ill and was forced to turn the government over to his vice-president, Conservative Ramón S. Castillo, who quickly undid all that Ortiz had accomplished. The Radical party did not enlarge its program in the direction of social and economic reforms, and its failure to do so was partly responsible for the successful intervention of the army a few years later. Party competition lost much of its vigor in the dismal days of the great depression.

From 1940 to 1943 Castillo ran the country with an iron hand. After the Japanese attack on Pearl Harbor in December, 1941, he used the extension of the war to the Western Hemisphere as an excuse to impose a state of siege, the easier to harass his enemies. He explained his action as necessary to preserve moral unity, to prevent inconvenient modes of expression—by which he meant pro-Ally declarations—and to safeguard neutrality and continental defense. The Argentine press, which had not yet been stifled, commented acidly on the suppression of individual guarantees as a means of defending democracy.

Castillo and his foreign minister, Enrique Ruiz Guiñazú, did not conceal their antipathy for the United States or their sympathy for Nazi Germany. When Chile called for a meeting of foreign ministers at Rio de Janeiro in January, 1942, Castillo used the opportunity to advance his country's plan for an Argentine-dominated southern bloc. Ruiz Guiñazú's overtures to other Latin American delegates were not well received, however; even the Chileans, who had special reasons for fearing a rupture of relations with the Axis at that stage of the war when Germany and Japan seemed to be winning, refused to take a neutral stand in support of Argentina. By steadily resisting pressure from other nations to agree to a severance of diplomatic relations with the Axis, Ruiz Guiñazú nevertheless won his point, and the conference ended by merely recommending such action. Argentina thus won a diplomatic victory, but one which was to cost her the respect and friendship of a large part of Latin America as well as the largesse that the United States was then bestowing on her friends in the form of economic and military assistance.

The rising cost of living and wartime shortages, coupled with harsh political measures, gradually increased opposition to the Conservative government and contributed greatly to Castillo's growing unpopularity. As the time for the election of 1943 approached, the Radicals and Socialists discussed the possibility of a coalition, though with little enthusiasm, for they were quite aware that even a majority of votes would not assure them either victory or possession of the presidency. Revolution seemed to be their only hope for gaining control of the government, but no revolution could succeed without help from the army. The Radicals still did not generate the policies and leadership that might have won them a large and enthusiastic following, and their apathy and failure to lead the way increased the general cynicism of all those opposed to Castillo's regime.

Castillo's choice of a successor was Robustiano Patrón Costas, the sugar baron of Salta, a most unlikely candidate. He had no following even among the Conservatives, but his election seemed certain because of Castillo's determination to force it on the country. The opposition desperately tried to subordinate factional differences to form a democratic union; the attempt itself only widened the rifts that separated the liberal elements. The election, however, was never held.

Early in the morning of June 4, 1943, the old era came to an abrupt but scarcely violent end. Except for a brief and bloody resistance by personnel of the Naval Mechanics School, an army coup succeeded smoothly and with little trouble. What had the earmarks of a typical barracks revolt carried in its wake enormous changes that were to alter the political and economic life of Argentina for years to come. Although not immediately apparent, the long domination of the cattle and agricultural oligarchy was drawing to a close. The military had moved in to stay, and their ideological baggage carried labels suggesting that extensive visits had been made to Mussolini's Italy, Hitler's Germany, and Franco's Spain. Argentina soon became the Axis powers' outpost in the Western Hemisphere.

General Arturo Rawson, one of the leaders of the military revolt, was no camp follower of Europe's fascist dictatorships. He seemed more concerned with Brazil's increasing military strength resulting from that country's close relationship with the United States and the latter's largesse with military and naval equipment for its allies. He hoped to secure some of the same benefits for Argentina and was willing to make conciliatory gestures toward the United States if that proved the necessary course to follow. Rawson's associates, however, had no such notions. They elbowed him aside and General Pedro P. Ramírez took over the presidency of the 'Provisional Government,' naming as his minister of war and vice-president General Edelmiro Farrell. The dominant military group was a small clique calling itself the Group of United Officers (GOU), and one of its key members was a young colonel, Juan Domingo Perón, to whom was assigned the post of chief of the war ministry secretariat.

Admiral Storni, the Argentine foreign minister, made a foolish move toward the United States in the summer of 1943 in spite of his government's ill-concealed preference for the Axis powers. He sent a note to Washington asking for military assistance as the price for Argentine adherence to her Western Hemisphere commitments and at the same time suggesting that American assistance to Brazil was upsetting the South American balance of power. Cordell Hull, Roosevelt's secretary of state, returned a heated reply which in essence suggested that his government did not place guns in the hands of its enemies. Although embarrassing Argentina, this exchange had the effect of strengthening the pro-Axis clique, for it made sympathy for the Allies appear almost unpatriotic. The ultra-nationalists now turned from what had appeared as a middle-class movement to seize power from the landed oligarchy to something far different. Argentina embarked on a program to dominate all of southern South America, and by force of arms if necessary.

Throughout the summer and early fall of 1943—winter and spring in Argentina—the Ramírez government sought to strengthen its position vis-à-vis the Axis powers. It asked Germany for arms, but bogged down in Russia and faced with an Allied invasion of the Italian mainland as Italian resistance collapsed, Hitler had no arms to spare and no time to devote to the requests of his would-be American associates. Ramírez, nevertheless, devoted increased resources to a build-up of Argentine military might, made threatening gestures toward Uruguay, from which country Argentine exiles were denouncing his suppressive measures, and generally flexed his muscles in the direction of such neighbors as Chile and Bolivia.

THE RISE OF PERÓN

General Ramírez soon discovered that he was on slippery footing. As Axis fortunes waned, Argentina saw that her increasing isolation threatened to cut her off from her usual sources of supply. Some industries were aided by the absence of foreign competition, but lack of replacement parts caused the transport system to grind slowly to a halt. A coup in Bolivia that Argentina helped instigate brought to power there a government with Axis sympathies, but Ramírez' movements were too transparent, and throughout the hemisphere feelings mounted against him. With Mussolini's imprisonment and Italy's surrender, the war was clearly running against the Axis, and Germany's defeat loomed as an inevitable consequence. President Ramírez decided to mend his fences, and on January 26, 1944, he broke diplomatic relations with the Axis powers. Clearly, however, his grip on the government had slipped. A new leader was required who was without the taint of former mistakes and who had not given in to Allied pressure. The moment for which Colonel Juan Domingo Perón had been waiting was almost at hand. In February Ramírez was pressured into retiring, and two weeks later he resigned, turning over the presidency to General Farrell. Perón became minister of war, and a few months later he also took over the vice-presidency. Farrell became putty in his hands.

Juan Domingo Perón came from an obscure middle-class family living in a small town of Buenos Aires Province. He was educated in the capital, but entered the Colegio Militar when fifteen years of age and from that point onward his development followed a strictly military pattern. Gradually he moved up in rank and by the middle of the 1930's he was a lieutenant colonel, had taught military history at the Army War College, and had served as an aide to the army chief of staff. Subsequently, he spent two years in Chile as military attaché, but the really important break in his career came when he was sent to Italy for further military training. He was in Europe at the outbreak of World War II, witnessed the tremendous early successes of the Axis powers, saw Mussolini's great popularity as he led his country into the war at the moment of French capitulation, and visited extensively among the Axis countries, as well as in Spain and Portugal. His European adventures were shared by a number of other Argentine officers, and after his return to Argentina early in 1941 Perón called upon the friendships made abroad in forming the core of his Group of United Officers.

Perón was a careful observer, and he witnessed many of the mistakes of the Axis leaders in both political and military strategy. He was also a student of history, as well as a teacher in that field, and he understood the political history of his own country very well. Unfortunately, he apparently never learned the fundamental concepts of economics, and in later years this turned out to be a lapse of major significance in his educational background.

Perón early developed political ambitions, and his European experiences apparently increased them, for he became an active force in military politics from the moment of his return. The military government of Ramírez at first sought to deal with the labor unions of Buenos Aires by repressing them. Shortly, however, a new National Department of Labor was created within the Ministry of Interior, and Perón was appointed to head it. Soon the department was raised to the status of a ministry, and little by little Perón strengthened the position of labor by decrees in its favor. At the same time he usurped control of the movement, brushing aside the older labor leaders while appealing to the rank and file. This control of the labor unions became one of the most important factors in Perón's rise to power. His firm grip on the secretariat of the Ministry of War guaranteed him freedom to maneuver in the labor field, for that ministry was headed by his close associate General Farrell during the seven months that Ramírez remained in power.

As Minister of Labor, Perón's fame grew rapidly, for he introduced long overdue reforms such as minimum wage laws for agricultural workers. He won general favor by forcing the British-owned railroads to grant wage increases, and by introducing tenure, retirement pay, and liability insurance into the public service. These reforms came at the expense of labor's independence, but only the Socialists protested. The military nationalists silenced the traditional parties and began the task of breaking the power of the great landowners. Industry was favored and encouraged not only to gain the support of industrialists against the landed class, but because industry was essential to what the nationalists considered the needs of national defense. By shrewdly stressing objectives neglected by the older political parties, such as nationalization of foreign companies, development of national resources on an unprecedented scale, and a vast program of social legislation, the nationalists won a large measure of popular support.

In 1944 and 1945 the government proceeded slowly with its economic and social reforms while solidifying its control. The goal of the GOU was a corporate state in the Hispanic tradition. Overtures were made to the church, and the government won adherence of the clerical hierarchy by reversing the law and decreeing compulsory religious instruction in the schools.

The economic program of the government was directed toward achieving independence of English industry, nationalizing the public utilities, developing mining in the Andes, building a vast industrial organization, and achieving an economic balance between wealthy Buenos Aires and the impoverished provinces. Underlying these aims was the primary goal—economic self-sufficiency and predominance in South America. Military preparedness on an unprecedented scale was an important part of the program, and by 1948 the appropriation for the armed services absorbed better than one-third of the total budget. The great stress on expanding the armed forces and arms production, plus the creation of many new garrisons on Argentina's borders, gave all neighboring countries cause for concern.

As the war in Europe and Asia drew to a close and the victorious Allies made plans for a new order in international organization, Argentina found herself in the difficult position of being left out. Other countries in Latin America, while not particularly sympathetic with Argentina's military government, saw a need to restore the country to good standing in the hemisphere. The departure of Cordell Hull from the American secretaryship of state facilitated a rapprochement, and early in 1945 secret arrangements were worked out to end what had become an embarrassing stalemate to the United States as well as to Argentina. Argentina was not invited to the Chapultepec Conference of American States held in Mexico City in March, but a belated declaration of war against Germany and Japan enabled her to sign the agreements reached there by the other powers, as well as to participate as a charter member in the forthcoming international conference in San Francisco that created the United Nations. For the moment, at least, hemispheric solidarity appeared to have been restored.

Perón's program of 'social justice' for the working man during his tenure as chief of the labor ministry made him many enemies as well as friends. Conservatives quite naturally felt that he had gone much too far and had granted excessive and unnecessary concessions to the laboring classes of Buenos Aires. Many in the military shared this view, while the old liberal intelligentsia had other reasons for opposing not only Perón but the entire military regime of which he was a part. When General Farrell finally relaxed control in 1945 by lifting the state of siege imposed four years before, anti-government demonstrations were mounted by all the opposition groups. So serious did the matter become that in October Perón resigned his various government posts and after a brief 'detention' on Martín García Island in the Plata river, returned on October 17 to address a mass demonstration from the balcony of the Casa Rosada, Argentina's presidential palace. The demonstration had been carefully organized by Perón's followers, and the dock and packing-house workers were present in overwhelming numbers. It became painfully clear to the Liberal and Conservative opposition that Perón held the poorer classes of the Argentine capital in the palm of his hand. With this kind of backing, plus significant support in the armed forces, Perón felt strong enough to reaffirm his resignations and stand back until the presidential elections were held in early 1946. Even without office he was in full view as Argentina's man of destiny.

During the presidential campaign, Perón skillfully increased his advantages by forcing employers to grant bonuses to employees, and by sending supporters to break up the meetings of his opponent, Dr. José Tamborini. Former United States ambassador to Argentina Spruille Braden, who had openly manifested his dislike for Perón during the months of his Argentina residence in 1955, openly sought to encourage Argentina liberals from his new post as assistant secretary of state for Latin American affairs. He spoke out strongly against Perón, while the Department of State published an account of the pro-Nazi activities and dictatorial methods of the military regime. The net result of this blatant political intervention was to strengthen the grip of the ultra-nationalists, for any voices raised against them were stigmatized as favoring outside interference in domestic affairs. Perón forgot about Tamborini and asked the Argentine people to choose between himself and Spruille Braden. Their answer was to give Perón a popular majority and an overwhelming victory in electoral votes. Since Perón's henchmen broke up Tamborini's meetings, and since Perón did not mention his opponent's name, many Argentines did not know who was running against Perón.

As president, supported by a strong majority in both houses of congress, Perón moved swiftly to fulfill his economic and social objectives. A Five Year Plan for industrialization was prepared, unions were placed under closer regulation, the Banco Central was nationalized, and a government trading agency, the Argentine Trade Promotion Institute (IAPI), was created to monopolize foreign commerce. The press was brought to heel by the use of newsprint quotas and intimidation. Educational institutions were forced into line by wholesale dismissals of teachers. In 1947 women were given the right to vote and hold office, and many of them became enthusiastic supporters of Perón and 'Evita,' his wife and astute political partner since 1945.

In 1946 a new constitution replaced that of 1853. Among its features was the authorization of two six-year terms for the president, a prohibition against forming coalitions of political parties, and a provision for severe punishment for anyone showing disrespect for the president or other public officials.

Perón was fortunate that his grandiose program was introduced at a time of unusual prosperity caused by heavy demands for Argentine products in Europe. In 1946 he called for the creation of the National Economic Council with wide powers in organizing and subsidizing industries, particularly mixed companies in which the government and private interests shared ownership. Air transportation and the national merchant marine were developed rapidly by the Council, for these were as essential as industry in furthering Argentina's aim of becoming the financial and commercial center of Latin America. The trade agency (IAPI) ended the era of free competition in grain and beef by monopolizing foreign sales. It purchased these commodities at prices that guaranteed little return to the producers, and sold them abroad at high profits for the government. This double-edged sword increased government revenues while forcing the

land-holding oligarchy to its knees. It also precluded virtually all re-investment in productive resources and set in motion a gradual but steady deterioration in the productivity of Argentine agriculture. The funds that this
maneuver made available were used to purchase and nationalize foreign-
owned public utilities, such as the British railways and the American telephone system. Perón bled Argentina's productive capability to procure
obsolescent facilities at exhorbitant prices in the cause of economic nationalism, and in the process Argentina became a creditor nation in the
artificial prosperity of the post-war boom. The high prices paid for Argentine beef and wheat lasted only until European agriculture recovered,
and soon the realities of high operation and maintenance costs of utility
and transport facilities began to undermine the economic benefits of Argentina's super-nationalism. The weaknesses of Perón's economic education became ever more apparent.

Perón named his program of economic nationalism and social integration 'Justicialism,' and called it a 'third position' between capitalism and
communism. Despite the frequent charges that it was simply an Argentine
form of European fascism, it was not a copy of the regime Perón had admired while living in Mussolini's Italy. It was called a blend of Rosas and
Mussolini with something new added, Perón's own original touch.

Under Justicialism regimentation flourished, just as it had a century before under the dictator, Rosas. Argentines, long committed to an individualistic, liberal way of life, chafed under the stifling cult of Perón, with
its strict censorship and thought control. The world-famous free press of
Argentina ceased to exist; in 1951 the country's famous newspaper, *La
Prensa,* was closed down and turned over to the General Confederation of
Labor.

As time for the presidential election of 1951 approached it was clear to
all that no one had a chance of defeating Perón. Suggestions of army opposition appeared in the 'voluntary' withdrawal of Señora Perón's candidacy for the vice-presidency and the abortive revolt of September 28.
Early rumors that Perón had planned the revolt himself for the purpose of
crushing his opponents were later believed to be erroneous, for the uprising apparently was a genuine if feeble bid of a dissident military clique to
seize power.

In the election of 1951 women exercised their right to vote in national
elections and to campaign for national offices for the first time. By encouraging women to participate in political affairs Perón showed again far
greater astuteness than the leaders of the traditional parties, and he won

enthusiastic support. The Radical party candidates could only make an oblique appeal to the army for aid, but to no effect.

Perón began his second term with far less optimism about the country's economy than before, for gold supplies and foreign credit reserves were low, and the huge profits formerly provided by meat and wheat sales had dwindled. Argentines, once celebrated for the prodigious amounts of meat they consumed, now endured meatless days, and in 1952 the country was forced to import wheat because of a two-year drought. Many businesses went bankrupt that year, and persistent reports of plots against the government kept political tensions high. By monopolizing the sources of agricultural and industrial profit, the government had polluted the fountain of national prosperity. Production declined in almost all sectors of the economy while expenditures on social services mounted.

THE UNIQUE ROLE OF EVA DUARTE PERÓN

The strange grip that Juan Domingo Perón had on the allegiance and affections of the Argentine masses was in major part attributable to the popularity of his wife, Eva Duarte Perón. An illegitimate child raised in poverty, 'Evita' achieved minor distinction as an actress when she moved from her provincial home into the capital, but her chief asset was her feminine attractiveness and her skill at employing it to establish herself in the company of important men. The most important of these was a handsome widower twice her age, Juan Perón, whose mistress she became in 1944. It was at the time of the major crisis in the late summer and early fall of 1945 when Perón's future was in doubt that Evita was discovered to have considerable political talent. She worked long and hard to get the union workers into the streets to trigger Perón's dramatic return from Martín García Island on October 17. She communicated with the workers and the poorer classes in their own language, the language of the hopeless and the oppressed, the *descamisados* or shirtless ones of the capital. She continued to communicate with them when, a few months later, married to Perón, she moved with him into the presidential palace as Señora María Eva Durate de Perón, the first lady of the land.

One of Evita's difficulties was that many did not consider her a lady at all. As a child she had been socially ostracized, and many of the capital social elite did not consider that a marriage certificate uniting her with the president necessarily changed anything. Evita thought otherwise, and she set about to prove it. As first lady she dazzled the country with her beauty and charm, as well as the luxury of her jewelry and clothing. Far more important, however, was her dedication to improving the welfare of the downtrodden descamisados. She created her own charitable foundation, the Eva Perón Foundation, snatching by government decree the old *Sociedad de Beneficencia* from under the condescending noses of the female aristocracy of Buenos Aires. Soon Evita's Foundation had more funds than anyone saw fit to keep track of. Not only was it supported by the unions, but industrial corporations, business houses, and private individuals wishing to keep in the good graces of the government made their regular contributions. Government subsidies were occasionally voted to augment its resources, and eventually a regular percentage of the income of the national lottery was paid into the Foundation treasury.

Regardless of the absence of controls to assure fiscal regularity and the many suspicions voiced as to the source of Evita's many extravagances, the Foundation spent enormous sums that contributed very tangibly to the welfare of the Argentine poor. The number of schools was greatly expanded, the number of hospitals in the country doubled, housing projects were constructed, and children were the recipients of benefits never before bestowed on them by the most magnanimous of charities. The Foundation came to the aid of the poor victims of natural disaster throughout the country and the continent, and on one occasion a shipment of food and clothing was even sent to aid the immigrants to Israel. Evita must particularly have enjoyed the consternation caused in Washington charitable circles by her shipment of clothing to the Children's Society of that city in January of 1949.

Eventually the Foundation became a monster that even entered the chain store business, retailing clothing and food in the Argentine capital at prices so low that the regular stores could not compete. All semblance of order in the provision of health and welfare services broke down, but the thousands or even millions who benefited remembered *la señora*. So did millions of Argentine women in whose behalf Evita struggled to secure social, economic, and political rights. The grant of woman suffrage in September of 1947 was directly attributable to her efforts.

In 1951 it became known that Eva Perón was ill, and less than a year later she was dead of cancer. Her death was a tremendous blow to the poor of Argentina who adored her. It was also a serious political as well as personal loss to her husband. Virtually from the moment of her departure Perón's political star began to wane, for he seemed to lose the fine sensitivities required for effective political manipulation. Nevertheless, his grip on the country remained firm in spite of the fact that it was becoming increasingly painful.

END OF THE PERÓN ERA

Perón's second Five Year Plan was designed to make Argentina self-sufficient in raw materials and to speed up industrial production. Like the first plan, however, it was not realized, and economic conditions worsened. Perón tightened his control, and Argentine exiles increasingly accused the police of terrorism and torture.

The General Confederation of Labor had early been converted into one of Perón's most powerful political supports. Under his rule the CGT controlled nearly all organized labor and enjoyed a privileged position with the government. It was a vital aid in holding the wage and price line, and the five million members were organized as a civilian militia, ready for action against Perón's foes. The army watched with growing displeasure, and the prominence given in the official press to stories of popular triumphs over the military in Iran and Bolivia suggested that Perón was possibly preparing to eliminate the army as a political factor. Jealousy between the army and labor leaders boded ill for the future.

In 1954 Perón seemed securely in control and less dependent on labor. A new wage policy announced during the year indicated that the days of favoritism toward labor were over. New wage increases, the president declared, would be granted only in cases of increased output. At the same time, an Employer's Confederation (CGE) was built up as a rival to the CGT. In congressional elections the Peronista party held its strength, although as usual opposition candidates had little opportunity to bring their names before the voters. After the election, Radical party leaders were arrested, ostensibly for violating the law against showing 'disrespect' to the president. A month later, however, Perón admitted that there were two main sectors of Argentine opinion, the Peronistas and the Radicals. He announced that the time had come for the 'depersonalization' of the revolution begun in 1943.

Before the end of the year Perón had to admit the existence of a third body of opinion, the Roman Catholic Church. He had become alarmed by the rapid growth of the Christian Socialist movement, and he warned the church against interfering with student and labor groups. Perón ordered an attack on the church despite its earlier support. The clergy had opposed the canonization of Evita proposed by her followers shortly after her death, but the president's anger was inspired more by the priests' encouragement of independent labor unions. Deliberately to offend the clergy, Perón pushed through the congress laws legalizing divorce and prostitution. Teaching by priests in the public schools was terminated, and a decree indicated that religious holidays would not be observed.

In June of 1955, after an eight-month battle with the church, Perón initiated action to separate church and state. He also threatened to tax church property. A vast Catholic demonstration took place in front of the Casa Rosada, followed by a march on the congressional palace. Intense violence followed. On June 16 naval air units rose in a brief rebellion in which the presidential palace was bombed. The army soon restored order, but Perón then unleashed his angered followers who attacked and burned churches throughout the capital. Appeals by the clergy were met with defiance. The Vatican thereupon excommunicated Perón and his immediate aides. The country was in chaos and it appeared that the president's touch had lost its magic.

Perón apparently sensed that he had gone too far. Church prestige remained strong, and the government offered to rebuild the church buildings destroyed by the violent acts of Perón's followers. In July the president offered an 'open hand' to his political opponents, and soon thereafter he resigned as head of the Peronista party. The opposition refused to accept the open hand, however, until constitutional guarantees were restored, the internal violence ended, and a general amnesty was granted to political prisoners and exiles. Perón made a gesture of resigning before his most devoted followers, and allowed himself to be persuaded to continue in office. Reassured, he announced a fight to the finish, promising to meet violence with greater violence. In September he sought to tighten his grip on the country by means of a congressionally approved state of siege. Again the sixteenth of the month proved a fateful day, for new uprisings broke out in the army and navy. Rebellious units swept all before them in spite of repeated announcements of government victories. Three days later Perón took refuge on a Paraguayan gunboat. An army junta took charge and submitted to the rebel demands. General Eduardo Lonardi declared himself provisional president. Perón departed into exile, finally establishing his permanent home in Spain.

THE POST-PERÓN ERA

General Lonardi did not long remain provisional president, for in November he gave way to General Pedro Eugenio Aramburu, who promised to accelerate the return to democratic processes and to hold free elections. He created a National Consultative Committee, an advisory body representing all major parties, except, of course, the Peronistas, whom he outlawed. Piece by piece he dismantled the Perón political regime, restoring the Constitution of 1853, freeing the press, including restoration of *La Prensa* to its previous owner, Gainza Paz, and re-establishing amicable relations with the church. Divorce was again made illegal and prostitution prohibited. Dr. Raúl Prebish, a distinguished economist, was called upon to guide Argentina back along the difficult path to economic stability and prosperity.

Several million Argentines, nevertheless, continued to maintain their allegiance to Perón, and from the safety of exile the former president stirred up trouble as best he could. His followers were not permitted to enter candidates in elections, and in retaliation they cast blank ballots. Some measure of Perón's continued strength was thus ascertainable, and the results were profoundly disturbing to his successors.

Argentine political party life had been greatly affected by the Perón era. Apart from Peronistas, the only significant political grouping that remained after the dictator's departure was the Radical party, and it was torn asunder by internal dissension. In the election for president of February, 1958, one group calling themselves the Intransigent Radicals (UCRI), supported Arturo Frondizi, who sought to restore political normalcy to the country by enticing the Peronistas back into effective participation. The other group, calling themselves the People's Radicals (UCRP), presented Ricardo Balbín as their candidate. The Intransigent Radicals were the younger and more vigorous group, and Frondizi's hints of restoration of political rights to all Argentines attracted much of the Peronista vote. With a last-minute assist from Perón himself, Frondizi won by an overwhelming majority.

By courting all elements of Argentine opinion during his campaign, Frondizi raised many expectations that could not possibly be satisfied. The Peronistas expected immediate restoration of full political rights and possibly even the return of Perón to Argentina. Political rights eventually were restored, but no president in his right mind would have dared allow the former dictator to return. Perón's angry blast suggested that a promise had been made and broken. Equally disappointed were those who expected an immediate return to prosperity and continuation of social betterment programs for the lower classes. The country was still virtually bankrupt, and only a rigorous austerity and foreign financial assistance offered promise of relief. Frondizi had little choice but to follow such a course, whatever may have been his political preferences, but he could hardly expect that his decision would be widely and popularly acclaimed. His decision to invite foreign petroleum companies to participate in the development of the country's oil resources ran directly counter to the long-standing view of the ultra-nationalists, even though significant economic benefits very shortly became apparent. His attempt to restore the army to the barracks and re-institute complete civilian rule disappointed many in the military class. However necessary Frondizi's course, he was soon to find himself traveling a lonely road. Strange sounds in the night suggested that his enemies were stalking him, waiting to pounce at the first sign of weakness.

Trouble in Utopia: Uruguay

Across the mighty waters of the Río de la Plata, Uruguay's semi-socialized economy did not escape the rigors of the great depression any more successfully than did the oligarchic agricultural system of her neighbor. The end of a world market for wool and meat created a crisis with which Uruguay's double-headed executive authority could not cope. President Gabriel Terra, the *Colorado* president elected in 1930, dissolved congress and the administrative council and governed with mildly dictatorial powers until a new constitution in 1934 established once again the principle of a unified executive authority. The government had entered the grain business earlier in an effort to assure satisfactory returns to farmers by establishing minimum prices at which it would purchase grain. The program proved costly, and public works and services had to be curtailed. Unemployment rose sharply, and the government placed restrictions on immigration and pared down its budget. Many other recovery measures were tried, such as exchange controls, restrictions on imports, and heavier taxes, but they had little appreciable effect. The problems were world-wide, not domestic. However, after 1934 exports began a slow recovery and both economic and political tensions relaxed. In that year an Import and Export Exchange Committee was created to balance imports, by means of a quota system, with available foreign exchange derived from purchases by each of the various countries from which imports were contemplated. This in effect created a modified barter system, but it stimulated the export market. A further reduction in the budget enabled the government to produce a modest treasury surplus by the end of 1935.

Terra's social programs were fairly well completed before his second term expired in 1938. Homes for workingmen were built and sold on easy terms; minimum wages, old age pensions, and health insurance benefits were increased. Terra's brother-in-law, Alfredo Baldomir, succeeded him in the presidency. He tried to strengthen national finances through a barter agreement with Germany, but World War II began and put an end to the plan's effectiveness before it had been in operation a year.

POLITICAL STRESSES OF THE WAR

During the war Uruguay was greatly troubled by Nazi activity, and the German embassy sought to create a strong local Nazi party. Many *Blancos,* following the nationalist—isolationist bent of their leader, Luis Alberto Herrera, openly demonstrated their sympathy for the Axis powers despite the government's consistent policy of close co-operation with the United States. Because of a troublesome senate in which the Blancos controlled half the votes, President Baldomir in 1942 abolished the congress and ruled by decree. He postponed the scheduled election and expelled all Blanco members of the administrative council, which he had re-created in an ill-considered step back toward the collegiate executive system. In an election held near the end of the year, Juan José Amezaga, a firmly pro-Ally lawyer, was chosen president. Baldomir had broken diplomatic relations with the Axis powers after Japan attacked Pearl Harbor in the Hawaiian Islands; Amezaga went the step further and war was declared on the Axis nations in 1945.

The Uruguayan political outlook during the war greatly irritated the Argentine government. Not only was the official policy contrary to that of the powerful neighbor across the river, but the oppression of the Argentine dictatorship caused increasing numbers of exiles to take up residence in Montevideo. Herrera's efforts were supported by Ramírez, Farrell, and Perón in the hope that he could establish a pro-Argentine government in

Uruguay, but without success. When the war in Europe and Asia was over, Perón still meddled; and when the Uruguayan election of 1946 was held he tried to influence the outcome by withholding wheat until a bread shortage occurred in the Uruguayan capital. Despite this aid to the Blancos, however, the Colorado candidates, Tomás Berreta and Luis Batlle, were elected.

RETURN TO THE PLURAL EXECUTIVE

Uruguayan political leaders seemed still to be fascinated by the concept of the collegiate executive. Internal prosperity seemed to bring forth this impulse. Baldomir toyed with the idea during the artificial prosperity of the war, but rejected it when the pressures of the opposition became difficult to withstand. Prosperity declined in the later years of the 1940's, and continued presidential leadership was considered essential. After the election of 1950, however, when Andrés Martínez Trueba had become president, prosperity revived under the stimulus of the Korean War. Again the plural executive was proposed, and in 1951 the Uruguayans voted to abolish the presidency in favor of a nine-man National Council of Government, whose chief exponent was the president in spite of the fact that the collegiate form would cost him his role as chief executive. The council assumed all executive powers. It was composed of six members of the majority party and three of the minority party. The presidency, whose incumbent was to do little more than chair the council, was to rotate each year to another member of the majority party, except that Andrés Martínez Trueba was to hold the post until the expiration of the term for which he had been elected initially. By this change Uruguay returned to the political course on which Batlle y Ordóñez had set the country in 1919.

THE HARD REALITIES OF ECONOMIC LIFE

With the end of the Korean War, Uruguay's artificially stimulated export market sagged again. Perón provided a further downward shove, for his dislike for Uruguay's press attacks upon him and the welcome given the exiles from his regime caused him to place a virtual embargo on commerce with his neighbor across the river. Argentines were forbidden to vacation in Uruguay, and a highly lucrative tourist market was thereby destroyed.

In 1957 the wool market fell sharply, and hard times again came to Uruguay. The government found itself unable to pay for the vaunted social welfare program that had caused some writers to laud the country as an almost utopian democracy. The government enterprises that operated the country's banks, insurance industry, utilities, petroleum, alcohol, and cement production found themselves in grave financial difficulties. Not only did business activity lag, but widely practiced featherbedding contributed to an extremely low productivity per worker. Nearly one-third of the labor force worked for the government or one of its public enterprises, and over two-thirds of the population were crowded into Montevideo and its urban area; these people were dependent on a public treasury that itself depended on an export economy that had collapsed. Inflation mounted rapidly, and labor troubles became acute. Frequent strikes further reduced worker productivity, and the coffee houses were crowded with people who disputed endlessly over political solutions to economic problems. Communist influence grew steadily, and numerous adherents were found among the poverty-stricken unemployed of Montevideo.

In the elections of 1958, the Blancos defeated the Colorados for the first time in nearly a century, but they had little to contribute that was constructive. The economy continued to slip slowly but steadily downward. In spite of American assistance in the form of financial support, many Uruguayans blamed their difficulties upon the United States. Had not the development of synthetic fibers by American industry destroyed the wool market? A visit by President Eisenhower in 1960 produced numerous demonstrations of anti-American sentiment. Unfortunately, no one seemed concerned that for years the quality of Uruguayan wool had been allowed to decline. Likewise, the quality of beef had not been maintained. No serious attempt at agricultural diversification had even been considered, although possibilities were highly favorable. A few observers of the Uruguayan scene began to question the basis of the country's enviable reputation abroad. Did almost everyone really belong to the middle class? Was there really no hunger, no poverty? Were the politicians really honest? Was the population really over 90 per cent literate? There had not been a census in fifty years. Clearly there was trouble in South America's 'most democratic' and 'egalitarian' republic.

The Chilean Struggle for Survival

For Chile, too, the problems of world depression were insoluble in the 1930's. The outlay required to service the foreign debt necessitated a critical reduction of the budget and a corresponding curtailment of public works projects. President Ibáñez sought to stimulate recovery through government controls over foreign exchange and trade, and he made a futile effort to sustain the price of nitrates through granting a monopoly of foreign sales to the Nitrate Company of Chile (COSACH). The government temporarily abandoned its export tax on nitrates, but the price continued to fall until it was below the cost of production. Financial collapse was imminent.

Carlos Ibáñez, whose government had enjoyed the easy money prosperity of the latter 1920's, struggled mightily to impose austerity and discipline in both the economic and political spheres. His regime became increasingly arbitrary, and outspoken opponents found it more and more convenient to launch their critical barbs from abroad. The government was forced to default on its bonded indebtedness, and the currency's value dropped almost to zero. Everywhere people were unemployed; hunger and starvation stalked the long, narrow country from one end to the other. Faced with widespread rioting and violence in the streets, Ibáñez fled the country in July, 1931.

After the failure of Ibáñez and his overthrow, Chile lapsed into a period of virtual anarchy. One group after another attempted to form a government, including the military, but each was equally unsuccessful. The repeated printing of useless paper money solved nothing. Labor and the unemployed demanded state ownership and control of basic industries, heavier taxes on the landowners and such other wealthy groups and individuals as could still be found, and nationalization of foreign-owned enterprises. However, a short-lived socialist regime solved nothing. Carlos Dávila, who headed the socialist effort, proposed a host of basic reforms that so frightened both conservative and liberal elements that they were roused to action. The army turned against Dávila and removed him from office, but the ideas he had fostered left a deep impression. The judicial power stepped into the picture and called a new election for December, 1932.

Former President Arturo Alessandri returned to office as a result of the 1932 election, but he was no longer the liberal Radical of earlier days. The old 'Lion of Tarapacá' had been living in Italy and his views had moderated considerably in the direction of conservatism, although he had hardly become the fascist that some of his enemies alleged. Alessandri now ruled with a firm hand, ignoring congress, stifling the press, exiling his enemies, and building his political support among the Conservative oligarchy. He chose as his minister of finance a wealthy Conservative, Gustavo Ross, a man to whom much of the credit must be given for the gradual economic recovery that followed Alessandri's election. The nitrate market was partially restored by new European demand, but the rigorous limitations on imports and government subsidy stimulated development of local industries producing products that formerly had been available only through imports. Measures popular with labor and leftist elements included acquisition by purchase of the British-owned railroad that ran over the Andes mountains to Mendoza in Argentina, re-organization of foreign-owned utilities to give Chileans and the Chilean government participation in both management and profits, and reconstitution of the nitrate extraction enterprise to increase benefits to the country. Such measures involved varying degrees of duress against foreign owners, and nationalistic as well as socialistic feelings were assuaged by the government's policy.

For a few critical years Alessandri's power was strengthened by the Republican Militia, an independent force of citizens committed to defending the existing order and constitutional government. The militia was assailed from all sides and resented by the army. In 1935 it peacefully disbanded, but it had served a useful purpose during a very critical time. The tide of anarchy that had threatened to engulf the republic had been stemmed.

Because of Alessandri's small enthusiasm for new social legislation, his open alliance with the Conservatives, and frequent allegations of his tolerance if not sympathy for fascist and Nazi causes and methods, the Radical party and labor abandoned him, ultimately to create a new Popular Front of liberal, socialistic, and even communistic views. By the end of his term the powerful demand for major social reforms was still unsatisfied. Additional credit had been made available to agriculture, industry, and mining, but nothing had been done in the cause of labor or to raise the workingman above a poverty level of existence. The most neglected group of all was the agricultural peasantry.

The Chilean Radical party, unlike its counterpart in Argentina, em-

404   *Hegemony and the Rise of Indigenous Nationalism*

braced a program of major social and economic change, and its abandonment of Alessandri in favor of the Popular Front changed the balance
among Chilean political parties. The rift was widened in 1936 by Alessandri's severity in suppressing a strike of railway workers. His zeal for maintaining internal security raised fears that he intended to establish a dictatorship, and it drove the variety of opposition groups to seek victory
through co-operation. Alessandri apparently had no such intention, but the
Popular Front was organized as a means of defeating him.

THE POPULAR FRONT

The Chilean Popular Front, through a coalition of moderate and left-wing
groups, broke the long domination of the middle and the right, the domination of land and wealth. None of Chile's many parties enjoyed a majority, but the combination, while it lasted, provided control of the presidency
and the congress for the Radicals. The Front was aided indirectly in its efforts to capture the presidency in 1938 when youths of the Chilean Nazi
party staged an uprising, were captured, and many of them shot without
trial. The anger of the Nazis helped the Front candidate, Pedro Aguirre
Cerda, to win the election by a slight margin over Gustavo Ross, Alessandri's able finance minister and an arch-enemy of the Radicals.

Soon after taking office, Aguirre Cerda had an opportunity to begin
carrying out his plans for economic and social rehabilitation as a result of
the devastating earthquake of January, 1939. The emergency relief program organized to restore the destroyed cities grew in a short time into an
instrument of state capitalism, the *Corporación de Fomento* or Development Corporation (CORFO). It came to constitute the Radicals' program
for promoting industry and conservation, and it was given wide latitude in
conducting economic studies, making loans, and encouraging the expansion
of old and the creation of new industries. It succeeded in speeding up industrialization, and eventually it set up a sizable iron and steel industry in
the south.

Once the Radicals and Socialists smoothed out their differences, the
greatest disturbances were caused by the Communist party and the fascist-
type groups that opposed it. After the Russo-German non-aggression pact
was signed, the Communists became violent in their attacks on the government which they ostensibly supported. The sharpest thrusts were reserved
for the Socialist ministers, whom they regarded as rivals for control of
labor rather than as partners in the Popular Front.

In 1940, while Aguirre was calling for a temporary suspension of strikes, the Communists intensified their agitation for labor disorders. When the conference at la Habana brought up the inevitable question of Chile's attitude toward the war, the Communists bitterly denounced the United States and stigmatized the Socialists as pawns of imperialism.

From the Nazi party came similarly vehement attacks on the government. Gustavo Ross and Ibáñez were known to be in Buenos Aires, and they were believed to be plotting the downfall of the Front, a suspicion that raised the hopes of the rightist groups. At this point the Spanish government of Francisco Franco offered indirect encouragement to them by severing diplomatic relations with Chile.

By early 1941 all pretense of unity within the Popular Front was at an end. The Socialists withdrew from it, and a few weeks later it formally dissolved. Differences of opinion on evolutionary methods as opposed to revolution and on hemispheric solidarity as opposed to resistance to 'Yankee imperialism,' the lack of success of popular front regimes in Europe, together with the Russo-German pact, were prominent factors contributing to the break-up of Chile's unharmonious coalition.

The most striking success of the Popular Front was in the stimulation of industry and raising the level of production. The Development Corporation's effectiveness was generally acknowledged even by those who loathed state participation in economic enterprise. Supplied with capital by the government and by the Export–Import Bank of the United States, Fomento modernized old industries such as fishing by re-equipping the fleet, and created new industries in a variety of industrial fields. In many cases the Corporation retained more than half the stock in the plants it subsidized, thus maintaining a continuing control over their policies.

SHIFTING POLITICAL ALIGNMENTS

After the Popular Front fell apart, the Radicals joined with the Democratic party and the radical Socialists for the approaching election, and the Communists threw their weight behind this union. The main body of Socialists, led by Marmaduke Grove and Oscar Schnake, refused to associate themselves with the Communists. When Germany attacked Russia the Communist tactics changed quickly, and for a time it appeared that the Popular Front would arise from the ashes stronger than before. At this juncture Aguirre Cerda died suddenly, and any hope of reviving the Front passed away with him.

Rivalry for leadership of the Radical party became intense between Juan Antonio Ríos, outspoken enemy of the Communists, and Gabriel González Videla, who was regarded as more cordial to the extreme left. Ríos won the Radical nomination for the presidency, and he called for a coalition of democratic and progressive forces, carefully excluding the Communists from either category. The Socialists nominated Schnake, and the Conservatives backed Ibáñez. Schnake subsequently withdrew his name and gave his support to Ríos.

Foreign affairs played a powerful role in the campaign, and the range of opinion regarding international commitments was so wide that the candidates could not express themselves freely without offending lukewarm supporters. In the campaign Ríos was portrayed as pro-democratic and anti-Nazi, while Ibáñez was branded with the opposite label. The campaign managers of Ibáñez hastily countered with claims of his friendship for the United States. Both men were careful to obscure their views as far as possible, but it was well known that the Chilean Nazis were ardent supporters of Ibáñez, and the triumph of Ríos was in part a victory for the cause of hemispheric solidarity. At the same time it indicated a swing toward the center and away from the extremes in domestic politics.

The splintering of Chilean political party life had begun more than a half-century before, but now new factors began to emerge that tended to clarify the political scene. Conservatives and Liberals had long since joined forces to reflect the unenlightened views of the land-holding oligarchy of the central valley, plus some of the older commercial interests. Alone they had insufficient support to win a national election. The Radical party had emerged to represent the newer commercial and industrial classes, particularly in the south of Chile around Concepción and in the northern desert region. It too could only hope for victory with the support of other groups, and increasingly it turned to the labor-supported Socialist party for coalition assistance. At times the Communists were included, as was true of the early period of the Popular Front. The Radicals were progressives, but they could hardly be said to favor major changes in the social structure, although they were pulled in that direction by their allies. The Nazi party was a passing phenomenon, reflecting the fascination which Hitler's rise to power in Germany had for many Chilean youths of German ancestry. Its strength was in the south of Chile where most of the German Chileans lived, but it is doubtful if its membership ever numbered more than a few thousand. It was highly visible, vocal, well led, and well financed from the German embassy. It was a factor difficult for Chileans to evaluate in a critical period when Germany seemed to be the master of Europe, Japan was in control of much of the Pacific, and neighboring Argentina clearly leaned toward the Axis powers.

The war, with its international overtones, aggravated many of the problems of the Chilean government, for the delicate balance among the many parties necessary to create an effective majority was barely possible without having to adjust to external ideological differences. Had the Radicals constituted a majority at the outset of the war, it seems likely that Chile would not have delayed breaking relations with the Axis for a year after the Rio de Janeiro conference. Compelling reasons caused her to hesitate —the acute cleavages of her multi-party system, her long coastline exposed to Japanese attack, and fear of trouble among her population of German descent. Chile's reasons for delay were appreciated by officials of the American government. A strain in relations developed, nevertheless, owing to Chile's lack of a serious effort to prevent Axis espionage agents from operating freely in the country until after January, 1943, when diplomatic relations with the Axis powers were finally broken.

The Communist party was not taken too seriously. Russia was not only no super-power, but Germany seemed to have her nearly defeated and occupied. Shifts in policy reflecting the changing orders received from Moscow did not help build a following. The Communists would become serious political contenders in Chile only after the war.

ECONOMIC BENEFITS OF THE WAR

During the wartime presidency of Juan Antonio Ríos the idea of government intervention in the economy flourished, for as the expansion of industry progressed, Chileans raised their sights to objectives undreamed of a few years earlier. The industrialist class rose rapidly in wealth and power under government protection, and the Radical party under Ríos swung away from its close alliance with labor to one with the industrialists. The temporary measures of economic nationalism begun during the depression were strengthened and extended. The country was prosperous, wartime demands for copper from Chile's mines providing a large part of the national income and government revenue.

In the election held after the untimely death of Ríos, Gabriel González Videla won the presidency. His administration was complicated by the post-war economic crisis which he inherited, and by the activities of the

Communist party. He began his administration by giving communists ministerial posts in his government, but he soon found it impossible to obtain their co-operation. He threw them out of his cabinet, persuaded congress to outlaw the party, and his government severed diplomatic relations with Russia.

Among the features of the González Videla administration was a reawakening of interest in the far south. In strengthening her historic interest in the area, Chile discovered oil in the Punta Arenas region and took measures to develop this new resource and bring wells into production. In 1947 an expedition was sent to the Antarctic continent to establish a Chilean base in the polar region, thus laying claim to a portion of the continent which was named O'Higgins Land. In the north the trans-Andean railway from Antofagasta to Salta was completed in 1948. Two years later the government celebrated still another signal achievement with the opening of the Huachipato steel works, near Concepción.

By the close of the González Videla administration, Chile showed remarkable progress. The dark days of 1931 and 1932 were forgotten. Politically, Chile had remained true to her traditions of constitutional government. Economic development had raised new classes to wealth and political power, and though the gains had been costly in governmental outlays, Chileans remained determined to base their hopes for the future on further industrialization. Only in agriculture did colonial anachronisms persist. In two decades the Radicals had been able to force through many of the changes they sought in urban areas, including substantial increases in wages paid to labor and in social benefits for the poorer classes, but the countryside remained unaffected. The powerful landowners of the south were traditionally members of the Radical party, but they teamed up with their Conservative associates farther north to check any movement toward change in the land tenure system.

Chile's friendly relations with the United States continued after the war, and by 1949 González Videla's government had received more than one hundred million dollars in loans for his program of economic development. Inflation remained the most threatening problem of post-war Chile, and one currency crisis followed another. After devaluating the peso late in 1949, González Videla was faced with the possibility of a general strike over the wage–hour freeze he proposed in February, 1950. His cabinet resigned and he was forced to withdraw the proposed measure. A copper price conflict with the United States ended temporarily in 1952 when the ceiling price for Chilean copper was raised, owing in large part to the new demands arising out of the Korean War. The contract was hailed by Chileans as strengthening their position for future negotiations, but copper sales remained a critical concern. Unfortunately, copper seemed destined to demonstrate one of the most elastic demand patterns on the international market.

THE RETURN OF CARLOS IBÁÑEZ

Politically, the key issue of 1952 was the presidential election, and inflation provided the primary point of argument. The main contenders were Pedro Enrique Alfonso, who was backed by the government in power, Carlos Ibáñez, the perennial Conservative candidate, and Arturo Matte. The now elderly Ibáñez waged a strongly nationalistic campaign, attacking the Radicals as being the lackeys of 'Wall Street.' Making the greatest possible use of the issue of chronic inflation, he promised a strong executive who could take effective action without having to placate various political groups or foreign governments, as González Videla most assuredly had had to do. One of Ibáñez' most enthusiastic supporters was Perón of Argentina; one Argentine consul was expelled from the country for meddling in the election.

The resounding victory Ibáñez won at the polls indicated disillusionment with the Radicals and their failure to check inflation. It also demonstrated the strength of Chilean nationalism, but it was hardly a victory for the Conservative party. Ibáñez had no strongly organized party support, during his campaign and subsequently, and soon he was setting new records in the number of people paraded through his cabinet in a vain effort to placate a sufficient number of the diverse political groups to gain support for this or that measure. Early fears that the former dictator would revert to his previous style of rule were reflected in a sharp drop in the American stock market when his election was announced, but such apprehensions proved unfounded. It was not so much Ibáñez himself who caused concern; it was his advisors, some of whom were reputedly ex-members of the Chilean Nazi party. The communists, too, cheered loudly for Ibáñez, for he had promised to annul the law ensuring the 'permanent defense of democracy' which proscribed the party. But those who expected the immediate nationalization of the American-owned copper industry were disappointed, for Chile's dollar-short economy could not stand so violent a shock, and Ibáñez knew it.

In February, 1953, Perón crossed the Andes for an official visit with Ibáñez, while Chileans watched fearfully for signs that their country was being drawn into the Argentine orbit. Argentine ambitions for continental hegemony were well known, and the strong Chilean nationalism that Ibáñez had so recently aroused made subordination to Argentina an unattractive prospect. It was necessary for the president to adjourn congress before Perón's visit to prevent embarrassing debate. Ibáñez soon reciprocated with a visit to Buenos Aires, and economic ties between the two countries were strengthened by a barter agreement and mutual reduction of customs duties on important products. The arrangements proved of little benefit to Chile, however, and Ibáñez was forced to yield more and more to firm opposition to anything approaching economic union with Argentina as visualized by Perón's followers.

By 1954 the Chileans who had expected the aging Ibáñez to perform a miracle and check inflation single-handed were beginning to display their disillusionment. Inflation, far from being stopped, continued at a faster pace than before. The ultra-nationalists, who longed for expropriation of foreign holdings, abandoned their erstwhile idol. Political tensions rose until the president declared martial law.

Having no majority party of his own to rely on, Ibáñez had increasing difficulty satisfying the miscellaneous and unharmonious following that had placed him in power. He was forced to appeal for the co-operation of all parties, including the Radicals, whom he had lately blasted with devastating charges of fraud and incompetence. He learned that it was far easier to capitalize on popular discontent than to eradicate its causes. He had come to power with a negative program rather than with constructive ideas. He had no plan for checking inflation, and it was not to be banished by good intentions. Devaluation of the peso continued and by 1958 the American dollar would buy over 1200 of them, a fourfold increase in three years. Those who suffered most were the workers and the pensioners, for their incomes simply could not keep pace.

The government's neglect of agriculture in favor of industry also had repercussions, for the deficit of 400,000 tons of wheat in 1954 was as large as any that had occurred, and shortages of other foodstuffs were also serious. A program to increase agricultural production was begun in 1951 with technical and financial aid from the United States, but its progress was hampered by inflation. A country that had once exported agricultural surpluses now could not even feed its own population. The misery of the people mounted.

In the election of 1958 no candidate received a majority, so the final decision was left to the congress. Its choice was Jorge Alessandri, son of the former president, as he had received the most votes, even though the total was far from a majority. Inflation was still rampant, and Alessandri was obliged to impose an austerity program, as international economists had repeatedly urged. The voters seemed to approve of Alessandri's actions in the local elections of 1960. In that same year, however, a severe earthquake and tidal wave struck the country, causing the death of several thousand people and enormous property damage. This natural catastrophe added considerably to Chile's economic and social ills.

In spite of the obstacles he faced, Alessandri was able to bring the inflation under temporary control. His austerity measures were rigorous, involving severe import limitations, a reduction in public employees, and sharp tax increases. These efforts were made in the face of sharply declining copper prices and the doldrum conditions in which the nitrate industry seemed destined to continue indefinitely.

A significant development in the 1958 election was a revised political alignment. Alessandri had been backed by the Conservatives, the Liberals, and what remained of the moderate Radicals. Leftist groups had formed a new coalition, the *Frente de Acción Popular,* composed of Socialists, Communists, and the more extreme Radicals. Its candidate had been Salvador Allende, regarded by many as a communist in belief if not by party allegiance. A third political force had also emerged, the Christian Socialist party, whose candidate was Eduardo Frei Montalva, an able lawyer with a platform calling for vigorous reform. Frei obtained only 20 per cent of the vote, but he loomed as a new and important force on the political horizon. The old Radical party had also presented its candidate, but his poor showing clearly indicated that most Radicals had voted for someone else.

Thirty Years of Travail

In the three decades between 1930 and 1960, South America's most European countries mirrored many of the problems that troubled continental Europe in the same era. Fortunately, Argentina, Chile, and Uruguay were spared the devastation of World War II, but the political and economic nostrums of fascism and Nazism penetrated the thinking of many of their leaders. Promises of a new social order and economic benefits for the

poor, the landless, and the unemployed were glibly advanced by demagogues who had little possiblity of fulfilling their commitments. Uruguay
and Chile both sought to move rapidly to a form of welfare state by legislative action without significantly increasing national productivity. Argentina greatly damaged its productive capacity by destroying the incentives
for re-investment while lavishly and prodigally expending the benefits of
prior development to buy political support. The results in each case were
disillusionment and national trauma. Popular expectations were nevertheless aroused, and they would not soon again be stifled.

The fragmentation of political life in Chile and Argentina mirrored the
parliamentary chaos of France's Third Republic and Spain before the rise
of Franco. Congresses were not strong, but they were powerful enough to
frustrate the efforts of any president seeking to govern in accordance with
democratic concepts. Uruguay's moribund parties and ill-considered system of executive stalemate provided no basis for the confrontation of basic
economic problems that increasingly took on crisis proportions.

In 1960 each of South America's European states was in the hands of a
civilian government chosen in accordance with democratic processes. Each
enjoyed basic political freedoms. Just below the surface, however, social
and economic ills festered; inevitably they would have to be treated in the
years ahead. Industrial development held out some hope, particularly in
Argentina and Chile, but all three countries continued to neglect their
basic resource—land. The future was obscure, frustrated nationalism stood
as a barrier to objective approaches to national problems, and the possibility of communist revolution could nowhere be entirely discounted.

17

Indian South America:
A Struggle Against Futility

Actually, the hope of the Andean countries, not only Peru but Bolivia and Ecuador as well, lies in the mountain regions with their masses of hard-working peasants.*

In the Sierra Indians generally sleep on the floor, most *mestizos* . . . on a bedstead on wooden boards, and "whites" on a bed with a mattress, while the poorer people on the coast use a hammock. . . .†

The Indian countries of South America contrasted sharply in many ways with most of their neighbors. Here the most distinct cleavages of race and class were to be found, the most flagrant examples of rule by clique, the greatest concentration in the ownership of land and wealth, and the most corroding examples of acute poverty among the mass of the people. In all of them, political instability and military intervention were chronic, despite occasional tyrants who were able to suppress opposition for a decade or longer. Most of the social, economic, and political ills generally ascribed to Latin America were found in these countries to an advanced degree. Their history between 1930 and 1960 was one of repeated violence and frequent governmental change. The conditions of the people changed only imperceptibly, and for many such changes as did occur were hardly viewed as improvements.

The problems of Peru, Bolivia, Ecuador, and Paraguay were similar in many respects, and efforts to solve them proved equally futile. In each country a large and neglected or maltreated Indian mass was the most numerous element of the population, and the conditions of the Indians had not improved significantly since the close of the colonial era. A basic need

---

* Allan R. Holmberg, "Changing Community Attitudes and Values in Peru: A Case Study in Guided Change," in Council on Foreign Relations, *Social Change in Latin America Today,* Harper and Brothers, New York, 1960, p. 78.

† Lilo Linke, *Ecuador,* Oxford University Press, London, for the Royal Institute of International Affairs, 1960, p. 11.

413

was to rehabilitate the Indians, to integrate them into national economic and social life, and to give them incentive and hope to raise themselves above the subsistence level at which most existed. The economic potentialities of the countries could not be approached while so large a part of their populations produced no more than for their barest daily needs.

In Ecuador and Peru the world depression added to the chronic political unrest and precipitated overthrow of the governments. In 1930 Colonel Luis M. Sánchez Cerro ended the Peruvian dictatorship of Augusto Leguía, and in the following year Dr. Isidro Ayora was forced out of the Ecuadorean presidency. Sánchez Cerro was assassinated in 1933; no one was able to remain long in power in Ecuador for years to come.

The Chaco War

International disputes among the Indian countries and with their neighbors led to further disharmony and chaos in the 1930's, in particular the senseless Chaco War between Paraguay and Bolivia. The vast, almost empty Chaco area had long been a subject of dispute, and fruitless negotiations had been carried on for years. Both governments upheld their claims with uncompromising zeal, although except for rumored oil deposits there was nothing at stake but national pride. Pride, however, proved a potent force.

Paraguayan troops provoked the conflict by a surprise attack on Fortín Vanguardia in December, 1928. Bolivians quickly retaliated by capturing the Paraguayan posts of Mariscal López and Boquerón. Diplomatic relations between the two countries were severed, but war did not break out in full fury until 1932.

Most Latin American nations sympathized at first with Paraguay, because the presence of a Standard Oil Company concession in Bolivia enabled jingoists to raise the irresistible cry of American imperialism. Standard Oil, with only a small operation in Bolivia, was accused of arming powerful Bolivia for aggression against weak and impoverished Paraguay. No evidence has been presented to indicate that the rumor was true, and Bolivian military preparedness was vastly overrated by Paraguayan sympathizers, for the Bolivian army had been trained for the parade ground rather than the battlefield. Upon leaving the altiplano for the unaccustomed rigors of the tropical lowlands, Bolivian troops suffered severe hardships.

In 1932, when fighting began in earnest, Argentine Foreign Minister Carlos Saavedra Lamas, reflecting the general delusion regarding the comparative strength of the contenders, obtained unanimous approval of the other American republics for a declaration that no territorial conquest would be recognized. Thus would Bolivia be shorn of the spoils of war should she persist in conquering Paraguay, as was believed likely. The declaration made the fighting fruitless, yet neither side would compromise. In the end it was Paraguay that gained disputed territory by conquest, and the declaration was conveniently forgotten.

The events of the wasteful and useless conflict are not significant, but its effect on the participants was demoralizing. An estimated 100,000 men were lost, and the financial condition of both countries became chaotic. By the end of 1934 the Paraguayan army was within striking distance of the Bolivian oil fields, but was held off by a desperate effort. Both sides were exhausted, and in June, 1935, a truce was signed, a truce negotiated by a mediation commission composed of representatives of Argentina, Chile, Uruguay, Brazil, and the United States. Three years later the two belligerent nations signed a treaty and agreed to arbitrate the boundary dispute under conditions that left Paraguay most of her conquests. Bolivia received token compensation in the form of access to the upper Paraguay river and free use of Puerto Casado in the Chaco.

AFTERMATH OF THE CONFLICT

In addition to disrupting the economies of the contestants and leaving many a family on both sides without a breadwinner, the Chaco War furnished both countries with a supply of ambitious army officers who made occasional bids for power in later years. Military interference in government became more frequent than before the war. Governmental stability and reforms were badly needed, but neither could be achieved. Champions of change arose among the military heroes of the war, some of whom were determined to restore order and to introduce radical programs. Paraguayan Colonel Rafael Franco and Bolivian Colonel David Toro seized power in their respective countries in 1936. Both attempted to introduce socialist regimes along authoritarian lines. One year later both proponents of change were ousted by *cuartelazos* or barracks revolts. Franco's downfall was caused by opposition to his program on the one hand, and by impatience with his inability to carry it out on the other. A law of 1936 authorized the government to expropriate land not under cultivation for distribution among the landless, but Franco did not dare move against foreign-owned holdings, most of which belonged to Argentines.

Toro's efforts to introduce a brand of national socialism in Bolivia were equally fruitless, and he was replaced by Colonel Germán Busch. As was the case with Paraguay, Bolivia's economic condition went from bad to worse, and none of her military dictators was able to check the trend. In 1937 Bolivia expropriated the Standard Oil holdings, but was unable to develop a domestic oil industry to replace the foreign company. Busch attempted to force the tin companies to invest their profits in Bolivia, but he was stopped by their threat to suspend mining operations. He considered seizing the mines, but was dissuaded by the knowledge that the tin interests also owned the only available smelters, and these were located in England. In 1939 Busch died a violent death officially reported as suicide.

Paraguay's Slow and Erratic Progress

Colonel Rafael Franco was replaced first by a provisional government, and in 1939 by General José Félix Estigarribia, the chief military hero of the war. Estigarribia's efforts to return Paraguay to the new course envisioned by Franco were defeated by the discordant elements among his supporters. In February, 1940, he issued a proclamation declaring that he had tried to restore political freedom and promote public works, but that the country was bitterly divided and on the verge of anarchy. Because of the impending chaos, he assumed total power. He saw his mission as one of starting the nation on the road to prosperity. While waiting for a new constitution to be written, he re-opened the university which had been closed, inaugurated public works, and resumed division of land among the landless. He had other plans for the country, including a new highway system, railway connections with Brazil, acquisition of a fleet of merchant vessels, and creation of a sound currency.

The new Constitution of 1940 gave the president ample power to intervene in the economy of the country. The senate was replaced by a state council composed of representatives of the army, the church, agriculture, industry, and government employees. The corporative tendencies in economic and social life were thus to be given political recognition. Estigarribia did not live to provide guidance for the new constitutional order, however, for he was killed in an airplane accident in September, 1940.

Higinio Morínigo, minister of war under Estigarribia, assumed control of Paraguay, and he remained in power throughout the years of World War II. After Morínigo's downfall in 1948, Juan Natalicio González, one of Paraguay's greatest writers, was elected president. He was opposed by conservatives and by pro-Argentine members of his own party, for they resented his enthusiasm for the construction of a railroad to link the country with Santos in Brazil as well as his cool resistance to overtures from Perón. He survived this opposition only half a year before he was ousted from the presidency.

CLOSER TIES WITH PERÓN

After a short interval, Federico Cháves, foreign minister under Morínigo and an admirer of Perón, assumed the presidency, and in 1953 he was elected for a five-year term. His supporters upheld his use of severe methods in restraining the opposition in the name of political stability and economic progress, despite the fact that he had promised to permit the traditional parties to campaign.

Paraguay began making a determined effort to achieve the degree of prosperity which her resources would permit. Cháves dedicated his efforts to increasing the production of cotton, beef, and quebracho extract, but his program also included plans for social legislation and for an extension of the highway system. The government also welcomed immigrants and provided loans and other assistance to farmers from Europe who wished to settle in Paraguay. Among the immigrant groups that came to the country were 700 Kalmucks, European descendants of the legions of Genghis Khan, who were given 9000 acres of fertile land and a supply of livestock.

Cháves remained an ardent supporter of *Peronismo* during his rule, and as a consequence Paraguay became the first country to adhere to the type of economic union proposed by Argentina in economic affairs. Argentines had invested heavily in Paraguayan agriculture, and Buenos Aires controlled the country's main access to the sea. But nationalism grew stronger in Paraguay, and with it a powerful undercurrent of resistance to Argentina.

Partly as a result of the growing antipathy toward Argentina, Federico

Cháves was ousted by the army in March, 1954, shortly before Perón was to visit Asunción. General Alfredo Stroessner, leader of the uprising, was elected to complete the unfinished term. Opposition parties did not participate. The overthrow of Cháves came at an awkward time for Perón, for the Argentine congress had ordered the return of all war trophies captured from Paraguay nearly a century earlier and had granted Perón a leave of absence from his presidential duties for the trip to Asunción and the trophy presentation. The visit had been expected to consolidate Paraguay's position within the Argentine economic bloc, and the up-river country's defection under Stroessner was a serious setback to Peronista dreams of Argentine hegemony in the south of the continent.

BEGINNING OF THE STROESSNER ERA

Once in power, General Stroessner gave every indication that he expected to remain there for the rest of his life, and he showed considerable skill in dealing with his opponents who might have other ideas. He faced many military uprisings, and he crushed them thoroughly and severely. With equal determination he crushed a general strike in 1958. In 1959 he was elected for a new five-year term, again without opposition as those not in support of the general remained away from the polls.

Stroessner sought and obtained from the United States considerable technical assistance and also military aid, but in general his policies were isolationist, intended to insulate Paraguay from political trends and movements in neighboring countries. He did not introduce sweeping social or economic changes, yet he promoted a modest amount of economic development while holding the currency at a stable level, no small accomplishment in his part of the world. The reports of Paraguayan exiles were filled with accounts of intolerable conditions—concentration camps and brutal treatment of political prisoners. As time passed, however, both the number of exiles and the vociferousness of their outcrys diminished. Stroessner spoke of preparing his backward country for political democracy, but observers looked in vain for measures likely to accomplish such a goal. The regime had little to commend it except a harshly imposed stability.

Bolivia's Social Revolution

In 1940 General Enrique Peñaranda, commander of Bolivian troops during the Chaco War, became president. He faced growing hostility and, branded as the tool of tin magnates and Yankee imperialists, in 1943 he was driven from office by a group of young officers led by Major Gualberto Villaroel. Behind Villaroel was a civilian group headed by Víctor Paz Estenssoro, the recently organized National Revolutionary Movement (MNR). The junta that replaced Peñaranda, and which Villaroel headed, professed itself to be the champion of the people, particularly the miners, against exploitation by the wealthy tin barons, Patiño, Hochschild, and Aramayo. It also promised to fulfill the country's inter-American obligations faithfully. It was the mid-period of World War II, tin prices were high, and recognition was needed from other hemisphere countries if prosperity and existing international trade arrangements were to be maintained. However, because of the well-known pro-Argentine and pro-Nazi leanings of junta members, the sincerity of the promises was doubted by the officials of other Latin American states. General recognition of the regime was delayed for six months; by that time Paz Estenssoro and others regarded as objectionable by reason of their real or supposed fascist connections had been removed.

In June of 1944 the junta called for elections, and when they were held several weeks later the MNR won an easy victory. Villaroel was installed as president. It soon became clear that the MNR was no typical political party attached to the personalistic ambitions of its leader. It was intensely nationalistic in outlook, viewed the mine owners and their international supporters as oppressors of the Bolivian people, and harbored a strong dislike for the United States. It also did not hesitate to employ terroristic methods to destroy political opposition, and the government soon became notorious for its savagery. Attempted revolts were suppressed with unusual severity. However, in July, 1946, a right-wing revolt led by another group of army officers succeeded in overthrowing the Villaroel regime. The mob that gathered at the national palace hunted down the now-hated Villaroel, threw him from a balcony and then hanged his body upside down from a lamp post in the plaza. Paz Estenssoro escaped and fled into exile, but others less fortunate were meted out a fate similar to that of the late president.

PRELUDE TO REVOLUTION

After the downfall of Villaroel and his MNR supporters, political chaos prevailed until Enrique Hertzog was elected president in 1947. Hertzog proved quite unable to end the chaos despite the fact that he declared a state of siege six times before he gave up and retired in 1949. The MNR, urged on by Paz Estenssoro from exile in Buenos Aires, was the principal instigator of the revolts, and it kept constant pressure on the government. The miserable conditions of the populace made them ready participants in any effort that held promise for improvement. Vice-President Mamerto Urriolagoitia replaced Hertzog, but a sharp drop in the price of tin added to the government's problems and intensified hostility toward it. Mines were closed and unemployment among miners became critical. In May, 1950, demands by La Paz teachers for pay increases led to serious mob violence, for the enemies of the government, whatever their grievance, seized the opportunity to demonstrate.

As the tin crisis mounted the government began encouraging oil production as a means of creating foreign exchange. The low world prices for tin and new sources of the mineral in Nigeria, as well as restoration of competition from the mines of British companies on the Malay peninsula, suggested that neither high profits nor substantial demand would soon again characterize Bolivian tin production. Attention focused more and more on Bolivia's eastern tropical lowlands in the hope of new oil discoveries and expanded agricultural resources. Refineries were planned for Cochabamba and Sucre to process crude oil piped from the lowlands, but justification of the plans from an economic standpoint was doubtful.

Lack of transportation facilities was one of the greatest obstacles to developing the eastern area, and the government negotiated a loan from the Export–Import Bank for building a highway from Cochabamba to Santa Cruz. At the same time Brazil completed an extension of the São Paulo Railroad to link it with Santa Cruz and ultimately with Cochabamba, while Argentina began building a spur line to Santa Cruz. Brazilian and Argentine construction activity was owing in large part to competition for the Bolivian oil, for both countries suffered from critical oil shortages. Argentina, fearful of being bested by Brazil, offered Bolivia financial assistance while charging that United Nations and American 'Point Four' aid merely cloaked Yankee penetration.

REVOLUTION UNDER THE MOVIMIENTO NACIONAL REVOLUCIONARIO

By the end of 1950, Bolivia's political and economic situation had become desperate. Four years of chaotic rule since the overthrow of Villaroel had accomplished little or nothing. Tin prices remained depressed, and the mining unions, led by able and articulate Juan Lechín, demanded higher wages and benefits as well as improved working conditions. Mine owners, such as the Patiño interests and British, Chilean, and American companies, had for generations demonstrated that they cared nothing for the welfare of the miners, and they were not about to make concessions in the face of a depressed market. Indeed, ugly rumors suggested that radicals such as Lechín wanted to take the mines away from the owners and turn them over to the workers.

The landless peasants working on the haciendas of the great landowners and the lesser landowners continued to be restless and to demand land of their own. The impoverished Indian of the altiplano remained on the verge of starvation, uneducated, illiterate, and without hope. Even the military were restless and disorganized, as one clique struggled against another for power. One voice held some appeal for all of these groups, except the mine owners, and that was the voice of Paz Estenssoro in Buenos Aires.

Paz Estenssoro was ably represented in Bolivia by numerous lieutenants, including Juan Lechín, the idol of the miners, and Hernán Siles Zuazo, son of a former president. When elections were held in May of 1951, Paz Estenssoro, running in absentia with Siles Zuazo as his vice-presidential candidate, won 40 per cent of the votes cast, the remainder being so divided as to give him a clear plurality. The total vote was only a little over 125,000, as only literate males enjoyed the franchise. It became the duty of congress to choose a president from among the three leading candidates, but Urriolagoitia and military leaders who had been severely treated by the Villaroel regime formed a military junta under General Ovido Quiroga, voided the election, and refused to permit Paz to return to the country. A little less than a year later, however, in a violent three-day battle, the junta was overthrown by an MNR rebellion in which tin miners, students, the military police, and school teachers and government employees all played important roles. Paz Estenssoro returned in triumph to take over the presidency he had won at the ballot box the year before.

There was not the slightest question that the MNR government was bent upon drastic changes in the Bolivian way of life. A fundamental political change was made by extending the right to vote to all persons over twenty-one years of age, female as well as male—whether or not they could read and write. A second major move was nationalization of the tin mines, accomplished toward the close of 1952. Soon after his inauguration Paz had created a government mining corporation as an adjunct of the Ministry of Mines and Petroleum, the latter headed by labor leader Juan Lechín. It would operate the mines once nationalization was decreed. A government commission established to study and recommend a procedure to be followed in taking over the mines advocated reimbursing the companies for their investments and equipment, but not for the value of tin still underground, for it presumably belonged to the nation. Partial payment was eventually effected.

Highly important to the revolution was the political re-organization of the country. Representatives of the MNR were placed in every town and village, and these individuals, some able and dedicated, others crooks who took quick advantage of their power role to enrich themselves at the expense of the populace, sought to replace established oligarchic power structures and guarantee to the masses the new rights which the revolution was to bring them. Of particular importance were freedom from debt peonage, the right to change jobs and work where one pleased, and freedom from obligatory service to employing landholders. In addition, the MNR representatives were to see that land redistribution was carried out fairly and in accordance with the procedures established by law.

The government's land reform program quickly got out of hand, and thousands of land-hungry peasants, both mestizos and Indians, simply seized the land of the *hacendados* by force and divided it up as best they saw fit. Many a landlord departed quickly for the capital to secure his personal safety; others fled abroad. Seizure of land was made relatively easy by reason of the government having distributed arms to thousands of peasants and tin miners to form a civilian militia whose purpose was to prevent overthrow of the revolution by reactionary forces. The regular army was disbanded, and peace throughout the countryside depended largely upon the ill-organized militia.

Eventually the government created a land reform commission, but the process of land redistribution to peasants on the great haciendas was never quite reduced to an orderly process. Land seizures by force continued, and eventually the government legalized property acquired by such action. One of the more significant accomplishments of the land reform program was the resettlement of many thousands of people from the altiplano to the lower lands of eastern Bolivia. This effort began in 1955 and was concentrated in the area around Santa Cruz at the outset. In part it was a response to dissatisfaction with the slowness of the government's land redistribution program, manifested by frequent Indian riots. At one point the town of Cochabamba was besieged by Indian hordes. There simply was not enough suitable land worth distributing on the altiplano and in the more accessible *yungas* areas.

The most powerful figure in the Paz government was Juan Lechín, the minister of mines and petroleum. He also served as executive secretary of the national confederation of labor unions. Lechín had risen to the top of the labor movement by gaining control of the tin miners' union during the Villaroel interlude, and his power had grown enormously thereafter.

INTERNATIONAL REACTION

The administration of Paz Estenssoro made a special effort to establish cordial relations with all of Bolivia's neighbors, but it also sought to avoid being drawn into a position of economic subservience to Argentina. Nevertheless, Bolivia's long-standing problem of an outlet to the Pacific was heightened by fears of Chilean reprisals for the expropriation of Chilean tin holdings. The election of Ibáñez as president of Chile diminished this danger, for he, like Perón, had applauded the proposed nationalization as a measure against 'foreign imperialism.' As a further gesture of support, Perón offered the landlocked country an outlet for its tin through the Argentine port of Rosario, though access to Rosario from the altiplano was even more difficult a transport problem than reaching the Pacific coast.

By the end of 1953 Bolivia and the United States had negotiated a technical assistance agreement for the purposes of increasing food production and expanding the network of roads. This action followed the working out of a satisfactory formula for compensating the dispossessed mine owners. In December of that year Paz Estenssoro and Getúlio Vargas met at Santa Cruz and Corumbá to celebrate the opening of the railroad line which gave Santa Cruz access to the Brazilian port of Santos.

Early in 1954 Bolivia, like Argentina, assumed a less hostile attitude toward foreign oil interests and granted a concession in the Yacuiba region to the American-owned Gulf Oil Corporation. The agreement marked a return of foreign capital to the Bolivian oil industry, following the expropriation of Standard Oil Company holdings in 1937, and it emphasized the tremendous difficulties and expense involved in developing and maintaining oil production. Both Gulf and the government petroleum company, *Yacimientos Petrolíferos Fiscales Bolivianos,* invested heavily in new exploration and in pipelines. Successful wells were drilled and the petroleum industry expanded sharply. Bolivia became an exporter of petroleum within a few years.

The state oil company remained in existence despite the achievements brought about by new foreign concessions, in contrast to its rather dismal failure to advance production since its creation years before. The government exercised care in obtaining technical and financial aid to avoid involvement with the most famous names among the foreign oil companies. The powerful current of nationalism made this precaution necessary, for Paz' administration was particularly careful to protect itself against the devastating charge of selling out to foreign interests. In this regard, Mexico's loan of oil experts to Bolivia was particularly helpful.

In spite of its openly revolutionary policies and programs, the MNR government received the blessing of the international community with surprising rapidity. Within a short time the United States was actively supporting the Paz regime with financial and technical assistance, in part, no doubt, to prevent the power center of the revolutionary movement from shifting from moderate hands to those of extremists and communists. Many United States policy-makers were anxious to demonstrate that American policy could support needed revolution as well as conservative dictatorship.

ECONOMIC AND POLITICAL PROBLEMS

The outstanding failure of the MNR revolution was its inability to manage the economy. The *Corporación Minera de Bolivia,* the government monopoly to which operation of the tin mines was entrusted, was quite unable to operate the mines profitably. The number of workers soon doubled while production decreased by 50 per cent. For eight years the extension of employment and workers' benefits in the face of falling production placed a severe strain on the economy and on the government budget. At the same time, agricultural production lagged as large estates were seized by land-hungry peasants and disorder and chaos spread throughout the countryside. The new landholders usually continued their subsistence production practices, as they were largely unaccustomed to raising crops for distant markets. A serious food shortage resulted, driving prices ever higher. The government's answer to such problems was to print money and more money. By late 1956, the *boliviano,* which stood at a ratio of a little under 200 to the dollar on the eve of the revolution, reached the apogee of worthlessness at over 15,000 to the dollar. Only heavy inputs of American budget support kept the MNR revolution alive and the country from anarchy. Finally, in 1957, with the assistance of the International Monetary Fund, the new president, Hernán Siles Zuazo, achieved a stabilized rate of 11,885 *bolivianos* to the dollar and was able to hold it there through the remainder of his term.

The MNR administration did not escape the usual outbursts of opposition. Nationalization of the tin mines and the threats of some labor groups in the party structure so alarmed conservative factions that they made numerous efforts to slow down or halt the government's programs. In January, 1953, right-wing elements of the MNR and a dissident army clique struck a blow against the government but failed to unseat it. The rebels were decisively defeated by the 'workers' militia' which had overthrown the junta in 1952, and by loyal elements of the army. The military had chafed at its exclusion from the government, the disbanding of many of its units, and the building up of a rival force in the civilian militia. One of the chief aims of the rebels was to remove Juan Lechín from the Ministry of Mines, for he was held responsible for many of the administration's policies that the conservatives found objectionable. The rebellion served to upset the delicate balance between the extreme groups that first comprised the MNR by crushing the right and leaving Paz supported largely by the left.

The election of 1956 was conducted under unusually peaceful conditions for Bolivia, and women voted along with the men. Vice-President Hernán Siles Zuazo won the presidency by a substantial margin. Siles was soon involved in a dispute with Lechín, who opposed the president's efforts to curb inflation and his insistence on greater productivity on the part of labor. Lechín resigned from the cabinet and went into the opposition, and the unions he controlled further decreased their productivity to add to the government's cares. The food shortage continued and became a chronic problem. Riots, strikes, and demonstrations became commonplace. Anti-American demonstrations, especially in 1959, reflected the national spirit of discontent and frustration and the well-established propensity to find a foreign scapegoat, particularly one with striped pants, a tall hat, a beard, and answering to the name of Uncle Sam.

The election of 1960, unlike that of 1956, was turbulent, and there were fears that the MNR was disintegrating. Paz Estenssoro, the party candidate, won easily, and Juan Lechín was presumably brought under control as vice-president. The administration's prospects were not bright, for most of the problems brought on by the revolution remained unsolved. The economy was in anarchy.

Peru

As indicated earlier, in 1932 Peru came dangerously near to war with Colombia over seizure of the Amazonian town of Leticia, which lay within the formerly disputed area conceded to Colombia by treaty in 1922. Peruvians resented the treaty, and in 1932 a group of adventurers seized Leticia and expelled Colombian officials. President Sánchez Cerro disavowed the act, but made it clear that Peru would resist any effort by Colombia to restore her authority. Both countries allocated large sums to the purchase of arms, but the assassination of Sánchez Cerro brought General Oscar Benavides to power in Peru and he calmed the feelings of the more aggressive of his associates. Benavides accepted the findings of a League of Nations commission and permitted the return of Leticia to Colombia.

DISPUTE WITH ECUADOR

In 1941 Peru sought compensation for her 'loss' of territory to Colombia by waging an undeclared war with Ecuador over disputed lands also in the Amazon region. At a conference held in Rio de Janeiro, Ecuador and Peru were persuaded to settle the boundary question by negotiation. As a result of the settlement Ecuador lost a large area she had claimed in the upper Amazon valley, for it was sacrificed in the name of hemispheric solidarity during World War II. Ecuadorians never really gave up hope of recovering the land, however, even though it is far down into the jungle and few Ecuadorians—or Peruvians, for that matter—have ever seen it. Inhabitants of the region are primitive but warlike Indian tribes living in much the same manner as their ancestors did before Columbus made his fateful first voyage to America. Every January 29 in Quito some form of demonstration still takes place in protest against the hated agreement signed that date in Rio in 1942.

POLITICAL STRIFE

The Aprista party of Peru, which Haya de la Torre had helped organize during the 1920's, continued to be constantly harassed by the Peruvian government. In 1931 APRA nominated Haya de la Torre for the presidency upon his return from exile. The government declared Sánchez Cerro the winner, although a general belief persisted that Haya had been defrauded. His followers were ready to carry him into office by force, but he declined to employ violence.

In 1933 the revolt that led to the assassination of Sánchez Cerro was used as justification for exiling Haya once more, and in 1936 APRA was not permitted to name a candidate on the grounds that it was an international organization rather than a legitimate political party. While the charge may have been technically true, APRA was essentially a Peruvian reform party. Denied a candidate of their own, the Apristas supported socialist Luis Antonio Eguiguren. Once more victory was snatched from their hands. The surprised supporters of the old regime discovered when the votes were counted that Eguiguren was the winner, but Benavides immediately voided the election and extended his own term until 1939.

In the election of 1939 Benavides was able to secure the presidency for his candidate, Manuel Prado y Ugarteche, by once more prohibiting the Apristas from participating. After Peru broke relations with the Axis in January, 1942, the Apristas offered to co-operate with the government, but their aid was not accepted. At the conclusion of the war, however, democratic sentiments were so powerful that the government was induced to hold one of the freest elections in Peruvian history. The Apristas, now known officially as the People's party, were permitted to take part, but not to run a candidate.

THE APRISTAS TASTE POWER

Just prior to the election, a coalition of political forces was formed with Haya de la Torre and former President Benavides as the principal leaders. The coalition, known as the National Democratic Front, supported a Conservative, José Luis Bustamante y Rivero, whom they elected easily. The

Apristas were the largest group of the coalition, but at first chose to remain outside the cabinet. Inasmuch as the coalition also controlled the congress, and the majority of congressmen were Apristas, it was possible to push through a variety of laws liberalizing the political system, extending individual rights, and extending the educational system. Wage increases were also voted for many classes of employment. These measures were bitterly resisted by opponents in congress and in the cabinet, and the government was torn by bitter antagonisms. There was no middle ground between those determined to preserve the status quo and those pledged to a platform of social legislation, including rehabilitation of the Indians. All that the Apristas prescribed was a serious threat to the old order.

One of the most astonishing actions of the Apristas was their forcing through congress a law to regulate the newspapers by requiring them to divulge certain information regarding ownership and finances. The vociferous and highly conservative newspapers of Lima challenged the act as a move to censor the press. President Bustamante refused to sign the bill and defended freedom of the press in convincing terms. To save the Apristas from embarrassment he signed their bill after another had been passed that rendered it ineffective. This episode, together with the furor over Aprista activities in the municipalities, weakened APRA's position.

In the process of restoring to municipal government the elective councils which Leguía had abolished in 1920, the Apristas had an opportunity to engage in practical foundation-building for the future. They were accused of general misuse of funds, a charge they stoutly denied, and which may have been merely an indication of their success. Bustamante apparently was convinced that the accusations were justified, for he ordered congress to omit subsidies to the municipalities from future budgets. The rift between the president and the Apristas widened.

If the Apristas were to remain in the government in the face of bitter opposition from the conservative forces, they needed to have at least a part of the army behind them. In order to maneuver Aprista officers into key positions they proposed lowering the retirement age and increasing army pay. The plan to retire a large group of officers aroused strong resistance; the pay increase passed but lowering the retirement age did not, and the resentment of the army toward the Apristas was aggravated.

In January, 1947, the publisher of the anti-Aprista *La Prensa* was murdered, and suspicion fell heavily on the party. Aprista cabinet members resigned and a wave of labor unrest swept the country. Bustamante selected a new cabinet composed largely of army and navy officers, for his most urgent task as he saw it was restoring order. The National Democratic Front was in complete collapse, and opposition members seized the opportunity to break down the government by absenting themselves from the senate so that a quorum was unattainable. The anti-Apristas in the chamber of deputies imitated the action, and legislative sessions could not be held.

This uneasy situation continued into 1948, leaving Bustamante in a position of having to govern without help from congress and with the growing enmity of the Apristas who had been instrumental in putting him in office. In October a part of the navy rebelled at Callao, and Apristas were accused of connivance in the plot. The uprising was quelled, and Bustamante retaliated by outlawing the Aprista party and arresting its leaders.

THE CONSERVATIVE RESTORATION

Conservatives were far from satisfied with Bustamante's moderate reprisals, and a few weeks after the naval revolt they persuaded the army to oust the president and destroy APRA. A junta of conservative officers headed by General Manuel Odría seized the government. Severe measures against the Apristas now followed, and by 1950 the party had been scattered and silenced so effectively that Odría was able to stage a presidential election in which he was named for a six-year term without opposition. His supporters seeking election to congress, however, found enemies of the regime fairly numerous and courageous.

When stern measures against the Apristas began, Haya de la Torre fled to the Colombian embassy in Lima. There he remained for five years while the two governments and the International Court of Justice at The Hague deliberated over his status. Finally, in 1954, Odría moderated his position and granted Haya safe conduct out of Peru. Previously he had maintained the position that Haya was not a political fugitive entitled to asylum but should be turned over to Peruvian authorities for trial as a criminal.

ECONOMIC GROWTH

Odría introduced an agricultural program designed to increase food production and to diminish the need for importing foodstuffs. Irrigation projects and machinery pools were established in the coastal area. The cost of the program, which began under the *Servicio Cooperativo Interamericano de Producción de Alimentos,* was originally shared by the United States and Peru, but the Peruvian government gradually assumed both the financial and administrative responsibility for the undertaking. Also inaugurated were housing projects, especially in the Lima–Callao area, but around Lima the miserable huts of the poor continued to spread until they became vast slums that increasingly disgraced the country.

In the development of industries, Peru under Odría made marked progress. In 1953 the *Corporación Peruana del Santa* was created to administer a program for industrial development of the Santa river valley. Because of her rich mineral and coal deposits, particularly of such metals as manganese and vanadium, Peru had the potential for producing special steels, and the government instituted plans for a steel industry. The Santa Corporation also devoted attention to transport problems by extending the system of highways and railroads.

Peru's moderate prosperity during the early 1950's was in part owing to the stimulation of high levels of American purchases of Peruvian products during the Korean War. Favorable trade balances made possible both maintenance of a stable currency and additional investments in industry and mining. Unfortunately, coupled with American military assistance, they also made possible heavy investments in new military equipment, naval vessels, and munitions plants. The need for expanding military power was unclear, for no one threatened Peru. Her neighbors viewed these developments with misgivings, recalling the country's historical tendency toward bellicosity.

When American war needs were no longer so great, Peru's export balances declined and as the end of the decade approached the Peruvian economy found itself on rather shaky ground. Inflation had eroded the value of the Peruvian *sol,* and development programs faltered. Continued poverty in the Sierra was attested to by the continuous stream of migrants moving into Lima and its environs, erecting their scrap wood and metal shacks wherever a spare piece of land was to be found. Vast *barriadas* spread over the hillsides and into the ravines that penetrated parts of the city, the miserable residents living without sanitary facilities or benefit of running water. Peru's social problems were thus laid bare for all the world to see, but the government seemed either disinclined or impotent to deal with them.

ODRÍA'S POLITICAL POLICIES

With the exception of a revolt in Arequipa in 1950, Odría's domination of the country was not seriously challenged. The revolt was inspired by the action of the National Electoral Board in nullifying the candidacy of General Ernesto Montagne, leaving Odría unopposed for the presidency. The Arequipa uprising, in which several hundred people were killed, was blamed on *Acción Cívica,* a minor political party, as well as on the communists, the Apristas, the Democratic League, in short, on any group opposed to the junta. In this way it was possible to stigmatize all opponents. Odría pursued the Apristas relentlessly throughout most of his term of office.

Odría justified his suppression of opposition on the grounds of necessity if governmental stability was to be restored and his programs of housing development, education, and social welfare were to be put into effect. These programs were organized for the purpose of capitalizing on sentiments favoring reforms already publicized by the outlawed Apristas, but without seriously disrupting the status quo.

Under Odría, free enterprise was encouraged and foreign capital and technical experts were welcomed. Increasing amounts of American capital did enter the country, for the potential wealth of the nation was obvious, the government stable, and the general investment climate favorable. At the same time the government made an honest effort to eradicate illiteracy all over the country, including long-neglected and isolated Indian communities.

Peru's hopes for industrialization and commercial expansion were enhanced by Argentina's efforts to create an economic union in the south and the development of the Colombia–Venezuela–Ecuador bloc in the north, for both groups hoped to include Peru. In August, 1955, Peru offered Bolivia unrestricted use of all her transportation facilities and ports, and the two countries laid plans for building additional railroads.

In 1956 Odría allowed an election in which women voted for the first time. Manuel Prado Ugarteche, who had been president from 1939 to 1945, was elected president once more. He continued Odría's development program, but allowed greater freedom. Prado even lifted the ban on the Apristas, and Haya de la Torre returned once more from exile to resume his oft-interrupted political activities. Soon the political pot was again boiling, and all factions looked to the 1962 election for vindication of their positions.

Ecuador

Ecuador's political history after 1930 was even more chaotic than that of Peru. After Dr. Isidro Ayora was forced out of the presidency in 1931 and his successor impeached two years later, José María Velasco Ibarra was elected. Velasco Ibarra struggled with insoluble economic problems, quarreled with congress and his supporters, and lost his influence with the army. In 1935 he tried to assume dictatorial powers and was forced to resign.

The military dictatorship of Federico Páez lasted two years, while unrest and military revolts continued. Páez finally withdrew in favor of his minister of war, Alberto Enríquez, who dissolved congress and issued a series of reform decrees including a minimum wage law and authorization for expropriating foreign holdings. Enríquez lasted only one year, and three more men held the presidential office briefly before 1940, when the liberal Carlos Arroyo del Río was elected.

Arroyo del Río's difficulties were heightened by wartime inflation and by the Peruvian seizure of Ecuador's Amazon territory in 1941. His government granted the United States the right to build bases on the Galápagos islands and the mainland as part of the defense system for the Panama Canal, and Ecuador in turn received a loan from the Export–Import Bank to be used for highway construction, the purchase of railroad equipment, and the eradication of tropical diseases. The government established a development corporation to carry out the program.

Political strife continued unabated, and in 1944 Arroyo del Río went the way of his predecessors. A loose alliance of opposition parties selected Velasco Ibarra once more, but he was soon at odds with many of those who had supported him. By 1946 his popularity had vanished because of his unpredictable actions, and in the following year the army sent him into exile. During his rule Ecuador's newspapers had instituted a program for eradicating illiteracy, in the hope that political and economic life would both benefit. The project, which was conducted by volunteers, provided daily instruction, and quickly spread over most of the country. Results, unfortunately, were insignificant.

GALO PLAZA LASSO

The victor of the presidential election of 1948 was Galo Plaza Lasso, candidate of the Independent Citizens party and son of former President Leonidas Plaza Gutiérrez. Plaza, whose family belonged to Ecuador's landowning aristocracy, had been born and educated in the United States and had served as his country's ambassador to Washington. He announced his goal of raising Ecuador's standard of living through improvement of agriculture.

Plaza's hopes for material progress were set back in 1949 by one of the worst earthquakes in the country's history. Thousands were killed, towns were completely destroyed, and roads were blocked by landslides. The president inaugurated a reconstruction program to rebuild the ravaged towns on new sites. Plaza proved himself an able statesman and developed a strong following among the middle and upper classes, but his power was regionally based. He was a *Quiteño,* and his principal support came from the northern Sierra. One of his outstanding achievements, unique because of its rarity, was to serve out his entire term of office. By a policy of moderation and of minimizing outbursts of opposition, he gave Ecuador her first taste of political stability in a quarter of a century. Plaza's following was largely personal. He did not found a new political party or institutionalize his support. Consequently, he lacked a vehicle by means of which to project his political influence beyond the one term of office to which he was constitutionally limited.

Many improvements took place during Plaza's administration, including the building of roads, a considerable extension of the school system, and increasingly successful efforts to eradicate malaria and other tropical diseases by which the country had long been troubled, particularly in the coastal area. Of great economic importance was the development of the banana industry. With Honduran banana plantations blighted by disease, Ecuadorean growers in the coastal valleys of the Guayas and Esmereldas rivers were able to capture a larger and larger share of the world banana market until eventually the country became the world's principal exporter of this fruit. Millions of dollars poured into Ecuador, and the economy was greatly stimulated. Only a small portion of the plantations were in foreign hands, and it was the Ecuadoreans themselves who benefited most as a result of the agricultural windfall.

JOSÉ MARÍA VELASCO IBARRA

Although he had twice been chosen president and twice had been forced from office before completion of his term, in 1952 José María Velasco Ibarra was once again elected president of the country. Velasco was an enigma to many. Some called him a demagogue, a man without principal, a seeker after power for its own sake. There was no question of his ability as an orator, particularly when campaigning before a large multitude, preferably speaking from a balcony to thousands assembled in a plaza below. The poor people loved him, for he was always able to convince them of his sincere interest in their problems and his determination to do something about them. The fact that he had been unable to keep his promises on previous occasions was invariably attributed to his enemies. Velasco in office was erratic, seemingly more motivated by whim and a love for the spectacular than by principle or policy. Invariably he fought with those around him, and a certain naïveté permitted his 'friends' to take advantage of him, sometimes at the expense of the public treasury.

After his election in 1952, Velasco, as usual, soon broke with some of his most powerful supporters, thus raising doubts as to whether he would be able to duplicate Plaza's feat and serve out his term of office. However, he helped stabilize Ecuador's finances by an agreement to settle the country's dollar debt, which had been in default since before the war. This move cleared the way for Ecuador to receive loans from abroad, and gave a belated boost to economic development. Velasco also launched a major road-building program to link the isolated Andean region more closely with the coast.

Velasco's international leanings were as erratic as his domestic tendencies. In 1952 he appeared to be an admirer of Perón, and in a general way he seemed to support Argentine moves for increasing hegemony in South America. Yet at the same time he welcomed American investment and economic assistance. Many viewed his lack of firm policies and shifting position as the cunning of a fox. In any case, he completed his term of office, and Ecuador's orderly transfer of power gave hope for increased stability in the future.

In 1956 the winner of the presidential election was Conservative party candidate Camilo Ponce Enríquez, the first of his party to hold the presidential office in over half a century. His victory was by a very narrow margin, and then only a plurality of the votes cast. His term of office was relatively uneventful. Commerce continued to expand as banana production increased, and large sums of money and many technical experts from the United States entered the country to modernize agriculture, improve health services, and to extend the highway system. Many projects were initiated that could not be completed during one presidential term.

The perennial contender for the presidency, Velasco Ibarra, was back again running for office in 1960. To the surprise of many Americans, he defeated Galo Plaza, who was thought by nationalistic Ecuadoreans to be too friendly with the United States. American admirers of Galo Plaza forgot Velasco's magic appeal to the poor, as well as his broader support throughout the country. Velasco capitalized on the powerful feeling of nationalism his campaign generated by becoming wildly nationalistic himself. One of his first acts was to denounce the 1942 agreement between Peru and Ecuador with respect to the Amazon territory. Thus Ecuador's claim was re-asserted and the dispute re-opened. Next he chose to ignore the traditional three-mile limit of territorial waters and to claim that Ecuadorean sovereignty extended 200 miles seaward. The waters included constituted a remarkably rich commercial fishing area, and Velasco intended to exclude the fishermen of other nations, or to make them pay a fee to fish in Ecuadorean coastal waters. Most of the foreign fishermen were Americans out of southern California ports fishing for tuna. Velasco and his government were headed for international as well as domestic difficulties.

The Widening Development Gap

The Indian countries of South America fell far behind the continental leaders during the thirty-year period ending in 1960. Paraguay was firmly held in the grip of an iron-fisted dictatorship, Bolivia was in the midst of revolution and anarchy, Peru had experienced some development but political life was in turmoil, and though Ecuador had passed through an unprecedented period of government stability, the only really promising sign of economic growth was the development of the banana trade. None of the countries was in a condition that gave much grounds for optimism about the immediate future. The root of their many difficulties was the colonial legacy of racial and class cleavages, failure to integrate the numerous Indian peoples into the national life, concentration of land-ownership and other forms of wealth, lack of economic opportunity, illiteracy, malnutrition, militarism, and inertia born of oppression. Each of the countries had made some gestures toward solving its basic problems, but only halfway measures were tried. The future was not entirely hopeless, but it could be made promising only by major effort and sacrifice.

SUGGESTED READING

R.N. Adams et al., *Social Change in Latin America Today.* New York, 1960.

R.J. Alexander, *The Perón Era.* New York, 1951.

S. Andreski, *Parasitism and Subversion: The Case of Latin America.* New York, 1966.

G. Arciniegas, *The State of Latin America.* New York, 1952.

M. Azuela, *Two Novels of Mexico.* Berkeley and Los Angeles, 1961.

J.R. Barager, *Why Perón Came to Power.* New York, 1968.

J.M. Bello, *A History of Modern Brazil, 1889–1964.* Stanford, 1966.

H. Bernstein, *Venezuela and Colombia.* Englewood Cliffs, 1964.

G.I. Blanksten, *Perón's Argentina.* Chicago, 1953.

P.B. Blanshard, *Democracy and Empire in the Caribbean,* New York, 1947.

E.B. Burns, ed., *A Documentary History of Brazil.* New York, 1960.

———— *Nationalism in Brazil: A Historical Survey.* New York, 1968.

J.L. Busey, *Latin American Political Institutions and Processes.* New York, 1964.

H. Cline, *Mexico: Revolution to Evolution, 1940–1960.* New York, 1963.

R.D. Crassweller, *Trujillo: The Life and Times of a Caribbean Dictator.* New York, 1966.

D.M. Dozer, ed., *The Monroe Doctrine: Its Modern Significance.* New York, 1965.

T. Draper, *Castro's Revolution.* New York, 1962.

V.R. de Dubnic, *Political Trends in Brazil.* Washington, 1968.

J.W.F. Dulles, *Vargas of Brazil, A Political Biography.* Austin, 1967.

R.H. Fitzgibbon, *Uruguay, Portrait of a Democracy.* London, 1956.

T. Gill, *Land Hunger in Mexico.* Washington, 1951.

R. Graham, ed., *A Century of Brazilian History Since 1865.* New York, 1969.

R. and L. Greenup, *Revolution Before Breakfast.* Chapel Hill, 1947.

H.M. Hamill, Jr., ed., *Dictatorship in Spanish America.* New York, 1965.

L. Hanke, ed., *Modern Latin America.* 2 vols., New York, 1959.

D.B. Heath and R.N. Adams, eds., *Contemporary Cultures and Societies of Latin America.* Austin, 1965.

A.O. Hirschman, ed., *Latin American Issues.* New York, 1961.

I.L. Horowitz, *Revolution in Brazil: Politics in a Developing Society.* New York, 1964.

J.J. Johnson, *The Military and Society in Latin America.* Stanford, 1964.

———*Political Change in Latin America: The Emergence of the Middle Sectors,* Stanford, 1958.

H. Kantor, *The Ideology and Program of the Peruvian Aprista Movement.* Berkeley, 1953.

J.L. Kuntz, *The Mexican Expropriations.* New York, 1940.

E. Lieuwen, *Arms and Politics in Latin America.* New York, 1961.

S.M. Lipset and A. Solari, *Elites in Latin America.* New York, 1967.

R.W. Logan, *Haiti and the Dominican Republic.* New York, 1968.

W. MacGaffey and C. Barnett, *Twentieth Century Cuba.* Garden City, N.Y., 1965.

S. Macy et al., *Costa Rica: A Study in Economic Development.* New York, 1952.

J.D. Martz, ed., *The Dynamics of Change in Latin American Politics.* Englewood Cliffs, 1965.

G. Masur, *Nationalism in Latin America: Diversity and Unity.* New York, 1966.

R.M. Morse, *From Community to Metropolis: A Biography of São Paulo, Brazil.* Gainesville, Fla., 1958.

S. Mosk, *The Industrial Revolution in Mexico.* Berkeley, 1950.

F. Ortiz, *Cuban Counterpoint: Tobacco and Sugar.* New York, 1947.

D. Perkins, *The United States and the Caribbean.* Cambridge, Mass., 1947.

F.B. Pike, ed., *The Conflict Between Church and State in Latin America.* New York, 1964.

L. Quintanilla, *A Latin American Speaks.* New York, 1943.

J.F. Rippy, *Latin America and the Industrial Age.* New York, 1941.

M. Rodríguez, *Central America.* Englewood Cliffs, 1965.

K.M. Schmitt and D.D. Burks, *Evolution or Chaos: Dynamics of Latin American Government and Politics.* New York, 1963.

T.E. Skidmore, *Politics in Brazil, 1930–1964: An Experiment in Democracy.* New York, 1967.

R.F. Smith, *Background to Revolution: The Development of Modern Cuba.* New York, 1966.

T.L. Smith, *Brazil, People and Institutions.* Baton Rouge, 1963.

——— ed., *Agrarian Reform in Latin America.* New York, 1965.

S. Snow, *The Pan-American Federation of Labor.* Durham, N.C., 1964.

J.R. Stevenson, *The Chilean Popular Front.* Philadelphia, 1942.

C.C. Taylor, *Rural Life in Argentina.* Baton Rouge, 1948.

W.C. Townsend, *Lázaro Cárdenas: Mexican Democrat.* Ann Arbor, 1952.

V.L. Urquidi, *The Challenge of Development in Latin America.* New York, 1964.

C. Wagley, *Amazon Town: A Study of Man in the Tropics.* New York, 1953.

N. Whetten, *Rural Mexico.* Chicago, 1948.

A.P. Whitaker, *Nationalism in Latin America: Past and Present.* Gainesville, Fla., 1962.

A.P. Whitaker and D.C. Jordan, *Nationalism in Contemporary Latin America.* New York, 1966.

A.C. Wilgus, ed., *The Caribbean at Mid-Century.* Gainesville, Fla., 1951.

———— *The Caribbean: Contemporary Trends.* Gainesville, Fla., 1953.

J.W. Wilkie and A.L. Michaels, eds., *Revolution in Mexico: Years of Upheaval, 1910–1940.* New York, 1969.

J.M. Young, *The Brazilian Revolution of 1930 and the Aftermath.* New Brunswick, N.J., 1967.

IV THE ABORTIVE ALLIANCE: FRUSTRATIONS AND DISILLUSIONMENT

18

Latin America's Urban Revolution:
Its Technological and Cultural Implications

> Those of you at this conference are present at an historic moment in the life of this hemisphere. For this is far more than an economic discussion or a technical conference on development. In a very real sense it is a demonstration of the capacity of free nations to meet the human and material problems of the modern world.*

The opening of the sixth decade of the twentieth century seemed to many residents of the Western Hemisphere a hopeful turning point for the entire region. To one optimistic author the end of tyranny and dictatorship in Latin America seemed at hand. Increasingly the forces supporting popular rule and democratic institutions appeared to be in the ascendancy. Military despotism had been banished even from so unlikely a place as Venezuela, inter-party strife in Colombia seemed close to an end as Liberals and Conservatives worked together under a long-term compact, Brazil and Argentina were governed by constitutionally elected presidents, and the miserable authoritarian regime of Trujillo was obviously losing its grip on the Dominican Republic. Then in the fall of 1960 the United States elected a Roman Catholic president for the first time in its history, a young and vigorous man who seemed to empathize with the Latin Americans and to understand their problems. He spoke of creating a new kind of alliance in the Western Hemisphere, an alliance dedicated to the progress of the region through economic development, amelioration of social ills, and a better way of life for all of its people.

* President John F. Kennedy in his message at the opening session of the Punta del Este Conference, August 5, 1961.

441

The Alliance for Progress

In August of 1961 at Punta del Este, Uruguay, the Alliance for Progress became a working agreement among the heads of state. A written charter pledged a joint effort to turn the 1960's into a decade of development. Financial resources in the amount of $20 billion would be contributed, more than half from the United States Government, as well as technical assistance and sympathetic support for the aspirations of Latin Americans. Resources would be drawn from private industry in the United States, from governments and industries in Europe and Asia, as well as from the American government and international lending and assistance institutions. In turn, the participating countries of Latin America pledged themselves to self-help programs of land reform, tax reform, administrative improvement, and a determined war on illiteracy, ignorance, disease, and poverty.

The Alliance involved more than mutual agreements and pious pledges of reform in exchange for funds to make development possible. New technological and organizational instruments would be utilized. An Inter-American Development Bank had been created in 1959 after long urging by Latin American leaders and years of opposition by the United States; now it would constitute a principal funding institution within the Alliance. Under the auspices of the Organization of American States, the Economic and Social Commission for Latin America was given broad responsibilities for setting national development standards, and a special committee of nine 'wise men'—the Inter-American Committee on the Alliance for Progress (CIAP)—was appointed to review individual country development plans to determine their suitability for support and financing by the Inter-American Development Bank, the International Bank for Reconstruction and Development (World Bank), or the United States Agency for International Development (AID).

Soon every national capital was bustling with planning activities, and the profession of economist became the *carte blanche* for entry into the inner sanctum of public policy making. For the first time, inventories of development needs and resources were assembled, growth rates were projected, priorities were established, and public and private investment policies were formulated to achieve specific sectoral development goals of both a long and short-term nature. Hopes were raised high that a new era had

dawned, that by the in-pouring of resources and by sustained and co-ordinated national efforts each country of Latin America might move rapidly
toward the promised land of material and social well-being, all within the
context of democratic political institutions.

THE ABSTENTION OF CUBA

One national participant was missing. The new decade had opened with
Fidel Castro firmly in power in Cuba, month by month demonstrating the
increasingly radical trend of his revolutionary movement. He would soon
indicate his allegiance to Marxism-Leninism and lead his country into the
communist camp, thus creating for the first time a Soviet enclave in the
Western Hemisphere. Castro refused to join the Alliance, and his representative at Punta del Este, 'Che' Guevara, predicted its failure. Instead,
Cuba's bearded leader made his own development deals with the Russians.
As the revolutionary movement in Cuba progressed, foreign-owned enterprises were confiscated and local business and commercial firms were nationalized. The country became a socialist state in the Russian pattern.
With help from the communist world, Castro too was planning a new era
in which a modern industrial economy would at least begin to offset the
century-old monocultural dependence on sugar.

THE GAP BETWEEN PLANNING AND ACCOMPLISHMENT

Elsewhere the bustling activity in newly created national planning offices
and the coming and going of international review teams, bankers, technical
assistance experts, program evaluators, and diplomats all served to give a
sense of motion and progress toward achievement even if little real development took place. In reality, the problems to which the eager economists,
technical experts, and development bankers addressed themselves were by
no means simple or easily solved. The planning effort itself required vast
amounts of data that had never been collected and were therefore unavailable. An air of unreality permeated the entire process, and gradually it became evident that the emerging national plans more often than not were
little more than page after page of pious hopes and extended shopping
lists. What the financial institutions termed bankable projects were few and
far between. Accomplishments soon lagged behind projections, and essen-

tial linkages between economic goals and administrative action to achieve them were frequently missing. Vast amounts of unexpended loan funds accumulated in what were euphemistically referred to as the 'pipelines' because basic conditions and commitments could not be met. Few governments possessed either the bold leadership or the popular support to carry out the needed social and economic reforms. Political necessity watered down the development commitments of most countries, including the United States. A skeptical American congress proved itself less than enthusiastic about voting the large sums of money in support of the American president's promises, and such grant funds as were appropriated in support of the international technical assistance program for Latin America increasingly were consumed by the large administrative staffs of the technical assistance missions. Years were consumed in the negotiation of loans, and strings attached to the funds to control the manner of their expenditure often injured national pride and made them excessively costly from the borrower's standpoint. The requirement that goods and equipment be purchased in the United States was particularly objectionable to those who knew that comparable items could be acquired in Europe or Japan at much lower prices. World Bank loans carried fewer restrictions, but they were seldom available except for projects whose financial soundness was beyond question. Many needed loans for infrastructure development were not of this character.

The middle of the decade had arrived before many of these difficulties had manifested themselves. In the meantime, the inspiring leadership of President John F. Kennedy had been eliminated by an assassin's bullet, and the successor in the White House demonstrated none of the charisma that had enabled the young leader to fire the imagination of millions of Latin Americans and draw the hemisphere into a closer bond of friendship than had existed for years. Increasingly, it became evident that the Alliance for Progress was foundering and that there was little hope of its objectives being realized. An economic growth rate of 2.5 per cent per capita over a ten-year period was potentially attainable, but rapid population increases would make it necessary for country after country to run very hard just to stay in the same place. Some countries would end the decade way out in front while others would lag far behind; few indeed would be those vigorous enough in pursuit of program goals to undertake and carry through the structural and social reforms called for in the Charter of Punta del Este. No one as yet foresaw the dismal record of almost universal failure that the Agency for International Development would have to submit to the American congress in support of its 1970 appropriation request. In nearly all sectors of development activity—education, housing, land reform, taxation, administrative improvement, strengthening of democratic institutions and processes—the problems remaining unsolved at the end of the decade loomed larger and more formidable than when confronted ten years before.

Generation after generation had struggled with the problems of the vast and often inhospitable region referred to as Latin America. They were not suddenly to be solved by application of the economist's magic. Racial and cultural differences still constituted major barriers to integration and development in all but a few countries, and the age-old issues of social structure and land tenure continued to trouble the large and small nations alike. The hope of the development planners rested upon the application of a new technology, a rational co-ordination of effort, and firm political determination to break through these barriers. In few cases were such conditions met, and nowhere fully so. Indeed, it sometimes seemed that external assistance created a false sense of accomplishment and reduced the urgency and resolution with which its recipient went about the task of facing the imperatives of his own situation.

Population Growth and Mobility

Early in the 1960's it became evident that older technologies were quietly but steadily producing a revolution of quite another sort. For over a decade substantial foreign aid as well as national resources had been going into road construction, malaria eradication, public health clinics, and hospitals. Radios, buses, and automobiles in ever greater numbers were familiar aspects of the daily lives of increasing millions of people. The impact of these elements of modernization proved cumulative. Suddenly, in the late 1950's and on into the 1960's, statistical indices began to demonstrate that the population of most of Latin America was reproducing itself at a much more rapid rate than ever before. They also demonstrated what everyone could see, that in country after country the population was on the move. Medical and public health technology had reduced infant mortality and lowered the incidence of disease. Families grew larger as more children survived to reach maturity and produce their own families. Pressure on the land increased, and ever larger numbers of people took to the newly constructed roads and began moving toward the large cities, the national capitals, and the centers of commerce and industry. Within a few years, teeming millions of dissatisfied agricultural workers and rural dwellers and their families left the countryside and headed toward what they hoped would be a better life with greater opportunity in the urban centers of the hemisphere.

A similar movement caused by much the same factors was transforming the rest of the world. The same technological changes reached into the remote hamlets of the Himalayas, into the Negro share-cropper hovels of America's Deep South, into India's vast countryside, as well as into the villages and pueblos of Colombia and the mountain valleys of Peru and Mexico. Few indeed were the countries that escaped the increasingly portentous phenomena of population explosion and internal migration.

THE NEVER-CHANGING COUNTRYSIDE

The years following World War II saw vast changes take place in agricultural technology in the United States and Europe. By the introduction of new and improved crop varieties and the application of fertilizers on an unprecedented scale, crop production mounted phenomenally for a large number of basic commodities. Increased mechanization at the same time sharply reduced the need for manpower in agricultural production while facilitating new approaches in organization and ownership to an increasingly capital-intensive activity. In the United States the small family farm began to disappear. In its place large corporate enterprises emerged with extensive landholdings, the most modern equipment utilized on a grand scale, and marketing and storage facilities of which the individual farmer of previous years could scarcely have dreamed. As a result, production mounted while the percentage of the population dedicated to agricultural pursuits declined sharply until only about 8 per cent were so engaged. Industrial expansion and the growth of service industries absorbed most of those who left the farm, and unemployment remained but a minor problem. Agriculture had become an industry rather than a way of life.

No such 'Green Revolution' took place in Latin America. With a few remarkable exceptions, such as in parts of Mexico, Brazil, and Colombia, the countryside remained essentially unchanged. In most places a few families holding vast amounts of land continued to dominate the rural scene, conducting their limited agricultural activities in the same manner as their forebears. Seldom was full utilization made of the land, seldom were better plant varieties introduced, fertilizer played little part in production, and hand labor by ignorant peons and share-croppers constituted the manner of working the fields. Farm management was entrusted to a *mayordomo* or *capitaz* who directed the work of the laborers. Seldom did such persons have any training in agriculture beyond that acquired by practical experience. Yield per hectare remained woefully low for such basic crops as maize, rice, cotton, and wheat. Characteristically, few young people were induced to seek an agricultural education, and often those who did so were from the city and upon completing their studies took desk jobs in agricultural ministries or went to work for implement or fertilizer companies. There were few if any job opportunities in agricultural production.

Exceptions to the all-too-common pattern were of course to be found. These were primarily in the export crop category and in particular countries or regions. Both domestic producers and foreign companies dedicated to the growing of coffee, bananas, and sugarcane strove to achieve high efficiency in the production of these items for export. Employment conditions for the workers remained extremely poor, however, particularly on the coffee *fincas* and sugar plantations where the annual harvest was completed in a few short weeks and little gainful employment was to be found the remainder of the year. Wages remained extremely low by almost any standard, and had it not been for subsistence crops grown on small marginal plots, millions of families in Central America, the Andean highlands, and northeast Brazil would have faced starvation.

Even in such potentially productive areas as Argentina, cereal crops and beef output lagged far behind capabilities, and the agriculturally based prosperity of former years did not return even after the ill-considered marketing monopoly of the Perón era was removed. Uruguay languished in agricultural depression, her poor-quality wool attracting few buyers in a market surfeited with synthetic fibers. Throughout Latin America as a whole, food production barely kept pace with population growth in the late 1950's and early 1960's, and in many countries it failed to do so.

Agricultural production for domestic consumption throughout much of Latin America had long been hampered by marketing conditions that had changed little since the days of colonial rule. Absence of storage facilities frequently left the producer, particularly the small one, at the mercy of middlemen who controlled transport facilities and thereby market access. Even in many of the more advanced metropolitan areas of Argentina, Chile, Uruguay, and Brazil, marketing practices continued to be chaotic and basic standards to protect both producer and consumer remained unenforced. Remarkable exceptions are today to be found in São Paulo, Brazil, and with respect to certain products in Mexico City and a few other centers. In many areas price controls to benefit the urban lower classes appeared after the Second World War, and during the 1960's they weighed heavily upon the producers of such basic items as meat and milk —and the problem was exacerbated by constant inflation. Prices to producers invariably lagged behind those charged the consumer. In some instances, countries that should have been producing surpluses of major commodities experienced absolute declines in domestic production and inauguration of the importation of these same commodities. In such circumstances, incentives for agricultural development remained minimal or disappeared altogether, even in the face of population increases that were staggering.

THE CAMPESINO ON THE MOVE

Obviously, there was little to keep the rural dweller in Latin America on the *hacienda,* the *estancia,* or the little plot of rugged hillside from which he eked out his meager subsistence. Generations before him had remained there in essentially the same conditions, but now suddenly, in the middle of the twentieth century, many more like him were overcrowding his limited *lebensraum.* The younger, the more energetic, the more venturesome left their homes in search of the glittering lights, the excitement, and the rumored greater opportunity of urban life. At first the movement was from the countryside and the rural village to provincial towns and cities. Later, the next step was taken to the national capital or to major industrial centers such as São Paulo or Monterrey. Increasingly, provincial towns and villages were by-passed as more and more *campesinos* migrated directly from the villages to the largest urban centers. As new generations took up the move, lesser towns and cities even began to lose population in some localities, and in few cases indeed did the growth of secondary urban areas keep pace with that of the capital city. A major population movement was under way, and it continued throughout the 1960's with accelerating momentum. In a few brief years, a number of countries that had been predominantly rural for centuries became predominantly urban. This was truly a revolution, for the way of life of millions of people was profoundly altered.

Many factors have influenced the patterns of urban growth throughout history. No single factor ever seems to predominate for long, and often the patterns are so complex and confused that it is difficult to trace their origins. Rapid urbanization in Colombia between 1950 and 1970 was owing in part to *la Violencia,* the lawless strife and butchery that prevailed in many rural areas for nearly two decades, but larger percentages of the rural population moved to the city in Chile and Brazil during the same period. In Guatemala, the balance between urban and rural population remained almost static during these years, and the pronounced growth that took place in the countryside as well as the capital city was largely attributable to natural increase rather than migration. Industrial employment opportunities no doubt accounted for the rapid growth of São Paulo, Brazil, but periods of drought and prolonged depression in the northeast states certainly contributed a share of the migrants who settled in the bustling metropolis that in a few brief years became the wonder city of the South American continent.

The principal cities of Latin America soon developed vast settlements of squatters, some occupying mountainside areas in the heart of the city, as in Rio de Janeiro and Bogotá, others scattered over the surrounding countryside. In Lima the in-flooding population occupied alleys and stream beds within the city and vast tracts of land virtually surrounding the urban area. Characteristic of the mushroom expansion of urban centers was squatter occupation of whatever vacant land was available, regardless of ownership, and the rapid erection of cheap dwellings of wood, bamboo, thatch, corrugated iron or zinc, metal from gasoline cans and oil drums, and whatever other material was freely or cheaply available. Clustered together in high density, without sanitary facilities, running water, or electric power, the houses of the squatters provided only the most rudimentary shelter from the elements. Such settlements created not only health and fire hazards, but became breeding grounds for vermin and major sources of pollution of near-by streams and lakes, where these existed. Upper-class residents and foreign visitors generally referred to the mushroom settlements as slums, and indeed they were densely populated areas marked by squalor and wretched living conditions. Local terms for them varied from country to country. In Chile they were called *callampas,* a type of mushroom, in Brazil *favelas,* in Peru *barriadas,* and in various localities *barrios pobres.*

For a time the problem of migration into urban areas was viewed as requiring for its solution construction by government agencies of large numbers of low-cost housing projects. During the 1950's and early 1960's singular efforts were made by various countries to meet the housing needs of their growing urban populations by such construction. Housing authorities soon discovered, however, that the problem was far more complex than had at first been realized, and that in any case there was not the slightest possibility of keeping pace with the expanding need. Political leaders and the officers of international lending institutions that initially had helped finance public housing construction threw up their hands in despair and frustration. By 1970 public housing programs had lost a great deal of their appeal and relatively fewer resources continued to be invested in them. Chile and Venezuela provided exceptions.

At first the mushrooming shantytowns were thought to be a temporary phenomenon, quarters into which migrants flooded until they could find more satisfactory and permanent accommodations in regularly constructed public or private housing. As years passed and the squatter areas continued to expand, and particularly as more permanent brick and adobe structures began to replace the makeshift houses first erected, political leaders and urban specialists began to realize the permanent character of what had been considered marginal settlements. By the latter part of the 1960's, serious efforts were being made to comprehend the culture of the shantytown dwellers, to understand the economic foundation of their existence, their social outlook and potential political role. Perhaps more research focused on Lima, Peru, than other urban areas because the barriadas constituted such a large proportion of the total community, accounting for approximately one-fourth of Lima's two million people. Other investigations were conducted in Rio de Janeiro, Santiago, Mexico City, and Bogotá, however, and gradually new and very tentative understandings began to emerge.

Many of the residents of the barriadas were found not to have come from rural areas at all, but from smaller cities and towns. Others have lived in the metropolitan area all of their lives, but had moved into their present quarters because they represented an improvement over an earlier location, or because they made possible ownership of one's own dwelling, however miserable it might be. On the other hand, there were instances in which a small village was found virtually to have transplanted itself from a distant rural area to form a part of a large barriada complex. In other cases, particularly in Central America, many new urban dwellers simply moved in from near-by villages and continued to move back and forth with great frequency. Ease of transport to and from employment was found to motivate many favela dwellers of Rio de Janeiro to remain in their miserable but centrally located hovels on a hillside rather than move to more desirable but distant homes which their income would have permitted them to afford.

The development of barriadas, or movement into new squatter areas, was frequently accompanied by opposition and occasional violence as the authorities attempted to block incursions into private or public property. If houses had been built by their owners one by one, police and other officials would have had little difficulty evicting trespassers. Anticipating opposition, however, the squatters frequently developed a substantial 'invasion' organization to mobilize the families, assemble materials, and move en masse into pre-selected areas, thereby presenting the authorities with a *fait accompli.* Mass trespass became a common overnight phenomenon in Bogotá, Lima, and many other cities. Such defiance of the law apparently did not carry over into the general mode of life of barriada dwellers in most urban areas, however. What little information is available on the subject would suggest that, with some exceptions, the poverty-stricken residents of the mushroom shantytowns have been remarkably law-abiding. Had the opposite been true, all semblance of law and order would have broken down in city after city, for local police forces would have been quite incapable of coping with so massive a problem.

THE ECONOMY OF URBAN POVERTY

The mass migrations into the urban centers of Latin America were not occasioned by the rapid industrialization taking place in those centers. São Paulo, Monterrey, and a few other cities provided exceptions, but in general the pace of industrialization and the creation of new jobs lagged far behind the burgeoning labor supply. The consequence of this lag was mass unemployment and underemployment. Domestic service provided jobs for many, and construction work gave irregular work to others, but very large numbers found no regular remunerative activity at all. A common source of meager income was found in operation of small shops and stores, street peddling, and similar forms of merchandising. Prostitution and begging continued to play their time-honored roles in an economy of poverty.

Thousands became dependent for food on their success in foraging on the garbage dumps, and land around such dumps became prime property for squatter dwellings.

A major problem of any human settlement is water, and as the barriadas expanded and multiplied, water generally had to be brought in from outside. Century-old practices of water-carting were revived, and the miserable residents were subjected to price manipulation and gouging by water peddlers at every opportunity. Local governments in many cases piped water into the barriadas to provide at least an occasional open hydrant, and this alleviated the problem in older settlements, but increasingly, local officials found it difficult to keep up with the need. The selling of water for whatever the traffic will bear remains a lucrative form of exploitation in shantytowns all over Latin America.

Large numbers of the barriada dwellers are without job skills or training for any form of urban-type employment. Many are also illiterate, although a few very preliminary studies suggest that literacy rates and educational achievement among the urban poor are somewhat higher than anticipated and on occasion approximate those for Latin American urban populations generally. This finding may be a reflection of the tendency of the more enterprising and better prepared to be the more mobile elements among small town and rural populations, and therefore the ones who migrated to the larger urban centers. It may also indicate the extent to which people who grew up in older urban areas joined the more recent arrivals in the barriadas to build their own houses on land for which they would not be obliged to pay any rent.

More commonly, however, residents of the barriadas constitute the poorest and least advantaged groups within the urban regions in which they dwell. The families are large with a resulting disproportion in age distribution in favor of the very young. Undernourished, hungry, and sickly children constitute the most visible product of barriada life. Infant mortality is high and disease common among all age groups. Most shantytown occupants have never had any form of medical attention and are unlikely to receive any throughout their lifetime. Equally unpromising is the prospect of educating the millions of children. High percentages are not currently attending any school, partly for lack of facilities and partly because of little interest, ill-health, and the instability of the population. In many barriada areas the people feel under constant pressure to move on in search of more favorable surroundings, better economic opportunity, or greater security from eviction by government or private owners. The result is a substantial floating population of families almost constantly on the move. Not only does this make difficult the rendering of public services, but it discourages community co-operation and self-help measures aimed at improving conditions of life in the local area. Although there are notable exceptions, participation in community organizations, political party life, and local government is low in the barriada areas of most Latin American cities.

Governments in a number of countries, faced with the obvious permanency of the mushrooming shantytown settlements, have taken steps to legalize some of the earlier 'invasions' by granting land titles to barriada residents. This procedure has generally been accompanied by efforts to regularize the size and patterns of land parcels, to establish streets, and to provide such minimal services as water, sewerage, and electric power. As a consequence, many of the older settlements have come to take on the aspects of 'regular' residential areas, with more permanent structures, additional rooms on the houses, small yards, and the presence of a few amenities. Thus cities continue to grow today in much the same manner as they grew in earlier periods of history. Orderly development, with professional construction in planned subdivisions and careful attention to land ownership, long ago came to characterize urban growth in stabilized Western communities; but Latin America today is in many respects a burgeoning frontier, and in many critical areas the rule book has been laid aside. The culture of the barriadas remains, nevertheless, a culture of poverty. If migration to the cities were to end tomorrow, it would be many years and several generations before the barriada dwellers could be assimilated into the economic and social mainstream of urban life. In the meantime, however, the influx continues.

The Changing Urban Culture

The mainstream of Latin American urban life has itself been undergoing dramatic change since the mid-1950's. Far more visible in most instances than the mushrooming shantytowns in and around the cities is the result of an enormous building boom that has converted formerly easy-going communities dominated by conservative, low-profile structures into vast metropolises of glass-walled, towering skyscrapers. Industrial and commercial expansion has in some areas been enormous, particularly in key centers of

Brazil, Mexico, and Venezuela, and a new and cosmopolitan urban culture has resulted from it. A very substantial middle class has emerged, with middle-class values, attitudes, and tastes. Vast new residential areas have been opened by private developers to meet the housing needs of middle-income groups, and luxury dwellings of the wealthy sparkle with architectural innovations in attractive suburbs of most principal cities. In some urban areas, particularly in Brazil and Mexico, heavy emphasis has been placed on construction of large apartment houses, thereby deriving maximum utilization of extremely costly land. New boulevards have been opened, expressways built, and urban subways are a recent development in a few major cities, although Buenos Aires has benefited from a major subway network for years. Despite these advances, the growing affluence of the urban population has so crowded the streets and boulevards with automobiles and buses that traffic jams in Lima, São Paulo, or Mexico City rival the problems of congestion in other densely populated areas throughout the world. Vehicles and factories have also filled the air with smog, and Santiago, Rio de Janeiro, and Mexico City compete easily in this regard with Los Angeles, New York, and Pittsburgh.

NEW PATTERNS OF URBAN LIFE

Urban life itself has taken on new dimensions. Industrial growth has produced a host of service enterprises, such as machinery supply houses, office equipment establishments, construction and architectural firms, data processing centers, banks and other lending institutions, real estate developers, transportation companies, freight forwarders, warehouse operators, import and export brokers, plus hosts of specialized service activities too numerous to mention. A part of the picture also are accounting firms, professional training schools, and management consulting organizations. Hosts of clerks, stenographers, draftsmen, and other office personnel are required in all such enterprises. Public services, particularly those at the municipal level, have expanded greatly to cope with the urban growth, and a constant problem is the endless battle to increase water supply, adjust the size and location of water mains, and provide sewerage lines in keeping with the ever-expanding demand.

All these developments mean that urban life has become an increasingly noisy, bustling, congested life. Vast numbers of people commute to work from considerable distances. The streets are crowded; the shops are full;

holidays and fiestas are celebrated with elaborate decorations and much activity. Sports events attract enormous crowds to new stadia built in every major metropolitan area; and vacant lots, stretches of beach, or convenient side streets are commonly converted into temporary football fields for the young people in the late afternoons day after day. The cities are where the action is. It is no wonder that the seemingly endless influx from the drab countryside continues.

With increasing urbanization has also come a great expansion of cultural life and facilities. The very process of expanding and building new cities had provided an enormous challenge to architects, engineers, interior decorators, sculptors, muralists, and painters. The response elicited has been dramatic. In originality and boldness, Latin American architecture is probably the best in the world. It has excelled particularly in the design and execution of such public buildings as university campuses, churches, government offices, museums, and stadia. Particularly outstanding are the university cities of Mexico and Caracas, the anthropological museum in Mexico City, and the Church of Saint Francis at Belo Horizonte in Brazil. Nothing in the modern world compares with the new capital of Brazil, Brasília. Plans for the city were the work of Lúcio Costa, and the chief architect was Oscar Niemeyer, whose outstanding designs for the capital structures brought him world fame. Individual buildings are masterpieces in themselves. The cathedral has been described by Gilbert Chase as 'the most revolutionary ecclesiastical structure in modern times.' Other outstanding buildings house the congress, the presidency, the supreme court, as well as the various ministries of government. Included in the construction, of course, was an entire city of apartment houses, commercial buildings, cultural facilities, and recreational areas. Brasília was begun in 1956, was inaugurated when only partially completed in 1960, and construction has continued throughout the past decade. Many structures remained unfinished in 1970, including the new airport terminal, but the principal government buildings were completed and occupied, although many major government offices continued to function in Rio de Janeiro. Rising from a previously barren plain and partially surrounded by a man-made lake, Brasília constitutes one of the most remarkable urban enterprises of all time.

Artistic development flourished not only in the creation and decoration of various types of edifices, important as this was, but art centers became significant elements of the cultural life of various urban areas. Painting, sculpture, and neofigurative designs attracted attention for their modernism and expressionism in Rio de Janeiro, Buenos Aires, Mexico City, Guadalajara, and São Paulo. Increasingly, creative effort departed from traditional modes—nationalistic and folkloric inspiration—and turned to more abstract or universalistic forms. Such trends have not been evident in all countries, but rather have been particularly associated with the more cosmopolitan life of the major cities. As might be expected, some of the smaller countries have shared few if any of these cultural and artistic developments. Major cultural enterprise has been a phenomenon of urban life throughout history, and this relationship is clearly evident in modern Latin America.

TECHNOLOGICAL LAG AND THE PROBLEMS OF EDUCATION

Urbanization, industrialization, and national development have created great demand for technically trained people. Unfortunately, the currents of Latin American culture run contrary to the creation of an empirically oriented scientific community. Intellectual life has traditionally emphasized humanistic and philosophic values, and approaches to science have been primarily metaphysical rather than empirical. Generations of *pensadores* or thinkers of a meditative bent have enriched the intellectual life of the region, but the discovery of truth through observation, classification, experimentation, and empirical verification of hypotheses has, with a few notable exceptions, been left to others. A departure from this pattern became noticeable in the closing years of Spain's colonial empire, but the emerging stream of scientific inquiry disappeared quickly in the barren sands of intellectual stagnation that followed the chaotic years of the wars for independence. It has been slow in returning to the surface.

Apart from deep-rooted attitudes regarding the objectives and methods of intellectual activity, the poverty against which Latin American educational institutions have struggled has constituted a major obstacle to the development of scientific inquiry. Humanistic and philosophical studies have required little more than a room, a few students, an instructor, and a few books. Laboratories, expensive equipment, and costly expendable supplies are not requisites for the conduct of the educational program. Few secondary schools have been able to equip themselves for effective scientific instruction, and most universities have done little better. Despite the limited numbers of students who are privileged to complete a university education in most countries of Latin America, few of those who do so have at any time in their studies personally performed a scientific experiment or developed the values and attitudes that would cause them to view such an endeavor as useful or desirable. It is no accident that few Nobel prizes in scientific fields have been awarded to Latin Americans.

The structure of the educational systems in most countries further contributes to the difficulty. While there are numerous variations, secondary programs of five or six years' duration are generally viewed as providing the culmination of general education. Upon entering a university, the student proceeds immediately to professional education. Rigidly prescribed curricula lead to degrees in engineering, law, economics, medicine, dentistry, pharmacy, agriculture, or education. In only a handful of institutions in the more advanced countries is it possible to obtain a degree in a pure science, such as physics, chemistry, biology, or geology. Few students elect such programs because of the frequently mistaken belief that only a professional degree leads to useful employment. Several countries of Latin America have never, in their own institutions of higher education, produced a pure physicist or a geologist.

The consequence of these patterns, tendencies, and attitudes is a dearth of national scientific talent. Students who go abroad for scientific study often remain in Europe or the United States where their talents are more appreciated and better remunerated. In the meantime, developing industry in Latin America is often forced to import scientific personnel from abroad, even in such countries as Brazil, Venezuela, Peru, and Chile. For the most part, Latin American higher education is largely unprepared to support the highly technical urban-industrial civilization that is emerging by furnishing it the scientifically trained personnel essential to its further evolution.

A further and perhaps even more serious difficulty arises from the lack of technically prepared sub-professional workers. Although technical and trade schools exist in major centers and technical assistance programs from abroad have attempted to expand their number, the output is small and the training often inadequate. Again, cultural factors impeded an effective response to needs arising from industrial development and growth. For generations, trades and handicrafts have been viewed as appropriate activities only for the lower classes. Sons of middle and upper-class families simply did not enter such occupations; whereas those of the lower classes who did often lacked sufficient educational background to progress beyond those skills requiring only manual dexterity. This pattern is slowly changing, but the gap in middle-level technology poses one of the most serious obstacles to rapid industrialization in every country of Latin America.

The urban revolution has presented many Latin American countries with educational opportunities of an unprecedented scale. Rural education has always lagged far behind that available in cities and towns. Often only three or four years of elementary school have been offered in smaller villages, and teachers in rural and village schools more often than not have had little more education than their pupils. Drop-out rates have been excessively high, and inappropriate examination systems have sometimes contributed to the problem by forcing children to repeat the same grade levels year after year. With mass migration to the cities, increasing numbers of children have come within the range of better developed educational programs. Only a few of the rapidly urbanizing countries have been able to expand city educational facilities fast enough to keep pace with the growing number of children needing an education, but the simple aggregation of the pupil population in major urban centers facilitates school construction and the assignment of better qualified teachers to them. Likewise, the upper levels of elementary and full secondary programs can be made available to thousands who could never hope for such opportunities in the rural countryside. The opportunity also exists to give special emphasis to trade school programs and technical education for the new urban residents, thus providing a relevance that the more traditional educational programs have lacked. In 1970 there was growing evidence that ministries of education in the more advanced countries were aware of their new opportunities and were attempting to respond to them. Major obstacles to be overcome, however, were inadequate budgets, lack of trained teachers, and bureaucratic and professional conservatism.

STUDENTS IN URBAN LIFE

Conflicts between 'town' and 'gown' are as old as the medieval universities of Europe and the pitched battles that sometimes raged between their students and the townspeople of the communities where they were located. *Tumultos* in which university students participated have been common throughout Latin American history, and student activism as a component of political protest continues to present governmental leaders of many countries with a vexing and sometimes profoundly unsettling problem. Increasing urbanization and rapid growth in secondary and university student populations have accentuated difficulties in recent years, and during the 1960's major confrontations occurred in Argentina, Brazil, Venezuela, Ecuador, Guatemala, and Mexico.

Causes of unrest, protest, and demonstration varied from increased bus fares to disagreement with government policies and outright attempts to overthrow an unwanted regime. Typically, protesters urged on by activists of various ideological persuasions marched from university cities or campuses down main thoroughfares to central municipal plazas to demonstrate and listen to speeches denouncing whatever was the subject of the protest. Violence would occur when unruly or more radical elements attempted to loot or destroy property along the line of march, or when the police or the army sought to disperse the demonstrators. In some instances physical attacks were directed against government buildings, foreign embassies, or a bi-national center or library of the United States Information Service. To control problems of student unrest and turbulence, government officials closed universities for varying periods of time, invaded campuses with military forces, and not infrequently accused students of manufacturing bombs and storing weapons on university property. Sometimes the charges were true.

To a greater degree than in most parts of the world, intellectual life in Latin America has had a university base. This is in part owing to the fact that educated leaders in political life and the professions have maintained university ties by occupying chairs in their specialty. The holding of a university professorship has constituted a mark of distinction and prestige, and such posts have been greatly sought after even though the remuneration was little more than a token. Correspondingly, the status of a university student has been highly valued, and society generally has accorded students an intellectual recognition not always merited. The intellectual community, both students and professors, has often found itself alienated from the political life of the nation, nevertheless, because the latter has all too often and for long periods been dominated by repressive and basically anti-intellectual military regimes. Tension and bitterness have resulted, and it is not surprising that an opposition-to-the-establishment bias tends to permeate university life. This is accentuated by youthful idealism and dissatisfaction with the obvious injustices of an oligarchic and anachronistic social system characteristic of so many Latin American nations.

Political leaders and demagogues, poignantly aware of the dominant value systems of their people, have been far from scrupulous in using the universities and even the secondary schools to their own advantage by urging students into the vanguard ranks of demonstrations, riots, and civil disturbances from which they hoped to reap political benefits. Alliances between right-wing politicians and communist student leaders have become commonplace, each seeking to promote his own cause through mutual collaboration in the fomenting of chaos and anarchy.

Communist efforts to take over the leadership of student movements in Latin America were greatly stepped up after the successful Castro revolution in Cuba. Numerous students were induced to participate in special training courses in subversion and sabotage conducted in Cuba. Upon completion of their indoctrination they were sent back to their own countries to become activists in student movements aimed at taking over university administrations and bringing about the downfall of existing governments. Such leaders were not infrequently paid regular retainers for their agitational services by their communist mentors. Varying degrees of success attended these efforts, depending largely on the extent to which noncommunist majorities of both students and faculty were willing to permit a few activists to dominate the political life and policies of their institutions. In several countries the system of university administration known as co-government, in which students participated equally with faculty and administrators in electing university officers, selecting faculty, and determining policy, facilitated the efforts of the radical elements by reason of their ability through better organization to win elections and dominate university councils.

Institutions with thousands and thousands of students, such as the University of Buenos Aires, the National University of Mexico, the National University of Colombia, and the National University of Chile, constitute increasingly potent social and political forces in their respective countries, quite apart from their academic purpose. In an urban world in which the streets and plazas may suddenly be filled with a hundred thousand screaming students and their supporters, student power assumes ominous proportions. In 1970 this fact was well known in most Latin American capitals and was rapidly being borne home to the political and intellectual leadership of Anglo-Saxon America as well.

THE POWER OF URBAN LABOR

Growing industrialization and urbanization have increased the ranks of labor enormously in the major Latin American countries. Strangely, these processes have not increased proportionately the power of the labor movement, although a great potential remains untapped. Except in those countries where organized labor has been closely identified with a dominant political party—such as Mexico, or Argentina during the era of Perón, and Bolivia during the years of MNR supremacy—labor leadership has had a relatively minor voice in the determination of governmental policy. Several factors account for this. One, no doubt, has been the constant struggle against inflation that has tended to absorb the energies of labor leaders in obtaining periodic massive wage increases to keep up with galloping price increases. Another has been the continual in-fighting among labor leaders themselves in such countries as Brazil and Argentina. The expansion of the labor force through the constant influx of migrants to urban areas has served as another restraint, for many of the newly arrived workers had little conception of union purposes and organization. They did not easily become disciplined union members. Finally, the lack of an effective and enforceable dues structure in most countries deprived labor leadership of the financial resources with which to promote labor solidarity.

For much the same reasons, Marxist influence in labor organizations has not expanded appreciably over the past decade, in spite of Cuban efforts to promote communist leadership of the labor movement throughout Latin America. On the other hand, in such countries as Uruguay, Chile, and Argentina the many social benefits voted labor over the past several decades by generous legislatures have seriously impeded industrialization and have become such a burden on industry and the national treasury as to place in doubt the economic viability of national economies. Labor featherbedding on the Argentine railroad system became so notorious as to constitute a national scandal, and it has caused the principal deficit in the national budget year after year. A legacy of labor favoritism during the Perón era, labor's dominant role in the commercial life of the Argentine capital, its constant demands for ever higher wages in the face of declining productivity, and the need for national austerity to control inflation have created the single most difficult problem for political leaders to cope with over the past fifteen years. Many other economic and political ills have their origin in this complex and unhappy situation.

In most of the rest of Latin America, the full potential of labor power remains far from realization, although at given moments it has had important and even decisive influence on political events, as seemed to be the case in Brazil between the fall of Vargas and the military deposition of João Goulart in 1964. With increasing urbanization, transport workers have come to exert excessive control over the main arteries of urban life. Employees in other key utility service areas are in position to bring potent pressure upon both government and industry through effective labor organization. Great urban communities are far more vulnerable to labor threats and work stoppages than less sophisticated but more self-sufficient smaller cities, and rural economic and political units. This fact will likely acquire increasing importance as the urbanization process continues throughout the hemisphere.

The Future of Urbanization

Much of Latin America must of necessity remain rural and agricultural. Vast urban complexes cannot exist without an agricultural hinterland and an effective industrial base. Many parts of Latin America have no potential for supporting large urban populations. Some of today's larger urban centers rest upon rather flimsy economic foundations, and endless expansion does not necessarily constitute the wave of the future for even the more fortunately situated. The urbanization process is far from having run its course, however. The 1970's will see much of Latin America become more intensively urban than heretofore imagined, and the lives of millions upon millions of its people will be revolutionized by the process. Many will be benefited, but as in all major revolutions, there will be those who suffer and those who die, for the process is profoundly disruptive. The necessary balance between needs and their satisfaction can never wholly be maintained in stable societies of relative abundance. Imbalance cannot fail to be greater in periods of turmoil and when resources are far from adequate to meet basic human demands. The faltering Alliance for Progress was all but at an end and could be of little help. Increasingly, the United States was turning inward to meet its own critical racial and urban crises. Her remaining international concerns were focused on such far-away places as Viet Nam, Cambodia, and the Middle East. Increasingly, the countries of Latin America were confronted with the necessity of meeting their problems with their own resources. The dream of hemispheric solidarity and mutual assistance seemed more remote than ever.

19

Castro's Cuba:
Communist Challenge in the Americas

> In our country the individual knows that the glorious period in which it has befallen him to live is one of sacrifice; he is well acquainted with sacrifice.
>
> The men in the Sierra Maestra, and wherever fighting occurred, were the first to become acquainted with it; later all of us in Cuba learned to know it. Cuba, as the vanguard of America, must make sacrifices, because she is pointing the way to full freedom for all the peoples of Latin America.*

Fidel Castro's triumphal entry into la Habana in January of 1959 was hailed throughout the world as a victory over tyranny and oppression. By the end of 1958 the brutal regime of Fulgencio Batista had lost all semblance of support both at home and abroad. Even Batista's erstwhile friends in the United States had turned their backs as the Twenty-Sixth of July Movement swept across the country and Castro's armies moved down from the Sierra Maestra and headed for the capital. Batista fled from the island and the bearded lawyer in the fatigue uniform held Cuba in the hollow of his hand.

Progress of the Internal Revolution

Few people knew what kind of revolution Castro had in store for Cuba. He had long promised restoration of the liberal Constitution of 1940, and a Fundamental Law issued by decree on February 8, 1959, did include many of its features. The structure of government, however, was altered to

* From a letter of Ernesto Che Guevara published in *Verde Olivo* (la Habana), April 11, 1965.

463

give virtually all authority to a council of ministers over which Castro presided as prime minister. The Fundamental Law also sought to legalize prior acts of the revolutionary regime before it came to power, as well as measures already being taken to punish large numbers of individuals associated with the Batista dictatorship. The process of consolidating power consisted essentially of placing trusted associates of Fidel and his brother, Raúl, in key political and managerial posts.

More violent aspects of the revolution were first revealed by a long series of public trials and summary executions of former Batista associates conducted during the early months of 1959. Some of these spectacles were televised, and a wave of revulsion swept from Cuba to the rest of the hemisphere. Clearly Castro's revolution was something deeper than a forceful change of leadership in the National Palace. Some light was subsequently shed on the violent aspects of the Twenty-Sixth of July Movement through accounts, principally written by Ernesto Che Guevara, of the rigorous discipline enforced by Castro among his followers during the hard years in the Sierra Maestra. Men who joined Castro and then used the association to loot or plunder for personal advantage were forcefully dealt with and frequently executed, however loud their protestations of loyalty to the revolution. Adherence to the Castro cause required absolute loyalty, personal sacrifice, and a rigorous morality in those matters involving public trust. Little mercy was shown weak or wayward supporters; avowed enemies and former opponents could hardly expect more.

Castro's early policies were far from clear. This was in part owing to the varying expectations of the many different groups that had supported his victory. Each read into the prime minister's actions and speeches what it hoped would be the outcome of the revolution. Moderates hoped for the restoration of political liberties, stimulation of industrial growth, and a return to the easy-going governmental system that had prevailed under Grau San Martín and Prío Socarrás. Others of a more radical bent applauded Castro's insistence upon land reform and his concern for extending economic, social, and educational benefits to the rural workers and their families. They had no difficulty accepting expropriation of foreign landholdings or even those of wealthy Cubans. In their view, fundamental reforms such as these were long overdue. Members of the *Partido Socialista Popular,* Cuba's Communist party, which had offered Castro sympathetic if not whole-hearted support since 1958, hoped to move into the leadership of the revolution and convert Cuba into a socialist state in keeping with the principles of Marxism-Leninism and Soviet communist doctrine. Castro's rebel army, while intensely loyal to the man who had brought it victory, contained officers who in some instances did not wholly disguise their ambition to share in the political rewards of military success.

The government formed in January of 1959 was predominantly civilian and moderate. Dr. Manuel Urrutia, a former judge, assumed the presidency in accordance with agreements reached some months before among the various groups supporting the revolution. Another lawyer and former dean of the Cuban Bar Association, José Miró Cardona, was appointed prime minister. Fidel Castro was officially designated as commander-in-chief of the armed forces. These arrangements were short-lived, for no one in Cuba could mistake the fact that Castro was personally directing the government. He made frequent and seemingly endless speeches, and wherever he went he attracted huge, enthusiastic crowds. He announced programs and policies as he spoke, ignoring his nominal superiors almost as though they did not exist. By the middle of February, José Miró Cardona saw the complete anomaly of his position and resigned in favor of Castro, departing shortly thereafter as ambassador to Spain. In 1960 he defected and went into exile in the United States where he became a leader in the anti-Castro movement.

The revolutionary leaders used a heavy broom. Cuba was given a more thorough sweeping than ever before in her history. Indoctrination programs in the armed forces and among the Cuban labor groups strongly emphasized communist ideology and revolutionary tactics in keeping with the views of Che Guevara and Raúl Castro, both of whom expressed more radical views than did Fidel. On the economic and social fronts, however, Fidel's policies of expropriation and nationalization soon resulted in the expulsion of foreign enterprises from the island; sugar plantations, refineries, a large nickel plant, plush hotels, and gambling casinos, all were taken over and their foreign personnel deported. Wealthy landowners of both urban and rural property saw their holdings taken from them and their life savings confiscated. Professionals were reduced from private practice to working for the government and paid at wage-level rates. Throughout 1959 and on into 1960 the process continued. Denunciations, labor disputes, almost any excuse was sufficient for the government to 'intervene' and take over the management and eventually the ownership of business corporations and even family enterprises. The entire economy was rapidly being socialized.

Political moderates who supported Fidel Castro enthusiastically at the outset became increasingly fearful of the path along which their bearded leader and his radical associates were proceeding. In July of 1959 Castro resigned from the premiership and appealed to the people in a dramatic gesture to force the resignation of Manuel Urrutia from the presidency, denouncing his associate and nominal chief of state for opposing the revolution. Upon Urrutia's departure, Castro resumed his former post as prime minister and had a radical supporter, Oswaldo Dorticós, named president. The ranks of the disillusioned and disaffected grew rapidly, as did colonies of Cubans in exile in Miami, Caracas, and Mexico City. The moderates were the first to discover that Castro's revolution was not their kind of revolution at all. They were not the last to make this discovery, however.

LABOR AND THE PARTIDO SOCIALISTA POPULAR

Cuban labor had been strongly influenced by the communist movement from the 1930's, and at various times particular unions had been under communist domination or leadership, including the Confederation of Cuban Workers which became a decisive force in the political life of Cuba for a number of years after its organization in 1939. However, after World War II communist influence in the labor unions declined, and by the time Batista outlawed the Partido Socialista Popular in 1953 the labor movement in Cuba was relatively free of communist control. After allying themselves with Castro's Twenty-Sixth of July Movement late in 1958, the communist leaders hoped to restore their domination of Cuban labor if and when Castro came to power.

Early in 1959 the Castro government assisted loyal Twenty-Sixth of July Movement leaders to take over the Confederation of Cuban Workers, and the communists were ignored. Subsequently, when elections were held for union offices, the workers themselves rebuffed communist initiatives and defeated the majority of the communist candidates. Cuban labor at this point remained relatively moderate in outlook and objectives. Later in the year, however, when national officers were to be chosen and it appeared that communist candidates would again be defeated, Castro proposed a compromise slate on which the communists were given significant representation. Just as the ouster of Urrutia a few months earlier had marked the departure of moderate elements from Castro's government, the breaking of the Twenty-Sixth of July Movement's domination of labor in favor of greater communist influence marked the beginning of the end of the Movement's influence in political circles. Another group of disillusioned revolutionaries discovered that they were in the wrong revolution. The stream of exiles headed for safer climes increased once more.

By the middle of 1959 and on into 1960 the terminology of the Cuban revolution had changed markedly from that employed in the earlier months after Castro's victory. The jargon of communism increasingly dominated Fidel's seemingly endless television speeches. Capitalism and the bourgeoisie were roundly denounced while the virtues of the workers and peasants were extolled. The class struggle was emphasized and all those who expressed even mild misgivings about the trend of political developments were categorized as enemies of the revolution. The press was rigidly controlled, and the freedoms that many had fought alongside of Castro to restore were once again denied and suppressed.

The Partido Socialista Popular soon became Castro's principal organized political support. Its leaders, Carlos Rafael Rodríguez, editor of the communist daily newspaper, *Noticias de Hoy;* Aníbal Escalante, secretary of the central committee of the party; and others of long-standing party association clearly enjoyed official favor. Castro did not, however, permit them to assume command positions. These he reserved for himself, his brother, his Argentine friend and fellow revolutionary from the Sierra Maestra, Che Guevara, Rolando Díaz Aztarain, and one or two other trusted associates. The revolution had become increasingly communistic in program and concept, but Castro still regarded it as his revolution and he had no intention of relinquishing control over it. The communist leadership also well realized that it was Castro, not the communist party, who had captured the loyalty and affection of vast numbers of the Cuban population. They had not taken over Castro; rather he had embraced them, and his charismatic leadership was indispensable to continuation of their prominent role in the revolutionary movement.

Many charged that Castro had betrayed the revolution, that he had turned on his former friends and associates, supporters who trusted him and believed in his purposes and programs as expressed in the Twenty-Sixth of July Movement. Perhaps he *had* betrayed them. On the other hand, as Fidel himself explained it, his views while still a rebel in the Sierra Maestra were immature, tainted with bourgeois ideas and misconceptions. The realities of carrying out the ideals of the revolution forced a clarification of his thinking, and this led him to the kinds of decisions that gave the revolution its increasingly socialist character. On the other hand, in May of 1961 Castro boasted of having established a 'socialist' regime 'under the nose' of the United States, thus suggesting that his intention all along had been to turn Cuba into a communist state. He was not yet ready, however, to identify himself as a communist. Fidel Castro's motivations were obviously both enigmatic and complex. While influenced by ideological considerations, it would be naïve and simplistic to assume that doctrinal beliefs alone dictated the course of his actions. Deep-seated animosities toward the United States and his general view of the world situation no doubt influenced his foreign policy and led him to seek close ties with the socialist powers at an early date. The further evolution of his domestic policies, however, suggests a developing commitment to remake Cuba totally, including the character and culture of its population. Elements of pragmatism persisted, but obviously much was borrowed from Soviet and Chinese models. He had no intention of simply handing his country over to international communist control; rather he sought to preserve the autochthonous character of his revolution and to incorporate in it his own contributions as well as those of Che Guevara and close associates.

CONCEPTS AND PRACTICES OF TOTAL REVOLUTION

In the decade from 1960 to 1970 the ultimate shape of the Cuban revolution emerged. The character of the Cuban population was obviously considered a matter of great importance. It was early apparent that many Cubans opposed Castro's socialist measures. They fled the island in increasing numbers until further departures were prohibited. By the end of 1961 several hundred thousand Cubans were living in exile, the largest group of them in southern Florida. Among the people who had chosen to leave Cuba were not only former landholders and businessmen but a large proportion of Cuba's professional classes: doctors, lawyers, dentists, engineers, economists, and scientists. Cuba became increasingly a country of workers and peasants, for the rest of the population had fled. In late 1965 the exit door was opened slightly again when Castro announced that persons with relatives living in the United States might join them by signing up for departure on a list of persons waiting to be flown to Miami. A plan was eventually negotiated whereby flights would be operated on a limited basis by Pan American World Airways, with the costs borne by the United States Government. Thousands signed up to depart in spite of the fact that they would be allowed to take nothing with them except the clothes on their backs, and they were dropped from any government payroll the minute their names appeared on the waiting list. Thousands subsequently departed on the flights. Hundreds sought to escape in fishing boats, rafts, and other small craft. Severe hardship and loss of life frequently attended these efforts.

In reality, the Cuban population was being purged. Those who would never be able to adjust to the revolutionary way of life were permitted and for a time even encouraged to leave. Eventually the departures will end, but the Cuban population will have been transformed and its culture profoundly altered, for those who remained were introduced to a new way of life and educated or re-educated for their role in it.

The educational emphasis of the Cuban revolution has produced what is in all probability the country's greatest achievement: an educated population. Within three years after Castro took power, extraordinary measures that literally turned the island into a massive classroom had reduced illiteracy to something less than 4 per cent of the population. Cubans who could not read constituted nearly one-fourth of the island's inhabitants in 1958. The formula used to accomplish such a dramatic reduction was basically a simple one: effective mobilization of all available human resources and their disciplined application to the problem. The process was continued, however, to provide the equivalent of a sixth-grade education for the entire population, a goal not yet attained but one toward which significant progress had been made by 1970. Massive adult education programs were created in rural and mountainous areas as well as urban centers, and education for the young was expanded to the point where Cuba could boast that more than 80 per cent of school-age children were in school.

The content of the educational program developed by the revolution constituted a basic shift away from traditional Latin American patterns. Technical and scientific education was emphasized at the expense of the humanities. At higher levels this was only made possible by the use of instructors brought in from Russia and other countries of the Soviet bloc. Cuba lacked native instructors for many fields of science and technology. Equally important was emphasis upon the indoctrination of all ages and educational groups in the goals and programs of the revolution. A simple little booklet, *Venceremos* or *We Shall Conquer,* provided the basic text of the literacy campaign, while other materials produced in large quantities and distributed throughout the island appealed to more sophisticated readers. Communist values were clearly asserted and the alleged evils of capitalistic imperialism laid bare.

Basic to the program of re-educating the Cuban people was the typical socialist stress on participation in revolutionary organizations, women's organizations, peasants' organizations, trade organizations, labor organizations, and, of course, the Communist party itself for those who could qualify. Educational efforts involved the channeling of instructional programs through such organizations, programs of health education, sanitation, technical improvement, and development of work skills. Teacher education became a major governmental thrust, for with such a basic and far-reaching program to be carried out, the preparation of qualified instructors assumed enormous importance.

Much of Castro's educational effort was at first characterized by haphazard methods and organization; enthusiasm and dedication substituted for competence and mastery of teaching skills. Results were nevertheless impressive, and evidence continues to mount that a significant transformation has taken place, not only in the knowledge and skills of the Cuban people, but in attitudes and cultural values as well. Sacrifice, long hours, hard work, and little reward have come to be accepted aspects of the Cuban way of life, at least for the apparent majority who continue enthusiastically to support the bearded leader whose own way of life differs little from their own.

Land reform was from the outset a fundamental promise of Castro's revolution. To carry out the program a special organization was created, the National Agrarian Reform Institute (INRA), and basic policy was set forth in an Agrarian Reform Act of May 17, 1959. Large estates were to be broken up, foreign agricultural enterprises were to have their property taken from them, and agriculture was to be organized on the basis of cooperatives and small holdings distributed to the peasants. Castro himself headed the Institute for a time, then in 1962 named Carlos Rafael Rodríguez, a long-time key figure in Cuban communism, to take his place.

Application of the agrarian reform program in the early years of the revolution achieved the confiscation of foreign holdings and break-up of some of the larger estates. It still left sizable amounts of good agricultural land in the hands of a relatively small number of well-to-do families, and among this group there were known to be persons who had little sympathy for Castro and his program. Also, relatively small amounts of land had been distributed to peasants. Sugar-growing land in particular was retained by the National Agrarian Reform Institute and farmed as a state enterprise, as it was doubted that sugarcane could be grown and harvested efficiently on the basis of small holdings. A further reform of the agrarian effort was therefore decreed in October of 1963 whereby a limitation of 165 acres was placed on all private holdings. Large amounts of land passed immediately into the hands of the Institute, not to be redistributed but to be converted to state-operated collective farms. A steady trend toward collectivization set in, with more and more private land passing into government ownership and operation as measures were taken to make private farming increasingly difficult. By 1966 the Cuban government reported that 65 per cent of the agricultural land was in public hands, and some estimates for 1970 run as high as 85 per cent. Principal crops still grown by private owners are vegetables, tobacco, cacao, and coffee. Eventually all commercial agriculture in Cuba would be conducted by the Institute. Peasants who had joined the Castro movement in the hope of becoming landowners had also bet on the wrong revolution.

Cuba's initial thrust after Castro came to power was in the direction of industrialization and economic diversification. Che Guevara was largely credited with setting these priorities, since he became Castro's principal economic adviser and president of the National Bank despite his professional background in medicine. Support for the industrialization effort was promised by the Russians, as well as by other communist-bloc countries. A hundred or more factories would be provided ranging from steel mills to electric power generating plants to manufactories of minor supplies and parts. An automobile plant would be included, as well as oil refineries, textile mills, and farm machinery factories. In the expectation of immediate industrialization, Castro's planners allowed agriculture to lag. Sugar production in particular slipped badly, and the acreage devoted to growing cane fell to considerably less than half of what it had been prior to the revolution. Loss of the United States market, low world prices, and unsalable sugar surpluses discouraged the government from emphasizing sugar production. The process of nationalizing cane land and sugar refineries also contributed to the decrease, for the first years of government ownership and operation were marked by considerable confusion.

The industrialization program proved far less successful than had been hoped. Many of the promised factories simply never were built, raw materials needed for production were not available and had to be imported for those that did, and as was common in many countries seeking to industrialize, the new products proved to be more costly produced locally than if imported. Cuba soon found itself with acute shortages of all sorts and little foreign exchange with which to purchase from abroad. Sugar production was too low to meet even the barter commitments with the communist-bloc countries. A re-emphasis upon agriculture was indicated, and particularly sugar production had to be restored. In 1963 Cuba's economic planners announced not only that sugar production would be increased and a new priority given to cattle raising, but as Castro put it, the cane fields and the cattle industry would become 'the pillars of [his] economy' until the end of the decade. A goal of 10 million tons of sugar was set for production in 1970. The attainment of this goal was repeatedly stressed by Fidel as a measure of the ability of the revolution to carry out its programs.

As 1970 approached, however, it did not appear that the goal would be met. Much stress had been placed for several years on getting everyone into the cane fields to participate in the harvest, a measure designed not only to dramatize the equalitarian character of the revolutionary regime but also to overcome the seasonal nature of the cane-cutting task. By mobilizing a large extraordinary work force from urban as well as rural areas during the season, large amounts could be cut quickly and at minimum cost. Castro made it a point to get out in the fields and cut cane himself, and other high-ranking officials followed suit. Getting in the harvest thus became a form of national service in which all, women as well as men, were expected to participate. In the fall of 1969 some 216 Americans, calling themselves the 'We Shall Conquer' Brigade, joined Castro and his fellow Cubans in the cane fields. Departing from Canada, another and larger group set out for Cuba early in 1970.

In spite of such efforts, it proved most difficult to increase the harvest substantially. Owing largely to a pair of very dry years, the production of sugar in 1968 reached only a little more than half of the 1970 target, a little over 5 million tons. The following year showed an improvement, but the elusive 10 million figure still remained somewhere off in the future. It appeared that the final 1970 harvest would yield between 8 and 9 million tons, possibly the largest output in Cuban history.

As in agriculture, so also in commerce and industry—government ownership and operation came to characterize the revolutionary regime. Private enterprise, even in the professions, gradually diminished and seemed destined to disappear. In the decade after Castro came to power Cuba became a totalitarian socialist state. All phases of life were regulated, operated, or controlled by the government. Only an official press was functioning by the end of the decade, and opposition to the regime was vigorously suppressed whenever it appeared. No legislature existed; Castro and his council of ministers made and carried out government policies, promulgated laws, and through public enterprises directed all phases of economic life. Weaknesses in management and lack of administrative competence continued to constitute major problems. As in other socialist countries, the task of centrally planning and directing a total economy was made enormously difficult by the complexities of co-ordination and the basic inertia of large-scale bureaucracy. Political energies and the urge to participate, on the other hand, were channeled into a vast array of organizations at all levels and in all fields of activity. This technique for keeping large numbers of people mobilized and involved has long been one of the key elements of communist strategy for guaranteeing the continued enthusiasm and support of the masses of the population. It makes privation and sacrifice meaningful and acceptable, for through their mobilized participation individuals are given a sense of usefulness and accomplishment toward the achievement of great causes. Western democratic countries have normally employed such organizational devices only in wartime, but in socialist states the struggle to revolutionize society throughout the world is viewed as a kind of continuous warfare.

In Cuba the continuity of the struggle was palpable. Food was rationed, with the meat allowance down to as little as one-half pound per person per month. A heavy dependence on starchy foods was noticeable, but even rice was rationed. Clothing was also rationed, as was gasoline. By the latter years of the 1960's the private automobile had all but disappeared, and some apologists for the regime viewed the almost total dependence on public transportation as a sign of socialist progress, for the private car was condemned for having created inequalities in society. Shortages of machine parts, supplies, medicines, and other commodities hampered the development effort. Economic blockade by the United States and most Western Hemisphere countries had forced Cuba into almost total dependence on Russia and other communist-bloc states for a variety of basic items, including gasoline. The refusal of Canada, Mexico, and a number of America's European allies to join in the trade embargo provided only minor help to Castro, for he had little foreign exchange with which to purchase their products. Cuba's economic independence as a socialist state was no greater —indeed, it was less—than when she had been an economic dependency of the United States.

Cuba's Role Within the Communist Camp

Both public opinion and official reaction in the United States were generally sympathetic to Fidel Castro when his Twenty-sixth of July Movement swept to victory in January of 1959. An experienced and able American diplomat, Philip Bonsal, was appointed as the new ambassador in la Habana only a month after Castro and his supporters took over the Cuban government. He assured the bearded rebel leader of American willingness to co-operate with him and provide assistance to his program of national development. Two months later, in April, Castro paid what he described as an unofficial visit to the United States, accompanied by a large staff, and he was received cordially by Washington officials, including the secretary of state. Already, however, his regime was being severely criticized in the American press for its summary trials and executions of Batista associates, and to this clamor was soon added denunciation of Fidel's announced plans to take over foreign-held property in Cuba. Officially the United States remained sympathetic and even conciliatory as the prime minister struck back at his American critics in public speeches, but it soon became clear that Castro's increasingly virulent attacks against his northern neighbor had deeper roots than reaction to critical journalists. Other leaders of the Twenty-Sixth of July Movement, such as Che Guevara, harbored memories of American involvement in the overthrow of Jacobo Arbenz in Guatemala; and Fidel's brother, Raúl, had traveled extensively in communist portions of Europe and had clearly indicated Marxist leanings on numerous occasions. Both were outspoken in their dislike for the United States.

DETERIORATION IN CUBAN-AMERICAN RELATIONS

As the weeks passed, the American ambassador found himself isolated and snubbed by the Castro government, while Fidel's television speeches to the Cuban people contained more and more vitriolic criticism of American imperialism and suggested that the United States was plotting his overthrow. Relationships between the two countries deteriorated rapidly. Members of Cuba's upper and middle classes, who at first had viewed Castro favorably, turned increasingly against him, and many professional and business people took refuge in the United States, accusing the prime minister of favoring the communists and following a disastrous political and economic course. Fidel charged the American government with fomenting such disaffection and with giving assistance to opponents who sought to sabotage his economic programs, set fire to the cane crop, and distribute anti-Castro propaganda, some of it dropped from the air by small Florida-based planes. Despite American efforts to curb flights over Cuba from Florida and to prevent acts of violence against the Cuban regime by refugees in the United States, Castro's denunciations increased. He attacked American policies throughout history, in the present, and for the future; he assailed President Eisenhower, likening him to various unsavory despots of the ancient world. In shocked amazement, many formerly sympathetic Americans turned against Castro and his revolution.

In September of 1959 Castro's government signed an agreement to sell over 300,000 tons of sugar to Russia. The sale itself was insignificant from an economic standpoint, but it marked the beginning of a long series of steps leading to closer and closer ties between Cuba and the Soviet Union. In February of 1960 a much broader trade agreement was negotiated providing for much larger Soviet purchases of sugar and the extension of $100 million of credit to Cuba for purposes of industrialization. Then in May, diplomatic relations were established between the two countries and a large Russian embassy staff appeared in la Habana. Four months later Cuba recognized the government of the People's Republic of China, at the same time severing relations with Chiang Kai-shek's government on Formosa.

In June of 1960 a number of Soviet tankers arrived in Cuba loaded with oil which Castro ordered American-owned refineries to process. When the Texaco refinery officials refused to do so, the plant was 'intervened' by the government, in effect confiscated. Two other American refineries were seized the following month. President Eisenhower, employing new powers granted him by the American congress, terminated United States purchases of Cuban sugar for the remainder of the year. Response to this was expropriation of all American properties in Cuba. Those still in American hands, or in which Americans owned interests, included banks, utilities, sugar refineries, agricultural lands, nickel plants, hotels, and an almost endless number of business and commercial establishments. In a matter of weeks American investors saw more than $1 billion of their assets wiped out by Cuban government confiscation. The United States further retaliated by placing an embargo on the shipment of goods to Cuba, excepting only certain pharmaceutical products and food items for which no subsidy had been paid to American producers. Virtually all trade between the two countries came to an abrupt end. The United States at the same time told tourists to avoid Cuba, but the number of visitors had already dropped drastically by reason of the unrest prevailing in the island. Furthermore, confiscation of luxury resorts, hotels, and country clubs had already removed most tourist attractions.

The United States had been Cuba's principal sugar market for years, and although quotas fixed by the United States limited the amount that could be sold there in any one year, prices paid were above the world market price and had long constituted a subsidy to Cuban producers. Despite the fact that many of these producers were American-owned companies that returned their profits to the United States, loss of the American market threatened the extinction of Cuba's principal industry and the source of most of her foreign exchange. The end of tourism further deprived the country of $20 million a year in net income from foreign sources. By the fall of 1960, Cuba and the United States, engaged in bitter economic warfare, had both fired their heaviest rockets and in the process exhausted their weaponry.

KHRUSHCHEV TO THE RESCUE

As Cuban relationships with the United States went from bad to worse, relationships with the Soviet Union went from non-existent to tentative to close. Premier Khrushchev lost no time in bringing his fishing equipment into play in the troubled waters of the Caribbean. His hook was well baited with tendered credit, a new sugar market, and assistance for Cuba's industrialization program. His net man sent to la Habana in February of 1962 was none other than the wily old bargainer, Anastas I. Mikoyan, vice-premier of the Soviet Union. The agreement Mikoyan signed with Castro assured the Cuban prime minister of at least a partial alternative to continued economic dependence upon the United States. Five months later, at the height of the Cuban-American economic battle, Khrushchev promised to buy every ounce of sugar that Castro could no longer sell to the United States. He also threatened the use of Russian rockets in support of Cuba's sovereignty, a gesture viewed as largely symbolic at the time.

Their economic weapons expended, Cuba and the United States stepped up their political warfare. All over the hemisphere Cuban diplomatic representatives did their best to stir up anti-American sentiment in the countries to which they were accredited, and in some instances they threw their support behind local communist groups or anti-American student movements, and organized demonstrations against United States business interests. Thousands of Latin Americans reacted with amused pleasure at American discomfiture, for few shared what they commonly regarded as the United States' neurotic phobia about communism. Indeed, the Eisenhower-Nixon administration was never particularly popular in Latin

America owing to its seeming favoritism for dictatorial regimes such as those of Pérez Jiménez, Somoza, and Trujillo; political liberals had little difficulty in applauding Cuba's 'David' as he unlimbered his slingshot in defiance of the American 'Goliath.' At a conference of American foreign ministers held in San José, Costa Rica, in August, delegates refused to accede to the United States' request for condemnation of Cuba as a recipient of Soviet military protection. Instead they voted a more innocuous resolution to the effect that American republics should eschew Russian or Chinese military support. A month later Castro delivered a four-hour speech at the United Nations in New York roundly berating the United States for her colonialism and the many sins he alleged she had committed against Latin America in general and Cuba in particular. During his speech he was repeatedly cheered by some Latin American delegates and representatives of former colonial states in Africa and the Middle East. It appeared to many that even the diplomatic battle was going in Fidel Castro's favor.

CUBAN VICTORY AT THE BAY OF PIGS

In January of 1961 Castro ordered the United States to reduce its embassy staff in la Habana to eleven people, far too few even to maintain the physical premises. President Eisenhower thereupon broke diplomatic relations with Cuba, closed up the embassy—which Castro subsequently confiscated —and asked the Swiss government to represent American interests in the island. Political and diplomatic warfare had reached a new stage.

Recalling American involvement in the overthrow of a leftist government in Guatemala in 1954, an event witnessed by Che Guevara, the Cuban leaders early anticipated some form of American military move against their socialist regime. They were not disappointed. Cuban refugees began training in Guatemala early in 1960, supplied with arms and technical assistance by the United States Central Intelligence Agency. A force of some 1500 men was thus assembled and prepared for action to overthrow the Castro regime, a development of which Castro and his aides were not unaware. Indeed, military supplies, including MIG fighter planes, were rushed from Czechoslovakia and the Soviet Union to shore up Cuban defenses.

Plans for the refugee force to invade Cuba from Guatemalan bases were prepared during the Eisenhower administration and were far advanced when President John F. Kennedy assumed office January 20, 1961. Kennedy had little enthusiasm for initiating his years in the White House by embarking on new American military adventures in the Caribbean, and some advisers urged that the plans be canceled. Both the CIA and the Joint Chiefs of Staff supported going ahead with the invasion, insisting on the feasibility of the plan and the urgency of executing it before Cuba's military strength was further augmented by the return of cadets sent to Czechoslovakia for pilot training. The CIA assured Kennedy that the Cuban people would rise against Castro and support the invaders as soon as they landed. The decision was made to proceed as planned.

On April 17 the invasion force reached Cuban shores and landed on the southern coast at a point known as the Bay of Pigs. Ambivalence on the part of the American leadership as to how openly the United States should support the action resulted in the absence of promised air cover. It would have made little difference, however, for the invaders upon going ashore found themselves in a miserable swamp under a blistering tropical sun. A disastrously inappropriate landing site had been selected. Within three days members of the refugee force had all been captured or killed by Castro's waiting militia, and the bearded prime minister in the olive-green fatigue uniform added a military victory to his already long list of economic and diplomatic achievements. No Cubans had risen to support the invaders, and the entire operation proved to be a grand fiasco. The inadequate intelligence sources of the CIA contributed to the debacle; far too much dependence had been placed on the wishful thinking of refugees in Florida and elsewhere, and Castro's internal support had been badly underestimated.

Among the 1179 prisoners taken by Castro's militia was a small group of Batista associates. The prime minister claimed to identify 100 of the former dictator's 'butchers' and he used their presence to demonstrate to the world the character of those who opposed him. Finding priests among the invasion force as well, Castro used their participation as an excuse to expel virtually all clerics from Cuba, leaving a mere handful to care for the spiritual needs of the Cuban people.

The abortive Bay of Pigs invasion caused a wave of sympathy for Castro and his revolution to sweep across Latin America while the American government and its new president were made to look foolish. United States prestige sank to a new low. Khrushchev chortled and sent messages of support to his friend, Fidel. He also sent large amounts of new weapons. In the months and years that followed Cuba became the best-armed country in Latin America.

THE NEW AND THE OLD COMMUNISTS

Obviously emboldened by his Bay of Pigs victory, Fidel Castro moved rapidly during the remainder of 1961 to solidify his relationships with the communist bloc. A necessary step was creation of an appropriate organizational apparatus. To bring together the various groups supporting the revolution, the prime minister announced in July the creation of a body to be known as the *Organizaciones Revolucionarias Integradas* or Integrated Revolutionary Organizations (ORI). Included in the new grouping were the Partido Socialista Popular, what was left of the Twenty-Sixth of July Movement, and a former revolutionary student organization which had long since ceased to have any significance. The ORI was to be the forerunner of a new proletarian Communist party which when organized would be called the *Partido Unido de la Revolución Socialista Cubana.* In effect, the ORI was little more than the old Communist party under a new name, and Aníbal Escalante, long-time secretary of the Partido Socialista Popular, was made secretary in charge of organization. To him was given the responsibility of selecting key individuals from among the revolutionary organizations and putting them in charge of cells to be organized throughout the entire social, economic, and governmental structure. Assisted by such old-line communists as labor leader Blas Roca and newspaper editor Carlos Rafael Rodríguez, Escalante moved rapidly to secure the Cuban revolution for communism and the international communist movement directed from Moscow.

Months passed while the old communist cadre moved in and took over the key positions within the ORI. Castro's old supporters from the Twenty-Sixth of July Movement and even such intimates as Che Guevara were brushed aside as the leadership posts in the party and then in the government were taken over by the vintage figures of Cuban communism. Castro continued to command the support and allegiance of the masses, but the ORI had assumed the principal role in applying the communist structural model to Cuba, and the prime minister seemed willing to stand aside while Escalante and his associates readied the country for full participation in the Soviet political association.

The economic programs of the revolution did not go well in 1961. The entire agricultural sector was in such disarray that much of the coffee crop was lost, sugarcane remained uncut in many areas, and a severe food shortage developed. Critics suggested a deliberate work stoppage by dissatisfied peasants and agricultural laborers, but in the light of subsequent events, disorganization of production and administrative incompetence would seem to provide a better explanation. After all, the year was devoted to education; perhaps everyone was in school. It became necessary for the government to point out to the populace that revolution and work were synonymous terms.

In November a new economic plan emerged, prepared not by Che Guevara but by Carlos Rafael Rodríguez, communist stalwart of the pre-revolutionary era. Fidel supported the plan, but he also went to considerable length to identify its source and in so doing effectively disassociated himself from its contents.

Despite his close ties with the communist countries and his growing economic dependence upon them, Fidel Castro had not yet clearly identified himself personally as a member of the communist fold. On December 1, 1961, he did so in a long speech in la Habana. He announced that he was a Marxist-Leninist and would remain one until the last day of his life. He went one step further by abjuring the cult of *personalismo,* indicating that in the future the destinies of Cuba would be guided by a form of 'collective leadership.' Castro was clearly pleading for full membership in the communist camp of Nikita Khrushchev.

The prime minister's announcement was received with glad cries by enthusiastic young Marxists in Cuba, as well as by many communist leaders in other parts of Latin America. A common reaction in the United States was, 'I told you so.' Liberals who had urged patience and understanding with respect to the Cuban revolution were mute, for Castro's assertion of long adherence to Marxism-Leninism made them appear to be dupes. On the other hand, in many countries of Latin America where uncertainty had long prevailed concerning the Cuban prime minister's intentions, his statement cleared the air and gave uneasy admirers the opportunity to change their minds.

If Castro expected Khrushchev to fly to la Habana and embrace him, he was doomed to disappointment. In Moscow the December 1 speech was greeted with a stony silence. Eventually it was reported in the press and still later an editorial in the official newspaper, *Pravda,* extended a lukewarm welcome. Obviously, some members of the exclusive club looked upon the bearded prime minister in the fatigue uniform as a rather crude interloper with forged credentials.

Fidel Castro now found himself in a very difficult situation. In order to gain full Soviet support for his revolution he had turned to communist economic and social policies and mechanisms, he had extolled to the Cuban masses the virtues of the Soviet Union and Communist China and the correctness of Marxist doctrine, he had given to old-line Cuban communists the key roles in organizing the island's party apparatus, he had declared himself a communist, he had gone the full length of the communist course. Now he discovered that the old-line communists—Blas Roca, Carlos Manuel Rodríguez, Aníbal Escalante, and others whose party membership stretched back over the years—were virtually in control of the revolution and, to make matters worse, were possibly more acceptable in Moscow than he. Indeed, in spite of all that he had done, indications were that he was suspect as a Johnny-come-lately opportunist whose conversion to communism was perhaps more convenient than genuine. The economy of the island was in chaos, serious food shortages threatened, and his own trusted associates from the Sierra Maestra had been brushed aside by the Communist party regulars. His own status was clearly threatened and his credibility questioned in Moscow. He faced one of the severest crises of his revolutionary career.

Castro's strength rested upon his popularity with the masses of the Cuban people. Were this base to be lost, his concept of the revolution would be rejected and his role in it would quickly be ended. Just when Fidel grasped the full import of what was transpiring on the Cuban political stage was not clear. Certainly he was cautious in November with respect to the authorship of Rodríguez' new economic plan. Moscow's cool reception of his speech of December 1 cannot have failed to suggest that some question existed as to who spoke for communism in Cuba. In any event, President Dorticós and Blas Roca traveled to the Russian and Chinese capitals later in December to negotiate new trade agreements, and relationships with the two major communist powers moved forward as if only sweetness and light obtained among Cuba's revolutionary leaders.

In the early weeks of 1962 Castro undertook a re-appraisal of the Cuban political situation. He found widespread dissatisfaction in several quarters, among the agricultural co-operatives, the private farmers, the army, and among his old comrades of the Twenty-Sixth of July Movement. Everywhere the complaint was much the same; namely, that long-time members of the Partido Socialista Popular had moved in and taken control. Key positions in the ORI, in government, in the military, in industry, and in agriculture were all occupied by persons whose communist militancy was unquestioned from the viewpoint of the Partido Socialista Popular. However, with few exceptions, the new bosses had no record of participation in the early, violent phase of the revolution and they had no base of support among the masses of the population. There was no particular reason to believe they had any loyalty to Castro. In case of a showdown, they might well be expected to take their orders from Moscow and the international communist apparatus, represented in Cuba by Aníbal Escalante, rather than from the real leader of the revolution.

Battle for control of the revolution was joined in March. Castro moved on both the political and administrative fronts, supported by his brother, Raúl, and Che Guevara. On March 8 the permanent membership of the National Directorate of the ORI was published. Former top leaders of the Partido Socialista Popular, including Aníbal Escalante, held ten of the twenty-five posts. Thirteen members named were lesser figures of the Twenty-Sixth of July Movement, and the remaining two were former participants in the Revolutionary Directorate, a small group of early Castro supporters. The old-line communist members, although outnumbered, seemed to be in a command position by reason of their stature and eminence.

Event followed event with lightning swiftness over the next two weeks. Fidel Castro began criticizing something he called 'sectarianism'; Che Guevara publically denounced Carlos Manuel Rodríguez' economic plan as absurd and ridiculous; the prime minister named trusted old friends and supporters of Sierra Maestra days to key posts in civil and military administration, including his brother, Raúl, as vice-premier; and when, on March 22, the Secretariat of the ORI was announced, the post of first secretary went to Fidel. The next most important posts were given to Raúl Castro and Che Guevara. Aníbal Escalante was thereupon dismissed as organizing secretary of the ORI and left hastily for Czechoslovakia. Finally, on March 26, Fidel Castro delivered a long radio and television speech explaining what had taken place and personally attacking Aníbal Escalante as the source of most of the 'sectarian' deviation from the principles of the revolution.

In essence, the prime minister accused the former Partido Socialista Popular membership of having come to constitute a sect within the communist movement in which they favored each other for all key posts and arrogated to themselves decision-making authority, even by-passing the heads of government ministries. Aníbal Escalante, as organizing secretary of the ORI, he accused of heading up the sect to build his own personal following. Castro sarcastically pointed out that 'old militants' of the communist movement in Cuba were hiding 'under the bed' when the real battles of the revolution were being fought in the mountains. No doubt speaking for himself, he insisted that communists were not better communists or more deserving of merit by reason of their long association with the party going back to pre-revolutionary days. In the future, there was to be no privileged sect within the revolutionary movement; the whole people, or its immense majority, had embraced Marxism-Leninism, and they were just as deserving of positions and opportunities under the revolution as those who flaunted their long record of party association. Fidel no doubt hoped that Comrade Nikita would read his speech carefully.

A year later the United Party of the Socialist Revolution was finally formed. It was composed of a carefully screened and selected membership in which the former Partido Socialista Popular members played a continuing but diminished role. In the fall of 1965, still another change was made. The party was renamed the *Partido Comunista de Cuba* (PCC), and the National Directorate was abolished in favor of a hundred-member Central Committee, of which the 'old militants' had less than one-fifth membership. A Secretariat and a Politburo were formed, thus creating essentially the same pattern of party organization prevailing in the communist countries of Europe. Total membership by the end of the decade was on the order of 50,000, essentially an elite group in which factory workers, government officials, and military personnel predominated. The agricultural, or peasant sector, was only lightly represented. The aging militants from the old Partido constituted a minor and disappearing element.

From the crisis of 1962 onward, Castro's control of the communist movement in Cuba was not seriously challenged. Aníbal Escalante returned from Europe after a prolonged absence and set about to prove that all the prime minister had said about him was true. Once again he tried to form a small group, with himself at its head, this time to oppose Castro's free-wheeling international policies that obviously were not always in accord with the Moscow communist line. After a secret investigation of their activities by a commission of the Central Committee of the party, Escalante and his small clique were arrested in January of 1968. A revolutionary tribunal in la Habana sentenced him to fifteen years in prison while his associates, numbering less than three dozen people, were given lesser terms.

THE MISSILE CHALLENGE TO THE UNITED STATES

Cuban revolutionary leaders were early convinced that sooner or later the United States would mount some form of military attack on the island to bring about the overthrow of Castro and his supporters. The Bay of Pigs invasion confirmed this fear even though it was a dismal failure. Any new effort would certainly be better planned and would surely involve the direct participation of American military forces. With Guantánamo Bay still in American hands as a naval base on the southeast coast of the island, the United States possessed a natural foothold from which an attack might be launched. Castro did not dare attack the base, although he did cut off its water supply for a time, thereby forcing the Americans to construct a desalination plant to guarantee themselves continued access to potable water. Overt action would have precipitated the very conflict he wished to protect himself against. The Cuban leader turned instead to the development of military ties with the Soviet Union. He even talked about joining the Warsaw Pact, the mutual defense treaty among the communist-bloc states of eastern Europe. Khrushchev, however, appeared to have no stomach for formalizing a mutual defense agreement with the meteoric and unpredictable Castro. He preferred to keep his options open, and neither he nor his successors saw fit to extend Cuba an invitation to join their defense club.

New trade agreements were negotiated with the Soviet Union in the spring of 1962, and in July, Raúl Castro, as Cuba's minister of the armed forces, visited Russia to talk with Khrushchev and other Soviet leaders. Just what was said and by whom during these conferences on the subject of joint military operations is not clear. Nevertheless, a build-up of Soviet military strength in Cuba gradually became evident as the year progressed. The total number of Russian military personnel on the island eventually reached about twenty thousand, and it was obvious that they were not all advisers, trainers, and technicians. Any attempt to invade Cuba would certainly have brought the invading force into combat with Russian as well as Cuban defenders.

Fortunately for the United States, a wary eye was kept on the Cuban military build-up. High flying reconnaissance aircraft, U-2's, took repeated pictures of what was taking place on the ground. In late August the construction of missile sites was observed, and an initial exchange between President Kennedy and Premier Khrushchev produced evasive denials and warnings against a new Cuban invasion from the Russian leader. The reconnaissance continued, and on October 14 a launching pad and a ballistic missile on the ground beside it were clearly revealed in aerial photographs. Not only had missiles been brought to Cuba, but the weapons were designed for offensive action against the United States or other parts of the hemisphere.

There followed a week of critical analysis and evaluation in Washington to determine what course of action should be taken. Immediate invasion of Cuba was urged by a number of military leaders, while congressional leaders, presidential assistants, and cabinet members, as well as the military chiefs, debated other alternatives and discussed their advantages and disadvantages with the President. Additional Russian ships were known to be headed for Cuba, and in all probability their cargoes included additional thermonuclear missiles.

The action eventually taken, beginning with a television announcement by the President to the American people on the evening of October 22, was a combined one involving a partial mobilization of military forces for an attack upon Cuba should it become necessary, plus imposition of an immediate blockade of the island to prevent further Soviet ships from reaching their destination. American forces were ordered to intercept vessels carrying 'offensive weapons' to Cuba if and when they sought to enter a designated zone around the island. Khrushchev thereupon ordered his ships to stay outside the zone, at least for the time being. There then followed a series of heated exchanges between President Kennedy and the Russian premier. The attention of the entire world was focused on the confrontation. It could mark the beginning of a nuclear holocaust, World War III. It was certainly one of the tensest moments in history. Its drama was heightened by the instantaneous communication that modern radio and television made possible.

On October 29 Khrushchev backed down. He sent a message to Kennedy promising to dismantle the missile installations and return the missiles themselves to Russia. The Il-28 bombers capable of carrying nuclear weapons would also be returned. On the other hand, the American president had given assurances that there would be no invasion of Cuba. A great sigh of relief was heard throughout the world. In la Habana, however, Castro could not help but feel let down. His Russian supporters had failed him. He could only grumble as he watched the Soviet technicians go about their work of preparing the missile systems and bombers for their return journey. In a few weeks the sites were bare, and Soviet vessels headed eastward across the Atlantic carried their strange cargoes lashed to the deck where they could be inspected by patrolling American warships and low-flying aircraft. The missile crisis was over.

What caused Khrushchev and Castro to decide upon the installation of atomic missiles on the island of Cuba remains a matter of much speculation and debate. Which of the two pressed for military escalation remains uncertain. A common interpretation of these events suggests that Khrushchev hoped to achieve a sudden and dramatic superiority over the United States and that he believed the Kennedy administration lacked the resolution to oppose his Cuban adventure. Another possibility is that Russia, behind in the development of long-range missiles, sought—through the deployment of intermediate-range missiles in Cuba—a strategic position comparable to that enjoyed by the United States. Obviously, the presence of American missiles in West Germany and Turkey irritated Soviet military planners who possibly saw in Cuba the opportunity to develop a countervailing presence in the Western Hemisphere. In any event, the effort failed. The Red Chinese government labeled Khrushchev's gamble pure 'adventurism.' The Russian premier suffered a marked loss of prestige while that of Kennedy mounted.

The missile crisis marked a turning point with respect to Castro's popularity throughout Latin America, for no country in the hemisphere was prepared to see Russian nuclear weapons introduced into the area. The presence of over 20,000 Soviet military personnel in Cuba was also viewed with misgiving. The Council of the Organization of American States had voted unanimous approval of Kennedy's moves to force Russian missile withdrawal, and it became increasingly evident that the Cuban revolution had disappointed a great many liberal leaders who favored social revolution but not at the cost of submission to Soviet domination.

CASTRO AND THE SINO-SOVIET SPLIT

Early in 1963 it was far from clear how closely the Cuban regime was identified with Russian as opposed to Chinese views on communist world policy. Castro in public speeches in January identified his position as midway between the two poles of ideological difference. Perhaps he was still peeved with Khrushchev over the missile debacle.

In April of 1963 Fidel made his first trip to the Soviet Union. He was received as a hero and as a member of the inner circle of communist leaders. On the occasion of the annual May Day parade, he stood beside Khrushchev to review the spectacle from atop Lenin's Mausoleum facing Red Square, taking a position of greater prominence than even Soviet leaders present for the occasion. The visit involved extended talks, Castro remaining in Russia for over a month. In the end, the Cuban prime minister placed himself and his country firmly in the Russian camp vis-à-vis China. In return for continued Soviet economic and military support, including food shipments and a better price for sugar, Castro expressed himself fully in support of Khrushchev's policy of peaceful coexistence, as opposed to Chinese insistence upon violent world revolution and continued defiance of the capitalist powers everywhere. It also became evident that after his Moscow visit the Cuban prime minister considered himself the spokesman for communism throughout Latin America. His trip had been a huge success.

In spite of his Russian support, which soon amounted to the equivalent of one million dollars a day and which was basic to the continued existence of Castro's communist regime, the bearded prime minister persisted in playing a relatively independent role. He sided with Albania and China in refusing to sign the nuclear test-ban treaty that the Soviet bloc supported. He made a variety of trade agreements with western European countries, purchasing buses from England, ships from Spain, and other commodities from France and Italy. To the extent that his limited foreign exchange permitted, he used Canada as a source of needed supplies. Clearly Fidel Castro wanted to be subservient to no one, yet his Soviet support was indispensable. He well recognized that Russia had made an important psychological investment in Cuba as well as an economic and political one, and that only a major act of disloyalty on his part would cause a withdrawal of support. He also knew, as did the Russians even after Khrushchev had been deposed and Aleksei Kosygin and Leonid Brezhnev had taken his place, that any intrigue to replace himself with a more docile and pliable leader would be unacceptable to most Cubans and would seriously endanger Russia's influence in Latin America. Castro enjoyed a considerable range of freedom, and he did not hesitate to take advantage of it.

A significant example of Castro's effort to exert significant influence over the communist movement was his convening of a major world conference in la Habana in January of 1966. Eighty-two countries were represented at what was publicized as a meeting to demonstrate the solidarity of the Asian, African, and Latin American people. The delegates, over five hundred strong, were mostly not sent by their governments, for they represented communist groups that in many nations were outlawed; rather they constituted a strange collection of Marxist-Leninist revolutionaries who denounced the United States, capitalist imperialism, and various regimes whose anti-communist attitudes they deplored.

Far more significant than conferences and resolutions, however, was Castro's continued effort to sow the seeds of revolution in country after country throughout the hemisphere, and, on occasion, even in Africa. Such a policy did not accord well with Soviet efforts to develop new and stronger commercial ties in Latin America. On the other hand, neither did it coincide with Chinese efforts to support revolutionary communism in various countries of South America. Castro and the Chinese had a falling out early in 1966 over failure of the Asian communist power to live up to its commitments to supply Cuba with rice. No doubt the Peking decision against completing its promised rice delivery was owing in part to Castro's apparent preference for the Russian brand of communist doctrine, as well as the Cuban leader's determination to plot his own course in fomenting revolution in the hemisphere.

The Exportation of Revolution

At the moment of victory over the Batista dictatorship in Cuba, Fidel Castro seemed to feel that his revolution contained a form of contagious virus that could easily be spread to other countries of the region. Enthusiastic supporters were indeed to be found in virtually every country of the hemisphere, and, as in Cuba, large numbers of these were liberals and leftists who felt the urgency of basic social and economic reform in their countries but who were not Marxist-Leninists and did not subscribe to communist ideology. As Castro turned to old-line communists for leadership at home and to the Soviet Union for support abroad, his international following diminished rapidly until eventually it came to consist principally of dedicated communist agitators and a host of young converts among student groups. The effort to spread the Cuban revolution thereafter took the form of carefully planned subversion.

The United States reacted to Castro-supported violence and revolutionary movements in other hemisphere countries by seeking to isolate the Cuban regime. Washington scored its first rather dubious success at a conference of foreign ministers held at Punta del Este, Uruguay, in January of 1962. A majority of states supported an American resolution to expel Cuba from the Organization of American States, but such major countries as Brazil, Argentina, Chile, and Mexico did not vote, thereby expressing disapproval of the action. Further efforts to isolate the hemisphere's communist enclave saw the United States urging the countries of Latin America to boycott Cuba economically and to break diplomatic relations with her, the latter in part to prevent use of Cuban embassies as centers for communist infiltration and subversion. Not much success attended this American initiative until the pattern of Cuban subversion became clearly revealed.

FOCUS ON VENEZUELA

Many regimes around the Caribbean might appropriately have been singled out by Castro for the introduction of subversive forces during the first several years after he came to power. Trujillo was still in power in the Dominican Republic, and some forays against his dictatorship were made. A comic opera kind of seaborne move was made against Panama, but no one took it seriously. In later years Castro-supported subversive groups were active in Guatemala, and their presence was still a serious problem in 1970. Strangely, the most oppressive dictatorship in the hemisphere after the fall of Trujillo in 1961, that of 'Papa Doc' Duvalier in Haiti, attracted little Cuban attention in spite of its proximity to the island's eastern shore.

Castro was after more important game than tiny republics with few resources. Venezuela was another matter. A country rich in oil and iron ore, resources—particularly the oil—which Cuba needed badly, Venezuela constituted an attractive prize for the communist powers. Furthermore, there was considerably less risk of United States' armed intervention there, should a communist victory appear imminent, than would be the case with a Caribbean island or a Central American state. Furthermore, an active communist movement existed in Venezuela, the *Movimiento de Izquierda Revolucionaria,* which, together with a guerrilla army, the *Fuerzas Armadas de Liberación Nacional* (FALN), posed a serious threat to the stability of the fledgling democratic regime of Rómulo Betancourt. Beginning in 1960 a deliberate program of terrorism, sabotage, and assassination was mounted by the leftist groups, including the Communist party. The intensity of the campaign mounted as the elections scheduled for December 1,

1963, approached. The Venezuelan police were particularly singled out as targets for assassination by the FALN, but the terrorist campaign became so intense that no one was really safe and the country was kept in mounting turmoil. The objective of the leftist groups seemed to be the creation of such chaos that a new intervention by the military would become necessary, thereby bringing discredit on the democratic regime of Betancourt.

Obvious links between the leftist demands for the overthrow of the government and support of those leftists by Castro caused the Venezuelan government to break diplomatic relations with Cuba in November of 1961. It seemed clear that the guerrilla forces were being supplied with arms and explosives from Fidel's arsenal. Incontrovertible proof of Cuban involvement was not forthcoming, however, until caches of arms were found along the coast. One of these, reported by a fisherman at Falcón, contained an assortment of weapons directly traceable to Cuba. These discoveries occurred in November of 1963, just prior to the election. Also found on November 4 among revolutionary elements was a plan whereby the weapons would be used to take over Caracas, block the national election, and extend control throughout the country. Public sentiment was strongly aroused against the communists and their Cuban supporters. Voters turned out in extraordinary numbers to give a smashing victory to the *Acción Democrática* candidate, Raúl Leoni.

Venezuela invoked the Rio de Janeiro reciprocal assistance treaty of 1947, charging Cuba before the Organization of American States with armed intervention and aggression. A special commission of the OAS was appointed to investigate the charges, and early in 1964 reported that the weapons were indeed of Cuban origin. The foreign ministers subsequently voted in Washington to break diplomatic relations with Cuba, and by the end of the year all OAS members except Mexico had complied. Castro had effectively isolated himself from official support in the hemisphere.

Castro's efforts to support a communist overthrow of the Venezuelan government did not end with his failure to prevent a significant democratic victory in the election of 1963. Many Venezuelan terrorist leaders were captured or killed and the FALN movement was virtually crushed by the middle of 1964, but the communist forces that remained carried on their activities in the mountains and remote rural areas. Castro continued to supply them from time to time. In May of 1967 two uniformed Cuban army soldiers were captured on their way to join guerrilla forces in the interior. They were part of a twelve-man landing party, consisting of four Cubans and eight Venezuelans, the latter having been to Castro's insurgency training program. The other two Cubans died in the landing from a sailing ship off the coast and in the brief battle that preceded capture of the entire invading force.

Che Guevara disappeared from Cuba in 1965. For over two years his whereabouts remained a mystery, and rumors abounded as to the reason for his disappearance. Some said he had been killed, and the black mourning attire worn by his wife lent credence to this story. Others reported a violent disagreement between Fidel and Che over communist strategy. Guevara was alleged to have favored Chinese views urging instant revolution throughout the hemisphere whereas Castro was supposed to have preferred the more cautious Russian approach to revolution by use of normal political processes wherever possible. Castro's speeches tended to support the story of a disagreement, and an alleged letter from Che purported to be a document of repentance.

In September of 1967 Che Guevara was discovered to be leading a small international guerrilla band in the jungles of Bolivia. Less than a month later the bearded communist romantic was dead. Bolivian army rangers, scouring the mountainous jungle in search of Che's guerrilla band, surprised them in a narrow ravine known as the *Quebrado del Yuro*. The small force of communist militants was completely surrounded and many were killed in a brisk but short encounter. Che was wounded and captured, then carried to the little town of Higueras. He was shot a few hours later upon orders of the military authorities in La Paz. Subsequently his body was cremated. It was a sad, dismal, but perhaps fitting end for the 39-year-old revolutionist whose exploits as a dedicated Marxist and charismatic military leader had made him a legendary figure throughout the world.

Che had enjoyed little success in Bolivia, as his own captured records demonstrated. He was far from the Sierra Maestra, and the Indian peasants of the Bolivian countryside showed no interest in joining his guerrilla band or in overthrowing their government. After some eight months of effort, his support was diminishing rather than increasing. His Bolivian venture had been a fiasco, and Che saw the end approaching even before he was captured and executed.

A French journalist, Régis Debray, had accompanied Che's guerrilla band. He was captured and put on trial for complicity in the rebel movement. In spite of numerous pleas from fellow journalists for his release, the Bolivian court sentenced him to a long prison term. A Marxist himself, Debray was all that remained in Bolivia of Che's futile effort.

The Cuban prime minister, as self-designated head of the communist movement in Latin America, did not send out his emissaries unprepared. Schools were set up in Cuba, initially by Che Guevara, to train not only Cubans but young people from all over Latin America in communist doctrine, subversive tactics, and sabotage. The exact number trained for revolution by the end of the 1960's has been estimated at more than 7000. Most are back in their own countries, many on university campuses. Others have infiltrated labor organizations, become school teachers, or found positions in government service. Some, of course, have turned their backs on Castro and his subversive ambitions. Nevertheless, in the event of civil unrest, well-trained Castro agents are prepared to lead revolutionary movements in country after country.

In Uruguay, Brazil, Colombia, and Guatemala, guerrilla bands, some of them operating in urban areas, commit acts of violence and terrorism regularly. From 1968 onward the kidnapping and ransoming of prominent figures became almost epidemic in its frequency. The American ambassador to Guatemala was killed in a 1968 kidnapping attempt. In 1969 the American ambassador to Brazil was kidnapped on a public street and held until the Brazilian government released and flew to Mexico a group of leftists being held in jail. Then in April of 1970, the West German ambassador to Guatemala was captured. When the Guatemalan government refused to release twenty-two political prisoners and pay a ransom of $700,000, the ambassador, Count Karl von Spreti, was murdered in cold blood.

Obviously, such violence and terrorism cannot all be credited to Castro and his trained guerrillas. On the other hand, whenever political prisoners have been ransomed successfully, they have usually headed for Cuba.

Another troublesome aspect of Castro's rule has been the long series of airplane hijackings that has resulted in dozens upon dozens of commercial airliners and their passengers being flown to Cuba. Planes and passengers have subsequently been released, but the number of hijackers residing in Cuban hotels has continued to grow. The airlines of the United States have been the most frequent victims, but those of Colombia, Brazil, Ecuador, and Venezuela have suffered as well. Most hijackers appear to be mentally disturbed persons or individuals seeking notoriety. A few have apparently been leftists seeking asylum in Cuba. Castro could put an end to the hijacking traffic quickly enough by imposing severe penalties upon those guilty of the crime, or by turning them over to the country of origin. So far he has refused to do so.

THE STRUGGLE AGAINST CASTRO

In its early years, Castro's Cuba was troubled by considerable counter-revolutionary activity. As time went on, however, domestic opponents were gradually eliminated. Some were killed, others captured and imprisoned. Many fled the island in small seagoing craft of all descriptions. Terrorist acts against the Cuban dictator and his government have nevertheless continued from bases outside of Cuba. Occasional forays by armed bands have gone ashore to set fire to warehouses and storage facilities near the coastline. Such raids have been conducted by Cuban refugees from the United States, for the most part; but the hundreds of uninhabited Bahama islands have provided ideal bases from which to launch the attacks.

Officially the United States has opposed acts of violence against Cuba being undertaken from American territory, or by residents of the United States, whether refugees or not. With several hundred thousand disgruntled Cubans living in south Florida, the policy has proved difficult to enforce. Indeed, there have been numerous incidents to suggest that American intelligence services have been involved in some of the actions. If so, there has been no acknowledgement. The Cold War continues, and so also does the long series of charges and counter-charges on both sides.

Cuba's Cultural Eclipse

The Cuban revolution had a confusing effect on Cuban cultural life. At first, exiles from the Batista oppression returned. Soon, however, intellectuals began seeking refuge abroad, and as the Castro regime became rigorously Marxist the dampening influence of doctrinal control drove more and more writers, artists, and musicians to leave the island. Soon newspapers and journals were under firm management by the government and many became outright organs of propaganda. The official organ of the revolution, the paper known as *Granma* (from the name of the ship on which Castro and his followers returned to Cuba in November, 1956), became the principal source of news and information concerning revolutionary programs and activities. *Bohemia* continued to serve as Cuba's principal news magazine, but it reflected only the views and policies of the government. Apart from those whose writings extolled the virtues of Castro and the revolution, the outlet for self-expression in Cuba dried up.

SUPPORTERS OF THE REVOLUTION

Oddly enough, two of the principal literary figures of the Cuban revolution were not Cubans at all. One, of course, was the Argentine doctor, Che Guevara, whose books and numerous other writings provide much of the intellectual and theoretical background of the revolution and its doctrinal progression. A lucid and able exponent of his views, Guevara frequently put his ideas and political concepts on paper. He even kept a diary of his abortive struggle to start a revolution in Bolivia. By 1970 many of Che's works had already been translated and published in English. To many they make fascinating reading.

The other literary figure was the former Guatemalan president, Juan José Arévalo, whose anti-American *Fábula del tiburón y las sardinas,* written in 1956, became a best seller in Cuba after Castro came to power. A later book, *Anti-Komunismo en América Latina,* was also widely read.

Cuban musical talent had been outstanding prior to the revolution, both in composition and rendition. Apart from José Ardévol and some of his pupils, who adapted easily to the revolutionary regime, most of Cuba's leading musical figures found life more pleasant and stimulating abroad.

Castro's Cuba fostered no significant architectural development. Indeed, very few new buildings were built during the decade of the 1960's apart from housing projects and schools. Certainly these were more needed than elaborate office buildings and hotels. New government structures were given low priority. These were not the objectives of the revolution.

One consequence of the communist cast of the Cuban revolution was the introduction of eastern European cultural influences. Touring Russian theatrical performances provided new forms of entertainment, and ballet assumed a popularity in Cuba it had never enjoyed before. Basically, however, the Cuban revolution focused attention on the practical, the technological, and the scientific aspects of development. Aesthetic values were for the time being subordinated to the remaking of Cuban society, and particularly the value system of the Cuban individual. Who could tell what would emerge when the ideological eclipse had passed.

20

The Developing Giants:
Mexico, Brazil, and Venezuela

Brazil is too big a country for small ambitions.*

The rich should be less rich and the poor less poor.**

The Institutional Revolutionary Party, in its various epochs, has conjoined the deepest aspirations of our people and has always sought to convert them into reality; it has been and continues to be not only a vigorous and active electoral instrument but also a genuine political institution of service to the entire Mexican people, without seeking to distinguish among those favored by the benefits of its action, for it does not have as its purpose rewarding its members for their merits, but service to all of Mexico.***

As the sixth decade of the twentieth century drew to a close, three Latin American nations stood on the threshold of major power status. For two of them, at least, such eminence was not surprising; it was long overdue. By reason of its vast extent, its great resources, and its growing population, the nation of Brazil was early destined to play a major role in the affairs of the hemisphere and of the world. It lacked only mobilization and effective integration of its capabilities to emerge as the outstanding power of the South American continent. By 1970 great strides had been taken to overcome long-standing weaknesses in economic and administrative policies and organization, and the results were astonishing. Mexico, formerly the richest gem in Spain's imperial crown, required over a century to forge its national ethos in the fires of war, revolution, and self-realization. Thirty-six years of steady progress under stable and self-renewing leadership were paying off handsomely as the sixth decade ended. National develop-

* President Emilio Garrastazú Médici, Oct. 7, 1969.
** Dr. Rafael Caldera, later president of Venezuela, in an address at the formation of his political party, COPEI, in Caracas in 1947.
*** President Gustavo Díaz Ordaz on the occasion of the fortieth anniversary of the founding of the PRI, Feb. 20, 1969.

ment had been spectacular, socially and culturally as well as economically, and while many difficult problems still persisted, Mexico could face the beginning of the 1970's with optimism and self-confidence.

Venezuela's decade of achievement was far less predictable. Generation upon generation of despotic military rule did not provide an auspicious background for the democratically elected government of Rómulo Betancourt, which was less than a year old when the ten-year span began. True, Venezuela was uniquely endowed with highly salable natural resources: iron ore and oil. There was little historical basis for believing, however, that the revenues derived from the production and export of these mineral assets would be devoted to national development. In the past, military dictatorships had preferred to use government income for lavish living, supporting a large military establishment, and building personal bank accounts abroad. Would civilian rule be different? Could it endure? Despite the apparent odds against it, by the opening of the 1970's Venezuela had twice transferred political power to new civilian leaders by orderly elections, her gross national product rivaled those of Mexico and Brazil, and a tremendous transformation had been wrought in the social and economic life of the nation.

The Continuing Dynamism of Mexico

Mexico's record of national development was impressive indeed by 1960. By 1970 it was even more so. Industrialization had progressed steadily and at an accelerating rate, domestic consumption had greatly expanded, and the nature and volume of Mexican exports demonstrated that no longer was the country trading vital raw materials for manufactured commodities. Mexico was producing primarily for her own domestic market and supplying that market with most of the agricultural and manufactured goods it consumed. Imports continued to run high, but they consisted mostly of new production goods rather than consumer items, and foreign investment in Mexican manufacturing enterprises was at record levels and growing. Much of the investment came from the United States, totaled well over a billion dollars, and constituted nearly 15 per cent of that country's total investment in Latin America. Foreign capital was continuing to flood Mexico at the rate of more than $200 million a year. The gross national product had increased at an annual rate of approximately 7 per cent during the decade, and manufacturing had finally caught up with commerce in its contribution to the total. Agricultural production had also shown steady increases, and annual gains equaled or ran ahead of the population growth rate. Significant agricultural exports included coffee, cotton, tomatoes, fruit, cattle, and meat products.

THE RANGE OF INDUSTRIAL GROWTH

Major manufacturing centers were well established in Mexico by the 1950's. The following fifteen years witnessed not only great expansion but large-scale modernization as well. *Altos Hornos de México,* the principal steel manufacturer, looked forward to installation of new German fabricating equipment at Monclova, in the state of Coahuila, which by 1972 should restore to Mexico the leadership in steel production in Latin America with an annual output of 4.2 million tons. Brazil had assumed production leadership in Mexico's place some years before with the creation of her extensive mills at Volta Redonda. Other Mexican steel plants were situated in Monterrey and Guadalajara, and these too were in the process of expansion in 1970. Mexico was also manufacturing sizable numbers of automobiles, and output was expected to reach 180,000 units in 1970, a 12.5 per cent increase over the previous year. Production costs were still high in comparison with those in Germany, Japan, and the United States, whose companies had invested heavily in the Mexican automobile industry. This was in part owing to the initial investments required to develop domestic parts plants following a government regulation of 1962 requiring that vehicles be of 60 per cent local manufacture.

The rapid increase in automobile manufacture and use, coupled with new and rapid highway development, provided the stimulus for a host of subsidiary industries and service facilities. Mexico's government-owned petroleum industry, Pemex, responded with its own expansion program, moving rapidly during the 1960's into the petrochemical field as well. The manufacture of tires and tubes likewise assumed major industrial importance.

Significant industrial growth also marked progress in textile production, leather processing, shoe manufacture, as well as development of synthetic fibers, plastics, and paints. Food processing followed a similar pattern. A great dairy enterprise emerged in northern Mexico, and large refrigerated milk tank trucks moved their liquid cargo daily to the capital and other principal cities. As in more advanced countries, some sectors of agriculture were beginning to show signs of becoming capital-intensive industrial activities.

EDUCATION AND HEALTH

By 1967 Mexico claimed 72 per cent of her population to be literate, indicating marked achievement in recent years. One-fourth of the national budget regularly was expended on educational and cultural services, and constant attention was devoted to improving and extending the educational system at all levels. Fewer and fewer Mexicans still found themselves beyond the reach of any available educational facility. Equally impressive were improvements in the health of the people, for by the end of the 1960's the general mortality rate was down to about 10 per thousand, close to that of the United States. Infant mortality had been reduced to something in the neighborhood of 50 per thousand as compared with 125 in 1940. Such impressive conquests in the field of health were matched by a marked increase in the population growth rate which by 1969 reached 3.5 per cent annually. By 1968, Mexico's people numbered over 47 million, of whom 56.6 per cent were under twenty years of age, and by 1980 a population of over 71 million was projected, almost fearfully. Those living in urban areas totaled 58 per cent by 1970, but a decade later it likely would be 70 per cent.

DISTRIBUTION OF WEALTH

Critics of Mexico's economic and political systems frequently pointed to a generally negative aspect of Mexico's phenomenal development, the great disparity between income levels of the poor and the wealthy—a disparity which appeared to grow steadily wider as the years passed. There could be no doubt that great poverty still prevailed throughout Mexico, that millions of people lived under conditions of grinding penury, with inadequate housing, no running water, absence of sanitary facilities, and only wood or charcoal with which to cook their limited supply of food. But these conditions had existed for centuries. More important was the fact that industrial laborers, greatly augmented in number, received a wage sufficient to support a modest standard of living, that a large middle class had emerged, that sufficient capital continued to be accumulated to provide the funds for new development, that increasing numbers of rural peasants had their own land, and that the total system possessed sufficient dynamism to carry on the development process.

The Mexican government continued to devote substantial attention to the sad plight of its rural population. More and more land was being made available for cultivation by extensive irrigation projects, and the process of distributing land under the agrarian reform program continued. Indeed, President Díaz Ordaz, who took office December 1, 1964, was able to announce by the spring of 1968 the distribution of some 26 million acres. This achievement placed him second only to Lázaro Cárdenas in the amount of land granted to farmers during his term of office, and his period of service was little more than half over. The tremendous increases in population continued to place serious strains on the limited amount of arable land available. In 1970 no relief from such pressure was in sight; it could only increase.

The poverty of the urban slum dweller constituted an equally serious and also a growing problem, for surplus population from the countryside continued to head for the larger cities. Insufficient jobs were available for the expanding work force in spite of the increasing pace of industrialization. Unemployment and underemployment have continued to characterize every major urban center of Mexico. The problem is, of course, highlighted for the visitor by the obvious affluence of the country's new industrial and commercial classes, whose fine homes in beautiful residential settings contrast vividly with the miserable hovels and the squalor of the crowded *vecindades,* or slum areas.

Despite such contrasts, which can be found in every major country of the world, Mexico's progress and development have been real. Faced with extremely rapid population growth, Mexico has nevertheless been able steadily to increase the proportion of her population participating in the benefits that hard work and modernization have made possible. That is a major achievement of which the country and its government may justly be proud.

POLITICAL DEVELOPMENT

Mexico's remarkable progress, economically, socially, and culturally, has failed to counteract mounting criticism of her political structure, particularly abroad. The apparently well-oiled machinery of the *Partido Revolucionario Institucional* has long provided a point of major criticism for many liberals in the United States and some other countries who have been prone to confuse the mechanics of democracy for its substance. As the decade of the 1960's passed and the year 1970 loomed as another milestone marking once again the orderly transfer of presidential power, the clamor of the cynics was to be heard once more. The same old process would be repeated for the seventh consecutive time; the party oligarchy would select their man, giving careful attention to the wishes of the outgoing chief executive, and the people would be asked to ratify the choice in an election that provided no contest or opportunity for real alternatives. To those who saw in seriously contested, free elections the only acceptable guarantee of popular self-government, Mexico's claim to democracy was fraudulent. When were the *people* to participate and make their own selection?

Simplistic views such as these failed to take into account how democratic processes functioned anywhere, including the United States. Effective participation in the democratic process had always required individual effort and dedication—eternal vigilance. Aggressive leaders would always dominate the political stage. The real issue was how open the system remained, whether those who wished to participate were free to do so. Would dissident voices be heard and their pleas given attention? Was policy, including the selection of leadership, responsive to appeals and pressure from the lower echelons? Were all sectors of opinion free to express their views and exercise their powers of persuasion? To these basic questions the Mexican political system provided a generally affirmative answer. Essentially, however, effective participation lay within the Partido Revolucionario Institucional—not through organizing opposition to it. Barring the use of violence, coercion, and demagoguery, the opposition route was open, but few but a minority of extremists of both the left and right chose to pursue it, for it offered little hope of success. So open was the system that few indeed were those who could not find satisfactory accommodation within it. It is noteworthy that the most persistent opposition political parties have been those of the extreme right, such as the National Action Party, and the National Sinarquista Union. The communist movement is small and badly splintered, its electoral element being the *Partido Popular Socialista* which in the last presidential election supported the PRI candidate.

Several indices suggest that the existing political structure of Mexico remains basically responsive to the wishes and needs of the Mexican people. The high level of popular support for the governing party is one. The pattern of taxation and the priority structure of public expenditures are others, for the income tax leads all other levies as a source of government income (45 per cent), followed by taxes on commerce and industry (27 per cent), and education consumes a quarter of all direct federal government expenditures. The next highest levels of expenditure are for such infrastructure needs as communications and transport and for welfare, health, and social security programs. The government taxes in accordance with ability to pay, and spends to develop the human resources of the nation. The military services receive a mere 10 per cent of the budget, and if some officers benefit personally as a consequence of lax financial controls over defense expenditures, as critics often suggest, the fiscal impact is hardly significant.

Equally significant has been the social mobility prevailing within the political system. Mexico's last three presidents all came from the lower middle class. Ruiz Cortines was the son of a customs officer, López Mateos the son of a small town dentist, and Díaz Ordaz a lawyer who began his career on the bottom rung of the judicial bureaucracy. Many others of the top leadership have also come up through the ranks from modest and humble origins. Mexico's politics is controlled by a small group at the center, but it is not a closed group and it does not represent an economic or social elite.

Dedication to Mexico's welfare and development has not prevented the political leaders from looking out for their own interests. Presidents since Miguel Alemán have promised 'moralization' of public administration, and some have indeed struggled to eliminate peculation and graft. Alemán himself set a poor example and left office a millionaire, but his successors have been less grasping and more sincere in their efforts to prevent private fortunes from being made from public office. As in many countries, including the United States, it has proven very difficult to prevent officials from associating themselves with or investing in enterprises favored by government contracts or purchases, or from accepting substantial gratuities for services rendered. Low salaries and poor working conditions for public employees continue to encourage the demanding of facilitating payments (the *mordida* or bite) for the processing of normal government business. This practice proves particularly irritating to businessmen and tourists and provides the basis for widespread criticism. Little progress has been made in eliminating it.

THE PRESIDENCY

In 1964 the popular and able Adolfo López Mateos turned over the nation's highest office to his PRI-designated and elected successor, Gustavo Díaz Ordaz. The new president had served as minister of government in López Mateos' cabinet. The two men contrasted sharply. Although both were of humble origin, as previously indicated, López Mateos was a handsome man of the world, a favorite of the ladies, and had enjoyed a distinguished career in education, government, politics, banking, public service, and international affairs. Avowedly left of center in his politics, he nevertheless maintained throughout his administration a governmental climate favorable to business growth and industrial development. Diaz Ordaz came to the presidency relatively unknown. His career had begun with the judicial system in the state of Puebla and included service in the national congress. As minister of government he came into contact with state and local officials and party functionaries, but his modest and unassuming manner kept him out of the limelight. He was small of stature, and his closest friends would hardly have described him as handsome. His administration was fraught with political problems, but he approached the end of his term with a solid record of accomplishment marking him as one of the outstanding presidents of modern Mexico.

In October of 1969 the leaders of the Partido Revolucionario Institucional named Luis Echeverría Álvarez, prominent 47-year-old attorney and Díaz Ordaz' minister of government, as their choice for presidential candidate. At the party convention the following month the selection was officially confirmed, and Echeverría set about the arduous task of visiting every nook and cranny of the republic to meet the people and familiarize himself with their problems. The election was scheduled for July and, barring a most unforeseen eventuality, the new PRI president would take office December 1, 1970.

THE DIFFICULT SUMMER OF THE YEAR OF THE OLYMPIAD

In the fall of 1968 Mexico became the first Spanish-speaking country and the first country of Latin America to host the international Olympic Games. To host this event is a major undertaking for any country, and Mexico became the first of the so-called 'underdeveloped' countries of the world to try. Usually considerable construction must precede the opening of the games, for the various facilities required for the many different events must meet exacting international specifications, and few cities in few countries find themselves so equipped. Mexico City was no exception. The stadium of the National University, with a capacity of 80,000, provided the site for many of the events, but other structures, including a huge swimming pool with seating capacity around it for 10,000 spectators, was built specifically for the games. In addition, a host city must have suitable hotel accommodations for both athletes and spectators from all over the world. A great deal of preparatory work had to be done, and hosting the nineteenth Olympic Games proved costly for Mexico. On at least one occasion President Díaz Ordaz and the organizing committee debated the wisdom of going ahead when the magnitude of the task confronting them became fully apparent. To have backed out, however, would have involved an enormous sacrifice of prestige, as well as loss of sizable tourist income and a variety of long-term, less tangible benefits, such as the stimulus to sports and physical fitness programs in Mexico. The decision was made to go ahead.

The games, held in October, proved a huge success, and Mexico distinguished herself as an excellent host. Many of the events and ceremonies were seen on television throughout the world. For a time during the summer and fall of 1968, however, it seemed that the entire affair would have to be postponed or called off altogether owing to violence and disorder in the national capital.

Trouble started on July 23 when riot police intervened to prevent a street fight between students of the National Politechnic Institute and those from a private preparatory school. Three days later students from the Institute conducted a long march through various streets of the city protesting the actions of the police and demanding that the force be disbanded and their leaders dismissed. Permission for the march had been obtained, and no attempt to interfere was made as long as the 6000 students remained orderly. In spite of some violence along the route, such as throwing of rocks and attacks upon photographers, the marchers reached their announced destination and most disbanded. A few hundred, however, decided to continue the demonstration by moving on to Mexico City's central square, the *Zócalo,* and these were joined by communist agitators carrying Cuban flags, shouting *vivas* for Castro, and denouncing the Mexican government. Soon buses were commandeered, property destroyed, windows broken, traffic tied up worse than it had previously been, and the central part of the city thrown into turmoil. Once again the police had to intervene, arrests were made, and a number of people were taken to jail, although bona fide students were released. It was early Saturday morning, July 27, before peace was once again restored. A sizable number of persons had been injured and considerable property had been destroyed.

The initial demonstrations and rioting proved but a prelude to over four months of disorder. Students from the National University joined with those from the secondary schools in mass meetings and demonstrations again and again in the days and weeks that followed. The army was brought in to assist the police, but for a time it seemed impossible to bring the situation under control. Thousands were injured in street fights between rioters and those sent to control them, and other thousands were arrested. Students demanded that the government release a number of alleged prisoners whom the authorities denied they were holding and whom student leaders seemed unable to identify. Military forces occupied various educational establishments, including the Autonomous National University whose rector, Javier Barros Sierra, and other officials denounced the blatant violation of their most prized academic value, autonomy. At one point the rector resigned, but his resignation was rejected by the governing board of the institution and he agreed to stay on.

As the rioting and confrontations continued, violence mounted. Again and again buses were commandeered by the rioters to move from one part of the city to another. Many were burned. Damage to property was enormous, and the economic life of the Mexican capital was brought to a virtual standstill. Inevitably more potent weapons than tear gas and night sticks were brought into play; rifles and bayonets were used with increasing frequency and the toll of dead and wounded increased rapidly.

The violence came to a head on Wednesday, October 2, when a pitched battle raged for over four hours in the *Plaza de las Tres Culturas,* with snipers with automatic weapons firing from balustrades of buildings and the army returning the fire from the street. A score of persons were killed and many more wounded, some of them innocent bystanders and members of the press. One of those gravely wounded was an army general.

The bloodletting of the tragic October 2 evening provided a climax to the disturbances. Thereafter they gradually subsided. However, a student strike council, organized to present demands on the part of the student groups, continued to insist upon a number of conditions being met before it would permit the re-opening of the university and other schools. These centered around the release of prisoners, both students and professors, modifications in the penal code, and removal of police and military personnel from educational premises. A gradual de-escalation of the conflict took place, making possible the successful staging of the Olympic Games, for which some 60,000 people converged on the Mexican capital in spite of the tense political climate. It was early December, however, before the various schools and the National University were again able to conduct classes.

The grim events of Mexico's student revolt made little sense. Clearly it was not communist inspired or communist led, although Castro supporters joined in the fray and pictures of the late Che Guevara were paraded through the streets on huge posters. Attacks against the government and the Partido Revolucionario Institucional were bitter, but such animosity developed with the violence and the government's attempt to suppress the marches and demonstrations. Political dissatisfaction was a factor, but opposition to the 'establishment' did not precipitate the unrest. Student appeals for support from labor and other groups within the population attracted little sympathy. Government measures to maintain order and to secure adherence to the law were on the whole moderate. Two thousand or more were arrested, but only a few of the more violent ringleaders were detained for extended periods of time. The remainder were released within hours.

Reactions abroad were strange. In Spain and France students demonstrated in support of their Mexican associates, but behind the alleged sympathy was opposition to their own inflexible governments as much as to that of Mexico. The press in the United States reported the troubles of its neighbor almost gleefully, devoting more space to attacks on Mexico's one-party political monopoly than to the events themselves or their causes. *Time* magazine decried the government's 'harsh and unnecessary repression' and suggested that hardening of the arteries affected a political regime that had been too long in power.* Mexico's highly successful management of the Olympic Games soon brought praise from around the world, however, and the country achieved new stature for its sportsmanship and its increasingly impressive role in international athletics. The student crisis receded into the background. Nevertheless, the difficulties dur-

---

* As student unrest mounted in the United States after 1964 and erupted into violence on campus after campus, culminating in the spring of 1970 with the slaying of four students by National Guardsmen at Kent State University in Ohio and two other deaths at Jackson State University in Mississippi, the American government displayed no greater wisdom or sensitivity than had that of Mexico.

ing the summer and fall of 1968 remained a firm reminder that Mexico's youth could not safely be kept on the periphery of the nation's political life.

MEXICO'S CULTURAL ASCENDANCY

Mexico made good use of her opportunity as host to the nineteenth Olympic Games to offer a wide variety of artistic and cultural presentations. She had much to offer, for Mexican cultural accomplishments since the Revolution had attracted attention and praise throughout the world. Of more immediate significance, however, were the many indications that the country had moved into a new cultural era. Folklore and patriotism centered on Mexico's revolutionary goals, and the struggle to achieve them had long provided dominant themes in art, literature, and music. By 1960 the old masters had largely passed from the scene and a new post-revolutionary generation was moving to the fore. Its members were rapidly demonstrating a new creativity that transcended the older nationalistic themes but that still reflected the distinctive character of Mexican life and values.

Augustín Yáñez continued to be regarded as Mexico's outstanding novelist. His *Al fila del agua,* written in 1947, was translated into English in 1963, and other works continued to flow from his pen, such as *La creación, La tierra pródiga,* and *Las tierras flacas.* However, younger men were increasingly demonstrating outstanding competence, and such names as Juan Rulfo and Carlos Fuentes had drawn attention with their interpretations of the contemporary Mexican scene. Rulfo's *Pedro Páramo,* written in 1955, showed the stylistic influence of Faulkner; and Fuentes' *La región mas transparente,* translated as *Where the Air Is Clear,* ridiculed the nation's growing class of wealthy entrepreneurs. Fuentes earned further fame in the 1960's with additional novels, translated into English as *The Death of Artemio Cruz* and *A Change of Skin,* the latter a psychological adventure interlaced with existentialist philosophy written seemingly with tongue in cheek. The first publications of a new writer of short stories and novels —Juan García Poncia—appeared on the scene in 1963, *Imagen primera* and *La noche,* both volumes of short stories distinctive for the descriptive power displayed and for the author's ability to capture and transmit a mood to the reader. Two novels also appeared from his pen, *Figura en paja* and *La casa en la playa.*

During the 1960's Mexico developed pre-eminence in the book-publishing field throughout the Spanish-speaking world. Mexico City's *Fondo de*

Cultura Económica had some years before deservedly achieved fame as a major publishing house of technical and professional materials as well as fiction. Early in the sixth decade many other major publishers were active in Mexico, and a number of them received substantial stimulus from the United States Agency for International Development's Regional Technical Aids Center which contracted with publishers and film producers for large quantities of technical materials. William A. Rogers, Jr., for several years director of the program in Mexico City, devoted his efforts to raising the quality standards of Mexican publications with respect to book manufacture and binding, as well as selection of material. Today the quality of book manufacture by principal Mexican houses compares favorably with that anywhere in the world. This has given Mexico a distinct edge in the publishing field.

A member of Mexico's older generation, Carlos Chávez, continued to dominate the field of Mexican classical music, but he long ago crossed over the bridge from nationalistic to universal themes. Organizer of Mexico's symphony orchestra in 1928, Chávez has contributed much to his country's musical development as an outstanding composer and director of symphonies.

Mexico in the 1960's could boast an outstanding ballet as well as a distinctive theater. Her movie industry dominated Spanish-language productions throughout large portions of Latin America. Ballet and theatrical performances drew heavily upon European materials, but Mexico's performers were outstanding. Movie productions displayed a more autochthonous character.

Jaime Torres Bodet, author, educator, and diplomat, remained Mexico's outstanding man of letters, while Jésus Silva Herzog, seemingly ageless interpreter of the Revolution, continued to write lucidly of his country's social and political scene. Octavio Paz, Mexico's distinguished poet and essayist, published a new poem, *Blanco,* in 1967, and it immediately won him additional acclaim in the Spanish-speaking world. His earlier fame was well established by numerous volumes of poetry and by his essay on the Mexican character, *El laberinto de la soledad.*

New painters, sculptors, and workers in plastics and other materials abound in Mexico today. Among the more outstanding are José Luis Cuevas, Alberto Gironella, Miguel Cervantes, Francisco Corzas, Pedro Friedeberg, and Jorge Hernández Campos. Mexico's greatest contemporary muralist is Juan O'Gorman, born in 1905. Examples of his artistic talent are to be found from the United States to Chile, and include a mural in natural-colored and enameled stones created for the 1968 Hemisfair in San Antonio, Texas. O'Gorman is an engineer and architect as well as painter and muralist, and his contributions to the design and decoration of Mexico's modern university city probably constitute his greatest work. Many achieved fame by their participation in the university city project.

Mexico has many outstanding architects whose modernistic structures adorn not only the capital but also such other metropolitan centers as Monterrey and Guadalajara. Félix Candela designed a new Sports Palace for the Olympic Games, and the dramatic structure will serve as an arena for a variety of events for years to come. Most significant, however, has been the work of Pedro Ramírez Vásquez who designed Mexico's National Museum of Anthropology, opened in Chapultepec Park midway in the decade. Ramírez Vásquez then produced another magnificent structure, the huge Aztec stadium with its soaring cantilevered roof. Constructed to hold over 105,000 spectators, it was completed in time for the Olympic soccer matches and other Olympic events. The stadium is considered a most unusual architectural work and one of the finest such structures in the world. The final play-offs for the world soccer cup were held there in mid-1970.

The opening of the National Museum of Anthropology marked one of Mexico's greatest cultural achievements. Dedicated to the preservation and presentation of the long and rich history of the nation's early peoples, the museum elicits the admiration of thousands who visit it every year. The quality of the exhibits is as outstanding as the building in which they are housed, and the museum is regarded by many as the finest anthropological exhibition in the world.

In 1970 Mexico remained a country of contrasts and contradictions. Industrial, cultural, and political progress had been enormous. Poverty nevertheless remained the lot of millions of the nation's people in spite of years of prodigious effort to overcome it. Rapid population growth was increasingly being viewed by thoughtful Mexicans as perhaps the greatest single obstacle to a more equitable distribution of the benefits of national development. New mouths to feed, bodies to clothe, and minds to educate canceled out major portions of the advances in food production, industrialization, and education, year after year. A land of limited natural resources, Mexico could not for long continue to double the number of its people every twenty to thirty years without reversing the development trend. In 1970 measures to control Mexico's population explosion were nowhere in evidence. A new national problem was clearly discernible on the horizon.

Brazil: Emerging Colossus of the South

Brazil's prospects were doubtful in 1960. Five years of extravagant spending had been accompanied by runaway inflation, huge budget deficits, and repeated recourse to the printing press. The governor of São Paulo, Jânio Quadros, was elected president in October, Brazil's first opposition candidate to achieve the honor in her relatively brief history of democratic selection of the chief executive. He was inaugurated on January 31, 1961. So also was his political opponent, João Goulart, whose successful bid for re-election to the vice-presidency was made possible by a strange provision of the constitution that permitted the presidential and vice-presidential candidates to run on separate tickets. The arrangement was fraught with peril, for apart from their political differences, the two men had little use for each other personally.

Quadros had been regarded as an able governor of São Paulo, but his campaign for the presidency raised many misgivings. He tried to be all things to all people, telling each segment of opinion precisely what he thought it wanted to hear. It was as though he had read a book on how to be a successful politician and tried to apply its nostrums mechanically. People wondered what he really had in mind. Many reform groups, impressed by his record, expected the new president to put Brazil's chaotic economic house in order; others were certain he would carry out long overdue administrative reforms in the national government. Still others looked to him for social reform, land reform, educational reform, currency stabilization, and a favorable balance of payments. The most skilled magician could not have pulled all these rabbits out of the hat.

'JANGO' TAKES OVER

Quadros went through his hatful of rabbits with amazing rapidity. He tightened up the budget, removed government subsidies on a number of key products, put a brake on spiraling wage increases, pulled Uncle Sam's beard by friendly gestures toward the communist powers, and, lacking support in congress, turned to the people to receive their applause. His act received only a stony silence. The resignation he had submitted to congress on August 25 was quickly accepted, the public did not rise to his defense, and his only recourse was to depart quietly for more favorable climes. Quadros' brief flirtation with charisma was over. Somehow it had eluded him.

Quadros' resignation and its prompt acceptance by the Brazilian congress caught political and military leaders by surprise. Stunned at first, the armed forces chiefs suddenly realized that the presidency was about to devolve upon João Goulart, a man whom they held in contempt and whose demagogic appeals to labor had led to suspicion of communist sympathy if not affiliation. Indeed, at the very moment, he was just completing a visit to Peking where he had expressed high praise for Mao Tse-tung. 'Jango' simply could not be permitted to take office.

The Brazilian congress, sitting in the new capital at Brasília, included many of Goulart's supporters in the Labor party; but faced with the possibility of a military take-over, it sought to resolve the crisis by amending the constitution so as to insulate somewhat the distrusted politician from day-to-day direction of governmental affairs by inserting a prime minister in the executive structure. This makeshift arrangement was reluctantly accepted, and Goulart was permitted to assume office. An old associate of Getúlio Vargas, Tancredo Neves, was selected for the prime ministership. Under the constitutional change, the president would be little more than the titular head of state. Government would be in the hands of the prime minister and his cabinet and they would be responsible to the chamber of deputies as in various European parliamentary systems.

Brazilian government under the parliamentary arrangement was essentially irresponsible. The country drifted. A fruitless struggle took place between Goulart and the congress. Repeatedly the president named ministers, including new prime ministers, only to have his appointees rejected by the chamber of deputies. Finally 'Jango' prevailed upon congress to submit to the voters the question of restoring full presidential authority and abolishing the prime ministership. A plebiscite was held in January, 1963, and although the voter turnout was small, the five to one margin by which 'Jango' was granted full executive authority left little doubt that the people were fed up with the endless deadlocks of the parliamentary experiment.

Brazilian economic conditions grew progressively worse, meanwhile, as inflation mounted out of control. No serious effort was made by the prime ministers, by the parliament, or by Goulart when full presidential powers were granted him to gain control over the nation's chaotic fiscal affairs.

Foreign capital increasingly avoided Brazil and even the international lending institutions showed no enthusiasm for funding Brazilian programs, projects, or the government's budgetary deficits. The cost of living rose several hundred per cent while the value of the *cruzeiro* in relation to stable world currencies dropped more than four-fifths. To make matters still worse, the president's brother-in-law, Leonel Brizola, who was governor of the state of Rio Grande do Sul, expropriated foreign-owned utility companies, including the telephone system. The parent company of the telephone network, International Telephone and Telegraph, was offered a token amount in payment for the value of the property. While still shaken by Brizola's action, foreign investors were dealt another blow when the congress restricted the freedom of foreign companies operating in Brazil by limiting profits that might be taken from the country to 10 per cent of invested capital. Near panic ran through Brazil's international financial community as fear of a general expropriation of foreign holdings mounted.

The country was wracked by strikes and public unrest with each new political crisis in Brasília. Goulart seemed to favor his communist friends while at the same time seeking to build a large political following among the laboring classes. Communist agitators were active throughout the country, and they were particularly energetic in the northeastern states where poverty was most acute. Goulart's decision to re-open diplomatic relations with the Soviet Union created further fear concerning the government's ideological orientation. Investors, foreign and Brazilian alike, sought convenient means of liquidating their holdings and depositing the proceeds in Swiss and American banks. A flight of capital took place and the economic crisis mounted.

GOULART TAKES ONE STEP TOO FAR

Goulart's ineffectual, drifting government showed no improvement, even after restoration of full constitutional authority. Cabinet memberships revolved endlessly. Fearful that the country was drifting into anarchy that would be exploited by the communists, the United States agreed to grant nearly $400 million in new credits early in 1963, insisting at the same time on Goulart's carrying out essential fiscal reforms. He could not do so, for he neither knew how nor cared to find out. He fired the finance minister whose efforts seemed to offer promise. The next one, Carvalho Pinto, set forth on a program of austerity and reduction in wasteful expenditures, but 'Jango' undercut him completely and by the end of 1963 the disgusted minister submitted his third and final resignation.

Faced with the implacable hatred of the country's chief military officers and constantly attacked by the able governor of Guanabara, Carlos Lacerda, who sought to rally other state governors to the opposition, Goulart became desperate. He proposed a broad constitutional revision enfranchising illiterates, transferring legislative powers to the presidency, and permitting presidential re-election. This only intensified the attacks upon him. In March, 1964, 'Jango' appealed to the enlisted men of the armed forces, supporting some 1400 of them in open mutiny against their superiors at the naval base in Rio de Janeiro. That proved the last straw. Throughout the country the military officers rose in revolt and took over the government. Goulart fled to Montevideo, Uruguay, leaving behind his large estates in Rio Grande do Sul as well as extensive properties he had illegally acquired in Mato Grosso. One point became clear. However inept 'Jango' had been at managing public finances, he had demonstrated remarkable ability in augmenting his personal fortune while in high political office. He seemed to have no difficulty reconciling personal capitalism with public sympathy for communist causes. Brazil was well rid of him.

REVOLUTION FROM THE RIGHT

Brazilians refer to the events of April, 1964, as the beginning of a far-reaching revolution. Many foreigners and some Brazilians, on the other hand, question the accuracy of this term, in part because the movement came from the right rather than the left and because it did not turn power over to the masses or even redistribute land to the peasants. If, however, a complete about-face in the political and economic life of the nation can be called a revolution, what occurred in 1964 in Brazil amply justifies application of the term. Brazil did an about-face, and six years later the country is still marching in the new direction.

In the confusing days following Goulart's departure, it was not immediately clear how the country was to be governed. Soon, however, the military leaders demanded extraordinary powers of congress, and the legislative leaders were urged to expel numerous members whose political records the military did not like. The congressional response was dilatory; the mood of the armed forces and their officers was not sensed and many politicians hoped to continue business as usual. On April 9, the chiefs of the three armed services ministries took matters into their own hands and, calling themselves the Supreme Revolutionary Command, they decreed an Institutional Act vesting in the chief executive extensive powers to propose modifications in the constitution which the legislators would have only thirty days to consider and which were to be approved by a simple rather than a two-thirds majority as provided in the 1946 document under which the country had been governed. Still more significant were the sweeping powers enabling the executive to deprive 'political undesirables' of their political rights for a period of ten years. Included among those to whom such action might apply were members of congress and of state and municipal legislative bodies. Finally, the Act provided that a new president and vice-president were to be chosen within two days, and military officers on active duty were made eligible.

The message came through to the legislators loud and clear. On April 11 they elected as the new president to fill out the unexpired term of Goulart, the chief of staff of the army, Marshal Humberto Castello Branco. He was inaugurated on April 15. Tension relaxed throughout the country, for bloodshed had been avoided and the deadlock between the executive and legislative branches was ended.

THE PRESIDENT USES HIS BROOM

The new Brazilian president, at 64, was a professional soldier who had spent most of his life in military service. He had enlisted as a private at the age of 17, was promoted to the officer corps several years later, and had seen combat duty on the Italian front in World War II. Of stocky build and possessed of the very short neck common to many from his native state of Ceará, Castello Branco was little known outside the military service. Those who were acquainted with him respected his honesty, his dedication, and his moderation.

It was the third quality that assumed greatest importance in the months immediately after the new president took office. Many of his military supporters favored a hard line that could possibly have resulted in a massive purge of Brazilian public life. Although many were arrested as political 'undesirables' and 'grafters,' relatively few were detained more than a few hours. Thousands might have been deprived of their rights, had the advice of the hard-liners been followed, but actually only 378 individuals were affected. Those who were arbitrarily sentenced to loss of political rights could not run for or hold public office for up to ten years, and they could not even participate in elections. Against this executive action, no recourse to the courts was permitted. Among those against whom the action was taken were a half-dozen state governors, fifty-five members of the congress, the head of the regional development organization for the Northeast, Celso Furtado, the communist organizer of the peasant movement in the Northeast, Francisco Julião, and, of most significance, the three most recent former presidents, Goulart, Quadros, and Kubitschek.

The president's arbitrary judicial power over the political rights of individuals expired on June 15, and Castello Branco himself refused to request its extension or to extend it on his own authority, although there was considerable pressure for him to do so.

EFFECTIVE GOVERNMENT OR CHAOTIC DEMOCRACY?

Castello Branco adopted an economic policy of rigorous austerity, tightened up the tax collection machinery, held the line on wages, eliminated import subsidies that had kept consumer prices down on gasoline and certain food items, and sought to balance his budget. He appointed two able and respected economists, Roberto Campos and Octávio Bulhões, to head the key planning and finance ministries. A new and detailed analysis of the Brazilian economy was prepared, revealing its many weak spots and leading to development of a new national economic plan. Celso Furtado had made a similar but less thoroughgoing study two years before, but Goulart had given him little support and the planning process foundered. This time the government stood firmly behind the economic reform measures. Pressures on foreign-owned enterprises were relaxed and steps taken to create once again a favorable investment climate. The new government assigned a much more significant role to the private sector in developing the country's economy than had been the case in Brazil in many years.

The Brazilian president's apparently firm resolve to cope with the nation's monetary and fiscal crises soon loosened the purse strings of the international banks and the American foreign assistance agency. Castello Branco further improved his position with the United States by breaking diplomatic relations with Castro's Cuba almost immediately after taking office and by sending a force of more than token proportions to support American and OAS peace-keeping operations in the Dominican Republic in 1965. Nearly a billion dollars were poured into Brazil to shore up the desperately sagging economy. The budget deficit for 1964 had amounted to more than half that amount, however. Much more assistance was needed.

If Castello Branco hoped that his firm hand at the economic helm would be appreciated by the Brazilian populace and applauded by electoral support for his candidates at the polls, he was soon to be disappointed. An early constitutional amendment extended his own term until March 15, 1967, but congressional and gubernatorial elections in 1965 showed the existence of a very substantial opposition in spite of wholesale and arbitrary disqualification of potential opposition candidates. A new Institutional Act was therefore employed to abolish the old political parties, the more important of which had been the Labor party, the Social Democratic party, and the Democratic National Union. In their place were created a government party known as the National Renovating Alliance and a so-called opposition party, the Brazilian Democratic Movement. Few political parties have ever been created successfully by fiat, and in the years following 1965 it did not appear that the Brazilian case would prove any exception.

In 1966 a further change was made in the constitutional system by providing that in the future, executive officers—the president and state governors—would be chosen by the respective national and state legislative bodies rather than by popular vote. Only members of the legislative bodies would be directly elected by the people. Under this arrangement, the congress in October, 1966, chose General Artur da Costa e Silva to succeed Castello Branco in the presidency on March 15, 1967. He would serve a four rather than a five-year term.

Under Castello Branco's stern rule the democratic processes in Brazil had been considerably restricted. He and his military supporters had made it painfully clear that the military revolution would be continued whether it had popular support or not. The electorate would simply be restricted and curtailed until only those willing to support the regime had a voice in the legislatures and at the polls. One of the president's least popular measures was a restrictive press law passed in the closing days of 1966. It prescribed severe penalties for printing reports tending to undermine confidence in the nation's financial institutions. Protests were immediately forthcoming from the Inter-American Press Association and newspapers in the United States and Europe, and the president-elect hinted that his government would not enforce the obnoxious press law.

A new constitution was prepared prior to Castello Branco's departure from office and approved by a special session of congress. It vested very extensive power in the chief executive, gave congress little more power than to ratify decree laws after they had gone into effect, and continued the system of indirect election of executive officers. The president and his military supporters were well aware that the restoration of popular democracy would result in his government being turned out of office, but they pointed to reviving Brazilian prosperity, a reduction in the rate of inflation from nearly 100 per cent annually to around 40 per cent, new road construction and industrial development achievements, and a relatively honest public administration. Even the blatantly crooked but popular governor of São Paulo, Adhemar de Barros, had been thrown from office and his political rights suppressed. The leaders of the military revolution placed the economic and social development of the country higher on the priority list than open, popular democracy. They had no confidence in Brazil's traditional political elite or the country's chaotic and splintered party structure. Limited democracy would be permitted, but the military would stay in charge.

GENERAL ARTUR DA COSTA E SILVA

Brazil's second president under the military revolution was, as his predecessor had been, a professional soldier all his life. No one questioned his honesty or his resolve to work for the benefit of his country. He was by no means a popular hero or a charismatic leader, however. Indeed, he seemed more drab than Castello Branco. However, he promised to 'humanize' the revolution, to consider the needs of the people as well as the stability of the economy. To many Brazilians this was a promise of moderation and possibly even a hint of return to more popular government. Such an assessment proved premature.

Costa e Silva continued most of the economic measures of Castello Branco, holding the line against labor pressures for inflationary wage increases and insisting on financial stringency in public expenditures and extension of bank credit. Roberto Campos was replaced as minister of planning. This, as well as other major shifts in cabinet posts, produced a significant pause in government programs to improve the fiscal system, interrelate the planning and budgetary processes, and tighten up revenue collections. Educational programs likewise languished and agriculture received virtually no attention. On the other hand, capital investment continued to mount, industrial production increased astonishingly, and the general economic situation improved greatly. By the end of 1968 the gross national product was rising at a rate of over 7 per cent annually and the inflationary spiral had been slowed to 24 per cent a year. Even in the economically depressed Northeast, new industrial plants were springing up in such key areas as Recife in response to carefully designed tax inducements.

Against such improvements there had to be weighed the growing dissatisfaction with the military government and its increasingly repressive measures to keep opposition under control. Student unrest spread throughout the universities and forceful action by the security police was taken again and again during 1968 to suppress student demonstrations. Outbreaks at the Universities of Brasília and São Paulo were met with firm action involving the arrest of many students and dismissal of a sizable number of faculty members. An increasing number of intellectuals were arbitrarily deprived of their political rights under the president's virtually unlimited power to control subversion. Heavy-handed press censorship was imposed from time to time during the heat of political disturbances, and highly esteemed newspaper publishers were arrested for their outspoken criticism of government excesses and over-zealous suppression of opposition activities. In spite of such measures, however, the press continued to maintain a lively independence, reporting acts of the authorities' with screaming headlines as soon as the censorship bans were lifted. Only editorial comment seemed tempered to the political climate.

Student and university unrest was by no means a Brazilian phenomenon, as troubles in Mexico City, Paris, and on many campuses in the United States amply demonstrated. Active opposition by the Roman Catholic clergy was quite another matter. In Brazil many priests seemed just as ready to oppose revolution from the right as their counterparts in other countries had so often opposed revolution from the left. A seemingly reform-minded church spoke out against government excesses and protested harassment of priests who urged violent social change. Archbishop Helder Câmara of Olinda and Recife was particularly outspoken and publicly opposed the government. Complaints to the Vatican produced a veiled warning in January of 1970 that the Pope was keeping a vigilant eye on the Brazilian controversy between church and state.

COSTA E SILVA DIES IN OFFICE

Toward the end of 1968, mounting congressional opposition provoked a new crisis. A member of the chamber of deputies, Márcio Moreira Alves, had become a painful thorn in the side of the government's military leaders. He had written a book denouncing the regime for torturing its political opponents, only to have the book temporarily banned from public sale. In September he surged to the attack again, urging the people to stay home and not attend Independence Day celebrations. Executive officials thereupon decided to remove him from office and suppress his political rights, and to make such action legal congress was asked to suspend his legislative immunity. By a surprising vote of 216 to 141 the deputies refused to do so. The military hard-liners were dumbfounded and enraged. Such defiance was not to be tolerated. Costa e Silva was persuaded to sign a new Institutional Act—the fifth—empowering himself to suspend the constitution, dismiss congress, and rule by decree. He might also establish a state of siege or suspend the political rights of any citizen. A new round of arrests followed and a sizable number of people ended up in jail. By the end of the year congress had been sent home and the 1967 constitution had been laid aside.

Untroubled by a noisy congress, Costa e Silva found 1969 a quieter year. His principal active opposition came from roving bands of urban guerrillas who committed acts of sabotage and terrorism in Rio de Janeiro, São Paulo, and other major cities. Although government police met terror with terror, the battle continued; and in September a guerrilla band kidnapped the newly appointed American ambassador to Brazil, C. Burke Elbrick, and held him captive for over three days until fifteen alleged political prisoners were freed and flown to Mexico City. The ambassador was then released unharmed while most of the recent prisoners flew on to la Habana.

Brazil's military presidents seemed plagued with misfortune. Castello Branco was killed in a plane crash only four months after he left office. In 1969 Costa e Silva was also struck down. He suffered a paralyzing stroke on August 31, just a week before he had planned to make an Independence Day announcement of a new constitution and plans for electing a new congress. For weeks he lay helpless, unable to speak; then, shortly before Christmas, he died.

GENERAL EMILIO GARRASTAZÚ MÉDICI

Immediately upon learning of their president's serious illness, Brazil's three military chiefs assumed responsibility for running the government until their leader recovered. When Costa e Silva failed to respond to treatment, a major political crisis loomed, for it became obvious that a new president would have to be named. The military triumvirate did not delay, however, until tensions had had time to build. Instead, they calmly made their choice of General Emílio Garrastazú Médici, another professional soldier and experienced army commander. The long-dismissed congress was then called back into session and asked to approve their choice. The 63-year-old military officer was elected without opposition, although some members abstained from voting. He assumed office in October, weeks before the ailing Costa e Silva passed away.

The new Brazilian president (another president from Rio Grande do Sul —the state of Costa e Silva, Goulart, and Vargas) was another military figure about whom very little was known among the populace. There was much speculation as to whether he would be a hard-liner or a moderate, whether he would lead the country back toward populist democracy or continue military dictatorship. The answer was far from clear, and as the early months of 1970 passed the question continued to be posed.

BRAZIL ENTERS THE NEW DECADE

Brazil entered the decade of the 1970's with considerable promise. Economically the country was in better condition than ever before. Its domestic industry was prosperous and expanding, producing both consumer and capital goods. The gross national product had expanded by over 9 per cent in 1969, a phenomenal rate by anyone's standard. Trade balances were favorable and the rate of inflation had been reduced to below 20 per cent annually. Vastly endowed with resources of all kinds, Brazil possessed tremendous potential and that potential was being increasingly realized. São Paulo had become one of the great industrial cities of the world; only its miserable transportation problems seemed unsolvable, for the urban giant of over six million people had grown like topsy—unplanned and in defiance of reason. Even Brazil's impoverished Northeast showed signs of recovery as industrialization began to make its impact and new highways opened up avenues of communication with Brasília and the rest of the country. Great development was taking place westward in Minas Gerais and Mato Grosso, where new farmlands were rapidly being opened to cultivation and people were pouring in. Brazil was on the move.

Brazil's military government suffered from a generally unfavorable press, both domestic and foreign. Interference with press freedom had produced widespread retaliation in the form of antagonistic reporting. Stories about Brazil and its problems dwelt heavily on the high rate of illiteracy among the 85 million people, of whom over 50 per cent could neither read nor write; the miserable favelas or shantytowns in and around all major cities; the low per capita income of approximately $300; the high incidence of disease and infant mortality rates that ranged up to 200 per 1000 live births in some areas of the Northeast; the hopeless and depressing poverty of the rural countryside; the sharp contrasts between opulence and penury in the great urban centers. There can be no doubt that Brazil has a very long way to go to raise the living standards of all her people to decent levels.

The military revolution has not brought popular democracy to Brazil. It has brought stability, order, and progress on many fronts. One of its worst faults has been a tendency to over-react to opposition and take highly repressive measures against individuals on an arbitrary basis. There is great need to establish a rule of law and to live within its parameters, whether they provide for a limited form of popular participation or a more broadly based democracy. The government has sought repeatedly to do this, but as of 1970 it has not yet found the magic formula.

In 1970 Brazil remained troubled with political unrest, but reports of wholesale dissatisfaction with the military revolution seemed exaggerated. True, the government had little support in intellectual circles or among the leadership of the former political parties. On the other hand, many of the signs of unrest such as student opposition and guerrilla activity were common throughout the hemisphere and by no means limited to countries ruled by right-wing or military dictatorships. Early in June, the Rio guerrillas struck again, kidnapping the German ambassador, Ehrenfried von Holleben, and holding him until forty prisoners were released and flown to Algeria. He was then released unharmed. The guerrillas called themselves the Popular Revolutionary Vanguard, and their leaflets and slogans, as well as their method of operation, suggested their communist orientation.

CULTURAL DEVELOPMENT

One of Brazil's greatest handicaps has been its chaotic educational system. The national education ministry has long constituted an overcentralized labyrinth of bureaucracy seemingly incapable of bringing about needed improvement. The military revolution has made little or no impact in this area of activity other than to purge the universities of 'undesirable' professors. The elementary school system remains hopelessly bogged down in irrelevant programs and procedures that leave enormous numbers of children stranded indefinitely in the first grade until they lose interest and drop out. The secondary system is largely in private hands, with many schools operated by the church, whereas the largely autonomous universities have failed to orient their instructional programs to national development needs. Cultural emphases on law and the humanities continue to attract the largest numbers of students to professional faculties teaching such subjects. At the same time, there are far too few higher education institutions to provide spaces for all those eligible to enroll. Many capable students must be turned away.

Weaknesses in Brazil's educational system have failed to inhibit the development of many forms of cultural expression. Contributions in the field of architecture have already been mentioned. Output in other fields is also impressive. In the decade of the 1960's Brazil's outstanding novelist was clearly Jorge Amado, the Bahian who first attracted attention two decades earlier with his *Terras do Sem Fin,* translated as *The Violent Land.* More recently his *Gabriela* was widely applauded for its rich portrayal of the captivating magic of life in his native bay region. In 1969 *Dona Flor* was published, together with an English translation. Amado's style and subject treatment have caused him to be referred to as the Bahian Hemingway. Another novel, *The Devil To Pay in the Backlands,* by João Guimaraes Rosa, also received wide acclaim.

In music, the nationalist tendency of Heitor Villa-Lobos continued on past his death in 1959, and was particularly represented by the compositions of Camargo Guarnieri. Claudio Santoro, another folkloric composer, abandoned the nationalist school in 1964, with his widely acclaimed *Eighth Symphony,* which established his reputation as Brazil's outstanding composer of symphony music. Extremely popular as an interpreter of Brazil's widely varied cultural background is the guitarist, Baden Powell, whose breadth of repertoire is tremendous.

Brazil's great naturalist painter, Cândido Portinari, died in 1962, but the expression of his outstanding talent will live for years in the murals with which he helped decorate the United Nations building in New York, the Library of Congress in Washington, and the beautiful education ministry building in Rio de Janeiro. In abstractionist painting, probably the outstanding Brazilian representative is Waldemar Cordeiro, whereas Mario Cravo, Jr. is widely noted for his abstract work in sculpturing.

Another major expression of Brazilian culture is to be found in the country's active movie industry. Outstanding films have won a number of international prizes. Culturally, Brazil is very much on the move in many fields of intellectual and artistic expression. Her exceedingly rich background cannot fail to find increasingly fecund manifestation in the years to come.

Venezuela's Phenomenal Modernization

Rómulo Betancourt had been a revolutionary most of his life. Of modest origins, he attended public schools and the Central University in Caracas. Soon he was active in opposing the military dictatorships that continued to plague his country, and the result was a long span of years during which he varied his schedule by languishing in prison or languishing in exile. He became a communist, changed his mind and left the party, and became a liberal dedicated to democracy and its institution in Venezuela where it had never really been tried. He helped found the political party, *Acción Democrática,* and held the presidential office briefly as its representative. He once more fled abroad after Marcos Pérez Jiménez established his unsavory dictatorship. Then, as the popularly elected president, he again assumed office in 1959, supported by a majority in both houses of congress. He was still a revolutionary, and he demonstrated it repeatedly during the five-year term he served.

Betancourt was determined to take full advantage of the brief time he had to revolutionize Venezuelan social and economic life and, in so doing, to provide a new and firm basis for political democracy that would render return to military dictatorship unlikely, if not impossible. Vast sums were devoted to education, and in a few brief years the number of elementary schools was doubled, as was their enrollment. University enrollment was expanded threefold and greater attention focused on useful rather than prestigious professions. At the same time, funds for public health were likewise expanded, and very substantial support was given to a broad industrialization program. A massive land reform effort was mounted, not only for the purpose of satisfying the desires of land-hungry peasants, but to increase food production and to slow down the migration of rural dwellers into the cities. Caracas had become a shantytown shambles with something approaching 40 per cent of its population living in hillside *ranchos,* as local squatter settlements were called. Betancourt's land redistribution program was unique in that it focused primarily on arable tracts that were not being utilized productively and expropriation was accompanied by compensation to the owners.

One of Betancourt's most difficult and remarkable accomplishments was keeping the military in check. This feat involved keeping the armed forces adequately supplied with funds and removing a few of the more politically minded leaders from the local scene by retiring them or sending them abroad on diplomatic missions. No doubt the communists helped the president quite unintentionally, for by their militant guerrilla activities they kept the armed forces occupied while at the same time they made of Betancourt a hero to all those who opposed the communist movement in Latin America, including many who might otherwise have viewed the government's reform activities as too radical.

The Venezuelan government's bloody and protracted struggle against foreign and domestic subversion made Betancourt's tasks doubly difficult, and nearly cost him his life in a bombing attack. The climax was reached just prior to the election of Betancourt's successor on December 1, 1963, when Castro's agents were foiled in an attempt to pull off a *coup d'état* and block the voting. The Acción Democrática candidate, Raúl Leoni, received a plurality of the votes in an open contest in which a very high percentage of the qualified electorate participated. On March 11, 1964, the new president was peacefully inaugurated.

What enabled Betancourt, and Leoni after him, to carry out a large-scale development program was one magic resource: oil. Venezuela had become the world's largest exporter of oil, and oil income accounted for 70 per cent of government revenues. The oil pool under Lake Maracaibo is enormous, and at long last the Venezuelan government was using it to promote the welfare of the Venezuelan people. The foreign companies that exploit the resource continued to make handsome profits in spite of the 67 per cent royalty and other charges paid to the national treasury. In time the various concessions would expire, and Betancourt's policy, as well as that of his successors, was to turn production over to the state-owned *Cor-*

poración Venezolana de Petróleo as the various dates arrived. In the meantime, no new concessions would be granted.

By making good use of its enormous mineral resources, the Venezuelan government under Betancourt and Leoni was able to perform something of a miracle. It mounted an impressive development program, paid off inherited debts from the previous extravagances of Pérez Jiménez, paid for expropriated agricultural land, held inflation to a minimum, and maintained the most stable currency in Latin America, if not in the hemisphere.

DEVELOPMENT OF GUAYANA

Venezuela's resources are by no means limited to oil. A mountain of iron ore known as Cerro Bolívar has opened up vast new industrial possibilities that have attracted new foreign corporations and substantial investments. Also available in both quantity and quality are aluminum, manganese, and coal. A huge hydroelectric potential had only begun to be exploited. The center of many of Venezuela's new industrial and mineral extraction activities is the city and region of Guayana, inland on the Orinoco river, some 350 miles southeast of the capital. The state-owned *Corporación de Guayana* has been organized to develop the region. In co-operation with such American business enterprises as United States Steel Corporation, the Corporación de Guayana worked with great rapidity during the 1960's to move Venezuela into the forefront of iron and steel production in Latin America. At the close of the decade, Venezuela loomed as a new industrial giant in Latin America, with a gross national product rivaling those of Mexico and Brazil and an annual growth rate of around 8 per cent.

VENEZUELAN POLITICS

Betancourt linked his Acción Democrática party with COPEI, a Christian Socialist type of party led by Rafael Caldera. Appointing numerous members of other groups to cabinet posts, including those from COPEI, Betancourt was able to govern with a democratic coalition that he considered highly important to maintain in the face of possible military opposition on the right and communist subversion on the left. The task was not easy, and minor groups kept splintering off to form opposition parties, many of them ephemeral and centered around an individual. President Leoni seemed less concerned with maintaining the coalition with COPEI, and the latter entered the opposition in congress after Leoni's inauguration. Thereafter it emerged as a major competitor to Acción Democrática.

COPEI, under Caldera's expert guidance, became a party heavily influenced by progressive Catholic reformist doctrines. Although it continues to attract many of the more conservative political elements in the population, its basic economic and social doctrines are little less socialistic than those of its principal rival. In 1968, campaigning on a platform of the need for *un cambio,* a change, Rafael Caldera won the presidency by a very small plurality, thus becoming the first opposition leader to win the presidential office through democratic processes in Venezuela's entire history as an independent nation. He was duly inaugurated on schedule without incident, and the event was widely hailed as evidence of the country's growing political maturity.

President Caldera faced a difficult period ahead, however. Congress was badly splintered and his Christian Democratic COPEI, while second, lacked even the numerical strength of Acción Democrática, and even that party fell far short of having a majority. It appeared that the old problem of legislative chaos, so common in Latin America and frequently fatal to progress through democratic processes, would pose serious problems for Venezuelan popular government in months to come.

Caldera sought to put an end to leftist resistance and guerrilla activity in the countryside by giving legal status to communist political groups and by entering into discussions leading to mutual accommodation. Some groups responded favorably, but the Armed Forces of National Liberation (FALN) declined to negotiate. Linked to Fidel Castro's program of international communist subversion, FALN continued to carry on its subversive terrorist activities. Before 1969 was over, renewed agitation on Venezuelan university campuses produced a virtual shut-down of the country's secondary and higher education systems. Caldera came to realize that his good intentions and resolve to employ processes of rational discussion had little to do with overcoming communist determination to take over the country.

CULTURAL DEVELOPMENT

The 1960's saw the passing of two great Venezuelan intellectuals, Mariano Picón-Salas, whose historical interpretations of Latin American culture had earned him considerable fame, and Rómulo Gallegos, statesman, one-time president, and Venezuela's greatest literary figure. No one would soon take their places.

Venezuela lacked the breadth and depth of cultural background possessed by either Mexico or Brazil, but as her urban culture flourished the prospects brightened. Outstanding architects had built the modern capital of Caracas and had designed the beautiful campus of the Central University. The work of Carlos Raúl Villanueva was particularly impressive in this regard. In some respects, Venezuela was still in the nationalistic stage of musical and artistic development. The country had only recently begun to find its national ethos.

The Long Road to Greatness

In the 1960's, Mexico, Brazil, and Venezuela had each made startling progress. Mexico's achievements represented the continuation of trends already well established. Both Venezuela and Brazil had executed an abrupt about-face to confront a destiny that had long lain dormant. Neither had as yet solved the basic problem of political stability, and a sudden upheaval could throw one or both of them into another period of chaotic deterioration.

All three countries possessed vast populations still living in misery and want. All three still had major battles to fight against disease, too rapid population growth, and inadequate medical attention. All three still lacked educational systems that met the needs of their populations and the requirements for continued development in an increasingly technological world, although Mexico was far ahead in this regard. The very size of the countries, the diversity of their resources, their regions, and their people rendered impossible the kind of uniform progress that small and more homogeneous nations sometimes attained. Nevertheless, each of the three was building rapidly an industrial civilization, a strong middle class, and an increasing capacity for self-sustaining growth. These were countries for the future, the coming giants of Latin America.

2 1

The Caribbean Trouble Zone:
Old and New Nations

> The American nations cannot, must not, and will not permit the establishment of another Communist government in the Western Hemisphere.*
>
> We are not Communists. How can we make the Americans understand that we are not Communists? **

Fidel Castro dominated the center of the Caribbean stage in 1960. Fear that the Cuban conflagration might leap across the waters to adjoining islands or even to the near-by mainland provided a source of great anxiety to American foreign policy planners and to numerous government leaders in the region. The fear persisted throughout the decade and was not entirely forgotten in 1970, although Castro's glaring failures in economic development, in agriculture, and political penetration abroad had greatly reduced his stature throughout the hemisphere. At several critical moments, however, the communist presence and its expansionist proclivities conditioned the nature and extent of reaction to political crises in the area and tended to magnify both the crises themselves and the seriousness with which they were viewed. Four significant areas of activity provided the locale for the more important developments of the ten-year period. The Central American nations sought to strengthen their program of regional integration, generally referred to as the Central American Common Market, and to promote as rapidly as possible their industrial development and social modernization. Panama struggled to achieve a new national identity and a more satisfactory accommodation to the continued presence of United States military and economic operations at the very heart of her physical being. The Dominican Republic overthrew a thirty-year-old dictatorship

* President Lyndon B. Johnson at the time of the Dominican crisis.
** Dominican rebels to feature editor of the *Saturday Review,* James F. Fixx, June, 1965.

528

and found it exceedingly difficult to keep her balance in the face of instability at home and violent pressure and even occupation from abroad. Finally, former British colonies found independent existence an exhilarating experience but by no means a solution to their many problems. They moved gradually to assert their influence and to achieve the status of full-fledged participants in the inter-American system.

Some localities, both on the mainland and among the Caribbean islands, remained dependencies of European powers. During the 1960's a greater measure of control over their own internal affairs was granted to a number of them by Great Britain, although such an arrangement proved unsatisfactory to the five thousand inhabitants of the tiny island of Anguilla. They preferred to 'go it alone' rather than in association with St. Kitts and Nevis, and eventually physical intervention by the British was necessary to restore order. France's *département* of Guyane, on the coast of northern South America adjoining Brazil, moved suddenly into the space age when late in the decade the French installed there a launching base for earth satellites. The influx of scientists and technicians created almost boom conditions and the first real excitement since the prisons that once made the colony famous, or infamous, were closed down in 1946. The French island of Guadeloupe achieved the dubious distinction of being the scene of repeated crashes of Air France jetliners trying to land at Pointe-a-Pitre.

On the west end of the island of Hispañola, the black Republic of Haiti continued in the iron grip of François ('Papa Doc') Duvalier and his *Tonton Macoutes,* or private strong-arm police force. Enduring hunger, disease, and fear, the miserable and ignorant Haitians lived and died without hope, trusting in the magic spells cast by voodoo priests. Not even Fidel Castro showed an interest in a country so devoid of prospects that it invariably appeared at the very bottom of any scale measuring progress or development in the Western Hemisphere. In 1970 'Papa Doc,' at the age of 63, gave no indication of willingness to relinquish his despotic control, despite constant plots against him. But even were one of the plots to succeed, nothing in the Haitian past or present offered much of a basis for optimism that a new regime would markedly improve upon the existing one.

The Notable Progress of Central America

As the five republics of Central America entered the decade of the 1960's, a movement among them was under way that was soon to prove highly significant in stimulating the region's economic and social development. On June 10, 1958, a Multilateral Treaty on Central American Free Trade and Economic Integration was signed by all five countries. It was the outgrowth of several years of effort of economists within the various governments as well as those from the Economic Commission for Latin America (ECLA), a United Nations' regional entity dedicated to promoting economic growth among all the Latin American states. The initial objects were to bring about the gradual reduction of tariff barriers throughout Central America and to encourage industrialization by enlarging the potential market available to manufacturers who would find the purchasing power of the residents of a single country inadequate to justify the establishment of a new enterprise. Costa Rica did not ratify the agreement, but El Salvador, Guatemala, and Nicaragua did, and later they were joined by Honduras. Some Costa Rican economists and political leaders feared that their country was too far removed from Central America's population centers to provide attractive sites for new industries. They also feared the competition of lower-paid laborers in the other countries. Consequently, they persuaded their government to withhold the necessary final approval that would have joined Costa Rica in the economic integration effort.

Initial progress toward integration was slow, and further discussions and negotiations led to the signing of a new General Treaty of Central American Economic Integration on December 13, 1960. This agreement, together with one providing for the creation of a Central American Bank, became effective in June, 1961. Again Costa Rica refrained from participating, but after an election had been held and a new government installed in San José a change in policy took place. Fearing exclusion from development programs financed by the Central American Bank, the Costa Ricans signed the integration treaty in 1963.

The new treaty was much broader and bolder in concept than the first one. It established *immediate* free trade in the region rather than listing items on which tariffs were to be reduced or eliminated among the participants over a period of time. Relatively few items were excepted, and some of these, though very important to the international trade of the member states, such as coffee and cotton, were unlikely to be interchanged locally in any case. The agreement also provided administrative machinery to carry out its provisions and to resolve disputes that arose among the parties. A rather complex network of supplementary relationships eventually emerged looking toward or establishing uniform duties on items imported from outside the region, a clearinghouse for the various currencies, and similar arrangements to facilitate intra-Central-American trade.

Benefits derived from the Central American Common Market, as the new regional relationship came to be called, were immediate and in some respects spectacular. Within four years intra-regional trade nearly quadrupled in value and more than doubled as a percentage of total imports by the five countries. By 1968 the total value of trade among the partners was almost eight times larger than it had been in 1960 and amounted to over $260 million. Particularly significant was the fact that the increase consisted overwhelmingly of industrial products. Fabrics, clothing, chemicals, tires and tubes, paint, and related items were the principal types of commodities involved. Many of the products had not been manufactured in the region at all prior to 1960.

Principal beneficiaries of industrial growth were El Salvador, Guatemala, and Costa Rica, but toward the end of the decade substantial increases in output were being registered by Honduras as a consequence of new factories established in San Pedro Sula area. Nicaragua also was experiencing some industrial growth, but progress lagged behind that of her partners.

CONSEQUENCES OF INDUSTRIALIZATION

Each of the countries sought to lure foreign investment by tax incentives and infrastructure inducements such as power, water, roads, and needed services. Thus encouraged, and with the entire Central American region as a prospective market, numerous foreign companies built plants. American capital predominated, but European and Japanese investment also entered the area. Local capital likewise accounted for some of the new factories, particularly in El Salvador. Results, however, had significant negative as well as positive aspects. Many factories imported machinery and raw materials duty free to produce import substitution products which then entered into the commerce of the region without paying any tariff duties.

The resulting declines in customs revenues adversely affected government budgets and at the same time the heavy importation of 'privileged' raw materials added to balance-of-payments difficulties. To make matters still worse, many of the plants were highly mechanized and automated, and employed very few people. Thus the countries struggling to industrialize their economies witnessed the construction of a host of new factories from which immediate tangible benefits seemed painfully disappointing. Governments were considering the revision of internal tax policies by the end of the decade to make the new industries bear at least some share of the cost of the industrialization program.

As the 1960's drew to a close, the pace of industrialization slowed. Initial benefits from the common market had been realized and further expansion would be at a slackened rate and more difficult. Despite the unfavorable features that attended significant parts of the industrialization program, the overall balance sheet showed a favorable result. Industrial production had risen from a very minor figure to approximately 15 per cent of gross national product in the region. True, there was considerable disillusionment with the common market, and its benefits had not been distributed equally among all the members; but initial expectations had been exaggerated and the economists had painted an over-optimistic picture. The danger in 1970 was that dissension among the participating nations would bring the entire structure of delicate relationships crashing to the ground.

POLITICAL PROBLEMS

It was remarkable indeed that the common market had progressed at all, given the political instability that continued to prevail throughout the area. El Salvador, Honduras, and Guatemala each experienced the overthrow of governments by force, and Costa Rica was for a time troubled by the inevitable deadlocks created by having a president of one party and a congress dominated by the opposition. Nicaragua continued as the fiefdom of the Somoza clan, although Luis left office at the end of his term in 1963 and a long-time associate, René Schick Gutiérrez, was elected to the presidency. Schick died in office in 1966, and a few months later, in February of 1967, Anastasio Somoza, Jr. was elected president. Luis Somoza's earlier talk of the family retiring from Nicaraguan politics thus went for naught. Shortly after his younger brother was installed at *la Curva,* Luis was struck down by a heart attack, leaving 'Tachito' to rule alone.

When the decade opened, José María Lemus was in the midst of his term as president of El Salvador but experiencing increasing difficulty. Left-wing and student opposition disrupted the peace of the capital and Lemus, stiff and austere, showed neither skill nor imagination in coping with the problem. A group of young and radical army officers seized the government and drove Lemus into exile. The junta was itself soon overthrown by a more moderate military group, headed by Colonel Julio Adalberto Rivera, who sought to put the country back on the road to progress that had been its course during most of the previous decade. A constituent assembly was called and it modified the 1950 constitution by reducing the presidential term of office from six to five years. In April, 1962, Rivera was elected president without competition, but opposition elements who ran no candidates complained bitterly about the 'fraudulent' election.

Julio Rivera reflected the same basic outlook of moderate but progressive military leadership that had characterized the Salvadorean government in the early years of the *Partido Revolucionario de Unificación Democrática* (PRUD), of which Lemus had been the second and rather unsuccessful representative in the *Casa Presidencial.* Rivera created his own official party, however, the *Partido de Conciliación Nacional,* and both as a member of the second junta after Lemus' departure and as president he took firm measures to speed reform. The national income tax was revised and the rates were adjusted sharply upward. Tax penalties were provided on uninvested capital whereas funds invested in new industries were exempted from taxation. These financial incentives were effective, and some members of the coffee aristocracy began shifting portions of their wealth into the industrial sector.

Rivera's five years in office were years of progress and development. Extensive resources were employed in expanding the educational system, in improving health facilities, and in providing new public housing. Laws were passed designed to ameliorate the lot of the agricultural worker, and a gesture was even made in the direction of distributing land to the landless. El Salvador's problem, however, was that there simply was not enough usable land to go around. The country's population of three million was literally bursting at the seams and spilling over into underpopulated Honduras. Unlike many countries in Latin America, El Salvador is characterized by intensive use of the land, including that of the small number of coffee growers who constitute the nation's agricultural aristocracy. To break up the *fincas* would serve only to convert the country from latifundia to minifundia; it would certainly not increase production. In the long run, El Salvador's hope for her people lies in limiting their increase and in finding other things for them to do than farm.

Rivera permitted a relatively open political system, despite stern measures to curb communist agitation and vandalism. A surprisingly strong Christian Democratic party emerged to challenge the government party, and in 1966 its colorful spokesman, José Napoleón Duarte, was elected mayor of San Salvador. Under a system of proportional representation, it also secured some fifteen seats in the national legislative assembly. In the 1967 presidential election, however, it was no match for the government party. The popular Rivera was able to project his cabinet member and close associate, Colonel Fidel Sánchez Hernández, into the presidential chair with little difficulty. Many Salvadoreans feared the candidacy of Fabio Castillo, a former rector of the national university and a civilian member of the radical junta that governed briefly after the overthrow of President Lemus. He was thought to be a communist and open sympathizer with Fidel Castro. In an election generally regarded as open and honest, Castillo ran third, well behind the Christian Democratic party candidate and far, far behind Sánchez.

PROGRAMS OF FIDEL SÁNCHEZ

Fidel Sánchez Hernández lacked the popularity of Julio Rivera, but he attempted to carry on the policies and programs of his predecessor, and El Salvador's development progress continued. A major effort in 1967 and 1968 involved the development of a new urban plan for the metropolitan region of San Salvador, which included the capital city itself and some twenty adjacent *municipios*. The work, done jointly by Salvadorean planners and contracted consultants from the United States, attempted to achieve an organizational structure as well as a plan that would assure the future interrelation of physical and economic development of the urban area. Financial assistance for the project was provided by the United States Agency for International Development, as was also the case with a very substantial program to develop an effective educational television system for technical education.

THE HONDURAN-SALVADOREAN 'WAR'

For a number of years a sizable migration of Salvadoreans into Honduras had been under way. Some went to engage in agriculture where land was more readily available; others became merchants; a few found jobs in Honduran factories. As the Salvadorean population mounted to about a quarter of a million, many Hondurans became alarmed. Frequently better educated and sometimes more industrious, the newcomers threatened to displace the local residents in their own country. Feelings became bitter on occasion. Such a situation occurred in June, 1969, when competition became so intense over a series of soccer matches that a final play-off was held in Mexico City to avoid the hazard of rioting and violence among local *aficionados*. The Salvadoreans were victorious, and some Hondurans vented their disappointment by attacks on Salvadorean residents of their country, with resulting damage to both persons and property.

Tensions mounted rapidly and charges and counter-charges were hurled back and forth between the two countries. On July 14, El Salvador launched an invasion of southern and western Honduras, presumably to teach its neighbor a lesson in sportsmanship. The invasion was not carried very far before bitter fighting occurred and heavy losses were inflicted by both combatants. Hondurans fled from border towns while long lines of Salvadoreans, fearing more and more reprisals, headed back into their own country. Meantime, the Organization of American States hastened to send peacekeepers into the area to stop the fighting and restore normal relationships. A peace was finally arranged and President Sánchez agreed to withdraw his troops from the Honduran territory they had occupied, but only after his government had been branded an aggressor and economic sanctions had been threatened. The entire affair was extremely unfortunate and served little purpose other than to rekindle the fires of excessive nationalism on both sides. Observers and peace-keeping teams from the Organization of American States reported few instances of actual mistreatment of each other's resident nationals by the neighboring countries. In the end the greatest sufferers were inhabitants of Honduran border towns caught in the fighting and the miserable Salvadorean refugees displaced from their Honduran homes.

Many people bemoaned the death of the Central American Common Market the moment Sánchez' army entered Honduras. It was already in dire trouble by reason of the Costa Rican national assembly's refusal to ratify a 1968 agreement increasing duties on imports from outside the area by 30 per cent and Nicaragua's retaliatory gesture imposing sizable duties on all Central American products entering the country. Now Honduras closed its portion of the Central American highway, thus cutting the truck route between El Salvador and Nicaragua. At the end of 1969 the road was still closed and prospects for reuniting the five republics in common economic and political endeavors appeared dim. A special meeting called by President Somoza in Managua looked for a way to restore harmony.

HONDURAN PROGRESS

By 1960 Honduras, under the presidency of Dr. Ramón Villeda Morales, seemed to be making definite progress toward a more vigorous and democratic political life. The Tegucigalpa doctor's Liberal party was seeking to build a broad popular base, and the country was governed in an atmosphere of free expression with civil liberties fully maintained. Economic progress was slow, but the new Common Market held out prospects for more rapid improvement.

A new presidential election was scheduled for 1963, but it was never held. Just before the appointed day Colonel Osvaldo López Arellano and a group of fellow officers seized the government and forced Villeda Morales into exile. Sixteen months later a hand-picked constituent assembly made López Arellano a general and voted him into the presidency for a six-year term. In 1970 he still held firm control of the government, his prestige enhanced by the outcome of the clash with El Salvador. It remained to be seen whether he would step aside when his term expired in 1971.

The policies of López Arellano have been far from progressive. His has been the rule of a traditionalist military officer who seeks to preserve the status quo, uphold the privileges of the officer corps, protect the landholders, and perpetuate himself and his friends in power. The reformist and liberalizing measures of Villeda Morales remain on the books, but they have been conveniently forgotten. Meanwhile, most of the country languishes in poverty and ignorance.

Honduras has experienced significant but localized economic growth despite the heavy-handed and administratively incompetent government. By the late 1960's San Pedro Sula had become something of a boom town, with a host of new industrial plants in production or under construction.

Local entrepreneurs were justly proud of their achievements and the growing prosperity of the area, situated inland from Puerto Cortés on the north coast. They only hoped that López Arellano would stay in Tegucigalpa and leave them alone.

GUATEMALA'S ENDURING UNREST

President Miguel Ydígoras Fuentes proved to be an unpopular chief executive in Guatemala despite the twists and turns he made to curry favor, first with this group and then with that. For a time he berated the United States, usually a popular gesture in Guatemala; then he welcomed stepped-up American aid under the Alliance for Progress. He expropriated large holdings of coffee lands owned by Germans, threatened to take Belize by force from the British, and engaged in other actions apparently intended to solidify nationalist feeling behind his corrupt and incompetent government. Bitterly opposed to Fidel Castro, he permitted a training base to be established on Guatemalan soil for the preparation of the Bay of Pigs invasion force. The dismal failure of that CIA-sponsored adventure did nothing to improve Ydígoras' standing or prestige at home.

The aging general managed to hang on to his office for yet another two years, but he could not maintain order. Disorders multiplied as guerrilla groups organized on both the extreme right and the extreme left of the political spectrum. In March, 1963, Dr. Juan José Arévalo returned from Mexico, where he had been residing, to campaign for the presidency, and it seemed likely that he would win. This was too much for the minister of defense, Colonel Enrique Peralta Azurdia, who in a quick *coup d'état* assumed both executive and legislative powers, expelled Ydígoras from the country, and chased Arévalo back to Mexico.

Peralta's expressed fear of communist power in Guatemala provided the basis for his arbitrary assumption of power and immediate cancellation of the impending election. If the restoration of law and order was a principal objective, however, he did not achieve it. Guerrilla activity was continuous in the countryside and sporadic in the capital. A principal tactic became the seizure of prominent and wealthy citizens and their detainment for ransom. Terror stalked throughout the country and hundreds of thousands of *quetzales* were paid into the war chests of rebel groups to procure the release of loved ones and friends. Peralta hung on to the government and gradually tightened his grip while the country was wracked with violence.

In spite of civil unrest, the Guatemalan economy showed signs of increasing prosperity. A favorable coffee market increased export income while new industrial plants were built and existing ones expanded to take advantage of the enlarged trading area provided by the Common Market. Guatemala became a significant beneficiary of regional economic integration.

RETURN TO CONSTITUTIONAL GOVERNMENT

Colonel Enrique Peralta followed the traditional pattern of political procedure after taking power by a *golpe de estado*: he called a constituent assembly into being and had the members write a new constitution to his liking, modifying the old one in only minor details, and then set a date for an election. In this case, the date was March 6, 1966. At this point, however, Peralta departed from the typical course by departing from the presidential office. He refused to become a candidate and he held an open and honest election. Nearly half a million people went to the polls in a hard-fought contest in which an early candidate was murdered and his brother took his place. The brother, Julio César Méndez Montenegro, dean of the law faculty at San Carlos University, polled over two hundred thousand votes, running well ahead of Peralta's candidate, an army colonel, and another military man supported by followers of the late Castillo Armas. Méndez Montenegro's Revolutionary party was fortunate to gain control of the legislative assembly, for the civilian law dean lacked a majority and the final choice had to be made in congress. The representatives elected Méndez by a substantial margin.

Guatemala's reign of terror was by no means eased as a result of the popular election of a president. On the contrary, the rebels intensified their efforts and stated their objective to be the overthrow of the regime and establishment of a 'people's' government. The ties to Fidel Castro and his training schools for Latin American revolutionists were clear. Guatemala had been a prime Castro target from the time Che Guevara witnessed the fall of Jacobo Arbenz and subsequently joined Fidel's band of revolutionists in Mexico. Ties with Guatemalan rebel leaders and communists were solidified and expanded.

Discouraged by the government's apparent inability to control communist revolutionary activity, Guatemalan rightists created a terrorist force of their own, *la Mano Blanca* or the White Hand. This extra-legal band arrogated to itself the task of seeking out and executing known communist and leftist leaders. Terrorism mounted, and bombings and shootings became commonplace on the streets of Guatemala City. Arson, sabotage, and pilferage were added to kidnapping and murder as tactics of the revolutionary forces. In November, Méndez Montenegro declared a state of siege, but the terror did not end. In January, 1968, two American military advisors were killed by assassins' bullets while driving through the city, and in September of the same year an attempt was made to kidnap the American ambassador, John Gordon Mein, while riding in his chauffeured automobile between his residence and his office. When Mein tried to run from his would-be captors he was gunned down in the street, the first American ambassador ever to be assassinated. The act was attributed to members of the *Fuerzas Armadas Revolucionarias,* a pro-Castro guerrilla band. This band was also responsible for kidnapping and executing the German ambassador, Count Karl von Spreti, in April, 1970. The Guatemalan government refused to release political prisoners or pay ransom money.

Despite the continued violence and disorder throughout his administration, Méndez Montenegro finished his term as president and turned over the government to an elected successor, a relatively rare event in Guatemalan history. On March 1, 1970, the election victory went to Colonel Carlos Arana Osorio, candidate of the National Liberation Movement and a 'law and order' advocate who promised the voters an end to leftist revolutionary terrorism. Colonel Arana's record as former commander of the Zacapa Brigade, which in bloody slaughter wiped out a large rural guerrilla band and perhaps some innocent people as well between 1966 and 1968, suggested that he would make a vigorous effort to carry out his promise. Arana polled only a plurality of votes, but his lead was substantial and the legislative assembly quickly formalized his electoral victory. He took office July 1, 1970.

GUATEMALA'S INTRACTABLE PROBLEMS

Colonel Arana Osorio faced a difficult task if he attempted nothing more than the maintenance of power and suppression of revolutionary violence. His country's five million people, scattered over rugged mountains and jungle, remained exceedingly poor. More than half of them were Indians who lived apart and participated scarcely at all in the economic life of the country. Many spoke only Quiché, rather than Spanish, and remained beyond the reach of the wholly inadequate educational system. Guerrilla groups and revolutionists recruited their supporters primarily from the *ladinos,* however, the white and mixed-blood portion of the population, who resented even more bitterly than the Indians the long-standing domination of the country by a small group of wealthy landowners and militarists. Such people found themselves caught in a seemingly hopeless social and economic situation. Governments traditionally supported the oligarchy even while striking out at foreign corporate landowners, such as the United Fruit Company; and when an exception did occur, as during the administrations of Arévalo and Arbenz, power passed quickly to the communists who attracted counter-revolution and foreign intervention from the United States. No way out of this dilemma seemed possible. No one expected the new president even to look for a way.

THE CONTRAST OF COSTA RICA

Francisco Orlich was elected president of Costa Rica in 1962, his victory marking the return to power of José Figueres' National Liberation party. Enjoying a majority in the legislative assembly, Orlich was able to carry the country into the Central American Common Market and obtain ratification of the essential agreements. Costa Rica benefited from the system both in new industrialization and increased trade with her neighbors, exporting substantially more than she imported as the volume of regional trade mounted.

Costa Rica received an unfortunate economic setback in 1963 and for several years following. The most prominent of her fifty volcanoes, 11,300-foot Irazú, situated southeast of San José and just north of Cartago, started a major eruption in March of that year, throwing vast amounts of volcanic ash into the air. Clouds of smoke and ashes filled the atmosphere, and a fine gray powder settled over the countryside killing coffee, corn, and other crops wherever it fell. Cattle died from eating grass and forage covered with the ash, and milk and beef production fell sharply. The eruptions continued at intervals over the next two years, but seldom was the mountain still. The streets of the capital filled with dust, and the miserable powder filtered through windows, got into the water supply, and caused respiratory and bronchial disorders among the population. When heavy rains fell, vast mudslides did further damage. Agricultural losses mounted into the millions of dollars while costs of removing the ashes and dirt fell heavily on national and municipal budgets. Finally the eruptions stopped, but the country had suffered a major disaster.

In 1966, by a very narrow margin of votes, the conservative opposition candidate for the presidency, José Joaquín Trejos Fernández, won the election. As had President Echandi before him from 1958 to 1962, Trejos faced a legislative assembly controlled by the National Liberation party of Figueres. He talked of giving greater support to private enterprise and reducing the dominant role of the government in the economy, but his record included no major changes. The legislature dragged its feet, however, on the ratification of Common Market tariff increase agreements.

As the 1970 election rolled around, 'Don Pepe' Figueres decided to get back in the saddle himself. He campaigned all over the country, visiting virtually every town and village, and he promised more social action, new reforms of the economic system, and more meaningful democracy. Costa Rica's 1,700,000 people listened, and in early February when over 500,-000 of them went to the polls, they returned Don Pepe to the presidency overwhelmingly. He led all opposition combined by over 70,000 votes. He also got a clear majority of 32 seats in the 57-man national assembly. He should experience little difficulty getting his reform program approved.

Once again Costa Rica had proved her adherence to democratic processes and political stability. In all of Central America—indeed in all of Latin America—no other country entered the decade of the 1970's with a firmer base of orderly government and a stronger determination to achieve social and economic progress for all of its people. Don Pepe was 64 years of age, but he insisted his ideas were as young and vigorous as ever.

Panama's Perpetual Plight

The decade of the 1960's proved a most difficult period for Panama. It was a period of repeated confrontations with the United States over the status of the canal and the Canal Zone. It was also a period in which the government of the republic responded to a rapidly intensifying nationalism that limited its range of flexibility and made compromise and accommodation all but impossible. Yet it was also a period in which there loomed new possibilities for an inter-oceanic waterway whose location held the potential for further developing the nation or for destroying it utterly. The decade closed with these issues still unresolved and with little prospect that they would soon be decided.

Egypt's nationalization of the Suez Canal in 1956 immediately suggested the possibility of a similar action to Panamanian leaders, but the realities of the two situations were very different. A major world power, the United States, was physically present in Panama with armed might and no other power was willing or prepared to challenge that presence. Furthermore, the United States and the Soviet Union had demonstrated their unwillingness in 1956 to see Egypt's action reversed by forceful intervention, but in her own immediate sphere of influence the American government applied quite different standards of international propriety. In addition, the cold reality was that the Panamanians lacked the strength even to seize the canal, much less make a seizure stand up during the international fireworks certain to follow any such action.

The attractiveness of nationalization faded after 1967 when the Suez Canal was indefinitely closed as a result of the Egyptian-Israeli War. Other Latin American nations, particularly those on the west coast of South America whose international trade passed through the Panama Canal in overwhelming quantities, were unlikely to support any move that might interrupt unhindered access and passage. Panama also had to consider the growing obsolescence of a waterway too narrow to accommodate many of the world's newer vessels. Her long-run interest seemed to lie in playing ball with the United States, getting a new canal constructed and getting it constructed in Panama. How difficult such a course would be was clearly demonstrated by the events of 1964.

THE FLAG CRISIS AND ITS AFTERMATH

The 1960 Panamanian election brought to the presidency Roberto F. Chiari, a member of the country's small oligarchy and a strong nationalist. Throughout his term of office the canal issue seemed uppermost in his mind, and he made some progress toward obtaining for Panama a more favorable treatment from the United States. A state visit to Washington in 1962 produced an agreement to fly the Panamanian flag at certain points within Zone and to apply withholding provisions of the Panamanian income tax law to persons other than United States citizens working in the Zone. Efforts to obtain a larger share of the canal toll revenues were in vain, however. The payment to Panama remained at $1,930,000 annually in accordance with an agreement negotiated by President José Antonio Remón in 1955.

Then in January, 1964, a ridiculous and costly riot occurred. The problem started when American and Panamanian high school students got into a tussle over which flag was to fly over Balboa High School, an institution located within the Canal Zone. Panamanian street crowds entered the battle and American troops were called to eject rioters from the Zone. Vicious encounters followed and American soldiers fired from within the Zone into the mob outside, causing a number of deaths and many injuries. The rioting mounted in intensity and mobs rushed through the streets of Panama City looting and burning American stores and business offices. After three days of violence and terror the crowds subsided and the destruction stopped. Hundreds were injured, several American soldiers were dead and more than a score of Panamanians had been killed.

The Panamanian government was outraged. It broke diplomatic relations with the United States and appealed to the United Nations and the Organization of American States. There followed a series of investigations by American and international authorities, but the results were of little value. Some blame was attributed to all parties, a perfectly obvious assessment of what had occurred. The basic problems still remained.

Panama faced a new presidential election in May. Although diplomatic relations with the United States were resumed in April, the election campaign was fought out almost exclusively on the canal issue, each candidate seeking to demonstrate his uncompromising stance and his determination to bring about a complete renegotiation of the canal treaty. Washington, refusing to respond to pressure, insisted that it would not negotiate. Marcus A. Robles won the election by obtaining a plurality of the votes. Although more moderate than his principal opponent, Arnulfo Arias, Robles had the support of Chiari and a coalition of more than a half-dozen so-called political parties. He was determined to secure a new and more favorable canal agreement with the United States.

THE LOST CAUSE: A TREATY THAT COULD NOT BE RATIFIED

Late in 1964 President Johnson indicated willingness to negotiate a new treaty with Panama. In part the decision was less a response to Panamanian demands than it was a recognition of the need to prepare the legal basis for construction of a new canal. Washington made clear its intention to include in any new agreement provision for another canal route, probably a sea-level route. There followed two and a half years of negotiations and discussions, perhaps drawn out deliberately to allow tempers to cool and the bitter events of 1964 to be forgotten. Finally, in June of 1967, it was announced that President Robles and President Johnson had reached agreement upon a new treaty. Negotiations had been conducted in secret, and now the treaty itself remained a secret, although the principal features of the agreement gradually became known. Actually, three separate but related treaties were involved, the first providing for joint administration of the existing canal, abolition of the Zone, and recognition of Panamanian sovereignty over the territory. The second provided for a new canal to be constructed on Panamanian territory and the third was an agreement providing for American defense of both canals.

As major terms of agreement became known, cries of anguish arose both in Washington and Panama City. American jingoists insisted that Johnson was about to give away the 'American canal'; at the same time Panamanian supernationalists charged Robles with having been 'duped' by the United States and of having 'sold out' to the 'Gringo'. A new election was coming up in both countries, first in Panama in the spring of 1968 and then in the United States in the fall. Submission of the proposed treaties to the United States Senate and to the Panamanian congress was delayed. Many doubted that either legislative body would ratify them, and there was some reason to fear that the very discussion of the agreements might precipitate further violence in Panama.

In May of 1968 Arnulfo Arias pulled a surprising upset in the Panamanian presidential election. Immediately after taking office he began reorganization of the *Guardia Nacional,* the country's quite professionalized military defense force. He accepted the resignation of its commander, Bolívar Vallarino, and attempted to move his own personal supporters into key positions. The consequences were dramatic. Within eleven days after his inauguration Arias found himself exiled to the Canal Zone without any country to govern; a military junta was in command in Panama City. Arias fled to the United States, the country he had so long and loudly denounced, where he was able temporarily to take over the Panamanian embassy while he pleaded for assistance from the Organization of American States to put him back in office. Needless to say, his efforts were futile.

GENERAL OMAR TORRIJOS

The military leaders who ousted Arias quickly tightened their grip on the government and gave every indication of an intention to stay awhile. The junta was headed by Colonel José Pinilla, who was supported by Colonel Bolívar Urrutia, Colonel Boris Martínez, and Colonel Omar Torrijos. Public statements by junta members hinted at possible social reforms and even at redistribution of landed estates to campesinos. More alarming to Panama's wealthy families, however, was a rigorous clamp-down on corruption in high places. Scores of people were jailed on charges of graft and misuse of public trust. Press and radio censorship was imposed, and particularly strong measures were taken against papers favorable to the deposed Arias. As time passed, the strong men of the junta were revealed to be Colonel Torrijos and Colonel Boris Martínez, both of whom were alleged by the conservative oligarchy to be left-wing sympathizers if not outright communists. The American aid program ground to a halt until the complexion of the new regime could be ascertained. Little evidence of pink was to be seen, however.

Early in 1969 a shake-up occurred and several key officers were packed off to the United States to occupy positions as Panama's representatives on the Inter-American Defense Board, a pleasant form of exile. Included among them was Colonel Boris Martínez, considered by many to be the most reform-minded member of the ruling military group. Colonel Omar Torrijos, thirty-nine years old, tough, and popular with the common people of Panama, moved clearly into the top role. He was even promoted to brigadier general.

Torrijos was firmly in control of Panama in 1970. An abortive attempt to seize the government was made in early January while the general was absent from the capital, but supporters almost literally carried him back into power on their shoulders. His popularity with the common people was thus firmly established. Perhaps he even had sufficient support to take up with the United States once again the ticklish question of a new canal treaty. Already, however, other plans were in the wind. A British-German-Italian combine had plans to construct an oil pipeline across the isthmus for the Panamanian government. Such a pipeline would greatly reduce the need for a new canal inasmuch as large tankers were among the principal vessels that found the present canal too small. With the problem of oil transport solved by a pipeline, the cost-benefit factors involved in excavating a new canal would be considerably altered. There was just a faint possibility that Panama's bargaining position with the United States was improving, and the country might free itself from utter economic dependence upon the existing canal. In any event, the treaties negotiated during the administrations of Robles and Johnson no longer seemed relevant. Neither country saw much to be gained by pressing for their ratification.

The New Dominican Intervention

The miserable dictatorship of Rafael Leonidas Trujillo Molina came to an end in the Dominican Republic May 30, 1961. All the efforts of Louisiana's Senator Ellender to buttress the failing regime of the 69-year-old despot failed to protect him from the wrath of his fellow countrymen. His enemies shot him down on the highway and riddled his body with bullets. Although no proof is available, some evidence suggests that the weapons were provided by the same interests who armed the refugee force that had tried to recover Cuba from Castro a few weeks before at the Bay of Pigs.

Trujillo's departure from the Dominican scene was not unexpected in neighboring countries of the Caribbean. The dictator's nearly successful attempt to have his agents assassinate President Betancourt of Venezuela had brought him official condemnation by the Organization of American States in August of 1960, and most states of Latin America as well as the United States had severed diplomatic relations with his government by the end of the year. Economic sanctions against the regime were being applied early in 1961, but efforts to block the Dominican sugar quota by the Eisenhower administration were frustrated in the Senate by Trujillo's Louisiana friends, particularly Senator Ellender. Trujillo's position was fast crumbling under external pressures, nonetheless.

Within the country, however, the great 'Benefactor' seemed more secure, and his sudden death left the people of the republic in a state of shock. Indeed, so paralyzed were they that no immediate moves were made to unseat the puppet government of Joaquin Balaguer, who was serving as Trujillo's hand-picked president. The dictator's clan quickly gathered: his brothers, his son from Paris, and family supporters whose fortunes and sinecures were suddenly threatened by the abrupt departure of the individual whose personal fortune included most of the proceeds of the Dominican

Republic's agriculture, industry, and commerce, as well as the public treasury. Was the international playboy, Rafael Trujillo, Jr., or 'Ramfis' as he was popularly known, capable of taking his father's position as the Somoza sons had done in Nicaragua? For a time, at least, it seemed that he would try. He took over the armed forces and tried to hunt down his father's killers.

JUAN BOSCH TO THE PRESIDENCY

Gradually the Dominican terror subsided as it became clear that Trujillo's heirs in control of the government had neither the will nor the stomach for carrying on the dead man's iron-fisted rule. President Balaguer took a moderate position pointing to a return to democratic government. The economic sanctions and international pressure continued as foreign governments watched and waited. Finally the Trujillo family got the message that their days were numbered and they sought a more healthful climate elsewhere. Ramfis suddenly remembered that Paris was a far more interesting city than Ciudad Trujillo—certainly not an astounding discovery. Besides, he and other members of the family had adequately supplied themselves with funds in foreign banks. Why should they hang around and risk the fate of the great Benefactor? By the end of the year they were gone.

President Balaguer's position likewise deteriorated, and he turned the government over to a Council of State which he chaired briefly and from which he then resigned. Tension mounted, strikes and rioting became widespread and frequent, and plots and counter-plots threatened the country with chaos. At a mounting tempo all reminders of the Trujillo regime were removed or destroyed, and these included an enormous number of statues, pictures, and plaques. The name of Ciudad Trujillo was changed back to the time-honored Santo Domingo. Finally, after the human carry-overs of the Trujillo era were gone, the other nations of the hemisphere lifted their sanctions and normal diplomatic and commercial relations were restored.

In December of 1962, just before Christmas, a democratic election was held. The popular Dominican intellectual leader Juan Bosch was elected president by a very substantial majority. Bosch had been living in exile for years, much of the time in Puerto Rico from which near-by island he had kept in close contact with affairs in his home country. He knew its sad plight. He hoped to build a responsible democratic system to replace the years of dictatorship and despotism.

The government of Juan Bosch lasted only seven months. The difficulties it faced were insuperable. After thirty years as the personal fief of Trujillo, the Dominican Republic lacked most of the ingredients necessary to self-government, to say nothing of democratic self-government. Treated as serfs on the estates of their master, the ordinary people were largely illiterate, ignorant, untraveled, and unorganized. They had had no experience in political participation, no useful experience even in labor movement activity. Nearly half of them were unemployed and many of the remainder were underemployed. Apart from a small oligarchy of landowners and businessmen whose fawning attachment to the great Benefactor had enabled them to keep or amass their property, there was no class or group capable of managing the affairs of government. The bureaucracy and the armed forces consisted largely of incompetent hangers-on to the Trujillo coattails. Years had gone by during which other countries sent their promising young people abroad for education and training in health, agriculture, business, pedagogy, engineering, and public administration. Trujillo had provided no such opportunities for Dominican youth nor did he permit them to avail themselves of opportunities offered by other governments or international organizations. He kept them at home where they were unlikely to become 'contaminated' with dangerous ideas. Bosch had a following who loved him and supported him, but they were largely incapable of assisting him in carrying out his programs of reform and development.

The small oligarchy of landowners, businessmen, military officers, and conservative clergy feared and hated Bosch, for he posed a threat to the way of life they had learned to enjoy under the man who to them had been a benefactor. They sought to undermine Bosch even before he took office. They accused him of communist leanings, of appointing 'unreliable' cabinet ministers, and of being hopelessly incompetent. In September of 1963 they overthrew him, sent home his congress, dropped his constitution in the wastebasket, and packed him off to Puerto Rico.

The military clique that took over from Bosch did even less well than he had done. Bosch had no doubt been naïve in his assumption that a country with no experience in democratic government could overnight acquire that experience and make it applicable. The freedoms and liberty he permitted were used precisely to subvert his authority and overthrow the democratic regime he had established. The new government returned to the corrupt, self-seeking ways of the Trujillo era, but it lacked the determined will and firm hand of the Benefactor. The economy deteriorated, smuggling became rampant, and the government faced bankruptcy.

Dismayed by the chaotic conditions prevailing throughout the republic, political groups that had backed Bosch formed a compact on January 30, 1965, to restore constitutional government and bring the ousted president back from San Juan. The military were undecided which way to turn. Some officers, predominantly the younger ones, decided to support the restoration movement; others chose to oppose it. Fighting broke out in April between the opposing groups, and Bosch's supporters seemed quickly to be gaining the upper hand in the capital.

The opponents of Bosch regrouped, however, formed a new government headed by a Colonel Elías Wessin y Wessin, who commanded the San Isidro air base, and quickly counter-attacked with most of the heavier military equipment at their disposal. Wessin y Wessin promoted himself to the rank of general, announced that his group constituted the 'loyalists,' and directed an effort to throw the 'rebels' out of the city. In this strange and confused situation, the so-called rebels were actually the group loyal to Bosch and bent on restoration of constitutional government, whereas the self-proclaimed loyalists were the heirs of the rebels who overthrew the legally established government in 1963.

UNITED STATES INTERVENTION

So much heat and acrimony developed over the unhappy events of 1965 in the Dominican Republic that politicians, government leaders around the hemisphere, and historians have been arguing over them ever since. Clearly the near-by presence of Fidel Castro and his communist regime in Cuba caused some American officials in key positions, such as Ambassador William Tapley Bennett, Jr., to see a Castro agent in almost every 'rebel' face. When the battle began on April 24, 1965, with seizure by the restoration forces of two army posts and the radio station in Santo Domingo, many American officials, including the ambassador, were absent from the island. Washington's initial reaction was to suggest approval of the restoration movement. However, reports soon came flowing in from the ambassador and other embassy officials after their return to Santo Domingo expressing grave fear that the 'rebel' forces were strongly motivated by pro-Castro sentiments and that American support should be thrown behind the 'loyalist' group of Wessin y Wessin. By April 28 the panic-stricken Bennett, faced with continued fighting between the two Dominican military forces, pleaded for the landing of United States marines not only to protect American lives and property but to make certain that a 'Castro-type solution' to the Dominican crisis did not eventuate.

Almost immediately American forces began landing and they quickly took up positions that drove a wedge between the Dominican combatants. Fighting had been vicious and bloody, and it did not end immediately upon landing of the intervention army. As the number of American troops mounted, however, the fighting was brought under control. Some 22,000 Americans participated in the occupation force. A number of units saw armed combat in moves clearly designed to defend the 'loyalists' and prevent a 'rebel' victory. Positions of the opposing forces then became stabilized and an uneasy and often violated truce settled over the city while the future of the republic was debated both in Santo Domingo and in Washington.

American military forces landed in the Dominican Republic without prior consultation with other member nations of the Organization of American States, although they were informed of what was taking place and the reasons for it. Such unilateral intervention violated basic inter-American defense agreements as well as long-standing policy. Washington hastened to 'legalize' its action ex post facto by persuading the members of the regional organization to create an Inter-American Peace Force that would take over at least nominal responsibility for the intervention action. A favorable vote was obtained on May 5, and within weeks military units from Brazil, Costa Rica, Nicaragua, and Honduras arrived to replace at least a portion of the American 'peace-keeping' force. A Brazilian general was placed in charge, and eventually troops from his country numbered over a thousand men. Meanwhile, the secretary general of the Organization of American States, Dr. José A. Mora, had virtually taken up residence in the Dominican Republic to see to his responsibilities on a day-to-day basis.

THE IMPOSED SOLUTION

Even as American military forces poured into the island, American officials sought to find a suitable Dominican leader to head the 'loyalist' government. Wessin y Wessin was discovered to be highly unpopular, and another military man, Colonel Pedro Benoit, was named head of the junta.

His popularity was even less than Wessin's, and Wessin was still calling the shots from behind the facade of the junta in any case. So widespread was the popular opposition to the 'loyalist' leaders that the American king-makers looked further. Who indeed should be more popular than a man who participated in the murder of Trujillo? General Antonio Imbert Barreras was picked to become head of a new junta. The 44-year-old 'hero' assassin was quickly sworn into office as a staunch anti-communist around whom the Dominican people would surely rally. They did not. Imbert was viewed as just one more crooked military opportunist eager to assume the role of the deceased Benefactor. Presidential envoys and factfinders from the United States came and went, and some were distinguished advisors and associates of Johnson, such as McGeorge Bundy, Jack Vaughn, Thomas Mann, and Cyrus Vance. Their efforts to find a new Dominican leader acceptable to all parties were quite unsuccessful, however. The impasse continued, interrupted from time to time by bloody skirmishes.

COLONEL FRANCISCO CAAMAÑO DEÑÓ

Leader of the 'rebel' constitutionalist forces from the outset was Colonel Francisco Caamaño Deñó, a 32-year-old officer of the Dominican army. American journalists quickly converted him into a 'murky' villain of unsavory background. His character was questioned because his father had been a Trujillo general and one-time commander of the secret police. He was labeled 'truculent' and 'opportunistic' in contrast to the clean-living, impeccable patriot-assassin Imbert. American officials contributed to establishing Caamaño's image by pointing out the possibility of his becoming a Dominican Fidel Castro.

There can be little question that from the outset American representatives on the scene opposed Caamaño's constitutionalist movement, and when American troops landed, their actions tended to protect the 'loyalist' units from defeat, gave them time to regroup, and supplied them with the equipment and moral support necessary to turn the tide against the 'rebels.' Their presence then served to provide a corridor protecting the Caamaño army, defeated and demoralized, from complete slaughter at the hands of Imbert. Frustrated and angry, Caamaño and his supporters condemned the landing of American marines, and his soldiers from time to time engaged American units in combat and sniped at them from protected positions. The 'rebel' leader likewise showed little enthusiasm either for surrender of his forces to American-selected 'puppets' or for rallying around compromise leaders whose principal attribute was a willingness to accept American guidance and uphold the nation's oligarchic system. Caamaño was no knight in shining armor or paragon of constitutionalist virtue. His escutcheon was no more tarnished, however, than that of Imbert, Wessin y Wessin, and Benoit. One of his greatest mistakes was to identify himself and his followers with Santo Domingo's urban poor people rather than the landed oligarchy.

THE GOVERNMENT OF HÉCTOR GARCÍA-GODOY

As the occupation continued, international opinion began to shift. General Imbert soon proved himself to be bloodthirsty and vindictive, quite willing to use his powerful position for personal revenge against his enemies. The American government had put him in office and financed him, but the wisdom of this action began to be questioned. He seemed determined to wipe out Caamaño and all of his supporters in a 'fight to the death.' Only the continued presence of the Inter-American military forces prevented him from attacking the central part of the city where the 'rebel' forces continued in control.

Also as the weeks went by the Caamaño forces looked less and less like the vanguard of a new Castroite movement, in spite of their bitter expressions of resentment toward the American occupation troops. Organization of American States' representatives from other parts of the hemisphere found it much easier to establish a dialogue with the 'rebels' than had American negotiators. Finally, at the end of August, a compromise leader was found. He was Héctor García-Godoy, an associate of Juan Bosch and foreign minister in his cabinet. Caamaño Deñó accepted the suggestion with little delay, but Imbert had by now become the difficult and truculent one, and he rejected the idea out of hand. He and his supporters—the fickle American press now referred to them as 'cronies'—required persuasion. The persuasion was simple. The Americans simply refused Imbert any more money and he resigned. García-Godoy was installed in the presidency on September 3, 1965.

Leaders of the principal military factions on both sides of the Dominican controversy were soon living abroad, most with diplomatic appointments that kept them far removed from the highly charged atmosphere of the national capital. Gradually calm returned, speeded by massive inputs of American financial support and technical assistance. Crucial to maintenance of the peace, however, was departure of virtually all military leaders from the island. Not one of them on either the 'loyalist' or the 'rebel' side could be trusted to abide by the truce and give civilian government a chance.

THE ELECTION OF 1966

García-Godoy proved himself an able and moderate interim ruler. His most difficult task was persuading all the military politicians to leave, but he had strong assistance from the Inter-American Peace Force and by early spring of 1966 the principal troublemakers were happily in exile. An election was called for June 1 to select a new president and restore constitutional government.

Although three candidates entered the electoral contest, only two of them really had a chance. The favorite was Juan Bosch, returned from Puerto Rican exile now that the fighting was over. The other was former President Joaquín Balaguer, chief executive at the time of Trujillo's assassination. Bosch disappointed his followers badly by conducting a weak campaign. Apparently fearing an attempt upon his life, he did not get out around the island but remained at home in Santo Domingo. His seclusion and failure to carry his program to the people even in the capital seemed cowardly to many people. Some began to ask themselves and each other why Bosch had remained holed up in San Juan during the bitter days of 1965 when the 'rebel' constitutionalist forces so needed his support. Furthermore, his public statements did not inspire confidence; they seemed erratic and even foolish.

Balaguer campaigned like the professional politician he had become, appearing everywhere and talking to everyone. His efforts paid off handsomely. The Dominican voters went to the polls and gave him 769,000 votes to 525,000 for Bosch. A month later Balaguer assumed office. Constitutional government had been restored and the Inter-American Peace Force withdrew, thus ending the occupation. The new president settled down to the difficult task of getting the country moving again on the path to progress.

Balaguer served out a full four years in office. Throughout his term he was repeatedly troubled by threats of subversive movements on the right and on the left. In spite of the absence of the old military leaders on diplomatic assignment in such attractive posts as London and Washington, the military still at home continued to pose a threat. The president had to coddle them to keep them quiescent by providing pay, equipment, and timely promotions. Leftist groups caused him much less difficulty, for they were badly split and lacked able leadership. Balaguer strode firmly down the middle of the road, and he made remarkable progress.

A bachelor who lived with his widowed mother, Balaguer devoted all his energies to governing his country. Provided with massive assistance from the United States Agency for International Development, he attacked such long-standing problems as lagging agricultural production, an extremely deficient educational system, little industry, and very high unemployment ranging over 20 per cent of the working-age manpower. He also sought through a variety of contracts to carry on a program that Bosch had already begun: the modernization of the country's public administration. Another step taken by the government had as its purpose the building up of strong institutions of municipal self-government throughout the nation, including the fostering of a municipal association. The favorable results of all these efforts became increasingly evident as new capital entered the Dominican Republic, the construction industry boomed, and a sense of patriotic dedication gripped the people for the first time in over thirty-five years. In May of 1968, municipal elections were held, and the vote was a tremendous demonstration of confidence in Balaguer's administration. His *Reformista* party won nearly 90 per cent of 77 mayorality and 488 city council posts that were contested. Observers considered the election to be an honest and fair one. Particularly significant was the clear indication of Balaguer's widespread support throughout the country as opposed to the capital, where his party was weaker.

President Balaguer did not develop any elaborate governmental apparatus. His rule remained a personal one in which he himself made most of the important decisions and many that were not so important. He worked as the country's first servant and not its master, however. Civil liberties were reasonably secure, but he did not allow such blatant troublemakers as

General Wessin y Wessin to return; and Juan Bosch, no longer content to live in the United States, which he had grown to hate, made occasional pronouncements from Spain. No one paid much attention to him or to his comments. His political power in the Dominican Republic seemed ended.

A SECOND TERM FOR BALAGUER

In April, 1970, Joaquín Balaguer announced his intention to seek a second term as president, legally possible under an amended constitution. An immediate hue and cry was raised by opponents on all sides. Politicians desiring a chance at the presidency themselves denounced *continuismo* and compared Balaguer to Trujillo, although there had been little resemblance between the two men or their governments. A heated campaign followed, and the republic's four million people once more were provided the spectacle of democratic processes at work. Balaguer won easily against four opponents, gaining more than 60 per cent of the vote on May 16. No other Dominican possessed the stature, the experience, or the dedication that Balaguer had demonstrated. Whether he would be able to keep the military in check for another four years was a serious question to ponder, however. He would need all the skill he possessed.

New Nations in the Caribbean

Several new nations appeared in the Caribbean area during the 1960's. These were former colonies of Great Britain, and continued ties with the parent country varied among the offspring. For the most part, the remaining ties were economic in character and enabled the new nations, as members of the British Commonwealth, to sell certain of their products in the United Kingdom at preferential prices. Jamaica and Trinidad were granted independence in 1962, and Guyana, on the northeast coast of South America, was granted similar status on May 26, 1966. Barbados achieved it a few months later in November, 1966. The attempt to develop a single West Indian Federation comprising the British insular possessions in the region, begun in 1958, collapsed totally in 1962, but it was dead when Jamaica indicated her intention to secede in 1961. As independent nations, Jamaica, Trinidad, and Barbados applied for membership in the Organization of American states, and it was granted them.

The remaining British possessions, islands of the Leeward and Windward groups, achieved a kind of associated status with Great Britain which was short of complete independence and yet provided a large measure of self-government. For the most part, the so-called associated states—Antigua, Montserrat, St. Kitts-Nevis-Anguilla, Dominica, St. Lucia, St. Vincent, and Grenada—lacked the economic resources to go their own, independent ways, yet a viable federation seemed always to elude them. In 1968 a Caribbean Free Trade Association was formed among the former British possessions and associated states, and tariffs among the members were to be eliminated on a prepared list of commodities over five and ten-year periods. Great Britain continued to constitute the principal market for most of the states, however, purchasing their sugar and bananas. Jamaica, nevertheless, had become the world's largest producer of bauxite, with most of the ore and alumina going to the United States, Canada, and Norway.

JAMAICA

The political life of Jamaica had for years been dominated by the striking, white-haired patriot, Sir Alexander Bustamante. The old statesman, respected wherever he was known, fought for self-government for decades. As prime minister he led his country to independence in 1962 and continued to preside over its fortunes for another five years. By 1967, however, the 83-year-old Bustamante was tired, ill, and nearly blind. In January he submitted his resignation and called for general elections. Six weeks later the Jamaican Labor party, which he had founded, won a strong parliamentary majority, but the People's National party, headed by Norman Manley, polled nearly as large a popular vote. The Labor party's victory gave the prime ministry to Bustamante's long-time associate and deputy, Donald Burns Sangster, a 55-year-old bachelor and financial expert.

Unfortunately, Sangster was struck down by a sudden illness only weeks after the election and died on April 18, a few days after having been knighted by Queen Elizabeth II. Hugh Shearer succeeded him in the prime ministry. These changes effected without incident reflected the relatively stable Jamaican political situation; parliamentary democracy with a strong two-party system seemed well established.

Jamaica's industrial growth over the past two decades has been substantial, particularly with the development of the bauxite and related refining industries. In addition, the small island nation has become an increasingly important tourist center, attracting visitors mostly from the United States. The country's two million people face a growing problem of unemployment as their numbers increase far faster than new jobs are created. Most Jamaicans are still employed in agriculture, and sugar remains the principal export crop. Industrial expansion has been retarded in some degree by efforts to delay mechanization that would reduce the number of available jobs. In 1969 the Aluminum Company of America announced plans to construct a new $120 million plant to convert bauxite into alumina, and new positions would be provided in the construction as well as operation of the plant. Jamaica was using up her bauxite reserves at the rate of 10 million tons a year, and new mines would speed up that rate considerably.

TRINIDAD AND TOBAGO

By far the most prosperous of the Caribbean region's new nations was Trinidad and Tobago. Boasting a gross domestic product of over $650 per capita, the new country seemed better off than any other island unit in the area except Puerto Rico. Unlike Jamaica, whose population is almost entirely black except for a few whites and people of mixed race, Trinidad and Tobago was the home of a large number of East Indians, that is, persons whose parents or more distant ancestors came from India. This group constituted some 35 per cent of the nation's 1,100,000 citizens. About 3 per cent were white and just under 50 per cent were black. About 15 per cent of the population was of mixed racial origin.

Trinidad and Tobago owed her relative prosperity to the same basic resource that was enriching her near-by neighbor, Venezuela: oil. A well-developed and diversified agriculture also helped, as the country produced large quantities of sugar, cacao, and coconuts. In addition, a relatively rapid industrialization had added greatly to the nation's total economic output. On the other hand, rapid population growth seriously threatened to outrun increased productivity of agricultural and industrial programs and contributed to a high rate of unemployment. The country hoped to speed its economic development by full participation in the inter-American system, drawing upon such credit resources as the Inter-American Development Bank.

Trinidad's political development was similar to that of Jamaica in that it was characterized by parliamentary government in support of which two major political parties predominated, the People's National Movement and the Democratic Labour party. Dr. Eric Williams, very able graduate of Oxford University, led the People's National Movement in its first victories in the 1950's, and he became prime minister of the new nation upon its independence in August, 1962. His leadership was again demonstrated when in the autumn of 1966 his party scored another major victory in a national election. Sharp-tongued and incisive, Dr. Williams seemed destined to play an increasingly significant role in inter-American as well as Caribbean affairs. In late April and early May of 1970, however, he faced a dangerous crisis at home as black militants rioted and a portion of his small army staged a brief mutiny. The 58-year-old prime minister understood well the task confronting him. He must at all costs prevent racial tensions, hitherto almost non-existent in Trinidad, from developing into the disruptive force that for so long had troubled his near neighbor, Guyana.

GUYANA

Racial antagonism and extremist politics in British Guiana long delayed the granting of independence to that unfortunate colony. The country's population of half a million is divided almost equally between blacks and East Indians, with the latter increasing at a faster rate. The majority of the East Indians have supported the demagogic Dr. Cheddi Jagan and his People's Progressive party. Forbes Burnham, a prominent black lawyer from Georgetown, worked with Jagan in the party for a number of years and helped give it control of the legislature. When he split with Jagan, however, Burnham took his black following with him and from that point onward the political life of the colony became polarized along racial lines. In the early 1960's violence flared frequently. During one riot in 1963 much of Georgetown's business district was burned to the ground. Long strikes produced repeated economic crises, and struggles among competing labor unions added to the chaos. In 1964 troops had to be flown in from Britain as violence wracked the countryside; hundreds of persons were injured and many killed.

Hoping to break Jagan's one-party rule, which together with his rigorous tax program falling heavily on black businessmen in Georgetown were principal causes of the unrest, the British government introduced proportional representation in an election held December 7, 1964. Jagan's party obtained the most votes, but he lacked a majority and there was little possibility of any group joining him in coalition. The governor therefore asked Burnham to form a government. Burnham was able to put together a coalition of his own People's National Congress and the small United Force, led by Peter D'Aguiar, which had polled 12 per cent of the vote. Jagan was forced from office and Burnham became prime minister.

Political and economic conditions both improved under Burnham's rule. In May, 1966, British Guiana became the independent nation of Guyana. The future, however, was far from promising. Well provided by nature with mineral wealth, principally bauxite, timber, and good land for growing rice and sugar cane, Guyana seemed likely to remain poor unless racial antagonisms could be overcome. Jagan remained in the background, biding his time. A new election might well provide him victory. In the meantime, he gave up all pretense of being anything other than an avowed communist. In June of 1969 he formally enrolled his People's Progressive party in the world communist movement. Should a new election bring him back to power, there would be a second communist nation in the Western Hemisphere.

The Hazards of Social Revolution

As the Caribbean region entered the eighth decade of the twentieth century, old problems still remained and new ones loomed on every side. Social revolution threatened in several countries; racial unrest troubled others. In the entire region rapid population growth consistently undercut rapid strides in economic development. It added new laborers year after year to an already underemployed labor force in nearly every country. It placed new burdens on educational systems that nowhere met adequately the existing demands. Country after country found it necessary to import major portions of the food supply.

The Dominican Republic's civil strife had been both instructive and frightening. The same sad story could easily be repeated in Haiti. Guatemala could present a similar crisis. Wherever oligarchic rule held the masses of the population in ignorance, poverty, and economic servitude, some form of social revolution seemed inevitable. Had it become impossible for revolution to take place without involving foreign intervention? Need a revolutionary movement in a small country turn that nation into a battlefield of competing international ideologies? Those who looked at the Dominican record wondered. They also wondered if the fear of another Castro would drive the United States inevitably to support landowners, rightists, and military opportunists. To many the prospects for a liberal, leftist, but non-communist revolutionary movement seemed dim.

22

Nature's Stepchildren:
The Andean Highlands

Integration is above all a problem of Latin American politics. We must show that we are capable of making the big change away from the colonial system.*

The Andean highlands are a rugged and discouraging area. Nature has made the region difficult for human habitation, breaking it up into high mountains, steep valleys, deep canyons, and rushing mountain torrents. Lowlands are hot and humid and historically have harbored such endemic diseases as malaria and yellow fever. Modern public health measures have alleviated the disease problem, but much of the land remains basically inhospitable to human progress and development.

More difficult than living in the Andean region is the problem of developing there viable, integrated national economies and political systems. The fractured land makes communication and transportation difficult and fosters petty regionalisms that defeat efforts to achieve national integration. Colombia, Ecuador, Peru, and Bolivia have struggled against these difficulties throughout their histories. In many respects they have been treated by nature as stepchildren.

The decade of the 1960's was a time of trouble, of political unrest, acute economic difficulty, and sporadic guerrilla warfare. Each of the countries entered the 1970's in a state of uncertainty: two were under military regimes, and in the other two civil rule was tenuous. Economic growth and social development over the previous ten years had been at best erratic, and in some instances productivity had declined, markets had been lost, or political turmoil had caused the clock of progress to be turned back.

The ills of the Andean highland countries are deep-rooted, stemming in

* Carlos Lleras Restrepo

561

part from the colonial legacy as well as from the inhospitable but strikingly beautiful landscape, and from the failure of the social system to have created in the outlook of the creole landowners a sense of public responsibility. None of these peoples has ever found a symbol to which they can devote the same loyalty their ancestors once gave to the king. As a result, they have never felt compelled to abide by their constitutions or respect their presidents. Each of the countries has produced able men who recognized the need to modernize their societies, but none has been able to overcome obstacles to change such as military intervention, the power of the oligarchies, or the innate resistance to change of the masses.

In the 1960's economic nationalism—the desire that all productive enterprises and public utilities be owned by citizens rather than aliens—became a powerful force, especially in Peru and Bolivia when military regimes were in power. Economic nationalism had come earlier to other Latin American nations, so it is not surprising that it belatedly arose in the Andean countries. Ever since Mexico's expropriation of foreign oil company holdings, oil has been the major symbol of economic nationalism, and in Peru and Bolivia it was foreign oil companies that were the first targets of the nationalists.

In none of the countries is the outlook promising. In 1974 the *Frente Nacional,* designed primarily to end *la Violencia* and to accustom Colombians to the orderly changing of parties in power, will come to an end. The Frente has survived so far, and it has surmounted serious challenges. But guerrilla warfare has not been entirely eradicated, and unless the economy and the living conditions of the masses both improve substantially, there is no reason to expect the guerrilla movements to disappear. In Ecuador few people expect intermittent President José María Velasco Ibarra to finish out his term if an effort is made to oust him, and even if he is able to survive, only a major re-organization could make the government effective and financially solvent. Only a thoroughgoing revolution might be able to accomplish such a re-organization because of the entrenched vested interests that resist attempts to introduce changes. Peru and Bolivia are under military regimes that have shown a tendency toward repressiveness as well as a cavalier willingness to flirt with economic disaster in order to appeal to the spirit of nationalism.

Colombia

Colombian politics have always been the private preserve of the small, wealthy oligarchy. As in several Spanish American capitals, this elite meets and discusses politics in an exclusive social organization, in this case the Jockey Club of Bogotá. This is where political decisions have been made, for although the oligarchs are of both Liberal and Conservative persuasion, the urbane members of the Jockey Club ordinarily do not allow political differences to interfere with friendships. But Colombian political contests have occasionally generated extreme bitterness and bloody strife between groups of civilians, and after the *bogotazo* of 1948 compromise between the traditional parties vanished in the repressive measures of Laureano Gómez and the anarchy of la Violencia. Violence was introduced by the Conservatives to prevent reforms; the Liberals responded with equal violence, and the destructiveness was soon beyond control by political leaders. The Liberals, who represented the majority of voters, were kept out of office by their own malignant factionalism as well as the Conservatives' powerful ties with the church and the army.

ALBERTO LLERAS CAMARGO

Alberto Lleras Camargo, who had served ably as director-general of the OAS from 1947–54, was the chief promoter of the Frente Nacional and also its first president, 1958–62. He was a fortunate choice, for he had been out of the country when political hatreds reached their greatest intensity. He believed in constitutional government, civil liberties, and free elections; he also enjoyed the confidence of the ruling elite. Because of his moderate policies, however, he was occasionally attacked by the extremists of both the Liberal and Conservative parties.

The Frente Nacional, under which Liberals and Conservatives were to alternate in the presidency and to share equally all national offices from 1958 to 1974, contained the basic weakness of all compromises—both sides accepted it as preferable to anarchy, but few were willing to make major sacrifices for its success. Latent splits between factions within both parties soon widened and deepened.

The Colombian congress has rarely been the instrument of the president that national legislatures have been in so many of the Spanish American republics. Perhaps remembering its years of compliance and subordination under Laureano Gómez and Rojas Pinilla, it has been especially assertive under the Frente. Unfortunately for the country, the congress has been more negative than positive, more concerned with blocking action than with producing legislation designed to meet the nation's problems. But since communications and ties between constituents and congressmen are limited, the legislators have not been, until recently, much concerned over public opinion.

The executive has always played the dominant role in government, for although he is prohibited from immediate re-election, his powers are substantial. On occasion his powers have been increased by the congress giving him temporary authority to legislate by decree. This should not be misconstrued as a generous or selfless act on the part of the congress. It takes such action only when there is some nasty business that must be dealt with by unpopular methods, at which times the congressmen are willing to let the president take the risks. The absence of strong ties between congressmen and their constituents makes this type of dereliction of duty possible.

The Colombian government is unitary and highly centralized. The president appoints the governors of the departments, and the governors appoint the mayors and other local officials. Local government is weak, with the result that laws cannot be effectively enforced, so smuggling, tax evasion, and similar illegal activities are carried on almost openly. The Violencia in the rural districts and the bombings in the cities and kidnapping of public figures during 1963–65 were reflections of the ineffectiveness of governmental authority. These kidnappings were embarrassing to the government for it seemed unable to bring law-breakers to justice. There were also a number of 'independent republics,' districts that were so firmly held by guerrilla bands that government officials dared not enter them. The frequent need to declare a state of siege simply reminded Colombians that their government was pathetically weak. People expected little from it in the way of services such as education, hospital care, and road building.

An obstacle to governmental effectiveness and respect for governmental authority is the condition of communications. Colombia is severely divided by three ranges of the Andes, and travel other than by air is slow and difficult. People in the isolated villages and hamlets learn of national issues by means of radio broadcasts, but few of the campesinos are able to keep informed on national issues and they see no logical connection between their well-being and that of the nation. And the idea that the nation's welfare is the responsibility of every citizen is foreign to them.

COMPETITION FOR PUBLIC OFFICE

Whenever the party in power changed in the past it meant a wholesale turn-over of civil servants. This spoils system raised serious problems; for government posts were fiercely fought over, because in a society that had a traditional contempt for manual labor and for trade, working for the government was one of the few acceptable and available ways of earning a living. It is not surprising, therefore, that men were willing to risk their lives to obtain or retain government offices. Competition for these posts has undoubtedly intensified political struggles on many occasions. The rank and file party members, well aware that their chances of preferment depend on their services to the party and especially to its leaders, subordinate their own desires. This is another factor in limiting political power to a few. As long as the executive is strong and the government is unitary, centralized, and ineffective, the spoils system will be a problem. It was partially solved temporarily by the Frente Nacional agreement to divide all government posts equally between Liberals and Conservatives. Another consequence was a fair amount of 'featherbedding'—two people employed where one was adequate. This arrangement, although greatly reducing strife over offices, will end in 1974, and presumably the bitter competition will then be revived. The division of posts has been a compromise solution, a treatment of the symptoms of the problem rather than the disease itself.

In 1960 the Liberals urged limiting the president's emergency powers because many of them had suffered from the excesses perpetrated by Laureano Gómez. Article 121 of the constitution was amended to require the president to convene congress any time he declared a state of siege. Congress is to remain in session as long as the state of siege lasts.

As the presidential election of 1962 approached, representatives of the two parties faced the task of finding among Conservative leaders a candidate acceptable to the contentious factions of his own party and to the Liberals as well. They labored under the threat of an army take-over should the Frente falter. The followers of the arch-conservative Laureano Gómez shared his obvious distaste for working with the Liberals, and their support for the Frente was often lukewarm. The Conservative most acceptable to the Liberals was Guillermo León Valencia, who was known to be a firm supporter of the Frente.

In the meantime, Conservative supporters of the Frente lost ground in the congressional elections of March, 1962. Followers of ex-dictator Rojas Pinilla formed a new group and won six seats in the chamber and two in the senate. Rojas, whom the senate had stripped of his political rights, obviously hungered for power once more, and, under the astute management of his daughter, María Eugenia Rojas de Moreno Díaz, he attempted to disrupt the Frente by appealing directly to the masses.

The presidential election in May was a crucial test for the Frente, for Liberal Alfonso López Michelsen entered the campaign despite the fact that the agreement called for a Conservative to replace Liberal Lleras Camargo. No one moved to prevent López from campaigning, even though the votes cast for him would not be counted. Rojas Pinilla also entered the contest, and the few votes cast for him were also rejected by the Electoral Court. León Valencia won 62 per cent of the total vote, giving the Frente renewed strength.

León Valencia, like Lleras Camargo, was determined to make the Frente succeed. In appearance and personality he was not a commanding figure, and he was criticized for both lack of firmness and for not fully comprehending the country's economic problems. In fairness to him, however, the coalition arrangement made compromise more appropriate than dynamic leadership. León Valencia did expand counter-guerrilla warfare, and banditry became a less romantic career when it was known that the army did not bother to take prisoners. The anti-guerrilla units destroyed or scattered most of the guerrilla bands, but they had a tendency to re-appear. At the same time the factions within the major parties and other pressure groups became more demanding and hostile toward the Frente. The popular base of the coalition declined steadily, and the number of votes cast became smaller by about half as thousands stayed away from the polls. The boycott proved embarrassing to the government, for it claimed to stand on a broad, popular foundation, a claim that the elections seemed to deny.

Challenges to the Frente continued. In the congressional elections of March, 1964, the main factions of the Conservatives worked in relative harmony, yet opponents of the Frente gained nearly one-third of the seats in the chamber of representatives. During León Valencia's administration the cost of living rose 60 per cent and the trade deficit doubled, which accounted for much of the public resentment.

In 1965 Laureano Gómez died. His repressive measures had helped create la Violencia, but this pact with Lleras Camargo made the Frente Nacional possible. While he lived, however, the memory of his oppressive regime lingered in the minds of many Liberals.

The first two presidents under the Frente had regarded ending and preventing the vicious civil strife and restoring orderly processes of government as the immediate, crucial tasks. The need for socio-economic reforms was obvious and recognized, but under the circumstances these reforms could not be given highest priority. Unless the Frente produced a reform program that gave some hope of curing the nation's social and economic ills, however, sooner or later it would be jettisoned in favor of a radical movement promising revolutionary changes or a military dictatorship dedicated to maintaining law and order. The leaders of the two major parties, being members of the social, political, and economic elite, were of the class that would lose most in case of revolution. They were obliged, therefore, to offer reforms that would lessen the appeal of more drastic solutions, modest reforms that would appease the masses yet not hurt the wealthy.

To achieve this goal the Frente leaders stressed economic development —increased production, diversification, and a slowing down of the inflation that had run rampant in the Rojas Pinilla era and that had continued ever since. As the elite saw it, if more wealth had to go to the masses it was preferable to create new wealth rather than to share their own. They called for restrictions on imports and the establishment of ceilings on prices and wages, measures which were certain to arouse resentment against the Frente.

Late in 1961, in compliance with Alliance for Progress guidelines, the government had presented its General Economic and Social Development Plan for the 1960's. Among its hopeful goals were increasing the nation's annual economic growth rate to 5.6 per cent and raising the per capita annual income by more than 60 per cent. Investments from private and public, foreign and domestic sources were expected to total as much as $10 billion. The Frente leaders also stressed support of regional development projects such as the Cauca Valley Corporation which, like the TVA of the United States, embraced programs of electrification, flood control, and irrigation.

Lleras Camargo and León Valencia made at least modest progress in economic development, but many serious unsolved problems remained. Both men counted on tax reforms and economic expansion to provide the means for raising the miserable living standards of the masses. Revising the tax schedule was also employed as a device for attracting private investments in projects on which the government placed a high priority. In 1960 a graduated income tax and a levy on the profits from real estate transactions had been enacted to provide revenue.

The Development Plan also called for a nation-wide school construction program and for the training of teachers. Since 1957 the government had been committed to allocating at least 10 per cent of the national budget for education.

Construction of housing was another part of the Plan, and it was to be carried on through the *Instituto de Crédito Territorial,* which had been created in 1942 as the public housing agency. By 1960 it had built 33,680 units, far short of the growing demands. The Development Plan called for the construction of an additional 332,000 units over the decade.

Because of the uneven development between village and city, the Plan proposed a major effort in community development. Community health centers were to be created, and water and sewage systems were to be installed or expanded in many towns and villages. But if economic development were to succeed, the communities would have to take the initiative, for the government's resources were inadequate. The communities were encouraged to undertake the needed projects with advice and assistance from government agencies.

The community development program had an important social purpose —to prevent a recurrence of la Violencia. The country people were slow to accept change, and many viewed with cynicism the proposals for co-operation that presumably would benefit everyone. To encourage the campesinos to work and hope for a better life, government agencies promoted the creation of marketing and other co-operatives. The *acción comunal* program was essential if the rural areas that had been depopulated during the Violencia were to become productive again.

The typical approach to community development was the assigning of a *promotor* and an *equipo polivalente,* the latter a team composed usually of a doctor, an agricultural technician, and a home economics teacher. After the promotor and his team learned what seemed to be a community's most urgent need, they organized a committee of townspeople to undertake the project. They provided information as to government or private aid available from various agencies and foundations. The hope was that the committees would continue to function in the solution of other local problems. In some regions the government's expectations were fulfilled, and the campesinos developed a measure of self-respect and became receptive to change. In other areas the communal action juntas found it impossible to stir the campesinos out of their apathy.

The most significant early socio-economic legislation of the Frente was the Agrarian Reform Law of 1961. It was also the most controversial, for opposition to it was widespread, and even those who were active in the Frente were not unanimously in favor of it. The law embraced both social and economic goals, but its passage was largely for political reasons. The Frente, as its leaders knew, would never have popular support unless it sponsored reforms that would attract the campesinos and distract their attention from the Castro revolution in Cuba. Because of the Castro regime and fear of Castroism spreading, no one in Colombia, not even the large landowners, openly opposed the idea of agrarian reform. The law called for the division of uncultivated private lands as well as of public lands. It encouraged the large landowners to cultivate and utilize their lands fully in order to avoid losing parts of them, and in this way it promoted increased agricultural production.

Private lands that were taken from their owners were paid for with government bonds. The campesinos who purchased the plots under the law's provisions were given 15 years in which to pay for them. The law also had provisions for consolidating the multitude of holdings that were too small to support families. The *minifundio* as well as the latifundio were social problems.

To administer the law, the *Instituto Colombiano de Reforma Agraria* was created. Because of powerful if silent resistance to the program, it failed to fulfill the hopes of its founders. The government was cautious and deliberate in administering the law, for if the opposition intensified and came out in the open it could destroy the Frente Nacional. If, on the other hand, no noticeable progress was made in land distribution, Cuban-trained guerrillas were sure to provide a more drastic solution.

The presidential election of May, 1966, was for the purpose of selecting a Liberal to succeed León Valencia. Able economist Carlos Lleras Restrepo won the nomination, for he had the confidence of many Conservatives as well as the members of his own party. Yet another Liberal, Jaramillo Giraldo, ran against Lleras as the candidate of the Popular Alliance (ANAPO), which opposed the Frente. The coalition survived a serious challenge once again, as Lleras Restrepo won 71 per cent of the vote.

As factional strife appeared to be intensifying rather than abating, the future of the Frente was clouded. If a majority of either of the major parties failed to uphold the coalition arrangement of alternating the presidency, then the pact was at an end. The violence in the countryside, which had never completely disappeared, was likely to burst forth in fury. This threat, together with the increasingly bitter factionalism within the two parties, made it extremely difficult for a president to secure passage of the major part of his legislative program. Those who had looked to the Frente for genuine socio-economic reforms became resentful and cynical.

STUDENT UNREST

In 1966, shortly after taking office, Lleras Restrepo was confronted with a student strike presumably led by communists. Lleras did not vacillate as his predecessor might have done in a similar crisis. He threatened to prevent the students from graduating and, despite the venerable tradition of university autonomy, he sent troops onto the campus of the National University in Bogotá. Because of such forceful government action, the university students have not been as effective a political force in Colombia as they have elsewhere in Latin America. Like León Valencia, Lleras sent special military units after the guerrilla bands that appeared from time to time.

In 1967 Colombia adopted the tenth constitution since independence. No provision was made in it for a vice-president. Every two years the congress elected a *designado* from the president's party, and should the presidential office become vacant the designado would complete the term unless, as might happen, a military coup resulted in a different solution.

ECONOMIC PROBLEMS

Early in 1967 the Colombian economy staggered under the effects of a long decline in coffee prices in world markets, for coffee continued to be the country's major export. Lleras Restrepo managed to stave off financial collapse by negotiating a $200 million credit with the International Monetary Fund and other agencies. In exchange for the credit, which was for the purpose of alleviating financial pressure while economic activities were expanded, Colombia was asked to devalue the peso. Lleras refused, for he knew that devaluation was a politically explosive issue. He skillfully employed the request in making austerity measures palatable by appeal to nationalistic sentiments. He introduced exchange controls and drastically curtailed imports. At the same time he urged everyone to buy Colombian rather than foreign-made products.

Lleras knew that he could only delay devaluation of the peso, for it could not be avoided indefinitely. He re-opened negotiations with the Fund and presented a plan that included devaluation of the peso within six months, but the painful process was so adroitly camouflaged that the disagreeable word was not even mentioned.

Under Lleras Restrepo the Industrial Development Institute, an autonomous government agency, became the country's leading investor of risk capital in new enterprises. Once the new companies begin to show profits, the Institute sells its shares to private investors. At a time when Peru and Bolivia were nationalizing foreign-owned holdings, alien investors felt secure in Colombia. Lleras did not discourage foreign investors, but he insisted that in new, major industries there must be substantial participation by native capital, private or public. He limited repatriation of profits to 14 per cent of the capital brought into the country, and he insisted that Colombian-based companies transport at least 50 per cent of the cargoes they shipped to and from the country in Colombian-flag vessels. There are many successful joint enterprises with companies from France, Mexico, West Germany, and the United States.

The petroleum industry has attracted foreign companies to Colombia. Early in 1970 *Ecopetrol,* the state oil company, was in serious financial trouble owing to a shortage of funds and a lack of technicians. Several American oil companies, hoping to avoid the possibility of expropriation as had occurred in Peru and Bolivia, negotiated profit-sharing plans that were acceptable to the government. A Mexican company, Protexa, S.A., laid a pipeline across the mountains between Salgar and Cartago and ended the need for shipping oil by way of the Panama Canal. Lleras Restrepo and Velasco Ibarra of Ecuador met in the spring of 1970 to discuss mutual problems, and they hinted at new demands on foreign oil companies.

Although efforts were made to increase per capita production between 1961 and 1968, the per capita GNP increased by only 1.5 per cent a year instead of the 2.5 per cent goal set at Punta del Este in 1961. By 1970 unemployment had risen to more than 20 per cent of the economically active population.

POPULATION GROWTH

Colombia's birth rate in recent years has averaged 3.2 per cent a year, which places heavy emphasis on increased production in order to prevent a decline in the standard of living. By 1970, Colombia had 24 cities with populations of more than 100,000. Unlike most Spanish American capitals, Bogotá does not dominate the country. In most of the other Spanish American republics the capital contains nearly one-third of the total population and one-half of the city dwellers. Bogotá, with its 2.5 million inhabitants, contains only about 12 per cent of all Colombians and 25 per cent of the urban population. And the population increase is uneven—only 1.5 per cent in rural areas and 5 per cent in the cities. This rapid population growth has created serious housing shortages in all of the cities.

In January, 1970, the government announced a program for eliminating illiteracy within four years. The literacy rate at the time was 60 per cent. Under the new plan all children are to be in school from age 7 through 14. A shorter school day has been prescribed so that campesino children may be able to attend school and still help their parents part of each day. New high schools are to be constructed, and these are to operate two shifts daily. Because many families could not afford to purchase textbooks, these are to be provided by the government. Owing to the shortage of trained teachers, schools to prepare instructors are also projected. Radio schools such as the one devised in 1947 by the Colombian priest, Joaquín Salcedo, will also be employed both to stimulate community action and to educate the campesinos. It appeared that a leaf was to be taken from Fidel Castro's book on how to educate the masses.

GUERRILLA WARFARE

Long after la Violencia was supposedly at an end, guerrilla bands remained in some mountain strongholds. The army's counter-insurgency units gradually reduced their number by killing off some of the more famous leaders. Any group that defies the government wins a certain amount of admiration and perhaps a little envy from the more docile members of society. Guerrilla leaders became local heroes known by such colorful nicknames as *Sangre Negra* (Black Blood), *Desquite* (Revenge), *Media*

Vida (Half Life), *Venganza* (Vengeance), *Triunfo* (Triumph), and *Tiro Fijo* (Sure Shot). The guerrillas fought with the extreme savagery they had learned during the Violencia, but the warfare was largely meaningless—a way of life rather than a struggle to achieve specified goals. The army sought to track down and annihilate the bands.

BY-PRODUCTS OF THE VIOLENCIA

The Violencia ended the isolation of many rural communities, and thousands of campesinos, who otherwise would never have journeyed beyond their native districts, were uprooted and made mobile. Old traditions were shattered and the peasants were able to observe conditions in other regions. The result was growing dissatisfaction with their miserable lot. Many of them, who had lived in the stagnant eddies of Colombian society, were now drawn into the mainstream to be assimilated; and at the same time Colombia entered a transitional phase. The transitional process was accelerated by the violence, but it is still far from complete. The nation must yet demonstrate its ability to throw off completely the burdensome colonial legacy and modernize its social structure as well as its economy.

All except those who profited by the violence finally realized that it was an insurmountable obstacle to any kind of progress. The destructiveness in some areas made investment in any enterprise except traffic in weapons unwise, and the cost of suppressing the guerrilla warfare and banditry drained the nation of funds that might have been employed more productively in economic development. The Violencia obviously was no solution to the problems of underdevelopment. Dissatisfaction with the violence spread among the campesinos, with the result that they changed from helping the bandits to helping the army locate them.

Because of the violent dislocations, Colombia is no longer a 'closed' society, and a new set of values is in the making. A trend toward secularism is visible, but it is too early to determine the final structure of the new nation that is emerging. The rural and urban masses were persuaded that the Frente Nacional compromise would produce not only domestic peace but a socio-economic revolution. By 1970 neither of these expectations had been fulfilled, and it seems likely that a day of reckoning may arrive when the Frente ends in 1974.

One of the unique developments in Colombia's guerrilla activity is the attraction it has for young priests whose labors among the poor make them fully aware of the desperate need for social reforms. Camilo Henríquez became a martyr to the cause when he joined a guerrilla band and was killed in battle in February, 1966. Other rebel priests have organized into two groups known as 'Golgotha' and 'Golconda,' and they invoke Camilo Henríquez' name in their demands for change. In April, 1969, the Golgotha priests issued a manifesto in which they stated their aim to bring about a 'true structural change which will eliminate the violence that hangs over everyone.'

In January, 1970, 215 men believed to be members of the Army of National Liberation were tried by court-martial. Of these 108 were found guilty, while the rest were let off because of insufficient evidence against them.

In March, a Spanish priest named Domingo Lain was to be expelled from Colombia for interfering in politics. Instead he fled to the mountains and joined the rebel force. He had been a member of the Golgotha Group, which was under attack for what the government considered its Marxist activities. By this time, however, most of the priests rejected violence, for they were convinced that it would accomplish nothing positive.

THE PRESIDENTIAL SUCCESSION OF 1970

As president, Lleras Restrepo had done much to cure the financial ills of his country by introducing more effective tax collection, a drive against inflation, agrarian reform, and a birth control program. He had proved able and responsible, always keeping within the constitution, and always employing moderate measures against foes of the Frente. In January of 1968, for example, his government restored the political rights of ex-dictator Rojas Pinilla. Rojas, again under the tutelage of his astute and forceful daughter, María, began a campaign for the presidency. Latin America has not seen her like before. María Eugenia and her husband are both senators, but she is a one-woman political army rather than part of a team. Her appeal is to the masses, and she has shared her popularity with her father.

Rojas campaigned vigorously for the presidency, but his election in 1970 would have meant the death of the Frente Nacional. The result of his campaign was that the masses were aroused as never before, so that the elite politicians were forced to take them into account for the first time. If they become a major political force, as seems likely, Colombia will probably undergo radical reforms that will be much more thorough and painful than the polite concessions the elite has made thus far.

During the election, Rojas and his daughter voiced ill-concealed threats of violence if he were deprived of the presidency. Lleras, who had tried to avoid taking sides during the campaign, remained calm and firm. He had insisted that all candidates have equal time on TV. It was Rojas' appeal to the masses that was the most effective, and though he lost the election it seems certain that his campaign will have a lasting and, despite his intention, positive effect on the government. When Rojas claimed victory and threatened violence, Lleras declared a state of siege, and the crisis passed.

MISAEL PASTRANA BORERO

Misael Pastrana Borero triumphed narrowly over Rojas Pinilla and two other candidates, and the Frente entered its last four-year presidential term. Lleras immediately urged the defeated candidates to enter a national agreement to maintain peace and orderly government, to support attempts to bring about social improvements, and to make the understanding between Liberals and Conservatives strong enough to withstand the stresses of political campaigns. His emphasis on the social aspects of the needed changes made it clear that he and his party were well aware of the meaning of Rojas' surprising strength in the election: the masses were desperately dissatisfied with living conditions and would support any candidate who promised improvements. Lleras also announced that when his term ended he would devote himself to reorganizing the Liberal party to give it a wide and popular base.

ART, LITERATURE, AND MUSIC

Modern Colombian painters and sculptors have won acclaim far beyond their own land. In 1969 the Museum of Modern Art of New York City arranged a direct exchange of exhibits with the Museum of Modern Art of Bogotá. In November the Boston Museum of Fine Arts held a showing of the paintings and sculpture of Edgar Negret, Monica Meira, Roberto Pizano, and others who best represented Colombia's impressive contributions. In May of 1970 Alejandro Obregón, Colombia's maestro of modern art, held a one-man show at the center for Inter-American Relations in

New York. One of the most popular sculptors and painters was Elma Pignalosa, who won fame while in her early twenties. Bogotá is one of the Latin American art centers expected to set art trends in the future.

At one time in the past many Colombians were opera-lovers, but the cost of bringing foreign opera companies was too high to be sustained. In May and June of 1970 a major attempt was made to revive the opera's popularity. Medellín staged an International Festival of Opera by bringing renowned opera singers from Europe and the United States. The cost of the entire program was paid by a business firm in Medellín.

Several Colombian novelists have won followings throughout the hemisphere, among them youthful José Stevenson, whose popular novel *Years in Asfixia* is an engaging picture of life in Colombia during the 1950's. *Cien años de soledad* (*A Hundred Years of Solitude*), by Gabriel García Márquez, is regarded as one of the most significant Latin American books of the decade. It is an account of 100 years in the life of an imaginary Colombian village.

Ecuador

Ecuador has ever been exceedingly difficult to govern, and since independence, governments have lasted an average of two years. Constitutions have been discarded on the average of one every eight and one-half years. Under these conditions there has been no continuity in anything but political instability and economic backwardness. Traditionally the military has overthrown the government, occasionally for reasons so obscure it appears to be merely a matter of habit. In most cases the military quickly restored 'constitutional' rule, though the man in the street might not notice much difference.

VELASCO IBARRA

The man to watch at the end of the decade in Ecuador was the veteran campaigner and sometime president, José María Velasco Ibarra. His has been one of the strangest political careers in Western Hemisphere history, for although his political philosophy is too elusive to classify he was elected president in 1934, 1943, 1952, 1960, and 1968. Only once did he serve the full term (1952-56), for on every other occasion he was forcibly deposed. His great gift of oratory enabled him to talk his way back into the presidency time and again. 'Just give me a balcony,' he asked. After each successful election he was soon at odds with those who had supported him, for he was a far better campaigner than he was administrator, and Ecuadorean political followings are fickle. Political conditions in Ecuador prevent any president from accomplishing much more than staying in office.

Vice-President Carlos Julio Arosemena Monroy apparently expected when he took office with Velasco Ibarra in 1960 that the latter would run true to form, be quickly deposed, and leave the presidency to him. By 1961 Carlos Julio was becoming impatient, so he decided to help things along a bit by denouncing the president. Velasco Ibarra should have sensed that once again the time had come for his departure, but instead he had Arosemena arrested. The military responded by also arresting the president and deposing him. The path into exile was well-worn, and Velasco Ibarra had no difficulty finding his way back to his other home in Argentina.

Even then, Don Julio almost did not make it. The army opposed him, whereas the air force supported him. After a brief skirmish in which the air force demonstrated it had a somewhat better view of the situation, Arosemena was installed in the *Palacio Presidencial*. The Guayaquil politician and son of a former president fared little better than Velasco Ibarra. He soon lost the support of everyone. He offended the church and the United States by re-establishing diplomatic relations with Cuba, which Velasco had severed. The military shared the church's sentiment and a delegation of officers soon convinced Arosemena of his error. Again relations with Castro were broken. More important, perhaps, than his erratic gestures toward the communist powers, was the president's seeming inability to move in any direction, except toward the bar. Arosemena found the presidency a nerve-wracking job, and he sought relief from its tensions by consuming prodigious amounts of alcohol. He carried a gun, and his drinking got him involved in unfortunate shooting incidents. Frequently he appeared in public in a condition little befitting the dignity of his office. Not only was he unable to act positively or decisively on matters of state, but his conduct was disgraceful to the nation.

After one incident too many, the military moved in and sent Arosemena packing on July 11, 1963. A four-man military junta took his place. Although it was nominally headed by Vice-Admiral Ramón Castro Jijón, its principal formulator of public policy during the thirty-two months it remained in office was General Marcos Gándara Enríquez, an able professional engineer as well as military officer. The junta took its responsibilities very seriously and determined to carry forward a policy of modernization in keeping with the objectives of the Alliance for Progress. A national development plan was already far advanced and the military government threw its full weight behind implementation. Substantial support was obtained from the United States' aid program, from the United Nations, and from the Inter-American Development Bank.

Few, if any, Latin American governments tried harder to meet its commitments under the Alliance than did Ecuador under the junta. Reform after reform was decreed to modernize public administration, expand the educational system, improve public health services, stimulate industrialization, and distribute land to the campesinos. A new tax law and better enforcement procedures greatly augmented income tax collections. A good start was made in installing a modern merit system within the government service. A beginning was made toward consolidation of the government revenues through centralization of tax collection, for autonomous institutions of all types and sizes had long received directly more than 65 per cent of all public income, leaving the central government with little control over expenditures or fiscal policy. The effort was only partially successful, but a somewhat larger percentage of income was brought under budgetary control.

The military junta also tried to re-organize higher education, intervening in the state-supported universities repeatedly to suppress communist activity among the students and to discharge leftist faculty members. A new constitution was prepared and other basic legislation was decreed with a view to correcting evils of the past and ensuring a solid base for future national development. Many of the measures were technically sound, but the manner of their development and imposition caused them to be attacked by all who opposed military rule, irrespective of their merits.

Some of the most needed and appropriate measures from the standpoint of promoting the economic development of the country contributed significantly to the junta's downfall. The government determined to place the customs service on a sound technical basis and collect duties on the real value of merchandise imported, as distinguished from inadequately supported declared values. New schedules were announced reflecting the changes in evaluation procedure. The result was a virtual uprising by the Guayaquil merchants, who employed the local Chamber of Commerce to declare a general cessation of commercial activity. The shutdown spread throughout the country, bringing commerce to a standstill. Too long in power and lacking popular support when these events occurred in the early spring of 1966, the junta struck out viciously at its opponents. A foolish attack upon Central University in Quito was ordered, and the army carried out the assignment with wholly unwarranted brutality. Within a few hours all support for the junta vanished, and its members had no alternative but to flee the capital and seek refuge in exile. Military government was at an end and the military itself was discredited in the eyes of the people. The date was the end of March, 1966.

The downfall of the junta had begun long before, when it assumed for itself the unpopular task of reforming the social, economic, and political life of Ecuador. It had no mandate from the people, no support from any group except the armed forces themselves, and no successful or even serious attempt was ever made to develop a significant following. Those who initially backed the junta because of disgust with Arosemena, fear of communist infiltration, or desire for stable and constructive progress gradually were alienated for many and varied reasons. A major basis for disaffection, however, was the increasingly obvious inability of the ruling military officers to set a firm and reasonable date for their departure. In the end, a vicious backlash destroyed virtually all the constructive achievements of their nearly three years in office.

RETURN TO CIVILIAN RULE

At the request of the armed forces, the various political parties of Ecuador suggested a temporary president. In effect, the transitional arrangement was negotiated by former Presidents Galo Plaza and Camilo Ponce Enríquez in collaboration with the Guayaquil merchants. The choice turned out to be Clemente Yerovi Indaburu, a wealthy Guayaquil businessman. Yerovi called for election of a constituent assembly, which met in the fall. A new constitution, Ecuador's seventeenth, was promulgated in May, 1967. General elections were scheduled for June, 1968. In the meantime, the constituent assembly elected Otto Arosemena Gómez interim president. It was he who a short time later caused consternation at Punta del Este, Uruguay, by denouncing the ridiculously complicated assistance procedures of the Alliance for Progress in front of the assembled hemisphere presidents.

The general elections held in June, 1968, were the first since Velasco Ibarra was chosen in 1960. Now seventy-five years old, he was back again, campaigning with his usual flair for oratory. He was elected for a fifth time. Not closely associated with any party (except his own Velasquista followers), he had no genuine program. As he had well learned in the past, his chief preoccupation would be to remain in office throughout his term rather than to develop and carry out government programs.

In May, 1969, after eight months in office, Velasco Ibarra had faced eight cabinet crises. Predictions were openly made that he would not be able to complete his term. The army was discredited and lacked a leader of sufficient prestige to lead a coup, and political party leaders admitted that they had made no move against the aging president because they could not be sure of retaining control of the government afterward. So Velasco Ibarra remained, partly through his own skillful maneuvering and partly because no one made a serious effort to oust him. In reference to his difficulties, he grumbled that 'these people cannot be governed; everyone wants to be president.'

In May, 1970, Ecuador and the Soviet Union belatedly exchanged ambassadors, after having agreed in 1943 to establish diplomatic relations. Trade possibilities between Ecuador and Russia and her European neighbors were explored, especially with regard to the possible sale of bananas. Ecuador's most important crop was having a difficult time competing in North American markets with that of a revitalized industry in the Caribbean borderlands. New markets were essential to the Ecuadorean economy.

One of the few hopeful signs for economic improvement in Ecuador was the opening of new oilfields east of the Andes along the Colombian border. A concession to Gulf-Texaco had proved fruitful, and by agreement these companies were to lay a pipeline to the port of Esmereldas by 1972. The companies also agreed to turn the pipeline over to the government eventually, and they paid $11 million in advance royalties. Even though the contract was favorable to Ecuador, oil is everywhere in Latin America a principal symbol of economic nationalism, and domestic opposition to the contract was voiced soon after it was announced.

ART AND LITERATURE

Jorge Icaza, whose novel *Huasipungo* (1934) was translated into seventeen languages and went through at least twenty Spanish editions, remains Ecuador's most famous literary figure, although his pen has been inactive for many years. *Huasipungo* concerned the miserable lot of the Indian peons on the great haciendas, and it stirred up widespread discussion. Many of the conditions he depicted have changed but little.

Ecuador's most famous painter is Oswaldo Guayasamín, one of whose most outstanding pieces of work is a large mural adorning one wall of the law faculty building at Central University in Quito. His paintings are many and varied, but frequently convey a social or political theme reflecting his revolutionary views in the tradition of a Diego Rivera. Eduardo Kingman Riofrío paints indigenous subjects, emphasizing the grotesque in the features of those he depicts. Both artists' works are in demand abroad as well as in Ecuador and have been shown internationally. Still another painter, Luis Crespo, who studied in Paris and Madrid, has had successful shows and has sold many of his works in the United States.

Peru

In the 1950's Peru belatedly began a program of industrialization and economic development, which was continued sporadically during the 1960's. Although the country had been generally conservatively oriented and resistant to change, most of the men who campaigned for the presidency during the 1960's offered reform programs. Before the decade was over economic nationalism intensified, and its instrument was the army. Politically, the army junta that displaced President Fernando Belaúnde Terry was increasingly repressive and insensitive to civil rights.

Manuel Prado's term as president expired in 1962, during a period of ferment inspired by the Castro revolution and intensive union organization in Peru by Hugo Blanco, a Trotskyite who was captured by government troops in 1963. In the campaign for the presidency the main candidates in 1962—Víctor Raúl Haya de la Torre, ex-president Manuel Odría, and Fernando Belaúnde Terry—all offered reform programs. No candidate received a majority, so the choice was left to the congress, where the Apristas joined forces with Odría's followers. The army, APRA's most relentless foe, refused to accept this arrangement, which would have brought Odría or Haya de la Torre to the presidency, and overthrew the government. A military junta staged another election in June of 1963. Belaúnde Terry won with about 39 per cent of the vote.

BELAÚNDE TERRY

Soon after Belaúnde's term began, APRA called for a 24-hour general strike ostensibly in 'indignation' over the dismissal of 300 workers at a ceramics factory in Lima and to protest police killings of Indian squatters on hacienda lands. The strike had a deeper meaning as well, for it was intended to serve as a warning to Belaúnde that APRA was still powerful and had to be taken into account. Belaúnde demonstrated political skill by persuading a communist-dominated division of APRA's union to ignore the strike in return for settling the ceramics workers' dispute. The strike failed, for only a small fraction of Lima's factory workers responded to the call.

In his campaign Belaúnde had promised to redistribute land, erect public housing, and to take effective action against the International Petroleum Company (IPC), a Canadian affiliate of Standard Oil of New Jersey that claimed ownership of the oil-rich La Brea and Pariñas basin. In November the government canceled IPC's concession, but did nothing more. Although IPC paid high wages and built a company town for oil workers, its contribution to the Peruvian economy was minimal, and its presence aroused intense nationalistic feelings. Belaúnde demanded a payment of $50 million and a 60 per cent income tax. There the matter rested, much to the dissatisfaction of many Peruvians. The army would eventually capitalize on this dissatisfaction.

In 1963, Indians began occupying hacienda lands in the sierra. In some cases they were able to hold the lands, but in others troops forced the squatters out and burned their shacks. Support for the Indians came from the 'New Left' composed of dissidents from APRA, the Communist party, and the students. The New Left itself was sharply divided into the *Movimiento de Izquierda Revolucionaria* and the *Ejército de Liberación Nacional,* and there was no agreement between them on goals or procedures.

The Revolutionary Movement of the Left was composed of ex-Apristas; the Army of National Liberation was largely communist.

In 1965 the two groups launched separate guerrilla movements. Too late they formed a National Co-ordinating Command, for the army's counter-insurgency units had already turned the tide against the independently operating units. The two groups had been fighting in the same general area, but they did not join forces. The Peruvian government knew that guerrilla forces had to be destroyed quickly, before they could win the confidence and support of the peasants, and it harassed the rebels relentlessly. By the end of 1965 the guerrilla movements were crushed and their leaders captured or killed.

Belaúnde's government pushed a number of socio-economic programs. In 1963 education was provided free of cost from primary school through the university. In the same year local self-government was restored and an agrarian reform law, much weaker than the one Belaúnde requested, was passed. Looking toward future development of the eastern lowlands, Belaúnde established a gunboat fleet on the upper waters and tributaries of the Amazon for the peaceful purpose of providing medical services for the isolated Indian villages.

One of Belaúnde's major programs was for an extensive road system to link all parts of Peru. He also planned an international highway—the Marginal Highway—along the eastern slope of the Andes, connecting Colombia, Ecuador, Bolivia, and Peru. This project he expected would open vast new fertile lands for settlement and at the same time provide a basis for co-operation and a reduction of nationalism among the nations involved. The Peruvian sections were already being laid out in 1965, but the proposed international highway intensified the very nationalism that Belaúnde hoped to diminish. The most heated arguments concerned the role that might be played by foreign companies, particularly those from the United States. The most pressing problem for Belaúnde was the popular demand for nationalization of the International Petroleum Company, for if that were to be done his highway project was lost. It could not possibly be completed without massive financial assistance from the United States, and nationalization of the oil company would undoubtedly preclude the possibility of such assistance.

Despite Belaúnde's intentions, Peru's land reforms were ineffective, and most of the Indians remained landless. Although 60 per cent of the labor force was employed in agriculture, in 1967 and 1968 the country spent $134 million and $154 million on food imports. Belaúnde employed the army in building roads, the navy in the health program for the Amazon region, and the air force in transporting supplies and officials. Yet for all his efforts Belaúnde fell from power over the nationalistic issue of the International Petroleum Company.

On October 3, 1968, the army deposed Belaúnde and sent him into exile, and a junta headed by General Juan Velasco Alvardo took over the government and ruled by decree. The junta immediately seized the International Petroleum Company's properties and expropriated them, and by this move won popular support for its usurpation of power. Relations with the United States were immediately strained, for under the 1962 Hickenlooper Amendment the United States government was required to halt foreign aid and preferential trade with any country that expropriated the property of American citizens without adequate compensation. This requirement was to take effect six months after the seizure unless satisfactory negotiations toward a settlement were under way.

Velasco protested that the seizure was legal under Peruvian law, and claimed that the company owed $690 million for oil extracted illegally in the past. October 9, the day of the seizure, was declared the 'Day of National Dignity.' Peru's state oil corporation, *Empresa Petrolera Fiscal,* began operating the expropriated refinery with the help of experts from Mexico. An initial decline in production was experienced at the former International Petroleum Company facilities. On the other hand, other foreign companies had been engaged in developing off-shore oil fields since 1965, and over-all production for the country continued to rise.

President Velasco offered to pay the International Petroleum Company $71 million for its equipment and refining facilities, abut this amount was to be deducted from the $690 million he insisted the company owed Peru for oil illegally extracted. When the time came for cutting off foreign assistance and ending the preferential purchase of Peruvian sugar, United States officials were reluctant to invoke the law. Instead they postponed action on the basis that negotiations were under way, inasmuch as the International Petroleum Company had filed an appeal that had not as yet been acted upon. Peruvian sugar growers were apprehensive, for the United States had been paying seven cents a pound for sugar from quota nations, while the price in the world market was less than one-third that amount.

The petroleum company case was only one source of tension between Peru and the United States. Peru, Chile, and Ecuador each claimed jurisdiction over the ocean area within 200 miles of the coastline, a claim recognized neither by the United States nor by other nations under international law. In February, 1969, a Peruvian gunboat seized an American-owned tuna boat within the 200-mile limit. In retaliation the United States suspended arms sales to Peru under the Pelly Amendment to the Foreign Sales Act of 1968. Velasco charged that the suspension violated the terms of the bilateral military trade pact between the two countries, and announced that the proposed visit to Peru of Governor Nelson Rockefeller on behalf of President Nixon was now 'inopportune.' He turned the arms sales ban into another issue of Peruvian nationalism and employed the anti-American sentiment thus stimulated to gain support for his military government.

Shortly after its *coup* in October, 1968, the Peruvian junta expropriated 600,000 acres of land belonging to the American-owned Cerro de Pasco Corporation, for which it agreed to pay compensation. In 1969 the junta decreed an extensive land reform program that involved expropriation of both foreign-owned and Peruvian haciendas. Among the holdings immediately nationalized were two highly productive plantations owned by W.R. Grace and Company, another United States firm. The extensive industrial properties of the Grace organization in Peru were not affected. The government agreed to pay cash for the installations and equipment and offered twenty-year bonds for the land. Subsequently, vast properties under German ownership were also taken over.

Although Velasco declared that 'the land must belong to the peasants,' many Peruvians saw as his basic purpose an attempt to break the power of the landed oligarchy. Belaúnde Terry had tried to push through an effective agrarian reform law, but failed owing to the resistance of the oligarchs. It is quite possible that Velasco had both purposes in mind, for his junta made no effort to placate the oligarchy. But unless the new workers' co-operatives were carefully managed, agricultural production would likely decline.

In the fall of 1969 the foreign ministers of the Andean group of nations met in Peru and signed an agreement known as the Declaration of Lima. It stated that in economic development, preference would be given to native capital and businesses. Colombia, Ecuador, and Chile were represented along with Peru. It was hoped that Venezuela would join at a later date. Then in April, 1970, Colombia, Chile, and Peru began importing free of duties and restrictions some eighty-five products of the Andean bloc nations. Bolivia and Ecuador were also expected to participate.

The policy of Peru's military junta concerning the International Petroleum Company and the tuna boats provided effective impetus for stirring ardent nationalistic sentiments and distracting attention from some of the regime's more distasteful domestic actions. The cutting off of United States' aid and preferential sugar purchases was not, however, the most serious threat to the Peruvian economy that might result from these actions. American banks usually assisted Peruvian industry with about $150 million annually in loans. These loans were sharply reduced after the International Petroleum Company expropriation, and many private investments were also held up pending final settlement of the oil company issue. In the long run, private reaction might prove more damaging to Peru's development program than any official measures the United States chose to take.

In May, 1970, the junta decreed guidelines for a new mining law that was intended to expand both mining and Peru's share of the profits. The junta planned to make the refining and marketing of copper a government monopoly because of dissatisfaction with the policies of some foreign companies that had resulted in the loss of revenue for Peru. In a reversal of its general anti-foreign tendency during 1968, the junta had signed a contract with a group of American mining companies for developing a $355 million copper deposit. Similarly, the junta granted new oil leases to the Texas Company and Occidental Petroleum in February, 1970, before an edict ending such leases went into effect. In both cases there was considerable opposition from nationalists and leftist groups who once again raised the cry of 'American imperialism.' The junta's inconsistency with regard to foreign investors suggests that its actions against the International Petroleum Company were based primarily on expediency. On the other hand, a fundamentally different legal basis for operation was involved in that the International Petroleum Company claimed ownership of the oil reserves as distinct from mere possession of a development concession. The Peruvian government was unwilling to recognize any such claim, and there were numerous historic reasons for such refusal going back to old Spanish law regarding subsurface mineral rights.

On December 31, 1969, the Peruvian junta, which had earlier seized the magazine *Carretas* and arrested its editor, decreed a 'freedom of the press' law which was in fact for the purpose of restricting press freedom and silencing the junta's critics. The law contained a provision that owners of newspapers and radio-television stations must be native-born *residents*. This was a crude device to muzzle the newspapers *Expreso* and *La Prensa*. *Expreso's* owner, Manuel Ulloa, former treasury minister under Belaúnde, was in exile, and his paper sharply criticized the junta's economic policies. *La Prensa's* editor, Pedro Beltrán, was also an ex-minister and was married to a woman who was born in the United States. Early in 1970 *Expreso* and *Extra* were seized and turned over to the employees to run. Both were published by Alberto Ulloa Elias, brother of Manuel Ulloa. The editors of two APRA papers, Eduardo Chando of *La Tribuna* of Lima and Julio Carrido Malaver of *Norte* of Trujillo, were arrested for protesting the junta's ban on an Aprista rally.

DIRECTION OF THE JUNTA

By 1970 the military regime had gained control over executive, legislative, and judicial powers, and it seemed determined to eliminate criticism and opposition by the conventional methods of authoritarian governments. Where the junta was taking the country was not clear to most Peruvians; it appeared that it was not even clear to the junta itself. There was evidence to support the views of those who saw as the outcome of the junta's policies the creation of a socialistic state. There was also evidence to support the contention that the junta's main purpose was to stay in power so as to exclude the Apristas. Certainly the junta employed nationalistic sentiments to curry popular favor, and its economic policies were too contradictory and confusing to be considered doctrinaire. Whether the junta had a basic plan or was merely bungling along on the basis of expediency was not yet evident. One matter only was beyond argument: a bold military junta could effect drastic changes far more easily than could a civilian regime dedicated to peaceful reform. On the other hand, Ecuador's recent experience suggested that any changes pushed through without popular support were apt to prove ephemeral. But then, the Ecuadorean junta had not attacked the landed oligarchy by confiscating its land. Velasco in Peru seemed bent upon such a course.

CULTURAL DEVELOPMENT

During the 1960's a principal Peruvian contribution to the field of contemporary art was made by the abstractionist Fernando de Szyszlo, whose themes from Peru's pre-Columbian past won him international recognition for use of bold color in conveying the mystic power of the Andes and their early peoples. Joaquín Roca Rey, an outstanding artist and sculptor, left some of his finest works in Panama, such as the José Remón Cantera Monument, completed in 1956, but his continued impact as a teacher in Lima was expected to develop significant talent among his pupils. In general, however, Peruvian output in the arts, in architecture, and in literature was modest.

Bolivia

Even after the movement to resettle families in the fertile lowlands of Santa Cruz province had been under way for a decade, three-fourths of Bolivia's four million people still lived on the inhospitable altiplano. Aymará and Quechua Indians for the most part, they lived by a barter or subsistence economy and contributed little to the nation. In discussing the possibilities for developing the lowlands, President Víctor Paz Estenssoro once declared: 'The old Bolivia is up here on the altiplano. The new Bolivia is down below.' The movement to the lowlands continues, and it is one of Bolivia's hopes for improving the living standards of her people.

THE CONTINUED POVERTY OF AGRICULTURE

Only an extremely small amount of Bolivia's land is used for farming—between 2 and 5 per cent—but nearly half of the labor force is employed in agriculture. The country has had to import food regularly, especially wheat, for the land used for farming is by no means the best available.

Eventually the development of the yungas and the lowlands is expected to result in greatly increased agricultural output. Since the 1952 revolution, most of the great haciendas have been broken up and redistributed, but most of the peasant proprietors have been unable to maintain production at previous levels. Far too many were totally unprepared to employ their limited agricultural skills in a market economy.

A principal problem in drawing the peasant population into the nation's economic life was the persistent, high level of illiteracy. Many of the Indians were not even taught Spanish, and efforts to instruct them in even simple rural tasks often proved futile. After 1952 the government began spending larger sums on education, and under Barrientos in 1966 more than a fourth of the national budget was allocated to education and the building of schools.

POLITICAL EVENTS AND THE FALL OF THE MNR

In 1960 Paz Estenssoro was elected president for a second time, and in the following year a new constitution was promulgated. Paz continued to maintain strong ties with the United States, and the American government provided substantial financial aid to Bolivia—more, in fact, than to any other Spanish American country. Other governments also gave assistance in various forms. American and European officials were anxious to see Bolivia's non-communist revolution succeed, but it cannot be said that the assistance program was carried on only by reason of their generosity. Much of the American aid, for instance, was in the form of loans that had to be used for purchases in the United States. Eventually the loans would have to be repaid. And in 1970, in an effort to check the flow of dollars from the country, United States' officials spoke of requiring Bolivia to spend in the United States sums equal to the amounts of American loans that were to be used in Bolivia. A new word was coined for this concept: 'additionality.' Bolivian officials pointed out that if this requirement were adopted the United States would literally be repaid double for its loans.

When the presidential term ended in 1964, Vice-President Juan Lechín expected to have a turn as president. At the MNR convention in January, however, no agreement could be reached, so Paz decided to run again. Lechín was expelled from the MNR, and he made an attempt to build an alliance of dissidents of the extreme left and right. Paz favored senate President Federico Fortún Sanjines for vice-president, but the MNR right wing wanted air force General René Barrientos Ortuño in the office. Barrientos, who had been sent in 1952 to fly Paz back to Bolivia at the time of the revolution, was assigned the post of ambassador to London to remove him from the 1964 election contest. Before departing on his assignment, Barrientos was ambushed and wounded, though not seriously. He was hastily flown to Panama for medical treatment. The attempt on his life was worth the injury and discomfort, for it increased his popularity and prestige so dramatically that Paz quickly asked Fortún to withdraw his candidacy and persuaded the MNR to name Barrientos as vice-presidential nominee.

Paz and Barrientos easily won the election, but opposition groups, urged on by would-be presidential candidates, abstained from voting. After the election they refused to acknowledge Paz as the winner. Strikes and rioting became widespread and soon turned into an armed revolt against the government. In the early stages, the army and the peasant militia defeated the followers of Juan Lechín, the university students, and a group called the Socialist Falange. However, the armed forces became convinced that Paz' usefulness was at an end; they asked him to resign. Paz refused, but now led by Vice-President Barrientos, the army defeated his peasant militia and forced him to flee. Paz attributed the defeat of his militia to the modern weapons with which the United States had supplied the army. In 1952 the MNR had disbanded the army and re-organized it completely, so that all officers were members of the party, but some vestiges of old-style militarism could not be eliminated completely. Paz vowed that if he ever returned to power the army would be abolished. For the time being, however, Barrientos took over the government.

PUTTING THE MINES IN ORDER

The government mining company (COMIBOL), which had taken over operation of the tin mines when they were nationalized, had been losing money at the rate of about $8.5 million a year. This was owing in large part to padded payrolls, inefficient methods, use of outdated machinery, fluctuating prices, but above all to featherbedding. In 1962 Paz had negotiated with the governments of the United States and West Germany, as well as the Inter-American Development Bank, for a $38 million loan to modernize the tin industry. The loan was granted on condition that the payroll be drastically reduced. When about one thousand men were laid off, the miners' union struck, but it soon gave up and the mines were put back in operation. Some 26,000 remained on the payroll, far more than were needed.

In 1965 Barrientos announced a plan for re-organizing the mining industry, which was still operating at a loss. Battles between miners and troops began. The president sent Juan Lechín into exile, canceled pay increases granted since August, 1964, and authorized COMIBOL to hire and lay off miners as needed. The fighting spread, and army General Alfredo Ovando Candia submitted to threats by the miners.

The army, which feared that Barrientos would establish a dictatorship, demanded that he share junta leadership with Ovando. Barrientos was quite willing to accept the arrangement; there is a possibility that he may have engineered it himself. It removed his chief rival from command of the army at a time when the troops were needed for a major confrontation with the tin miners. In May, 1965, the showdown came, and Barrientos used the army to break the power of the miners' union. This accomplished, he reduced COMIBOL's payroll by 4000 men. In the following year COMIBOL at last began to show a profit, and in the presidential election of the same year Barrientos was elected easily. He was master of the situation. Luis Adolfo Siles Salinas was made vice-president. In 1967, Bolivia's sixteenth constitution was promulgated. Barrientos no longer was identified with the MNR. He and his supporters called themselves the Bolivian Revolutionary Front.

CHE GUEVARA'S BOLIVIAN FIASCO

In early 1967 a Castro-oriented band of guerrillas, largely of foreign nationality and led by Che Guevara, began attacking Bolivian army patrols. Apparently the Castroites had decided that Bolivia would serve as a strategic center of operations for a continent-wide revolution. Barrientos quickly sent counter-insurgency units after the guerrillas, and to strengthen his regime he invited Paz, Siles Zuazo, and Lechín to return to Bolivia. He need not have bothered. All declined, and he did not really need their support anyway. In April troops captured a French revolutionary journalist and guerrilla warfare veteran, Régis Debray. He was shortly sentenced to thirty years in prison. In October Guevara himself was captured and executed, and the guerrilla movement subsided. The guerrillas had had no success in winning over the Bolivian peasants. Bolivian communists, divided into a number of factions, refused to co-operate with Guevara. They saw nothing in it for them. Most were sidewalk revolutionists anyway; jungle fighting did not appeal to them.

Defeat of the guerrilla movement strengthened Barrientos' position, and he pushed ahead with socio-economic programs. Oil production was doubled, 20,000 miles of road were opened, and numerous schools, hospitals, and clinics were built. The highway expansion, plus improvement of the railroads, greatly facilitated internal trade, which had always been hampered by the difficulties of transportation. The school construction program was aided by the Bolivian Union of Christian Students, which worked out a program with high schools in the United States to raise funds for use in building high schools in Bolivia. In 1968 and 1969 the Union built seven schools and had two more under construction.

DEATH OF BARRIENTOS

In April, 1969, Barrientos was killed in a helicopter crash. Vice-President Siles Salinas assumed the presidency and reinstated the 1967 constitution which Barrientos had suspended. Almost immediately the Bolivian Gulf Oil Company was subjected to attack, no doubt mirroring what was taking place in Peru. Gulf Oil had been Bolivia's major producer for ten years, and not only supplied domestic needs but also crude oil for export. The company had laid a pipeline to Arica on the Pacific coast and had contracted for a pipeline to the Argentine border, to be paid for by Gulf and a World Bank loan. Gulf had made Bolivia an oil-exporting nation, and although it paid relatively low taxes and royalties, the issue was nationalism and Siles Salinas' desire to popularize himself; it had little to do with more profits for Bolivia.

In September General Ovando began preparing for the presidential election in May, 1970. Siles Salinas maneuvered for his own candidate, retired General Armando Escobar. When it was rumored that Gulf Oil Company, which was having so much difficulty with Siles Salinas, was contributing heavily to General Ovando's campaign chest, Ovando was aroused to precipitous action. He ousted Siles and seized power.

GENERAL OVANDO'S RULE

Apparently in hope of winning support for his illegal take-over by further arousing nationalistic feeling over the oil issue, General Ovando quickly emulated Velasco Alvarado of Peru. He abrogated the petroleum code and expropriated Gulf Oil holdings. Bolivia would pay Gulf only for plants and equipment, Ovando announced, not for its other investments, such as initial exploration costs. Like Velasco Alvarado, he was willing to play fast and loose with the nation's economy in order to secure popular support for his regime. A propaganda campaign against Gulf as the only private oil producer in Bolivia had prepared the way for expropriation. Among the more extravagant charges was that of ex-Minister of the Interior Antonio Arguedas Mendieta, who had been forced to flee the country when it was discovered that he had sent Barrientos' copy of Che Guevara's diary to Fidel Castro at a time when the Bolivian government was negotiating for its sale. Arguedas solemnly declared that Gulf Oil was financing a campaign against him. If this appeal to nationalism was not enough to exonerate him, he added that the CIA had planned to publish a revised version of the diary.

After expropriation of the Gulf holdings, part of the Bolivian press attacked the government for what it considered an unwise action. Work on the pipeline to the Argentine border, which would have earned Bolivia upwards of $10 million a year, halted soon after the seizure. No oil could be sold abroad. The economy, which had improved steadily under Barrientos' control, now faltered.

Ovando's campaign against Gulf and his hasty expropriation created problems he apparently had not anticipated. He found it impossible to sell oil or gas, and he was unable to get work resumed on the pipeline despite Argentina's offer to help with the financing. In the spring of 1970 Gulf negotiated an agreement with the Spanish government for one of its state-owned companies to operate the Gulf plants in Bolivia. By this arrangement oil production and work on the pipeline would be resumed, and Gulf would share in the profits. Although Ovando had little choice but to accept the offer or continue losing the revenue from oil production, his campaign against Gulf had conditioned the public against a compromise, and he was accused of selling out.

The Bolivian public was as much confused over Ovando's intentions as

Peruvians were over Velasco Alvarado's. To some Bolivians Ovando was trying to establish a socialist dictatorship; to others he was becoming the lackey of 'imperialistic capitalism.' Still others, who perhaps viewed the regime more charitably, did not try to attach a doctrinaire label. Ovando was not to blame for the confusion, they asserted, for his policy was actually quite simple and clear-cut: he bought old Peruvian newspapers and read them to determine what step his government should take next.

Prospects Uncertain

In none of the Andean republics was the outlook particularly bright as the decade of the 1970's opened. Colombia's inter-party compact might endure through 1974, but the 1970 election had demonstrated such strong opposition to it that further continuation seemed most unlikely. The future beyond the compact was anyone's guess, and many were pessimists. Ecuador was once more in the shaky hands of Velasco Ibarra, and in June of 1970 another political crisis caused him to assume dictatorial powers, arrest many people, and close the universities because of student opposition. The military had reportedly refused to let him resign.

Nature once more grimly informed the Peruvians of her supremacy in their troubled land. May 31, 1970, in the middle of the afternoon, a devastating earthquake struck along a 600-mile stretch of Peru's north coast and into the mountains. Chimbote, Chiclayo, Trujillo, and Huarás were all severely damaged, and some towns, such as Huaylas, were virtually leveled to the ground. Dams broke and water flooded the valleys, carrying away hundreds of people. Huge mud slides buried others. The toll mounted as aid was rushed to the region and the extent of damage assessed. Some estimates placed the dead as high as 30,000. Many more were homeless. Peru had been dealt a catastrophic blow. Once again to the problems of mere people had been added the grief imposed by a relentless and overpowering nature.

23

The Urban South:
Political Unrest and Economic Stagnation

> The origin of the present Argentine problems is without any doubt political, but the problems cannot be attacked with political procedures but rather with a renovation of structures.*

Southern South America is preponderantly urban. In Uruguay and Argentina the focus of national life has been in the principal cities for decades; in Chile it is a more recent but growing phenomenon. Paradoxically, each of these countries is famed as a producer of agricultural or animal products. Argentina and Uruguay in particular are justly renowned for their excellent farm and grazing land. They have virtually constituted the bread basket of South America. Despite Chile's fame as a mineral exporter, her wines are known throughout the entire world and numerous varieties of fruit grown in her central valley were at one time exported along the Pacific coast.

Today over 72 per cent of Argentina's 23 million people live in urban areas; 6 million of them—one-fourth of the population—live in Buenos Aires and its immediate metropolitan area. The pattern is even more accentuated in Uruguay where 73 per cent of the country's 2.5 million inhabitants are urban dwellers and over 50 per cent of the entire population resides in the metropolitan region of Montevideo. Of Chile's 9.2 million people, 27 per cent live in Santiago and neighboring communities and 68 per cent of the national population is urbanized. Such concentrations of people in cities have profound social and political consequences. Unfortunately, they also reflect a basic economic illness in each case. Rural life in

* Ex-president of Argentina, General Juan Carlos Onganía, in an interview with *Visión* editor, Igor Gordevitch. *Visión,* September 26, 1969. General Onganía was still in office as president at the time of the interview.

all three countries is depressed, neglected, and carries far less than its appropriate share of the nation's economic burden.

Heavy urban concentration would be readily understandable if the cities were major industrial centers requiring a large labor force. Buenos Aires is such a center, but neither Montevideo nor Santiago really qualify. Even in Buenos Aires the labor force far exceeds the available employment opportunities; many people are without work much of the time. The Argentine capital has also long been notorious for featherbedding practices in industry and transport services. Inevitably the per capita productivity of the urban labor force is low. Much of the urban population of both Buenos Aires and Montevideo has in part lived off government largess and social benefit payments of one kind or another for years. The consequences have been detrimental to economic development and have placed severe strains on national budgets. Frequent and prolonged labor strikes have been commonplace, often ended by massive increases in wage rates and the beginning of a new round of seemingly incessant inflation. The Chilean experience has varied somewhat from the pattern just described, and the causes have been somewhat different, but the economic and monetary consequences have been much the same.

An unusual facet of the urbanization problem in Uruguay and Argentina is the absence of a high population growth rate. In both countries it has amounted to no more than 1.5 per cent per year, and by 1968 and 1969 Uruguay was actually experiencing a population decrease as emigration exceeded the growth rate. Chile's rate of population growth is around 2.5 per cent a year, relatively high but far lower than that of such countries as Ecuador, Costa Rica, or Mexico. In southern South America it would seem that the principal cause of rapid urbanization has been and continues to be internal migration from the rural areas to the city.

Available data suggest that the population engaged in agriculture in Uruguay and Chile may be declining absolutely as well as relatively. In Argentina it is growing very slowly, if at all. Similarly, agricultural production in the three countries, while subject to substantial fluctuations in some years, has not increased on a per capita basis over the past ten years. For a number of basic agricultural products total production has increased but slightly or remained stationary over the same period. The agricultural potential of southern South America is not being realized and national governments, dominated by people with an urban outlook and faced daily by major urban problems crying for solution, have given far too little attention to the rural countryside and its development. Unfortunately, the resources with which to meet the needs of the city populations can come only from a higher level of national productivity. The quickest way to get it may well be to refocus national attention on agricultural development. No one seems to be thinking in these terms.

Argentina: A Retreat from Greatness

By all odds Argentina should stand at the apex of broad national development in Latin America. No country in the area can match Argentina's literacy rate,* the percentage of her population engaged in higher education, the size of her middle class, the per capita income of her population (apart from Venezuela's oil-inflated and deceptive figures), and the general well-being of her people. Argentina's industrial development is substantial and goods manufactured within the republic meet a very large proportion of consumer requirements. Despite these advantages, to which a few years ago many others could have been added, the country languishes. Her economy is depressed, inflation mounts year after year, and able professionals emigrate to other countries where greater freedom prevails and their accomplishments are more appreciated.

Many Argentines and not a few foreign critics blame the problems of the republic and its failure to keep pace with Brazil, Mexico, and Venezuela on Juan Domingo Perón and the legacy of social and economic imbalance that his regime bestowed on Argentina. There can be little doubt that throughout the seventh decade of the century Argentina still reflected the political consequences of the bread and circus policies employed by Perón and his wife, Evita, to build a huge popular following among the laboring people and the impoverished lower classes of the Argentine capital. Nevertheless, a basic imbalance existed long before Perón. It can be traced far back into the last century to the long struggle between the capital and the provinces, to the growing preponderance of Buenos Aires in Argentine life and culture, and to the mounting concentration there of thousands upon thousands of people who found underemployment and poverty in the great port city more tolerable than the backwardness and penury of the rural countryside. María Eva Duarte was herself one of these, and her

---

* Uruguay's 1964 census largely exploded the myth of that country's vaunted literacy, revealing that one-eighth of the population had never been to school and that 40 per cent were still functionally illiterate.

ready rapport with those of comparable experience and outlook made her an invaluable political ally to Perón when she threw in her lot with him. The social situation in the Argentine capital was ready-made for Evita's rise to power, and she and her husband made the most of it. The Peróns are gone, but the social problems persist, exacerbated by the recollection of hundreds of thousands of Argentines that for them, at least, life was a bit better while Juan Domingo and Evita were in charge at the *Casa Rosada.*

No one could have tried harder to cope with the legacy of Perón and the overurbanization of Argentina than Arturo Frondizi, elected to the presidency in 1958. The odds against which he struggled proved insuperable, and he must have felt an immense sense of relief—as well as bitter disappointment—when on March 29, 1962, he was forcibly removed from the presidency and taken to temporary exile on Martín García island. Frondizi fought inflation with a program of rigorous austerity. To increase domestic oil production he brought foreign companies back into the picture for exploration, drilling, and pipeline construction, in spite of campaign denunciation of foreign oil interests. He was highly successful in relieving the country of the need to import oil and gasoline, but the economic benefits were counteracted by the political losses he suffered for having 'sold out' to the foreign interests.

Frondizi took firm measures to decrease importation of luxury commodities, to reject wage increases not based upon higher productivity, to put an end to featherbedding in the transport industry, and to limit the extension of easy bank credit. The peso was devalued and an attempt made to put the national budget back in balance. His economics minister, Alvaro Carlos Alsogaray, was soon known throughout the hemisphere as somewhat of an economic wizard, and upon the strength of his management role the international financial community extended credit and support in substantial quantities. The Argentine nation seemed determined to overcome past mistakes and set a steady course for the future. Outsiders welcomed Frondizi to the ranks of liberal, democratic leaders who were moving their countries into a new age of national development. It was not Frondizi's fault that the gesture was premature; the difficulties were too great for any man to overcome.

Frondizi's austerity measures were unpopular with the urban masses, particularly his efforts to hold the line on wage and salary increases. His arrangements with foreign petroleum companies angered the extreme nationalists while his credit restrictions turned the construction industry and businessmen against him. The military looked on with misgiving, fearful that the president, in his effort to please with political favors those whom he had antagonized with his economic policies, would allow left-wing or Peronista elements to regain political power. Antagonisms mounted, and as is often the case when a political leader seeks to play a balancing game, Frondizi found his enemies steadily increasing in number while his friends and supporters disappeared. He was forced to dismiss Alsogaray early in 1961, and the action startled the international banking and financial community. Confidence in Frondizi diminished at home and abroad.

FRONDIZI'S POLITICAL GAMBLE

Frondizi was really on a tightrope anchored at one end by the military and at the other by the labor unions and the urban masses of Buenos Aires. If he went too far in either direction the opposite end of the rope would be dropped; at the same time, if he lost his balance he would fall in any case. This was no time for anyone to shake the rope, and that was precisely what the United States did. At a Punta del Este meeting of foreign ministers in January of 1962 the American representative, Secretary of State Dean Rusk, asked for denunciation of Cuba and her expulsion from the Organization of American States. Caught between his military supporters who favored a hard line against Cuba and his left-wing and Peronista supporters who tended to admire Fidel Castro, Frondizi tried to satisfy both groups. He supported denunciations of the Cuban regime but refused to back the expulsion resolution. The rope was nearly dropped at both ends simultaneously.

Under pressure from both left and right the Argentine president did his obeisance first to one side and then the other. He reversed his position on Castro and broke diplomatic relations with Cuba; then he permitted the Peronistas to present candidates in the forthcoming congressional and provincial elections. The result was disastrous. The Peronistas won a plurality of the votes cast (almost 32 per cent), captured forty-five seats in the national chamber of deputies (86 out of 192 were open to election), and took the governorship of nine provinces, including that of Buenos Aires. The immediate result was chaos. The military arrested the president, annulled the election, dismissed congress, put José María Guido, the provisional president of the senate, in as temporary chief executive, and then fell to fighting among themselves.

Argentina was almost without a government for over a year. Cabinet ministers came and went with such frequency that even the most ardent politicians lost track. Government programs ground to a halt, the cost of living rose drastically, and the peso collapsed, falling nearly 70 per cent in relation to the dollar in a matter of months. Virtually all confidence in the Argentine economy was lost as new foreign investment came to an end, production declined, business after business failed, and strikes and disorders brought the country to the verge of anarchy.

The military was badly split between hard-core, anti-Peronista conservatives, who rejected any participation whatsoever by Perón's followers in Argentine political life, and more moderate officers who sought to maintain some semblance of democratic government and popular participation in the electoral process. Efforts to revise the electoral machinery foundered as the two groups, calling themselves *Colorados* and *Azules,* or Reds and Blues, struggled for supremacy. In September of 1962 General Juan Carlos Onganía, commander of the motorized cavalry, moved his tanks into the capital city and ended the domination of the *Colorados.* President Guido then called for new elections, and on July 7, 1963, a vote was held. The election laws had been drastically revised by the introduction of proportional representation to minimize Peronista strength, and various manifestations of Peronista political organization had been outlawed as they appeared in different guises. Most of the ardent supporters of the absent dictator cast blank ballots in protest.

The 1963 election results were worse than inconclusive; they were farcical. Candidates abounded, as did old and new political parties. The largest vote for president went to the candidate of the *Unión Cívica Radical del Pueblo,* an obscure physician from Córdoba province, Dr. Arturo Illia. He had only 27 per cent of the presidential vote, but the group of electors cast their ballots for him since no one else had even come close. President Illia was inaugurated for a six-year term on October 12, 1963.

THE PATIENT GROWS WORSE

Dr. Illia's prescriptions for Argentina's illness not only failed to help the patient; they nearly killed her. He canceled the oil development contracts negotiated by Frondizi, canceled a major international loan agreement for expansion of the capital city's power supply, refused support of the International Monetary Fund to stabilize the peso, and started up the printing presses to meet the government's financial commitments. These nostrums discouraged new capital investment, caused a sharp decrease in domestic oil production, and set in motion a new round of dizzying inflation. Huge deficits mounted from the operation of the railroad on whose payroll were thousands who performed no work. Fares were not even collected on local commuter runs whose daily costs were enormous. Public services deteriorated and construction and maintenance activities on public works came to an end. Foreign debt charges absorbed exchange reserves while the internal debt increased at a staggering annual rate. Of course no measures were taken to improve the economy, speed industrialization, or modernize agriculture.

While Dr. Illia tended the patient, General Onganía, commander in chief of the armed forces, waited outside the door hoping for a sign of progress. He did not intervene when the good doctor made conciliatory gestures toward the followers of Perón who were repeatedly stirred by statements and promises of their exiled leader from Madrid. Indeed, Perón announced his intention to return to Argentina late in 1964 and actually got as far as Rio de Janeiro by plane. He seemed much relieved when the Brazilian authorities would not let him proceed southward without the appropriate documentation and put him on a return flight to Spain. His followers, organized as the *Unión Popular* party, were permitted to vote once more in March of 1965 when a new congress was elected. Again they scored a substantial victory, but their members were less strident in their demands for Perón's return, and *Peronismo* seemed to pose a diminishing threat.

As the end of 1965 approached, General Onganía became increasingly concerned over the condition of the patient and the competence of the physician. He broke with the doctor and resigned his post. On June 28, 1966, a military junta dismissed Illia and put General Onganía in office as provisional president. Once more Argentina was back in the care of the military.

THE ONGANÍA DICTATORSHIP

General Juan Carlos Onganía had for several years played the role of defender and upholder of the constitutional order, preserver of the processes of democratic rule, and guarantor of moderation in the treatment of Peronista supporters. Now suddenly it appeared that he had reached the conclusion that his position had been utterly futile, that there was really no hope of trying to restore liberal constitutional democracy in Argentina.

Upon assuming the presidency, Ongania's actions were anything but constitutional, democratic, or moderate. In a virtual orgy of released frustration, he abolished the constitution, dissolved congress, intervened in the provinces to dismiss the legislatures and place his own men in the governorships, abolished and declared illegal all political parties, replaced the judges of the judicial power who were not to his liking, and even put an end to co-education in the elementary schools of the capital. Drastic as these measures were, most had been taken before by military governments within the memory of millions of Argentines. Virtually without precedent were two additional measures: dismissal of thousands upon thousands of surplus personnel and featherbedded hangers-on in the national, provincial, and municipal governments, as well as in public enterprises such as the railroads; and equally severe, the unheard-of practice of collecting commuter fares on the trains, and at higher rates. Residents of Buenos Aires were shocked right down to their pocketbooks.

Millions of Argentines applauded Ongania's wisdom and, above all, his nerve. People were totally fed up with weak and vacillating civilian rule, endless inflation, and constant political bickering. Many people, including hundreds of thousands who had been taking advantage of the system, understood perfectly well what evils were dragging the country to ruin. They simply had not believed that anyone would feel himself sufficiently secure to tackle them head-on. If corrective measures were honestly and equitably applied, many would support the man in the Casa Rosada even though temporarily hurt by the resulting economic displacements.

President Ongania made few promises and, on the whole, had very little to say. He did not spin theories about *'justicialismo'* or a 'third force'; he did consider his actions somewhat revolutionary, however. Ongania was a man to be judged by what he did rather than what he said. He did plenty, and not all of it attracted new supporters or made people applaud his actions.

One of the first areas to feel the force of the general's wrath was university life. Argentina, the seedbed of university 'reform' in Latin America, saw its universities interfered with, university autonomy ended, *co-gobierno* or student participation in the management of university affairs abolished, and hundreds of professors dismissed. Many professors and students were arrested, often on trumped up charges of communism and left-wing associations, and soon thousands of intellectuals were fleeing the country.

In only a few months after Onganía came to power, the universities throughout Argentina were brought under rigorous governmental control. Catholic universities, while not interfered with, joined in the clamor in defense of autonomy and independence in higher education. By the end of 1966 Onganía had alienated the intellectual class of Argentina and a large percentage of the clergy. Many of Argentina's ablest scientists and scholars were seeking or had found employment abroad.

Although the military president devalued the peso and raised the wages of labor, his basic economic orientation was in support of industry, business, and the banking community. He was soon in conflict with organized labor. Efforts to consolidate the General Confederation of Labor, long split between the Peronistas and anti-Peronistas, produced a series of power struggles and ineffectual calls for general strikes early in 1967. Onganía cracked down hard, blocking access to union funds, terminating the legal status of a key transport union, and threatening recalcitrant workers with induction into the armed forces. With such measures he kept the unions in check for many months, but he lost the support of much of the labor movement.

THE CRISIS OF MAY, 1969

In the spring of 1968 (October), a number of strikes and labor conflicts troubled worker relationships in the petroleum industry, in the wine industry, and in agriculture. Complaints were made against the government for having frozen wages rather then against employers. Then in May, 1969, a series of incidents involving both students and labor created a serious national crisis. The difficulty began in Corrientes province where university students protested a rise in cafeteria prices, and in the ensuing disorders a policeman killed a student. Protests spread throughout the country and workers joined the university groups in voicing their complaints. Raimundo Ongaro, head of a faction of the General Confederation of Labor that opposed the government, called a general strike. Workers left their jobs all over the country. In Córdoba a serious incident occurred when police fired on a column of laborers moving on the governor's headquarters. More than a dozen were killed and many more were injured. Subsequently a major riot wracked the city, and for hours an unbridled mob controlled much of the downtown area. As the police struggled to regain control of the situation further deaths and injuries occurred, and not all of them were on the side of the laborers.

Ongaro was arrested and jailed for having called the general strike, and Onganía shook up his cabinet, seemingly to tighten his grip on the labor movement. A month later Agusto Vandor, long a leader of a Peronista labor faction that had taken a generally co-operative position toward the government, was assassinated. Ongaro, still in jail, became not only a new hero but the chief leader of the labor movement as his rival, Vandor, passed from the scene. The government's relations with labor were generally weakened by all these events.

ONGANÍA'S THREE-STEP PROGRAM

For some time after General Onganía took over the presidency it was not clear whether his rule would lead back to civilian government or whether he intended to occupy the position of chief executive indefinitely. Gradually a concept emerged that consisted of three phases: economic stabilization and recovery, social renovation, and a restructuring of the political system. At the end of the third phase some form of constitutional democracy would be reinstituted. The timing of these phases remained vague, but by late 1969 Onganía spoke of the economic phase as having been completed. Presumably a year or two more would be required for the social phase, additional time for the political phase, and a return to constitutional democracy would take place some time in the mid-1970's.

By 1969 the accomplishments in economic stabilization were impressive. Inflation had been reduced from an annual rate of more than 30 per cent to less than 5 per cent. Onganía had brought foreign oil companies back into the Argentine production scene as one of his first acts, other foreign investment was encouraged, and strong relations were once again established with the international banking community. Loans poured in to bolster the Argentine economy. In 1965 and early 1966 the country was stagnant, as among the populace there prevailed an obvious attitude of 'Who gives a damn? The country is beyond help anyway.' By early 1968 a marked change had occurred. Argentina was once more on the move and people felt themselves to be participants in national development and progress. In spite of Onganía's battles with students, intellectuals, labor unions, and some of the clergy, many felt that the president's stern measures had long been overdue. Perhaps Argentina too had a strong, silent majority.

Onganía's economic program had restored public and international confidence in Argentina's fundamental soundness. His so-called social program, however, remained unarticulated and obscure. From his take-over in 1966 the military dictator had set himself up as the arbiter of public morals and decency, and it was clear that his standards would have been considered a bit rigorous even by Queen Victoria, had she been around. Indeed, some critics detected in Onganía's outlook a bit of nineteenth-century anti-Semitism. Efforts to woo organized labor had failed miserably, and everyone was aware that the nation's education budget had been drastically curtailed. There was no move toward land reform or modernization of Argentina's obsolete agricultural establishment. What Onganía had on his mind when he spoke of the social phase of his program just did not come through. His political phase was just too far off in the future even to be considered.

OUSTER OF ONGANÍA

On June 8, 1970, the three chiefs of Argentina's armed forces, Lieutenant General Alejandro Lanusse of the army, Admiral Pedro Gnavi of the navy, and Brigadier General Juan Carlos Rey of the air force, informed General Onganía that his days as president were at an end. He resisted briefly behind a barricade of twelve hundred loyal members of the presidential guard who surrounded the Casa Rosada, but after a few hours he had himself driven to army headquarters where he turned in his resignation. The new junta then informed the Argentine public that Onganía had been removed because of his refusal to provide a 'political solution' to the country's governmental leadership. Other stories subsequently appeared suggesting that Onganía leaned too far toward fascist corporate state concepts, that he had failed to crack down on extreme right terrorist groups, and so on. In any case, the stiff-necked authoritarian was quickly replaced by another general, Brigadier General Roberto Marcelo Levingston, a 50-year-old army officer who had been serving as an Argentine representative on the Inter-American Defense Board in Washington. Levingston was inaugurated as president June 18, but for the time being, at least, he would share power with the military junta composed of the three chiefs of the armed services.

Uruguay: The End of Utopia

After many years of Colorado rule, the Blancos came to power in Uruguay early in 1959. The change in party, voted the previous November, reflected marked public dissatisfaction with the sad state of Uruguayan affairs. There was good cause for complaint. For years the government of Uruguay had been 'robbing Peter to pay Paul.' Peter was the miserable farming population of the country scattered across the monotonous landscape north of Montevideo, living in abject poverty and employing agricultural methods that would have seemed outmoded at the turn of the century. Sheep and cattle were the principal commercial items produced, and while grazing land was basically good, little was done to keep it so. The animals and their offspring deteriorated in quality over the years, and the poor grade of wool cost the country the loss of export markets she once had dominated. Beef was plentiful, but hoof and mouth disease dragged down the productivity of meat and dairy animals alike. In spite of these problems, however, the country had for generations lived off the export of meat and wool, and the proceeds had been substantial.

Paul was the urban population of the Uruguayan capital, over 50 per cent of the nation's inhabitants, whose easy living, social security benefits, pensions, short working hours, and high consumption of food—particularly beef—were the envy of the world and gave to the country the illusory appearance of a South American utopia. Visitors saw the metropolitan south of Uruguay as an extended area of middle-class development, noted fine beaches attractive to Argentine and occasional European tourists, and obtained an over-all impression of urbane sophistication and stable democracy. Slums there were, down along the waterfront in the older part of the city, but they hardly resembled the barriadas of Lima or the favelas of Rio. Few of those who ascribed to Uruguay a resemblance to Switzerland or reported the high standard of living of her people ever ventured into the northern countryside. The roads were too poor or non-existent; there were no large cities or even pleasant small ones; fine hotels were nowhere to be found; mostly there were just poor people living in poor hovels that would have provided only meager hospitality for the visiting observer.

The Colorado party had been primarily responsible for the 'Peter to Paul' transfer, for its continuation in office depended on the enduring support of the large urban middle class. The middle class was a kept class, however, dependent on the government for benefit payments, subsidies, pensions, jobs that required no work, and opportunities to engage in all sorts of petty graft. So long had the situation existed that no one questioned its continuation. Even the slightest infringement upon a privilege or benefit was met with outraged resistance, increasingly in the form of a strike. To do business in such an economy was unlikely to be profitable, and it was not entirely owing to the semi-socialistic government policy that most important enterprises were operated by the state, usually at a loss. The most preliminary feasibility study would have convinced almost any business enterprise that there were better places in the world to invest money than Uruguay.

COLLAPSE OF THE ECONOMY

During the 1950's Uruguay's agricultural productivity stood still or declined. Wool production remained relatively stationary, but the export of beef and beef products fell off drastically from an earlier average of over 140,000 tons annually to less than 35,000 tons. In 1958 and 1959 many sheep were drowned as a consequence of heavy rains, and wool production declined by over 25 per cent. More important was the decline in demand for Uruguayan wool and the lower prices obtained on the world market. Synthetic fibers were rapidly replacing wool in the garment industries of Europe and the United States, and only the best grades of wool could be sold at a profit. Uruguayan exporters could not meet the competition, and export earnings declined.

As Uruguay's international trade faltered, government deficits mounted, increased by heavy losses in state-operated industrial enterprises. Investments in new industrial capacity required more capital, but with decreasing exports and mounting social benefit payments to the country's urban working class, no surplus funds were to be found. The Blancos came into office promising economic reforms, restoration of a sound currency, and an end to inflation.

Uruguay's Blanco party had been out of office for nearly a century. It presumably represented the conservative land-holding and business interests, those who had long viewed with misgivings the endless extension of social benefit programs to the urban working and middle-class people. A program of austerity was anticipated when the party took office.

The heavy rains and floods of 1959 created one problem after another calling for immediate government attention, and it was not until January of 1960 that the Blanco-dominated national council, Uruguay's collegiate executive, got its reform program under way. The program did not amount to much. It imposed import restrictions, eliminated subsidies for some consumer products, and devalued the peso. It did not remove surplus employees in government enterprises, reduce or eliminate social benefit payments and pensions, step up productivity goals in industry, or introduce longer working hours and compulsory attendance on the job.

Prices continued to rise and round after round of higher wages were demanded in one industry after another. When higher productivity offered the only hope for slowing the inflationary spiral, the country was virtually paralyzed by work stoppages. The government was unable to meet its payrolls and state enterprises likewise fell behind. Each payday brought a new labor crisis followed by more strikes and a further deterioration of the economy. The country staggered along from month to month as prices mounted and the peso sank lower in value. Printing additional paper money only added to the inflation. Occasionally a loan was obtained from abroad, but there was little confidence among international lending institutions in Uruguay's economy or financial stability, and more and more frequently the bankers turned a deaf ear to pleas from members of the council, any one of whom, including the council president, might or might not have been able to speak for the others. By 1965 the country was bankrupt. Payments on the foreign debt were defaulted and the only possible way to meet domestic payrolls was by printing new and valueless pieces of paper.

THE END OF COLLEGIATE RULE

Uruguay got through 1965 and the early part of 1966 primarily by repeatedly calling on the armed forces to operate public services while the regular workers were out on strike. Stronger measures to curb wage increases, limit imports, and restrict credit were made partially effective by the vigorous efforts of the national council under the leadership of its president, Washington Beltrán. At the same time, Blanco spokesmen uniformly denounced the collegiate executive system and blamed it for the party's failure to lead the country back to stability and prosperity.

When the elections of November, 1966, came around, the public was more than convinced that the plural executive had to go. A new constitution was adopted restoring presidential government and giving to the president extensive powers, including that of initiating legislation and declaring it in effect if the two-house legislative body failed to act within a specified time on emergency matters. He might even dissolve the legislature and call for new elections in case of a deadlock between the executive and legislative powers. The constitution represented a drastic change, but the Blancos were not to benefit from adoption of the proposals they had long recommended. The same voters who adopted their constitution turned them out of office and elected a retired air force general, Oscar Gestido, president for a five-year term. Gestido was a Colorado. So was the complexion of the new legislative body. Gestido was inaugurated on March 1, 1967, and the problems he faced seemed almost too much for any man to bear. The country was still bankrupt, industry and public services were at a standstill, and the urban population of the capital was still demanding new wage increases. Even food shortages appeared as strikes stopped production and paralyzed transport. Gestido struggled with the situation manfully for nine months, then on December 6 he died suddenly of a heart attack.

JORGE PACHECO ARECO

Upon Gestido's death, the presidential power passed to the vice-president, Jorge Pacheco Areco, a journalist by profession and 48 years of age when he assumed office. Pacheco extended austerity measures adopted earlier by Gestido. He froze both wages and prices indefinitely, virtually stopped all imports, put new technical people in his cabinet in place of politicians, and took stern measures to assure that people went to work on time and did indeed put in a day's work on the job.

Pacheco's austerity measures were met by the usual strikes and work stoppages. For weeks during 1968 much of the capital was in darkness as electric power was curtailed because of a utility strike. Kerosene and gasoline lanterns appeared, but these had to be used sparingly because of fuel shortages. After years of economic chaos and depression, endless strikes, and uncontrolled inflation, the physical appearance of the capital showed marked signs of deterioration. The people became sullen and embittered. Predictably, Argentines and Brazilians began finding pleasanter places to take their vacations, and Uruguay's tourist business slackened sharply. After all, who wanted to take his vacation in a rundown country suffering from constant shortages and unpredictable public services?

As President Pacheco struggled to impose austerity on his bankrupt nation, recurring questions were posed regarding labor unrest and the endless pattern of work stoppages. How far had communist leadership and ideology infiltrated the unions? Were the strikes merely irresponsible actions of local unions or were they being called from abroad to disrupt the country and prepare the way for a communist take-over? Such questions were not easily answered. The National Labor Convention, the country's largest union, representing some 500,000 workers, was generally conceded to be in communist hands, but that in itself did not of necessity imply responsiveness to some kind of international conspiracy. The Soviet Union had long employed its Montevideo embassy as a main dissemination center for communist pay-offs and propaganda in Latin America, but that it provided headquarters for a plot to bring the Uruguayan government and the national economy to a state of complete collapse was far from demonstrable. Pacheco sought to gain control over the unions and put an end to the strikes, but he did not attribute his problems to a communist conspiracy.

Communist control of the unions was only one possible indication of subversion. A much more tangible attack and clearly a subversive one was made by a strange band of urban guerrillas known as the *Tupamaros*. Organized earlier in the decade, the Tupamaros, thought to be named for an Inca revolutionary of the eighteenth century in Peru, devoted their early efforts to large-scale hold-ups and robberies. On occasion their actions turned up information on illegal activities on the part of business enterprises, and the evidence was subsequently presented to the government. In other instances, funds taken in raids were used for the benefit of 'little people' whose savings were jeopardized by the robberies. Their actions seemed more designed to build up reserves and embarrass the government than to create violence.

Toward the end of the decade, however, the pattern began to change. The Tupamaros had obviously become a large organization with possibly a thousand or more well-trained and rigidly disciplined members. Their actions became more violent. Kidnapping and then murder became regular tactics. In April of 1970 they murdered the head of the Uruguayan police intelligence department, and he was the seventh police officer to die at their hands in less than a year. Occasionally members of the Tupamaro bands were killed or captured, and large caches of arms were found. Prisoners proved highly disciplined in maintaining silence under interrogation, but it was learned that the organization functioned through a series of cells in the established communist pattern. Some of the leaders, only a few of whose identity became known, were believed to have undergone terrorist training in Castro's Cuba.

Faced with continued labor stoppages and disorders, challenged by urban terrorists, and still struggling with a disorganized and depressed economy, President Pacheco increased the size of the army, imposed a limited state of siege, and began a strict censorship with respect to reports of Tupamaro activities and measures taken against the terrorists. A major problem was the fact that many Uruguayans, particularly young people, regarded the Tupamaros as romantic defenders of the downtrodden.

The austerity measures of Pacheco brought inflation virtually to a standstill by late 1969. They did not, however, improve Uruguay's position in the export market for wool and beef. Rather, they brought down the standard of living of the urban population and gave it a more realistic relationship to national productivity. How long the urban population would accept their more austere form of living was difficult to predict. It made little difference to the rural dwellers, for they had never enjoyed prosperity anyway. The basic imbalance still remained, and with limited resources apart from its soil the future of Uruguay appeared bleak.

The Country up the River

Far up the vast La Plata river system, on beyond where the Paraná comes in from Brazil, the city of Asunción huddles on the east bank of the Paraguay river. Although one of the earliest cities founded by the Spaniards in South America, the capital of modern Paraguay has been throughout much of its history isolated and cut off from the rest of the world. Landlocked and virtually inaccessible until recently except from the river, Paraguay has often lived in political as well as physical isolation. This has been the state of affairs for the past sixteen years during which General Alfredo Stroessner has presided over the fortunes and misfortunes of the republic. Paraguay remains a military dictatorship in which political rivalry is largely suppressed and one-man rule upheld with a firm and not-too-gentle hand.

Paraguay's two million people, all but a small percentage of whom are mestizos, enjoy but few of the amenities of twentieth-century life, and Stroessner has done little to improve the situation. He has drawn substantial sums from the United States' foreign aid program, much of it used to combat disease, increase agricultural production, and educate more of his people, but progress has been slow because the country is poor. New roads have been built, however, and they now connect Asunción with both Brazil and Bolivia. Paraguay agreed in 1968 to participate in an international effort with Argentina and Bolivia to develop the Plata river basin, but what tangible projects might emerge from this endeavor remained to be seen.

General Stroessner began his fourth term in office in August of 1968. A new constitution was prepared by a constituent assembly in 1967, and under its provisions the president was made eligible for two additional terms of office. There was little doubt that he intended to seek them both in spite of endless plotting against his rule. Many of the would-be insurrectionists lived abroad and after sixteen years of rule the still vigorous general had already outlived scores of them.

Christian Democracy in Chile

Chile, like Argentina and Uruguay, had become by 1960 a highly urbanized nation. In the latter years of the 1950's, however, the economy did not prosper. Industry expanded, but not remarkably, while agricultural production actually diminshed on a per capita basis in the face of a rapidly increasing population. Owners of Chile's great *fundos* or landed estates paid no attention to government admonitions to increase production. Much of their land remained idle while primitive methods prevailed in the utilization of those plots that were farmed. Characterized by a stagnant economy, rising prices, and unfavorable international trade balances, Chile was in trouble economically and therefore politically. A decline in the standard of living was experienced by almost everyone but the most wealthy. Although personally popular, President Jorge Alessandri rapidly lost political support as he allowed the country to drift. By 1964 every segment of the population was ready for a change.

THE ELECTION OF EDUARDO FREI MONTALVA

The presidential election of 1958 had seen a left-wing socialist, Salvador Allende, run a very close race with Jorge Alessandri. In 1964 he was back again, supported by FRAP, the *Frente de Acción Popular,* a coalition of socialist and communist groups and other left-wing elements. It constituted a powerful combination, and political observers around the world tended to equate its possible victory as a potential decision by Chilean voters to choose a communist course. Moscow's enthusiasm for Allende was openly displayed.

In the opposite corner was another left-of-center group, the rising Christian Democratic party headed by Eduardo Frei Montalva. The two principal candidates, Allende and Frei, both offered the Chilean people essentially the same platform: land reform through break-up of the large fundos and redistribution to the Chilean peasant, the poverty-ridden *inquilino;* government ownership of utilities; and a taking-over of the copper mines. Differences lay primarily in the manner by which the two political leaders proposed to carry out their program. Allende talked of seizure and expropriation, Frei of legal purchase and gradual 'Chileanization.' Allende was vigorously anti-United States, Frei was anti-communist and quietly friendly toward his North American neighbor. It was a dramatic contest between what appeared to be two distinct approaches to revolution. That a revolution was necessary not even many of the conservatives any longer questioned.

Frei's victory was decisive. He obtained over 1.4 million votes to less than 1 million for Allende, 56 as against just under 39 per cent of the votes cast. The Chilean people, including large numbers of the laboring classes and rural peasants, had expressed their preference for orderly procedures and gradualism in bringing about the needed changes. Many conservatives and liberals no doubt voted for Frei out of fear of a communist victory rather than as an expression of support for his program, but they gave little attention at the polls to the one rightist candidate, Julio Durán. Durán received only 125,000 votes.

THE DIFFICULT CHILEAN CONGRESS

Eduardo Frei as candidate had made many promises, but Eduardo Frei as president found that carrying them out was quite another matter. He took office on November 3, 1964, and shortly he and his party presented a host of measures to congress to bring about the reforms he knew hundreds of thousands of people expected of him. Even a constitutional amendment was proposed to permit a popular referendum on government proposals rejected by the legislative body. Frei's program got nowhere. The congress had been elected in 1961 and the Christian Democrats held only a few seats in either house. Conservatives and FRAP members joined forces and refused to pass any of Frei's proposals. The Christian Democratic revolution was stalled, at least for the time being.

The following March brought new congressional elections, and Frei focused his efforts on getting a congress elected that would support his program. The results were dramatic. The Christian Democrats scored an astonishing victory, capturing control of the chamber of deputies, the first time a single party had accomplished this feat in the twentieth century. Gains in the senate were also impressive, but they fell short of giving Frei's party a majority, for not all the seats had been up for election. Failure to win control of the senate proved to be the Achilles' heel of Frei's administration. Some reforms were approved, but others were held up indefinitely by rightists and communists who climbed into the same bed to embarrass the Christian Democratic government.

CHILEANIZATION OF COPPER PRODUCTION

Over 60 per cent of Chile's export income has long been derived from copper. The mines, however, were owned almost entirely by American companies, the most important being El Teniente mine owned by the Kennecott Company. Frei proposed a plan whereby the Chilean government would buy up interests in the mining enterprises over a period of years. In the case of El Teniente, a new company would be formed to operate the mine, and 51 per cent ownership would be held by the government with Kennecott keeping 49 per cent. The American company was to receive some $80 million as purchase price of the Chilean government's share. Both the government and Kennecott would invest new sums so as to increase production and thereby produce new export earnings and new revenues for the Chilean govèrnmènt's land reform, housing, and educational development programs.

Months of legislative discussion followed, as well as extended negotiations with the copper companies. Agreement was finally reached and the new arrangements were approved by congress early in 1966. One major problem could not be solved by Frei, the companies, or congress, however, and that was the problem of world demand and the world market price. Both demand and price had a long history of wild fluctuation, and regardless of what ownership arrangements prevailed the Chilean economy remained partially dependent upon these unstable factors.

OTHER FEATURES OF FREI'S PROGRAM

Eduardo Frei encountered much greater difficulty with his land reform program, for rather than attacking the interests of foreigners it struck directly at the small clique of landholders whose fundos comprised over three-quarters of all the arable land in Chile. Passage of land reform was accomplished in the chamber of deputies in May of 1966, but another full year was required to get approval in the senate where the rightists who wanted no reform joined with the FRAP members who wanted outright confiscation, and together they blocked all progress. Finally the measure was approved in July, 1967. The victory was a dear one for Frei, however. Not only had he lost valuable time, but the bitter controversy centering around the land reform bill cost him many friends and weakened the unity of his own party.

By the beginning of 1969 some 5 million acres of land had been expropriated, but much of it was not the best land and some was barely marginal. Nearly sixteen thousand families had been settled on their own farming plots, although ownership titles had been conferred on a much smaller number. Perhaps equally important was the rapid growth of union organizations among farm workers. Nearly 200,000 members were claimed by unions and farm locals known as *comités de fundo*.

A new ministry of housing and urban development was created by Frei's government, and by 1968 over 50,000 new low-income units had been constructed, many of them in the Santiago area. Progress was also made in extending the country's educational system, and a particular effort to emphasize science and technology in higher education began to produce benefits as the end of Frei's term approached. All taken together, the Christian Democratic 'revolution' had accomplished a great deal, and against substantial odds.

As the decade drew to a close, Chile was still struggling with Frei's Chileanization program. Successful arrangements had been completed and prices agreed upon for nationalization of foreign-owned utility companies. With the mining industry, however, there was still trouble. The El Teniente agreement was criticized as having been too favorable to the Kennecott Company. A number of people felt that the government had paid too high a price for its share of the company. In the meantime, negotiations with Anaconda, the world's largest copper-producing company, were encountering great difficulty. Anaconda at first resisted Chileanization, and when discussions finally began the formulas worked out were highly complicated and Chilean benefits heavily dependent upon continuation of a satisfactory world price. More and more voices were heard demanding outright nationalization.

THE 1970 ELECTION

As the 1970 election approached, the two-party polarization of Chilean politics seemed to have broken down. Municipal elections in 1967 had gone heavily against the Christian Democrats, and as the end of Frei's term drew near, conservative and leftist factions within the party divided on many issues, including that of party leadership. It was all Frei could do to hold the party together, and in 1969 he failed even to do that as a large left-wing segment seceded.

The Christian Democrats chose as their next presidential candidate a former senator and Frei's first ambassador to the United States, Radomiro Tomic. Tomic was known as far to the left of Frei, not friendly toward the United States, and inclined to court the Marxists. His speeches were demagogic in comparison with Frei's moderate and reasonable approach to the public, and he seemed to be determined to capture the leftist support that in 1964 had gone to Allende.

The Socialist party persuaded Salvador Allende to run again, but early in 1970 the Frente de Acción Popular was in disarray and split among a variety of minor parties. As the months passed, however, Marxist groups began to coalesce behind him, but it was difficult to tell just how much of an inroad had been made by Tomic among them.

A new party of the right, the *Partido Nacional,* made up of former Conservatives and Liberals primarily, chose as its candidate former President Jorge Alessandri, now 74 years of age. Highly respected and wealthy, Allessandri was expected to unite moderate and conservative strength, including the more rightist elements of the Christian Democratic party who could not abide Tomic's radicalism. Three months before the election, to take place in September, the outcome was very much in doubt.

Cultural Development

Southern South America during the 1960's continued to lag behind Mexico and Brazil in architectural accomplishment and in various artistic fields. This was owing in part to economic stagnation and endless inflation that discouraged investment in costly physical construction. Early in 1970 there were signs that this situation might be about to change, at least for Buenos Aires, as a number of huge new hotels were being planned for the city. They were badly needed and long overdue.

Buenos Aires continued her pre-eminence in the Spanish-speaking world, however, with respect to many fields of cultural development. Eduardo Mallea remained one of Argentina's outstanding novelists, his *La razón humana* being published in 1960. Ernesto Sábato and Beatriz Guido also demonstrated outstanding talent during the decade. Two books published by Miss Guido were *El incendio y las vísperas* and *La mano en la trampa*. The former was translated in 1966 as *End of a Day*. A combination of philosopher-theoretical physicist, Mario Bunge, published a number of works during the 1960's. Outstanding titles included *Causality: The Place of the Causal Principal in Modern Science* and *Intuition and Science*.

Argentine leadership in music was amply demonstrated by the contemporary composer Alberto Ginastera. In addition to a number of outstanding compositions for orchestra and vocalists, he wrote a *Concerto for Violin and Orchestra* under commission by the New York Philharmonic Orchestra. In 1964, he wrote a grand opera, *Don Rodrigo,* under commission from the city of Buenos Aires. It was premiered at the *Teatro Colón,* Argentina's most famous theater and concert hall. The opera was subsequently presented in New York.

Ginastera was for some time closely associated with one of Latin America's most unusual institutions, a cultural center in Buenos Aires known as the *Instituto Torcuato Di Tella*. The Institute sponsored not only musical studies but a great variety of artistic endeavors. Located on Buenos Aires' famous Calle Florida, it became known throughout the world for its presentations, displays, exhibits, and scholarships for budding young artists and musicians. Created by the wealthy Di Tella family in 1958, the Institute flourished for a decade, attracting substantial support from the

Ford Foundation after the Di Tella family fortunes began to slip. In June of 1970 it was announced that the Institute was closing its doors for lack of funds. With its passing would go one of Latin America's truly unique contributions to the arts.

Throughout the 1960's Latin America's most distinguished poet was still claimed by Chile. Neftalí Ricardo Reyes, known to the world as Pablo Neruda, was famous not only for his poetry but also for his outspoken support of communist ideology. In 1970 the Chilean Communist party sought to nominate him for president, but he declined the honor.

Uruguayan architecture came prominently to the fore in 1965 with the construction in Washington, D.C. of the new home of the Pan-American Health Organization. Designed by Román Fresnedo Siri, the building has been widely acclaimed as one of the most beautiful and functional in the American capital, despite its rather unfortunate location at the intersection of major highways. It deserves a far better setting. Latin American artistic talent has much to offer the world, and the new health organization building stands as an extraordinary example of what that talent can do.

SUGGESTED READING

L.C. Aguilar, *Marxism in Latin America.* New York, 1968.

N.A. Bailey, *Latin America in World Politics.* New York, 1967.

H. Béjar, *Peru 1965: Notes on a Guerrilla Experience.* New York, 1970.

R.E. Bonachea and N.P. Valdes, *Che: Selected Works of Ernesto Guevara.* Cambridge, Mass., 1969.

P. Calvert, *Latin America: Internal Conflict and International Peace.* New York, 1969.

L.J. González and G.A. Sánchez Salazar, *The Great Rebel: Che Guevara in Bolivia.* New York, 1969.

I.L. Horowitz, ed., *Masses in Latin America.* New York, 1970.

L. Huberman and P.M. Sweezy, *Socialism in Cuba.* New York, 1969.

J. Maier and W. Weatherford, eds., *Politics of Change in Latin America.* New York, 1962.

H. Mitchell, *Contemporary Politics and Economics in the Caribbean.* Athens, Ohio, 1968.

M. Mörner, ed., *Race and Class in Latin America.* New York, 1970.

M.C. Needler, *Political Systems of Latin America.* New York, 2nd ed., 1970.

C. O'Loughlin, *Economic and Political Change in the Leeward and Windward Islands.* New Haven, 1968.

J.H. Rodrigues, *The Brazilians: Their Character and Aspirations.* Austin, 1967.

S.R. Ross, *Is the Mexican Revolution Dead?* New York, 1966.

R. Ruiz, ed., *Interpreting Latin American History from Independence to Today*. New York, 1970.

J. Suchlicki, *University Students and Revolution in Cuba, 1920–1968*. Coral Gables, 1969.

R.D. Tomasek, ed., *Latin American Politics*. New York, 1968.

V.L. Urquidi, *The Challenge of Development in Latin America*. New York, 1964.

Index

Cuevas, José Luis, 508
Cundinamarca, New Granada, 91
Cunha, Euclides da, 172, 255, 267
Cuzco, Peru, 17
Czechoslovakia, 478, 482

Darío, Rubén, 171, 232
Dávila, Carlos, 402
Daza, Hilarión, 189, 190, 206
Debray, Régis, 491, 492, 591
Debt peonage, 11, 226
Declaration of Panama, 352
Degollado, Santos, 136, 139
De Lesseps Company, 166
Delgado Chalbaud, Carlos, 345
Del Valle, Aristobulo, 195
Department of Press and Propaganda
   (D.I.P.), Brazil, 368
Derqui, Santiago, 174
Descamisados, Argentina, 284, 393
Díaz, Felix, 243
Díaz, Porfirio, 138, 141, 143, 158, 223–
   43, 247, 283, 304, 314
Díaz Aztarain, Rolando, 467
Díaz Ordaz, Gustavo, 500, 502, 503, 504
Díaz Soto y Gama, Antonio, 241
'Dollar diplomacy,' 282, 333
Dominica, island of, 556
Dominican Guard, 357
Dominican Republic, U.S. intervention
   in, 232, 515; end of Trujillo regime in,
   546–55, 559; mentioned, 28, 165, 329,
   330, 346, 347, 357, 358, 360, 489, 528
Dorrego, Manuel, 73
Dorticós Torrado, Oswaldo, 356, 466, 481
Duarte, José Napoleón, 534
Dulles, John Foster, 333
Durango, Mexico, 248, 309, 321
Dutch, 5, 7, 23, 352
Dutch Guiana, 154
Dutra, General Eurico, 366, 370, 374
Duvalier, François ('Papa Doc'), 357, 360,
   489, 529

East Indians, in British Guiana, 550; in
   Dutch Guiana, 154; in Trinidad-Tobago,
   557
Ecclesiastical courts, 118, 136, 182
Echandi, Mario J., Costa Rica, 338, 541
Echenique, José Rufino, 105
Echeverría, Esteban, 77
Echeverría Alvarez, Luis, 503
Economic colonialism, 169, 172, 279
Economic Committee for Latin America
   (ECLA), 299
Economic nationalism, in Argentina and

Chile, 181; in Mexico, 240; in Peru and
   Bolivia, 562; mentioned, 279, 290,
   333
Economic and Social Commission for
   Latin America, 442
Ecuador, colonial, 4, 9, 14–16, 26; under
   García Moreno, 106–8, 207–10; pact
   with Peru, Bolivia, and Chile, 186;
   dispute with Peru, 426, 427; after
   1930, 432–35; in 1960's, 561, 562, 571,
   576–81, 583, 585–88, 596; mentioned,
   40, 85, 86, 89, 93, 98, 102, 156, 168,
   202, 203, 217, 343, 371, 413, 414, 459,
   493
Education, in colonial era, 20; after independence, 44, 45; in Argentina, 72, 78,
   195, 285, 603, 605; in Bolivia, 100,
   589, 592; in Brazil, 69, 254, 255, 364,
   372, 517, 522; in Chile, 59–61, 69, 182,
   183, 614, 615; in Costa Rica, 231; in
   Cuba, 469, 470; in Dominican Republic, 548; in Ecuador, 208, 578; in El
   Salvador, 341; in Haiti, 232, 537; in
   Honduras, 343; in Mexico, 114, 137,
   249, 250, 311, 318, 319, 499; in New
   Granada and Colombia, 88, 90, 93, 234,
   235, 348, 351, 568; in Paraguay, 62; in
   Peru, 105, 213, 583; in Uruguay, 184,
   198; in Venezuela, 222, 347, 523; men-
   tioned, 151, 152, 295, 340, 456–58
'Effective Suffrage and No Re-election,'
   242
Egan, Patrick, 191
Eguiguren, Luis Antonio, 427
Eguren, José María, 217
Egypt, 339
Eisenhower, Dwight, 340, 346, 356, 401,
   475–77
Ejido, 247, 283, 309, 315, 319
Elbrick, C. Burke, 519
El Salvador, 111, 123, 125, 229, 231, 278,
   300, 331, 340, 341, 530–36
Encomienda, 11, 24, 35
England, 23, 81–83, 94, 127, 134, 140, 151,
   238, 269, 281, 384, 416, 487
English, 5, 152, 153, 154, 177, 228, 254,
   283, 389
Enlightenment, the, 21
Enríquez, Alberto, 432
Entail, 31, 52
Entre Ríos province, 82, 83, 174, 187
Errázuriz Zañartu, Federico, 192
Escalante, Aníbal, 467, 479, 481–83
Española, 5
Estado Novo, Brazil, 284, 363–70
Estigarribia, José Félix, 416, 417